THE ROUTLEDGE HANDBOOK OF SHAKESPEARE AND INTERFACE

The Routledge Handbook of Shakespeare and Interface provides a ground-breaking investigation into media-specific spaces where Shakespeare is experienced. While such operations may be largely invisible to the average reader or viewer, the interface properties of books, screens, and stages profoundly mediate our cognitive engagement with Shakespeare.

This volume considers contemporary debates and questions including how mobile devices mediate the experience of Shakespeare; the impact of rapidly evolving virtual reality technologies and the interface architectures which condition Shakespearean plays; and how design elements of hypertext, menus, and screen navigation operate within internet Shakespeare spaces. Charting new frontiers, this diverse collection delivers fresh insight into human–computer interaction and user-experience theory, cognitive ecology, and critical approaches such as historical phenomenology. This volume also highlights the application of media and interface design theory to questions related to the medium of the play and its crucial interface with the body and mind.

Clifford Werier is Professor of English at Mount Royal University, Canada. His recent publications investigate time across media in Shakespearean jokes and the application of meme theory to the spread of contagious ideas in *Coriolanus*. He is the co-editor of *Shakespeare and Consciousness* (2016) and is the interface team leader on the Linked Early Modern Drama Online project.

Paul Budra is Professor of English at Simon Fraser University, Canada. He has published six books and numerous articles on early modern drama and contemporary popular culture. He is the director of SFU Publications and a past president of the Pacific Northwest Renaissance Society.

ROUTLEDGE LITERATURE HANDBOOKS

Also available in this series:

THE ROUTLEDGE HANDBOOK OF SHAKESPEARE AND GLOBAL APPROPRIATION
Edited by Christy Desmet, Sujata Iyengar and Miriam Jacobson

THE ROUTLEDGE HANDBOOK OF SHAKESPEARE AND ANIMALS
Edited by Karen Raber and Holly Dugan

THE ROUTLEDGE HANDBOOK OF LITERARY TRANSLINGUALISM
Edited by Steven G. Kellman and Natasha Lvovich

THE ROUTLEDGE HANDBOOK OF STAR TREK
Edited by Leimar Garcia-Siino, Sabrina Mittermeier, and Stefan Rabitsch

THE ROUTLEDGE HANDBOOK OF SHAKESPEARE AND INTERFACE
Edited by Clifford Werier and Paul Budra

THE ROUTLEDGE HANDBOOK OF ECOFEMINISM AND LITERATURE
Edited by Douglas A. Vakoch

THE ROUTLEDGE HANDBOOK OF NORTH AMERICAN INDIGENOUS MODERNISMS
Edited by Kirby Brown, Stephen Ross and Alana Sayers

THE ROUTLEDGE HANDBOOK OF VICTORIAN SCANDALS IN LITERATURE AND CULTURE
Edited by Brenda Ayres and Sarah E. Maier

For more information about this series, please visit: https://www.routledge.com/Routledge-Literature-Handbooks/book-series/RLHB

THE ROUTLEDGE HANDBOOK OF SHAKESPEARE AND INTERFACE

Edited by Clifford Werier and Paul Budra

Routledge
Taylor & Francis Group
NEW YORK AND LONDON

Cover image: David Budra

First published 2023
by Routledge
605 Third Avenue, New York, NY 10158

and by Routledge
4 Park Square, Milton Park, Abingdon, Oxon OX14 4RN

Routledge is an imprint of the Taylor & Francis Group, an informa business

Library of Congress Cataloging-in-Publication Data
A catalog record for this title has been requested

ISBN: 978-0-367-42088-8 (hbk)
ISBN: 978-1-032-28686-0 (pbk)
ISBN: 978-0-367-82172-2 (ebk)

DOI: 10.4324/9780367821722

Typeset in Bembo
by Taylor & Francis Books

To Sabrina Reed for her love, friendship, and editorial acumen. CW.
For the Lavamen. They know why. PB

CONTENTS

FIGURES

CONTRIBUTORS

Erika Mary Boeckeler is Associate Professor of English at Northeastern University, USA, and the author of *Playful Letters: A Study in Early Modern Alphabetics*. Her other publication topics include printers' devices, poems on combs, and text in engraving and painted portraiture. Her current research is on typographic race and gender.

Meaghan Brown is a program officer at the National Endowment for the Humanities and managing editor of *Papers of the Bibliographical Society of America.* She received her PhD from Florida State University, USA. Her research has been published in *Book History, Papers of the Bibliographical Society of Canada*, and most recently, in the essay collection *Book Parts* (2019).

Paul Budra is Professor of English at Simon Fraser University, Canada. He has published six books and numerous articles on early modern drama and contemporary popular culture. He is the director of SFU Publications and a past president of the Pacific Northwest Renaissance Society.

Anne Burdick is a designer, scholar, and founder of the Knowledge Design Lab at University of Technology Sydney, Australia. Her collaborative design-writing-interface projects include: *New Variorum Shakespeare* (2021); *Digital_Humanities* (2012); designer, *Writing Machines* (MIT Press, 2002); design editor, *electronic book review* (1997–2012).

Rebecca Bushnell is the School of Arts and Sciences Board of Advisors Emerita Professor of English at the University of Pennsylvania, USA, and has written on subjects including Greek and Renaissance tragedy, humanist pedagogy, English gardening, and time in drama, film, and videogames. She is a former President of the Shakespeare Association of America.

Sarah Connell is the Assistant Director of the Women Writers Project and the NULab for Texts, Maps, and Networks at Northeastern University, USA. Her research focuses on text encoding and computational text analysis, medieval and early modern historiography, and pedagogies of digital scholarship.

Heidi Craig is Assistant Professor of English at Texas A&M University, USA, editor of the *World Shakespeare Bibliography*, and co-editor of *Early Modern Dramatic Paratexts*. Her first monograph, *Theater Closure and the Paradoxical Rise of English Renaissance Drama,* is under contract.

Kurt Daw is Professor at San Francisco State University, and is the author of *Acting: Thought Into Action* and *Acting Shakespeare and His Contemporaries* and numerous other publications. He is a past president of the Association for Theater in Higher Education. Daw has directed over 50 theatrical productions, including numerous Shakespeare plays.

Gabriel Egan is Professor of Shakespeare Studies, Director of the Centre for Textual Studies, and Director of English Research at De Montfort University in Leicester, England. He is a General Editor of the *New Oxford Shakespeare* and teaches the arts of letter-press printing and the computational analysis of text.

Laura Estill is a Canada Research Chair in Digital Humanities and Associate Professor of English at St. Francis Xavier University, Canada. She is the former editor of the *World Shakespeare Bibliography,* the author of *Dramatic Extracts in Seventeenth-Century English Manuscripts,* and co-editor of *Early Modern Studies after the Digital Turn* and *Early British Drama in Manuscript.*

Daniel Fischlin is Professor in the School of English and Theater Studies at the University of Guelph, Canada, and Founder and Director of the influential Canadian Adaptations of Shakespeare Project. He is also the General Editor of the Shakespeare Made in Canada series (Oxford UP/Rock's Mills Press).

Mary Hartman worked as a professional actor, director, and teaching artist before devoting her professional energies to community education and engagement. After spending more than a decade with Shakespeare & Company in Lenox, Massachusetts, Mary joined Bard on the Beach Shakespeare Festival in Vancouver, BC as Director of Education.

Eric Johnson is the Director of Digital Access at the Folger Shakespeare Library, where he heads the Digital Media and Publications division. He manages the Folger's various digital initiatives, and oversees the journal *Shakespeare Quarterly* and the Folger Shakespeare Editions series of Shakespeare's complete works.

Laurie Johnson is Professor of English and Cultural Studies at the University of Southern Queensland, Australia. His most recent book is *Shakespeare's Lost Playhouse: Eleven Days at Newington Butts* (2018), and he is completing a history of the Earl of Leicester's Men and the early evolution of the Shakespearean playing companies.

Alexa Alice Joubin is Professor of English, Theater, Women's, Gender and Sexuality Studies, International Affairs, and East Asian Languages and Cultures at George Washington University in Washington, DC, where she co-founded and co-directs the Digital Humanities Institute. She is the author of *Shakespeare and East Asia* (2021), co-author of *Race* (with Martin Orkin, Routledge, 2018), and co-editor of *Shakespeare and the Ethics of Appropriation* (2014).

Mark Kaethler is Department Chair, Arts, at Medicine Hat College, Canada. He is the author of *Thomas Middleton and the Plural Politics of Jacobean Drama* (2021) and a co-editor of *Shakespeare's Digital Language: Old Words, New Tools* (2018). He has published several articles and chapters on early modern drama.

Shoichiro Kawai is Professor at the University of Tokyo, Japan. He received his PhDs from the University of Cambridge and the University of Tokyo. He contributed to *The Routledge Companion to Directors' Shakespeare* (2008), *Shakespeare Survey 62* (2009) and *64* (2011), and *The Cambridge Guide to the Worlds of Shakespeare* (2016).

Jonathan P. Lamb is Associate Professor of English at the University of Kansas, USA. He is the author of *Shakespeare in the Marketplace of Words* (2017) and many articles. He is currently writing a book called *How the World Became a Book in Shakespeare's England.*

Laura Mandell is Professor of English and Director of the Center of Digital Humanities Research at Texas A&M University, USA. She is also Director of the Advanced Research Consortium, general editor of The Poetess Archive, and author of *Breaking the Book: Print Humanities in the Digital Age* (2015).

Gretchen E. Minton is Professor of English at Montana State University, Bozeman, USA, and the co-founder of Montana InSite Theater. Her monograph *Shakespeare in Montana* won a High Plains Book Award and the Montana Book Award. Other publications include Arden editions of *Timon of Athens, Twelfth Night*, and *The Revenger's Tragedy.*

Rebecca Niles is an independent consultant with a focus on developing digital resources for the study of early modern texts and textual artifacts. She is the lead developer for The Folger Shakespeare, DIY First Folio, DIY Quarto, and Before Farm to Table, and Managing Editor of the Folger Shakespeare editions.

Stacey J. L. Redick is the Digital Strategist at the Folger Shakespeare Library, where she manages the user experience and information architecture of the Folger Shakespeare website and other digital products. She advocates for human users of digital products by centering them in design and development.

Simon Ryle is an Associate Professor at the University of Split, Croatia. His research focuses on intersections of literary infrastructures and ecopoetics. He has recently edited an issue of the *Journal for Cultural Research* on the topic of "Minor Shakespeares." His first monograph, which concerns Shakespeare and cinema, was published by Palgrave Macmillan.

Lauren Shohet is Professor of English at Villanova University, USA. The author of *Reading Masques: The English Court Masque and Public Culture in the Seventeenth Century*, she recently edited *Temporality, Genre, and Experience in the Age of Shakespeare*, and, with Kristen Poole, *Gathering Force: Early Modern English Literature in Transition 1557–1623.*

Bruce R. Smith is Dean's Professor of English and Theater at the University of Southern California, USA, and has published seven books, including *The Acoustic World of Early Modern England* (1999) and *Shakespeare | Cut: Rethinking Cutwork in an Age of Distraction* (2016). His current work is focused on the intersection of literature and sound studies.

Suzanne Tanner is currently a PhD candidate at the University of Kansas, USA. Her areas of study include early modern and medieval literature, book history, the history of reading, material culture, and media studies. Her dissertation, in progress, is titled "Shakespeare's Stage and Page as Interfaces."

Bryan Tarpley is Associate Research Scientist of Critical Infrastructure Studies at the Center of Digital Humanities Research at Texas A&M University, USA. He is also the Associate Director of Technology for the Advanced Research Consortium. Dr. Tarpley's recent software development includes the Corpora Data Studio, to be released open source in 2023.

Gary Taylor is Dahl and Lottie Pryor Professor of Shakespearean Literature at Florida State University, USA, where he has been Department Chair since 2017. He is Senior General Editor for the *Oxford Middleton* (2007) and the *New Oxford Shakespeare Complete Works* (2016–17) and *Complete Alternative Versions* (forthcoming).

Katayoun Torabi is Project Manager of The New Variorum Shakespeare Series at the Center of Digital Humanities Research and an Instructional Assistant Professor of English at Texas A&M University, USA. She specializes in Old and Middle English Literature, with research and teaching interests in the Digital Humanities. Dr. Torabi has designed and taught courses for the Graduate Certificate in Digital Humanities.

Michael Ullyot is an Associate Professor of English at the University of Calgary, Canada, and author of *The Rhetoric of Exemplarity in Early Modern England* (2022). His research also includes articles and chapters on algorithms for detecting rhetorical figures (with Adam J. Bradley); on a quantitative model of the English-language sonnet; and on archives and artificial intelligence.

Clifford Werier is Professor of English at Mount Royal University, Canada. His recent publications investigate time across media in Shakespearean jokes and the application of meme theory to the spread of contagious ideas in *Coriolanus*. He is the co-editor of *Shakespeare and Consciousness* (2016) and is the interface team leader on the Linked Early Modern Drama Online project.

ACKNOWLEDGMENTS

Work on this volume began just before the Covid-19 pandemic exploded, but shortly thereafter its influence profoundly shaped every element of the workflow of both authors and editors. Most of the contributors to this volume are academics who had to pivot quickly and become online teaching experts while juggling their research and writing projects and shifting personal circumstances. As a consequence, everything about this volume was delayed from our original timeline, as evolving circumstances forced us to request extensions. At the same time, these unprecedented events became a unique feature of several chapters in this collection as interfaces (such as Zoom) evolved to meet changing performance conditions.

We would like to thank our authors for their commitment to this collection, despite the profound personal and professional challenges of lockdowns. We also want to acknowledge the risks that some authors took in undertaking an examination of Shakespeare through a new critical lens with which they were initially unfamiliar. The results are truly gratifying.

Finally, we extend special thanks to Bryony Reece at Routledge, for her patience and unflagging belief in Shakespeare and Interface, notwithstanding our emails pleading for more time. We hope it was worth the wait.

A version of Erika Boeckeler's chapter, "The Hamlet First Quarto (1603) and the Play of Typography," first appeared in *Early Theatre: A Journal Associated with the Records of Early English Drama*, vol. 21, no. 1, 2018, pp. 59–86.

INTRODUCTION

Clifford Werier and Paul Budra

The inspiration for this collection began with a seminar on "Media, Interface and Cognition" which we led at the Shakespeare Association of America (SAA) conference in Los Angeles in 2018. At the 2019 conference in Washington, DC, Meaghan Brown offered a seminar on "Navigating Early Modern Interfaces," while at 2020's virtual conference Lauren Shohet led a seminar on "Shakespeare Studies and the Idea of Interface." This unprecedented consideration of interface at three successive SAA conferences suggested to us that interface had found its moment in Shakespeare studies. After successfully proposing a collection on Shakespeare and Interface to Routledge, we put out a call for papers to a diverse assortment of scholars—none of whom had written previously on the topic of interface—and were delighted by the enthusiastic response. Clearly, the idea of approaching Shakespeare through interface theory had ignited imaginations, although many authors needed guidance in the initial phases of their thinking because interface, as we discovered, can be difficult to define and conceptualize.

In our initial call, we asked our authors to differentiate media from interface, as we recognized that the distinctions between these two categories were crucial to the unique approach of the collection. Past scholars had considered how Shakespeare manifests across traditional and new media, but little scholarly attention had been paid to the ways in which cognition and design cohere in a user's engagement with those media. The mediating function of the Shakespearean interface—that elusive liminality between media and cognition—had, in all its multifarious forms, been largely ignored. For this reason, almost every chapter in the collection begins with its author attempting to define and theorize what is meant by interface, to offer some reflections on interface theory generally, and to distinguish interface from a more traditionally mediacentric approach, such as Shakespeare and the book, Shakespeare on film, or digital Shakespeare. Interface, an established field of inquiry in media studies, gave our authors an innovative theoretical lens that allowed them to reconsider both the Shakespearean media artifact or performance space and the corresponding user experience.

Prominent interface theorists such as Alexander Galloway, Branden Hookway, and Joanna Drucker are cited throughout the collection, as all our authors gesture toward working definitions of interface before applying them to examples of Shakespearean media. The reader of this collection should gain a deep understanding of interface theory just by reading the discussions which begin every chapter. *This* introduction, therefore, will not attempt to summarize the many complex definitions of interface offered in the collection, except to establish the following general principles which should apply to every example:

DOI: 10.4324/9780367821722-1

1 Interfaces condition every contact with Shakespeare.
2 Interfaces represent and/or activate media containers, both explicit and hidden.
3 Interfaces provide a mediating function that conditions users' access to media.
4 Interfaces are activated where design meets cognition.
5 Interfaces are never neutral.

It may be useful to note the active verbs which structure this list of principles, such as "condition," "mediate," "represent," "activate," and the noun "access," confirming what Alexander Galloway has called "the interface effect." According to Galloway, "Interfaces are not things, but rather processes that effect a result of whatever kind" (vii). The list of principles above describes the actions and conditions of the interface, confirming Galloway's contentions by describing what it does, but not what it is.

Part of the pleasure of applying an interface approach to Shakespeare begins with a recognition of how interface functions grammatically as both noun and verb; demonstrating the rhetorical trope of anthimeria, one can interface with an interface, but this linguistic flexibility serves only to make things more complex. The original meaning of the noun derives from nineteenth-century physical sciences: "The term *interface* denotes a face of separation, plane or curved, between two contiguous portions of the same substance" (*OED*). The word was first used figuratively to denote "A means or place of interaction between two systems, organizations" (*OED*) by Marshall McLuhan in his book, *The Gutenberg Galaxy* (1962). It began to be used as a verb in the late 1960s to describe the connection between pieces of technology, such as Selectric typewriters and computers. As we shall see, to this day, much interface theory is largely driven by technological (and especially digital) innovation, though the figurative use of the word has crept into the vocabulary of university administrators and business leaders. A Shakespeare scholar might be more inclined to observe how the prefix "inter" combined with the root word "face" suggests both apparent surfaces and literal human faces which are interconnecting or participating in an act of mediation between or among objects—an apt description for points of contact between the Shakespeare media artifact/experience and the face/senses of the user.

The first principle described above—interfaces condition every contact with Shakespeare—emphasizes the necessary (but sometimes hidden or seemingly invisible) function of the interface as the point of access. Any Shakespeare media example will serve to illustrate this point—whether in live theater, cinema, books, or digital instantiations, now or in the past. Each media type, considered as both a technology and a user experience, utilizes an interface to condition access to the multifarious manifestations of Shakespeare's works, both as static objects and animated expressions. As Brandon Hookway suggests, "the interface is the zone of relation that comes into being between human beings and machines, devices, processes, networks, and even organizations" (39). This "zone of relation" can also be understood as both a point of contact and an invitation to initiate an effect, for while the interface is a way "into" a medium, it can also anticipate predictable outcomes created by shifts of attention or other cognitive habits through the activation of interface features.

From another perspective, Shakespeare's plays as both artifact and performance are always accessed through a technology which requires a point of contact for human users. Understood in this way, the interface functions as a cognitive activator which opens access to Shakespeare: without the interface and the media containers that it controls, there is no Shakespeare, or to use a visual metaphor, Shakespeare is always viewed via the lens of the interface through which the user's access is necessarily channeled. To paraphrase McLuhan, the medium may be the message, but that message is mediated through the interface. Take the book page from a typical scholarly edition as a working example of this hypothesis. The

Shakespeare play and accompanying paratext are laid out in page spaces designed with the anticipation of user requirements, such as the playtext, footnotes, marginal word glosses, collations, headers, and other interface page features, some of which require specialized kinds of interface literacy in order for them to be useable. Somewhere, seemingly "behind" the interface, lie multiple Shakespeare containers—such as source texts and previous editions—which the interface represents using a collation shorthand which can be activated by shifts in the user's attention between text and paratext (for more detail, see Werier's Chapter 1 in this volume). The interface holds all of these elements together by virtue of its design features based on assumptions about the user's desire to experience the plays and access supplementary information along the way.

The necessary role of the interface in conditioning the Shakespeare experience is perhaps most obvious in its digital forms, as many of us have become hyper-aware of how the affordances of graphical interfaces operate in our daily interactions with phones, tablets, and computer screens. This idea of interface affordances is another feature of the discussions in this collection. Donald A. Norman defines the actions of affordances as providing "strong clues to the operations of things … Knobs are for turning. Slots are for inserting things into. Balls are for throwing or bouncing" (9). A well-designed affordance provides a recognizable sign which signals an expected outcome. If you, for example, hover your mouse over an underlined or highlighted word in a Shakespeare digital edition with this design feature, you will activate a word gloss which appears in an accompanying textbox. Once the user recognizes that highlighting activates word glosses, the affordance becomes normalized as a sign which should deliver an expected outcome. In optimal design, such interface fluencies become enmeshed in consciousness and embodied in somatic responses, such as in the seemingly automatic finger gestures of phone operating system navigation. At that point, users may forget that an interface exists at all and assume that their access to the content of the digital container is transparent.

The overarching idea behind this collection is that such assumptions are incorrect. As the first principle listed above makes clear, interfaces condition every contact with Shakespeare. Shakespeare's works cannot be accessed or experienced unless they reside in some kind of media container—whether that container be a book, a website, a live theatrical performance or a cinematic rendering—and the contents of that container can only be accessed through an interface. Alexander Galloway describes the nested effect of such containers within containers and its importance in establishing a theory of interface:

> What is video but a container for film. What is the Web but a container for text, image, video clips, and so on. Like the layers of an onion, one format encircles another, and it is media all the way down. This definition is well-established today, and it is a very short leap from there to the idea of interface, for the interface becomes the point of transition between different mediatic layers within any nested system.
>
> *(31)*

In each case, some form of media contains the play within its boundaries, and the interface defines a point of contact through which users can access and experience the overall Shakespeare gestalt or channel attention toward the activation of discrete features. And so an audience member's interface with *The Tempest* at the reconstructed Globe on a sunny afternoon will be very different than the experience of the RSC *Tempest* featuring computer-generated animation of Ariel in an indoor space with access to special effects. In both cases, the spectator's consciousness of the theatrical spectacle is partially conditioned by the fit between cognition and design, just as it would be in the viewing of a virtual reality *Tempest* in which the spectator feels fully immersed in the theatrical illusion projected into the eyes through a headset. Put another way, human users connect with the theatrical container in order to interface with unique cognitive wavelengths, the spectator seemingly plugging into the available frequencies mediated by the interface. Or, as Gretchen Minton demonstrates in her description of a walking outdoor production, in Chapter 21, even a natural setting such as a park can function as a theatrical interface which channels theatrical and ecological cognition and attention.

While it may seem as if the source texts which provide the content of any Shakespeare version function as a kind of pure Platonic form which are mirrored by the cave-like shadows of various containers, even the source texts themselves are media objects which display interface features designed to channel cognition. The First Folio, with its two columns and large, unwieldy size manifests an interface conditioned by the manufacturing standards of early modern paper production, printing house technologies, market economics, and user demand. It is not an interface that supports portability, for example, nor can it be read easily in bed or even while sitting on a chair, as it requires a table or lectern. And presumably Shakespeare's original manuscripts were conditioned by the interface constraints of goose-quill pens, ink, and paper, as were the various copies used by compositors of the quartos who set the type. In every case, modern and contemporary, the Shakespeare container is held, interpreted, and accessed through interface signs, including such seemingly neutral apparatus as lists of *dramatis personae*, stage directions, and speech prefixes.

An interface approach takes these often-normalized features of Shakespeare cognition and makes them problematic; or, put another way, it recognizes that the experience of Shakespeare depends on the fit between the user and the container of Shakespeare, and that the interface will always channel cognition in order to facilitate a user experience which anticipates the fulfilment of desire. This is what we mean when say that "interfaces are never neutral." An unprofessional reader encountering the First Folio today would likely experience serious difficulties with the interface because of its archaic spelling, punctuation, lack of act and scene divisions, and missing annotations which have come to be an expected feature of Shakespeare comprehensibility. Without the crutch of the modern paratext, most amateur readers will stumble as they attempt to make the plays meaningful in the act of reading. Likewise, a print edition which makes lavish use of illustrations from past productions will inspire the reader to imagine a relationship between silent reading and theatrical and cinematic possibilities. In both cases, the user's experience of Shakespeare is profoundly conditioned at the point of contact between an interface which mediates cognition and the play itself.

The theoretical approach that we have presented in this Introduction is influenced by cognitive criticism, an area of Shakespeare theory that began in the early 2000s and was shaped by the works of scholars such as Evelyn Tribble, John Sutton, Mary Thomas Crane, and Amy Cook who pioneered the idea that cognitive engagements with literary objects are legitimate areas of critical inquiry. In Evelyn Tribble and John Sutton's influential paper, "Cognitive Ecology as a Framework for Shakespeare Studies," for example, the authors describe how systems of distributed cognition can reveal something new about the ways in which early modern performances were mounted through a shared collective consciousness: "Cognitive ecologies are the multidimensional contexts in which we remember, feel, think, sense, communicate, imagine, and act, often collaboratively, on the fly, and in rich ongoing interaction with our environments" (94). And Mary Thomas Crane, in her seminal book, *Shakespeare's Brain*, argues "the brain constitutes the material site where biology engages culture to produce the mind and its manifestation, the text" (35). In a previously published collection, *Shakespeare and Consciousness*, we took up one strand of cognitive criticism in order to investigate how the study of consciousness could generate new ways of approaching Shakespeare:

> Because consciousness, neuroscience, the brain, mindfulness, and other cognitive categories are ubiquitous in today's print and electronic media—and cognitive science continues to capture the attention of scholars across disciplines—we hoped to harness some of this energy by deploying Shakespeare and consciousness together, allowing scholars to explore the synergies that emerged.
>
> *(3)*

One feature of cognitive literary criticism that ties it to theories of consciousness and neurocognition is an emphasis on phenomenological descriptions. Phenomenology offers scholars another way to observe media-specific reading practices. Bruce R. Smith recently undertook a phenomenological consideration of a text read through Early English Books Online (EEBO) and the same physical book accessed at the Huntington Library:

> The attention that I have devoted here to the differing configurations of space and time between encountering a text on EEBO and encountering it in a library is a concern with the phenomenology of knowledge: its texture, its temporality, its relationship to me as the possessor of a body as well as a mind, its relationship with perceptions communicated to me by other people.
>
> *(29)*

An interface approach naturally moves toward the phenomenological and cognitive because it coheres around an experienced effect or process—"the differing conditions of space and time"—which can best be captured descriptively, and this arises in almost every case study of a Shakespeare interface observed in this collection, whether it be a book, a video game, a digital edition, or a live performance. This tendency toward the observation of human beings engaged productively with the Shakespeare interface also aligns with the movement known as User Experience Design (UX or UXD), which has been ubiquitous in the design and testing of software applications. A user experience approach assumes that the user will make choices linked to interface affordances which activate particular results, and that the interface can be refined and improved through testing and observation. This approach is taken up in this collection by Kurt Daw, in Chapter 15, who describes the design assumptions and processes of making a digital Shakespeare version of *A Midsummer Night's Dream* that meets the multiple needs of theater practitioners by applying UX principles. Likewise, in Chapter 17, Eric Johnson and Stacey Redick describe how the Folger Shakespeare uses UX processes to test interface prototypes and assess usability.

Consider, for example, the number of interfaces that a hypothetical user must pass through in order to experience a streaming theatrical rendering of Prospero's famous speech toward the end of *The Tempest*, where he proclaims that he will "abjure" his "rough magic" and "drown [his] book" (5.1.59–51, 57). First, the user needs a machine to access the internet. Let us imagine that our user, after pressing the start button to activate a MacBook Pro, confronts a narrow horizontal window that asks for a password, a security interface that hides but eventually allows access to the computer's desktop with its strip of menu bar icons, all mediated by the hidden and visible elements of the Apple operating system. From a somatic perspective, fingers must interface with the computer, by typing a password but also through trackpad gestures that have already created familiar pathways which allow easy access to cursor movements and associated "click" activations. The user's eyes find the Chrome browser icon which, after clicking, opens to reveal a home screen—perhaps the familiar Google search web page. After entering the URL for a university library and pressing "return" to navigate there, the home screen from the library provides a number of search options, including one for databases. Into yet another search window, the user enters "Bloomsbury Drama Online," knowing that it is a service which is available. After activating a link button, the user "arrives" at the Bloomsbury Drama landing page, where the "Plays" link gives access to both the Globe on Screen and RSC Live streaming services. Having clicked the RSC Live button, the user chooses *The Tempest* from a range of play links, which open to a small viewing window (that can be maximized with another click on the appropriate icon), where (after some trial and error) the user activates the slider bar at the bottom in order to fast forward to the 1 hour, 59 minute and 42 second position, where Prospero prepares to drown his book and break his staff.

The user, then, passes through multiple interfaces with associated nested containers in order to access streaming Shakespeare: the computer operating system, browser architecture, library website applications, specialized database designs, and the window through which a digitized Shakespeare performance is finally accessed, all contained within the rectangular frame and bezel of the computer screen (rectangular containers are a crucial feature of most interface design, whether it be a codex or digital page, a theatrical proscenium or a computer monitor). All Shakespeare artifacts and performances must be contained or channeled through a technology, and the interface defines the point of contact through which the human body, mind, and senses establish access to those artifacts and performances. Every encounter with Shakespeare, then, should be understood as requiring an interface or functioning by virtue of the interface's role in mediating cognition "into" the Shakespearean media object or experience. And hence the Parts in this Handbook which all describe interactions between Shakespeare and the user as mediated by an interface or nested series of interfaces, and which all recognize an active cognitive engagement with both surface features and underlying operations that channel the user's intention.

For example, Part I, "Media and the Embodied Mind" considers the implications of how bodies and senses make contact with a diverse range of Shakespearean media, or, in the case of Bruce R. Smith's Chapter 4 on "Voice as Interface," with the energizing power of the human voice to fill spaces within bounded environments which condition such vocalizations. As Smith argues, "thinking of the voice as an action catches the transactional nature of interface" across and within bodies and worlds, such as theater buildings and their acoustic spaces and the ways in which characters construct and understand their own vocalizing. Likewise, in Chapter 2, Rebecca Bushnell and Michael Ullyot consider how Shakespearean media and associated interfaces—in theater, cinema, and virtual reality—negotiate and manage space differently. Unlike the bounded theatrical proscenium or film screen, VR's frameless interface creates opportunities for audience engagement which are conditioned by the limitations and design specifications of a technology and associated programming, but which, nevertheless, allow for agency and immersion in a more open and user-centered space mediated by the VR headset. The point of contact between the mind, body, and interface is similarly discussed in Chapter 3, in Mark Kaethler's consideration of the videogame controller and the ways in which a user's choices are mediated by the constraints of the game and its opportunities for the user to exercise volition at key junctures. Unlike the more passive spectating associated with traditional media, the videogame controller allows the player to interface with the Shakespeare game world directly, providing somatic points of contact, but more importantly, allowing for opportunities to make choices which not only influence game play but also highlight the ethical implications of what might happen if a button is pressed. The notion of the user's volition is also featured in Clifford Werier's Chapter 1 on the cognitive load associated with reading the sometimes overwhelming scholarly Shakespeare page, with its interacting textual and paratextual spaces. Unlike a videogame controller, the affordances of a Shakespeare media object designed for codex reading are accessed through recursive shifts of attention between various page fields which may create an extraneous cognitive load that disrupts reading fluency. In all of the chapters in Part I, spaces and boundaries are mediated by the interface, whether it be the acoustical properties of voice in a theatrical machine, the seemingly open world of the virtual reality performance, the ways in which a user interacts with a game narrative through a controller, or the reader's cognitive engagement with digital and codex page frames and affordances.

Our contention that "interfaces are never neutral" is emphasized by the authors who contribute to Part II, "Apparent Designs and Hidden Grounds." The contrast between apparent surfaces and operations which happen seemingly underneath or beyond interfacial contact points is explored by Daniel Fischlin, in Chapter 5, who offers a political reading which reminds us that the designs of the interface are often self-serving, such as the friendly Google search field which hides a network of data collecting algorithms that mines personal information for profit. The *Shakespeare Effect*, defined by Fischlin as a "vast swathe of adaptive uses of Shakespeare in which material objects and aesthetic re-devisings ... overtake the flesh-and-blood authorial source with an ever-expanding simulacrum of distributed authorship(s)," may resist such exploitation by manifesting sites and associated interfaces which sustain difference and promote a more transparent and accessible engagement. The argument for accessibility is echoed by Gabriel Egan, in Chapter 6, who also considers the "power relations that modern technologies are made to serve." The hidden grounds of coded zeros and ones which capture stored information and associated processes are channeled by creators whose interface designs condition access and utility. After describing the history of interfaces, Egan supports the Open Access movement which includes both open-source software and open standards as a way of making interfaces more durable and democratic.

The distinction between apparent designs and hidden grounds is given a very different twist in Chapter 7, in Gary Taylor's reflections on the role of the Shakespeare editor in the design process of creating a critical edition. While Taylor reminds us that "editing has always involved re-designing old forms," editors often "do their work in a volume, or series, that has been designed by someone else." Taylor tells the story of his 40-year involvement with editing and designing Shakespeare containers and interfaces, emphasizing how evolving designs respect the editorial tradition while adapting to the requirements of contemporary users. Similarly, in Chapter 8, Jonathan Lamb and Suzanne Tanner consider Shakespearean abstractions as under-appreciated containers that represent the "Shakespeare system" and make it accessible. Lamb and Tanner identify abstracted frames, such as "prefaces, playbills, introductions, footnotes, summaries, diagrams, cartoons, illustrations, videos, adaptations, and many more" as examples of such abstractions. These abstracted forms and associated interface gateways may be dismissed as inauthentic, but in reality they serve the needs of users who require partial access to the overall system, such as students who access plot summaries or theater-goers who read a playbill before the performance. In both examples, the abstracted information of the summary and its hidden ground functions as an interface which gives access to the apparent design of the play as a whole and makes it more comprehensible.

In Part III, "Surfaces and Depths," authors consider both the visual play of typography in early modern printed works and the underlying codes that express, support, and catalogue digital Shakespeares. In Chapter 9, Erika Boeckeler examines how orthography and typography "generate textual dynamism that conditions readers' encounters with the text" by looking closely at Q1 *Hamlet* and the ways in which the early modern eye was influenced by such things as orthographic puns which would be lost in a modern version with corrected spelling. Likewise, in Chapter 10, Simon Ryle observes how typographic interfaces can be read as participating in a "poetics of the material letter that charts and contests the newly emergent subjectivities of the print era." Ryle considers Geofroy Tory's manual of typographic design, *Champ Fleury*, observing how the interface of letters maps onto the human form and the world of things. In this regard, Ryle, echoing Tory, isolates the individual letter, exploring this basic interfacial unit of typography and its ability to carry multiple meanings and associations. This concern for the letter is also applied to V and A in Shakespeare's *Venus and Adonis*, as letters, bodies, and sexual violence are figured in typographical signs. While Ryle's chapter focuses on the smallest unit which constitutes the printed surface of the early modern book, in Chapter 11, Sarah Connell focuses on markup systems, such as XML, which usually function as the code that resides beneath the digital edition or database but which can be productively read in its own right as a container that holds and displays information. Readers who possess a fluency with TEI markup standards can read its signs as if it were "a direct interface for reading" while also making use of the computational potential of searching and cataloguing that we usually associate with such editions.

In Part IV, "Display, Navigation, and Functionality," authors continue to emphasize the non-neutrality of the interface, observing how its design features and affordances control browsing, searching, and reading. In Chapter 14, Heidi Craig and Laura Estill consider the functionality of *The World Shakespeare Bibliography* as a case study in interface usability. After surveying browsing and searching as traditional categories of information retrieval, Craig and Estill describe the ways in which the *WSB* interface has evolved to reflect "the changing state of Shakespeare studies" by expanding topic categories and taxonomies to include new areas of inquiry and specialization. This interface always shapes available results. In using a searchable interface to harvest information about Shakespeare, how granular can we expect the results to be? In Chapter 12, Rebecca Niles investigates "the systems that we use to interact with increasingly minute particles of Shakespeare's texts, and the editorial decisions that shape these systems." Modern textual indexing systems have the potential to account for and measure increasingly fragmented bits of text, while historically the plays have resisted such attempts, as the earliest versions lacked even rudimentary navigation systems such as act, scene, and line numbers. However, a computer's ability to manage minute fragments may create an information overload that must be mediated by an interface mechanism which makes such tiny units comprehensible.

Digital editions, of course, are conditioned by the technologies that underlie their display and the programming that captures the early modern artifact and makes it legible and searchable. This often requires designers to develop a template or standard which becomes the interface for all future editions, but what happens when a play does not fit the data model? This question is posed by Meaghan Brown, in Chapter 13, who describes the development of the Digital Anthology of Early Modern English Drama (EMED) developed at the Folger Shakespeare Library, and the ways in which Ben Jonson's *Bartholomew Fair and The Staple of News* breaks or resists this standard. A one-size-fits-all interface cannot always handle typographical outliers. In all of the chapters in Part IV, display and functionality figure prominently, as interface designers grapple with the kinds and quantities of information required by users and the ways it is displayed and navigated.

A similar concern with functionality is explored in Part V, "User Experience." This section begins with Chapter 15, Kurt Daw's case study of a Shakespeare interface design for a digital edition of *A Midsummer Night's Dream* which meets the needs of theater practitioners. After surveying the limitations of existing print editions, Daw describes the steps employed by User Experience Design (UX), that begins with empathy for the user's requirements, moves toward a detailed definition of the user's needs, continues through the ideation of problems inherent in existing versions, and culminates in the development of a testable prototype. Daw provides examples of a new digital text and an associated interface that attempts to meet the unique needs of an under-served demographic of readers. In Chapter 17, Eric Johnson and Stacey Redick mine similar ground in their examination of the Folger Shakespeare website and how it displays and makes available a range of digital texts. Digital Experience Design (DX) is another way of managing UX principles, as designs tested against user needs and expectations are an essential element of a development cycle that incorporates interaction design, information architecture, and user experience/usability. The evolution of the Folger Shakespeare interface benefits from a wealth of data that captures users' interests and which helps to shape the development of future prototypes. The complex requirements of displaying information in useable formats is also highlighted by the work of Anne Burdick, Katayoun Torabi, Bryan Tarpley, and Laura Mandell, in Chapter 16, who tell the story of the open-access digital version of *The New Variorum Shakespeare* (and its complex design challenges) as the visually dense and complex presentation of information in the print version was translated into a digital medium with user-friendly web pages. Like Daw, Johnson, and Redick, the authors describe a process which results in a useable interface and the ways in which the digital medium can handle complex information better than the static printed page. This is accomplished in a dynamic interaction between the back-end database (Corpora) which contains and manages information and the front-end display (Variorum Reader) that provides the search functionality. In such complex digital interface spaces, editors and users must learn a new type of fluency that takes advantage of such increasingly sophisticated remediations.

While digital humanities scholars appear to understand an interface approach intuitively—as people working in digital environments have used some form of interface language since the earliest days of computing—the fit between interface theory and theater may not be as immediately apparent. The contributors to Part VI, "Staging the Interface," consider the implications of performance and associated spaces, properties, languages, and theatrical conventions. In Chapter 18, Laurie Johnson attempts to bridge this gap in his comprehensive analysis of early modern theatrical spaces as interface access points for audience engagement with the plays. Johnson emphasizes the embodied experience which conditions individual access to theatrical systems and "the full array of sensory stimuli that audience members experience in fitting their bodies to the playhouse environment." To access the early modern theatrical spectacle, the user becomes self-consciously enmeshed in a matrix of interconnected interfaces that includes the body, the physical properties of the theatre, and the sounds and smells of the world beyond. Similarly, in Chapter 20, Shoichiro Kawai compares the bare thrust stage of an early modern theater, such as the Globe, with the property-less stage experience of Japanese Noh and its accompanying comic theater, Kyogen. Kawai considers the ways in which playwrights and actors adapt to the minimal stage interface by using vocal and gestural conventions that establish location and movement from place to place in order to cue audience imagination. Shakespeare and Kyogen come together in translated productions that adapt Shakespeare to the Kyogen form and utilize the bare thrust stage in both new and traditional ways. Unlike Johnson and Kawai's emphasis on embodiment and performance, in Chapter 19, Lauren Shohet aligns interface theory with textual scholarship in her reading of *Cymbeline*, comparing the mediating heuristics of digital interfaces with linguistic structures, such as rhetorical figures, that also exist on the boundaries where different systems of meaning cohere. Focusing on Drucker's notion of the interface as an "in-between space ... where two worlds, entities, [and] systems meet" (n.p), Shohet offers the example of the trunk where Iachimo emerges to spy on the sleeping Innogen, an interface connecting the disparate realms of Roman Britain and Renaissance Italy, as one example of a theatrical object that can be understood as a mediating heuristic between worlds.

A consideration of such shifting worlds figures prominently in Part VII, "Interfacing with Performance," where contributors grapple with the implications of human users accessing a variety of performance media through embodied points of contact with interface gateways, sometimes under the disorienting conditions of the global pandemic. In the summer of 2020, Gretchen Minton helped to mount "Shakespeare's Walking Story," a production that integrated the performance of selected speeches from Shakespeare's plays at fixed stations, focusing on the theme of imprisonment and freedom, with a guided walk in a city park in Bozeman, Montana. Taking its inspiration from open-ended, site-specific performances like *Sleep no More*, "Shakespeare's Walking Story" was "intended to offer a much-needed space for reflection" on what being-in-the-world means in the Covid-restricted summer of 2020. In Chapter 21, Minton provides a detailed description of the user's experience and the influence of an ecological interface—such as the weather—that becomes a crucial yet unpredictable feature of the experience and its spaces for reflection. Likewise, Paul Budra describes the proliferation of online Shakespeare productions during the height of Covid lockdowns, focusing on the use of the Zoom platform as a performance interface. In Budra's Chapter 24, all of the principles identified in this Introduction are in evidence, especially in the places where the interface's design limitations and mediating functions condition a spectator's cognitive engagement. Here the notion of media containers bounded by interfaces is explicitly rendered in the Zoom grid and its associated boxes that frame both performers and spectators. In order to engage with such an interface, Zoom theatre "requires new and unfamiliar cognitive processes" that force audiences to imagine and interact with Shakespeare in new ways.

Even familiar Shakespearean media, such as cinema, can be reframed as Alexa Joubin does in Chapter 22, in her consideration of the meta-cinematic power of screens within screens, tracing complex interfaces and fragmented renderings through which old and new media and past and present performances are juxtaposed, integrated, and disrupted. In Almereyda's *Hamlet*, for example, a series of filmic intertextual screen echoes continually intrude on the action, as Hamlet is portrayed as a film maker, film watcher, and screen aficionado. Audiences interface with the cinema screen on which *Hamlet* is projected, but also on the other screens which proliferate within it. While Joubin describes diverse styles of connection with Shakespeare, her examples are mostly passive: the user is a consumer who experiences Shakespeare through a screen interface, whether at the cinema or at home. Mary Hartman, on the other hand, offers a more immediately engaged version of the Shakespeare interface in her Chapter 23 on enactment, as she asks the question, "what happens when we shift our perspective from that of passive observer to that of active participant?" As a theater practitioner, Hartman has trained many non-professionals to experience Shakespeare directly, unhindered by the need to prepare and mount a performance. As Hartman suggests, "When our own bodies become the container for Shakespeare's text and our understanding comes through enactment, that is the bringing of text to life by actively personating it." In this way, participants become the interface and the performance simultaneously, as their somatic and immediate immersion provides direct contact with all that is signified by "Shakespeare." Unlike Hartman's fully embodied enactments, many of the interfaces investigated by the authors in this collection can be classified as screens or frames which somehow hold or contain Shakespeare and provide points of contact for the user, whether a cinema screen, a computer screen, a Zoom grid, a book page, or a theatrical proscenium. Looking into a framed lens, like a pair of glasses, alters vision and shapes perception. It is our hope that the concept and experience of the interface allow a diverse collection of authors to cast a fresh look on Shakespeare and imagine how design choices and interface interventions provide differing points of access into Shakespeare. Whether through an embodied engagement with a performance medium or in the searching and accessing of textual artifacts and digital platforms, the idea of the interface illuminates the sometimes invisible power of the mediating structures that condition our understanding of reality. We hope that this collection generates much thought and conversation, and that whether you are reading this in a book or on a computer or tablet screen, you never again take that interface for granted.

References

Budra, Paul, and Clifford Werier, editors. *Shakespeare and Consciousness*. Palgrave, 2016.

Crane, Mary Thomas. *Shakespeare's Brain: Reading with Cognitive Theory*. Princeton University Press, 2001.

Drucker, Johanna. *Introduction to Digital Humanities*. Available at; http://dh101.humanities.ucla.edu/2013.

Galloway, Alexander R. *The Interface Effect*. Polity Press, 2012.

Hookway, Branden. *Interface*. MIT Press, 2014.

McLuhan, Marshall. *The Gutenberg Galaxy*. University of Toronto Press, 1962.

Smith, Bruce R. "Getting Back to the Library, Getting Back to the Body." In *Shakespeare and the Digital World*, edited by Christie Carson and Peter Kirwin, CUP, 2014, pp. 24–32.

Tribble, Evelyn, and John Sutton. "Cognitive Ecology as a Framework for Shakespearean Studies." *Shakespeare Studies*, vol. 39, 2011, pp. 94–103.

PART I

Media and the embodied mind

1

READING SHAKESPEARE

Interface and Cognitive Load

Clifford Werier

When I first studied Shakespeare as an undergraduate in the late 1970s, my professor assigned plays to be read from our massive textbook, *The Riverside Shakespeare*, which I dutifully lugged to class twice each week. So when I began my career as a Shakespeare teacher, I automatically ordered the same textbook with which I had become so familiar. I gave little thought to its size, its editorial policies, or its two-column playtext interface with footnotes, assuming that it would serve my students' needs. These days, however, choosing an edition for undergraduates has become more nuanced, as I factor in the specialized styles of cognition and strategies of information processing which structure their reading experience.[1] This, of course, applies to any reading act, as successful users must adapt to both the difficulty of the content and the interfacial presentation of words in pages or on screens whose cognitive load conditions learning and presumably establishes a cognitive fit which serves the reader's preferences and requirements. For example, while I use a Kindle e-reader for fiction, I prefer codex paper books for research and non-fiction reading, and I tend to print important PDF articles rather than read them onscreen. Likewise, I still collect a paper edition of the *Globe and Mail* ("Canada's National Newspaper") from my front step, while my wife prefers to read the same *Globe* on her iPad. In each case, the chosen medium and associated interface establish a personal cognitive fit between mind and words. As Maryanne Wolf reminds us, "each reading media advantages certain cognitive processes over others" (7) and each demographic has a history of differing media, interface and reading practices.

Increasingly, my first Shakespeare class focuses not only on what we read—including theories of transmission that have resulted in the textbook editors' choices—but more importantly on how we read, or on the cognitive processes through which we make the text meaningful and access supplementary information which promotes understanding. This chapter will consider both the cognitive fit and cognitive load imposed by the Shakespeare reading interface as an under-theorized and under-valued feature of understanding and enjoying the plays. Both interface theory and cognitive load theory illuminate how the plays, understood as information mediated by an interface, make specialized cognitive demands on a user who is attempting to make them comprehensible. The challenges of such cognitive operations are a function both of the inherent difficulty of reading drama—as the medium of text attempts to represent the medium of performance by facilitating the construction of a play within the reader's mind—but also of the difficulties associated with the historical, poetic and editorial elements of Shakespearean drama and with the need for paratextual materials to

DOI: 10.4324/9780367821722-3

facilitate comprehension or provide scholarly supports which can be productively accessed while reading the playtext.

Interface and Cognitive Load Theory

The design features of the page interface anticipate the unique cognitive and imaginative challenges of reading drama.[2] The minimalist conventions of dramatic typography condition the reading experience: speech prefixes denote speakers, indented text indicates speeches, and stage directions describe settings, contexts, entrances, exits, speech directions (who is speaking to whom), and other actions. While reading drama, the stage directions, speech prefixes, and speeches structure the reader's imagined performance, in which voices, bodies, spaces, and properties held in the reader's mind interact to create the play.[3] The process of reading drama is uniquely active because the descriptive cues are minimal, unlike the explicit and sometimes lavish world-building of prose fiction. If the reader has seen the play performed previously, then the reading act may be strongly influenced by the memory of a past production, and the voicing of characters in the mind may be imagined more fully. However, the challenge of reading a play for the first time is greatly amplified if we have never seen it performed. In the successful reading act, we may become actors, directors, costume, set, and lighting designers, and stage managers, although the inexperienced reader may need to be trained in order to imagine these elements. In the act of reading one speech followed by another, our imaginations must bridge the many gaps created by the interface of the playtext which, in most cases, does not indicate mood through any explicit narrative cues, except in the occasional aside, soliloquy or reflective comment, in addition to the usual interpretive challenges associated with the decoding of language and rhetorical figures. Thus, the reader of Shakespeare is situated in a paradoxical cognitive space, as both actor and audience, director and spectator, reader and auditor.[4]

While an enthusiastic reader may simply dive into the reading experience of the playtext and ignore the accompanying notes, most readers will take advantage of the many paratextual elements which editors have included in order to help mitigate difficulties or provide supplementary information. Gérard Genette describes the paratext as a "threshold," "vestibule," or "fringe" which functions as "a zone between text and off-text, a zone not only of transition but also of *transaction* … at the service of a better reception for the text and a more pertinent reading of it" (2). As Thomas L. Berger and Sonia Massai have demonstrated, the paratexts of early printed drama in English include such extra-dramatic features as "title-pages, dedications, addresses to the reader, lists of dramatis personae, prologues and epilogues, stationers' notes and errata lists" (xi). However, the paratextual features which contemporary readers have most come to rely on are the accompanying notes and glosses which explain or interpret difficulties—features which have become normalized as an essential part of the Shakespeare reading interface.

The special place of the editor as mediator, interpreter and authenticator hinted at in Heminge and Condell's preface to the First Folio is taken up by the editors of the great eighteenth-century Tonson editions, who began to regularize editorial concerns through recognizable interface features. For example, Samuel Johnson's 1765 *Works* has been characterized as "the first variorum edition" (Walsh, "Editing and Publishing," 31), a term that has come to be associated with comprehensive editorial collations of previous editions, including chronologically arranged textual variations and explanatory annotations, usually featured in extensive footnotes or endnotes. Marcus Walsh emphasizes how eighteenth-century editors "thought of themselves as interpreters, who set out to construe and communicate the author's sense, and who developed, often consciously, a theory and practice of interpretation" (Walsh, *Shakespeare*, 29). Johnson describes categories of difficulty which the editor must address and the ways in which his text and annotations offer editorial or interpretive interventions which respond to the reader's potential perplexity: "The notes which I have borrowed or written are either illustrative, by which difficulties are explained; or judicial, by which faults and beauties are remarked; or emendatory, by which depravations are corrected" (lviii).

In re-engineering Shakespeare, Johnson and subsequent variorum editors created a new category of difficulty based on the reader's cognitive challenge of navigating the page and interpreting its interface spaces. All readers of scholarly Shakespeare must determine a strategy of attention, as the eyes move from text to footnotes or glosses and back again in a potentially disruptive process. Johnson anticipated this cognitive difficulty by reflecting on the choice to either read the notes or ignore them, a process that applies equally to today's readers:

> Notes are often necessary, but they are necessary evils. Let him that is yet unacquainted with the powers of *Shakespeare*, and who desires to feel the highest pleasure that the drama can give, read every play, from the first scene to the last, with utter negligence of all his commentators. When his fancy is once on the wing, let it not stoop at correction by explanation ... And when the pleasures of novelty have ceased, let him attempt exactness, and read the commentators.
>
> *(lxix–lxx)*

I have already alluded to the more general difficulties associated with reading drama, and the need for readers to manage the imaginative challenges of translating printed play texts into a coherent reading experience. M. J. Kidnie suggests that "readers still need to be trained to engage with scripts not as fiction but specifically as drama—as dialogue existing in space and time" ("Text, Performance," 466). But the interface features of critical editions, influenced by Johnson's variorum-style division between the play above and notes below, create a new type of difficulty based on the need to scan and process multiple fields of information while potentially being overwhelmed by the cognitive load. In later variorum editions, the playtext itself is invaded by collations and annotations which take over the page; scholarly apparatus in this case may subsume dramatic content, as in the great variorum collection of Furness, or even on many pages of third series Ardens. The relationship between editorial intention, as set out in the preface, and interface design is described by Paul Eggert:

> The edition's condition as text-critical argument soon unfolds, for the editor, into the strategic question of the architecture and interface of the volume. The edition's internal organization, declared conventions, and page layout become the systematic embodiment of the editorial argument.
>
> *(97)*

In such cases, the editor's intention to mitigate difficulty by providing annotations and collations may result in a paradoxical increase in difficulty driven by the cognitive challenge of navigating the page. As Kidnie suggests, understanding the busy page of a critical edition requires a specialized kind of training, especially when pages are divided between text and notes. Some elements, such as the obscure editorial abbreviations found in collations, cannot be understood by the lay reader, as they are intended for trained specialists.

Whether Shakespeare is consumed through codex books, digital screens, or performance structures, users must engage with a technology through its associated interface, and that interface inevitably mediates cognition. Such a consideration echoes N. Katherine Hayles' call for a "media specific analysis" which recognizes "literature as the interplay between form and medium," observing how "the materiality of those embodiments interacts dynamically with linguistic, rhetorical, and literary practices to create the effects we call literature" (69–70). Such material interplays always require structures to make accessible the words, images, and dramatic phenomena which constitute a literary artifact, such as the plays of Shakespeare, and whereas editorial theory concerns itself mainly with questions related to the recovery, reconstruction and transmission of Shakespeare's plays, an interface approach begins with the assumption that the mediating designs and affordances that channel cognition necessarily impact access to content, and shape/direct interpretation and understanding.

The question of what constitutes an interface and its crucial relationship to media has not been a feature of Shakespeare studies, as such considerations have mostly been in the purview of human computer interaction (HCI) specialists, user experience (UX) analysts, program and page designers, and media theorists who may function outside of the usual range of theoretical inquiry. Branden Hookway reminds us that the etymology of interface "suggests how the interface may be opened up to theoretical description even as it resists such description": "The prefix *inter-* connotes relations that take place within an already bounded field, whether spatial or temporal. It pertains to an inward orientation, an interiority" (7). The "inter" in interface always implies a mediating position: "The interface would be defined according to its between-ness, its amongness, its duration-within" (8). By contrast, "the etymology of *face* points toward an outward orientation and an exteriority … it is also the means by which that thing may project itself forward and outside itself" (8). Hookway brings these two halves together in a consideration of the interface's simultaneous looks in both directions: "In combination, the interface is both an interiority confined by its bounding entities and a means of accessing, confronting and projecting into an exteriority. It is defined by its bounding entities at the same time that it defines them" (9). These paradoxical notions of interiority co-existing with exteriority are further complicated by the grammatical flexibility of interface functioning as both noun and verb. For example, it is possible to interface with an interface, to interconnect the human face and its senses with technologies which mediate a connection between a surface and something that exists seemingly beneath. This "site of contestation between human beings and machines" (ix) is further described by Hookway as "a form of relation that … only comes into being as these distinct entities enter into an active relation with one another" (4).

Hookway's emphasis on interface as "a form of relation" involving humans and machines is echoed by Alexander Galloway, who interrogates the idea of the interface as a doorway or window into something else, rather than just a border or surface: "an interface is not something that appears before you but rather is a gateway that opens up and allows passage to some place beyond" (30). Galloway also considers the problem of differentiating media from interface, as the two are often bound together, yet a close analysis reveals key distinguishing features. Echoing McLuhan, Galloway describes a remediated model of media "wherein media are essentially nothing but formal containers housing other pieces of media." The interface exists "at the point of transition between different mediatic layers within any nested system" (31), always functioning in a liminal capacity:

> The interface is the state of "being on the boundary." It is that moment where one significant material is understood as distinct from another significant material. In other words, an interface is not a thing, an interface is always an effect. It is always a process or a translation.
>
> *(33)*

Similar to Hookway's insistence that the interface allows "distinct entities" to be in "active relation with one another," Galloway captures this crucial interface function in a pithy dictum: "not media but mediation" (36). Thus, the door or window model of interface is inadequate to explain the embedded function of something that activates something else and exists as a part of the thing that it opens or sets in motion, leading Galloway to conclude that "the interface is a palimpsest" because it functions through a "reprocessing of some other media that came before," while "the layers of the palimpsest themselves are 'data' that must be interpreted" (45).

Johanna Drucker also resists a mechanistic theory of interface, eschewing the simplistic door or window analogy used by HCI specialists in favor of a humanist approach which substitutes "the idea of a 'user' for that of a 'subject' whose engagement with interface in a digital world could be modeled on the insights gained in the critical study of the subject in literary, media, and visual studies" ("Humanities Approach," 1). Drucker uses the graphical reading practices of Scott McCloud, the frame analysis theories of Erving Goffman, and constructivist theories of perception to question the intimate connection between "the future of reading and the nature of interface" (15): "Interface theory has to take into account the user/viewer, as a situated and embodied subject, and affordances of a graphical environment that mediates intellectual and cognitive activities" (8). In this, Drucker explicitly references reading and the active role of the interface in mediating the reader's ability to access information, calling the interface "a dynamic space, a zone in which reading takes place" (9). Like Galloway, Drucker sees the interface, not as a mechanistic operation, but as a threshold of access or potentiality: "Interface *is what we read* and *how we read* combined through engagement. Interface is a provocation to cognitive experience" (9). According to this model, the interface is not neutral: it is not simply a button that activates something or a frame that passively reveals: "We know that the structure of an interface *is* information, not merely a means of access to it" (9). Drucker applies this insight to the question of reading through or by means of an interface, arguing that "interface and its relation to reading has to be theorized as an environment in which varied behaviors of embodied and situated persons will be enabled differently according to its many affordances" (12).

While such ideas may be more obviously applied to reading hyper-mediated digital texts, the same principles apply to the codex book. Like digital screen interfaces, book pages display a number of objects which invite attention. According to Drucker, "The purpose of headers, footers, page numbers, margins, gutters, indentations, tables of contents, indices, and every other bit of text and paratext is to structure our reading" (*Graphesis*, 162). Both Johanna Drucker in *Graphesis* and Bonnie Mak in *How the Page Matters* examine the evolution of the page, from manuscript to codex to digital instantiations, and the ways in which the principles of organization and cognition transfer from interface to interface. Bonnie Mak's comments about page design are particularly instructive:

> The architecture of the page is thus a complex and responsive entanglement of platform, text, image, graphic markings, and blank space. The page hosts a changing interplay of form and content, of message and medium, of the conceptual and the physical, and this shifting tension is vital to the ability of the page to remain persuasive through time.
>
> *(5)*

The organization of page information is also entangled in the cultural systems which produce it, as Peter Stoicheff and Andrew Taylor remind us that page architectures "are related to the ideologies that otherwise structured the cultures that designed and read them" (4). Thus, the page reflects both designers' assumptions about users' requirements and the historical conditions of a particular moment which may include questions related to literacy and accessibility.

The theories of Hookway, Galloway, and Drucker are based on the experiences of human users who engage with or activate the interface, however it is imagined, understood, or engineered. Every interface activation is a cognitive act which requires the resources of mind and memory in order to generate an expected effect. When I use the trackpad to move the cursor-arrow and click the ABC icon at the top of my Word screen, I expect the activation of spell-checking processes, based on my memory that this is the correct sequence for a previously learned outcome. When I encounter a difficulty in trying to interpret a passage of Shakespeare while reading, I consult the notes at the bottom of the page interface in the expectation that I will find information to help mitigate the problem, before shifting attention back to the text. Thus, every engagement with the reading interface is a complex cognitive act which harnesses limited resources of memory and other forms of information processing and learning. Whether we understand the interface as a window, a gateway, container, or an effect, it mediates or activates Shakespeare in the reader's immediate experience—it is the design of information that presents and supports understanding and enjoyment. Correspondingly, when the interface is poorly designed, it can impede not only the reading experience but cognition itself.

Cognitive load theory (CLT) offers an explanation of why learning sometimes is impeded by poorly designed interfaces or instructional design elements. It considers how the cognitive capacity of working memory (formerly called short-term memory) "is limited, so that if a learning task requires too much capacity, learning will be hampered. The recommended remedy is to design instructional systems that optimize the use of working memory capacity and avoid cognitive overload" (de Jong 105). The "human cognitive architecture" described by CLT "refers to the manner in which the components that constitute human cognition such as working and long-term memory are organized" (Sweller et al. 15). Kalyuga describes how the interplay of working memory and long-term memory function together to structure learning and facilitate understanding. Working memory has a "limited capacity and duration" because "we can consciously process no more than a few items at a time for no longer than a few seconds. If these limits are exceeded, working memory becomes overloaded and learning inhibited" (1). Long-term memory, on the other hand, "acts as a very large store of information" contained in schemas, "a cognitive construct that permits us to classify multiple elements of information into a single element according to the manner in which the multiple elements are used" (Sweller et al. 22). For example, when we are learning to read, we begin by processing the sounds associated with individual letters: "With increasing practice, we acquire automated schemas for individual letters but still may need to consciously process the groups of letter that constitute words" (23). Thus, learning can be understood as an interaction between the limited resources of working memory and an unlimited long-term memory, as successful instruction uses the resources of working memory to "increase the store of knowledge in long-term memory" and its schemas (24).

Cognitive load theory has developed a classification system which recognizes three main types of cognitive load imposed on working memory: (1) intrinsic cognitive load; (2) extraneous cognitive load; and (3) germane cognitive load. Intrinsic cognitive load "is defined by the intrinsic complexity of information that is to be learned. It depends on the interactivity of elements" (Hollender et al. 1279). Such interacting elements are features "that must be processed simultaneously in working memory because they are logically related. An element is anything that needs to be learned or processed" (Sweller et al. 58). Hollender gives the example of learning a foreign language as a task with high element interactivity, "as it requires an understanding of different parts of speech and their sequencing" (1279).

Extraneous cognitive load "is caused by an inappropriate presentation of the learning material or by requiring students to perform activities that are irrelevant to learning" (1279). Finite working memory resources can be consumed by extraneous features of a poorly designed instructional system or interface, interfering with learning outcomes. Finally, germane cognitive load refers to "working memory resources that are devoted to information that is relevant or germane to learning" (Sweller et al. 57). Germane cognitive load, therefore, recognizes the "effortful construction and automation of organized knowledge structures or schemas and the corresponding cognitive activities that directly contribute to learning" (Kalyuga 3). For the purposes of this discussion, extraneous cognitive load can be considered as a "bad" load because it diverts "cognitive resources to activities that are irrelevant to learning," whereas "good" intrinsic load "is associated with processing the essential interacting elements of information" (3). As Sweller concludes, "The primary, though not sole, aim of cognitive load theory has been to devise instructional procedures that reduce extraneous cognitive load and so decrease the working memory resources that must be devoted to information that is extraneous to learning" (68).

Cognitive load theory includes a number of observed effects, defined as "an experimental demonstration that an instructional procedure based on cognitive load theory principles facilitates learning or problem solving compared to a more traditional procedure" (87). The cognitive load effects most relevant to a discussion of Shakespeare and interface are the split-attention effect and the expertise reversal effect, although future scholars may wish to revisit the other effects to see whether they can be productively applied. According to Sweller et al., "split-attention occurs when learners are required to split their attention between at least two sources of information that have been separated either spatially or temporally" (111). For example, understanding a chart with explanatory components on another part of the page requires significant working memory resources in order to hold and consolidate two unlinked pieces of information required for learning, resulting in extraneous cognitive load. Roodenrys et al. observe that CLT research has helped to develop "alternative instructional formats that physically locate related information and join them together in order to avoid extensive searching and matching and thus reducing extraneous load" (878). The expertise reversal effect acknowledges that information which may be essential for novice learners has the potential to generate extraneous load for expert learners:

> As learners acquire more expertise in a specific area of knowledge, the information or activities that previously were essential may become redundant, causing increased levels of extraneous cognitive load. As a consequence, instructional technique effective for novices may be become ineffective for more expert learners due to redundancy. Conversely, techniques ineffective for novices may become effective for more expert learners. These changes in the relative effectiveness of instructional procedures according to levels of expertise underlie the expertise reversal effect.
>
> *(Sweller et al. 156)*

Anyone familiar with Human Computer Interaction and User Experience principles will immediately recognize the influence and applicability of CLT to the design of effective user interfaces. In fact, the idea of anticipating and meeting the needs of multiple users and levels of expertise is at the heart of all three approaches. As Hollender et al. observe, "the fact that human working memory can hold only a limited number of items at a certain time is common knowledge in user-interface design," resulting in the desire to "decrease cognitive load for users as much as possible" (1281). As we shall see in the following examples of Shakespeare interfaces, the extraneous cognitive load of the page or screen is often present for readers, as Shakespeare interface designers must contend with high element interactivity, often resulting in split-attention effects. At the same time, expert users who have been trained to manage the cognitive load may adapt to the split-attention interface which is no longer an extraneous feature of their working memory.

Application of CLT to Shakespeare and Interface

In the final section of this chapter, I use cognitive load theory to discuss how select Shakespeare interface designs manage Shakespearean difficulty, offering some speculations about the ways in which a reader's working memory and long-term memory engage with the Shakespeare page or screen. This distinction between Shakespeare (paper) page interfaces and Shakespeare (computer, tablet or phone) screen interfaces—between reading a codex book and reading a digital, online version—is crucial, as the interface differently mediates and manages the cognitive load based on the affordances of the particular medium.[5] For example, affordances which are possible in a digital format—such as a button which activates a hypermedia link—cannot function in codex book. This interaction between interface features and media affordances must always condition the reading experience. E-readers, such as the Amazon Kindle, provide a useful example of interface limitations linked to a medium, as the Kindle interface artificially simulates the spatiality of the book and its pages by estimating the time required to finish a chapter, indicated by a small field at the bottom left of the screen interface. If the reader wants to navigate back to a remembered page which has not been previously bookmarked, then he or she must navigate to the Table of Contents and hope that a chapter title will offer a location clue or else engage in a frustrating process of navigating backwards or forwards, screen by screen, in order to find the desired material. While the minimal Kindle interface works well for the simple demands of reading fiction, it does not support the more complex processing needs of scholarly reading which requires controlled movement between separated pages. Codex books, on the other hand, are a fast, efficient, and proprioceptive medium, as hands and eyes experience the book's material gestalt and manipulate its physical information spaces with practiced ease (e.g. with two fingers in different sections), or the book's binding may simply open fortuitously to the previously consulted page.

Notwithstanding interface differences linked to discrete media affordances, certain interface features have evolved across all Shakespeare media to mitigate a reader's experience of difficulty, most obvious in the dynamic relationship between text and paratextual annotations. If the reader did not require supplementary information, then the playtext could be enjoyed independently without supports, the reader presumably encountering no major difficulties to disrupt the reading. But because Shakespeare poses so many vocabulary and interpretive challenges to modern readers, paratextual information has become a requirement for structuring comprehension and supporting a complex learning task, resulting in the normalization of cognitively busy interfaces in most Shakespeare editions. The four main paratextual components which have been a feature of the Shakespeare interface since the Tonson editions are (1) explanatory notes; (2) word glosses (often incorporated with the notes); (3) editorial collations; and (4) act, scene, and line numbers or other navigational features.

A quick scan of a typical codex Shakespeare page reveals familiar interface divisions: the playtext is featured in the main block (either single or double column) with footnotes usually underneath and line numbers on the side. Collations may be placed below the footnotes (as in the third series Ardens), immediately following the playtext, at the back of the book in a "textual variants" section, or even in a separate volume, such as *William Shakespeare: A Textual Companion* which provides detailed notes to accompany *The Complete Oxford Shakespeare*

(1986), or they may left out entirely. Act, scene, and line numbers may occur in a running header with the play title, while line numbers are typically placed on the right or left side of the page in five-line increments. Marginal spaces may be used for word glosses parallel to a marked word in the text, as in the *Norton Shakespeare*, or for more extensive information, such as the detailed marginal performance notes in *The New Oxford Shakespeare* (Modern Critical Edition). One assumes the need for the same paratextual content in digital versions, but the interface properties of computers and tablets offer the potential for a more dynamic activation based on the interactive affordances of the digital medium. For example, the static codex book interface places paratextual annotations in fixed page spaces: notes can be found at the bottom, in the margin, on a facing page, or at the back, as endnotes. However, in digital versions, the annotations can be activated by a mouse click or touch which may cause them to hover temporarily in a textbox beside or above the passage in question. Likewise, word glosses in digital texts can be activated simply by clicking on or hovering over a problematic word, instantly revealing a definition in a proximate textbox. In fact, the permutations and combinations of digital interfaces offer much more flexibility and design possibilities than the fixed paper book page.

The main Shakespeare interface fields—playtext, notes, glosses, and collations—are accessed on the basis of immediate needs. In reading a codex book, the reader activates the page's interface fields through shifts of attention and ocular focus. Typically, a passage is read serially until a difficulty or interpretive question arises to stop the process, and then the reader's focus may shift away from the playtext to a paratextual field where the reader hopes to find supplementary information to support reading comprehension. At the very least, the paratextual symbol will create a decision point which may briefly interrupt reading fluency, even for a micro-second. According to cognitive load theory, the problem passage and associated difficulty must be held in working memory while the note or gloss is consulted. Reading the annotation requires the user to hold both fields in working memory, possibly by shifting attention back and forth (up and down) between the source text and the note until the information is assimilated temporarily into working memory or until the explanation is integrated into a long-term memory schema.

The split-attention required for this maneuver arises when a lengthy and dense passage defies the reader's comprehension. How can the reader hold both the dense passage and its paratextual explanation in working memory when the two elements are spatially separated? A similar problem arose when I recently taught *Paradise Lost*, a text which holds a particularly high degree of difficulty. I chose the Oxford World Classics, *John Milton: The Major Works*, (Milton et al. 2008) because it was inexpensive, but I neglected to inspect the book prior to assigning it for my class. Unfortunately, my students and I soon discovered that the extensive notes for *Paradise Lost* in this edition are located at the back of the book. While the split-attention effect is problematic for separated text and notes on the same page, it is almost impossible to manage when the notes are relegated to the back pages. Students must either place a bookmark or finger at the site of the endnotes and navigate back and forth between pages or print the endnotes so that they may be more physically proximate to the passage under consideration. In the case of reading *Paradise Lost* and its significant requirements for reader support, the decision to locate notes at the back creates an extraneous cognitive load that consumes huge resources of working memory. Chuck Zerby, in his history of footnotes, describes this process in detail:

> First you must fix in your mind the number of the footnote, say 27, then you have to remember the page number on which footnote 27 appears, say page 85. Then you must turn to the back of the book, trying to keep your place with an inserted

> finger, and scan page after page until you discover one headed "Footnotes for Pages 81–107." By this time you have forgotten the footnote number so you must scramble back to the original page and seek it out again.
>
> (2)

Zerby observes that the decision to place notes at the back of the book may be chosen by publishers because it is cheaper to produce such books compared to the complex interface features of displaying footnotes on the same page as the primary text, leading to unusable print versions with a significant extraneous cognitive load based on the split-attention effect.

Sometimes the reader is invited to play a guessing game concerning whether the footnote explanation below the playtext will be proffered to match the reader's current difficulty, as many editions do not indicate the expectation of a note with a superscript number. Instead, the common practice (e.g. third series Arden, New Cambridge, New Oxford, and Oxford World's Classics) is to tag footnotes with line numbers while offering nothing explicit in the playtext (such as bolding or superscript numbers) to indicate the expectation of a footnote. Presumably, the reader is invited to remember the line number when a significant difficulty is encountered and to hold both the nature of the difficulty and the content of a potentially lengthy passage in working memory while shifting attention to the note, usually at the bottom of the page (the Folger Shakespeare Library versions offer annotations on the facing page, while the Broadview and Norton versions include superscript numbers in the playtext field matched to matching numbers in the footnotes). Following a line number, the third series Arden footnotes begin with a bolded keyword which helps to signal the expectation of a specific word gloss or as a mnemonic link to the problematic passage above. Presumably the bolded footnote keyword matches the same word held in the reader's working memory, and its bolded interface allows the reader to remember the difficulty which prompted the shift of attention. The split-attention effect remains in play, as information is presented in two separated fields that require significant working memory resources, resulting in extraneous cognitive load.

Certainly, the "as above, so below" cognitive footnote formula has worked for generations of readers who have learned how to activate and hold the two main interface fields in working memory. However, many times I have had to read and re-read the playtext and explanatory annotations, moving my attention up and down and back up again, as I try to remember how the passage has been glossed while reading below the playtext, and then hold that interpretation in working memory when I shift focus back to the playtext in order to see whether I can apply the explanation to solve the interpretive dilemma. In some instances, I have shifted attention to the footnotes, only to be disappointed that the editor has not anticipated that my difficulty warranted an annotation, but because the edition did not use superscript numbers in the playtext interface, I had no way of knowing whether a numerically linked explanation would be available below until I interrupted my reading and shifted attention.

In a codex interface, book designers have few choices about where to place the notes: either below the playtext, in the margin, on a facing page or at the back. But as I have already indicated, the digital medium and its many interface features offer a much broader range of dynamic possibilities: the annotation may be displayed in forms which are much more proximate to the difficulty found in the playtext, such as a textbox that opens beside or above the playtext field. In such a case, the integral cognitive load is managed more efficiently because the resources of limited working memory are not strained by split attention. Likewise, annotations may be color-keyed to levels of difficulty, differentiating the information requirements of novice or experienced readers as a way of mitigating the expertise reversal effect.

While acknowledging that designers of digital Shakespeare interfaces can leverage the many interactive affordances of a more flexible medium, the refractive properties of the screen and its problematic ergonomic fit may compromise ease of comprehension for some readers. For the same reason that I print many PDF articles because I do not like reading complex works on a computer screen, readers may avoid digital versions of Shakespeare plays because of the reading experience. For example, I have never read an entire Shakespeare play in an online or digital version, either on a monitor, laptop screen, or iPad. Part of the problem has to do with eye fatigue caused by the backlit screen compared to the easy reflectivity of a paper book illuminated by a lamp, overhead light, or window and held at multiple angles on lap, in hand, or on a desk surface. While the interface of the digital edition may offer ways of overcoming extraneous cognitive load caused by split attention, its problematic optics may deter certain readers. Likewise, my paper editions of Shakespeare, particularly the ones that I use for teaching, are heavily annotated with my own marginal comments in ink or pencil, much like early modern readers who routinely marked texts with notes and commentary.[6] This customized interface—personal annotations which I superimpose on the text interface in my own hand—adds a layer of information directly to the book page that helps me to navigate and mitigate my own cognitive load. Certainly the Apple Pencil and iPad combination can replicate the palimpsestic graphic book marginalia, and for some readers such personal digital notes can complement the affordances of the digital interface.

In all of these examples, the interface functions as a mediating cognitive structure which allows readers to access Shakespeare. Whatever metaphor we employ to describe the function of the interface—whether we look through it to find Shakespeare "underneath" or participate in an interface effect which activates discrete features—the interface, operating within the constraints of a particular medium, channels cognition. While designers of reading interfaces try to anticipate the general or specialized needs of users, they may not always pay sufficient attention to the cognitive load required to make Shakespeare meaningful, making extraneous demands on the reader's attention. It is important to remember that Shakespeare versions always assume a target audience, designing the interface and marketing their texts selectively. I would never, for example, assign a third series Arden to an undergraduate class, as the extensive annotations and collations, sometimes taking up most of the page, would probably get in the way of reading comprehension. Such a complicated interface is not conducive to fluent reading, but it beautifully supports the requirements of researchers and expert readers who have been trained to manage the cognitive load or have acquired specialized expertise through practice and memory development. The *Norton Shakespeare*, on the other hand, obviously targeted to undergraduate students, offers a readable single column text with word glosses in the right margin and a carefully selected number of footnotes, striking a balance between playtext readability and requirements for consulting supplementary information.

In all of these examples the interface performs a mediating function through which the reader engages with text and paratext, shifting attention to specialized information spaces or activating digital affordances in a complex cognitive dance that moves at the speed of thought. Hookway's notions of interiority and exteriority are realized in every cognitive engagement with the Shakespeare interface, as annotations displayed inside the page frame point to documents beyond the text, and both exist in active relation to one another and to the user. Galloway's theory of the palimpsest captures the idea of a form containing traces of something that went before it, such as notes which point to an important spelling variant or to source text and editorial variations. The interface represents these complex layers, not by superimposing one version on another in a series of transparencies (like the Hinman collator), or by physically juxtaposing one edition beside another (although this may be possible to display in a digital version), but by using an interface shorthand, such as collation abbreviations which allow the reader to imagine these differences existing in palimpsestic layers outside of the immediate experience of the modernized text. Drucker's insights about the relation between what we read and how we read and her instructions that "all the graphic features of the book have functions" (*Graphesis*, 162) are particularly instructive here, as interface signs condition the reader's engagement with every feature of Shakespeare including paratextual structures that complicate the reading and make it more intelligible.

Every time we open a book or engage a screen version of Shakespeare with the intention to read, we are connecting the many cognitive mechanisms of senses and mind to a particular Shakespeare interface, anticipating a functional fit and a manageable cognitive load. Our eyes must interpret and operate the interface possibilities signified in the organization of information and expected affordances. The better the cognitive fit for a particular reading expectation, the smoother and more satisfying the experience. The interface of a high school Shakespeare like the Cambridge School Shakespeare, with its facing-page lessons keyed to teaching problematic performance and textual elements in the accompanying playtext, will not serve the purposes of a professor or graduate student engaged in textual studies, and the interfaces of editions pitched to different markets reflect this expectation. The interface matters because it profoundly conditions the reading experience and information requirements, as one size does not fit all. And while digital Shakespeare reading interfaces can be customized, so that the element interactivities are better integrated to reduce extraneous cognitive load, if readers are averse to the optics of backlit monitors and tablets, they will not be used by some demographics. Likewise, codex books may be ignored by Shakespeare readers who became so familiar and fluent with digital interfaces that they eschew the static affordances of books as being insufficiently flexible. Future research might investigate the media and interface reading preferences of undergraduate Shakespeare students in order to determine how they are managing the cognitive load of popular print editions or whether they would feel more engaged reading digital versions from laptop or tablet screens. If the reading of Shakespeare still matters pedagogically, then publishers and designers must seriously consider how the interface—on page or screen—can be better aligned with cognition and learning to maximize pleasure and mitigate difficulty.

Notes

1 See Manarin 1:

> Students cannot, we hear and sometimes say, read well enough to master disciplinary knowledge. Faculty members from different areas and institutions identify student difficulty with reading as a major barrier to learning. They talk about a necessary 'transition' to college reading and college reading expectations, a transition with which many students struggle.

2 See Kidnie "Text," 460:

> Roman Ingarden describes dramatic text as consisting of the unity and interaction of two discrete, unequal elements: the *haupttext* (dialogue) and the *nebentext* (side text). The *nebentext* includes those features that distinguish drama from a genre such as prose fiction, the most important being stage directions; although as essential as dialogue to the coherence of the script, the *nebentext* is ancillary, as the term suggests, to the *haupttext*. Ingarden's terminology has proven influential partly because it articulates and systematizes a commonly shared perception of dramatic text.

3 See Kidnie "The Staging," 158–177, for an examination of the configuration of stage directions on the page and their cognitive impact:

> A playwright cannot tell the reader every detail of the theatrical and fictional spaces, every actor's tone of voice and gestures, the build and costuming of each character ... There will always be elements that are left undescribed, that a reader may choose to fix in a particular way in his or her imagination—or indeed, may choose to leave unfixed, open. Comprehensiveness of direction is impossible, and so we are cast back to what, as readers, we might consider an acceptable 'bare minimum' of direction in a play-text. (159)

4 For a discussion of the intersection of stage and page, see Wright 159–169; Berger 69–83.

5 Bruce R. Smith offers a phenomenological consideration of digital and print Shakespeares:

> The ideal state of knowledge, it seems to me, is one that combines the accessibility and search capability of electronic texts with the multidimensionality of the books and manuscripts that the digital images represent ... On the computer screen I see a fragment of experience, part of a larger, more elusive whole, and I remain conscious of what has been lost as well as what has been made so readily available. (30)

6 Sherman reminds us that the habit of marking books in early modern reading culture was primarily a way of managing memory requirements: "Such annotations are, then, first and foremost, an aid to the memory" (4).

References

Berger, Harry. *Imaginary Audition: Shakespeare on Stage and Page*. U of California P, 1989.

Berger, Thomas L., and Sonia Massai, editors. *Paratexts in English Printed Drama to 1642*. Cambridge UP, 2014.

de Jong, Ton. "Cognitive Load Theory, Educational Research, and Instructional Design: Some Food for Thought." *Instructional Science*, vol. 38, no. 2, 2010, pp. 105–134.

Drucker, Johanna. "Humanities Approaches to Interface Theory." *Culture Machine*, vol. 12, 2011, pp. 1–20.

Drucker, Johanna. *Graphesis: Visual Forms of Knowledge Production*. Harvard UP, 2014.

Eggert, Paul. "Apparatus, Text, Interface: How to Read a Printed Critical Edition." *The Cambridge Companion to Textual Scholarship*, edited by Neil Fraistat and Julia Flanders, Cambridge UP, 2013, pp. 97–118.

Farmer, Alan B., and Zachary Lesser. "The Popularity of Playbooks Revisited." *Shakespeare Quarterly*, vol. 56, no. 1, 2005, pp. 1–32.

Galloway, Alexander R. *The Interface Effect*. Polity P, 2012.

Genette, Gérard. *Paratexts*. Cambridge UP, 1997.

Hackel, Heidi Brayman. "The 'Great Variety' of Readers and Early Modern Reading Practices." *A Companion to Shakespeare*, edited by David Scott Kastan, Blackwell, 1999, pp. 139–157.

Hayles, N. Katherine. "Print Is Flat, Code Is Deep: The Importance of Media-Specific Analysis." *Poetics Today*, vol. 25, no, 1, 2004, pp. 67–90.

Hollender, Nina, *et al.* "Integrating Cognitive Load Theory and Concepts of Human–computer Interaction." *Computers in Human Behavior*, vol. 26, no. 6, 2010, pp. 1278–1288.

Hookway, Branden. *Interface*. MIT P, 2014.

Johnson, Samuel. "Mr. Johnson's preface to his edition of Shakespear's plays." London, 1765. *Eighteenth Century Collections Online*. Available at: link.gale.com/apps/doc/CW0114034679/ECCO?u=mtroyalc&sid=bookmark-ECCO&xid=150ad5bc&pg=67.

Kalyuga, Slava. "Cognitive Load Theory: How Many Types of Load Does It Really Need?" *Educational Psychology Review*, vol. 23, no. 1, 2011, pp. 1–19.

Kidnie, Margaret Jane. "Text, Performance, and the Editors: Staging Shakespeare's Drama." *Shakespeare Quarterly*, vol. 51, no. 4, 2000, pp. 456–473.

Kidnie, Margaret Jane. "The Staging of Shakespeare's Drama in Print Editions." *Textual Performances*, edited by Lukas Erne and Margaret Jane Kidnie, Cambridge UP, 2004, pp. 158–177.

Lynch, Jack. "The Dignity of an Ancient: Johnson Edits the Editors." *Comparative Excellence: New Essays on Shakespeare and Johnson*, edited by Eric Rasmussen, and Aaron Santesso, AMS P, 2007, pp. 97–114.

Mak, Bonnie. *How the Page Matters*. U of Toronto P, 2012.

Manarin, Karen, *et al. Critical Reading in Higher Education: Academic Goals and Social Engagement*. Indiana UP, 2015.

Massai, Sonia. "Early Readers." *The Oxford Handbook of Shakespeare*, edited by Arthur F. Kinney, Oxford UP, 2012, pp. 143–161.

Milton, John, *The Major Works*. Edited by Stephen Orgel and Jonathan Goldberg, Oxford UP, 2008.
Murphy, Andrew. *Shakespeare in Print*. Cambridge UP, 2003.
Roodenrys, Kylie, *et al.* "Managing One's Own Cognitive Load When Evidence of Split Attention Is Present." *Applied Cognitive Psychology*, vol. 26, no. 6, 2012, pp. 878–886.
Shakespeare, William. *The Riverside Shakespeare*, edited by G. Blakemore Evans, Houghton Mifflin, 1974.
Shakespeare, William. *The Norton Shakespeare*. Edited by Stephen Greenblatt, *et al.*, 3rd ed., Norton, 2015.
Shakespeare, William. *The New Oxford Shakespeare: Modern Critical Edition*. Edited by Gary Taylor, *et al.*, Oxford UP, 2016.
Shakespeare, William, and Charlton Hinman. *The First Folio of Shakespeare*. 2nd ed., Norton, 1996.
Sherman, William H. *Used Books: Marking Readers in Renaissance England*. U of Pennsylvania P, 2010.
Smith, Bruce R. "Getting Back to the Library, Getting Back to the Body." *Shakespeare and the Digital World*, edited by Christie Carson and Peter Kirwan, Cambridge UP, 2014, pp. 24–32.
Smith, Emma. *Shakespeare's First Folio*. Oxford UP, 2016.
Stoicheff, Peter, and Andrew Taylor, editors. *The Future of the Page*. U of Toronto P, 2004.
Sweller, John, *et al.Cognitive Load Theory*. 1st ed., Springer, 2011.
Walsh, Marcus. *Shakespeare, Milton, and Eighteenth-Century Literary Editing: The Beginnings of Interpretative Scholarship*. Cambridge UP, 1997.
Walsh, Marcus. "Editing and Publishing Shakespeare." *Shakespeare in the Eighteenth Century*, edited by Fiona Ritchie and Peter Sabor, Cambridge UP, 2012, pp. 21–40.
Wells, Stanley, *et al.Oxford Shakespeare: William Shakespeare: A Textual Companion*. Oxford UP, 1987.
Wolf, Maryanne, and Catherine J. Stoodley. *Reader, Come Home: The Reading Brain in a Digital World*. 1st ed., Harper, 2018.
Worthen, William B. "Reading the Stage." *Shakespeare Bulletin*, vol. 25, no. 4, 2007, pp. 69–83.
Wright, George T. "An Almost Oral Art: Shakespeare's Language on Stage and Page." *Shakespeare Quarterly*, vol. 43, no. 2, 1992, pp. 159–169.
Zerby, Chuck. *The Devil's Details: A History of Footnotes*. 1st ed., Touchstone, 2003.

2

SHAKESPEARE AND VIRTUAL REALITY

Rebecca W. Bushnell and Michael Ullyot

Ever since Herbert Beerbohm Tree inaugurated Shakespeare on film (*King John*, 1899), and Orson Welles' "Mercury Theater on the Air" adapted Shakespeare for radio, recording technologies have transformed audiences' cognitive experience of Shakespearean performance. Film substituted the camera's eye for the spectator's, and the framed screen for the three-dimensional space of the theater. Radio, in turn, brought the disembodied voices of actors into domestic spaces. Virtual Reality (VR) platforms have now begun to extend this remediation, extending beyond analog sound and image to immerse the spectator in a digital rendering of a 360-degree performance. VR, even more than film, has a natural affinity with theater. As Sita Popat observes:

> Theater has always been a space of virtuality. The action on the stage exists as neither what it is actually nor what it is pretending to be; instead, it bridges the actual and the imaginary to create a virtual world in which performers and viewers are complicit.
>
> *(357)*[1]

With the recent trend toward immersion and audience engagement in live theatrical performance (see Machon, 2013; Biggin, 2017), the analogy between theater and VR has become even more apt. While it may appear more like film in its reliance on recording and projecting image and sound, a VR performance is in fact more like immersive theater, insofar as it is unbound by a frame or a single point of view, and as it summons up an illusion of a space that the spectator inhabits beyond the "real world."

This chapter explores aspects of the present and future of Shakespeare performance in VR, investigating the interface of theater and VR technology that mediates a spectator's engagement with a recorded performance. While there are many ways to approach interaction and engagement in a VR context, we focus on the ways in which VR constructs the experience of location in space and the negotiation of audience perspective. After considering the relevance of the interface for discussing VR performance and its production of audience immersion and engagement, we briefly review the history of immersion and the uses of framed and unframed space as an aspect of stage performance of Shakespeare, from early modern performances at the Globe Theatre to non-linear spatial theater like Punchdrunk's *Sleep No More*. Since VR uses cameras, we then turn our attention to the ways in which,

DOI: 10.4324/9780367821722-4

both in general and in Shakespeare adaptations, the medium of conventional film negotiates space and audience perception at the interface of the framed screen. We then turn to an analysis of the most complete, widely available version of a VR Shakespeare play to date: *Hamlet 360: Thy Father's Spirit* (2019), a VR performance produced by the Commonwealth Shakespeare Company in Boston in collaboration with Google and the VR company Sensorium. Although VR is a medium that relies on the technology of the camera's eye, in VR performance the interface of human and machine frees spectators from the screen frame and appears to move them into a central position in stage and story, with important implications for spectators' sense of their agency.

Theater, Virtual Reality, and the Interface

As Branden Hookway has reminded us:

> while the interface might seem to be a form of technology, it is more properly a form of relating to technology, and so constitutes a relation that is already given, to be composed of the combined activities of human and machine.
>
> (3)

The experience of VR is produced by complex technology involving (at minimum) a 360-degree camera recording live-action spaces and events and rendered in a virtual-reality headset worn over the audience's eyes using stereoscopic screens to give the illusion of three-dimensional space.[2] It is illusory because the cameras, arranged concentrically, actually capture contiguous shots with overlapping edges, before software stitches them together into a seamless continuity. A spectator's involvement in virtual space happens through the mediation of technology that connects the actions in the play space—the "real-world" space in which their body (or at least their head) moves—and movement in the virtual space, as perceived through a headset. This engagement in VR may merely invite the spectator into a passive 360-degree viewing experience, entering a recreated illusion of another place or world, as if entering into a film—but it may also offer the possibility to interact with that world. VR can thus provide the thrill of inhabiting a world in which one can look and even manipulate or create now realities. In Gabriella Giannachi's words:

> Virtual reality offers fluid and open forms that allow for the viewer simultaneously to be inside and outside the work of art … So, not only do the viewers become part of the larger narrative of virtual reality; they also become actively involved in it. In other words, they do not so much perform in it as perform it.
>
> (123)

In this sense, the human-machine relationship that Hookway defines as the interface appears to dissolve in the medium of VR, through the experience of sensory immersion.

However, the world generated by VR technology is hardly unconstrained. Hookway also defines the interface as a site and relationship that involve control and power, insofar as "agency, or the will or means to action, is a capacity at once mediated by and produced upon the interface" (18). The spectator who enters into a VR world may experience the illusion of freedom, whether in being free to view an event or object from various orientations, or in interacting in virtual space by manipulating objects and causing events in the virtual world. As Jeremy Bailenson has commented, it may feel like "virtual reality is a democracy. You can look wherever you want, whenever you want. In film, the director is a dictator, one who controls your senses, and forces you to look where she wants, when she wants you to" (location 3039). However, in VR, that viewpoint is always bounded by the conditions of the technologies that capture and represent the performance. In Hookway's term, a sense of agency is produced at the interface constituted by VR theater, but it is also directed by that interface.

The VR experiences that this chapter addresses are 360-degree films of discontinuous performances, edited into a seemingly continuous flow. These performances unfold in a seemingly real environment, not a digital one in which sets and props are computer-generated and where actors wear motion-capture suits. Aside from obscuring the camera tripod and other production necessities like the overhead lighting rig, that is the extent of the software's work. This is not *Hamlet on the Holodeck*, as Janet Murray titles her seminal 1997 book on cyberspatial narratives. In those environments the audience can wander freely, examining and interacting with digital objects and characters from multiple orientations. In VR recordings of live performance in contrast, the viewer's position is fixed, and the view is limited to the sides of objects and actors that they present. However, viewers can look in any direction, much as the members of a theater audience can.

While the technology might thus be seen to define the possibilities of VR for immersive theatrical performance, theater itself has the power to shape the VR environment and our experience of it, bringing its time-tested methods to this new medium. Theater designers, producers, actors, and directors know how to orient audiences toward the staged performances using design cues like lighting, sound, and seat orientation. Myriad design choices and social cues direct the audience's attention toward the stage, all of which depend on both theater's design choices and our co-identification with other spectators. However, because we currently experience VR as solitary spectators, only the implicit and explicit design features of the experience and its interface can nudge us to look at the action. As a frameless medium, VR lacks film's ability to force the spectator's eye to look at events and objects in limited space. Theater's ability to compel an audience's attention is thus key to designing virtual environments where the viewer's eye might wander.

Theatrical Space and Immersion

In his view of past and present theater seen from 1968, Peter Brook begins with space: "I can take any empty space and call it a bare stage," he writes: "A man walks across this empty space whilst someone else is watching him, and this is all that is needed for an act of theater to be engaged" (9). In this most basic definition, theater requires an actor and spectator located in a defined space. However, no space is ever truly empty, and the architectural and design features of theater space constitute interfaces that have the power to construct a complex relationship between the watcher and the watched; amphitheaters, platform stages, proscenium arch theaters, and black boxes all differently direct audience point of view and either divide or connect spectators with staged actions.

In his lifetime Shakespeare would have seen and acted in plays performed in very different and often elaborately designed spaces. He may have seen the revivals of the mystery plays still performed in the streets of England, as the performances moved on wagons throughout the towns. His own plays were acted in the spacious outdoor amphitheaters, to be sure, but also in the indoor, more intimate spaces of the Blackfriars Theatre, Middle Temple Hall, royal courts, aristocratic households, and more modest venues when the acting companies took to the road during times of plague.

Each of these places defined multifaceted relationships between actors and audience, with the audience itself not uniformly positioned. With their capacity of several thousand spectators, the outdoor theaters necessitated an acting style and blocking that communicated broadly and widely to differently located groups. The groundlings who clustered at the edges of the platform stage stood closer to the action and were more mobile than the spectators in more distant galleries (while Tiffany Stern argues that those in the galleries could move as well [211–16]). The indoor theater allowed all spectators to be closer to the stage action (while a different angles), because of the smaller size of the space itself. John Russell Brown claims that those theaters' "low-capacity and end-on stages," "with their more direct and intimate visual relationship with audiences, enabled spectators to pick up clues in the writing that are lost on a larger, three-sided stage" (115). In both the indoor and outdoor theaters, spectators might also be seated on the stage themselves, both watchers and watched, a phenomenon alluded to the chaos created in Francis Beaumont's *The Knight of the Burning Pestle*, when a grocer, his wife, and his apprentice ascend to the stage to join in the action. In all of these performance sites, the platform stage and the visibility of the audience must have created a strong sense of the theater as a shared space, what the former director of Shakespeare's Globe Theatre in London, Mark Rylance, calls an "imaginary space between audience and actors" shaped by theater architecture (Shaughnessy n.p., citing Rylance 171, 175).

That communality and a sense of at least an imaginary immersion were largely lost with the rise of the proscenium arch, which created both a division between audience and actors and a frame in which to enclose the spectacle. Later the audience itself became enveloped in darkness, thus increasingly invisible to the players. Much of Western theater practice of the past half-century has been devoted to undoing this division and the structure of the frame, redefining stage spaces to reconnect actors and audience and to expand the extent of the playing area. More radically, in the last 60 years, actors and directors have experimented with versions of a truly immersive theater, reimagining theatrical space and, within that space, the spectator's role as actor. Richard Schechner made that reinvention of space one of the axioms of his new "environmental" theater: "The bifurcation of space must be ended. The final exchange between performers and audience is the exchange of space, spectators as scene-makers as well as scene-watchers" (Machon 32, citing Schechner xxvi).

How has this redefinition of the theater space affected Shakespearean performance? Most notably, stages designed to recreate the early modern outdoor and indoor theaters have risen around the world. One can also experience Shakespeare in a multitude of alternative venues, from public parks to deconsecrated churches. However, while in many places the frame of the proscenium arch has been broken up as much as the architecture of older theaters allows, all of these venues have still largely replicated the spatial division between immobile spectators trapped in the "watcher's" space and the mobile actors on a stage. For most directors of classic theater performance, fully eroding the boundary between spectator and player has been a step too far.

The most notable experiment in a fully immersive or "environmental" Shakespeare has been Punchdrunk's production of *Sleep No More*, an adaptation of *Macbeth* filtered through a film-noir and Hitchcockian aesthetic. This wildly successful production takes place in an old warehouse recreated as the McKittrick Hotel, a six-floor building of perhaps a hundred rooms through which silent and masked spectators wander, following the actors while also exploring the elaborately decorated sets. Audience members are free to engage with *Sleep No More* in whatever way they want, albeit with consequences. They are not permitted to speak or interact with the actors, unless invited into a private or one-on-one encounter in special locked areas. But for the most part, the hundred or so rooms are open to everyone.

To experience *Sleep No More* as a narrative connected to the plot of *Macbeth*, one must follow a character or several throughout the building's multiple floors, and in so doing, join the crowd that follows them. There is a randomness to these encounters, which *Sleep No*

More tries to make up for by having each character repeat the same actions (more or less) in three one-hour loops. Following a character with the crowd does enforce a kind of forward movement in space, in contrast to free exploration. Felix Barrett, one of the production's directors and designers, has claimed that there is no one way to "experience" *Sleep No More*: "Some people choose to explore the space methodically, while others follow actors. Some people treat it as theater, others as an art installation. There's no one right way to do it" (*Sleep No More* playbill 29). However, many participants who come to it as theater express a sense of frustration at their inability to follow a story, or to experience *Macbeth*, if that is what they have sought in this performance (for an analysis, see Dailey, 2012; Worthen, 2012; Hunter, 2018).

As the audience members travel through *Sleep No More*'s rooms, we are also invited to touch, read, and contemplate the thousands of objects that fill them. There may or may not be a purpose to those objects: some hold clues to the plot; some realize metaphors, images, or scenes derived from *Macbeth*; and some just contribute to creating the 1930s environment and atmosphere that *Sleep No More* so richly evokes. In foregrounding these objects, *Sleep No More* does seek to translate the experience of *Macbeth* into apprehending the play materially, as much as they do in following and watching the actors. As William Worthen comments, as "the audience enters the space rather than observing it," interacting with the objects, "each spectator's progress creates a poetic, associative narrative" (82). The ability to thus engage directly and freely in space and with things does allow each spectator to create their own interpretation of *Sleep No More*, and with that, Shakespeare's play itself; however, it can also lead to a sense of profound disorientation.

Many critics have compared *Sleep No More* to the experience of playing a videogame, in which interaction with the environment produces a new experience each time. However, a comparison with VR is just as suggestive.[3] The medium of VR represents to many people the next phase for immersive theatrical—and Shakespearean—performances, because it breaches the theatrical frame created by the proscenium arch and division of audience and actors, creating a new interface between performance and the spectators' minds and senses. VR can profoundly change the spectator's relationship to theatrical space, by visually immersing the spectator in that space. Having a 360°-experience of space rather than being directed to the action at hand, VR's viewers have greater visual freedom than conventional theater spectators do, in a way that can be both generative and disorienting. Further, with the spectator's proximity to objects that create the setting, their immersion in virtual space may create the illusion of a different relationship with the setting's materiality than is experienced in traditional theater settings: objects appear close at hand, available to be explored or studied, rather than simply part of a framed design.

However, the technology fundamental to production of VR is still the camera, however complex and multi-faceted that camera might be, and the sense of presence and materiality is still, in the end, an optical illusion. Thus, the next step in our analysis is to describe the negotiation of space, point of view, and the frame in film, and the ways in which film adaptations of Shakespeare have experimented with the representation of narrative space, anticipating the affordances of VR.

Film, Space, and Interface of the Frame

Film, like the proscenium-arch theater, is a framed medium. The choices of directors and production designers govern film's *mise-en-scène*; those of cinematographers its shot composition, orientation, distance, and movements; and those of editors its succession of shots into scenes and sequences. While there are multiple other contributors to a film's evocations of space, including its sound designers, the visual elements are critical to this discussion: what spectators see in the frame, and how and when we see it.

Frames in film, as in theater, constrain both the audience's agency (to observe events and objects beyond them) and the narrative's range (to depict the same). In film, the interface of the frame confines the range of camera shots and orients audiences toward those subjects and spaces that its directors/cinematographers permit them to see.[4] The frame is thus an overt example of how an interface limits the film audience's agency, and affects their cognitive grasp of the represented space.

Editors' arrangements of two-dimensional shots create an imagined three-dimensional space around film subjects.[5] Editors do this with continuity edits, smooth transitions between different views of a plausibly continuous time and space—even if the shots are of discontinuous times and spaces. Whether or not audiences recognize it, we fill in the gaps between these edits when their continuities are subtle and suggestive: we see only what we see, partial sets and actors from particular camera angles, but our minds interpolate missing details. For instance, when an establishing shot of an exterior daytime building transitions to an interior with suitable light streaming through the windows, we readily imagine that they are contiguous spaces. The conditions of the first shot imaginatively beget those of the second, particularly when we see a character enter the building and then exit an elevator. The second shot happens a moment later onscreen, but it is certainly more than a moment later in the real world of locations, soundstages, and production schedules. The resulting continuity is a fiction of editing, but it also depends on design choices; that kind of exterior must be plausibly continuous with this kind of interior, and the actor must look identical in both shots for the transition to be seamless. Viewers are so accustomed to these conventions that we may notice them only if a film violates them.[6]

The interface between audience and narrative spaces is a constraint on the audience's agency, a limited set of sensory channels through which the audience can cognitively grasp that narrative space (Cooper 142). A film spectator, for example, watches a sequence of shots, images of real space, and maps them onto what André Gardies calls "mental space," or the cognitive grasp of a place represented through a visual medium, whereas a video-game player, for example, navigates through a virtual space using the interface of a controller, which constrains the player's agency to move only on the plane(s) that the program permits. Both media construct plausible fictional worlds, illusions that seem real because our glimpses of them follow rules of continuity that our minds recognize from our understandings of real space (Levin and Wang 26).

Silvana Dunat adapts Gardies' term "mental space," to mean the spectator's cognitive grasp of represented space, their sense of the conditions and limits of the film narrative's environment. The spectator's eye watches a screen displaying the projected images that a camera's lens has captured. The spectator's observations of images on that screen combine with their knowledge of the world, and of film conventions, to translate the camera's images of real space into the mind's conceptions of space. Dunat thus accounts for how film's two-dimensional, framed images of discontinuous action are edited into a sequence that turns them into the viewer's interpretive sense of three-dimensional images of continuous action (485–6).[7]

Space, Audience, and Agency in Shakespeare Film Adaptations

Film adaptations of Shakespeare plays present a rich opportunity to explore the linkages between the representation of theatrical space and the kind of space conjured up in film, and, with that, the experience of audience agency. Anticipating our analysis of the VR production of *Hamlet 360*, we will explore the implications of how film positions the viewer. In the process, we will discover how audience agency is constrained not only by media, but also by narrative exigency: events must unfold in a certain way in order for a production to credibly posit itself as an adaptation of two of Shakespeare's plays: first *Hamlet*, and then *Henry V*. Yet within these two constraints there is latitude to productively complicate these plays' events and our cognitive grasp of them—primarily, as our analysis will show, by manipulating or liberating the audience's sense of space. Shakespeare directly engages audiences to exercise their agency over what we see, what we think, and what we do; our analysis of these films and then of the VR performance of *Hamlet 360* will show how directors, designers, and performers are aware of the interfaces' possible and actual implications for that agency.

When film audiences watch a sequence of shots comprising a scene, we are cumulatively gathering those shots into an understanding of space: how it envelops the objects and characters and which parts are contiguous. This understanding relies on "[o]ur experience of space," which André Bazin in 1967 described as "the structural basis for our concept of the [cinematic] universe" (108). That universe is usually a secondary background to the primary events in the foreground, adds Ross Exo Adams; it "provides a basic topography in which the central plot can take root and develop" (14). Some film plots are confined to relatively fixed confines, like the apartment and the courtyard of Alfred Hitchcock's *Rear Window* (1954). Other films depict more complex, unstable spaces, as Jean-Luc Godard does in his 1963 film, *Contempt* (*Le Mépris*).[8] For the sake of coherence, we address only those departures from norms that occur in Shakespearean adaptations, making broad claims about film methods that are conventional and common rather than experimental departures from norms. To say that films present a series of singular views on represented spaces and events is not to deny experimental films' split-screen multiple views, but ignores them in favor of prevailing conventions, particularly among Shakespeare film adaptations.

Every film depicts spaces that audiences are charged with imagining, stitching together separate shots and *mises-en-scène* into a mental compilation. They depict those spaces by capturing them with a camera, which stands or moves among events and objects in different *positions* and with different *orientations*. We use these two terms deliberately, as they distinguish film from frameless media (VR and theater not defined by the proscenium arch), so definitions are in order. *Position* means the placement of the viewer/audience relative to performed events in represented space: before, beside, behind, above, beneath. *Orientation* means the direction of the viewer/audience's eyes relative to those events, but also to represented and real space. In framed media, our eyes must be oriented toward the frame or we miss everything visual about the performance. In frameless media, we can look at many possible elements and at different scales of the performance; if we turn away from the primary action we may see details of the production or of its represented spaces (sets) or real spaces (e.g. theaters) that the designers prefer us to ignore. Thus, in frameless media, the designers use overt or subtle techniques to direct our orientation toward the action and objects that they consider primary.

The film audience's position and orientation relative to represented spaces and events are wholly subservient to the camera. It is conventionally a singular view, or a series of singular views, even as it shifts positions and orientations through movements and edits.[9] Camera and editing techniques give audiences the illusion of omnipresence, of looking onto or into events or places from multiple perspectives simultaneously, or at least in quick succession—perspectives that owe, imperceptibly, to the deliberate arrangement of cameras around the subject's periphery.

In contrast, the theater audience's position and orientation can be flexible. In conventional theater, of course, audience members occupy a set of multiple fixed positions (seats in an auditorium, say). Immersive and processional theater gives audiences far more agency and consequently more complex, interesting conceptions of space. The spectator's eye can take in anything visible within three-dimensional space; production-design cues like lighting and sound induce us to look toward the action onstage, but even if we follow those deliberate cues, we are still free to observe different facets and details of the setting or action.

The interface generated by the medium of film thus constructs its audience's sense of space, and this sense impacts the audience's agency: to look, to conceive, and to act. This agency is constrained by the positions and orientations that audiences can take relative to spaces and performances, and by the narrative exigencies of Shakespeare's plays. Film adaptations address the audience's agency to look at and conceive of their spaces and performances.

Hamlet is an appropriate play for film adaptation, and for the use of experimental camera techniques to capture and represent characters in space, because it is so preoccupied with the agency of characters to evaluate each other's thoughts and actions, and the dangers of passivity in light of this revealed knowledge. While a film viewer is incapable of acting on their knowledge, characters like Horatio and Hamlet are surrogate agents: we viewers project our powerlessness onto these characters and will them to act on what we see. This begins with Horatio's confirmation of the sentries' sight of the ghost on the battlements, and culminates with both characters' looking at Claudius in the Mousetrap scene—the play within the play that encapsulates the film as a whole, provoking the king's guilt just as *Hamlet* provokes our sympathy and outrage.

Gregory Doran's (2009) BBC television adaptation of a (2008) Royal Shakespeare Company production foregrounds the ubiquity of surveillance in *Hamlet* by starting with grainy CCTV footage of the sentries' encounter with the ghost. A more explicit instance of a camera intervening between spectators and spectacles is in its staging of "The Mousetrap." Hamlet (David Tennant) wields a handheld video camera throughout the scene, training it on Claudius (Patrick Stewart)'s and Gertrude's (Penny Downie)'s faces to capture their reactions to the inset play—particularly its lines about second husbands. (He is at stage left, they downstage, with the performers in between.) When Lucianus poisons the sleeping Gonzago, courtiers like Horatio visibly turn to look at Claudius with alarm before the king rises and disrupts the performance.

Tennant's camera recalls the brooding experimental filmmaker that Ethan Hawke gave the world in Michael Almereyda's (2000) *Hamlet*, addressing soliloquies in a Blockbuster Video outlet—an unwitting relic of its time—and directly into a camcorder lens. Tennant does the latter, too. However, the (2009) film's stronger resemblance is to the Mousetrap scene in Laurence Olivier's (1948) *Hamlet*, when the cinematographer Desmond Dickinson's camera encircles the royal spectators to suggest that courtiers grow increasingly aware of the king's response to the incriminating play. This dolly shot makes the camera a surrogate character in the film, turning like Hamlet and Horatio from the performance to the spectators. Whether the cinematographer or a character onstage wields the camera, the movements and scale of its frame constrain the viewer's agency to look where we will—to powerful effect.

Kenneth Branagh's *Hamlet* (1996) is the most ambitious film adaptation of Shakespeare's play, at least in terms of its scope; the screenplay aggregates every line from the quarto and folio editions into a record-breaking 238-minute production. Cinematographer Alex Thompson depicts an equally epic, lavish world of wintry exteriors (on location and Blenheim Palace in Oxfordshire) and lush interiors befitting the Danish royal court. Thompson's techniques pay tribute to those of Freddie Young, who shot David Lean's *Lawrence of Arabia* (1962) and *Doctor Zhivago* (1965) (Crowl 66–8). For instance, in 4.4. when Hamlet meets Fortinbras's Norwegian captain and learns that their army of 2,000 men pursues a worthless "patch of ground," the camera focuses tightly on Hamlet's face when he begins his ensuing soliloquy, "How all occasions do inform against me" (9.8, 9.22). The camera zooms gradually outward while Hamlet addresses the prescience of his Creator, "looking before and after," and man's need to overlook his paltry circumstances and act, "greatly to find quarrel in a straw" (9.27, 9.45). By the soliloquy's close, he has enlarged both his rhetoric and his intentions, and spreads his arms wide to declare that "My thoughts be bloody or be nothing worth"—yet the camera has considerably diminished his stature (9.56). He seems no larger than the troops massing in the background, imaginatively absorbed into their ranks. Ultimately the film spectator sees the prince, whose inner mental workings compel so much of our attention, in a vast and indifferent landscape.

Film adaptations of *Hamlet* have thus sought to engage and control viewers' perceptions of people, spaces, and events in ways that parallel the play's own interplay of seeing and knowing. Their deliberate manipulations of camera movements and scales, and the presence of cameras onscreen, make viewers aware of how films position viewers as spectators through a frame. These and other precedents anticipate the potential of frameless 360-degree VR films, specifically to thrust the viewer into a more entangled position within the space of Shakespearean plays.

A Shakespeare play that is more pointedly invested in its spectators' agency is *Henry V*, which grants us the agency to realize its representational ambitions. The Chorus introduces every act of the play with apologetic appeals to the audience to suspend their disbelief: to "Work, work your thoughts, and therein see a siege" at Harfleur (3.0.25); and to "Piece out our imperfections with your thoughts," which "now must deck our kings [and] / Carry them here and there" (Prologue.23, 28–9). Similarly, in his Prologue to Act IV, the Chorus regrets that "we shall much disgrace / With four or five most vile and ragged foils, … / The name of Agincourt" (49–52). Audiences since 1599 have thus been told to exercise their faculties to compensate for the inadequacies of Shakespeare's representations, no matter how sophisticated. Let us now consider how two twentieth-century film adaptations of this play negotiate how new media addresses those inadequacies, while provoking the audience's active imagination.

Film directors have suggested that their own representations obviate Shakespeare's apologies for the limitations of his stage. In 1989, Kenneth Branagh's film adaptation of the play begins with the Chorus (Derek Jacobi) lighting a match in his apostrophe to "a muse of fire," before he trips an electrical mains switch with a dramatic flourish (Prologue.1). This gesture floods the space with light, a space where the sets and properties that will create the film's illusory world of palaces and war are starkly visible. From the outset, then, Branagh asserts film as a medium that surpasses theater, as electricity surpasses fire's brightness—and he is unashamed about revealing the mechanics of film's illusions. When Jacobi's Chorus emerges into the film's opening scene, he opens the doors into a brilliantly illuminated space. This takes spectators from behind-the-scenes to center stage, the place where film's façades are presented to spectators as a vivid simulation of reality. Branagh thus draws attention to film's representational superiority to theater, even if he is just humble enough to lift its veil of illusion.

The more visual information a medium supplies, the less it demands of audiences—and concomitantly, the less agency it grants to audiences. Yet the case of *Henry V* belies this tidy formulation. A film by Branagh's forebear and model Laurence Olivier, his (1948) *Henry V*, illustrates the necessity of spectators' thoughts to "deck our kings," among other feats. Olivier appears to share Branagh's conception of film's superiority to theater, but has greater respect for his audience's agency. At the start and at the close of his film, he overtly locates the Chorus's speeches in Shakespeare's Globe Theatre in 1599. Where Branagh shows his love of film techniques, Olivier exercises them to greater effect (in his time): moving past the Globe's rowdy spectators cheering and booing the actors, and into a soundstage set with Henry's ship, loading at Southampton. The backdrops are painted, and the sets are vivid in the same pseudo-medieval aesthetic of his *Richard III* (1954), resembling medieval manuscripts. To our modern eyes they look unconvincing, but to wartime spectators they were the height of film wizardry. Olivier seems so enamored of the idea that film surpasses theater that he presents a scene of Falstaff's deathbed, an event that theatergoers must imagine through the Hostess's description; Branagh would also intersperse his narrative with such flashbacks. Later, our scene moves to a location (in Ireland) standing in for the Battle of Agincourt, where whole battalions of soldiers on horseback leave little to our imagination. And yet the film closes in the Globe Theatre once more, where a rapt audience hears the Chorus's epilogue before erupting in applause for their conquering hero. All the locations that film audiences have seen, Olivier implies, were in the mind's eye of a theater audience.

By progressing through the locations of the Globe, the soundstage, and the fields of Ireland, Olivier suggests that more sophisticated and elaborate film techniques will supply what theater wants. However, by returning to the Globe at the close, he reasserts the illusory nature of those images, and Shakespeare's reliance on his audience's agency: to look where we will, to identify with characters as we will, and to conceive of stories' images as we will. In so doing, he also anticipates the power of VR to create a heightened illusion of immersion in space, even while the spectator is rooted in place. The dynamics and constraints of the interface created by film performance are transformed in VR, when the frame disappears. Yet as we will indicate in our description of a VR Shakespeare performance, those dynamics and constraints are reconstituted by other means.

Space and Agency in a VR *Hamlet*

Experiments in VR *Hamlet*, and Shakespeare in general, have been limited. The American Shakespeare Center has created a 360-degree immersive documentary introduction to their Blackfriars playhouse, accompanied by VR films of two speeches from *Hamlet*, putting the viewer in the position of a spectator of a play in action. In this experience, we can turn our heads around 360 degrees, although overall our position is fixed. This virtual experiment does provide a sense of the proportion and sight lines of this stage, meant to evoke the stages of indoor performances in Shakespeare's London; however, our only agency is in seeing. These experiences seem motivated to introduce viewers to a specific playhouse comparable to the interior theater space for which Shakespeare wrote many plays. One must say, however, that these short films are more successful at this than the Royal Shakespeare Company's brief film of Alex Hassell in his 2015 role as Henry V. As he delivers the St. Crispin's Day speech to an empty stage and stalls at the RSC's Swan Theatre, we viewers hover overhead at an unnatural height that no real-world audience would ever inhabit. In both productions, it would have been worthwhile to give us the option of sitting in the stalls or on a balcony—though multiple positions around live performances would require postproduction removal or concealment of the other cameras.

The Blackfriars and RSC examples evidence how the interface created by VR alters our perceptions of these performances. The viewer's eyes watch two stereoscopic screens side by side in a head-mounted display designed to create the illusion of three-dimensional moving images. Stereo audio sonically reinforces this illusion. Both video and audio outputs use tracking sensors to respond to movements of the viewer's head—so when we look up or down, right or left, the audiovisual feeds respond to those motions to suggest that we are watching and hearing things in real space. However, these feeds have been recorded from a fixed position relative to the action, so our illusion of real presence only extends so far.

Trying to move around a live-action VR performance simply exceeds the system's boundaries.

In contrast to these short experiments reproducing the view of a spectator in a conventional theater space, Steven Maler's hour-long (2019) VR film *Hamlet 360: Thy Father's Spirit,* produced by Sensorium and featuring the Commonwealth Shakespeare Company for WGBH Boston, does reconceive how Shakespeare's play can be performed and viewed by mixing theatrical and cinematic techniques. The Mousetrap scene, suitably enough, relies on theatrical conventions to induce viewers to watch the players. The camera is positioned between Hamlet and Gertrude who watch, alongside others, from the stage of a disused theater. The players, brilliantly illuminated, perform on a platform above the orchestra pit and the bare floor of the auditorium. This inversion reminds us of the mirrored nature of this spectacle, and of our divided attention between the play and its royal audience. Further, the theatrical setting of the whole VR production is a nod to the time-tested methods of some of *Hamlet 360*'s predecessors. Claudius is in shadows until he calls out for a theatrical method ("Give me some light!") and the whole set illuminates.

The production's derelict proscenium-arch theater underscores this inheritance: paint peels from fading pillars, and the auditorium's seating has been removed. This bounds the action to an open space perhaps 30 meters square, with the aforementioned elevated stage spanning one side and an irregular platform the other. In this space are several large properties—a car, a four-poster bed, a bathtub, a large immersion tank—and several chairs, oriental carpets, and occasional tables topped with Art Nouveau-esque lamps. In an echo of the audience's experience of *Sleep No More*, when watching the performance a spectator is tempted to pause the film to examine the space and the objects littered about it, leaving the actors frozen in place.

While *Hamlet 360* thus evokes the presence of theater space and uses the theatrical effects, in creating it, the producers were also aware of how the camera technology they used could shape their staging and interpretation of the play. The director, Steven Maker, and the cinematographer, Matthew Neiderhauser have both commented on the complexity of staging and filming a performance in VR, in which they were "synchronizing 17 different camera feeds at the same time in order to complete a 360-degree image." They also have spoken of how the technology itself potentially shaped the imagery that they wanted to use, when they were tempted, for example, to put a camera inside of Yorick's skull. However, while they did go so far as to film underwater, they pulled back from any camera trick with Yorick's skull: they reminded themselves that technology is helpful only when you know why you are using it, and "how that technology is advancing narrative" ("*Hamlet 360*; Virtual Reality Shakespeare").

Hamlet 360 uses film techniques, in addition to theatrical techniques, to nudge viewers to look toward the performers rather than in other directions. At moments of great pitch and magnitude, like Claudius's confession soliloquy, a red-shift and zooming effect have been added in post-production to force our perspective. It is powerfully suggestive, but not constraining: we need only turn our heads to either side to see other distorted and curved set features which could have been darkened altogether. Given the freedom to position viewers anywhere in relation to the action, a key question for VR's production designers is whether and how to induce us to orient ourselves toward it.

Another feature that VR shares with theater is the pace of its transitions, typically between scenes but occasionally within scenes. Unlike theater, *Hamlet 360*'s transitions often include a shift of position—but as in theater, the pace cannot be overly jarring or sudden, lest viewers become literally disoriented and lose their sense of place and space. In *Hamlet 360* the editors make liberal use of the film techniques of fade-outs and -ins to smooth scene transitions, and to signal a shift of position using a ghostly swirling-smoke effect to surround the viewer, evoking the typical image of the Ghost on the foggy battlements of Elsinore. There are also a few less graceful mid-scene shifts of position, including one in the final sword-fight when Gertrude is mid-sentence; however, for the most part, these transitions are gradual and rare enough to resemble theatrical ones. The two most striking mid-scene shifts of position are underwater: we join Hamlet in the bathtub in his suicide attempt in the midst of the "To be or not to be" soliloquy; and we witness Ophelia's drowning from beneath her corpse. Such shifts are surprising, to good or ill effect, and reinforce our earlier claim that Shakespeare VR performances are in their experimental infancy.

In inviting a spectator into a fully realized illusion of three-dimensional space, *Hamlet 360* VR tempts the spectator into trying to engage with objects and people inhabiting that space. When we are confined in a seat in a traditional "real" theatrical performance, we know the rules of engagement: stay seated, be as quiet as possible, and follow the cues as to where to direct our gaze. In immersive theater experiences like *Sleep No More*, the audience may move and explore, but even then, there are rules: wear your mask, do not speak, and do not touch the actors unless asked to do so. In VR the seat disappears and we are alone, apparently immersed in the stage space. But what can we do? Where can we go? What kind of agency do we have then?

Some VR experiences go beyond sight to give the spectator agency to play or engage with the virtual world through the use of controllers or more sophisticated haptic devices. As the technology works now, making things happen in VR means mastering a set of stylized gestures involving the hands manipulating the controls. The player is not free to control the effects of those gestures, which are governed by both the device and the program. In Oculus VR games, for example, even when one is free to move, play is restricted to a space defined by "guardian" limits set up to prevent the participant from crashing into furniture or walls when we sense that we are elsewhere. As Brandon Hookway has observed, control is inherent to the concept of the interface, insofar as "interface describes a zone of contestation that extends from the relation that holds between a user and apparatus to a notion of control and power" (16). In the interaction of human and machine, agency is complexly constituted in tension between interface constraints and volition. VR experiences that do allow the player to move in and affect the environment offer the sense of agency in the virtual world, but that effect is only possible by mastering the mechanisms that allow movement, and within the space permitted by the program.

While the producers of *Hamlet 360* did not aspire to this kind of interactivity, they did attempt to give the viewer a sense not only of the space and the spectacle of *Hamlet*, but also of its problem of what constitutes action by bringing the viewer into the play through the presence of the ghost of Hamlet's father. Maler sees *Hamlet* "very much as a father and son story," observing that he "really leaned into that in terms of this adaptation of the material. That intimacy between father and son is something that I thought would really translate well into the medium" ("*Hamlet 360*; Virtual Reality Shakespeare"). To emphasize this theme, the creators decided to make the viewer literally inhabit "Thy Father's Spirit" as the subtitle suggests: the ghost of King Hamlet, omnipresent throughout the play, who interjects his presence and his words at decisive moments. Viewing the action in the ghost's persona provokes questions of why he intervenes when he does, yet restrains himself from intervening at other moments—like the drowning scenes, when our position underwater seems inconsistent with the ghost's role. At perhaps five discrete moments in this condensed and rearranged version of Shakespeare's play, the otherworldly voice of the ghost emanates from the viewer, addressing characters (usually Hamlet alone) who react in amazement and wonder. Here there is a perceptible shift of atmosphere: the lamps flicker, and a soundtrack of bass notes signals the ponderous mood. The ghost also makes at least three appearances to the viewer's eye: two reflections in mirrors during his speeches, and one wordless sequence at the play's close, when we witness him walking among the dead, seemingly reflecting on the carnage his vengeance has wrought.

Further, there are two significant moments in *Hamlet 360* that seem to go beyond just observation or presence to grant the ghost a kind of agency, even where there is no real interaction with the play world. In one moment in the final scene of the duel, Laertes is distracted, apparently by a vision or at least a sense of presence of the ghost. This hesitation allows Hamlet to stab him (while it is not the final blow). When Gertrude drinks the poison, she also looks directly at the spectator as the ghost, implying a kind of awareness or connection with the ghost spectator. In these two instants, as the ghost the spectator feels a sense of connection with the action, and even a kind of effect on it. At the play's end, when the spectator once again changes perspective, finally seeing the ghost of Hamlet's father in third person below, and thus splitting from him, we are now left to judge the ghost, and his culpability in the disaster, in turn: *his* vengeance, that is—not ours.

If we, the viewers of *Hamlet 360*, are complicit in the ghost's vengeance it is only by proxy, only by the strength of the production's assertion of our coextensive similarity to King Hamlet. This is a 360-degree video performance, after all—not a video game whose controller lets us exercise our will, or a holodeck whose interface lets us direct the course of action. In a *Star Trek: The Next Generation* episode (Season 3, Episode 10: "The Defector"), when Lieutenant Commander Data performs Henry V's perambulatory reflections on the eve of Agincourt, he cites Laurence Olivier as one of his models. We viewers of Shakespeare in VR today can exercise none of Data's agency, interact with no other characters, because our agency in this production is illusory. At this point in VR's technological history, we have no freedom to act in either the performative or the interventionist sense; however, VR does grant us greater freedom to think than any other medium.

In this chapter we have witnessed multiple ways, across formats and interfaces, that decisions by Shakespeare's adapters alter spectators' conceptions of his stories, ideas, and characters. We have paid particular attention to those decisions about the audience's spatial positions, orientations, and movements because space is a construct of our imaginations, produced at the interface of human and machine, and based on the representations that a medium offers to our eyes. The VR performances treated in this chapter will someday, we expect, seem as foundational as the Lumière brothers' first moving images, including the film of a train arriving at La Ciotat (1895) that provoked astonishment and alarm.[10] Increasingly multi-directional capturing and rendering technologies may yet give VR's dislocated spectators an experience like the highly localized *Sleep No More*, in which we wander freely through the spaces of unfolding scenes.

During the time in which we wrote this chapter, the world was gripped by the coronavirus pandemic and millions of people turned to virtual experiences to connect with each other and experience theater. For instance, in July 2020, the Disney+ streaming service offered a live recording of the Broadway musical "Hamilton," originally slated for theatrical release in October 2021; and London's National Theatre released more than half of its 30 NTLive productions, intended for cinema broadcast and paywalled streaming services, for free on YouTube from April to August 2020. Such experiences were largely limited, once again, to camera recordings enclosed in the frame of the flat screen. There are preceding counter-examples of virtual presences incorporated into Shakespearean theater spaces: in 2016, the RSC included projections of a digital avatar of Ariel, played by Mark Quartley in a motion-capture suit, in the company's stage production of *The Tempest*; and, in 2019, the company produced Robert Gilbert's recitation of the "Seven Ages of Man" speech from *As*

You Like It in augmented reality. In the most innovative use of virtual reality to screen Shakespeare to date, in 2020–21, the Tenderclaws production company produced a live virtual reality recreation of *The Tempest*, in which the spectators entered as avatars into an animated version of Prospero's island, where they cast spells and performed roles in scenes from the play as directed by a live actor. In this case, the spectators were engaged fully in interacting with the space, as well as with each other. Future mediated reproductions of immersive performances will further negotiate with space—the final frontier—by obviating the frame of media to shift the audience's frame of mind.

Notes

1 For other recent discussions of the intersection of VR and theater, see Giannachi (2004); Charlton and Moar (2018); Lan (2003); and Lewis (2017). As Giannachi notes, VR can be "delivered in three forms":

> through goggles, gloves or suit, in which you feel you are inside a virtual world; on a "desktop," in which you view "a 3D world through a screen," or as a third-person view, "steering an avatar through a virtual world" (9). Antonin Artaud is credited with introducing the term "virtual reality" in *The Theatre and Its Double* in 1938.

2 For a recent analysis of five live-action VR Shakespeare performances and potential directions for the medium's future, see Ullyot.

3 As of June 2020, an initiative had started to create an augmented reality version of *Sleep No More*: https://www.wired.com/story/niantic-punchdrunk-augmented-reality-collaboration/

4 "The act of framing or cutting the space out of its environment is a semantic act by which a view is transformed into an image and consequently into a signifier that refers to something signified" (Dunat 476).

5 Mark Garrett Cooper argues against the traditional view of shots constituting space, as if editing is the way that viewers perceive a fictional space.

6 See, in particular, the "180-Degree Rule" elaborated in Levin and Wang (26–8) and its violation in the 1988 film *Twins* (32–4).

7 She compares film's framing of space within broader environments to that of painting or photography: their frames isolate and localize views onto a broader terrain, like views through a window onto an exterior world (475–6). She contrasts, however, their static images with film's evoking a cognitive sense of *space* from dynamic, discontinuous views of *place* using Gardies' theory of the "mirror ball" or *boule spéculaire*.

8 Godard makes "very subtle, yet seemingly precise alterations to the ... standard relationship between the actors' drama and scenic background. The effect ... [is] to destabilise the smooth cinematic experience" (Adams 15).

9 Andrei Tarkovsky has written that "The dominant, all-powerful factor of the film image is rhythm, expressing the course of time within the frame" (113).

10 Reports that spectators feared the train would come through the screen and collide with them are a founding myth of cinema, writes Martin Loiperdinger.

References

Adams, Ross Exo. "Foreground, Background, Drama: The Cinematic Space of *Le Mépris*." *Critical Quarterly*, vol. 53, no. 1, 2011, pp. 14–28.

American Shakespeare Center Virtual Reality Theatre Tour and Performances. Available at: https://americanshakespearecenter.com/vr/.

Bailenson, Jeremy. *Experience on Demand: What Virtual Reality Is, How It Works, and What It Can Do*. Norton, 2018. Kindle.

Bazin, André. *What Is Cinema?* U of California P, 1967.

Biggin, Rose. *Immersive Theatre and Audience Experience: Space, Game, and Story in the Work of Punchdrunk*. Palgrave Macmillan, 2017.

Brook, Peter. *The Empty Space. A Book about the Theatre: Deadly, Holy, Rough, Immediate*. Atheneum, 1968.

Brown, John Russell. "Staging Shakespeare's Plays: A Choice of Theatres." *New Theatre Quarterly*, vol. 26, no. 2, 2010, pp. 115–120.

Charlton, James Marton, and Magnus Moar. "VR and the Dramatic Theatre: Are They Fellow Creatures?" *International Journal of Performance Arts and Digital Media*, vol. 14, no. 2, 2018, pp. 187–198.

Cooper, Mark Garrett. "Narrative Spaces." *Screen*, vol. 43, no. 2, 2002, pp. 139–157.

Crowl, Samuel. *Shakespeare and Film: A Norton Guide*. Norton, 2008.

Dailey, Alice. "Last Night I Dreamt I Went to *Sleep No More*: Intertextuality and Indeterminacy in Punchdrunk's McKittrick Hotel." *Borrowers and Lenders*, vol. 7, no. 2, 2012.

Dunant, Silvana. "Film Space as Mental Space." *Semiotica*, vol. 207, 2015, pp. 475–487.

Gardies, André. *L'espace au Cinéma*. Meridiens Klincksieck, 1993.

Giannachi, Gabriella. *Virtual Theatres: An Introduction*. Routledge, 2004.

Hamlet. Directed by Laurence Olivier. Two Cities Films, 1948.

Hamlet. Directed by Kenneth Branagh. Castle Rock Entertainment / Columbia Pictures, 1996.

Hamlet. Directed by Michael Almereyda. Miramax Films, 2000.

Hamlet. Directed by Gregory Doran. BBC, 2009.

Hamlet 360: Thy Father's Spirit. The Commonwealth Shakespeare Company in Boston in collaboration with Google and Sensorium. 2019. Available at: https://www.youtube.com/watch?v=Jc88G7nkV-Q.

"'Hamlet 360: Virtual Reality Shakespeare.' Interview with Barbara Bogaev, Steven Maler and Matthew Niederhauser." Available at: https://www.folger.edu/shakespeare-unlimited/hamlet-virtual-reality.

Henry V. Directed by Laurence Olivier. Two Cities Films, 1944.

Henry V. Directed by Kenneth Branagh. BBC Films / Renaissance Films, 1989.

Henry V 360. Royal Shakespeare Company and the Google Cultural Institute, 2015. Available at: https://www.youtube.com/watch?v=SDcMHzUrIQc.

Hookway, Brandon. *Interface*. MIT P, 2014.

Hunter, Elizabeth. "Enactive Spectatorship in Contemporary Productions of Shakespeare's Plays." PhD dissertation. Northwestern U. 2018.

Kaye, Nick, and Gabriella Giannachi. "Acts of Presence: Performance, Mediation, Virtual Reality." *TDR*, vol. 55, no. 4, 2011, pp. 88–95.

Lan, Yong Li. "Shakespeare as Virtual Event." *Theatre Research International*, vol. 28, no. 1, 2003, pp. 46–60.

Levin, Daniel T., and Caryn Wang. "Spatial Representation in Cognitive Science and Film." *Projections*, vol. 3, no. 1, 2009, pp. 24–52.

Lewis, William W. "Performing 'Posthuman' Spectatorship: Digital Proximity and Variable Agencies." *Performance Research*, vol. 22 no. 3, 2017, pp. 7–14.

Loiperdinger, Martin. "Lumière's Arrival of the Train: Cinema's Founding Myth." *The Moving Image*, vol. 4, no. 1, 2004, pp. 89–118.

Machon, Josephine. *Immersive Theatres: Intimacy and Immediacy in Contemporary Performance*. Palgrave Macmillan, 2013.

Popat, Sita. "Missing in Action: Embodied Experience and Virtual Reality." *Theatre Journal*, vol. 68, 2016, pp. 357–378.

Rylance, Mark. "Playing the Globe: Artistic Policy and Practice." *Shakespeare's Globe Rebuilt*, edited by J. R. Mulryne and Margaret Shewring, Cambridge UP, 1997, pp. 169–176.

Schechner, Richard. *Environmental Theatre*. Applause Theatre Books, 1994.

Shakespeare, William. *Henry V: The Norton Shakespeare: Essential Plays*, 2nd ed., edited by Stephen Greenblatt, *et al.* Norton, 2009a, pp. 833–910.

Shakespeare, William. *Hamlet: The Norton Shakespeare: Essential Plays*, 2nd ed., edited by Stephen Greenblatt, et al.Norton, 2009b, pp. 1080–1168.

Shaughnessy, Robert. "Immersive Performance, Shakespeare's Globe, and the 'Emancipated Spectator'." *The Hare*, vol. 1, no. 2, 2012. Available at: https://thehareonline.com/article/immersive-performance-shakespeare%E2%80%99s-globe-and-emancipated-spectator.

Sleep No More. "Playbill." Purchased April 2020.

Stern, Tiffany. "'You that Walk i'th the Galleries': Standing and Walking in the Galleries of the Globe Theatre." *Shakespeare Quarterly*, vol. 51, no. 2, 2000, pp. 211–216.

Tarkovsky, Andrei. *Sculpting in Time: Reflections on the Cinema*. Translated by Kitty Hunter-Blair, U of Texas P, 1989.

Ullyot, Michael. "Infinite Space: Notes Toward Shakespeare's VR Future." *Shakespeare and Virtual Reality*, edited by Stephen Wittek and David McInnis. Cambridge University Press, 2022.

Worthen, W.B. "'The Written Troubles of the Brain': *Sleep No More* and the Space of Character." *Theatre Journal*, vol. 64, no. 1, 2012, pp. 79–97.

3

ALL THE GAME IS A STAGE

The Controller and Interface in Shakespearean Videogames

Mark Kaethler

Introduction: Controlling as Performance

Videogames have been commonly misconstrued as passive, mindless sources of entertainment that result in people becoming detached from reality and demonstrating aberrant behavior,[1] presumptions that are not altogether dissimilar to critiques of the early modern theater from Puritanical authorities who claimed it was a distraction from God's original works in favour of false idols and other vices. In his *Anatomy of the Abuses*, Phillip Stubbes draws an early connection between gaming and playgoing insofar as both are corrupt pastimes: "Are not vnlawfull games, playes, Enterludes, and the like euery where frequented?" (sig. A4r). Both theater spectatorship and early modern game playing worked reciprocally, as audiences adapted the practices of both pastimes to interpret and comprehend the material circumstances and dynamics of the playhouse. Gina Bloom has recently identified, for instance, that theatrical conventions regarding audience engagement, response, and participation in the Shakespearean theater were generated out of similar methods of play that spectators were accustomed to in games they had played previously (2018, 3). Bloom's historical research and Stubbes' anxieties point toward the ways in which new media, such as the commercial early modern theater, build upon extant forms of play, such as outdoor games, and how anxieties about entertainment shift and evolve, as new technologies and distractions emerge.

In the past few decades, videogames have been increasingly recognized as a serious art form worthy of critical examination in its own right and in ancillary readings of gaming and literature.[2] In Shakespeare studies, videogames have been a regular topic of scholarly conversation,[3] leading to the development of educational or experiential videogames, especially those that replicate theatrical experiences and the game-like aspects of Shakespearean theater. This experiential focus, however, has led to a general neglect of Shakespeare in mainstream videogames and the interface implications of videogame consoles. In this chapter, I will examine the ways in which the videogame controller and its interface features establish new theatrical conventions as an essential component of the user's videogame experience. The tactile technology the gamer uses to shape and experience the digital world reflects Andrew Galloway's notion that the interface "makes the apparatus visible" (40),[4] as the controller functions as a reflexive interface which guides and structures the gamer's experience with the gaming world. Further, the Brechtian dimensions of videogames allow for an interrogative

 DOI: 10.4324/9780367821722-5

dynamic that draws attention to the separation between player and played while also rendering the game mechanics familiar through connections with users' lived conditions. The second mode of interface explores how the controller generates affect according to Gregory J. Seigworth and Melissa Gregg's conception that "[a]ffect arises in the midst of *in-betweenness*: in the capacities to act and be acted upon" (1).[5] This definition of affect as "in betweenness" speaks to Branden Hookway's theorization of interface as liminal or Joanna Drucker's conception of the interface as a "space between human users and processes that happen according to complicated protocols" (Hookway 4; Drucker 138).[6] The interface is therefore not simply the technologies gamers use to interact with the game; it also participates in emotional networks between player and played, similar to the circulation of emotions in theatrical spectatorship.

Console and computer videogames alter the theatrical experience by allowing users to be both audience members and actors; they simultaneously situate gamers as spectators of cinematic sequences and makers of the world with which they interact.[7] Their agency depends upon conventions to facilitate cognitive processes, much as performance relies upon audiences conditioned to the habits and customs of the theater. The gamer is therefore not the stereotypical mindless consumer or button masher conceived by adversaries of the game industry, but rather what Valerie M. Fazel and Louise Geddes term "the Shakespeare user," an active party in the renegotiation of Shakespeare (14). Users' agency allows them to manipulate Shakespeare through digital technologies in an "experimental activity" that breaks free "from the hegemony of the 'educative and civilizing agencies' of academia and theatre" (3). The technologies thus allow users to refashion literature and literary icons while also performing work on themselves through the affective process of playing through and creating those narratives. Hence, the controller functions similarly to Elizabeth Grosz's notion of a "prosthesis," an extension of the body and self.[8] It establishes the enhanced interface wherein players *are* the avatar rather than *feeling as though* they experience and connect with stage personae; moreover, they make and participate in the storyline rather than imagining as though they are involved in the creation of the narrative. Whereas an audience's hands can only free Prospero through applauding Shakespeare's drama, the videogame user's hands can direct Prospero's every motion within the parameters of the game-world through the controller.

Videogame technology's potential to facilitate this active and engaged creative process—especially in the adaptations of Shakespearean drama's metatheatrical dimensions—has not been sufficiently explored for its ethical and affective capabilities. This chapter attends to two sustained appropriations of Shakespeare in mainstream videogames, *Final Fantasy IX* (2000) and *Life Is Strange: Before the Storm* (2017). Both of these games allow characters to enact but also guide Shakespearean narratives. In bringing the videogame frame into the foreground through the integration of the theatrical medium, they perpetuate the concept of *theatrum mundi* while signaling the ways in which this notion alters with the interface of a videogame. All the game's a stage, and all the world's a game. This chapter therefore argues that Shakespearean videogames expose the ways in which seemingly passive videogame technologies contribute in active ways toward the facilitation of an ethical and affective experience that reflects the early theater while transforming the ways in which Shakespearean drama is made and played by users.

Learning and Performing Ethically: *Final Fantasy IX* and Shakespeare

Theater historians have illuminated the complex ways in which the stage cultivated audience reception. This topic has been explored through studies of repeated conventions (Lopez 133), print media circulation (Stern 5–6), and cognitive habits developed through technologies and habits of memory (Tribble 50). In short, playgoers learned how to use and interpret the theater as genre and platform by interfacing with actors who guided them to understand the space and its productions. As this first section will show, *Final Fantasy IX* highlights the commonalities between the standard yet multivalent control tutorial and theatrical participation in meaning-making onstage. While actors instruct audiences and guide their cognitive interpretation of events, theatrical spectatorship simulates the *feeling* of being a player rather than allocating an audience the full power to play along with actors.[9] The videogame, on the other hand, involves the user in the embodied cognitive processes of the physical controller to maneuver an avatar. Although the interface differs depending upon the media in question, it is the prosthesis of the controller that distinguishes the user's relation to Shakespearean theater within videogames from traditional audience engagement.[10]

The videogame user is rendered into an actor but may still remain part of the audience, depending on whether the game is collaborative or not. Previous scholarship has remarked upon this dual function of the gamer. Katherine Rowe examines the network of interactions between avatars in *Second Life*'s Shakespearean theaters, observing how users often experience the play as an avatar they have created rather than purely as an audience member experiencing the drama that unfolds before them (61–2). The rendering of the stage in the game therefore changes its interface, as users can now make theater. Theatrical performance in videogames no longer functions according to traditional theatrical conventions, and its narrative and cognitive structures involve users as active participants. Instead, the new interface grants the user liberty to be an actor as well as an audience and to focus on crowd interaction instead of the more passive reception of a staged play.

Although similarities have been drawn between the performative aspects of the stage and videogames, these accounts tend to study kinesthetic technologies that rely upon motion capture. Bloom begins to mark these differences by distinguishing between those games that "center on trivia," which she defines as "*scholar-making games*," and "*theater-making games* … in which the player essentially inhabits or controls a Shakespearean character" (115). Both of these categories differ from the mainstream, controller-based platform games discussed in this chapter, and they tend to focus on or recreate Shakespeare predominantly within the realms of theater and academia. Arguably the most successful theatrically or academically engineered Shakespeare videogame thus far is Bloom's *Play the Knave*, which allows users to act out scenes together in a virtual stage. A Kinect v2 motion sensor affiliated with the Xbox One console functions as the interface that projects the user's body onto a stage they have selected on a screen. Analyzing the ways in which the technology contributes to the project, Bloom claims that "the motion capture interface … makes it seem that the avatar is mirroring the player's movements in real time" (14). The idea that the avatar *seems* to be doing this action stresses the theatrical and imagined nature of Bloom's interface between player and avatar. This raises the question of whether or not *Play the Knave* is a simulation or a game. The interplay of multiple users creates a dynamic sense of play but without a standardized set of rules to win or complete it. Sandbox games possess varying open-ended worlds with optional questlines or missions. There is typically a lack of narrative or at least narrative linearity. Examples include *SimCity, Second Life*, and to a lesser extent the *Grand Theft Auto* series. Essentially, sandbox games resist structural features that dictate the path of gameplay and instead allow the user fuller control over the circumstances of play. Virtual reality interfaces have likewise led to innovation in audience participation and creation in the worlds of videogames. Stephen Wittek's *Shakespeare-VR* project at Carnegie Mellon University, for instance, simulates the experiences of the Blackfriars Theatre.

Bloom's work emphasizes this view with respect to Shakespearean theater and videogames when she distinguishes between "the physical mechanics of most games" and "the *phenomenological* experience of theater-making" (117). As discussed already, Bloom's *Play the Knave* helps users experience some of the ways in which the early theater operated. However, Bloom's and other scholars' proclivity to privilege this kind of technology above other gaming interfaces has caused a dearth of attention concerning the transmutations of theatrical conventions and their cognitive processes in games created by non-academic professionals that are nevertheless inspired by Shakespeare.[11]

Square Enix's *Final Fantasy IX* demonstrates one of the most sustained early engagements with Shakespeare's canon. The opening sequence introduces users to the various characters who will form their party of four for the remainder of the game, and the game uses a theatrical performance reminiscent of *King Lear* to unite the various plotlines of the individual avatars. The gamer enters into a world whose buildings and layout resemble early modern London, and the narrative provides cues for users to situate themselves in this historical period. When encountering a statue in the marketplace, the user reads an inscription: "The Three Heroic Knights of Pluto: The statue was built to commemorate the three knights who fought bravely in the 15th Lindblum War, in 1601." The uncertainty of when the current narrative takes place leaves the distance between this date and the unspoken present time of the game world uncertain, but the inclusion of a year within the scope of Shakespeare's dramatic career persuades the user to make an association between the early modern theater and the game's stage. The game's opening focus on the theater with a ticket booth in the center of the marketplace augments the chronological connection. While a separate ticket booth in a market square would not have existed for early modern playgoers, this one nevertheless contains manuscripts with what appears to be early paleography and features coats of arms that are indicative of an early modern setting. The user plays as Vivi who possesses a ticket to the show. The title of the play does not bear a Shakespearean name, but its characters nevertheless resemble those from *King Lear.* Shakespearean references are not limited to the performance either, for Vivi later encounters a character named Puck who mischievously helps him watch the play from the rooftop when he discovers his ticket is actually a forgery.

Fans have noted additional correspondences with Shakespearean theater. A user under the name of GameMage on YouTube offers an informative overview of the ways in which Shakespeare and the theater influence *Final Fantasy IX* (GameMage), thereby demonstrating Fazel and Geddes' point that the digital allows space outside the traditional academic sphere to theorize and discuss Shakespeare. For example, the vlogger comments on the game's allusions to characters from *A Midsummer Night's Dream* and *King Lear,* and he makes some cursory reflections upon the ways in which early overviews of battle mechanics function as a kind of rehearsal for later stage combat.[12] There is more to be said, however, concerning the framing of the game's action and narrative in relation to the theater. The prospective kidnappers, for example, engineer their strategy to abduct Princess Garnet, and during this sequence their leader, Baku, visualizes this plan through the use of prop dolls. These function as avatars that Baku controls, and this action takes place during a cut-scene or cinematic depiction of the game's storyline advancing that the user views rather than makes. By framing the sequence in this manner, the user is positioned at this point as an audience member witnessing a metatheatrical unfolding of their plan. The angle by which the segment is framed positions the user in the seat of an audience member watching the action between the puppets unfold, and this point of view likewise establishes Baku as a godlike figure directing the events. The user is oriented to pay attention through questions and pauses along the way, wherein Baku asks if the crew are paying attention to him. The rehearsal thus functions to prepare and educate a user in a manner akin to how the early theater operated.

Videogames establish these quandaries alongside a compulsion to act. This dynamic corresponds with Shakespearean drama but also with the ideas of modern theorists of theater like Bertolt Brecht, who were inspired and influenced by Shakespearean techniques. Metatheatricality, for instance, is an effect used across the work of these playwrights, and the effect occurs through a critical engagement that results from the medium bringing the frame into focus.[13] Regardless of whether examples are metatheatric or metaludic, they draw the interface between fiction and reality into the frame by making the user cognizant of the fact that in these moments they are between worlds. In discussing the ethical implications of videogames, Galloway draws attention to the manner by which the Brechtian "aesthetic of incoherence" facilitates these reflections (48). Looking more carefully at Brecht's concepts and terminology helps us better understand the ways in which this occurs in videogames. The "Not-But" effect of Brecht's vision of theater generates the incongruencies that spur ethical action, since for Brecht the concept allows the playgoer to be "able to look at what takes place in such a way as to be able to affect it" (197). Thinking about this in relation to videogames, this is arguably always the case, as the player controls the avatar; however, it is important to distinguish regular controlling habits from moments of control that have a gravity to them. The latter instances in the games studied in this chapter are remarkable for their ability to instigate reflection through the "Not-but" effect. At these moments, users are led to see themselves as player not played, but nevertheless they are still drawn to see their lived experiences as gamelike, as played. The incoherence of this theatrical technique thus informs the interface between player and played, which can facilitate important ethical reflections. The dissonance that results from the "Not-But" effect therefore has an ethical and emotional purpose that ideally translates into action on the part of the user. In the case of videogames, these actions are more likely to transpire both in general and as acts of volition, given that the videogame player, unlike the playgoer, has to perform the narrative through the avatar.[14]

In the case of *Final Fantasy IX*, the knowledge that users will later control an active variation of this cut-scene puppet stage business beckons them to remember that the game characters are also akin to puppets. Zidane is effectively a puppet of the user guided through the controller, much as Princess Garnet is a puppet manipulated by Baku in the cut-scene. The game's more cartoonish representation of characters in relation to earlier installments in the *Final Fantasy* series emphasizes this dynamic since they appear less human and more toylike.[15] The ethics of kidnapping, however, structures an interrogative moment for users regarding their own treatment of the avatars as objects. The mock puppet theater brings the additional frame of the videogame user's puppeteering into focus, thereby instigating a blurring of the play-world and audience reality and potentially spurring critical reflection. The Brechtian nature of this metatheatrical engagement is a product of its interface, reflecting Andrew Galloway's observation that interfaces often "make the apparatus visible" (40). In this case, the game makes the theatrical interface visible within the game interface. The game's attention to itself as theater and its encouragement of the user to be reflexive guide the metatheatrical experience within the game, preparing the user for what is to unfold. GameMage's observation that users know Shakespeare and his theater from high school shows that a familiarity with the theatrical interface allows users to become readily familiar with stage conventions, but *Final Fantasy IX* simultaneously deploys unfamiliarity by compelling users to question their actions, thereby fully executing the "Not-But" effect.

The involvement of Shakespearean users in a videogame is thus complicated by the ways in which they are simultaneously spectator and actor, as both the viewer and creator of the story, at different intervals. This interpretive and ludic dynamic establishes the Brechtian dimensions of the interface that mirror those of the theater but adds a novel or perhaps enhanced agency to the user's experience. By returning to the kidnapping plot sequence, we can perceive this dynamic at play. Although the cinematic cut-scene plays out a familiar dramatic sequence, in which plots are revealed in advance of the events transpiring, the metatheatrical dimensions of this event are different. The dimension of unfamiliarity comes from the recognition that this is not an entirely immersive experience as users are reminded that they are controlling avatars to engage in unethical behavior, resulting in potential discomfort with the kidnapping plot. The videogame's ability to draw attention to the ethical implications of the interface between player and played therefore relies upon theatrical conventions, like metatheater, made apparent through the incorporation of one medium in another.

Pushing Your Buttons: Affect and *Life Is Strange: Before the Storm*

Although ethical interpretation functions as the basis for this Brechtian assessment of videogames, it is prompted by affect as well. Videogames are located at an intersection of player and played or reality and game-world that triggers an emotional response similar to theater but with perhaps an increased investment, as users spectate and play simultaneously. Galloway identifies the ways in which the computer draws us in with an immersive interface rather than having users tilt their heads back and reflect, as they would with a film (12). This assessment, however, neglects the ways in which videogames function as a hybrid of active gameplay and film viewing (i.e., cut-scenes without any ability to guide the events), and it presupposes that the experience of using a computer never prompts users to take a step back. Galloway later clarifies that videogames are ethical playgrounds, but like film they also bring their users' lives to bear on the event and connect through embodied affect. The PlayStation 4 (hereafter PS4) in particular prompts somatic responses that have the capacity to cause or work in tandem with affective ones as well. The controller vibrates when action occurs to the user's avatar and buzzes with a sound emitted through the controller in closer proximity to the user than a television sound system. The PlayStation 5 controller advances this embodied technology by detecting sweat through sensors that work in concert with the user's affective responses to increase the anxiety-inducing effects of the game. The cognitive mapping of a videogame is therefore embodied and extended. In his examination of *Political Affect*, John Protevi explores the ramifications of 4E cognition on affect,[16] examining the technical assemblages that provoke affect and disrupt the epistemological concept of an ideal self (4). By this logic, the controller becomes an extension of the body or an organ unto itself, rendering the interface into prosthesis.

Aside from these features, the buttons on the controller, of course, orchestrate actions in the game world. Previously disregarded for their supposed passive nature, the buttons of the technology are used according to the events of the videogame narrative to generate targeted affect in the user. Jonne Arjoranta's examination of embodied cognition and videogames identifies the manner by which the PS4 in particular simulates embodied experiences. Players are often required to wield their controllers in ways that engage their own bodies with the actions or environs of their avatars. The ability for sounds to emit from the controller likewise connects more directly with the user's senses in closer proximity than the typical soundtracks coming from a television or sound system, the quality of which varies while the controller's technology is a constant.[17]

This outlook challenges previous assumptions about videogame controllers or videogames in general. Videogame controller buttons have been commonly associated with the idea of clicking, mashing, and selecting (Best 29). They bear a resemblance to the computer interface that Galloway discusses insofar as they draw users into the screen in a similarly guided manner. While not all games have a straightforward pathway from which the user can easily divert, the two games studied in this chapter do provide a linear trajectory, even if there are efforts to unsettle that outlook through multiple temporalities or choices. In such a case, the game's multiple yet limited pathways, as with a website URL, have been predetermined for users. The number of buttons corresponding with these pathways (four in the case of the PS4 controller) are what confine the number of choices and put parameters around the potential outcomes of the videogame's narrative. However, the idea that button pressing simply facilitates the user's mindless movement through a singular linear sequence is predicated upon the belief that buttons are insignificant. In the case of choice-based videogames, there are in fact multiple pathways available that draw the user into the narrative and place emotional weight and investment upon which button is pressed. This assumption derives from the notion that the buttons have no relation or connection to the events that transpire in the game-world. J. R. Parker, for instance, perceives buttons as automated and incapable of achieving meaningful attachments between player and played, particularly through what he perceives as "natural" modes of play through technologies like the Nintendo Wii, which was capable of replicating real motions in game worlds. Although he ultimately concludes that "[c]urrent buttons are not suitable for intimate, performance-based play," Stephen N. Giffin nevertheless acknowledges the Nintendo Wii interface's historical achievement of rendering the player an active participant: "It was instrumental in the transformation of pinball from a game of chance to a game of control … players were finally able to control the roaming protagonist of pinball's stylized worlds." However, Sara Shamdani identifies the affective pathways of videogames that can be facilitated through non-kinesthetic technologies. Drawing upon Seigworth and Gregg's aforementioned definitions of affect and emotion, Shamdani perceives affect as drawing attention to "something that is found in the in between-ness, in the intensities that pass through the body, between bodies and their environment." It is thus possible to determine the ways in which the tangibility of the videogame controller and its buttons is actually capable of stimulating affect rather than remaining passive.

Life Is Strange: Before the Storm's implementation of Shakespeare's *The Tempest* demonstrates how buttons not only replicate theatrical conventions but also emulate theatrical responses.[18] *Life Is Strange* is narrative-focused and choice-based, which means that it is comprised primarily of cinematic cut-scenes which are triggered by the user's choices and reactions. The game's interface presents these choices at various points in the game by offering three or four options associated with different buttons on the controller. The game also frames certain moments as pivotal by slowing time. These instances emphasize the augmented consequences of the choice in question by visually changing the colour scheme as well. The moment passes very slowly with a fuzzier resolution and an ominous soundtrack. All of these elements collectively signal the importance of this choice, thereby stressing for users that the button they push will cataclysmically alter or direct the plotline. The results of these climactic choices seriously alter the events of the narrative, the fate of the user's avatar, and the events of the characters in the game world. By utilizing affective triggers and changes to the game's sensual interface that place considerable weight on the button's ability to influence the narrative and relations of the game world, the interface executes a Brechtian effect of reflection that causes the user to consider the ramifications of a given choice. At the conclusion of chapters, users can also reflect on how their choices align with those of other users who have played the game, which allows them to see how their response contributes to that of a larger collective. What is important, therefore, is that the game's interface presents pushing a button as a choice with considerable gravity and frames this design for the user through affect.

Life Is Strange: Before the Storm's narrative—in which Chloe and Rachel's budding relationship culminates in a Shakespearean performance—deploys metaludic or metatheatrical techniques to prompt users to reflect upon the manner by which their own lives operate by similar choices. Chloe is presented as a character who has experienced drastic changes in the past and expectations that similar changes will occur in the future. As she continues to deal with the trauma of losing her father in a car accident, she becomes interested in Rachel, a popular and successful student at her high school who is playing Prospero in *The Tempest*. Chloe learns about theater and theatrical games from her as well as tactile role-playing games from her other high school acquaintances. These pastimes help Chloe work through her traumatic past, which she returns to through theatrical, dreamlike sequences over the course of the game.

Chloe eventually must play as impromptu substitute for Ariel's actor, as neither the actor nor her understudy is able to perform. The game prepares the user for this additional interface of avatar (Chloe) and avatar's avatar (Ariel) that brings the frame of gamer and avatar into the user's perspective. This Brechtian effect takes shape in multiple instances when the videogame user plays as Chloe playing games. Before turning to *The Tempest*, then, it is important to examine these prior episodes. Early in the game, Chloe encounters some peers engrossed in a role-playing game that closely resembles *Dungeons and Dragons*, and she is asked to join. As the role-playing game unfolds, the camera frames the friends seated at the picnic table looking down on the figurines, which represent their *Dungeons and Dragons* avatars. The scene is therefore similar to one people would play in everyday life with the various role-playing paraphernalia. In this scene, then, the user plays as Chloe who plays as an elf barbarian. The design allows the user to remember that they are experiencing a connection with Chloe that is similar to that which Chloe shares with her barbarian avatar. The emotional connection between character and user is stressed, however, when Chloe sacrifices her barbarian character to save her friend's avatar and states, "I actually feel sad right now." The investment and attachment to the avatar prompt users to reflect upon their own affective tie to Chloe or other characters in *Life Is Strange: Before the Storm* or games in general. The tactile control of a figurine through Chloe's hand thus draws the user's attention to their own manual operation of her with the controller.

Characters within the narrative foster intimate and meaningful bonds between one another as well through games, as shown later when Chloe and Rachel develop their relationship after they steal away on a train car. They play "two lies and a truth," and then an improvisation game that Rachel states she learned through her theatrical education, claiming "I like games." *Life Is Strange: Before the Storm* therefore overtly builds a bridge between gaming and theatrical performance, and much like in *The Tempest*, games are utilized to develop and frame the relations between the characters. Miranda and Ferdinand are discovered to be playing chess near the play's denouement, for instance, and Gina Bloom has noted that the Brechtian quality of this event "engages theatre spectators' embodied knowledge of the game" (421).[19] This dynamic of play and engagement makes *The Tempest* an ideal play for *Life Is Strange: Before the Storm* to adapt and appropriate in order to execute similar resonances between users and fictional personae. Chloe's relations with other characters are likewise defined by the contours of games. If the user opts to work on mending relations with Chloe's militant and chauvinist stepfather, Chloe will define this action as, "reset button pressed." The user is therefore repeatedly reminded of the fact they are playing a game, much as Shakespeare's audience are reminded that they are watching a play. But the user also sees their reality in terms of buttons through watching the avatar understand and define her life through them, much as Shakespeare's audience was directed to see their world as a stage. Buttons thus become an interface not only for gameplay but also for understanding and processing life events. The concept of hitting reset on life as one would on a game console exemplifies the extended analogy of the interface's buttons to life. The ongoing efforts to make users cognizant of this fact prompt them to reflect upon the effect, but also affect, of what they are watching as well as creating.

After aligning the videogame with the theatrical in the entire first episode and a half, *Life Is Strange: Before the Storm* then turns its Shakespearean performance into a game. The story's arc prepares the user to see the production of *The Tempest* as the central event. *Life Is Strange: Before the Storm* is the prequel to the initial instalment, *Life Is Strange*. In *Life Is Strange*, the user plays as Max, who has returned to the town where she grew up and becomes reunited with her past friend Chloe. Among the various plotlines in this first game of the series, a deadly storm encroaches on their small Oregon town, which remains the setting for the prequel. *Life Is Strange: Before the Storm* establishes the origins of this storm with Rachel's fury at her father's infidelity spurring a forest fire and anticipates the continuance of this thematic content of natural disaster later by including a high school production of *The Tempest*. Rachel plays Prospero in the private school's production of the play, and the chemistry between her and Chloe emerges from their shared witnessing of Miranda and Ferdinand's romance played out by teenage actors who are rehearsing the scene. As the actors rehearse lines, both Chloe and Rachel are framed as spectators watching the drama, and questions of delivery and purpose unfold between them. The actor playing Ferdinand seeks counsel for his motivation in delivering the lines to Miranda, as from his perspective he seems to be professing true love but has previously "been bragging that" he (Ferdinand) has "been banging all the ladies." Rachel asks Chloe what she thinks about the circumstances, thus bringing her into the fold of the performance. The fact that Rachel asks her the question coupled with the user's knowledge that Chloe has a budding romantic interest in Rachel, however, defines the contours of the player's affective response to the situation, as it will determine in some ways the course of their own relationship. Thinking back to the earlier *Dungeons and Dragons* episode, which the user plays only moments earlier in the videogame, it is possible to see a parallelism. Much as Chloe experiences affect toward her elf barbarian that she maneuvers, her watching the actors and guiding their motivation through her interpretation of the circumstances is likewise influenced vicariously through her desire for Rachel. By not only committing to an investment in the Shakespearean characters and the actors' motivations but also working through her own emotions for Rachel in the process, Chloe lives vicariously through Miranda and Ferdinand's relationship to comprehend her own feelings.

The videogame's framing of the theatrical interface as affective and interrogative technology prepares users to see the performance of *The Tempest* that will follow as a game, one they must play out in the game narrative. When the actor playing Ariel cannot make it to the performance because of the fire encroaching on the town, Chloe is the only person who can fill the role, and Rachel suggests that she is suited for it because of her knack for the theatrical improvisational games she has played with her. Once Chloe reluctantly accepts the role and after the cinematic sequence ends, users find themselves as Chloe costumed as Ariel backstage. Looking around the space, users have the opportunity to read the script beforehand. They may opt not to do so, but if they read it, they will find lines and cues for Ariel in 1.2 of the play. At this point, the videogame user prepares for the event according to the techniques and mechanics of the stage, wherein they must memorize and prepare their delivery by knowing when and what to speak. The user has the choice of whether or not they will adhere to this stage practice, but other than the fact Chloe now dons a raven costume as Ariel and is ostensibly going onstage soon, there is nothing to dictate she must peruse the script or prepare. The user must also anticipate this game of language and stage business beforehand and listen for cues to deliver their lines. As the second scene of act one commences, Chloe as Ariel receives her cue from Rachel as Prospero and enters onstage. During the dialogue, the user has the option of three possible lines to respond with, and their ability to do so depends upon their prior knowledge of *The Tempest*. The game therefore replicates the live anxieties and pressures of the actor whose ability to recall the play's lines properly can result in the success or failure of the play. The buttons on the controller are aligned with these choices, and the affective experiences of performance are translated into the interface of the game. In this climactic moment, then, the conventions and cognition of Shakespeare's Globe and its bearing on game tutorials, as shown previously in *Final Fantasy IX*, are exhibited, but their representation in *Life Is Strange: Before the Storm* renders them into instances that generate affective experience through choice and buttons in ways similar to the theater.

Conclusion: Reading and Writing the Screen's Page

While buttons can be an immersive, automated method of gameplay, the appropriations of Shakespeare in these games prove that the interface of the controller has possibilities for generating meaningful affect that replicates the reflective aspects of the theater. The Brechtian potential Galloway links to videogame interfaces and their ability to produce an ethical playground mean that the avatar's actions resonate for the user in ways that establish quandaries that are choice-based and render selection into a consequential action rather than a cognitively passive push. The orchestration of buttons and instructional features of the videogame console's interface prompt these affective cognitive processes, but they also train the user to comprehend the gaming interface in a manner similar to the cognitive ecology of the Shakespearean theater and its reliance upon theatrical convention to guide audience reception. The replication of previous theatrical media and gaming conventions with which the user is familiar produces this process of comprehension. However, these lessons apply to actors as well as audiences, since the videogame user is both of these parties at different intervals. The videogame interface therefore renders the Shakespearean audience into actors and alters the experience of his drama in the process, but in turn it generates a critical and self-reflexive component.

Whereas Shakespeare's theater's interface taught its audience by virtue of the *theatrum mundi*, the videogame interface leads its users to perceive that all the world's a game. In doing so, it revises the page on which those performances survive. By exploring a pre-print history of the page and considering it in relation to current digital technologies, Bonnie Mak reveals that "the page need not always be physically circumscribed as it is in the codex" (10). In the game world of *Life Is Strange: Before the Storm*, the user can summon Chloe's journal with the click of a button, complete with photographs, drawings, and words that Chloe has included as a result of the user's actions. In this way, the game world becomes the page, but one that determines and rewrites Shakespeare as well. Chloe's actions not only define the writings in her journal but also function as acts of graffiti and writing on her world, for which she and the user are rewarded through trophies associated with gameplay for these expressions. The game interface therefore asks us to reconceive Shakespeare, not only as performance, but also as page through the videogame and its user's manipulation, creation, and production of his art as well as himself. The controller empowers Shakespearean users to perceive the entire dramatized and written world they experience and maneuver as Shakespeare's but also Chloe's and therefore in part the user's own page and stage.

Notes

1 The 1993 and 1994 congressional hearings on videogames and violence, particularly the intense violence and gore of *Mortal Kombat*, spurred a system of censorship through an implemented ratings system as well as moral concern. These concerns escalated after news media linked the events in

Columbine to the videogame industry, especially the game *DOOM* (Lukas 75–6). The direct correlation between videogame violence and subsequent real actions, however, is tenuous. In assessing the association between sociopathic behavior and violent media, Grimes and Bergen conclude that arguments about art as spurring violent activity ultimately derive from "a socially, politically, and morally based agenda, not a scientific one" (1151).

2 Game studies, of course, stretches back much further with Johan Huizinga's *Homo Ludens* and other major prior studies, but videogames in particular have become increasingly accepted alongside other studies of play in more recent years.

3 The earliest discussion seems to be Best's brief overview of the current state of educational Shakespearean videogames (29, 37). Murray's *Hamlet on the Holodeck* (1997) examines Shakespearean narratives in the Star Trek series' representations of digital game worlds, but this earlier instance does not address actual Shakespeare-based videogames.

4 Although Galloway is preoccupied with avant-garde artistic concepts, he applies these to *MAD* magazine among other art forms' interfaces. His discussions of videogames likewise allow for applications to this medium by focusing on the overlooked analytic potential of bringing the frame into focus here as well.

5 This contemporary theoretical angle aligns with Brian Massumi's similar notions of affect and emotion as rendering persons open to that which they act upon, which Amanda Bailey and Mario Digangi have applied to the early modern world to understand emotion "as the subjective, embodied manifestation of the interface between individuals or between individuals and their environment" (4). In this manner, the chapter's investigation of interface is diverging from the psychoanalytical definition of "affect" and instead using these concepts from affect theory that have been previously applied to early modern literature.

6 In attending to the interface, Galloway makes a similar observation when he states that it is a "middle … not a medium" (18).

7 Thabet acknowledges the agency of creation in videogame narratives, but this understanding should still be tempered with the cinematic experience of viewing events that unfold without the user's guidance or input, even if these scenes draw them in and potentially influence how users play afterward (9).

8 Grosz asks, "[d]o prostheses function because the body lacks something, which it uses an external or extrinsic object to replace?" (147). This chapter adopts this line of questioning in its approach to prosthesis rather than viewing it as corrective or making the body whole, so that regardless of whether or not the user identifies as able-bodied, the controller is an extension of their self and body, though this is not to assume that all console videogames are accessible.

9 Garner explores the cognitive phenomenology of the theatrical interface through the German concept of *Einfühlung*, "which means 'in-feeling' or 'feeling into'" (147). As a consequence, audience members live vicariously through witnessing the kinesthetic motion of others onstage.

10 The embodied experience likewise extends beyond the prosthesis of the controller. Yee identifies the ways in which users' connections with videogame avatars and their actions have ramifications for players' somatic experiences during and after they have finished playing (152–3). The imagined embodied experience of the avatar may become the real embodied experience of users, even if it does not equate with their lived experience. For example, one may feel taller or be able to experience the world differently as a result of having interfaced with characters who possess those traits in a game.

11 Exceptions to this statement include Harrison and Lutz's exploration of videogame adaptations and appropriations' "exercise in choosing not to be Hamlet" (24); Bushnell's *Tragic Time in Drama, Film, and Videogames*; Roberts-Smith, DeSouza-Coelho, and Malone's foray into mainstream videogames "such as *Heavy Rain* (2010) or *Journey* (2012), where players become affectively invested in non-playable characters" in foregrounding the discussion of their approach to engineering the pedagogy and gameplay of their *Staging Shakespeare* (4). Forthcoming work from Bushnell comparing gaming in *Hamlet* to the mechanisms of *The Wolf Among Us* (2014) and on the ways in which videogames based upon *Hamlet* offer a means to develop new theories of adaptation also seek to remedy this gap in present scholarship.

12 When initially playing as Zidane on the airship prior to the band of thieves and actors' arrival at the castle, their boss (Baku) dons a dragon mask and fights them in disguise. This event functions as an early means to teach users role-playing game mechanics. The rehearsal aspect that GameMage identifies here, then, is apt, given Tribble's account of the ways in which the stage guides and instructs spectators.

13 Brecht's *Verfremdungseffekt* is one technique that can be said to produce this state by not allowing for a complete immersion into the theatrical world as real, which he associates with "Western actor[s]" (93).

Chinese artists' different tendency to observe themselves results for Brecht in a theater that stops the spectator from "losing himself in the character completely" (93).

14 It is worth noting that although Brecht encouraged a lack of emotional connection with characters onstage, he did not eschew affect or ethical considerations. He acknowledges that audiences are "bound to release emotional effects," so theatergoers have "to adopt a critical approach to [their] emotions" (101). Moreover, Brecht argues that the "crude aesthetic thesis that emotions can only be stimulated by means of empathy is wrong" (145). The compulsion to act and acknowledge the gravity of those actions can therefore involve emotion and spur affect.

15 This is not to say that it leads to a more disaffected relation between the user and the avatar. If anything, the less box-like bodies from *Final Fantasy VII* create avatars that more closely resemble the user's own embodiment. Moreover, Bissonnette theorizes the ways in which "cognitive and sensory extensions" are formed between the viewer and animated figures through the interface of the screen to produce what she terms "'becoming-animated'" (3). The film adaptation of the *Final Fantasy* game series is also one of the examples she uses of this phenomenon (1; 64–5). In other words, just because the animation prompts a puppet-like dimension to the characters, it does not limit the potential for a user to establish a meaningful connection with the avatars or other figures in the game's narrative.

16 4E Cognition entails extended cognition, embodied cognition, embedded cognition, and enacted cognition. This chapter primarily explores embodied cognition and will offer more on this topic later.

17 Although these features distinguish the controller from less sensual technologies like television remotes, it is important to note the historical role these other tactile devices play in users interfacing with narratives. Paulsen notes ways in which "[v]iewers touching the buttons on their clunky remote controls intervened in the current of event reception, to make it, even if in a minor way, a current of event production" (138). By considering the interface history of TV remote controls in relation to the affective dimensions she uses to conceptualize "[i]nterfaces" as "caus[ing] problems for distinguishing the here from the there" (15), Paulsen's work can be deployed to think about videogames as a later development that more readily connects the user with the "there" of the game world while rendering the user into an actor rather than just a conductor. The PS4 controller therefore simply enacts a fuller vision of the affective theory of interface Paulsen's slashed title *Here/There* implies in its exploration of television: "It is a place where opposites touch" (15).

18 On the affective similarities between theatrical and videogame media, see David Owen's discussion of his past experience directing and performing for the stage and his reflections on videogame play (1–4).

19 Poole remarks upon the unique qualities of this particular game in the Shakespeare canon, as it is the only occasion in which a "Shakespearean play-within-a-play goes uninterrupted" (52).

References

Arjoranta, Jonne. "Games & Embodied Cognition: What Is It Like to Be a Cat-Person?" *First Person Scholar*, 2014. Available at: http://www.firstpersonscholar.com/games-and-embodied-cognition/.

Bailey, Amanda and Mario DiGangi. "Introduction." *Affect Theory and Early Modern Texts: Politics, Ecologies, and Form*, edited by Amanda Bailey and Mario DiGangi, Palgrave Macmillan, 2017, pp. 1–24.

Best, Michael. "Electronic Shakespeares: Which Way Goes the Game?" *The Shakespeare Newsletter*, Spring/Summer 2008, pp. 29, 37.

Bissonnette, Sylvia. *Affect and Embodied Meaning in Animation: Becoming-Animated*. Routledge, 2019.

Bloom, Gina. "Videogame Shakespeare: Enskilling Audiences through Theater-Making Games." *Shakespeare Studies*, vol. 43, 2015, pp. 114–127.

Bloom, Gina. "Time to Cheat: Chess and *The Tempest*'s Performative History of Dynastic Marriage." *The Oxford Handbook of Shakespeare and Embodiment*, edited by Valerie Traub, Oxford UP, 2016, pp. 419–434.

Bloom, Gina. *Gaming the Stage: Playable Media and the Rise of English Commercial Theatre*. U of Michigan Press, 2018.

Bloom, Gina. "Theatre History in 3D: The Digital Early Modern in the Age of the Interface." *English Literary Renaissance*, vol. 50, no. 1, 2019, pp. 8–16.

Bloom, Gina, Sawyer Kemp, Nicholas Toothman, and Evan Buswell. "'A Whole Theater of Others': Amateur Acting and Immersive Spectatorship in the Digital Shakespeare Game *Play the Knave*." *Shakespeare Quarterly*, vol. 67, no. 4, 2016, pp. 408–430.

Brecht, Bertolt. *Brecht on Theatre: The Development of an Aesthetic*. Translated and edited by John Willett, Hill and Wang, 1964.

Bushnell, Rebecca. *Tragic Time in Drama, Film, and Videogames: The Future in the Instant*. Palgrave Macmillan, 2016.

Bushnell, Rebecca. "Videogames and *Hamlet*: Experiencing Tragic Choice, and Consequences." *Games and Theatre in Shakespeare's England*, edited by Tom Bishop, Gina Bloom, and Erika T. Lin, Amsterdam UP, 2021, pp. 229–254.

Drucker, Joanna. *Graphesis: Visual Forms of Knowledge Production*. Harvard UP, 2014.

Fazel, Valerie M. and Louise Geddes. "Introduction: The Shakespeare User." *The Shakespeare User: Critical and Creative Appropriations in a Networked Culture*, edited by Valerie M. Fazel and Louise Geddes, Palgrave Macmillan, 2017, pp. 1–22.

Final Fantasy IX. Square Enix, 2000, Playstation.

Galloway, Andrew R. *The Interface Effect*. Polity P, 2012.

GameMage. "GAME DESIGN: *Final Fantasy IX* – The Influences of Shakespeare." YouTube, 2016. Available at: https://www.youtube.com/watch?v=xJ5nJnIV8Hk.

Garner, Jr., Stanton B. *Kinesthetic Spectatorship in the Theatre: Phenomenology, Cognition, Movement*. Palgrave Macmillan, 2018.

Giffin, Stephen N. "Push. Play: An Examination of the Gameplay Button." *Loading... The Journal of the Canadian Game Studies Association*, vol. 2, no. 2, 2008, pp. 1–5. Available at: https://journals.sfu.ca/loading/index.php/loading/article/view/37.

Grimes, Tom and Lori Bergen. "The Epistemological Argument Against a Causal Relationship Between Media Violence and Sociopathic Behavior Among Psychologically Well Viewers." *American Behavioral Scientist*, vol. 51, no. 8, 2008, pp. 1137–1154.

Grosz, Elizabeth. *Time Travels: Feminism, Nature, Power*. Duke UP, 2005.

Harrison, Matthew and Michael Lutz. "South of Elsinore: Actions that a Man Might Play." *The Shakespeare User: Critical and Creative Appropriations in a Networked Culture*, edited by Valerie M. Fazel and Louise Geddes, Palgrave Macmillan, 2017, pp. 23–40.

Hookway, Branden. *Interface*. MIT Press, 2014.

Life Is Strange: Before the Storm. Square Enix, 2017. Playstation 4.

Lopez, Jeremy. *Theatrical Convention and Audience Response in Early Modern Drama*. Cambridge UP, 2007.

Lukas, Scott A. "Behind the Barrel: Reading the Video Game Gun." *Joystick Soldiers: The Politics of Play in Military Video Games*, edited by Nina B. Huntemann and Matthew Thomas Payne. Routledge, 2010, pp. 75–90.

Mak, Bonnie. *How the Page Matters*. U of Toronto P, 2011.

Owen, David. *Player and Avatar: The Affective Potential of Videogames*. McFarland, 2017.

Parker, J.R. "Buttons, Simplicity, and Natural Interfaces." *Loading... The Journal of the Canadian Game Studies Association*, vol. 2, no. 2, 2008, pp. 1–11. Available at: https://journals.sfu.ca/loading/index.php/loading/article/view/33.

Paulsen, Kris. *Here/There: Telepresence, Touch, and Art at the Interface*. MIT Press, 2017.

Poole, William. "False Play: Shakespeare and Chess." *Shakespeare Quarterly*, vol. 55, no. 1, 2004, pp. 50–70.

Protevi, John. *Political Affect: Connecting the Social and Somatic*. U of Minnesota P, 2009.

Roberts-Smith, Jennifer, Shawn DeSouza-Coelho, and Toby Malone. "Staging Shakespeare in Social Games: Toward a Theory of Theatrical Game Design." *Borrowers and Lenders: The Journal of Shakespeare Appropriation*, vol. 10, no. 1, 2016, pp. 1–19. Available at: https://www.proquest.com/docview/1803822776?pq-origsite=primo&accountid=13800.

Rowe, Katherine. "Crowd Sourcing Shakespeare: Word and Screen Play in Second Life." *Shakespeare Studies*, vol. 38, 2010, pp. 58–67.

Seigworth, Gregory J. and Melissa Gregg. "An Inventory of Shimmers." *The Affect Theory Reader*, edited by Gregory J. Seigworth and Melissa Gregg. Duke UP, 2010, pp. 1–25.

Shamdani, Sara. "Affect at Play: Politics via Videogames." *Loading... The Journal of the Canadian Game Studies Association*, vol. 10, no. 16, 2017, pp. 1–14. Available at: https://journals.sfu.ca/loading/index.php/loading/article/view/175.

Stern, Tiffany. *Documents of Performance in Early Modern England*. Cambridge UP, 2009.

Stubbes, Philip. *A Critical Edition of Philip Stubbes's Anatomie of Abuses*. Edited by M.J. Kidnie. The Shakespeare Institute, 1996. Available at: https://etheses.bham.ac.uk/id/eprint/4435/1/Kidnie96PhD_redacted.pdf.

Thabet, Tamer. *Video Game Narrative and Criticism: Playing the Story*. Palgrave Macmillan, 2015.

Tribble, Evelyn. *Cognition in the Globe: Attention and Memory in Shakespeare's Theatre*. Palgrave Macmillan, 2011.

Valera, Francisco J., Eleanor Rosch, and Evan Thompson. *The Embodied Mind: Cognitive Science and Human Experience*. MIT Press, 1992.

Way, Geoffrey. "Shakespeare Videogames, Adaptation/Appropriation, and Collaborative Reception." *Games and Theatre in Shakespeare's England*, edited by Tom Bishop, Gina Bloom, and Erika T. Lin. Amsterdam UP, 2021, pp. 255–273.

Yee, Nick. *The Proteus Paradox: How Online Games and Virtual Worlds Change Us—And How They Don't.* Yale UP, 2014.

4
VOICE AS INTERFACE

Bruce R. Smith

Variants of *voic* occur 211 times in Shakespeare's plays and poems. The text with the most occurrences is *Coriolanus*, with 35 iterations. I arrived at these statistics by interfacing with my computer. I pulled up Open Source Shakespeare and entered a search for *voic*. Since *The Two Noble Kinsmen* is not included in Open Source Shakespeare's database and no searchable text seemed to be available via a Google search, I pulled up the Folger Shakespeare Editions website, downloaded the e-text, converted it into a pdf file, and again searched *voic*. The whole operation took three minutes 52 seconds. In doing these operations with my computer I (and it) created an interface. The situation felt like it was just the two of us, with nothing but air between us: my face *here* looking at the screen and deciding what questions to ask, the computer's "face" *there* bombarding my face with phosphorescent answers. We—I and my computer—transacted our business in a liminal space/time in which neither of us was in full control. The mechanics of our transaction made me feel as if I were in control, but my power over the computer was only an illusion: the computer was giving me commands all the while. I had to know which sites to pull up, how to search (*voic*, not *voice*), the necessity of converting an html file to a pdf file The resulting tabulations of *voic* was a collaborative effort, perhaps indeed a *competitive* effort.

You, of course, have entered into an interface with a page or a screen to read what I have written.

My investigations of voice as interface in this chapter are informed by Branden Hookway's theorizing of interface as a fluid state in which two entities create between them a new habitation: "The interface is a liminal or threshold condition that both delimits the space for a kind of inhabitation and opens up otherwise unavailable phenomena, conditions, situations, and territories for exploration, use, participation, and exploitation" (5).

Like most people, when I conceptualize an interface, I think visually, in terms like Hookway's "threshold," "space," "opening up," "territories." What happens when I try to re-imagine interface in terms of voice? Lungs, cartilage and muscles in the throat, tongue and teeth in the mouth: those I can visualize. But voice as something that these physical parts produce? That's harder. Voice is invisible, ephemeral. Contemporary digital technology can turn voice into something seeable. Using an update of Dictaphone technology of the 1880s, I might have dictated this chapter, with my computer doing the work of a typist. My voiced words would have become visual letters. The one-sidedness of speech-into-print applications offers—for me at least—none of the "conditions, situations, and territories for exploration" that Hookway celebrates as the essence of interface. There is more scope for interactivity in

 DOI: 10.4324/9780367821722-6

the "Shax App" possibilities that W. B. Worthen describes in *Shakespeare, Technicity, Theatre* (68–103).

Instead of trying to visualize voice as interface, we come closer to Hookway's dynamic model if we turn the noun into a verb: *to voice.* Astonished at Timon's pitiful state, Timandra exclaims, "Is this the Athenian minion whom the whole world / Voiced so regardfully?" (*Tim* 4.3.82–83).[1] To voice something or someone is to bring it into presence (*OED*, "voice, *v.*," 1). Thinking of voice as an action catches the transactional nature of interface. An additional advantage is that the verb describes what *actors* do: they *voice* words that someone else has written. They operate in the interface between writing and performance. To consider voice as interface in Shakespeare's plays is to enter the space that actors have created—and on that space's terms.

Hookway's coordinates of interface in space and time can help us get our bearings. With respect to space, Hookway imagines interface as *bounded*:

> As a threshold condition that extends into and incorporates the environments that it bounds, the interface demands of the entities or states that enter into relation with it a surrendering of claims of self-sovereignty and of identities distinct from the threshold, as it is the threshold that becomes the standard by which these are defined and the source from which their agency is derived.
>
> (16)

In the exploration I am undertaking in this chapter I am imagining the boundedness of interface within five environments, each imagined as a closed circle:

1 the human body with its vocal apparatus;
2 the inhabitations of Shakespeare's fictions;
3 theater buildings as acoustic spaces;
4 the space between texts and readers' eyes;
5 the "field" that binds us as theorists/scholars/critics to "Shakespeare" as a cultural construct.

Within each of these interfaces I will attempt to situate voice as an energy force and human actors as competitors.

That task is complicated by our historical distance from each of these sites: from early modern models of human physiology, from the site-specificities of the Globe and the Blackfriars theatres, from the oral reading practices of early modern readers, from the sonic horizons encoded in early modern fictions, from early modern ways of speaking about literature. Hookway's temporal coordinates of interface—the counterparts to his spatial coordinates— prove useful in negotiating these challenges:

> A theory of the interface is a theory of culture … the interface describes a cultural moment as much as it does a specific relationship between human user and technological artifact … Culture here is not given from without but rather produced within moments of encounter.
>
> (15–16)

The human body

In our post-human cultural moment it will not seem far-fetched to anatomize the human body and its apparatus for voicing in terms of computer technology. The biological—along with the social, the material, and the technological—is one of the "realms" within which Hookway locates human interfaces. The materiality of vocal body parts is a topic in early modern anatomy books like John Banister's *The History of Man* (1578). Banister details all the physiological components that go into the production of speech:

> This larynx is the organ, by which we receive and put forth breath, as also of making and forming voice … For to the forming thereof commeth not only bones … but also cartilages, ligaments, muscles, and membranes: besides that I omit both veins, arteries, and nerves.
>
> *(sig. F4v; spelling modernized)*

To think so precisely about the mechanics of voice, in Shakespeare's time as in ours, can result in two opposite outcomes: a heightened control over voice or a loss of voice. Shakespeare's characters usually take for granted the ability of lungs, larynx, and mouth to sound out thoughts and feelings. Only when these mechanisms fail, usually in times of conflict, do characters recognize the pent-up breath in their lungs, the tightness in their throats, the failure of their mouths to utter the words and the feelings they have within. Hamlet is the most famous example. Awed by the traveling player's ability to voice Hecuba's passion so forcefully, Hamlet berates his own inability to speak—even as he outdoes the just-departed player in an outpouring of words that threatens to burst the constraints of iambic pentameter:

> What would he do
> Had he the motive and that cue for passion
> That I have? He would drown the stage with tears
> And cleave the general ear with horrid speech,
> Make mad the guilty, and appale the free,
> Confound the ignorant, and amaze indeed
> The very faculties of eyes and ears.
>
> (Ham *2.2.456–462)*

We witness in these words a translation not just of interior feelings into external words—a relay process—but of soundless interior feelings and the physiological restraints on externalizing those feelings in speech: a reflexive process. Inner feeling presses for expression in sounded words, but lungs, throat, tongue, and mouth refuse to do Hamlet service. He experiences a struggle between inner feelings and outer words.

In this fraught interface between inner and outer, Hamlet enacts the etymology of the word *interface* unpacked by Hookway:

> The prefix *inter.*- connotes relations that take place within an already bounded field, whether spatial or temporal. It pertains to an inward orientation, an interiority … *Inter-* holds its bounded condition as already given, as a priori to the relations it describes.
>
> *(7)*

Face, as Hookway explains,

> is derived from the Latin *facies*, meaning like the English face a visage or countenance, as well as an appearance, character, form, or figure; *facies* in turn is derived

> from the verb *facere*, meaning to act, make, form, do, cause or bring about. A face, then, is the aspect of a thing by which it presents itself.
>
> *(8)*

In Hamlet's case, the interface between inner and outer is conflicted. In their jerky shifts and loose syntax the words that result are akin to noise, in both its semantic and technological senses.

Hamlet finds his own voice by projecting his interior feelings onto voices outside himself, the actors' voices. This reflexive interaction breaks out of the relay model of vocal production. Interface, as a point of exchange, lets us correct the uni-directional concept of voice assumed by physiology (voice is the vibration of vocal chords in the larynx), physics (voice is air molecules vibrating at certain frequencies), and psychology (voice is the perceived sense of the speaker in the listener's ears and brain). In the field of sound studies, this relay sequence has been calibrated as a series of "transductions" in which one form of energy is transformed into another (Helmreich). Thus vibrations in the larynx become sound waves in the air, which become electrical signals in the listener's ear. The concept of interface changes this relay model into an exchange model: uni-directional action becomes reciprocal *inter*-action. The failure at voicing experienced by Hamlet stands as critiques of the uni-directional relay model that informs much scholarly writing about voice and speech.

In digital computing, the interface between mechanical hardware and its software applications is an operating system. In the early modern body the operating system had been designed by the second-century CE Greek physician Galen, with updates from early modern anatomists and physicians (Park 464–84). It is a system in which brain, mouth, and heart are interconnected via a vaporous spirit coursing through the human body (Park). *Spiritus* was to early modern bodies what electrical signals are to modern computers.

In the schema of early modern psychology, voice could be sounded forth according to the feelings of heart or the dictates of head—or a combination of the two. Thought begins in sensations, which are communicated by *spiritus* to the heart, which incites a feeling of moving toward (in the case of objects felt to be good) or shrinking away (in the case of objects felt to be bad). Only then do the heart's responses get communicated, via *spiritus*, to the brain, which in turn dictates the person's responses, including the person's *vocal* responses.

Galen's hydraulic model of the human body has a curious affinity with Hookway's tracing the term *interface* to James Thomson's work in hydrodynamics in the 1880s. It is from Thomson's physics model that Hookway derives his concept of interface as a fluid state in which two energies compete for control (59–119). Applying Hookway's theory to Galen's physiology, we might think of the hydraulic human body as the interface between heart and brain, between thorax and head, with the throat in between as interface.

To voice is to *ex-press*, to press out the energy of air from the lungs. Beyond the instantaneous energy of exclamations like "oh," "no," and "fuck," we ordinarily think of the voiced energy as being shaped by the brain before coming out the mouth—yet another instance of the uni-directional relay model of communication. How is that common idea changed when we think instead of the two-way energy of an interface? We must then take into account the reciprocal power of the environments within which the voicing happens. In what follows I begin by considering Shakespeare's fictions as one such environment. I then attend early modern theater buildings as giant interfaces for the production, reception, and return of voiced sounds. Next comes a sounding of the physically smaller but operationally more complex interface between texts and readers' eyes.

These physical interfaces provide physical grounding for considering next the vocal interfaces implicit in Shakespeare's fictions. We set up our own interfaces with these vocal environments, interfaces that are situated within another environment, the "field" of Shakespeare studies. A brief consideration of the place of voice in this field concludes this chapter.

Fictions

Dramatic fictions are interfaces bounded not in space but in time. In Hookway's terms, they are "inhabitations" in which the participants are bodies-with-voices. The characters *inhabit* dramatic fictions; so do we as we insert ourselves into the fiction as observers, as listeners. *Their* acoustic interface becomes *our* acoustic interface as we listen in the theater, as we imagine while we read. Early modern actors understood their art to be a matter of "personation." To *personate* was to "sound through" (*per-sonare*) (Roach 23–58). In their own persons-as-bodies (*OED*, "person, *n*.," II.4.a) actors took on the passions—physiological and psychological—of persons-as-characters (*OED*, "person, *n*.," I.1). Different passions involved different voices as well as different appearances. As interfaces, voices in dramatic fictions operate with closed systems of communication, systems that contain just so many bodies, and perhaps within with just so much quanta of energy. We can chart the negotiations of voices within these systems in terms of four particular conflicts or (in computing terms) tasks:

feeling | | words
voicing | | writing
voicing | | *de*- and *im*-personating
individual voice | | group voice

Within the closed energy-systems of dramatic fictions these tasks are not totally separable. They entail one another.

Feeling | | words

Shakespeare's dramatic fictions offer a catalogue of ways *to voice*. That catalogue can be organized under various headings: formal types of dramatic speech (dialogue, soliloquy, aside), speech genres (conversation, oration, letter), register (high, medium, low), ethnicity (English, French, Welsh), prosody (blank verse, rhymed verse, prose), and so on. Characters within the fictions exist not as independent entities but in relationship to each other. With respect to voice, the interface in dramatic fictions is a contested space in which voices compete with another. Onstage they literally "face off." Shifts in the energy of one character's voice cause changes in the energy of other characters' voices. At stake in their voicings is the "self-sovereignty" that Hookway specifies as a feature of all interfaces.

We can hear that struggle with special acuity in characters whose voices resist or refuse the dominant speech culture. In general, characters in early modern English plays are seldom at a loss for words. That would include Hamlet, who may keenly feel the tension between interiority and exteriority but nonetheless has more lines to speak than anyone else in the fiction, much of them in soliloquy rather than dialogue. Hamlet's speeches end, however, in a failure of lungs: "The rest is silence" (*Ham* 5.2.316). Horatio, more adept as a participant in the vocal interface of Elsinore, then speaks for Hamlet. The last word, however, is Fortinbras's. A different situation arises when characters refuse speech, when they silence their voices. In every instance the refusal disrupts the interface. Cordelia's "Nothing, my lord" in response to Lear's demand for verbal affirmation of her love is a signal example of this disruption (*Lr* 1.1.73). Lear's shocked response ("How? Nothing can come of nothing. Speak again" [1.1.74]) gradually gains in volume, rhythm, and pitch to fill the acoustic gap left by

Cordelia's refusal. Other such silences, also on the part of women, occur in Isabella's lack of verbal response to Duke Vincentio's proposal of marriage in *Measure for Measure* and Hermione's failure to address her husband Leontes in "the statue scene" of *The Winter's Tale*. In each case, as with Cordelia, it is a male character (Duke Vicentio in *MM*, Leontes in *WT*) who supplies the missing vocal energy by speaking over the silence. The entire acoustic interface alters when characters refuse to speak. The balance of power shifts. Refusals of voice upset the equilibrium of the vocal interface within the system and set up waves—air-waves—of sonic turbulence.

Vocal reticence can work a similar effect, as with the last speech in *Lear*. Whether it is spoken by Albany or Edgar, the sentiment "Speak what we feel, not what we ought to say" (*Lr* 5.3.320) reverberates in the play's final silence. In such instances, the marks and remarks of a character (which means literally a mark made on a surface [*OED*, "mark, *n.*," I.1]) *exceed* words. The gap between surface and depth is felt but not voiced, intuited but not heard.

Voicing | | *writing*

For all its shock value, Derrida's argument that difference-marking must happen before speech can happen adheres to the uni-directional relay model of communication. Thinking of speech and writing as an interface within dramatic fictions allows for much more complexity and negotiation. The appearance of a piece of writing in the midst of a dramatic fiction—which is, after all, a process of turning a written script into vocal sounds—can seem intrusive. Within his dramatic fictions Shakespeare often plays up the physicality, permanence, and authority of written words as opposed to the ephemeral sounds of speech. Air is a less durable medium than paper. At the same time, the inscribed words lose the truth-value of written words. The writing down of voiced words and the voicing of inscribed words call attention to differences between air as a medium and paper as a medium. Once taken away or taken down from a speaker, words become subject to dissimulation. The result is an estrangement of voice. In speech-to-text and text-to-speech apps such transactions sometimes end in laughably approximate results. In Shakespeare's plays the faulty interfaces are often laughable, as with most of the "notings" in *Much Ado About Not(h)ing*, especially Dogberry's deposition (*Ado* 4.2). Conversion of speech into letters and back into speech have tragic consequences in the letter Edmund drafts in the likeness of his brother Edgar's hand and gives to Gloucester to read aloud. What is presented as a transcript of Edgar's voice is sounded out in Gloucester's voice, with disastrous consequences for all concerned (*Lr.* 2.1.51–52).

Voicing | | **de-** *and* **im-***personating*

The dissociation of voice from body is another form of disruption in the vocal interface of dramatic fictions. A separation of voice occurs when a character's voice is absent (the ghost in the first scenes of *Hamlet*), unseen (the ghost under the stage in *Hamlet* 1.5), uncanny (the voice Macbeth hears crying, "Sleep no more. / Macbeth does murder sleep" [*Mac.* 2.2.32–33]), or anatomically dislocated (the wounds on Caesar's body that Mark Antony says "like dumb mouths, do ope their ruby lips, / To beg the voice and utterance of my tongue" (*JC* 3.1.264–265). In such instances the voice becomes an object with nowhere to *be*.

This voice-isolation effect in Shakespeare is most obvious when a character disguises his or her voice—*im*-personating someone else. This particular interface is a stock feature of Shakespeare's romantic comedies, including Portia/Balthasar in *The Merchant of Venice*, Rosalind/Ganymede in *As You Like It*, Viola/Cesario in *Twelfth Night*, and Helena/pilgrim in *All's Well That Ends Well*. Each of these visual disguises does not necessarily involve a change in voice.

"Thy small pipe," Orsino tells Viola/Cesario, "Is as the maiden's organ, shrill and sound" (*TN* 1.4.32–33). A disjunction between image and voice seems to have been part of the joke.

Misplaced voices figure largely in the subplot of *Twelfth Night* as well. The raucous singing of Maria, Sir Toby, and Sir Andrew is lambasted by Malvolio for being out of place:

> Have you no wit, manners, nor honesty, but to gabble like tinkers at this time of night? Do ye make an alehouse of my lady's house, that ye squeak out your coziers' catches without any mitigation or remorse of voice?
>
> (TN *2.3.75–78)*

Their revenge on Malvolio, once he has been locked away "within" as a lunatic, involves a change of voice on Feste's part. Donning the gown of a priest, Feste impersonates Sir Topas the Curate not only in a priest's gown but in an exotic voice. Before speaking to Malvolio—who, let us remember, cannot see him—Feste first tries out his new voice on Sir Toby, perhaps in a Spanish accent:

> *Bonos dies*, Sir Toby, for, as the old hermit of Prague, that never saw pen and ink, very wittily said to a niece of King Gorboduc, 'That that is, is.' So I, being Master Parson, am Master Parson; for what is 'that,' but 'that,' and 'is,' but 'is'?
>
> (TN *4.2.11–14)*

One "that" is Feste's visual disguise; the other "that" is his voice. Later in the scene Sir Toby commands Feste, "To him in thine own voice, and bring me word how thou find'st him. I would we were well rid of this knaver" (*TN* 4.2.52–53).

Individual voice | | group voice

A final point of contestation within the vocal interfaces of Shakespeare's dramatic fictions concerns clashes between individual voice and political voice. One reason *Coriolanus* contains more iterations of the word *voice* than any other play by Shakespeare is the synecdoche of "voice" for "vote." The essential conflict in this intensely political play is a matter of voice. The play begins in a cacophony of voices: "*Enter a company of mutinous citizens, with staves, clubs, and other weapons*" (*Cor* 1.1.1 SD). The first of the mutinous citizens has to shout to be heard. The multitudinous voices of the angry citizens are countered, first by the politic voice of Menenius, then by the contemptuous voice of Coriolanus. His first extended speech is a vocal assault: "He that will give good words to thee will flatter / Beneath abhorring" (1.1.149–150) and so on for another 23 snarling enjambed lines. The cacophony of this scene establishes the highly wrought state of the acoustic interface in this play. Noise threatens to out-decibel everything else; bodily assault is always at hand.

Coriolanus is, by his own estimate, not a man of words: "When blows have made me stay, I fled from words" (2.2.65). Coriolanus *acts*; others must *speak* his acts. At the beginning of the play Coriolanus exists (for the audience at least) only as other characters inscribe him in letters: a spy letter that Aufidius reads aloud in 1.2 and a letter from Titus to Volumnia in 2.1 about Coriolanus's victory at Carioles. When Coriolanus is being put up as a candidate for consul, it is up to Cominius to give voice to Coriolanus's heroism: "I shall lack voice. The deeds of Coriolanus / Should not be uttered feebly" (2.2.75–76). Coriolanus's one soliloquy—his one opportunity to speak as an individual—comes late in the play (4.4) and is focused on social relations, on his banishment from Rome and his turn to his former enemy Aufidius:

O world, thy slippery turns! Friends now fast sworn,
Whose double bosoms seem to wear one heart,
Whose hours, whose bed, whose meal and exercise
Are still together, who twin, as 'twere, in love,
Unseparable, shall within this hour,
On a dissension of a doit, break out
To bitterest enmity.

(4.4.12–18)

Angry voicing is implicit in "dissension." Perhaps the letter of resignation that Coriolanus hands Menenius at 5.2.82 is his most eloquent verbal act in the play. But the audience does not get to hear it. Despite Coriolanus's refusal to voice feelings beyond pride and anger, a failed negotiation at the interface of individual voice and public voice proves to be the material cause of his tragedy. From his heroic entry alone into Carioles in 1.5 to his donning the white robe of candidacy in 3.3, Coriolanus presents himself as a *body*. His *voice* is often supplied by others: by Cominius in the case of his battle report, by the consuls when they tell Coriolanus what to say to the tribunes and the plebians, by the plebians when they turn on him and refuse to hear his wounds "speak," by Volumnia when she persuades him to abandon the Volscians in 5.3. In that scene Volumnia repeats her role from 3.2, when her voice overpowers her son's voice and sends him into the marketplace to solicit the people's votes. Volumnia urges upon him an alienation of voice from his physical and psychological person:

CORIOLANUS: Why force you this?
VOLUMNIA: Because, that now it lies you on to speak to th' people,
Not by your own instruction, nor by th' matter
Which your heart prompts you, but with such words
That are but rooted in your tongue,
Though but bastards and syllables of no allowance
To your bosom's truth.

(3.2.51–57)

Standing at this interface of individual voice against group voice, Coriolanus ultimately loses his individual voice entirely. He is ventriloquized by voices not his own, by the consuls' voices, by Menenius's voice, by his mother's voice. He is out-voiced one final time in the "Kill, kill, kill, kill, kill him!" of the Volscians (5.6.130), incensed that he has abandoned their cause. Aufidius is the last character to usurp Coriolanus's voice and calmly creates an equilibrium among voices—an equilibrium that has been missing since the noises of the citizens' revolt in 1.1. In computing terms, his voice—like the voices of Duke Vincentio and Leontes—establishes itself as the default voice.

Theater buildings

The characters in Shakespeare's fictions are, of course, hypothetical persons, and the interfaces they engage with their voices are hypothetical interfaces. The hypothetical becomes the actual when actors *personate* characters by "through-sounding." In the process of personating, actors become a living example of the interface between private voice and public voice. The conceptual interfaces of Shakespeare's fictions become the acoustic interfaces of performance. In the Globe and the Blackfriars theatres Hookway's interface as "threshold" took shape as physically and temporally bounded spaces for turning articulations of lungs, larynx, tongue, teeth, and mouth into speech that filled the ambient air.

A theater may be, literally, a "viewing-place" (West), but with respect to voice, it is first and foremost an acoustic space. The Theatre in Shoreditch, the Globe on the South Bank, the Blackfriars Theatre in the City, the great hall of Whitehall Palace, provincial courtyards, chapels, and town halls: all of these performance venues provided the hardware (literally *hard* since they were made of wood and/or stone) for interfaces between competing voices. The sessions usually lasted two hours or more. They were powered by air. Like other interfaces, these bounded physical environments were also social, political, and psychological environments. In all of them what was being negotiated was, as Hookway puts it, self-sovereignty. Within early modern theater buildings we can identify three interlocking interfaces with respect to voice:

actors | | architecture
individual actor | | other actors
actors | | audience

As Hookway would predict, each of these three interfaces is implicated in the other two.

Let us explore them one by one.

Actors | | architecture

The temporal interfaces in dramatic fictions become physical interfaces in early modern theater buildings. "Playing the house" is a later addition to theater lingo, but the acoustic designs of the all-wood Globe and the mostly-wood Blackfriars theatres invite us to consider these structures as sounding-boards that actors could play upon in the same way a viol-player would play the sounding-board of a viol (B. Smith 1999, 206–45). In each case a wooden structure acted as an interface between bodily actions on the performer's part and the sending of sounds through ambient air. In the case of a viol-player, the physical action was pulling a bow across strings; in the case of an actor, forcing it through the vocal cords and shaping that sound with the mouth. With an actor, as with a viol-player, the quality of the sound being produced was a function of several factors: physical force behind the action, volume, speed, pitch, rhythm, varying qualities of tone, and the positioning of the instrument—viol or voice—within the performance space.

Within the architectural interface not all players of the space were equal. Mladen Dolar, in *A Voice and Nothing More*, proposes several ways of describing voice-as-voice: "Another way to be aware of the voice is through its individuality. We can almost unfailingly identify a person by the voice, the particular individual timbre, resonance, pitch, cadence, melody, the peculiar way of pronouncing certain sounds" (22). The contestation of voices within a particular acoustic interface is thus a complex matter. Placement on the platform is a crucial factor.

Until the reconstruction of Shakespeare's Globe in London, theater historians had assumed that the position of greatest power was a visual matter. The edge of the platform, closest to the audience, was thought to be the place of acoustic power (Styan 81–108). The experience of actors at Shakespeare's Globe has suggested the position of power is an aural matter: the middle of the platform, under the middle of the canopy.

The physical positioning of the actor playing Richard II is an example. The loudness of the voice of the actor "through-sounding" Richard undergoes a huge metamorphosis from the play's opening scene to its closing scene—each change of voice being coordinated with a different implied position vis-à-vis the sounding-board interface. "We were not born to sue, but to command" (1.1.196): Richard's dissolving of dispute between Mowbray and Bolingbroke continues the oratorical command that Richard has assumed over the acoustic space from the very beginning, from a central position under canopy, farther back on the platform than Mowbray and Bolingbroke occupy. The result is a heightening of Richard's voice in physical force, volume, speed (likely slower as Richard establishes command at the beginning of the scene, faster as he grows impatient), tone quality, and perhaps pitch. "Down, down I come like glist'ring Phaëton" (3.3.177): Richard's visual descent from "above" to "below" in 3.3 comes with vocal consequences, a diminution in force, volume, speech, and likely tone quality as the actor personating Richard moves closer to the audience, into the acoustic position of soliloquies and asides. The looking-glass scene, so intensely visual in Richard's calling for a glass, speaking to his mirrored image, and shattering both glass and face, likewise involves a drastic shift in vocal interface from his acoustic position in the beginning. "Was this face the face / That every day under his household roof / Did keep ten thousand men?" (4.1.127–129). The voice that speaks into the looking-glass asks a series of five questions, each of which extends by several lines the querulous cadence and amplifies Richard's loss of acoustic power in his loss of political power.

Individual actor | | other actors

Another anachronistic term, "air time," points up the implicit competition of one actor with another within the sounding-board interface of the theater. Asides, dialogue, soliloquies, orations: in ascending order, each of these speech types gives actors a greater degree of temporal and acoustic space. The boundedness of this interface can be measured in the relatively small number of actors involved in performing one of Shakespeare's dramatic fictions: on average, 12 (Gamboa 108). For individual actors there really was a limited supply of air time. A signal instance of such competition happens when Lear asserts vocal dominance over Kent, who has counseled Lear not to banish Cordelia: "Hear me, on thy allegiance hear me!" (*Lr* 1.1.149). Cordelia, when asked to speak, refuses the competition for air time with her simple "Nothing, my lord" (1.1.73). The loud talkers in the play—Goneril, Regan, Edmund—eventually lose the competition, to be replaced by the reticent Albany and Edgar. Cordelia's voice time in the play's opening scene is complicated by the double-casting of her role with the Fool's role, setting the stage of her much larger voice-share in the last third of the play.

Actors | | audience

Noise, in computing terms, is unwanted signals in the electronic system, signals that disrupt and distort information-transfer. Noise, in theatrical terms, is unwanted sound signals that can drown out information-transfer via actors' voices. Early modern theaters were notoriously noisy places. Josua Poole in his writers' guide, *The English Parnassus, or, A helpe to English poesie* (1657), provides under the heading "theater" a very suggestive list of adjectives: "Publick, spacious, thronged, crowded, open, populous, peopled, crammed, well-fill'd, mirthfull, joyous, noisefull, clamarous, applausive, pompous, gorgeous" (515). When Shakespeare's company attempted in 1596 to move into the indoor Blackfriars Theater—a space they had spent large sums to outfit—neighbors in the parish of St. Anne's Blackfriars complained to the Bishop of London that performances there would be too noisy: "the same Playhouse is so neere the Church that the noyse of the Drummes and Trumpetts will greatly disturbe and hinder both the Ministers and the Parishioners in tyme of devine service and Sermones" (Nelson). The loud acoustic scene of London's theaters is evoked in a taunting speech Philip the Bastard makes to Louis the Dauphin in *King John*. The Bastard's 38-line harangue at last bursts into noise:

Indeed your drums, being beaten, will cry out;
And so shall you, being beaten. Do but start
An echo with the clamour of thy drum,
And even at hand, a drum is ready braced
That shall reverberate all, as loud as thine.
Sound but another, and another shall
(As loud as thine) rattle the welkin's ear
And mock the deep-mouthed thunder.

(Jn *5.2.168–172)*

All of these sounds, including backstage thunder, were common effects in performances, particularly performances of history plays. For actors and playgoers alike, these sounds were *not* heard as noise. They carried semantic meaning. Drums and brass instruments could, in fact, "speak." They had voices. Early modern brass instruments lacked valves, so that differences in pitch had to be articulated by the player's lips and tongue. There were different articulations for military charges, for retreats, for the entries of important persons. The sword-fight between Edmund and his disguised brother Edgar is arranged through trumpets. Preparing to defend his knighthood against the disguised Edgar's charge of treason, Edmund commands a trumpet to sound: "This sword of mine shall give them instant way / Where they shall rest for ever. Trumpets, speak!" (*Lr* 5.3.143–144). Early modern drums may have lacked articulation but they, too, could communicate characters' identities and signal their movements. In *Coriolanus*, while awaiting news of the battle for Carioles, Volumnia imagines the unseen battle through trumpet sounds. She tells Coriolanus's wife Virgilia, "Methinks I hear hither your husband's drum, / See him pluck Aufidius down by th' hair" (*Cor* 1.3.23–24).

The most persistent noises in the architectural interface were not what the Blackfriars' neighbors thought. The main source of noise in the strict sense of unwanted signals came not from the actors but the audience. Several writers comment on how unruly early modern audiences could be, with their restlessness, their crunching on hazelnuts, their boos, their hisses, their shouts, their applause. Internal evidence of the noisiness of the theatrical interface is provided by the scripts themselves: prologues that command attention ("O for a muse of fire," *H5*, Pro. 1), epilogues that plead for applause ("But release me from my bands / With the help of your good hands,: *Tem* Epi. 9–10), opening scenes that begin with a loud male voice ("Now is our winter of discontent / Made glorious summer by this sun of York," *R3*, 1.1.1–2), loud sound effects ("*A noise of thunder and lightning heard*" (*Tem*, 1.1.SD). All of this evidence points up aural conflict in the interface between actors' voices and audience's voices. In Hookway's terms, the struggle is for control, for self-sovereignty. A speech by Ulysses in *Troilus and Cressida* uses the example of an actor playing for applause to get Achilles back into action:

no man is the lord of anything—
Though in and of him there is much consisting—
Till he communicate his parts to others;
Nor doth he of himself know them for aught
Till he behold them formèd in th'applause
Where they are extended, who, like an arch, reverb'rate
The voice again.

(Tro *3.3.114–119)*

We can witness this conflicted dynamic in verbs associated with ears. "Friends, Romans, countrymen, lend me your ears" (*JC* 3.2.65) functions here as synecdoche for modes of listening—and refusing to listen. The actions associated with ears in Shakespeare's fictions had their counterparts within Shakespeare's theaters. Ears can be "pierced," "cleaved," and "struck," in that order of frequency. Listeners can "give," "lend," "incline," "close," and "open" their ears, again in that order of frequency. In live performance this situation is an interface in which actors and listeners compete. Gina Bloom, in *Gaming the Stage*, analyzes stage performances in early modern England as "playable media" that invite strategizing of a spectator's physical position in the theater and consuming plots as moves in a generic game. Bloom has experimented with a videogame called "Play the Knave," in which users can project themselves virtually into scenarios taken from particular Shakespeare plays (Bloom "Theater of Others").

The concept of interface, as Hookway points out, derives from hydraulic engineering: two forces of water crashing into one another (59–61). With voice in the theater, two currents of air meet in the middle of "the wooden O," one emanating from actors, the other from the audience. The result, as Hookway insists, is violence, fluidity, and the establishment of an equilibrium.

Texts

Discussing how users of computers learn to read and use the icons on a screen, Johanna Drucker in "Reading Interface" insists that icons read the reader as much as the reader reads the icons:

> In the constitutive exchange, the effect is not merely efficient tasking but also cognitive adaptation and change. Interface is a space of individual and collective subject formation. Our notions of privacy, property, identity, and even *individual voice and self* are modified constantly in the exchange, bound to the cognitive modeling of experience through experience.
>
> *(217, emphasis added)*

Textual and literary readers, Drucker notes, have been reluctant to consider "the graphical dimensions of texts" as constituting an interface no less powerful than an electronic digital display (217). In each of these interfaces, voice and the reading self are implicitly being modeled.

Since the publication of the First Folio in 1623, there has been good reason that scholars have not thought of texts on the page (and now on the computer screen) to be inert, available, energyless. The First Folio is presented to the reader as a collection of texts passively to be taken in with the eyes: Shakespeare's engraved portrait on the title page is faced by an address, "To the reader," and a prefatory epistle by Hemminge and Condell, "To the great variety of readers" ends with the exhortation "Read him then, again and again" (Shakespeare *Comedies, Histories, and Tragedies*, sigs. flyleaf verso, A3). Paratexts are provided to guide the reader's eye: horizontal and vertical rules frame the text as a visual object, act and scene divisions deliver the text in discrete visual units. Readers are invited to cast their vision on the text (E. Smith). Many of the texts printed in handier quarto format during the earlier half of Shakespeare's career invite more active reading. The text is presented on the title pages "as it hath often been acted" or other words to that effect. An example is:

> *M. William Shakspeare: His True Chronicle Historie of the life and death of King Lear and his three Daughters … As it was played before the King's Maiestie at Whitehall vpon S.*

> *Stephans night in Christmas Hollidayes. By his Maiesties seruants playing vsually at the Gloabe on the Bancke-side.*
>
> *(1608)*

To see such a performance in one's mind's eye, to hear the voices in one's mind's ear, creates an active interface between reader and text, an interface in which the reader accepts the energy emanating from the text and negotiates its challenges

Jennifer Richards in *Voices and Books in the English Renaissance* has assembled evidence of just how common the practice of reading aloud was in early modern England and has studied the ways in which early modern literary texts were *designed* to be read aloud (37–75). Some books, I would argue, were more amenable to being voiced than others. In a chapter on "Early Modern Books and Phonography," I lay out a continuum stretching from books intended to be sounded out at one end (abcedaries, *The Book of Common Prayer*) to knowledge-in-folio at the other (Cook's *Institutes of the Laws of England*, Crook's *Microcosmographia*). Printed playscripts fall toward the middle of my continuum (B. Smith forthcoming). All of these reading situations involve an interface—literally a face-to-face encounter between facing pages and the reader's face—but voice-forward texts confront the reader. For a reader to deny the interface is to assume a false sense of mastery over the text. It is a matter of mistaking one interface for another.

The Shakespeare field

Academic "field" is, so to speak, an *entrenched* metaphor. Doing scholarship is imagined to be like working a plot of land that is set apart from other plots of land. Farmers know better, but the metaphor assumes that the actor here is the ploughman, not the land. There is a second sense of "field," however, that recognizes the two-way dynamics of plotting out a field and ploughing it: classical field theory. Like interface, field theory attends to environments, boundaries, temporalities, motion, fluidity: the very essence of an interface in Hookway's analysis. Thinking of Shakespeare studies in terms of fluidity acknowledges the pressures of supposedly "outside" forces like gender, sexuality, colonialism, social justice, and media. The self-identities of scholars who enter into this force field cannot remain stable; those identities must constantly be negotiated and renegotiated. With respect to voice in particular, the shift in orientation is from voice-as-object to voice-as-energy.

Note

1 This and all other quotations from Shakespeare are taken from *The New Oxford Shakespeare* and are cited in the text with abbreviated titles by act, scene, and line numbers for plays and line numbers only for poems.

References

Banister, John. *The History of Man*. London, 1578.

Bloom, Gina. *Gaming the Stage: Playable Media and the Rise of English Commercial Theater*. U of Michigan P, 2018.

Bloom, Gina, *et al.* "'A Whole Theater of Others': Amateur Acting and Immersive Spectatorship in the Digital Shakespeare Game Play the Knave." *Shakespeare Quarterly*, vol. 67, no. 4, 2016, pp. 408–430.

Derrida, Jacques. *Of Grammatology*. Translated by Gayatri Chakravorty Spivak, Johns Hopkins UP, 2016.

Dolar, Mladen. *A Voice and Nothing More*. MIT Press, 2006.

Drucker, Johanna. "Reading Interface." *PMLA*, vol. 128, no. 1, 2013, pp. 213–220.

Folger Shakespeare Editions. Available at: shakespeare.folger.edu/shakespeares-works.

Gamboa, Brett. *Shakespeare's Double Plays: Dramatic Economy on the Early Modern Stage*. Cambridge UP, 2018.

Helmreich. Stefan. "Transduction." *Keywords in Sound*, edited by David Novak and Matt Sakakeeny, Duke UP, 2019, pp. 222–231.

Hookway, Branden. *Interface*. MIT Press, 2014.

Nelson, Alan. "Neighbors' Petition of November 1596 against a Playhouse in Blackfriars." Folger Shakespeare Library, Shakespeare Documented. n.d. Available at: shakespearedocumented.folger.edu/resource/document/neighbors-petition-november-1596-against-playhouse-blackfriars.

OED (*Oxford English Dictionary Online*). Available at: www.oed.com.

Open Source Shakespeare. Available at: opensourceshakespeare.org. Park, Katherine. "The Organic Soul." *The Cambridge History of Renaissance Philosophy*. Cambridge UP, 1988, pp. 464–484.

Poole, Josua. *The English Parnassus, or, A helpe to English poesie*. London, 1657.

Richards, Jennifer. *Voices and Books in the English Renaissance: A New History of Reading*. Oxford UP, 2019.

Roach, Joseph R. *The Player's Passion: Studies in the Science of Acting*. U of Delaware P, 1985.

Shakespeare, William. *Mr. William Shakespeare's Comedies, Histories, and Tragedies*. Isaac Jaggard and Edward Blount, 1623.

Shakespeare, William. *The New Oxford Shakespeare*. Edited by Gary Taylor, et al., Oxford UP, 2016.

Smith, Bruce R. *The Acoustic World of Early Modern England: Attending to the O-Factor*. U of Chicago P, 1999.

Smith, Bruce R. "Early Modern Books and Phonography." *The Oxford Handbook to the History of the Book in Early Modern England*, edited by Adam Smyth, Oxford UP. [forthcoming]

Smith, Emma. "Shakespeare's Early Modern Books: Printing, Paratext and Text." *The Arden Research Handbook of Shakespeare and Textual Studies*, edited by Lukas Earne, Bloomsbury, 2021, pp. 94–110.

Styan, J. L. *Shakespeare's Stagecraft*. Cambridge UP, 1971.

West, William N. *Theatres and Encyclopedias in Early Modern Europe*. Cambridge UP, 2002.

Worthen, William B. *Shakespeare, Technicity, Theatre*. Cambridge UP, 2020.

PART II

Apparent designs and hidden grounds

5

SHAKESPEAREAN INTERFACES AND WORLDMAKING

Buried Narratives, Hidden Grounds, and the Culture of Adaptive Practice

Daniel Fischlin

I. Interfacial Economies and Shakespeare

This chapter explores the hidden grounds of the Shakespearean interface as a form that, in some cases, subverts and offers resistant practices to what has been normalized by interfacial economies where scale, aggregation, branding, data extraction, and monetization are key drivers. The chapter unpacks some of its implications within the context of theorizing interfaces through the lens of the Shakespeare effect, that vast swathe of adaptive uses of Shakespeare in which material objects and aesthetic re-devisings across multiple media and cultural sites of production overtake the flesh-and-blood authorial source with an ever-expanding simulacrum of distributed authorship(s) working across multiple worldmaking epistemes.

Interfaces are cultural constructs wherein hidden design, buried narrative, controlled access to content, and end-user experience align with assumptions and ideologies presented as an opaque surface. The Facebook interface emblematizes design neutrality even as, in one of its notable outcomes, it subsumes, disseminates, and monetizes malevolent worldviews. Hence, an interface mutating toward monetizable duplicities (Fakebook) and its meta-relation to the virtual engagements that drive its business models (Meta)—a simulacral shaping of the imaginary community of netizens where community is an expression of algorithmic, if not mercenary, self-interest. The Google interface presents as pure "search" function even as its search-centered public functionality fronts for advertisement-driven monetization algorithms that remain hidden from end-users, the interface quietly tailoring users' choices to suit Google's profitability. And Amazon's panoptic interface gives the illusion of a plethora of choices tailored to the omnivorous consumers it aims to create even as its sales functions shape choice and feed an invisible supply chain predicated on effaced material realities of all those workers and the all-but invisible lived circumstances that determine what is on offer.

In each of these scenarios a formula is at work: interactivity is streamed through a portal (interface, or mediating technology) whose algorithmic and machine learning design principles are less than transparent—even as every one of these examples' business strategies reaps the most valuable commodity on the planet: personal data. The unity of the portal and its

DOI: 10.4324/9780367821722-8

apparent neutrality are contingent on the pliability of the end-user to accept design functions over which there is no option for control, no real capacity to alter deep functions related to monetization and data-reaping, and no choice other than to accept the interface that abjects the agency of users to its subsumed design functions. As such, the interface is a potent form of worldmaking, of reality creation in which virtuality produces material effects associated with the design intent set by the creators of the interface.

Where interface theory has posited a notion of the interface as a convergence of distinct realities, a plane in which abrasions and differences are made explicit, the movement toward pan-global corporate technologies that putatively connect has transformed abrasion and the sustenance of difference into the remaking of the end-user in the form that the interface allows the user to take. The operations of the interface to produce this outcome, via operating systems and back-end design functions, are largely invisible and untouchable. This transaction, between end-users and normative surface features that obscure the design realities of an interface, smooths difference. Smoothing aligns with monocultures of intent tied to the self-serving designs of the interface. This version of the interface is, in the thesis of this chapter, what predominates, even as other forms of interface operate to subvert that hegemony, sustaining the abrasions, hidden designs, and the capacity to modulate use-value in relation to end-user controls and interests. The Shakespearean interfaces that have emerged in the last two to three decades, such as the Canadian Adaptations of Shakespeare Project (CASP; of which more later), the Internet Shakespeare Editions, Folger Digital Texts, MIT Shakespeare, Open Source Shakespeare, and so forth, are a response to the digitization of a vast ecology of knowledges. From Google Books to Wikipedia, and a host of lesser-known sites that agglomerate epistemes and align with different worldmaking ideologies, an abyss has opened between those interfacial entities extending colonization and imperial self-interest and counter-worldmaking interfaces that present a radically different set of values.

This chapter explores the hidden grounds of the Shakespearean interface as a form that, in some cases, subverts and offers resistant practices to what has been normalized by interfacial economies where scale, aggregation, branding, data extraction, and monetization are key drivers. Further, it unpacks some of its implications within the context of theorizing interfaces through the lens of the Shakespeare effect, that vast swathe of adaptive uses of Shakespeare in which material objects and aesthetic re-devisings across multiple media and cultural sites of production overtake the flesh-and-blood authorial source with an ever-expanding simulacrum of distributed authorship(s) working across multiple worldmaking epistemes. Shakespearean interfaces, drawn from a range of examples discussed below, trouble ideological conventions around what an interface is and what it can be.

The Shakespearean interface aligns literariness with the preconditions for virtuality embedded in its interface. By this, I mean, for instance, that a rhetorical trope like epizeuxis (the repetition of a word to create affect) can move from its sounding in a theatrical context to the intimacies of affective impact it produces in an audience, a kind of virtual transaction that uses literary coding to inhabit the imaginary of the listener. Lear's infamous lines spoken on the death of Cordelia and just before he dies—"Never, never, never, never, never" (5.3.372)—translate the spoken words with the virtual experience of Lear's inexpressible pain and loss to an audience, a virtual transfer of affect achieved by literary/rhetorical means. Literariness defines an imaginary, interpretative relation to a signified, in this case, the repeated word "never" that leads to loss, mortality, and pain. In so doing, literary effects produce ambiguity, nested narratives, affective realities, and opaque patterns of meaning. Shakespeare and the Shakespeare effect, then, rely on literariness as grounding conventions of their capacity to make meaning and to proliferate virtually.

The interface presents as a portal through which end-users' desires—for information, for entertainment, for sex, for product, for companionship—are mediated, with those desires determinative of the use-value of the interface. But the pact between end-user and interface, where the latter subsumes and satisfies the inclinations and needs of the former, where the gaze of the end-user penetrates the screen through which the interface makes itself available, is a deception. In surrendering appetite and the patterns of need produced by appetite as data points to the Cyclopean screen, end-users themselves become the content that instrumentalizes the viability of the interface as a worldmaking mediation between surveillance technologies and human pliability. To pass through an interface is to make a fundamental decision about subjectivity, agency, exchange economies, and autonomy and self-sovereignty—a decision that is tied to pan-global structures of worldmaking enabled by digital platforms and the epistemic flows they instrumentalize.

The interface presents as an inevitability and, as such, remains hermetic to scrutiny and readability in terms of its algorithmic premises and intent, its first principles of design, and its impact on a complex set of relations that unfold when human agency is entrapped in its deep structures of metadata, a form of semantic harvesting. As the signifier increasingly displaces the signified in a set of abstractions at multiple removes from the signified, the function of the aggregator, represented by the interface portal, as a determinant of meaning is assured via unseen transactions between the user and the interfacial monolith. Algorithms, the set of computational instructions governing how the interface behaves—data intake and assessment, outputs and automated reasoning, calculation, and design intent—are key to the interface. Yet algorithms are also zealously guarded intellectual property, largely unscrutinized, as part of sustaining the asymmetrical power relations that dominant interfaces of the kind cited above exercise over their end-users.

In this scenario it is important to emphasize what systems biologist Yarden Katz says about algorithmic accountability:

> viewed as a recognition that the internal structure of data-hungry computing systems encodes politics. But algorithmic accountability can also be a sleight of hand, an epistemic forgery. The oft-repeated notion that 'algorithms exercise their power over us' obscures the fact that algorithms alone don't do things in the world; people do. Algorithmic accountability places a veil over institutions that enact violent decisions and create the conditions for the decisions to be made in the first place. This burial works to naturalize incarceration.
>
> *(123; emphasis mine)*

This last trope of burial is of especial importance for this chapter in the sense that it identifies the carceral elements of design, the hidden grounds, that are obscured in interfaces, naturalizing the meta-verse of the interface as a simulacrum of epistemic freedom even as the interface "buries" its ideological contexts, design intents, and the controls these exert over end-users. The interface in this sense mimics the humanity, for better or worse, of its designers.

As a form, in many dominant interfacial structures, of virtual carcerality, interfaces manifest surfaces of convergence that obscure what lies coded beyond the superficiality of its digital façade and superstructure. The design principles and the origins of the dominant interfaces mentioned earlier, for instance, are tied to the emergence of artificial intelligence constructs "formed in the largely white military-industrial academic complex" reproducing the "shape of whiteness as an ideology" and "steered by the aims of empire and capital" (Katz 15–16). But the trope of burial cuts both ways. Embedded in the proliferating interfaces that netizens can access are a range of hidden grounds and nested narratives that resist or mutate these dominant realities. These alternative narratives not only operate in the here and now, but they are also anticipated early in the familiar construct most associated with Shakespeare's oeuvre, the 1623 First Folio, itself arguably an early modern prototype of what was to become the digital interface.

Consideration of Shakespearean interfaces offers useful examples, as I will argue below, of some degree of alternative to the dominant interfacial ecosystem. The rationale that was shared with me in the invitation to contribute to this book suggested

> that Shakespeare is always accessed through a mediating technology—the interface—the design features of which structure every cognitive engagement. While scholars have long considered problems of Shakespeare's text and transmission, less attention has been devoted to studying the design elements and theoretical implications of pages, digital platforms, and the other media that channel Shakespeare through complex interactions and affordances. While such media-specific operations may be largely invisible to the average reader or viewer, the interface properties of books, screens, and theaters structure Shakespeare in ways that are never neutral and have a bearing on reading, spectating, and, therefore, understanding.
>
> *(Budra and Werier, personal correspondence, 2 August 2019)*

Shakespeare's proliferative modelling powers for cultural production, then, are of especial significance for how they arise from the compressed information and epistemes gathered in his "work," most often thought of in relation to the First Folio. The title points to a kind of supremacy if not primacy of the book—it is designated as the First. But the First Folio's artifactuality has also had important repercussions on the changing nature of the interface as a site where epistemic compression and ideological coding are interactively determinative of forms of understanding and cognition, and hence of worldmaking. At the very moment in which corporations emerge as an anticipation of advanced capitalism (East India Company, Royal Charter granted 1600), then, so too arises the early modern English entertainment industry (the King's Men given its Royal Patent on 19 May 1603)[1] associated with the theater and by extension via the First Folio, with the history of the book, another interfacial mediating technology. The connection between Shakespearean theater and the emergence of corporate culture is not to be diminished, with theater scholar Andrew Gurr noting that Shakespeare "besides being a poet faithful to his company ... was an exceptionally good businessman" (28), a fact borne out by his long-standing connection to aristocratic patronage, which included, among others, notable aristocrats like Henry Carey, the first Lord Hunsdon and King James VI and I and his long-term association with what Gurr calls the "highly profitable business of playhouse owning" (146). I mean to draw attention here to early modern literariness as a technology, the rise of corporate capital culture tied to colonial encounter and imperialism (let alone to Shakespeare and early modern English theater culture), and to how these intertwined modes of cultural production have continued to produce new ways of asserting hegemony via evolutions in how interfaces encode political relations of dominance and subjugation.

The conceptual framework for interfaces arises from "nineteenth century fluid dynamics" articulated in the work of physicists James Thomson and James Clerk Maxwell, before influencing "thermodynamics, information theory, and cybernetics" (Hookway 6). In this origin story, the interface has a "particular relevance to complex, dynamic systems, within which it describes the possibilities of agency and governance" (Hookway 6). I point to these historical resonances in relation to the emergence of corporations associated with entertainment and colonialism and the ways in which complex dynamic systems impact on agency, governance, and thus worldmaking. The role of emergent forms of interface like the First Folio devises an albeit illusory notion of collectability, comprehensivity, and compression of information (36 plays in one book) into an aggregate form. The three—collectability, comprehensivity, and compression of information—are key determinants of value, talismans of what will become foundational aspects of imperial, corporate, and institutional systems—to the extent that at a certain point the value of the content will be displaced by the value of the system that gathers the content. Or, as David Graeber summarizes: "from inside the system, the algorithms and mathematical formulae by which the world comes to be assessed become, ultimately, not just measures of value, but the source of value itself" (41). Value requires assessment and assessment requires tabulation, that is, collectability into aggregate form. The more comprehensive, the more searchable, the more compressed, the better the aggregate. What that aggregate represents, then, beyond it being a metonymy for literariness, itself an extension of British imperial cultural value, is worth considering in Shakespearean contexts in light of the notion of dynamic systems and how interfaces operate.

In the case of the First Folio, as Emma Smith argues, "Shakespeare's own reputation can be mapped, economically and geographically, against the distribution of [the First Folio] … [and] the value of First Folio copies and the imperial spread of Shakespeare were in … step" (34). As an interfacial object, then, the First Folio codes empire, economic power, literary achievement, and monolithic, dominant cultural presence—measurable achievement based on a database (the First Folio) that can be mined for information, aligned with worldmaking interpretative gestures of authority, and set up as a standard for comparative assessment with lesser acts of worldmaking made subordinate to its primacy.

The notion of a "collected works," which subsumes a version of comprehensivity and compression into its design, arises in English literary culture precisely at the moment when the First Folio appears. Comprehensivity and compression, or the illusions thereof, are at the core of the design of interfaces, predicated as they are on the capacity to be a singular entry point, a haecceity that is also a through-point to all the things for which the haecceity stands. Monocultural singularities like these are a recipe for dissimulation and distortion, for laying the hidden grounds that align with asymmetries of power. In the case of the First Folio, for example, despite its proclamations to be the first of its kind, it emphatically was not—a fact that points to the interface as a site of not only the struggle to assert authority, but also of the potential duplicity it manifests in the service of its own interests.

James VI and I, who had issued the King's Men their 1603 Royal Patent, had preceded, if not anticipated the very same notions—collectability, comprehensivity, and compression. He did so from within the frame of a literate monarch advancing an ideology of sovereign power closely tied to the sovereignty of words that his collected writings—the *Workes*, published seven years prior to the First Folio in 1616—exemplifies. Moreover, in the same year as James published his *Workes*, the poet and dramatist Ben Jonson, more of whom below, also published *The Workes of Benjamin Jonson*, itself an example of yet another early modern folio interface laying claim to collectability, comprehensivity, and compression. The artificiality of the interfacial construct and its power to create, if not subsume, a reality of its own is at stake in all these works and deeply tied to questions of power, legacy, primacy, and authority—not to mention the degree to which these publications associate wealth and cultural influence with literariness, the linguistic and semantic algorithms that are guarantors of power, prestige, and the capacity to influence and worldmake through rhetoric and oratory.

Ben Jonson famously makes a pre-emptive appearance in Shakespeare's First Folio. His poem "To the Reader" is the first text one reads upon crossing the threshold of this interface itself laying claim to its firstness. The lyric is especially important as it appears facing the frontispiece (splash) page (see Figure 5.1) featuring the infamous Martin Droeshout engraving of Shakespeare. What is fascinating about Jonson's appearance in this position is how his text provides a sophisticated statement, avant la lettre, about interfaciality. The apostrophe to the image that Jonson's lyric is (inter)facing outlines a theory of representation and how to read what is quite literally the face of the interface that gives one access to Shakespeare's oeuvre:

> This Figure, that thou here feest put,
> It was for gentle Shakespeare cut;
> Wherein the Grauer had a strife
> with Nature, to out-doo the life:
> O, could he but haue dravvne his vvit
> As vvell in brasse, as he hath hit
> His face; the Print vvould then surpasse
> All, that vvas euer in brasse.
> But, since he cannot, Reader, looke
> Not on his picture, but his Booke.

The lyric and the engraving, then, co-compose an interface (portal) to the First Folio, bringing visual and textual coding into relief with each other as the start of the reader's experience of the artifact—much like current digital interfaces devise similar intermedial (branding) entanglements on splash pages.

While the Droeshout image is aesthetically challenged, the poem is not. Jonson takes pains to outline a theory of the face that is the interface, suggesting that the engraved image is in "strife" with the life it represents. The lyric lays out a series of cascading contrastive realities that put to the question what is more real: from the figure or image representing the flesh-and-blood author, to the abstracted wit and imagination of the author now represented as an engraved face, to the

To the Reader.

This Figure, that thou here feest put,
It was for gentle Shakefpeare cut;
Wherein the Grauer had a ftrife
with Nature, to out-doo the life:
O, could he but haue drawne his wit
As well in braffe, as he hath hit
His face; the Print would then furpaffe
All, that vvas euer vvrit in braffe.
But, fince he cannot, Reader, looke
Not on his Picture, but his Booke.
B. I.

Mr. WILLIAM
SHAKESPEARES
COMEDIES,
HISTORIES, &
TRAGEDIES.
Publifhed according to the True Originall Copies.

LONDON
Printed by Ifaac Iaggard, and Ed. Blount. 1623.

Figure 5.1 Verso and Recto first pages of First Folio. Folger Shakespeare Library. Copy 68.

printed words of the author unsurpassed by the brass figurations devised by the engraver, to the oppositional binary that concludes the poem between the picture and the book, all in relation to "Nature" and "life" that cannot be outdone. Jonson's poem, in short, maps a signifying hierarchy tied to the interface and to the mediating technologies that provide a gateway into the First Folio.

The undercurrent of references to the battle for authentic representation and the degree to which there are nested truths about which reality should take precedence is a key component of the poem. The message is clear: be wary of the worldmaking claims of representation and its avowal to represent life and Nature. The poem's closing lines, moreover, echo, in the negative, famous Shakespearean lines found in *Hamlet* 3.4.63–64 where Hamlet speaking of an image of his father and uncle (Claudius), states: "Look here, upon this picture, and on this, / The counterfeit presentment of two brothers." The echo reminds that intertexts are always at work in how interfaces resonate. Jonson's overwriting of the line from *Hamlet* allows him another form of pre-emptive primacy: not only is he saying that the book takes precedence, he is also saying, quite literally, "don't look at this image of Shakespeare"—a not-so-subtle undercutting of the very person with whom he is, in the historical moment, in direct competition as an icon of English literariness. Again, forms of worldmaking are at stake. Representations can be skewed to mean different things. Battles to trump and usurp differential forms of authority reveal self-interest. What is presented as real may not be so.

Between Jonson's admonition not to look at the picture of Shakespeare and Hamlet's demand that his mother look upon a picture that represents a counterfeit, an imitation, of Hamlet's father and uncle, a struggle emerges around representation itself. Even as the description of Hamlet's father unfolds as a "truth" to be known about his virtues by comparison with Claudius, the argument Hamlet makes also exposes the duplicities of his uncle to his mother. So, the truth of the image is, if read as Hamlet suggests, that it reveals, by contrast, the dissimulative nature of the reality that has entrapped his mother. The interface, even when presented as a version of the real, cannot fully access the layers of interpretation it stands in for and is thus always already compromised, or ready to be compromised, as a form of representation.

The hidden ground of the interface, evident in early Shakespearean contexts, then, is one in which dissimulation, representational struggle, and duplicity are enmeshed. This frame lays the foundation for the theoretical and embodied (un)doings of the digital interfaces that were sourced—however partially—in the originary discourses situated in early modern Shakespearean contexts. At the core is how authority and dissimulative representations of reality align to shape the cognitive events that proceed from the convergence of reader/end-user and interface. And Jonson is explicit: the image or picture that stands for the interface is not to be confused with the book itself—"Reader, looke / Not on his picture, but his Booke"—suggesting that the originary mode for interfaciality requires the critical acumen to make such a distinction. Even as the interfacial image calls for acceptance of itself on its own terms, its duplicities and failure to represent the fullness of experience for which it stands are poised in opposition to that assumption.

II. The Shakespearean Avatar of Extended Humanity

Shoshana Zuboff makes explicit how "every time we encounter a digital interface we make our experience available to 'datafication,' thus rendering unto surveillance capitalism its continuous tithe of raw materials" (234), a world of the "robotized interface where technologies work their will, resolutely protecting power from challenge" (225). Zuboff's ideas resonate with Canadian media theorist Marshall McLuhan's notion that

> the 'content' of any medium blinds us to the character of the medium. It is only today that industries have become aware of the various kinds of business in which

> they are engaged. When IBM discovered that it was not in the business of making office equipment or business machines, but that it was in the business of processing information, then it began to navigate with clear vision. The General Electric Company makes a considerable portion of its profits from electric light bulbs and lighting systems. It has not yet discovered that, quite as much as A.T. & T., it is in the business of moving information.
>
> *(Understanding Media 8–9)*[2]

Even while McLuhan's content/character binary is dated, his reading stands: the apparent content that the interface references acts as a screen to camouflage the design realities and intents, the information flow, made imperceptible, or barely perceptible, by the interface.

McLuhan references the "extensions of man" [sic] in the sub-title to his book *Understanding Media*, a reference to the final phase of humanity in which the "technological simulation of consciousness" occurs and "when the creative process of knowing will be collectively and corporately extended to the whole of human society" (3). As examples of these extensions McLuhan cites Shakespeare, selections from whom

> [a] fairly complete handbook for studying the extensions of man [sic] could be made ... Some might quibble about whether or not he was referring to TV in these familiar lines from *Romeo and Juliet*: 'But soft! what light through yonder window breaks? / It speaks, and yet says nothing.'
>
> *(9)*

Citing other examples of Shakespearean prescience, from *Othello*, *King Lear*, and *Troilus and Cressida*, McLuhan locates Shakespeare at the center of the notion of "people transformed by illusions" (9). Illusion is a form of worldmaking. In this context it is not surprising that McLuhan turns to Shakespeare, whose fictions and storying created immersive dramatic illusions that necessarily take place in the consciousness of the reader/end-user/audience member by virtue of linguistic interfacilities.

Literariness provides a portal to the illusive realities it creates and requires the interpretative frames that interfacilitate exchange between the seductive world of the interface and the audient/reader/end-user. Shakespeare's skill at creating extended narratives, illusions felt to be real, then, invite adaptation across media and technologies—precisely the work of Shakespearean simulacra and the Shakespeare effect, captured in the prescient trope of the light breaking through a window (or screen), speaking yet saying nothing. Here it is helpful to distinguish between two usages of McLuhan's notion of "extended humanity": the first notion expands what it means to be human in the material, quotidian world of the real. The second elaborates ways in which the plays, understood as simulacra, create such fully imagined worlds that they transcend their illusory status becoming simultaneously real and unreal types of extended humanity—a frame for interfacial sentience that models the further evolution of this simulacral economy via technologies yet to be developed.

So, McLuhan's turn to Shakespeare here is in direct and continuous relation to the claims the First Folio makes for itself (discussed in Section 1) as a source of the illusions that are in dynamic relation to systems of authority, cultural value, and pre-eminence. Shakespearean literary and theatrical interfaces, then, anticipate and imagine technologies capable of simulating consciousness, a prototype of Artificial Intelligence and the phases of development leading to the merging of human-generated metadata with the machine learning that extrapolates from that to full simulacral awareness. As an extreme example of this extended humanity, philosopher Nick Bostrom discusses the research into neurocomputational versions of personhood where whole brain emulation, using a sufficiently powerful computer, results in

> a digital reproduction of the original intellect, with memory and personality intact. The emulated human mind now exists as software on a computer. The mind can either inhabit a virtual reality or interface with the external world by means of robotic appendages.
>
> *(36)*

Capture of information at this level of neuronal detail produces a new simulacrum, a new (dis)embodiment of an extended humanity that begins to shift away from carbon chauvinism to other forms of extended being yet-to-be-made manifest.[3] Again worldmaking. Shakespeare's place in this kind of thinking is as an iconic, canonic, recognizably branded site where linguistic interfaciality is the ground for an early expression of extended humanity (print)—one that anticipates trends toward digital hyperextensions of the same. Shakespeare, then, can be read in such a context as the avatar of an extended humanity predicated on illusions, simulations, and an imaginary fully anticipatory of the final phase of transformative media that will simulate consciousness. Yet even as these technologies point toward a future where knowing is potentially extended to all human society, the very technologies of knowing subsume the "nothing" associated with speaking in the simulacrum, where Shakespeare's imagined window refracting light is a McLuhanesque trope for the screen that illuminates while emptying itself of meaning.

The unspoken element in McLuhan's voicing is the degree to which the very anticipation of these technologies also foreshadows the resistances, the hidden grounds that identify the illusory "nothing" of the simulacrum as a site of an extended humanity that is also restricted by the hidden designs that allow for the extension. The early turn to Shakespeare in McLuhan's prescient work on media-extended humanity, then, is not accidental. It frames an aporia at the heart of idealized notions of technology extending human consciousness at the same time as it produces a deceptive field of vision that restricts that very humanity.

Interfaces are tied to brand cultures that require aggregation to be profitable and Shakespeare's canonical centrality is key to the ways in which the connections between brand and interfacial use-value are established as an effective form of cultural production serving often competing values. A brand requires/is an interface, the portico and infrastructure under which design principles are occluded even as its seemingly benign, neutral presence is an invitation to submit to its hidden internal logics. For all the talk of the public-facing nature of the best-known interfaces, there is a profoundly anti-public design logic that obscures the intentional machinations that produce a certain version of human agency tailored to the needs of the interface. The interface, then, understood in this way, is a metonymy of the illusion of aggregation and comprehensivity, the delusory capacity of a portal to mediate a totality of experience that occurs when passing through the interface into the content for which it putatively stands. Interfaces naturalize brand. They serve to expand a brand's reach and its dissociation from anything but its own self-interest. They normalize comprehensivity and monocultures of occluded design ideology even as they weaponize these in the name of their own utility and self-interest. Interfaces, to be profitable and to expand their influence, require and depend on convergences between their own self-interest and those of their end-users.

McLuhan notes how:

> In Europe and England alike the extreme specialism of the industrial revolution created a massive retrieval of medieval sensibility in the arts and crafts, and in

religion. This was the new hidden ground that entered into abrasive interface with the pronounced figure of the dominant new industrialisms.

("Hidden Environments" 84; original emphasis)

McLuhan's insight—that of someone who taught Shakespeare at the Jesuit St. Louis University in Missouri—suggests that in moments of mass undertaking like the Industrial Revolution, reactive and counterbalancing sensibilities emerge to challenge dominant new narratives, a form of oppositional, if not reparative, worldmaking. These latter are in tense interfacial relation with the dominant new narrative(s) and require a retrieval of historical materials, the buried narratives and hidden grounds, that now enter into subversive relation with the new hierarchy.

The subversive interface engages with the dominant interface, producing a culture of adaptive use that sustains the hidden grounds, but does so in ways that reshape, critique, and repurpose the dominant ethos looking for supremacy. And, as McLuhan foresaw, Shakespeare literariness and the Shakespearean imaginary played and continue to play a significant if nuanced role in extending the simulation of human consciousness. I say nuanced because the First Folio, as we have seen earlier, offers the grounds for its own undoing as a simulation: not only does Jonson's poem expose the (dis)simulative nature of the interface, but the very structure of Shakespearean discourse is also predicated on linguistic algorithms that compress and proliferate interpretative ambiguity as a condition for entering the simulation that is the theatrical playscript turned into a static book. So, the tension between "specialism" and "sensibility" that McLuhan outlines in relation to the Industrial Revolution proffers the conditions for undoing and subverting the primacy of the "pronounced figure" of interfacial worldmaking designs.

If such was the case in the Industrial Revolution, it is also the case in the Digital Revolution. The latter has proliferated virtual interfaces—from the hardware and accompanying system software of PCs and mobile screens found on phones, pads, household appliances, and the like and now even beyond the screen itself via hologrammatic meta-screens found in cars and elsewhere. The proliferation observes the law of this kind of technology, which is to heighten the simulacral real to the point it is the norm via which the interfacial defines and limits realities. This expansive heightening that is also a limitation returns us to David Graeber's point, discussed earlier, that value lies less in the content of a system than in how the system metricizes that content, makes the content capable of assessment (as is the case with digital aggregators like Spotify, YouTube, and the like). The interface, not the creator, becomes the site of ownership and value. This displacement is consistent with Graeme Webb, Max Haiven and Xenia Benivolski's read of Amazon, pace bell hooks, that "advanced capitalism is affecting our ability to see and imagine. Our world, and hence our future, has become something not to be created, but to be owned … we must learn to see beyond our cognitive horizons" (n.p). If the interface becomes the cognitive horizon, then, how to escape the limitations it imposes on our capacity to see and imagine, the very core of how worldmaking possibilities manifest?

The hidden ground, by contrast, exposes the artificiality of that which presents as the interfacial real; and this ground, as I've argued, is present in the very consideration of the interface that emerges in Shakespeare's First Folio and how it provides the conditions of its own interrogation. It interfaces with the new face of the real, or the meta-real, as a way to challenge reductive forms of reality-making that limit and direct end-users' agencies. It offers formal and interpretative ambiguities and anti-reductive orientations that sustain abrasion and subversion, regardless of the seemingly limitless powers unleashed against these core aspects of human agency. It exposes duplicitous, uncritical, and reductive practices for what they are via this sustained abrasion, a convergence that is marked by dissonance, tension, and subversion.

Further, this form of oppositional subversion to the work of corporate digital interfaces is always already embedded in the etymological and intertextual (Shakespearean) contexts from which the word interface itself has emerged. In Shakespearean usage, the noun "face" carried within it, among other meanings, a sense of feigning, of duplicity, what Samuel Johnson's 1755 *Dictionary* defines as "to carry a false appearance, to play the hypocrite" (To Face. v.n. [from the noun]; Vol. 1), as in Suffolk's line from *Henry VI* (5.3.141–142), "Fair Margaret knows /That Suffolk doth not flatter, face, or feign." Schmidt's lexicon reveals a plethora of senses associated with "face" that underlines how it tropes superficiality, a difference between intrinsic and extrinsic signifying, an unquestioned truth that can always be undone (the "face value" of something). The preposition "inter" merely exacerbates the sense of being caught "between" appearances. All of which suggests a hidden ground to the notion of interface used in digital contexts that arise from well-documented plays of meaning embedded in Shakespearean signifying practices. These Shakespearean meanings range from "oppose," to "brave," to "bully," to "trim" (as in to dress a façade, to ornament or edge a garment), "to uphold a false appearance, to lie with effrontery," and "to get through one's business by effrontery" (Schmidt; "Face"). Taken together, this play of meaning adds yet another dimension of Shakespearean context to the work of the interface, with the lexical content of the word pointing to the very ways in which it codes its own potential undoing.

III. Shadow Libraries: Adaptive Practices of Generative Difference, Pluriversal Worldmaking

If the potential for undoing is always already self-present in the interface, then what might that undoing look like and where might Shakespeare sit in the mix? In this last section I argue that undoing, which is to say resisting dominant trends in interfacial surveillance technologies, is predicated on adaptive practices of difference that can produce generative forms within interfacial simulacra, all part of structures of pluriversal worldmaking of which the Shakespeare effect is but one instance.

The McLuhanesque tension between emergent forms of digital industry and sensibilities that sit outside the cultural forms it imposes is one that continues to mutate as the scale of the struggle between digital commons approaches to the interface come into conflict with corporate spaces working to neoliberalize those commons. Shakespeare is one site among many where this work occurs. An underlying dynamic remains in which new technologies and those who use them act on a continuum that extends from full-on conformity to critical engagement and subversive, adaptive uses of the technology in the name of sustaining difference and expanding the digital commons.

The non-Shakespearean example (even though it subsumes Shakespearean content) of UbuWeb, "a web-based educational resource for avant-garde material available on the Internet, founded in 1996 by poet Kenneth Goldsmith" and offering "visual, concrete and sound poetry, expanding to include film and sound art mp3 archives" (UbuWeb) is instructive. Arts-based repositories of digital information, using the ubiquity of digital interfacial connections that the Web allows, offer up a substrate of subversive and adaptive use alternatives and practices to the dominant forms of interface predicated on monetization, self-interest, and an abjected end-user experience that circumscribes agency. On the twenty-fifth anniversary of its launch (1 November 2021), UbuWeb posted to Twitter the following: "UbuWeb started 25 years ago today, November 1, 1996. No permission, no money, no copyright, no ads, no cookies, no data collection, no marketing, no mailing list, no donation box, no terms & conditions. Ever. Thank you. #custodiansonline #piratecare."

The tweet underlined UbuWeb's subversive relation to aggregating content by outlining the disruptions the site models to normative (business) models of the interface: so, no monetization, no attention to copyright, no use of the suffocating ads that clog the digital metaverse, no terms, no conditions, no extraction of personal data, and so forth. Of especial importance is UbuWeb as a form of shadow library:

> [an] alternative system ... that provides access to its materials to anyone regardless of affiliation and free of charge. We don't track what you have downloaded, how much time you spend on the site, or where you have clicked. Who you are and what you do are no business of ours.
>
> *(Goldsmith 38)*

Goldsmith's project envisions a distributed network of shadow libraries that offset for-profit, corporatized forms of data reaping and information flow. As he says:

> Taken individually, each of us is small; taken wholly, we're substantial.; taken locally, we barely exist; taken globally, we're huge. Each of these shadow libraries provides something different from the others ... Together we're out to combat the ever-mounting stupidity, commercialism, and surveillance capitalism that the web has become, offering models of resistance that can hopefully inspire others to do the same. There are vast numbers of us out there preserving those works that are marginal, forgotten, yet crucial ... toiling to preserve the 'memory of the world.'
>
> *(140)*

The hashtags in the UbuWeb tweet point readers toward the notion of the web interface not as a digital economy but rather as a custodial online space, a digital commons where the function of aggregation is free dissemination and sustenance of alternatives liberated from the machinations of extractive portal sites like those discussed at the beginning of this chapter. Moreover, the #piratecare hashtag references the transnational research project Pirate Care:

> a network of activists, scholars and practitioners who stand against the criminalization of solidarity & for a common care infrastructure. Pirate Care reflects and brings together those care initiatives which are taking risks by operating in the narrow grey zones left open between different knowledges, institutions and laws, inviting all to participate in an exploration of the mutual implications of care and technology that dare questioning the ideology of private property, work and metrics.
>
> *(Pirate Care)*

In short, UbuWeb embodies an alternative vision of what the interface can be: a hospice for materials freely available; a custodial and generative space with no interest in circumscribing or monetizing its end-users; a form of common care infrastructure, or a digital commons, where access to knowledge and epistemic difference are aligned with solidarity and mutual implication; an embodied interrogation of the very notions of property and metricization that are at the core of the most powerful interfacial entities on the planet, including Twitter, YouTube, Google, Amazon, Facebook, Spotify, and the like. UbuWeb, then, was an early model of how to produce interfacial resistance and alternative worldmaking strategies via attention to specialized fields of differential cultural production, in this case, the avant-garde. Moreover, UbuWeb's model played a crucial role in envisioning core principles related to the design of the Canadian Adaptations of Shakespeare project site (CASP), launched in 2004 (see Caldwell),[4] one of the earliest and most elaborated digital interfaces for the study of Shakespeare to emerge in the early phases of digital humanities scholarship.[5]

A key premise of the site was to embed in its self-description the very terms for its undoing: thus "Canadian" seen as an illusory descriptor for a national entity that reductively subsumes multiple differential realities related to immigrancy, indigeneity, and linguistic and cultural otherness; "adaptation" as a simulacrum for proliferative cultural productions and epistemes that are inherently differential; and "Shakespeare," a fluid signifier for an adaptive, ever-mutating effect of cultural production deracinated from its incarnate source. The site's self-titling presents as an interface that subsumes the interrogations of stable notions of what the national entity known as Canada signifies; what an adaptation is; and the cultural constancy and coherence of who and what Shakespeare constitutes. In fact, one of the lessons the creation of the site under these terms afforded was:

> [how] pre-conceptions around premise terms such as ... Shakespeare, adaptation and Canada, will inevitably be put to the test by the archive produced—especially in a web-based environment where serendipitous and powerful search functions combine to produce new knowledges that inevitably push the conceptual limits underlying a project such as this. What makes a play Canadian? How to define Canadian-ness? What are the limits of adaptation? Is a single line-change sufficient to refigure a play as an adaptation? How to measure Shakespearean presence? How to define theatricality? Are stagings and productions governed by specific directorial interventions worth considering as adaptations? Numerous archival examples of work that put these questions to the test have become part of the daily routine for the CASP team ... a rigid and inflexible conceptual model for addressing these questions would have made the archival work a great deal simpler, if not less responsive to the range of materials that have become the archive.
>
> *(Fischlin et al. 96)*

If adaptation is the simulacrum for knowing and producing difference, then the interface that archives adaptation requires practices of generative difference predicated on inclusion, accessibility, and attention to expansive notions that, in Pirate Care terms, question the "ideology of private property" at the same time as they exemplify a form of solidarity at odds with the alienation effects subsumed in corporate for-profit interfacial economies. A Shakespearean interface focused on adaptation within a national context whose very coherence is put to the question by differential representations is one that moves away from individuated single author originary narratives to more complex notions of source materials and how they are generative. Thus, the splash page statement that fronts the CASP Version 2 site, reflecting the "ongoing commitment to blending the best practices of humanities research, new media, online publishing, accessibility, and online engagement" (Fischlin) is shown in Figure 5.2.

The splash page of the CASP site, which uses the controversial Sanders Portrait of Shakespeare as its signature image (itself a signifier of differential, hidden ground interfaces at odds with normative, authoritative assumptions gathered around the Chandos portrait, NPG1, the founding portrait of the National Portrait Gallery, itself a powerful emblem and interface of British history and culture), signals how the notion of a subversive interface self-presents. The less than conventional design choice leads into multiple other adaptive narratives that the CASP interface projects, unsettling the colonial/settler and asymmetrical power dynamics that big data interfaces continue to proliferate. Hence, a spotlight page on the vast network of indigenous adaptation practices, significant attention to French Canadian adaptation, women, marginal and local theater, youth experience, literacy, multicultural experience,

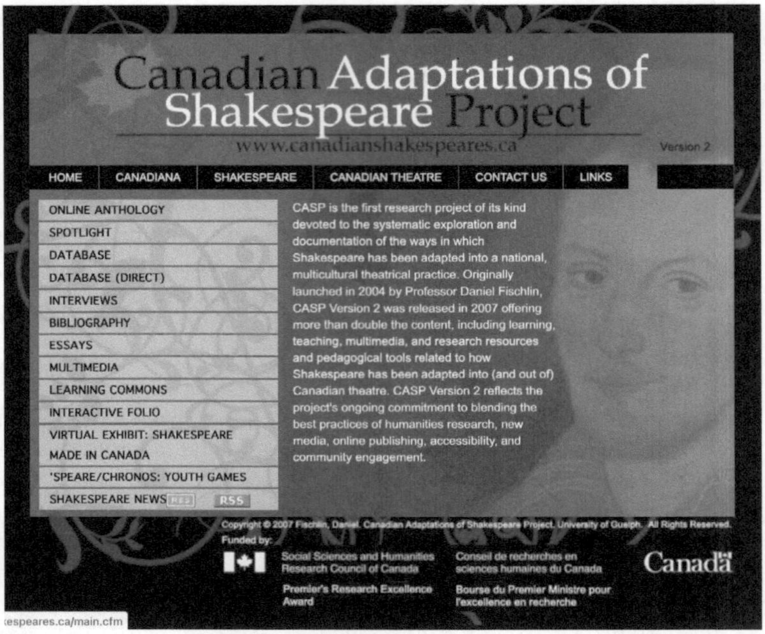

Figure 5.2 Splash page, Canadian Adaptations of Shakespeare Project

and so forth. And again, following on the UbuWeb model of a custodial and generative space in which no advertising or monetization occurs; no tracking of individual use occurs; no metricization; no marketing; no terms and conditions; no donation button; and no copyright. Moreover, no attention to search engine optimization (SEO); a consistent commitment to open-source software wherever possible; no self-promotion or concern for competitive advantage over other Shakespearean sites, many of which monetize or have access to substantial institutional support; and an almost complete focus on content creation, democratization of access, and expansive models of adaptive practice (as in the online literacy game 'Speare created for the site, which uses online gameplay to teach literacy skills to youth).

The CASP site, whatever its limitations and its impact, then, participates in a network of shadow libraries where these sorts of archival materials gather, in all their idiosyncratic manifestation of diverse worldmaking possibilities. As a modest example of such, it models an archive aligned with adaptive practices of generative difference that point toward more extended pluriversal forms of worldmaking. The pluriverse, as Arturo Escobar explains, embraces "ontological difference" (17) whether biotic, epistemic, or cultural. It is "*a world where many worlds fit*" (17). And it is an "ethical and political practice of alterity that involves a deep concern for social justice, the radical equality of all beings, and nonhierarchy" (17). If "both design and difference are about the creation of form" (17), then the difference built into the design of the Shakespearean interfaces discussed in this chapter points to expansive possibilities. These remain to be made in the name of a pluriversal nonhierarchy in which alterity, resistance, solidarity, and resistance to interfacial hegemonies of self-interest are modeled and sustained. Such an interface takes the rightfully suspect canonic centrality of Shakespeare and remakes it differentially as a pluriversal shadow library in which autonomy, adaptation, creativity, self-sovereignty, and the critical pursuit of public commons spaces interface with other forms of generative worldmaking.

Notes

1 Royal Charters and Letters Patent could both be used as legal instruments to grant rights, powers, and status to individuals and corporate identities such as the East India Company, the King's Men, and other public bodies such as universities and guilds. They played a critical role in the emergence of corporations in early modern England involving transfers of powers to entities authorized by sovereign divine right. In the case of the King's Men, a Privy Seal warrant (18 May 1603) based on a Signet Bill that was issued the day previous (17 May 1603) allowed for the Letters Patent that was enrolled in the Patent Rolls (19 May 160s). The text gives some degree of evidence of the latitude to conduct business that was afforded the King's Men to "exercise publicly to their best commodity":

> To all Justices, Mayors, Sheriffs, Constables, Headboroughs, and other our officers and loving subjects, Greeting. Know ye that we of our special grace, certain knowledge, and mere motion, have licensed and authorized, and by these present do license and authorize, these our servants Lawrence Fletcher, William Shakespeare, Richard Burbage, Augustine Phillipps, John Hennings, Henry Condell, William Sly, Robert Armyn, Richard Cowley, and the rest of their associates freely to use and exercise the art and faculty of playing comedies, tragedies, histories, interludes, morals, pastorals, stage plays, and such other like as they have already studied or hereafter shall use or study, as well for the recreation of our loving subjects as for our solace and pleasure when we shall think good to see them during our pleasure. And the said comedies, tragedies, histories, interludes, morals, pastorals, stage plays and such like to show and exercise publicly to their best commodity, when the infection of the plague shall decrease, as well when their now usual house called the Globe, within our County of Surrey, as also within any town, hall, or moot halls, or other convenient places within the liberties and freedom of any other city, university, town, or borough whatsoever within our said realms and dominions. Willing and commanding you and every of you, as you tender our pleasure, not only to permit and suffer them herein without any your lets, hinderances, or molestations during our said pleasure, but also to be aiding and assisting to them if any wrong be to them offered, and to allow them such former courtesies as hath been given to men of their place and quality, and also what further favour you shall show to these our servants, for our sake, we shall take kindly at your hands.
>
> *(Nelson and Folger Shakespeare Staff)*

2 Since McLuhan identified General Electric's "electric light bulbs and lighting systems" business as fronts for the "business of moving information," G.E. has announced that it would split into three companies, reflecting its interests in aviation, healthcare, and energy (Lohr and de la Merced). G.E.'s marketing tagline—"We bring good things to life"—embeds a Frankensteinian trope of bringing the thing it produces to "life," also a convenient way of describing interfacial economies predicated on screens and objects that contain virtual worlds an end-user can inhabit.

3 In theory, this notion of being defined by informational flows of neurons and electrons can mutate away from incarnate interfaces to AI interfaces in dialogue with forms of extended humanity (using AI prosthetics) and beyond that to AI interactions with other artificially intelligent agents. Elon Musk's Neuralink version of this interfacial economy clearly outlines a first step in this expanded direction predicated on virtual spaces tied interfacially to hardware: "We are creating the future of brain interfaces: building devices now that will help people with paralysis and inventing new technologies that will expand our abilities, our community, and our world" (Neuralink).

4 Full disclosure: I am the founder and director of the CASP site.

5 Another key influence on the core principles associated with the CASP site design was an experience of publishing, with Mark Fortier, *Adaptations of Shakespeare: An Anthology of Plays from the 17th Century to the Present.* Frustrated with the limitations of print technology and the commercial demands of academic publication, not to mention keenly aware of the rapidly changing flow of new information related to adapting Shakespeare, the limitations on inter- and multimedial representation that print conventions imposed, and the impossibility of gathering enough of a representative spread of differential texts into one volume, plus the restricted access associated with the high cost of academic publications, it became very clear in 2000 that web-based publication was a reasonable way to proceed in order to circumvent these obstacles. In short, the self-evident limitations of print interfaces by comparison with what online digital interfaces afforded played a key role in the development of the CASP site.

References

Bostrom, Nick. *Superintelligence: Paths, Dangers, Strategies*. Oxford UP, 2014.

Caldwell, Rebecca. "When Pucks Collide." *The Globe and Mail*, 24 April 2004. Available at: https://www.theglobeandmail.com/arts/when-pucks-collide/article997637/.

Escobar, Arturo. *Designs for the Pluriverse: Radical Interdependence, Autonomy, and the Making of Worlds*. Duke UP, 2018.

Fischlin, Daniel. *Canadian Adaptations of Shakespeare Project*. U of Guelph, 2004. Available at: http://www.canadianshakespeares.ca.

Fischlin, Daniel, and Mark Fortier. *Adaptations of Shakespeare: An Anthology of Plays from the 17th Century to the Present*. Routledge, 2000.

Fischlin, Daniel, Dorothy Hadfield, Gordon Lester and Mark A. McCutcheon. "'The Web of Our Life Is of a Mingled Yarn': The Canadian Adaptations of Shakespeare Project, Humanities Scholarship, and ColdFusion." *College Literature*, vol. 36, no. 1, 2009, pp. 77–104.

Goldsmith, Kenneth. *Duchamp Is My Lawyer: The Polemics, Pragmatics, and Poetics of UbuWeb*. Columbia UP, 2020.

Graeber, David. *The Utopia of Rules: On Technology, Stupidity, and the Secret Joys of Bureacracy*. Melville House, 2015.

Gurr, Andrew. *The Shakespearean Stage, 1574–1642*. 4th edition, Cambridge UP, 2009.

Hookway, Branden. *Interface*. MIT Press, 2014.

Johnson, Samuel. *A Dictionary of the English Language*. 2 vols. London, 1755.

Katz, Yarden. *Artificial Whiteness: Politics and Ideology in Artificial Intelligence*. Columbia UP, 2020.

Lohr, Steve, and Michael J. de la Merced. "G.E. Breaks Up with Its Storied Past." *The New York Times*, 9 November 2021. Available at: https://www.nytimes.com/2021/11/09/business/general-electric-break-up.html.

McLuhan, Marshall. "Hidden Environments Reshape Their Makers." *Essential McLuhan*, edited by Eric McLuhan and Frank Zingrone, Anansi, 1995, pp. 84–86.

McLuhan, Marshall. *Understanding Media: The Extensions of Man*. Gingko Press, 2013.

Nelson, Alan H. and Folger Shakespeare Library Staff. "Warrant under the Privy Seal for The Issue of Letters Patent Authorizing Shakespeare and His Companions to Perform Plays Throughout the Realm under Royal Patronage." Folger Shakespeare Library, Shakespeare Documented. Available at: https://shakespearedocumented.folger.edu/resource/document/king-james-establishes-kings-men-warrant-under-privy-seal.

Neuralink. "About." Available at: https://neuralink.com/about/.

Pirate Care. Available at: https://pirate.care/pages/concept/.

Schmidt, Alexander. *Shakespeare Lexicon*. Georg Reimer, 1902.

Shakespeare, William. *First Folio*. Folger Shakespeare Library, copy 68. Available at: https://www.folger.edu/first-folio-number-68.

Smith, Emma. *Shakespeare's First Folio: Four Centuries of an Iconic Book*. Oxford UP, 2016.

UbuWeb. Available at: https://twitter.com/ubuweb/status/1455154328910577668

Webb, Graeme, Max Haiven, and Xenia Benivolski. "From the Belly of the Beast: Amazon Workers, Sci-Fi and the Space Between Utopia and Disaster." *The Sociological Review*, 9, 2021. Available at: https://thesociologicalreview.org/magazine/november-2021/methods-and-methodology/from-the-belly-of-the-beast/?s=09.

Zuboff, Shoshanna. *The Age of Surveillance Capitalism: The Fight for a Human Future at the New Frontier of Power*. PublicAffairs, 2019.

6
WHAT ARE INTERFACES FOR, REALLY?

Gabriel Egan

In almost all modern computers, everything is represented by zeroes and ones that exist as physical states of matter. This can be as electricity present or absent in circuits, as magnetized poles on the surfaces of disks, and as electrical charges pumped into or drained from capacitors. The meaning of these zeroes and ones is given by their context rather than being inherent. The same binary sequence 01000011 might in one context represent the age of a person in years (being equivalent to 67 in decimal counting), yet in another context represent the upper-case letter "C" (as it does in the ASCII encoding scheme), and in another context again be an instruction to the processor to move data from one memory cell to another (as it is in the Intel 8080 processor instruction set). In computing, context is everything.

To show what this means for how we conceive of and use human-computer interfaces, this chapter will sketch the technical innovation that gave rise to the context-dependency of digital representations and chart how, over time, accreted layers of meaning-making contextualization have obscured it. At the most fundamental level, the zeroes and ones in a computer are merely representations (when created) and interpretations (when read), since physical states of themselves bear no meaning and matter does not, in any case, exist in the sharply distinguished states that match the sharply distinguished mathematical concepts of zero and one. In computer design, any electrical pressure above an arbitrary voltage is treated as a one and any pressure below another arbitrary voltage is treated as a zero. The permitted limits of variation—known as tolerances in engineering—map the realities of the physical components to the abstraction of the binary system.

The software programs that we call interfaces are the same kinds of abstractions as the content they appear to contain and mediate to us: they are '"made" (in the abstract sense) of exactly the same kinds of zeroes and ones. The interface/content distinction is, to that extent, illusory. Tracing the history of this illusion will take us to a consideration of four digital datasets widely used by Shakespearians showing the best and worst of what is possible with this technology. What we find is while at the lowest level everything we are discussing exists merely as streams of zeroes and ones, the illusory interface/content distinction is nonetheless strictly policed, for reasons that must be understood in terms of the power relations that modern technologies are made to serve.

DOI: 10.4324/9780367821722-9

Context as meaning

The context-sensitivity of digital representations did not feature in the earliest digital computers. The Harvard Mark I computer completed in 1944 was the culmination of earlier work on mechanical calculating machines and it embodied in physical form (as a strip of paper tape punched with holes) a series of commands about the automated movement between memory cells called registers of the numbers representing the intermediate results of a series of calculations, and it also embodied in physical form (as paper cards punched with holes) the data upon which the calculations would start (Priestley 102–7). The two physical embodiments—of instructions, on one hand, and data, on the other—were kept separate and used different media: paper tape and punched card. What effect does this separation have in a computing machine? Crucially it made it impossible for the result of a calculation to form the basis for a new instruction, as happens when instructions are treated as if they are numbers.

In 1945, John von Neumann, responding in part to his experiences using the Harvard Mark I computer, came up with a revolutionary innovation in the design of computing machines (see Von Neumann). Virtually every digital computer since then has been a "Von Neumann" machine and nothing essential has changed: they have simply become faster each year. Von Neumann's innovation was to put the data being worked upon and the instructions for what to do with the data into the same storage medium, the same memory space, rather than keeping them separate. In this view, instructions are just data—specifically, data about what the machine should do next—and, conversely, data can be expressed as instructions, so, for example, instead of storing the number pi as a constant, it can be algorithmically calculated afresh each time it is needed.

The fact that the meaning of binary strings in computers is thoroughly contextual should alert us that the content/form distinction made in the Text Encoding Initiative (TEI) application of eXtensible Markup Language (XML), the distinction between a text and the DTD or schema that describes its parts and their inter-relations, is only the outermost of a series of nested contextualizations. A string of binary digits stands for a particular letter of the alphabet only in the context of an encoding scheme, such as the ASCII encoding scheme (now part of the UTF-8 scheme) first approved by the American Standards Association in 1965 (MacKenzie 211–97), in which the binary number 01000001 is designated as "A," 01000010 is designated as "B," 01000011 is "C," and so on. The ASCII context can be understood as providing metadata: data about the data, or a comment made about it. The contextualization may end at this single level of metadata. The world's oldest collection of free online digital texts, Project Gutenberg begun in 1971, standardized on ASCII encoding on the principle that this would give its texts the greatest possible longevity and widest reusability, since all computers understand this first level of contextualization and will correctly display as letters and punctuation a text encoded this way. ASCII encoding relies upon a context that every computer manufacturer has agreed to implement so that the processing of the string 01000001 is bound to result in the letter "A" being displayed, printed, or transmitted.

Project Gutenberg has been criticized for the decision to use this minimal encoding, most influentially by the co-creator of XML and TEI, C. M. Sperberg-McQueen, who objected that without additional metadata providing additional layers of context—textual apparatuses and descriptions of sources and principles of transcription—such impoverished texts cannot be the basis for serious scholarly work (see Sperberg-McQueen). The XML/TEI approach applies such an additional layer of contextualization, taking the writing beyond the mere imperative to interpret 01000001 as an "A" that arises from the ASCII context. XML's additional metadata assert that one part of the string of binary digits be understood as a verse line, another as a prose paragraph, and so on. This metadata can be embedded in the same file as the character data (as "tags" around the content words) but need not be: the XML metadata may reside in a separate file and merely point to the parts of the character data that it comments upon, in the technique called standoff markup.

As merely layers of additional commentary upon the text, all such metadata are in a sense various kinds of literary criticism. Even the choices to normalize to a single space the variety of spaces found in manuscript and printed sources, or to preserve the line-breaks in verse and to reflow paragraphs of prose, are kinds of micro-criticism. Digital texts allow us to see more easily than we can with printed texts that without the lowest level of metadata—in computers, the ASCII context—the content we call writing is inherently meaningless. In printed texts the letters and words are mere ink marks that acquire meaning only when we apply a context by choosing to understand them as standing for letters within a particular alphabet, and then apply a further layer of context to understand the resulting collection of letters as words within a particular language. In digital texts there are rather more layers of contextualization separating the underlying physical substrate—the active and inactive transistor circuits representing zeroes and ones—and the final image that human eyes and brains make sense of as writing.

It is common to refer to the last stage of this process as the human-computer interface but we should recognize that everything we see on a computer screen—the pixels we switched on by typing our text and the pixels switched on by the text-editing software to create frames that surround and contain our text—is all, at origin, merely the expression of strings of zeroes and ones. A text encoded in the internal format used by the Microsoft Word software is, at the lowest level of matter, indistinguishable from the software that created it: each is just a long binary number. Bearing this in mind disables the false interface/content distinction that clouds our habits of thinking about digital text. This interface/content distinction is especially pernicious when exploited in the power relations between creators and consumers of digital texts and other creative works, as I hope to show.

Habituation to particular practices of, and tools for, reading and writing—that is, habituation to our interfaces—makes those practices feel natural and effortless and makes the tools seem to disappear. When our interfaces to reading and writing are changed, our interactions with them feel at first unnatural and onerous. As the philosopher Martin Heidegger observed, our tools tend not to appear to us as they really are so long as we are usefully employing them, or as Terry Eagleton summarized him "when the hammer breaks, when we cease to take it for granted, its familiarity is stripped from it and it yields up to us its authentic being" so that a "broken hammer is more of a hammer than an unbroken one" (Heidegger 68–81, 149–52, 342–4; Eagleton 64). A consideration of the history of our interfaces with computers will help illustrate the technology's progress toward effortless utility and invisibility.

A brief history of human-computer interfaces

The earliest Von Neumann computers scarcely had a human interface to speak of. For those directly operating the computer the interactions were mediated through paper tape and punched cards, modified teleprinters, and large banks of switches and lamps by which individual binary numbers could be entered into the machine or read from it. In some cases the state of the hardware of an early Von Neumann computer could even be directly read by human operators without the need for intermediary lamps and switches (Lavington 13, 17–19, 65–6; Bashe 104–8).

The dominance of the punch card as the primary human interface in the early history of literary and linguistic computer projects can largely be explained by IBM's popularization of this medium in business data processing before the invention of the digital computer, and in that light the punched card might seem something of an obstacle to progress. But to individual users in Humanities departments, the punched card had distinct advantages over newer media that called for a closer relationship with the computer and those who looked after it.

Until the microcomputer revolution of the late 1970s, the long-term storage of a digital text on a magnetic medium such as disk or tape required ongoing interaction with a computing centre, which typically for an academic user was the computing service of her university. Such magnetic storage was relatively costly. By contrast, a digital text stored on a paper medium (tape or cards) could be kept in the user's office and its maintenance required only the minimal protection from water and extremes of temperature and humidity that books require.

Although it is technically possible to punch a new paper tape by hand without access to a computer, the task is time-consuming and intricate, and the resulting tape cannot easily be altered once it is punched. But because each card contains just one line of characters, a deck of punched cards holding a digital text could, by contrast, be easily extended by interlarding additional cards and could be edited by replacing existing cards with new ones. These tasks could be performed by the user without recourse to a computer, using desk-size electro-mechanical punching machines. A batch of punched cards offered a digital surrogate for the literary-historical text that gave the Humanities investigator an autonomy over the creation and editing of a text that came close to the autonomy that handwritten and typewritten files provided.

Working on the collation for the New Variorum Shakespeare edition of *A Midsummer Night's Dream*, R. L. Widmann reported such autonomy as a prime consideration:

> We use an IBM 029 key-punch. I have rented one of these, at $62 a month, for use by my three part-time student assistants, who are paid $2 an hour … Punched cards were chosen as in input medium since I anticipated difficulties in correcting paper tape or magnetic tape without the help of professional staff.
>
> *(59n1)*

This model of local curation of texts still holds in some projects of computational stylistics in the sense that much of the investigator's time is spent on the relatively mundane tasks of creating and refining the large textual corpus on which the work is founded and relatively little time is spent actually processing it. Such curation of a text is non-computational in the sense of "computation" used by the early, mathematically oriented, pioneers of the new technologies. But these days this work of curation is itself largely undertaken using computers to run the various software aids provided by tools such as XML editors. Notice that Widmann's concern was to manage his text without needing the help of professional staff, and that the medium of punch cards empowered him in his relationship with the institutional providers of computing services. The historical account of technological development presented here is intended to show that particular technologies and ways of working shift the balance of power toward the user and, as we shall see, that others shift it away.

Histories of the development of academic computing services usually contrast the inconvenience of batch-mode data processing involving forms and punched cards with the interactive, conversational, interfaces that succeeded them. For example, Joy Lisi Rankin began her account of the liberating spread of teleprocessing—the ability to control a computer from afar over telephone lines—by contrasting the six-hour round trip that a mathematics professor at Dartmouth College had to take in 1958 to run a program that he hand-delivered to the Harvard University computer centre on punched cards with the ease of remote, conversational access available to a Dartmouth undergraduate student ten years later (12–13).

In a conversational interaction, the user operates what is known as a terminal: originally an adapted teleprinter, later a visual display unit comprising a keyboard and a video screen. The computer presents on the terminal's printer or screen a prompt, meaning an invitation to enter an instruction, and in reply the user types a short sentence that commands the computer to perform a particular action, for example, an imperative verb such as "RUN" followed by an accusative noun specifying the object to be acted upon such as "PROGRAM1." The results of executing a program might be the creation of new data within the computer and/or the production of a report or data presented on the printer or screen. After completing the commanded task, the computer presents a fresh prompt to invite the user to enter a fresh command. This interaction is sometimes also called command-line processing.

Such conversational interaction was always a possibility for the operators present in the same rooms as the earliest computers, but it later became viable as a mode of interaction for the wider user community only after the development of timesharing computer systems powerful enough to serve the needs of multiple simultaneous users. Timesharing computers give each user the illusion of dedicated access to the computer by the method of time-slicing: attending to each user for only a fraction of a second in a rotation rather as a busy waiter serves multiple tables in a restaurant. Timesharing computers could be accessed via terminals which might be in the same building as the computer or else connected remotely over conventional telephone lines. The first timesharing computers were large and expensive mainframe machines, but by the late 1960s cheaper minicomputers—most notably Digital Equipment Corporation's PDP-10 (see Bell et al.)—also supported such multiuser operation, albeit with fewer simultaneous users.

The conversational model dominated the teleprocessing revolution described in Rankin's history and formed the earliest computing experiences of the pioneers of the microprocessor computing revolution of the late 1970s, including Bill Gates, who later co-founded the Microsoft corporation (Manes and Andrews 23–36). Bringing the computer even closer to the user—putting it physically on her desk—the new microprocessor-based personal computers adopted the conversational model: the software used to operate the earliest personal computers, their primitive operating systems, expected the user to type commands onto the command line to execute programs and create and move files of data.

Most influential of the new microcomputers was the IBM Personal Computer (PC) introduced in 1981. Its operating system—called PC-DOS and effectively equivalent to the MS-DOS sold separately by its creators Microsoft—used a command-line interface. Programs running on a PC could themselves provide a Graphical User Interface for further interaction with the user, but the native operating systems of all microcomputers used a command-line conversational model until Apple introduced the Macintosh computer in 1984. The Macintosh's operating system was designed to be wholly graphical and used the metaphor of a desktop instead of a conversation and required users to manipulate iconic representations of objects (documents, storage devices, a wastebin, and so on) using a pointing device (the mouse) instead of typing their names at a command line (see Hertzfeld). The new visual metaphor rapidly replaced the conversational metaphor when Microsoft copied Macintosh's design to create its Windows operating system for the PC (Manes and Andrews 214–28).

The desktop metaphor transformed the user's visual tracking of what happens on a computer screen. With a command-line interface the user focusses intently on the single instruction sentence as she carefully types it, since even small errors of spelling or punctuation cause a command to be rejected or, worse, initiate an unintended operation. In this mode of close reading and writing, the screen space above the line currently being typed contains the sentences of previous commands and can be ignored other than as a reminder of what has just happened and a guide to what to type next.

The desktop-metaphor interface, by contrast, requires a visual scanning of the entire screen since the interaction could in theory transform any part of it. Close reading was replaced by visual scanning. For those charged with providing help to computer users this meant that the instructions to make something happen could no longer be conveyed as a series of commands to be carefully typed and instead required accurately describing in words a moving picture and a set of gestures the user should make with the mouse.

With the rise of Graphical User Interfaces, users came to expect that interactions with computers would involve visual scanning of a screen comprising relatively fixed furniture such as menus and persistent borders within which changeable contents appear. This kind of interaction intensifies a false content/form distinction as the fixed parts of the interface seem to give shape to the malleable data—words, numbers, pictures—that appear within them. For instance, the bounding boxes topped with menus and so-called ribbons that are the screen furniture provided by Microsoft Word appear to give shape to the user-chosen words typed within them, and to provide the means to reshape those words by changing the typeface, margins, and so on.

In truth, the apparently fixed screen furniture of an interface is as much the consequence of patterns of zeroes and ones inside the machine as are the apparently more malleable data held within the furniture. This becomes clear when the user inadvertently selects to alter or hide a part of the furniture. The anxiety displayed by computer users when their interfaces change, either by their own accidental instructions or because the manufacturer changes the design, is witness that the illusory permanence of the screen furniture has become deeply embedded in the cognitive expectations of computer users. If the change was initiated by the user, the knowledge of how to restore the lost furniture goes some way toward assuaging the anxiety, although it is not uncommon to hear users complain that it ought to be impossible to so easily harm such fundamental components of their interaction with a computer. If the change was initiated by a manufacturer and the users are powerless to reverse it, the anxiety amongst users may become intense and be collectively expressed.

The fundamental relations giving rise to anxiety about human-computer interfaces are ones of power and knowledge. At the lowest level inside the computer all representations are equal and the zeroes and ones are moved around by mindless processes that invoke no implicit meanings. Whatever meanings attach to the binary digits—assigning this stream the status of an instruction and that stream the status of data—arise solely from context. Such meaning-bearing contexts are nested one within another, so that the instructions that comprise a complex software package will designate some streams of binary digits as representations of the screen furniture and others as representations of the contents to be displayed within that furniture.

The worst kind of computer software reifies such high-level distinctions in the meaning of binary digits so that it feels as if some parts of the interaction really are fixed, the parts forming the interface, and that only the remaining parts are within the user's control. The choice to make software behave in this way reflects the power relations that inhere in the use of computers and resistance to it requires the assertion of power by the users of computers and better knowledge of how their machines actually operate. To illustrate this point, and show that bad choices are not exclusive to either the commercial or the publicly funded realm, we will now consider four illustrative examples of the publication of digital resources of special interest to Shakespeare scholars.

Four cases: The Oxford Complete Works of Shakespeare Electronic Edition (1989), Literature Online (LION, 1997–), the Henslowe-Alleyn Digitization Project (2005–), and the Database of Early English Playbooks (DEEP, 2007–)

Two of our illustrative examples are commercial products, the Oxford Complete Works of Shakespeare Electronic Edition and Literature Online, and require a purchase or subscription, and the other two are publicly funded and are free at the point of use. Our first example, the Oxford Complete Works of Shakespeare Electronic Edition (1989), predates the widespread adoption of Graphical User Interfaces in personal computing, coming as it does from the MS-DOS era of 1981 to about 1995.

The dominant transportable storage medium in the MS-DOS era was the floppy disk, available in two physical sizes—5¼ and 3½ inches wide—using a number of partially compatible file formats. This variety of standards gave each disk a capacity from 160 kilobytes (in the first IBM PC) to 1,440 kilobytes in the last format commonly in use before floppy disks became obsolete in the late 1990s. Floppy disks were used to distribute computer software but could also contain significant quantities of text, and Michael Best has documented the commercial projects to sell Shakespeare's works in this format. A practical constraint was the inherently small overall data capacity of the floppy disk: even in the most capacious format it could hold only four or five plays so that a large authorial canon might require a set of disks.

As detailed by Best, almost all the editions of Shakespeare made available on floppy disk, and later on CD-ROM, were based on out-of-copyright Victorian editions, most commonly the Globe Shakespeare (see the Shakespeare 1864 edition). An important exception was the Oxford Complete Works of Shakespeare Electronic Edition, based on the printed edition of 1986–87, which appeared in 1989 as a set of floppy disks for the IBM PC and compatible computers (see the Shakespeare 1989 edition). There were 20 disks in the 5¼-inch set and 10 in the 3½-inch set and each work, such as a play, occupied one text file on a disk, encoded in the ubiquitous ASCII file format that made them usable by every program for text display, processing, and editing.

The manual accompanying the Oxford Complete Works of Shakespeare Electronic Edition explained the markup conventions used within the files, which employed the system of COCOA tags that was first developed specifically for use with the COCOA concordance software and later the Oxford Concordance Program (see Russell; Hockey and Martin). The manual illustrated how this COCOA tagging provided information not available in the printed edition. For example, the printed works' type-layout convention for distinguishing prose from verse put the first line of speech on the same line as the speech prefix, if it was prose, and on the line below the speech prefix, if it was verse. While marking the start of a speech unambiguously, this convention cannot show transitions from verse to prose or vice versa occurring within a speech, which can—depending on vagaries of sentence and line length in relation to the width of the printed book's measure—be impossible to detect by sight. The electronic edition eliminated this ambiguity by providing explicit markup tags for all transitions from verse to prose and vice versa.

Likewise, there is no indication in the printed edition (beyond the lines being perhaps somewhat short) of occurrences of a run of three verse lines being amphibious in the sense that either the first and second or the second and third could together form a complete metrical unit. In the digital edition this was also explicitly marked up. Most usefully of all, since the 1986–87 Oxford Complete Works of Shakespeare was ground-breaking in its theorizing and practice regarding Shakespeare's collaborations with other writers, the digital text explicitly marked changes of author within the body of a work. This pioneering digital edition gave users what must have been for most their first sight of textual markup used to convey literary-critical assertions, in this case about changes of author and versification. The COCOA's system's relatively transparent and unobtrusive nature—Shakespeare's text is readily readable between the tags—and the edition's encoding in the universally understood ASCII format enabled anyone to make use of the extra information. This digital edition is the high watermark of openness in the commercial publication in electronic form of Shakespeare's works edited to the highest modern standards, and in that aspect at least, it has not yet been surpassed.

A standard floppy-disk drive is capable of writing a disk as well as reading it, so that turning a blank disk into a copy of one purchased from a publisher was cheap and easy for users to do. Indeed, the single command needed to do this was built into all personal computers' operating systems. There was nothing inherently suspicious about taking such a copy, and the Oxford Complete Works of Shakespeare Electronic Edition advised doing so for backup purposes, and its manual explained how (see Shakespeare 1989, ["Manual"] 1). From the publishers' point of view, the new CD-ROM physical format that became standard on PCs in the 1990s had one special advantage over the floppy disk as a distribution medium: it was read-only. Until the early 2000s, the CD-ROM drives in most computers could not write to disks, so copying a publisher's disks was beyond the ability of most users. A second advantage for publishers was that because each CD-ROM could hold as much data as about 400 floppy disks there was room not only for a copious text—plus images, and sound, and short video streams—but also for software.

Including software with the texts on a CD-ROM enabled publishers to disguise or even encrypt the raw texts so that instead of viewing them from the supplied disk with an interface of her own choosing, the user could reach them only via a publisher-supplied software application that had to be installed on her computer. With such a CD-ROM the user was paying not just for the raw data, the texts of Shakespeare, but also the means to inspect—to read or process—that data. Indeed, with most such CD-ROMs there was no other way to get at the Shakespeare works. They could not be simply extracted from the disk because, disguised and/or encrypted, they were invisible even to the user's operating system other than as inscrutably encoded files. The only way to see the texts within was to run software provided by the publisher that undisguised and/or unencrypted them for display.

The shift from floppy disks that simply carried texts that the user could manipulate with any software she already had to CD-ROM disks whose contents could be examined only with the software provided on the disk itself was a substantial transfer of power from the user to the publisher. The appropriate analogy with old technology would be the invention of printed books that produced blank or garbled pages when photocopied and could be read only using spectacles supplied by the publisher. To pursue this analogy a little further, it was as if each publisher's spectacles worked only with one publication so that the user had to acquire as many different spectacles as she had books. The balance of power shifted slightly toward the user again when CD-ROM drives capable of writing to blank disks became cheap enough to be installed in most new computers from the early 2000s, since this at least allowed the user to make multiple copies of an expensive CD-ROM to use in different locations, such as the home and office.

Although CD-ROMs gave publishers more control over what users did with their publications than they had with floppy-disks, the very fact that these CD-ROMs, like floppies, placed all the data in the user's hands at one time and in one physical object made it relatively trivial for advanced users to release the data from the digital enclosures the publishers put them in. The transition to predominantly online delivery of published materials in the early 2000s marked a much greater shift of power in favour of the publishers, since the user's computer need never contain all the data at one time. If the data are sent over the network in piecemeal fashion, so that at any one time the user's computer is given only part of the object under examination (say, one scene of a Shakespeare play), then it is technically more challenging for the user to create on her machine a complete copy of the entire object (the whole play).

This principle is used in video streaming over the Internet, for example from Google's YouTube service, in which the user's computer receives only a few frames of the moving image at any one time—just enough to display it while the next few frames are being sent—and hence never possesses the entire recording all at once. To reconstruct the whole of the original recording, a streaming-video user has to capture the frames as they are sent and locally recombine them to replicate the complete recording they were drawn from. As we will see, two of the four digital resources examined here use exactly this piecemeal approach to restrict access to the raw materials they present, allowing the user to examine only a small part of them at any one time.

The advantage, from the publisher's point of view, of online content delivery was readily apparent to Charles Chadwyck-Healey whose company (later bought by ProQuest) sold as standalone CD-ROM products the datasets it called *English Poetry, English Verse Drama, English Prose Drama, Early English Prose Fiction*, and *Editions and Adaptations of Shakespeare*. "My concern," Chadwyck-Healey wrote, "was that an English professor would borrow a set of *English Poetry* from the library and spend the weekend making copies to give to his/her students" (Chapter 20, "Literature Online [LION]"). As well as duplicating disks, users could transfer the contents to their local hard disks (by a process called virtualization), which, because they have shorter access times, make the process of retrieving information from the disks faster.

The Chadwyck-Healey company consolidated their literature CD-ROM collections into a single online service called Literature Online (LION) in 1997, accessible only to those with an institutional subscription. In place of physical disks that generated one-off sales and could be copied by the users to reproduce entire datasets, Chadwyck-Healey would now sell a service that generated an annual fee for letting users see only a part of the data at any one time. Charles Chadwyck-Healey was explicit about the benefits and the power relations:

> even if a user downloaded some texts, they would only be a small part of a much larger whole ... We would also know if there was unusual activity on the website, as we were able to monitor the usage of the data on our servers.
>
> *(Chadwyck-Healey Chapter 20, 'Literature Online [LION]")*

With the online service, the time taken for a result to appear on the user's screen is determined not only by the power and speed of the user's computer but also, and to a larger extent, by the power of Chadwyck-Healey's servers and the speed of the network connections between those servers and the user. Although LION does not block users from downloading the whole of a literary work, one work is the most her computer can possess at any one time. The user never possesses a full set of works as she did with the CD-ROM versions, so she cannot repurpose that full dataset for her own ends. This might seem a trivial consideration to many users, but such a transfer of the power to search the dataset from the user to the provider has severe consequences if the provider decides to reduce the range of searching options or unintentionally disables features in its own searching software.

Such unintentional disabling of features is not merely a hypothetical concern. On 28 June 2014, Chadwyck-Healey's parent company ProQuest changed the software that delivers LION to its users, inadvertently breaking LION's proximity-searching and variant-spelling features, and in the worst way possible for investigators who rely on them. After the change, the search results returned from the website are wrong, so that, for example, the counts of hits are untrue, but nothing visible on the screen indicates this fault and no error message is produced. This silent disabling of LION's advanced search options brought a halt to the work of researchers who rely on these features, and at the time of writing (November 2020), the fault has not been fixed. Such things cannot happen when users rely solely on their own computers and locally attached sources of data, and keep them unchanged.

LION is not the worst example of how online delivery gives the providers of datasets far-reaching power over their users. The Henslowe-Alleyn Digitization Project took digital photographs of the collection of papers belonging to the early modern theater impresario Philip Henslowe and his son-in-law, the actor Edward Alleyn, which are kept at Dulwich College in South London, and placed them online for free viewing. Copyright law exists to protect acts of originality and creativity, which for these documents means the originality and creativity of Henslowe, Alleyn, and the other early modern persons who contributed to the documents. Being about 400 years old, any copyrights subsisting in these documents have long since expired, but of course what the Henslowe-Alleyn Digitization Project gives its users are digital photographs of the documents, and the application of copyright laws to new media requires interpretation.

The landmark case of Bridgeman Art Library versus Corel Corporation established in 1999 that under American and British law the photographing of a flat surface containing an image or writing in order to provide the most faithful reproduction of it for viewers or readers constitutes an act of slavish copying, not originality. The United Kingdom Government's Intellectual Property Office published a notice in 2015 confirming this interpretation, remarking that "copyright can only subsist in subject matter that is original in the sense that it is the author's own 'intellectual creation'" and observing that it would be hard to see how anyone could claim copyright "if their aim is simply to make a faithful reproduction of an existing work" (Intellectual Property Office 3).

The Henslowe-Alleyn Digitization Project was funded by a number of private charities and directly by the people of the United Kingdom via the British Academy, which is itself funded by the British government. Despite being made with public money, the Project's website asserts that all the materials it provides are "copyrighted and cannot be downloaded, reproduced, copied, circulated or otherwise used" without the Project's permission and that "The copyright of all manuscripts in the Henslowe-Alleyn Papers belongs to the Governors of Dulwich College" (Ioppolo, "Copyrights, Reproductions, and Permissions"). Neither claim appears to be true under British law. The habit of treating the possession of a document as if this conferred copyright—which as the Berne Convention makes clear arises from originality and creativity not ownership—is deeply and harmfully ingrained in the culture of museums, libraries and archives.

In the case of the Henslowe-Alleyn Digitization Project, this culture of institutional irredentism has practical ramifications because from its inception in 2005 until a technical refurbishment released on 5 March 2020 the project provided access to the digital photographs using proprietary software (Zoomify and Adobe Flash) that prevented the user's computer from receiving the whole of a picture at once. Instead, the user was given a small movable window that revealed only part of the photograph at a time. The Henslowe-Alleyn Digitization Project chose a window 630 pixels wide and 450 pixels deep, which by 2020 was about one-sixth of the typical computer's screen size. The specious assertion of copyright in this case went hand-in-hand with a practical, intentional impediment of the user's freedom to exploit the materials as she would wish.

The Henslowe-Alleyn Digitization Project's reliance on the proprietary Adobe Flash format was the main reason it had to be refurbished. The Adobe Flash software is so poorly written that it provides an easy route for malicious software to infiltrate and take over its user's computer, and by 2020 all the major web-browser manufacturers had announced that for this reason they would stop supporting Flash later that year. Without remedial work, the Henslowe-Alleyn Digitization Project materials would simply disappear from view. The refurbished website uses the Open Source image viewing software called Open SeaDragon (Caton, personal correspondence, November 16, 2020) and the viewing window is now as wide as the user's screen rather than being artificially constrained to a small portion of it. The user is now able to download a single image in the resolution at which she is viewing it—so the better her computer screen, the larger the image she can download—but not to download the image at the full resolution at which it exists on the project's web-server. Nor is the user able to download more than one image at a time. Thus this publicly funded project continues to limit what users can do with its materials and make specious claims about copyrights.

The Database of Early English Playbooks (DEEP) contrasts with the Henslowe-Alleyn Digitization Project in almost every particular except that it too was built with public money by academic subject specialists and is free to use (Farmer and Lesser 2007–). Where the Henslowe-Alleyn Digitization Project asserts its creators' copyrights, DEEP makes its contents available under a Creative Commons Attribution Non-Commercial Share-Alike licence. Where the Henslowe-Alleyn Digitization Project explicitly forbids downloading the project's underlying data, DEEP explicitly encourages it by putting a "Download DEEP Data" link on its homepage, which leads to a page that offers the project's entire contents in HTML, Comma-Separated Values (CSV), and XML form.

Nothing in the design of the DEEP website is intended to limit the user's ability to work with the data, as the Henslowe-Alleyn Digitization Project does. Nothing in the DEEP website relies upon proprietary software, the main search functionality being provided by the language JavaScript, which conforms to an International Organization for Standardization (ISO) standard for scripting languages. Built in this way on open standards, DEEP has an excellent chance of remaining in good working order with minimal maintenance for many years to come.

Conclusion: Open Access, Open Source, Open Standards, and interfaces

Across academia, the Open Access movement is a response to the privatization of public goods and the limitation of users' freedom to do what they wish with these goods. In the publishing of academic journals and books the movement encourages writers to make their materials free at the point of reading, either by paying publishers to publish it (the so-called Gold option, favoured by most publishers) or by putting it on unfettered personal, or subject-centered, or institution-centered websites (the Green option, favoured by most writers). The Open Access movement took much of its inspiration from the Open Source movement in computer software, which promoted the sharing of computer programs in their full-text form, called source code. This is the form in which computer programs are originally written and in which anyone can make sense of them if she knows the particular computer programming language used.

Much of the infrastructure of the World-Wide Web runs on Open Source software, most notably the Apache webserver used by about half the world's websites and maintained by a team of volunteers. With proprietary software the purchaser is not allowed to see the source code and has to trust the supplier's assertions about what it does and how it works, whereas use of Open Source software ensures that many pairs of eyes examine it and can confirm that it does what it is supposed to do. The Open Source model has proved itself to be the best approach for creating robust and maintainable computer systems that last for a long period of time, whereas proprietary software is notoriously prone to rapid obsolescence, as with the Adobe Flash software used by the Henslowe-Alleyn Digitization Project.

Open Standards are the third desideratum of durable digital projects. All digital files are merely strings of zeroes and ones and, to that extent, all are merely long binary numbers. This is equally true of the binary files representing the works that belong to everyone—the texts of Shakespeare's plays, the images of early theatrical documents—and those over which particular individuals legitimately (albeit unhelpfully) claim ownership, most especially the interfaces to that content. This distinction between numbers that belong to everyone and numbers that are private property is invidious, giving rise to the bizarre notion of illegal numbers such as the large prime number used to decode the encrypted video signal on DVD films. The owners of such privatized numbers claim that merely communicating one of them to another person is a crime, and indeed arrests have been made for this supposed offence (see González).

When Shakespeare scholars plan a project to create new content, such as the digitization of a collection of records, they typically design a new interface to present that content to users, and most commonly these days it is a website. It is clear why they do this, since they want to make it as easy as possible for users to access and exploit the new resources. There is, however, a powerful argument that creators should not make new interfaces but should instead merely make the raw materials available on the web and let others pull these together howsoever they wish, as Peter Robinson argued. Such an approach gives users the kinds of freedom they have with the Oxford Complete Works of Shakespeare Electronic Edition.

A compromise alternative to Robinson's position would be to do both: construct interfaces for those who want them but also enable direct downloading of the raw materials by those who want to use them in their own ways. This is what DEEP does, because it is typical of the best Digital Humanities projects and all the best ones do this. Ideally, the raw materials should be encoded using Open Standards so that the user is not confined to any one set of software for making sense of them. But there exists a compromise alternative to this ideal too, which takes into account the reality that not all Open Standards are widely used. The open video format standard called Ogg, for example, is much less widely used than ones based on proprietary formats such as MPEG-4. If a proprietary format is widely used and there are many different tools for consuming and editing materials in this format, its lack of openness need not be especially problematic.

The standards for any digital encoding are merely the rules for making sense of a string of zeroes and ones; they are merely a statement of the contexts within which the various parts of a long binary number have particular meanings. The rules for how to make sense of long binary numbers differ from format to format. The rules of ASCII and PDF encoding (and others) tell us how to turn them back into simple digital texts, the rules of WAV and MP3 encoding (and others) tell us how to turn them back into sounds, the rules of JPEG and TIFF encoding (and others) tell us how to turn them back into pictures, and the rules of MPEG-4 and AVI encoding (and others) tell us how to turn them back into video streams.

We already have many digital tools for decoding texts, sounds, and still and moving pictures that work well for our scholarly and entertainment purposes. These tools are our interfaces. Oftentimes we have so many different tools for turning the binary digits of a particular format into readable and listenable words and pictures that these tools, even the proprietary ones, effectively cease to function as interfaces. If we dislike the way that one tool decodes or allows us to edit a TIFF-encoded file, we simply discard it and use another. With so many tools to choose from, we are tied to none. The only really dangerous encoding formats are those for which there is no rich variety of tools but rather just one proprietary tool for decoding it, as is the case with Adobe Flash.

When we have a wealth of different interfaces for each of our digital file formats, we are liberated from reliance on any particular one. This is the situation we enjoy with files encoded in the formats ASCII, PDF, WAV, MP3, JPEG, TIFF, MPEG-4, and AVI files, which between them represent a large proportion of the total means by which human culture is nowadays created and disseminated. But the files used for digital artefacts in the field of Literary Studies are still not always provided to us in such unfettered formats. The history of digital Shakespeare is littered with failed and broken interfaces that frustrated the scholarly endeavour. There is no reason this has to continue.

References

Bashe, Charles J., et al. *IBM's Early Computers*. 3, MIT Press, 1986.

Bell, C. G., A. Kotok, T. N. Hastings, and R. Hill. "Evolution of the DECsystem 10." *Communications of the Association for Computing Machinery (ACM)*, Special Issue on Computer Architecture, vol. 21, no. 1, 1978, pp. 44–63.

Best, Michael. "Shakespeare and the Electronic Age." *Shakespeare and the Text*, edited by Andrew Murphy, Blackwell, 2007, pp. 145–161.

Chadwyck-Healey, Charles. *Publishing for Libraries: At the Dawn of the Digital Age*. Bloomsbury, 2020.

Eagleton, Terry. *Literary Theory: An Introduction*. Basil Blackwell, 1983.

Farmer, Alan B. and Zachary Lesser. "Database of Early English Playbooks (DEEP): A Database of Bibliographical Information Delivered Over the Internet." 2007–. Available at: http//deep.sas.upenn.edu.

González, Andrés Guadamuz. "Trouble with Prime Numbers: DeCSS, DVD and the Protection of Proprietary Encryption Tools." *Journal of Information, Law and Technology*, vol. 3, 2002, pp. 1–31. Available at: https://era.ed.ac.uk/bitstream/handle/1842/2273/troublewithprimenumbers.pdf?sequence=1&isAllowed=y.

Heidegger, Martin. *Being and Time*. Translated by Joan Stambaugh, revised and with a foreword by Dennis J. Schmidt, State U of New York P, 2010.

Hertzfeld, Andy. *Revolution in the Valley: The Insanely Great Story of How the Mac Was Made*. Foreword by Steve Wozniak, O'Reilly, 2005.

Hockey, Susan, and J. Martin. "The Oxford Concordance Program Version 2." *Literary and Linguistic Computing*, vol. 2, 1987, pp. 125–131.

Intellectual Property Office. "Digital Images, Photographs and the Internet: Copyright Notice Number 1/2014." United Kingdom Patent Office, 2015.

Ioppolo, Grace. "Henslowe-Alleyn Digitization Project." 2005–. Available at: https://henslowe-alleyn.org.uk/.

Lavington, Simon. *Early British Computers: The Story of Vintage Computers and the People Who Built Them*. Manchester UP, 1980.

MacKenzie, Charles E. *Coded Character Sets: History and Development*. Addison-Wesley, 1980.

Manes, Stephen, and Paul Andrews. *Gates: How Microsoft's Mogul Reinvented an Industry and Made Himself the Richest Man in America*. Simon & Schuster, 1994.

Priestley, Mark. *A Science of Operations: Machines, Logic and the Invention of Programming*. Springer, 2011.

Rankin, Joy Lisi. *A People's History of Computing in the United States*. Harvard UP, 2018.

Robinson, Peter. "How We Have Been Publishing the Wrong Way, and How We Might Publish a Better Way." *Electronic Publishing: Politics and Pragmatics*, edited by Gabriel Egan. ITER Press, 2010, pp. 139–155.

Russell, D. B. "'COCOA' Manual: A Word Count and Concordance Generator for Atlas." Atlas Computer Laboratory, 1967.

Shakespeare, William. *Works [The Globe Edition]*. Edited by William George Clark and William Aldis Wright, London, 1864.

Shakespeare, William. *The Complete Works*. Edited by Stanley Wells, et al., electronic edition prepared by William Montgomery and Lou Burnard, Oxford UP, 1989.

Sperberg-McQueen, C. M. "Textual Criticism and the Text Encoding Initiative." *The Literary Text in the Digital Age*, edited by Richard J. Finneran, U of Michigan P, 1996, pp. 37–62.

Von Neumann, John. "'First Draft of a Report on the EDVAC: Contract Number W-670-ORD-4926 between the United States Army Ordnance Department and the University of Pennsylvania'. A Report from the Moore School of Engineering at the University of Pennsylvania. U of Pennsylvania, 1945.

Widmann, R. L. "The Computer in Historical Collation: Use of the IBM 360/75 in Collating Multiple Editions of *A Midsummer Night's Dream*." *The Computer in Literary and Linguistic Research: Papers from a Cambridge Symposium*, edited by R. A. Wisbey, Cambridge UP, 1971, pp. 57–63.

7

INTERFACE DESIGN AND EDITORIAL THEORY

Gary Taylor

> Never leave well enough alone.
>
> *Raymond Loewy*

1 Editions are designed material interfaces that contain earlier designed material objects.
2 The design of the containing material interface differs, by definition, from the design of the contained material object.
3 Even when the edition/interface represents itself as a "mere" (or "transparent" or "faithful" or "scholarly" or "accurate") representation of the original object, the material design of the container inevitably transforms the material design of what it contains.
4 Designers use particular tools to design material objects for designated/imagined users, who have particular resources, needs, and expectations.
5 The greater the temporal, geographical, and/or cultural gap between the container and the earlier object, the greater the mentalité gap between the makers and users of the interface/edition/container and the makers and users of the contained object.
6 The greater the technological gap between the container and the earlier object, the greater the material gap between the designed interface/edition/container and the original material object it contains, transmits, transforms, and transformats.
7 Both material objects (container and contained) are artiginal, in that they result from designed modifications of pre-existing forms, based on the material affordances and constraints of such forms.
8 The potential artiginality ("originality proper to artisans") of the editorial interface designer may be expanded by new technological forms, but it is also limited by user-resistance to departures from traditional and familiar forms.
9 The more widely, highly, and traditionally valued the original designed objects are (which is to say, the more fetishized the earlier objects are), the more initial resistance there will be to modifications of interface design.
10 But failure to redesign the editorial interface for new users will inevitably result in a decline in the commercial and cultural value placed on the earlier contained object(s).

DOI: 10.4324/9780367821722-10

11 Resistance to transformission/translation accelerates the decline of usability and the loss of radiant energy generated by and through past objects, culminating in the degree-zero heat-death of dead languages and dead cultural achievements.
12 Interfaces die, unless they are collaboratively redesigned for new environments.

***

These dozen design axioms apply equally to the 1623 folio edition of *Mr. William Shakespeares Comedies, Histories, & Tragedies* (designed by the publisher Edward Blount and the Jaggard printing firm) and to the 2017 online edition of *The New Oxford Shakespeare: Complete Works* (designed by Oxford University Press and a team of Shakespeare scholars it had commissioned). Like all intervening Shakespeare editions, the 1623 and 2017 editions were posthumously produced objects, designed by persons other than the designer of the original material objects. Whether or not the 1623 edition accurately represents the textual intentions of William Shakespeare, faithfully transmitted by his former theatrical colleagues John Heminges and Henry Condell, the material object containing those 36 plays was created by craftsmen in the Jaggard printing shop, and the 1623 container's design differs radically from the design of all earlier material incarnations of Shakespeare's work—and all earlier material incarnations of other commercial London playbooks—produced during Shakespeare's lifetime. The 1623 edition was produced for different users, with different financial resources and different expectations, than the users of earlier manuscript, oral, and printed forms of those 36 plays. Users of the designed container first sold in 1623 resembled previous users of Shakespeare's texts less than they resembled previous users of material objects designed and sold by the publisher Edward Blount (Taylor, *Comedies*).

The "Guidelines for Editors" of the Committee on Scholarly Editions does not describe editorial work in terms of design theory, design problems, or the affordances of forms. Its reading list does not encourage design-thinking, or recognize the relationship between, say, modernist New Bibliography and Bauhaus industrial formalism. Particularly, in the history of Shakespeare's text the editors most conspicuously and personally invested in the visual design of their books—Alexander Pope and Thomas Hanmer—are generally despised for their editorial policies. It is therefore easy to assume that visual intelligence is inversely proportional to editorial innovation. But editing has always involved re-designing old forms. As Laurie Maguire concludes, in her recent study of *The Rhetoric of the Page*, "we cannot ignore the relations between textual appearance and meaning—not just in the early modern world but in today's academic world where our representational (i.e. editorial) media are changing" (248).

Although I have been working on scholarly editions since 1978, I did not begin to conceptualize an edition as a designed *container* until 2019, and did not understand it as a designed *interface* until 2020. An edition, like a container, like an interface, is "a relation with technology, rather than a technology in itself" and "a boundary condition that is at the same time encountered and worked through toward some specific end" (Hookway, ix); each "is a mediating structure that supports behaviors and tasks" and "a space between human users and procedures that happen according to complicated protocols" (Drucker, 138–9). In the case of William Shakespeare, or Thomas Middleton, the terms "boundary" and "space" directly connect these definitions of edition, container, and interface to the boundary spaces of the early modern theater, which contained and connected literal faces. The acting company and the acting space were the interface that mediated between playwrights and playgoers. The technologies that constructed that theatrical interface were primarily those of pre-modern manuscript culture, pre-modern architectural form, and pre-modern oral and musical performance. The playhouse scriptorium produced "licensed playbooks, actors' parts, musicians' scores, prologues, epilogues, scenarios, backstage plots, perhaps scrolls and letters to be read onstage, scribal copies for fans and patrons … account books, inventories of costumes and properties, contracts, and advertising copy for playbills" (Taylor "Artiginality" 8; Greg 1931; Stern 2009). These manuscript technologies made it possible for the playwrights' words to be memorized, embodied, costumed, and choreographed by performers, who orally and physically transmitted them to audiences. Bonnie Mak describes the page as an "integration of physical and cognitive architectures" (18), but that formula is even more obviously relevant to the architectures of purpose-built playhouses of the late sixteenth and early seventeenth centuries: built infrastructural spaces specifically designed for the efficient and precise transmission of sound and meaning to large human gatherings (Smith; Deutermann).

My belated recognition of the theater as an interface is inspired by a biographical detail in Brendan Hookway's *Interface* that has usually been ignored by the media scholars who quote him. Hookway's "theoretical exploration of the interface" began "as an introduction to a dissertation on the airplane cockpit as a paradigmatic twentieth-century environment" (ix). This unexpected origin narrative no doubt affected me so powerfully because my father was a flight engineer, who introduced my childhood to the cockpit of a C-124, my adolescence to the cockpit of a small private plane, and my adulthood to the cockpit of the Space Shuttle. My chief collaborator for the last ten years, Terri Bourus, is also a licensed pilot, who trained as a "Citizen Astronaut" to pilot the Space Shuttle, before the Challenger disaster abruptly terminated that program. I therefore immediately recognized Hookway's description of the cockpit as "at once a space of inhabitation, an ergonomics of use, an assemblage of mechanical articulations … and a threshold between human and machine." But I also recognized "The Cockpit" as the name of a performance venue in early modern London, originally designed for commercial exhibitions of cockfighting, which in 1616 was transformed into a commercial indoor theater (Berry). So I could immediately connect Hookway's description of the modern aeronautic interface to the early modern theatrical interface—which, like the one my father worked in, "encompasses a multiplicity of derivations … and simulations" (ix). Like the cockpits of the C-124 and the Space Shuttle, the early modern Cockpit was a designed collaborative workplace, which depended for its effective functioning on multiple human agents, working simultaneously, moving through a four-dimensional spacetime arena.

Technologically and experientially, the early modern theatrical cockpit interface overlapped only minimally with the early modern print interface. But the commercial success of the theatrical interface created a population of theater fans who proved to be interested in printed playbooks. The remediation of theater-interface to print-interface provided only a thin synecdoche of the sensory richness of the multi-media performance-complex. Nevertheless, the printed playbook, as a genre, was commercially exceptionally successful (Farmer and Lesser). This success depended not only on the literary quality of early modern drama, but on the fact that "the codex itself is an exemplary portable storage and retrieval technology" (Borsuk 159). Once purchased, a printed play could be repeatedly accessed, whenever and wherever the owner wanted to experience it again; they did not need to wait for a theatrical revival, or pay to attend one. They could also skip ahead in the text, or go backward, or reread, or annotate the text, as they pleased. In all these respects, print freed them from the theater's control of time. Most importantly, late Elizabethan and early Stuart playgoers could themselves supplement the printed text: they had been to that theater, they had seen and heard those actors. They brought to the boundary space of the printed book their own memories of specific performances, or at the very least of generic conventions, individual performers, and particular playing spaces.

Moreover, the playbook interface, like the theatrical interface, was being constantly redesigned, in manuscript and print, throughout the sixteenth, seventeenth, and eighteenth centuries (Howard-Hill; Taylor, Daileader, and Bennett; Bourne; Maguire). This does not mean that the textual contents of printed plays became more accurate, or that the plays themselves improved. It means only that the playbook interface was adjusted to make its design more user-friendly for readers of printed plays.

***

My own career at the interface between editors and publishers, creating new interfaces for readers, has lasted more than 40 years: a short time in the history of editing, or even of Shakespeare editing, but a period of rapid transformation in editorial and interface design. In January 1978, I was interviewed for a job at Oxford University Press, producing an edition of Shakespeare's *Complete Works* that would eventually be published in 1986–87 (Wells and Taylor). I worked as an OUP employee from March 1978 to June 1986; by the time I left Oxford, I had already signed a contract with OUP to produce, for them, acting as a freelance agent in the gig economy, an edition of Thomas Middleton's *Collected Works*, which finally appeared in late 2007 (Taylor and Lavagnino). A few months before the Oxford Middleton was published, I was invited by OUP to produce, for them, a new edition of Shakespeare's works. *The New Oxford Shakespeare: Complete Works* was published, in print and online, in modern-spelling and old-spelling forms, in 2016–17 (Shakespeare, *New Oxford Shakespeare*). But the project that we began to design in 2007 will not in fact be completed until we publish the printed and online, modern-spelling and old-spelling, incarnations of *The New Oxford Shakespeare: Complete Alternative Versions*. We originally planned to publish the *Complete Alternative Versions* simultaneously with the *Complete Works*, but it has now been significantly redesigned to prioritize its online interface. My editorial career has consisted, almost entirely, of an overlapping series of collaborations with a single publishing organization, designing editorial containers for early modern objects.

Most editors do their work in a volume, or a series, that has been designed by someone else. Contributors to the Arden Shakespeare, Cambridge Shakespeare, Norton Shakespeare, Penguin Shakespeare, Variorum Shakespeare, Internet Shakespeare, and Oxford World Classics Shakespeare, are all contracted to produce a text that fits into a pre-existing container. Within the given templates, the editor fills in the blanks with introductory materials, modernized texts, collations, notes etc.—all placed within the frame of the predetermined interface. So it is not surprising that most modern editors have paid little attention to design. They regard accepting a publisher's house design as the price of admission to play the editorial game. But unlike most editors, some general editors may be able to influence a publisher's design of the container. Stanley Wells is one such general editor.

In 1978, I did not think of myself as a fledgling collaborative interface-container-designer. I could never have imagined that the *MLA Handbook: Eighth Edition* would refer to editions as "containers." In my 1978 interview, I was not much interested in the OUP representative (John Bell), whom—I must confess—I hardly remember. I was not thinking about what it meant to work for an international publishing company. Though Oxford University Press is a registered charity, it is required by its owner (the University of Oxford) to turn a profit. "I have yet to encounter a publisher," Stanley Wells wrote in 2006, "who was oblivious to financial considerations" (367). OUP competed then, and competes now, not only with other academic presses, but also with other commercial publishing conglomerates.

In retrospect, I realize that Bell was instrumental to the whole project, and to OUP's innovative investment in editorial infrastructure. In retrospect, I realize that in January 1978 I was being recruited by a profit-seeking multinational corporation—one suffused with a sense of its academic and cultural mission, one controlled by the oldest university in the English-speaking world, but a corporation nevertheless, built and managed by Anglo-Saxon elites, sustained by branches in former British colonies, and trafficking in the mass-produced commodity fetishism so reviled by my Marxist colleagues. In retrospect, I recognize that Bell was introducing me to the world described by the so-called "father" of industrial design, Raymond Loewy:

> The industrial designer never works alone … a mass-manufactured product needs to be perfected from first sketch to completion by a team of men [*sic*] and in a welter of unavoidable interferences such as suggestions, countersuggestions, criticisms, and technical restrictions.

But at the time I was wholly focused on the senior Shakespeare scholar in the room, Stanley Wells, who had proposed the new edition, was its general editor, and was seeking to employ an editorial assistant. I was shown what might be my (smaller) office, right next to his, and told that, if hired, I would be working alongside him five days a week for—OUP thought at the time—five years. As I soon discovered, we both saw Shakespeare as a theater-maker; we both rejected the dominant Fredson Bowers model of scholarly editing, which elevated bibliography over all the other forms of intellectual labor that might be relevant to the understanding and transmission of early modern texts. Most heretically of all, we both recoiled from the whole concept of a "definitive edition." Just as no performance of a Shakespeare play would ever be definitive, no edition could be. A live or filmed performance (like Olivier's *Richard III*) might set a standard, against which subsequent performances would have to compete; but no past performance would ever satisfy all future spectators. Toward the end of the interview, I asked him whether we would "act" (perhaps unintentionally, an ambiguous word) upon our own conclusions, and do something that no previous edition had done, if we decided that all previous editions were wrong. Wells said "yes." Neither of us, then, had any inkling of how different our edition would be from its predecessors.

Wells was undoubtedly more aware than I was of the relationship between these editorial principles and the material design of an edition for and by a publisher. His 2006 essay, "On Being a General Editor," traces the early evolution of his collaborations with publishers, beginning in 1964 with discussions about the New Penguin Shakespeare series. That beginning, and all subsequent negotiations with publishers, included "aspects of design"—and, in particular, aspects of editorial design that would appeal to a "general reader" or a "popular market." From the publisher's point of view, such issues are inseparable from calculations about the number of potential customers, print runs, and profit margins. But Wells did not come from an elite background, and neither did I; for us, such commitments were inseparable from an idealist and—in my case at least, naïve—desire to make great artistic achievements accessible to the greatest possible number of readers. Notably, the Oxford *Complete Works* published in 1986 won an industry award for its design. The award went to the then-young and very talented OUP designer Paul Luna; but, having been present at early discussions with Wells and Luna, and having seen a series of draft versions, I would say that Wells deserves at least some of the credit for the "elegant simplicity" of that design.

Wells certainly deserves all the credit for the edition's elegant simplification of spelling and punctuation, which affected the appearance of virtually every line in the text. In "Modernizing Shakespeare's Spelling" (Wells 1979) and then again in *Re-Editing Shakespeare for the Modern Reader* (Wells), he exposed the absurdity of the editorial tradition of preserving some early modern spellings (or some early modern punctuation), while systematically modernizing others. This policy, championed by W. W. Greg, had reached its epitome of absurdity in the

1974 Riverside edition, edited by G. Blakemore Evans. Unlike virtually every other aspect of the Oxford edition, its treatment of spelling and punctuation has had almost no detractors—perhaps because the modern spelling *Complete Works* (1986) was complemented by an *Original Spelling Edition* (1987), which let readers choose which system of spelling and punctuation they preferred.

But if the overall design, and the systematic innovation which affected more of the text than anything else, were both so successful, why did the 1986 edition generate so much resistance? Some resisters challenged, intellectually and compellingly, particular theories and practices embodied in the edition; like all editors, like all human beings, we got some things wrong. (If I believed we got everything right in 1986, I would not have agreed in 2007 to produce a completely new edition of Shakespeare.) But some of the resistance to the 1986 edition was generated by the fact that it was simply too new. Not too new in its *mise-en-page*, and not too new in its spelling and punctuation (which made readers more comfortable). But it was demonstrably too new in the way that it designedly reshaped what "Shakespeare" meant, and in the process made visible the disturbing global consequences of the editorial labor that usually remains comfortably hidden inside the academic black box. Hookway notes that the social power of interfaces depends in part on the fact that its inner workings are a "hidden background noise" (87). A radically new interface makes those inner workings conspicuous, and therefore uncomfortable. Probably the most notorious Shakespearian example of such a radically new interface is "the notable failure of Edward Capell's mid-eighteenth-century editions of Shakespeare" (Bourne 284). Many of Capell's emendations and explanations have been adopted by subsequent editors; his conjecture that *Edward III* should be included in editions of Shakespeare's works is now widely accepted. But Capell's "extremely prettily printed" edition, with its innovative system of glyphs, was simply frustrating and messy for most readers, who would have needed to access other books by Capell to decipher the glyphs and to understand the reasoning and evidence that underlay his textual decisions. Because of the overambitious, user-unfriendly design of his edition, it took centuries for Capell's intellectual achievement to be fully appreciated.

The 1986 Oxford Shakespeare was not as unfriendly as Capell's: the overall design by Luna and Wells ensured that. But the edition did make some readers uncomfortable. For example, the edition's organization of contents not by genres but by chronology challenged the assumption that there was anything tidy about Shakespeare's own formal investments. Its emphasis on performance challenged the canonical perception of Shakespeare as a "literary" dramatist. Its resurrection of unfamiliar early titles (displayed not only in the Table of Contents but in running titles atop hundreds of pages) challenged the entire editorial and critical tradition. Its unavoidable visualizations of authorial revision (most conspicuously in two versions of *King Lear* and of some sonnets) challenged the posthumous mythology of Shakespeare warbling "his native Wood-notes wilde" (Milton), producing a Poetry that "comes … as naturally as the Leaves to a tree" (Keats 1:239). The Oxford Shakespeare's restoration in *1 Henry IV* of the original name "Oldcastle" (rather than "Falstaff") exposed the operations of Elizabethan censorship—thus challenging the political mythology of an Elizabethan golden age; more disturbingly, "Oldcastle" denied the aesthetic unity of one of Shakespeare's most famous and beloved characters, and also denied the unity of the "Second Tetralogy", the four plays central to E. W. M. Tillyard's claim that the history plays constituted a patriotic "epic" whole. Tillyard's model was also challenged by the restoration of original titles (which identified some of the "history" plays as "tragedy") and by the chronological sequence (which made *1 Henry VI* a later "prequel", rather than the first installment of an ambitious, original, early pre-planned trilogy). The edition's "Reconstructed Text" of *Pericles* made visible the logical consequences of the then-almost-universally-accepted theory of memorial reconstruction: if editors are supposed to use their specialist knowledge to correct mistakes in the early editions, then should they not emend more frequently the texts that they insist are more pervasively corrupt?

Even if all these innovations had been indisputably correct, in combination, they violated Loewy's most famous axiom: a "visual engineer" designing a mass-produced product must recognize that "The adult public's taste is not necessarily ready to accept the logical solutions to their requirements if this solution implies too vast a departure from what they have been conditioned into accepting as the norm." Loewy's solution to the problems created by this consumer "tug of war between attraction to the new and fear of the unfamiliar" was to seek the "Most Advanced Yet Acceptable" (MAYA) design (326). Capell's glyphs were clearly "too vast a departure", then and now. What Paul Luna did with the *mise-en-page* of the Oxford Shakespeare was clearly an "acceptable" innovation; so was what Stanley Wells did with its spelling and punctuation. The organization by chronology instead of genre would also probably have provoked some grumbling but no profound resistance, especially in a period when various forms of historicism and critical theory were systematically rejecting formalism. For instance, the chronological principle was accepted by all three Norton Shakespeare textbooks (1997–2016). But the sheer number of overlapping innovations in the Oxford Shakespeare apparently put the edition into what Loewy called "the shock-zone" (325).

As a demonstration of the validity of Loewy's principle, contrast reactions to the Oxford Shakespeare (1986–87) and the Oxford Middleton (2007). The Middleton edition won the MLA prize for a Distinguished Scholarly Edition and the Elizabeth Dietz Award for Outstanding Publication in Early Modern Studies; it has also been a much more significant commercial success than Oxford University Press anticipated. Academic reviews were overwhelmingly positive. But the Middleton edition was far more adventurous than the Oxford Shakespeare, 20 years before. It not only included two complete versions of two plays; but for one of those two plays, the edition aligned the two versions as parallel texts in adjoining columns, and for the other it gave one version in modern spelling and the other in an original-spelling transcription from manuscript sources. The running titles not only featured unfamiliar titles; they randomly rotated variant spellings and variant versions of the titles. In *The Old Law/An Old Law*, the edition rotated the visual relationship of text to commentary and textual notes. The occasional poems juxtaposed photographs of the earliest texts with modernized texts. *The Black Book* was printed in a different type-face, to emphasize the purposeful distinctiveness of its original black letter font. Middleton's pageants were treated as events, rather than texts, with the "official" texts juxtaposed with diplomatic reports of what actually happened. In all these ways the edition systematically abandoned the norm of editorial monovocal uniformity and embraced a self-consciously "federal" practice, highlighting the fact that the introductions were written from a great variety of critical and theoretical perspectives, and that some commentaries focused on different aspects of vocabulary.

Why then was the 1986 Oxford Shakespeare shocking, and the 2007 Oxford Middleton celebrated? Simply because potential users of the Oxford Middleton had no strong expectations about what a Middleton edition should look like. Until 2007, there had never been a one-volume "collected works" of Middleton. The last collected edition had been published 120 years earlier, and anyone interested in Middleton knew how unsatisfactory it was. Moreover, the design innovations of the 2007 edition directly and obviously reinforced its declared purpose: to emphasize Middleton's artistic originality, and to introduce him in his totality to new readers, who had very little sense of the scale or range of his achievement. A new scholarly edition of an as-yet non-canonical author has much more freedom to experiment with new designs. (That freedom includes the freedom simply to duplicate the design of traditional scholarly editions, and therefore claim the authority of a standard model.)

By contrast, new editions of Shakespeare, or other already-canonical authors, have to be designed to appeal to a different kind of customer: one who already has a strong allegiance to traditional values, a strong sense of the author's importance, and strong convictions about what makes him important. Such readers have already seen editions of Shakespeare, and consequently they think they already know what an edition of Shakespeare *should look like*. That is obviously a problem for postmodern editorial designers, who are intellectually dissatisfied with those old designs, or simply bored by them. But it was also a problem for Edward Blount. Before 1623, Shakespeare had been a successful commodity in the book trade, but that success had taken the form of individual quartos. Blount's vision of an elite, complete, expensive, double-column, Folio Shakespeare-interface eventually triumphed: all three (or four) subsequent seventeenth-century editions reproduced that format, and established Shakespeare as England's dominant dramatist. But, in 1623, no one had ever seen anything like it. And, in 1623, not many book-buyers liked it. Blount as a result was almost driven in bankruptcy. It took years for his business to recover.

Pity the pioneer.

What most disturbed Shakespeare-consumers about the first Oxford Shakespeare, and what still disturbs them about the New Oxford Shakespeare, is that those postmodern interfaces are designed to challenge Blount's design. Both resist the monologic appeal of traditional interfaces, which contain visually uniform single texts of the works of a unified single author, who never changed his mind and never collaborated. This kind of container appeals to what is perhaps our most basic definitions of form: "Totality. Unity. Containment. Wholeness." Caroline Levine argues: "For many critics, these words are synonymous with form itself." That 1623 monologic design, that material embodiment of unity and wholeness, was further entrenched by two evolving editorial conventions. Beginning in 1709 (Rowe), an expanding abundance of editorial stage directions, embedded in the text, gave readers instructions on how the plays should be staged. Beginning in 1899 (Dowden), professorial introductions, prefacing each work, gave readers instructions on how to interpret each text. When the professorial interpreter was also the editor, a single professorial monologue became the dominant feature of the interface.

The most radical design features of the *New Oxford Shakespeare* interface challenged both these conventions. To begin with (literally), the professorial monologue was replaced in the *Modern Critical Edition* by a montage-introduction. The montage consisted of a deliberately non-chronological bricolage of many varied quotations and images, underlain with time-lines (of various kinds) and concluding with a tiny toolbox of historical information. The double-column montage juxtaposed, vertically and horizontally, competing interpretations and competing genres of authority: scholars, critics, poets, novelists, playwrights, actors, politicians, directors, artists, photographers, cinematographers, and designers. This opening dialogue between interpreters was then followed, in the text itself, by a dialogue about performance options. Uncontroversial editorial supplements to the original stage directions—adding a required name in a group entrance, for example, or a direction for words to be sung, or spoken "to" someone in particular—were added, and square-bracketed, within the body of the text column. The bracketing called attention to the editorial intervention. These marked interventions were distinguished from performance options discussed in the margin: noting, for instance, that Desdemona's "unpin me here" might refer to her hair, or some article of clothing, or a necklace (*Othello* 4.3.19), or that some editors mark Cleopatra's "Excellent falsehood!" as "an aside, but some performers make it part of Cleopatra's open mockery of Antony (sometimes with a pause after 'Excellent')" (*Antony and Cleopatra* 1.42). As Laurie Maguire notes, the "visual relationship" of such side-notes (in contrast to footnotes or endnotes) foregrounds a "dialogue" between them: the marginal note "is itself on the edge of the text, negotiating the boundary between author and reader, between text and response" (208–9).

The *Critical Reference Edition* also combined square-bracketed emendations to the text with marginal notes. Press-variants in the copy-text were recorded in the margin of the edited text, representing visually the dialogue between different exemplars of the initial print-run. The design of the old-spelling edition thus distinguished variations in the original printing from later emendations. Unlike press-variants, emendations to the stage directions of the original document were square-bracketed in the text, then recorded and discussed in the footnotes of the *Critical Reference Edition*, which treated them as no different from emendations of the to-be-spoken text: in each case, an emendation needed to be justified by evidence of compositorial or scribal error.

Both the *Critical Reference Edition* and the *Modern Critical Edition* were designed to force readers to engage with Shakespeare's texts dialogically. But the relationship between those different components of the New Oxford Shakespeare was also dialogic. Theoretically, that could be said of the earlier Oxford Shakespeare as well, which also published both a modern-spelling (1986) and an old-spelling (1987) edition. But the line-numbering of those earlier printed editions made it extremely difficult to compare them. By contrast, the New Oxford Shakespeare uses the same line-numbering system for both, and each volume cross-references the other. Even more importantly, both the *Critical Reference Edition* and the *Modern Critical Edition* were designed to cohabit in *Oxford Scholarly Editions Online*. In the digital environment, you can open the old-spelling edition (and its paratext) side-by-side with the modern-spelling edition (and its paratext). The online interface thus allows each edition to become part of the paratext of the other. It also allows readers to juxtapose the editorial text with digital visual images of the relevant page (or opening) of the early modern copy-text. Every play and poem has its own digital identifier (DOI), and every line its own URL.

Like the most successful innovations in the 1986 edition, these design innovations in the New Oxford Shakespeare interface did not originate with me. The montage introductions and side-by-side performance notes were suggested and developed by my fellow general editor Terri Bourus (the most prize-winning teacher on the team, and also the one who, as a theatermaker, has the best grasp of visual design). Another general editor, John Jowett, contributed more than anyone else to the design of the *Critical Reference Edition*. The latest addition to the general editorial team, Gabriel Egan, has been instrumental to the evolution of the Online Edition, including aspect-ratio options that make it possible for students to read it on their smart phones, and hyperlinks that will allow readers of the forthcoming *Complete Alternative Versions* to move easily to any passage in the digital *Complete Works* cross-referenced in a note, letting readers easily access the dialogue between different Shakespeare texts. The emphasis on dialogue, in the New Oxford Shakespeare interface design, itself reflects the dialogue between members of the editorial team.

It might seem obvious that anyone interested in the works of a great playwright should also be interested in dialogue. But dialogue always includes conflict. The New Oxford Shakespeare bricolages include some negative assessments of individual works (and, in the general introduction, some negative assessments of Shakespeare). Such reactions are part of the historical record, and Shakespeare has survived them; indeed, they have often stimulated new interpretations and defenses of his work. In my experience, they always generate lively classroom debates. But they were inevitably magnified by the "rival salesmen" described by Loewy, who "say to the prospective customer, 'I wouldn't buy that stuff, it is too extreme. You won't like it'" (327).

In particular, the innovations of the 1986 and 2016 Oxford editions offend users whose drug of choice is a single author. (Revision is also a form of collaboration, in which a living author in the present collaborates with a no-longer-living other self.) To attribute some portion of a play to another playwright is perceived, by such consumers, as "taking something away" from Shakespeare. It is also, perhaps more profoundly, perceived as a kind of disloyalty to Shakespeare. Someone who is not loyal to Shakespeare should not be editing his work. Of course, one might just as easily argue that someone truly loyal to Shakespeare would not attribute to him work (by a "lesser artist") that he did not do. Likewise, loyalty to the historical Shakespeare should be distinguished from loyalty to a posthumous editorial tradition. But the emotional appeal of loyalty, in such cases, has more to do with familiarity than logic. Josiah Royce, author of the most sustained articulation of a philosophy of loyalty, recognized that loyalty joins "many persons into the unity of a single life," and hence is "at once personal and … superpersonal." A shared loyalty to Shakespeare creates a community of Shakespearians just as a shared loyalty to the Bible creates a community of Christians. Both communities are "people of the book"—notably, as the definite article assumes, a single book, imagined as the work of a single divine intelligence. If, as Heidegger claimed, "To think is to bind together" (367), then the binding together of many works into a single designed material container-interface also has the potential to bind together an otherwise diverse collection of individuals into a community of loyal user-readers. Too great a change to that designed object of veneration therefore threatens the cohesion of that community, which means that it is likely to be labeled, by at least some of the faithful, as an act of heresy or treason.

But Royce also recognized that loyalty could be a virtue only if it coexisted with what he called "a loyalty to loyalty." Consequently, "in so far as my cause is a predatory cause, which lives by overthrowing the loyalties of others, it is an evil cause, because it involves disloyalty to the very cause of loyalty itself." A moral loyalty to Shakespeare thus also entails a willingness to recognize the legitimacy of someone else's loyalty to his collaborators: to Thomas Middleton, Christopher Marlowe, John Fletcher, Thomas Nashe, George Peele, George Wilkins—and perhaps to Thomas Heywood and Thomas Watson too. Any container designed to give us the "whole works" of Shakespeare must also contain fragments that overlap with the "whole works" of other writers. In this way, as Royce promised, "Without giving up old loyalties I shall annex new ones. There will be evolution in my loyalty."

Such evolutions are a necessary corollary of the fact that the designed editorial container, the designated boundary of the editorial interface, requires a double loyalty in its designers: a loyalty to the past and a loyalty to the present. This double loyalty forces us to "reconceptualize editorial theory as a specialized subset of translation theory" (Taylor *In Media Res* 98). As the temporal, geographical, and cultural gap between one side of the interface and the other increases, the strain created by those competing loyalties intensifies. Which matters to us more: the current community of Shakespearians, or the community that Shakespeare himself inhabited? Is it possible to design an interface that will satisfy both?

References

Berry, Herbert. "The Phoenix." *English Professional Theatre, 1530–1660*, edited by Glynne Wickham, Herbert Berry, and William Ingram, Cambridge UP, 2000, pp. 623–637.

Borsuk, Amaranth. *The Book*. MIT Press, 2018.

Bourne, Claire M.L. *Typographies of Performance in Early Modern England*. Oxford UP, 2020.

Committee on Scholarly Editions. "Guidelines for Editors of Scholarly Editions." Modern Language Association, 2011.

Deutermann, Allison K. *Listening for Theatrical Form in Early Modern England*. Edinburgh UP, 2016.

Dowden, Edward, editor. *The Tragedy of Hamlet*. London, 1899.

Drucker, Johanna. *Graphesis: Visual Forms of Knowledge Production*. Harvard UP, 2014.

Farmer, Alan B., and Zachary Lesser. "The Popularity of Playbooks Revisited." *Shakespeare Quarterly*, vol. 56, no. 1, 2005, pp. 1–32.

Greg, W.W. *Dramatic Documents from the Elizabethan Playhouses*. 2 vols, Clarendon Press, 1931.

Heidegger, Martin. *Being and Time*. Translated by John Macquarrie and Edward Robinson, Harper, 1962.

Hookway, Branden. *Interface*. MIT Press, 2014.

Howard-Hill, T. H. "The Evolution of the Form of Plays in English During the Renaissance." *Renaissance Quarterly*, vol. 43, no. 1, 1990, pp. 112–145.

Keats, John. *The Letters of John Keats: 1814–1821*. 2 vols., edited by Hyder Edward Rollins, Harvard UP, 1958.

Levine, Caroline. *Forms: Whole, Rhythm, Hierarchy, Network*. Princeton UP, 2015.

Loewy, Raymond. *Never Leave Well Enough Alone*. Simon & Schuster, 1951.

Maguire, Laurie. *The Rhetoric of the Page*. Oxford UP, 2020.

Mak, Bonnie. *How the Page Matters*. U of Toronto P, 2011.

Middleton, Thomas. *The Collected Works*. Edited by Gary Taylor and John Lavagnino, Oxford UP, 2007.

Milton, John. "L'Allegro." *Poems*. Humphrey Moseley, 1645.

Rowe, Nicholas, editor. *The Works of Mr. William Shakespear*. 6 vols. London, 1709.

Royce, Josiah. *The Philosophy of Loyalty*. Macmillan, 1908.

Shakespeare, William. *New Oxford Shakespeare*. Edited by Gary Taylor, *et al.*, Oxford Scholarly Editions Online, Oxford UP, 2017. Available at: https://www.oxfordscholarlyeditions.com/nos.

Smith, Bruce R. *The Acoustic World of Early Modern England: Attending to the O-Factor*. U of Chicago P, 1999.

Stern, Tiffany. *Documents of Performance in Early Modern England*. Cambridge UP, 2009.

Taylor, Gary. "In Media Res: From Jerome through Greg to Jerome (McGann)." *Textual Cultures*, vol. 4, no. 2, 2009, pp. 88–101.

Taylor, Gary. "Artiginality: Authorship after Postmodernism." *The New Oxford Shakespeare: Authorship Companion*, edited by Gary Taylor and Gabriel Egan, Oxford UP, 2017a, pp. 3–26.

Taylor, Gary. "Comedies, History, & Tragedies (and Tragicomedies and Poems): Posthumous Shakespeare, 1625–1728." *The New Oxford Shakespeare: Complete Works: Critical Reference Edition*, 2 vols, Oxford UP, 2017b, vol. 2, pp. xvii–lxix.

Taylor, Gary, with Celia R. Daileader and Alexandra G. Bennett. "The Order of Persons." *Thomas Middleton and Early Modern Textual Culture*, edited by Gary Taylor and John Lavagnino, Oxford UP, 2007, pp. 31–79.

Taylor, Gary and Lavagnino, John. editors. *Thomas Middleton and Early Modern Textual Culture*. Oxford UP, 2007.

Tillyard, E.M.W. *Shakespeare's History Plays*. Chatto and Windus, 1944.

Wells, Stanley. *Modernizing Shakespeare's Spelling / Stanley Wells; with Three Studies in the Text of Henry V / Gary Taylor*. Clarendon Press, 1979.

Wells, Stanley. *Re-Editing Shakespeare for the Modern Reader*. Oxford UP, 1984.

Wells, Stanley. "On Being a General Editor." *Shakespeare on Stage and Page: Selected Essays*, edited by Paul Edmondson, Oxford UP, 2016, pp. 367–380.

Wells, Stanley, and Gary Taylor, editors. *William Shakespeare: The Complete Works*. Oxford UP, 1986.

8

ABSTRACTION AS SHAKESPEAREAN INTERFACE

Jonathan P. Lamb and Suzanne Tanner

In Act 2 of *Hamlet*, Shakespeare suggests that actors are like interfaces—or perhaps that they *are* interfaces. Hamlet exhorts Polonius to treat the players visiting Elsinore well because "they are the abstract and brief chronicles of the time; after your death you were better have a bad epitaph than their ill report while you live" (*The Norton Shakespeare*, 2.2.446–448). Whatever "the time" may refer to, Hamlet indicates that the players give us special access to it, just as the mediation of Polonius by the players' "ill report" would embarrass him more effectively than stone or paper inscribed with a "bad epitaph." Players, like icons on a computer desktop or the interactive virtual environment of an internet browser, give us access to, say, Aeneas's tale to Dido, itself a report of the events of the Trojan War. Although of course Hamlet does not use the term, actors in his description function as *interfaces*, which Johanna Drucker defines as a "constitutive boundary space" between systems (Drucker, "Reading Interface" 216). In Hamlet's admittedly simplified formulation, players make up a constitutive boundary space between their audiences and "the time" they chronicle.

Interfaces frequently work by way of abstraction, and Hamlet's players are no exception. Interfaces "isolat[e] properties or characteristics common to a number of diverse objects, events, etc., without reference to the peculiar properties of particular examples or instances" (Oxford English Dictionary Online "abstraction, n. 3a"). The icon we click to activate an application does not represent the actual structure of a memory drive; what we click is an abstraction of the computing action taking place, even when the icon somehow mimics that action (when, say, a folder icon appears to open). A second, more general, kind of abstraction typical of interfaces is "the action of taking something away; the action or process of withdrawing or removing something from a larger quantity or whole" (Oxford English Dictionary Online "abstraction, n. 2a"). Interface removes something from one system and makes it available to the other, often the only access users ever have of that other system. A search interface, for instance, gathers partial information from a large dataset and renders it, graphically, in a way it does not actually exist in the dataset. The point here is not that interfaces *are* abstractions, but that they work by them. Interfaces abstract the system they mediate on behalf of the users they address, often with the goal of making complex systems accessible.[1]

Likewise, Hamlet suggests that the players make an account of ("chronicle") but do not comprehensively represent "the time." They also give audiences constitutive access to the play they present. Some editors have glossed Hamlet's "abstract" as "summary," so that

 DOI: 10.4324/9780367821722-11

Hamlet is saying the players offer *summarized* and brief versions of complex and detailed events. Others, noting that the First Folio text reads "abstracts," have glossed the Second Quarto's "abstract" as a noun, so that Hamlet is saying the players present *generalizations* or *idealizations* of concrete events. Either reading clarifies Hamlet's point that actors work as a "mediating scrim," another term Drucker uses to define interface ("Reading Interface" 216). To the audience, the actors *are* the play—practically, though not in reality.

Taking a cue from Hamlet, in this chapter we explore how Shakespeare's plays are necessarily accessed through a variety of interfaces, including not only actors on stage but a whole range of "abstracts."[2] Let us expand the analogy to the interface of the personal computer: on one side is the "system" of the physical computer drive and the data stored on it, working in concert with other hardware components, such as the processor. On the other side is the "system" of the human user with expectations, needs, faculties, limitations, and a body. Various interfaces mediate the two systems to each other: the physical media of the screen and keyboard, the deep medium of the operating system, the surface medium of the graphical user interface (or GUI), the highly interactive internet browser, and so on. These layers facilitate communication and access along a continuum between the human system on one end and the computer system on the other. Importantly, these overlapping interfaces constitute the computer system for the user by way of abstraction. The user does not spare a thought for the file system until something goes wrong with the interfaces' ability to abstract computational processes. To the user, the interfaces *are* the computer—practically, though not in reality.

We want to suggest that, like this computer system, users know the system of Shakespeare's plays in and through interfaces working by way of abstraction. These users' primary point of access to the "Shakespeare system," as we will call it in this chapter by analogy with the file system of a memory drive, is the interface of language. Although the Shakespeare-computer analogy breaks down at some point, we might regard language as a kind of operating system, the deepest layer of interface. But Shakespeare has more interfaces than language alone, as a generation of bibliographically minded scholars has taught us.[3] Accessing Shakespeare has long meant interacting with frames—icons, we might say—that make possible our comprehension of the plays and poems. A moment's thought calls to mind such frames, built on or around Shakespeare's language, that promise access to his writings: prefaces, playbills, introductions, footnotes, summaries, diagrams, cartoons, illustrations, videos, adaptations, and many more. In this chapter, we argue that these frames make up a diverse set of interfaces which constitute the Shakespeare system for users by abstracting it. Rather than attempting to define the "true," "authentic," or "real" Shakespeare on the other side of the interface (as many scholars still aim to do), or declaring the impossibility of such an attempt (as others seek to do), here we discuss how the great variety of interfaces, working by way of abstraction, creates different kinds of access to Shakespeare and, in doing so, makes different Shakespeares for users.

As in computer interface design, user experience governs the creation of Shakespeare interfaces. A scholarly edition, for instance, facilitates the study of "advanced" users, much like some computer users often prefer the speed of keyboard shortcuts and the command-line interface over slower point-and-click interaction. By contrast, a desire to avoid Shakespeare's language has given rise to SparkNotes's much-maligned "No Fear Shakespeare" paraphrases, which promise a less challenging experience. In this chapter, therefore, we take user experience as a prompt for interpreting Shakespearean interfaces: organizing our inquiry around different types of users, we examine a cross-section of paratexts, summaries, formats, and other interfaces to expose what kinds of user experience they produce, and how they abstract Shakespeare on behalf of that experience.

The Student User

Consider what a student in a high school or university course needs to "get out" of Shakespeare. Initially, students need to know and remember the names of major characters, to understand the major points of the plot, and usually to be able to identify major themes or points of critical interest so that they might write a coherent paper and achieve a passable grade. Ideally, students are expected to achieve these ends by reading the actual text of the plays, but the scrim of archaic language, cultural and social references four hundred years out of context, and plots and characters that confound even highly trained Shakespeare scholars hamper access to the system of Shakespeare (Blank). Asking students to grasp everything about a Shakespeare play on first reading is like asking them to open a computer drive to point out exactly where a file is stored. Just as the computer search interface (such as the Mac Spotlight feature) makes it possible for users to find and use those stored computer files without having to know much (or anything) about the drive system, so too have various types of interfaces been developed to help the student user access the Shakespeare system—that is, to get what they need from Shakespeare, but also to learn what they need. Each of these interfaces is composed of various levels of abstraction.

One common abstraction, under the second definition of "removing something from the larger quantity or whole" is the gloss or footnote. A footnote takes a word or phrase out of the play and explains it. Moreover, footnotes are visual abstractions on the page, paratexts that "decorate" the margins, but also abstractions in the reading experience, causing (inviting, forcing) readers to pause in the flow of their reading to step out of the play and digest a piece of information that is separate, not part of the "larger ... whole." These linguistic abstractions function as an interface by mediating between the original language of Shakespeare and modern readers. Considering that a primary goal of interface is "access," what exactly is being accessed through this interface of footnotes? What part of the "system" of Shakespeare? Generally, the assumption is that footnotes attempt to provide a more user-friendly access to the content of Shakespeare by offering translations of archaic word usages, contextual historical information, stage direction clarification, and even plot clarification. However, the complicated history of editorial theory has taught us that what footnotes actually provide is far less straightforward. Paul Eggert argues that footnotes, or more accurately, all editorial interventions, make and materialize an argument about the work's textual transmission over time (109). Thus, in an attempt to provide more user-friendly access to the content of Shakespeare, editors generally end up providing access to the history of editorial debate and textual transmission of a Shakespeare play. M. J. Kidnie also argues that editorial intervention, particularly where stage directions are concerned, provide access mostly to an individual editor's favorite staging or mental visualization of a play, rather than leaving the text open or ambiguous as original quartos or Folios seem to be (473). While the main goal of footnotes may be providing clarification, or a more "complete" understanding of the entity of Shakespeare, often these abstractions end up supplying as many boundaries as they may remove (Hoffman).

Readers of Shakespeare interact with footnote interfaces, and this interaction constitutes Shakespeare for users while also constituting Shakespeare users. For instance, readers of *The Merchant of Venice* may puzzle over what Portia says after the vain and self-conscious Prince of Morocco chooses the wrong casket: "A gentle riddance. Draw the curtains, go. / Let all of his complexion choose me so" (Shakespeare 2.7.78–79). A modern reader may well ask: doesn't "complexion" mean skin color? Is Portia's line racist? Does that make Shakespeare racist? And does it make me racist for reading Shakespeare? Some editions such as the Norton 3 omit a footnote altogether, while other editors provide glosses with which readers interact.

The sixth edition of David Bevington's *Complete Works of Shakespeare* glosses "complexion" as "temperament (not merely skin color)" (2.7.78–79n). This is abstraction at its most basic. The gloss offers readers the philological reassurance of the broader semantic range of "complexion" while parenthetically accepting that this range includes skin color (Desai). Portia may be racist, the implication goes, but she's not *that* racist. Our point here is not to enter the debate about *Merchant*'s vexed history but to emphasize that the footnote shapes access to Shakespeare, even as it fashions a Shakespeare user, now comforted by the abstraction of the footnote. Glosses function less as a doorway or threshold through which students walk to Shakespeare's language and more as a boundary space that actually constitutes that language, for better and worse (Genette; Drucker, "Reading Interface").

Footnotes and glosses entail a user experience in helping students grasp Shakespeare's language at the local level. Other types of student aids, such as Cliff's Notes, SparkNotes, Wikipedia entries, and other plot summaries and character lists, function as more general and, indeed, abstract interfaces by which users access Shakespeare. These summaries, perhaps more familiar to undergraduate students than to their instructors, present themselves as user-friendly interfaces that allow easy access to Shakespeare. Consider, for instance, the first paragraph of SparkNotes' "Plot Overview" of *Othello*:

> *Othello* begins on a street in Venice, in the midst of an argument between Roderigo, a rich man, and Iago. Roderigo has been paying Iago to help him in his suit to Desdemona. But Roderigo has just learned that Desdemona has married Othello, a general whom Iago begrudgingly serves as ensign. Iago says he hates Othello, who recently passed him over for the position of lieutenant in favor of the inexperienced soldier Michael Cassio.

This counts as abstraction in the sense already established—"summary" is a synonym for "abstract"—but it also fits the less common definition of abstract as a "thing regarded as … representing the essence of … the characteristic qualities or features of something much larger (Oxford English Dictionary Online "abstract, adj. B.3.a"). The descriptive language here may be correct—"begrudgingly … hates … inexperienced"—but it is also retrospective: Iago's begrudging service and his hatred for Othello, as well as Cassio's inexperience, emerge in the course of the play, but here they are conferred as pre-existing conceptual categories. In many cases, the materials not only abstract the plot in summary (as above) but highlight and briefly discuss specific themes, point out and define symbols, and provide relevant critical, social, and historical information. These abstractions, representing the "essence" of the whole play in easily consumed and palatable formats, offer student readers exactly what the designers think their users need without any of the extra work of decoding archaic language or slogging through clown scenes irrelevant to the student's need to pass a quiz or write a paper.

Instructors and advanced readers have long deplored these aids as poor substitutes for the "real thing," presumably based on the conviction that students *really* need to understand the full system of Shakespeare. Such justified dismissiveness, however, ignores the way these summaries function as interfaces by which readers come to understand the plays and poems.[4] To return to the computer metaphor, it seems almost as unreasonable to ask students to jump into an advanced reading of Shakespeare as it does to ask beginner computer users to locate the physical location of their documents in the file system.[5] If, however, we view these summaries and paratextual aids as interfaces, we can value them as sites of initial contact, in which both users and Shakespeare get acquainted. Here is SparkNotes' description of *Othello*, 4.1:

> Through Iago's machinations, Othello becomes so consumed by jealousy that he falls into a trance and has a fit of epilepsy. As he writhes on the ground, Cassio comes by, and Iago tells him to come back in a few minutes to talk. Once Othello recovers, Iago tells him of the meeting he has planned with Cassio. He instructs Othello to hide nearby and watch as Iago extracts from Cassio the story of his affair with Desdemona.

Let us assume, optimistically, that students do not take this abstraction as gospel truth but turn to the scene instead. There, they find that this roughly accurate abstraction obscures the most exciting and powerful features of the scene: Iago's arresting insinuation that Cassio has lain "with her, on her; what you will," and Othello's sudden break out of verse and into prose to mark the "trance" into which he falls. But if our reader second-guesses the summary, noting that the play text never says Othello "writhes on the ground" and that it is Iago who calls the trance "epilepsy," they have been positioned to do so *by way of* that very same summary. Used as an interface rather than a mere substitute, this abstraction can help students become more critical and attentive.

Diagrams often accompany written summaries, and they too constitute the plays for readers in a non-neutral manner. Unlike a text summary, which can adapt and reconfigure the language and narrative movement of a play, character diagrams typically present a static set of relations. In doing so, they abstract not just events but the temporalities in which those events occur. The Cliff's Notes character map of *The Tempest* offers a taste of how these dual abstractions function (see Figure 8.1). The graph literally centers Prospero, emphasizing (for better or worse) that he functions as the play's master signifier. Characters' relationships with others, even when labeled, remain secondary to relationships with Prospero. Moreover, the diagram labels relationships with simple terms: Sebastian "covets" Alonso; Ariel "helps" Prospero; Caliban "hates" him. These terms abstract the action of the play into a temporally unspecified state. While Miranda and Ferdinand's double arrow, labeled "loves," refers to their mutual state at the end of the play, Antonio's arrow to Prospero, labeled "hates and envies," refers to his state at the beginning of the play. Likewise, Stefano and Trinculo "seek to injure" Prospero, but from the perspective of the end of the play, they *fail* to injure him. We might rightly critique these abstractions as misrepresentations. For instance, to say that Ariel merely "helps" Prospero overlooks the dynamic of extortion, coercion, and deferred compensation that plays out over five acts. When we view these diagrams not merely (or even primarily) as representations but as interfaces by which users access abstractions of Shakespeare's play, then we see more clearly how they operate on those users.

Digital media facilitate many more types of student interfaces, whose abstractions add layers of cultural and technological scrim. One popular series is the "Thug Notes" YouTube series. Clearly adapting the titles of Cliff's Notes and SparkNotes, the channel's videos feature a short summary of plot followed by general analysis highlighting key themes and questions. In addition to the difference in medium, what makes Thug Notes particularly distinct from the traditional student aids discussed above is its use of African American Vernacular English (AAVE) to remediate Shakespeare summary and analysis into terms and concepts that sound, or are, far more modern and unexpected. For instance, the Thug Notes summary of Shakespeare's *Hamlet* begins, "Da shit's gone whack up in the kingdom of Elsinore. The old King's brother Claudius gone and married the king's old breezie Gertrude, and Queen Gertrude's son Hamlet getting all crunk since his mama actin like a ho" ("Hamlet (Shakespeare) – Thug Notes Summary and Analysis"). Unlike the more traditional student aids, these remediated forms of abstraction seem to be far more popular with educators (Wood).

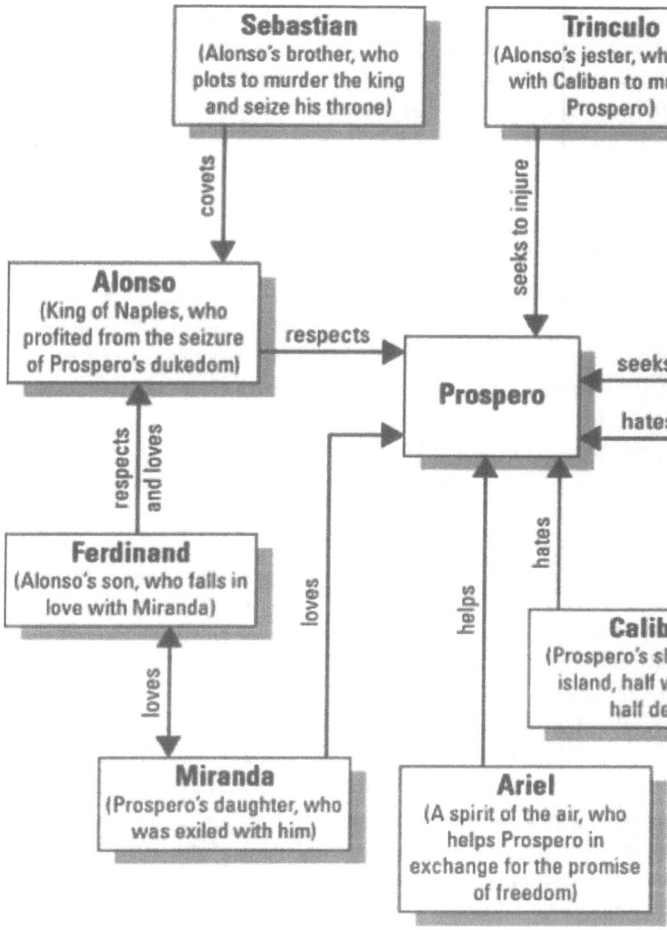

Figure 8.1 Cliff's Notes' diagram of *The Tempest*
Source: https://www.cliffsnotes.com/literature/t/the-tempest/character-map.

"Thug Notes" offers a complex form of interface abstraction to create its distinct, effective user experience. It's hard to deny that "Thug Notes" is effective: high school teachers and college professors alike bring the videos into the classroom not just as a way to gain student attention but because the videos serve as an effective interface, producing access to the Shakespeare system in a language and visual medium that, at least anecdotally, communicates effectively.[6] The abstraction at work is the familiar one of plot summary and analysis, by which students grasp basic information about Shakespeare's plays in a user-friendly form of access. But this interface does far more than just simplify access; it also adds layers of sociocultural interpretative possibilities that enrich one's experience. This abstraction relies on the willful disjunction of Shakespeare's perceived cultural whiteness and elitism with the familiar and often politically charged use of AAVE. Gertrude both is and is not Claudius's "old breezie," and that dual consciousness is the point of the term. Moreover, the abstraction may be so thorough that readers need an additional interface to understand this interface. We double-checked the terms "breezie" (good-looking girls) and "crunk" (crazy and drunk, though this is debated) ("Urban Dictionary"). The description constitutes Gertrude's character by way of a label that makes its abstraction legible to students. Rather than disappearing the questions of racial politics surrounding Shakespeare's plays, "Thug Notes" videos encode those questions directly into the interface. They create points of contact that both simplify (certain) user access and also complicate and enrich the user experience with a call for a more critical focus.

The Casual Consumer

What about Shakespeare readers and viewers with no pedagogical motivations? Such users have neither assignments, quizzes, and grades, nor would scholarly debates necessarily excite them. In fact, this group might be the most varied with the most wide-ranging and hard-to-pin-down access needs. A casual consumer may simply want to enjoy a performance of a Shakespeare play, occasionally collect Shakespeare editions, or may just be looking for a pithy quote to make a point or impress their colleagues. An internet user, bookstore browser, or playgoer interested in Shakespeare's plays and poems has requirements that are different from those of students or scholars, and interfaces have been created to meet and shape those needs.

Consider, by way of transition, the popular Folger Shakespeare texts, available online (folger.shakespeare.edu). This digital edition provides a helpful distinction between student and casual users and the interfaces that both respond to and make possible those experiences. Unlike the codex Folger Shakespeare Library Editions, from which the digital texts have been taken (one might say abstracted), the digital texts necessarily cast a broad scope for readers ("The Folger Shakespeare"). Due to copyright constraints, by which editorial labor such as footnotes belongs to the publisher of the printed texts, the digital editions lack the features more familiar to student users than to general ones. Rather than a digital version imitating the paper codex, the site offers a digital version of unannotated text, now memory-resident on computer or tablet. As often happens, intellectual property rights have determined user experience. In this case, the Folger made a virtue of necessity, recasting the website to appeal to consumer-readers across the world, promising that "there are other great things to find in our online plays! Keep your eye out for pictures, recordings, and videos from the Folger's vast holdings" ("The Folger Shakespeare"). The site features an "FAQ" site, which abstracts the granular work of scholars into very short essay answers. For instance, to the question "What were the different ticket costs to go to a play in Shakespeare's time?" the answer runs to just six short sentences, noting that the Globe's price of one penny "went up to about sixpence" in the seventeenth century ("Frequently Asked Questions, What Were the Different Ticket Costs to Go to a Play in Shakespeare's Time?"). These features do some of the abstract work of footnotes, allowing more user-friendly access to the casual consumer, just in a different form that may not meet the needs of other users, such as students.

In the theater, a diverse range of experiences function as interfaces working by way of abstraction. A visitor to the 2010 Globe performance of *Macbeth*, for instance, encountered signs reading, "PLEASE NOTE THAT THIS IS A GRUESOME PRODUCTION OF A BRUTAL PLAY" (see Figure 8.2). This sign does little to summarize, analyze, or interpret *Macbeth*, but it does abstract certain features of both the play text and the production to promise—and, indeed, to guarantee—a particular kind of user experience. In this case, the warning was warranted, even though abstract: the production was, in fact, gruesome, and the play therefore recognizable as brutal. These abstractions provide cover for the violence of the production, working as a boundary between theatergoer and production. By way of this sign, ticketholders become *spectators* and the play becomes knowable as "brutal." Signs like this may seem completely unlike the icons and links we click on a computer interface, but they function in strikingly similar ways.

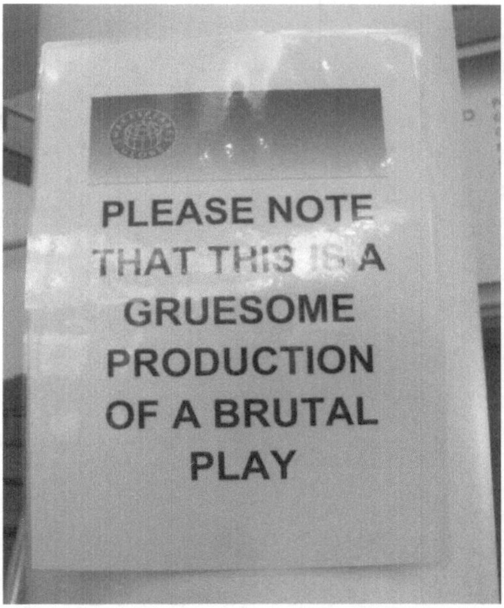

Figure 8.2 A sign posted at the front door of the Globe Playhouse in London, warning potential spectators about the 2010 production of *Macbeth*
Source: Photo by Jonathan P. Lamb.

A more common abstraction in the theater is the playbill or program, a magazine provided or sold before a theatrical performance. Playbills work as an interface for the entire system of Shakespeare, but more specifically, they provide access (or interface) to the performance of a particular play. Playbills mediate the play before, during, and long after it has been performed by providing a set of abstract but essential details. These include the dates and locations of performances, scenes and entertainments to be expected, and most importantly, a dramatis personae accompanied by the list of actors playing each role. The first and early purpose of playbills was to mediate the play before it had been performed. Playbills originated in the eighteenth century as sometimes handwritten, sometimes printed advertisements for upcoming productions, and they included relevant information about the production, including a list of actors and the roles they would be playing. Gillian Russell argues that "playbills were a kind of contract with the public[,] and managers varied them at their peril" as audiences could get rowdy if they were not delivered the actors or scenes expected ("1796 Theatre Playbill – the Earliest Surviving Document Printed in Australia"). Often, a popular actor had a bigger draw than the play itself. Consider the case of an 1821 production of *Macbeth* at the Oswestry Theater (see Figure 8.3). The playbill for this production includes a brief summary of the plot in a stilted, almost bullet-point format:

> This excellent piece commences with the execution of the Thane of Cawdor; and the Treacherous Prognostics of the Weird Sisters. The Barbarous Murder of their good King Duncan. The Coronation of Macbeth, the Assassination of Banquo, and the Appearance of the Ghost at the Royal Banquet. Hecate's Cave. A Mystic Dance of Witches around the Burning Cauldron, into which the Evil Spirits throw their Charms and Magic Spells; and the Several Apparitions of Eight Kings!
>
> *("A Collection of Playbills from Miscellaneous Theatres")*

Figure 8.3 Playbill advertisement for an 1821 production of *Macbeth* at the Oswestry Theatre
Source: Courtesy of the British Library.

This list serves as an advertisement, assuring a potential audience already familiar with the play that their favorite scenes will be presented. The advertisement provides access to what the potential audience member needs to know about the performance and shapes that audience's experience by managing expectations.

If we look at a more contemporary playbill from the 2008 production of *Macbeth* starring Patrick Stewart, we see a new user function emerge ("Macbeth Broadway @ Lyceum Theatre – Tickets and Discounts | Playbill"). Much of the same information remains, including cast lists (see Figure 8.4). The draw is still the headlining actor: Patrick Stewart had better be the actor on stage or the audience may feel cheated of their ticket fees. But the function of the Playbill itself has changed from that of an advertisement (an unnecessary function when the playbill is handed out after the tickets have already been purchased; instead, it is full of ads for other products and productions), to a kind of login: a boundary or obligatory ritual that enfolds the playgoer into the theatrical experience and confers on it the status of entertainment and art. Moreover, the Playbill serves the user function of souvenir. Much of the real value of contemporary playbills lies in their ability to be saved once the performance is over, and to evoke the experience—the *user experience*—in memory. These ephemeral articles of print and paper often serve as the only record of Shakespeare's plays in performance and allow scholars of performance studies the briefest glimpse of access to the repertoire performance. Playbills mediate on behalf of a moment in time, providing access to a system that can otherwise no longer be accessed at all.

For the casual Shakespeare consumer interested in savoring the Bard outside of the playhouse, illustrated editions of Shakespeare's text serve as another popular form of abstracted interface by guiding visualization of the text and comprehension of the story. While many might assume that illustrations provide a user-friendly type of interface, a closer look reveals that, as abstractions, illustrations both ease and complicate the access they provide to the Shakespearean system. Illustrations function as abstractions in a variety of ways. First, in some cases, illustrations can summarize portions of a text. They mediate the "essence" of the language of the text, but they also remain separate, distinct from it. Illustrations function as both paratexts that interpret and comment on texts and as texts in their own right open to interpretation. This dual operation makes illustrations a key form of interface, as interfaces themselves also function as both paratext (object providing access to another text) and text (object worthy of study and consideration in its own right) (Drucker, *Graphesis*). In the same way,

Figure 8.4 Playbill cover for the 2008 production of *Macbeth* at the Lyceum Theatre
Source: Available at https://www.playbill.com/production/macbeth-lyceum-theatre-vault-0000007082.

for example, that the icons in a GUI may be said to illustrate aspects of the computing process at the same time as they produce the computing environment, illustrations work as icons, both mimicking and producing a particular, iconographic environment. Viewed as the work of an interface, illustrations arise out of a sense of user need (that is, readers find it both useful and interesting to see illustrations), but they also shape the user experience by guiding interpretation (here's how to think about the setting, the story, etc.).

Consider the example of John Bell's 1776 editions of Shakespeare, in which two illustrations accompany each play, one portraying a real, named actor in costume from a contemporary London production of the play and the other depicting the imagined story world space of a specific scene, captioned with a line from the play (Figure 8.5). Bell's dual images are unique in that most illustrated versions of Shakespeare will only include one or the other type of image (either a story world illustration or a depiction of a staged production). The inclusion of both these types of visual images represents the unique visualization process that a reader experiences. The text of a play invites two options for visualization. First, a reader has the option of imagining the play as they would a novel, with the characters inhabiting a fully-fledged, diegetic story world. Second, the reader may choose to imagine the play as a performed production on a stage.

The dual images represent both these possible visualizations and, as an interface, guide the reader in constructing both types of visualizations while they read. The eighteenth-century reader of Bell's *Antony and Cleopatra* may use the provided illustration of the actress Miss Younge, arrayed in a beautifully elaborate late eighteenth-century costume that would look at home in any ballroom of Europe, to imagine the play as produced on a London stage, with the actors and actresses in contemporary costumes. At the same time, using the first illustration as a guide, the reader may also choose to imagine Cleopatra in more historically accurate flowing robes, inhabiting a more historically accurate classical world of columned

Figure 8.5 Illustrations accompanying *Antony and Cleopatra* in John Bell's 1776 edition of the collected plays

Source Photograph by Suzanne Tanner. Courtesy of Kenneth Spencer Research Library, University of Kansas, Lawrence, KS.

buildings, acting and living in a fully-fledged classical story world. While these illustrations serve as interface guides aiding in visualization and comprehension, they also complicate that visualization process, illustrating (literally and figuratively) the multiple visualizations allowed and demanded by the activity of reading a play. Again, the illustrations both make possible and complicate access to the Shakespeare database.

Just as Bell's illustrations construct how readers experience the plays, Shakespeare podcasts produce a user experience that both is and is not pedagogical, permitting us to query the distinction between student and consumer users of Shakespeare. Many podcasts, drawing on scholarly expertise of one kind or another, appeal to broadly pedagogical aims by creating mediating scrims between users and plays. Oxford Professor Emma Smith's "Approaching Shakespeare" podcasts, for instance, comprise Smith's lectures on Shakespeare, recorded and remediated in serial podcast format (Smith). Despite the retention of pedagogical markers, this act of remediation changes the user experience by changing the users. In the podcast on *Much Ado About Nothing*, for instance, Smith begins with the question, "Why does everyone believe Don John?" when he claims that the lady Hero, Claudio's betrothed, has had sex with another man. The answer, she goes on to argue, is that the play is "structured by male relationships." The play substitutes male-male relationships for male-female relationships, and thus Don John's claims receive credit even though he had already tried and failed to foil the marriage once before. The reading is so persuasive and thorough that it becomes difficult to see the play in any other terms—the mark of an interface that has successfully abstracted one system on behalf of another. Someone who listens to the podcast and then reads *Much Ado* will inevitably interact with Smith's claims.

How far does this approach take us? Are all mechanisms of access to Shakespeare best understood as interfaces? We acknowledge there may be limitations, but our point here is to emphasize the fruitfulness of the category of interface for studying a diverse set of materials. Even prologues and prefaces attached to plays since their earliest circulation function as interfaces. While typically regarded as paratexts or thresholds, these liminal structures do not simply work as doorways the reader passes through (*limen* actually means doorway) but as sites of interaction. They work, to be precise, as interfaces by which audience and play become known to one another (Bruster and Weimann). The well-known Prologue to *Romeo and Juliet*, for example, starts the play by abstracting the features of the narrative and of the theatrical experience:

> Two households, both alike in dignity,
> In fair Verona, where we lay our scene,
> From ancient grudge break to new mutiny,
> Where civil blood makes civil hands unclean.
> From forth the fatal loins of these two foes,
> A pair of star-crossed lovers take their life,
> Whose misadventured piteous overthrows
> Doth with their death bury their parents' strife.
> The fearful passage of their death-marked love
> And the continuance of their parents' rage—
> Which, but their children's end, naught could remove—
> Is now the two hours' traffic of our stage;
> The which, if you with patient ears attend,
> What here shall miss, our toil shall strive to mend.
>
> *(Prol. 1–14)*

The Prologue tells us what happens, where it is supposed to happen, and what its consequences are in the imaginary world of the play. It also relays crucial theatrical information, also in abstractions: how long this will take (two hours), what is expected of the audience ("attend"), and what the actors promise ("to mend"). The Prologue, we might say, offers us not a doorway to step through but a vehicle to climb into. These lines become the sonnet-shaped mechanism by which we access the rest of the play's events. The same might be said of the Prologue to *Henry V*, which offers spectators and, in another sense, readers a tutorial on how to interface with the persons and events represented. Moreover, the witty preface epistle to the 1609 Quarto *Troilus and Cressida* offers a value-laden interface to readers:

> So much and such savored salt of wit is in his comedies that they seem, for their height of pleasure, to be born in that sea that brought forth Venus. Amongst all there is none more witty than this, and had I time I would comment upon it, though I know it needs not, for so much as will make you think your tester well bestowed, but for so much worth as even poor I know to be stuffed in it. It deserves such a labor as well as the best comedy in Terence or Plautus.
>
> *(Pref. 18–26)*

The author does not even pretend to be representing the play in what Hoffman calls a "veridical" way, and that is the key point: this preface is not *representing* the play at all but abstracting its features into a form of entertainment value, worthy of the effort one would put into Terence or Plautus. By abstracting rather than representing, these prologues mediate plays to the imagination, like the series of icons and sounds mediating your email to you.

The Shakespeare Scholar; or, Conclusion

We Shakespeare scholars may think ourselves immune to interface. Surely a group of highly self-critical, decorously educated, constantly peer-reviewed experts have immediate access to Shakespeare. We scoff at SparkNotes, deign to read Playbills, and only listen to podcasts for, ahem, pedagogical reasons. We need no mediation! But this obvious fiction calls attention to scholars' abiding dependence on interfaces, old and new. And ours is a professional dependence: Early English Books Online, JSTOR, Project Muse, and the World Shakespeare Bibliography mediate our access not just to the "Shakespeare system" but to the sprawling system of scholarly work on Shakespeare and early modern English drama. Interface wraps up and makes possible a whole professional ethos.

Consider one last example: the collation formula, staple of advanced scholarly knowledge, which we ought to regard as an interface to our benefit. For the scholar trained in bibliographical methods, such a formula may seem transparent:

πA^6(πA1+1 πA5+1.2) A-2B^6 2C^2 a-g^6 X2g^8 h-v^6 x^4 "gg3.4"(± "gg3") ¶-2$¶^6$ 3¶1 2a-2f^6 2g^2 "Gg^6" 2h^6 2k-3b^6

This is, of course, the collation formula for Shakespeare's 1623 First Folio, as encoded by the Folger Shakespeare Library ("The First Folio's Collation Statement"). (Didn't you know?) To the initiated, this formula represents the material configuration of a particular copy of the folio. Or rather, it does not represent but *abstracts* the assembly and printing process of a particular book copy. This is abstraction at its most refined, from one system of codes to another. As with all of the interface-abstractions we have discussed in this chapter, this scholarly interface offers access to Shakespeare by way of a particular experience of use. It shares with footnotes, Thug Notes, and SparkNotes the unavoidable and necessary capacity to mediate Shakespeare's plays to us, and us to Shakespeare.

Studying the many pathways of access to Shakespeare as a set of interfaces raises the stakes for how scholars, editors, teachers, and performers present Shakespeare's writings to different publics—that is, to users and groups of users. In particular, the concept of interface makes us aware that these are not merely liminal or threshold spaces through which users pass, but sites of constitutive interaction, in which Shakespeare and his users become knowable and distinct. Interface is inevitable: we cannot avoid approaching Shakespeare by way of interfaces and the abstractions on which they depend. Rather, the interfaces surveyed here suggest that an effective Shakespeare user experience adds and complicates the facets of mediation. These interfaces enrich by abstracting the system on the other side of the screen.

Notes

1 See Hoffman; Drucker, "Humanities"; Galloway; Drucker, "Reading Interface"; Drucker, *Graphesis*.
2 On surface in the context of textual scholarship, see the seminal essay by De Grazia and Stallybrass as well as Eggert's more recent work on editorial interface.
3 See, for instance, Smith and Wilson, and especially Werier.
4 This dismissiveness also wrongly assumes that there is any immediate access to Shakespeare. See Orgel.
5 Cf. the character Hanson in the film *Zoolander*: "The files are *in* the computer?"
6 See the many comments on Thug Notes, "We Are the Team behind Thug Notes, Yo' Main Hookup for Classic Literature Summary and Analysis."

References

"1796 Theatre Playbill – the Earliest Surviving Document Printed in Australia." *Radio National*, 25 June 2008. Available at: https://www.abc.net.au/radionational/programs/archived/bookshow/1796-theatre-playbill—the-earliest-surviving/3258552.

"A Collection of Playbills from Miscellaneous Theatres: Nottingham – Oswestry 1755–1848 Collection Item." The British Library. Available at: http://access.bl.uk/item/viewer/ark:/81055/vdc_100022589132.0x000002.

Blank, Paula. *Shakesplish: How We Read Shakespeare's Language*. Stanford UP, 2018.

Bruster, Douglas, and Robert Weimann. *Prologues to Shakespeare's Theatre: Performance and Liminality in Early Modern Drama*. Routledge, 2004.

De Grazia, Margreta, and Peter Stallybrass. "The Materiality of the Shakespearean Text." *Shakespeare Quarterly*, vol. 44, no. 3, 1993, pp. 255–283.

Desai, R. W. "'Mislike Me Not for My Complexion': Whose Mislike? Portia's? Shakespeare's? Or That of His Age?" *The Merchant of Venice: New Critical Essays*. Edited by John W. Mahon and Ellen Macleod Mahon, Routledge, 2002, pp. 305–323.

Drucker, Johanna. "Humanities Approaches to Graphical Display." *DHQ: Digital Humanities Quarterly*, vol. 5, no. 1, 2011. Available at: http://www.digitalhumanities.org/dhq/vol/5/1/000091/000091.html.

Drucker, Johanna. "Reading Interface." *PMLA*, vol. 128, no. 1, 2013, pp. 213–220.

Drucker, Johanna. *Graphesis: Visual Forms of Knowledge Production*. Harvard UP, 2014.

Eggert, Paul. "Apparatus, Text, Interface: How to Read a Printed Critical Edition." *The Cambridge Companion to Textual Scholarship*. Edited by Julia Flanders and Neil Fraistat, Cambridge UP, 2013, pp. 97–118.

"Frequently Asked Questions, What Were the Different Ticket Costs to Go to a Play in Shakespeare's Time?" The Folger SHAKESPEARE. Available at: https://shakespeare.folger.edu/frequently-asked-questions/what-were-the-different-ticket-costs-to-go-to-a-play-in-shakespeares-time/.

Galloway, Alexander R. *The Interface Effect*. Polity Press, 2012.

Genette, Gérard. *Paratexts: Thresholds of Interpretation*. Translated by Jane E. Lewin, Cambridge UP, 1997.

Goodman, Nelson. *Languages of Art: An Approach to a Theory of Symbols*. 2nd ed., Hackett, 1976.

Goodman, Nelson. *Fact, Fiction, and Forecast*. 4th ed., Harvard UP, 1983.

Greetham, D. C. *Textual Scholarship: An Introduction*. Garland, 1994.

"Hamlet (Shakespeare) – Thug Notes Summary and Analysis." YouTube, 2011. Available at: https://www.youtube.com/watch?v=A98tf9krihg&t=32s.

Hoffman, Donald D. "The Interface Theory of Perception: Natural Selection Drives True Perception to Swift Extinction." *Object Categorization*. Edited by Sven J. Dickinson*et al.*, Cambridge UP, 2009, pp. 148–166. doi:10.1017/CBO9780511635465.009.

Kidnie, Margaret Jane. "Text, Performance, and the Editors: Staging Shakespeare's Drama." *Shakespeare Quarterly*, vol. 51, no. 4, pp. 456–473.

Levine, Caroline. *Forms: Whole, Rhythm, Hierarchy, Network*. Princeton UP, 2015.

"Macbeth Broadway @ Lyceum Theatre – Tickets and Discounts | Playbill." Available at: https://www.playbill.com/production/macbeth-lyceum-theatre-vault-0000007082.

Mack, Peter. *A History of Renaissance Rhetoric, 1380–1620*. Oxford UP, 2011.

Mann, Jenny C. *Outlaw Rhetoric: Figuring Vernacular Eloquence in Shakespeare's England*. Cornell UP, 2012.

Orgel, Stephen. *The Authentic Shakespeare, and Other Problems of the Early Modern Stage*. Routledge, 2002.

"Othello: Plot Overview." SparkNotes. Available at: https://www.sparknotes.com/shakespeare/othello/summary/.

Oxford English Dictionary Online. "Abstract, adj. B.3.a.", June 2020. Available at: https://www-oed-com.www2.lib.ku.edu/view/Entry/766?redirectedFrom=abstract.

Oxford English Dictionary Online. "Abstraction, n. 2a.", June 2020. Available at: https://www-oed-com.www2.lib.ku.edu/view/Entry/766?redirectedFrom=abstraction.

Oxford English Dictionary Online. "Abstraction, n. 3a.", June 2020. Available at: https://www-oed-com.www2.lib.ku.edu/view/Entry/766?redirectedFrom=abstraction.

Shakespeare, William. *The Complete Works of Shakespeare*. 7th ed. Edited by David M. Bevington, Longman, 2013.

Shakespeare, William. *The Norton Shakespeare*. 3rd ed. Edited by Stephen Greenblatt, Norton, 2015.

Smith, Emma. "Approaching Shakespeare | University of Oxford Podcasts – Audio and Video Lectures." Available at: https://podcasts.ox.ac.uk/series/approaching-shakespeare.

Smith, Helen, and Louise Wilson, editors. *Renaissance Paratexts*. Cambridge UP, 2011.

"The First Folio's Collation Statement." Available at: https://www.folger.edu/sites/default/files/Collation_statement.pdf.

"The Folger Shakespeare." Available at: https://shakespeare.folger.edu/.

Thug Notes. "We Are the Team behind Thug Notes, Yo' Main Hookup for Classic Literature Summary and Analysis." Available at: https://www.reddit.com/r/IAmA/comments/1xnwdf/we_are_the_team_behind_thug_notes_yo_main_hookup/.

Urban Dictionary. "Breezie." Available at: https://www.urbandictionary.com/define.php?term=breezie.

Weimann, Robert. *Author's Pen and Actor's Voice: Playing and Writing in Shakespeare's Theatre*. Edited by Helen Higbee and William West, Cambridge UP, 2000.

Werier, Clifford. "Getting the Joke: Shakespeare, Time, and Interface." *Shakespeare*, vol. 15, no. 3, 2019, pp. 252–261.

Wood, Peter. "Celebrating 2013 in Education." *NAS*. Available at: https://www.nas.org/blogs/article/celebrating_2013_in_education.

PART III

Surfaces and depths

9

THE *HAMLET* FIRST QUARTO (1603) AND THE PLAY OF TYPOGRAPHY

Erika Mary Boeckeler

Early modern textuality is a culture of orthographic variation. This chapter argues that fluid early modern spelling and typography collude in the first printed *Hamlet* playtext to generate dramatic and poetic action unavailable to playhouse audiences. Typography is a textual interface, a space of encounter that emerges as it is actively worked through (Hookway 17). This zone of engagement is not a thing, but rather a set of prompts to read in particular ways, construing readers but also construed by readers (Drucker 157–8).[1] Orthography and typography, while operating to materially constitute the text, generate textual dynamism that conditions readers' encounters with the text. Poised between the oral stage and the non-theatrical visual page, and between poetry and prose, early printed playtexts forge the dramatic readerly experience through the unique affordances of spelling, letterforms, and graphic organization.

It is perhaps not a coincidence that both typeface and interface contain the word "face." In his theorization of interface, Branden Hookway defines the face as a threshold for the marshaling of interior energies into an exterior-oriented communicative form (8–9). Sixteenth-century typographer Geofroy Tory took this facing off between reader and piece of type, this inter-face, so literally that he modeled his Roman letterforms on the proportions and sensual experiences of human heads and bodies in his celebrated *Champ Fleury* (1529). His imagining of textual agency as words capable of staring back at their readers drives at the idea of an interface facilitating the process of mutual construal. But one of the remarkable features of an interface is that it slowly effaces itself as it becomes naturalized through experience. By the early twentieth century, the self-effacement of typography was widely regarded as the typographer's goal: Beatrice Warde famously compared a well-printed text to a crystal—as opposed to golden—goblet containing wine, emphasizing that the goal of printing is to convey the intoxicating ideas of authors' minds to other minds in the most unmediated way possible (11–18).[2] The apparent invisibility of typography, like the standardization of spelling, is due to a conventionalized interface that has become so naturalized that it practically does not register with readers.

Early modern textual interfaces turn Warde's crystal goblet back into gold. They present scholars accustomed to texts crystalized in contemporary forms with a unique opportunity to see the work that typography and orthography do to generate the semantic energies of a text, putting pressure on Ward's conceit of a textuality independent of its material instantiations.

DOI: 10.4324/9780367821722-13

This chapter argues that orthography (spelling) and typography (in the graphic design sense that includes page layout and individual letterforms, like f and ſ and s) shaped poetic practices and the semiotic experiences of readers, and that early printed playtexts generated performances of their own through the play of typography. The focus play of this chapter, *Hamlet* in the first printed edition from 1603, known as Quarto 1 or Q1, looks very different from today's Shakespearean playtexts, which are characterized by centuries-old graphic conventions. In centering poetics, I take a different tack from the important recent study on the origins of such theatrical print conventions, Claire Bourne's *Typographies of Performance in Early Modern England* (2020), which centers the playtext's relationship to the stage in its examination of evolving typographic features. The present chapter rather examines the ways in which early print interfaces unlock supplemental or alternative dramatic and poetic action available only through the reading experience.

The scholarly disciplines have inconsistently heeded D.F. McKenzie's call in 1986 to consider how the specific forms of words contribute to scholarly interpretation. His examination of typography in William Congreve's 1710 play *The Way of the World*

> bears upon the most obvious concerns of textual criticism – getting the right words in the right order, on the semiotics of print and the role of typography in forming meaning; on the critical theories of authorial intention and reader response; on the relation between past meanings and present uses of verbal texts.
>
> *(21)*

Scholars have likewise ignored the ground-breaking but challenging suggestion made by Margreta de Grazia and Peter Stallybrass in 1993 that we attend to the semantic fields prompted by spelling variation, despite the fact that we now have better tools than ever to aid us in that goal (266).[3] Early modern theater provides a particularly rich environment for thinking about the culture of orthographic variation: when it appears as a print genre, drama lies at the crossroads of oral performance and privately read text as well as at the generic crossroads between poetry and prose. In particular, my approach considers the visual features of the First Quarto *Hamlet* as rich sources of meaning-making for early modern readers who could work out connections that might disappear on stage.

We cannot definitively know where intentionality lies in early modern typesetting. Myriad influences can produce the way the words appear on a printed page: printing conventions for vernacular dramatic works, in-house printing conventions, attempts to protect delicate pieces of type or save paper, justification of a line to fit into the page, availability or scarcity of type, difficulties in reading copytext handwriting, incomplete copytext, printing house practices at an oral proofing stage, individual compositors' spelling preferences, carelessness of compositors and proofers, perceived importance of a job by printing house professionals, copy text abbreviations, disparities in regional dialects, shifts in pronunciation between the time of performance and the event of printing, formal schooling and writing/reading practices, and varying respect for etymology as well as compositors'/proofreaders'/authors'/publishers' deliberate exploitation of spelling to create visual and aural resonances. And still other influences could have conjured up this quintessence of playfull type called Q1.

I will suggest sources of intentionality specific to Q1, but for the most part my argument necessarily takes a readerly approach, keeping in mind that authors and publishers are also readers. In the fluid world of early modern spelling and allographic pieces of type, the early modern eie saw visual relationships between seemingly unlike words much like those the eare heard, and the Quarto typesetting often works to activate visually and aurally similar words and phrasings. Does it matter that *Hamlet*'s first print public saw "To be, or not to be, I there's the point" (D4v), in a speech about why the self, or the I, persists in the face of adversity?[4]

Why Q1 *Hamlet*?

Although the following analysis might be relevant to any early modern literary text, I use the Q1 *Hamlet* as an example for two primary reasons. Although Q1 is equally authoritative as a *Hamlet* text, scholars have not traditionally valued its literary qualities in the ways they have the Second Quarto (Q2, 1605) and the First Folio (F1, 1623) versions. Responses typically read it: (1) as a way of making sense of the other *Hamlets* we "really" care about; (2) as an exercise in analytical and historical bibliographic questions surrounding the plays; (3) in terms of source questions; (4) as primarily a performance text; or (4) as part of a New Historicist tissue in the cultural *Hamlet* web.[5] The 2008 work of Zachary Lesser and Peter Stallybrass opened new avenues for thinking about the literariness of Q1 and its performance on the page in light of book historical research.[6] In looking at orthography, typography, and page layout to highlight the texture and literary experiences of this culturally important playtext, my approach intervenes into traditional responses while still taking them into account. My readings do not necessarily provide a radically different view of Q1 but rather point to subtle ways in which the text's visuals enhance thematic concerns. Homographic words from vastly different parts of the lexicon, for example, efficiently link disparate ideas: power and pour (both *powre*) link the power-grab with poison. Visual wordforms may nuance character and character relations, such as the orthographically expressed brother-sister parallelism between the *aloofe* Ofelia and the *abroode* Leartes. Or format and homophonic printing can tease out crucial statements of identity, calling for a rereading of the iconic "To be or not to be" speech.

A second reason to focus on Q1 is to provide a model for considering the critical challenges and pitfalls of normative standards more generally. The interface of today's standardized typography haunts every contemporary reading of Q1. But this text also confronts us with the near impossibility of reading unconstrained by a First Folionic or a Q2 norm—a practice that early moderns may have grappled with themselves given *Hamlet*'s publication history. Once upon a time, for a fleeting moment in 1603, this text was the only printed *Hamlet* game in town. Less than a year after Q1's publication, the Q2 *Hamlet* title page lays claim to a prior originary status with the boast that it is "enlarged to almoſt as much againe as it was, according to the true and perfect Coppie."[7] That said, in terms of performance the going theory argues that Q1 was the last of the three to come into creation, making it, oddly, both the alpha and omega *Hamlet*. Certainly it has served as the alpha and omega of *Hamlet* readings as the first available *Hamlet* text in the early seventeenth century and the last one "rediscovered" at the bottom of a closet in 1823.

The play has symbolically functioned as an interruptive force in *Hamlet* studies. The performance, publication, and textual transmission histories of the three versions are so intimately imbricated that no critic can afford to ignore Q1. Holding out as potentially the final vndiſcouered *Hamlet* country, the questionable Q1 offers both the promise of tantalizing new text-based readings and, equally, of their impossibility. Thinking about Q1 from the perspective of typography suggests a new avenue of corrective disruption in interpretive practices. I ask what our critical and orthographic norms both reveal and conceal about an early modern playtext.

Why haven't the texture and literary experiences of Q1 been valued? The general attitude toward the Quarto assumes that Q1's poetry and its nuances are comparably weaker, and that Q1's impact as a performance text is comparably good or at least adequate since it moves at a quick pace with stagecraft flourishes and the length is playable. These two judgments have shaped the critical response with the exception of character studies; most critical analysis has hardly focused on the kinds of poetic, psychological, and philosophical questions about the other two versions that have excited centuries of readers. The virtues of Q1 as a performance text lie behind the first editorial decision to include it in a major contemporary scholarly Shakespeare series. The 2006 Arden edition asserts that "Q1 has now acquired enough of a theatrical history to have a claim to an edition of its own" (Thompson and Taylor 505). No doubt such decisions come as part of an ongoing feedback loop that involves the genesis theories of Q1 as an actor's (or actors') memorial reconstruction and/or a stage adaptation, theories promoted by the title page of Q1's note that it has played in London, Cambridge, and Oxford, among other places. But even at its supposed moment of textual ascendancy, Q1 retains its derivative status: the Arden edition presents Q1 either as a bibliographic oddity that must (along with the First Folio) defer its annotations to the Q2 control text or as a text primarily accessible through its onstage performance history. In the latter case, Q1 generates its value through the very virtue of being perceived as an inferior other. The chronicled success of these performances, in other words, relies primarily on their novel deviation from a familiar First Folionic or Q2 norm. As a performance text, Q1 is still better and worſe. But what if we evaluate it based on its on-page performances, rather than its translatability to or from the stage?

Scholars have widely acknowledged that the three *Hamlet* texts are separate versions interesting on their own terms only in the past 15 years or so, and several diplomatic editions do replicate orthographic features, though not necessarily all typographic ones. In 2016, operating with a primarily undergraduate audience in mind, the Norton online edition of Shakespeare's collected works began offering all three *Hamlet*s along with the edited hybrid that appears in their print version, but with many regularizations and modernized typography. At the more advanced scholarly level, early modern citation practice puts its object of study under frequent typographical erasure: see, for example, *Early Theatre*'s paleography guide ("the standard and elongated forms of 's' are uniformly transcribed as 's'") or *Shakespeare Quarterly*'s style pages ("Retain original capitalization, spelling, and punctuation in titles and quotations from early modern sources, except for the long s. Do not modernize"). Because of such scholarly conventions, we miss important visual connections between words, like the typographically expressed logic between distance and the preservation of virginity: Ofelia must "keepe a **looſe**" (C2[r]), since "that we thinke / Is ſureſt, we often **looſe**" (D4[r]). How much do we lose in our distance, and how much richer might our arguments be if we account for the play of typography?

I do not insist that intent lies behind the readings I suggest below, although I do propose that authors, printers, publishers, and readers were primed to compose and read in such a way. Textual interfaces facilitate a cultural feedback loop in which graphical organization is shaped in part by the habits of readers and likewise provides a provocation to read, interpret, and author in particular ways. To Johanna Drucker, "authoring absorbs and depends on provocations coded into the graphical space that maps relations among one bit of text and another" (173). In the following analyses of textual examples, I seek to articulate connections motivated in multiple, reinforcing ways, whether through plot, rhyme, metrical stress, or repetition.

Visual Powre

We can never replicate an early modern reading experience, armed as we are from early literacy with a sense of standardized spelling. But we can become more sensitive to how our norms operate to direct interpretation. My initial example examines the anagrammatic **power/powre**. Our contemporary word "pour" is entirely absent in Q1, although with the w sometimes appearing typographically as the double uu (hence the letter name), the early modern word subtly exudes an underlying u.[8] "Powre" works synonymously as our power and pour, while "power" only ever refers to the meaning we typically assign today to that combination of letters.[9] To take proper account of the former word's orthographic and semantic power, we mark it in action referring to: (1) supernatural might, as in "vniuersall **power**" (G1^{v}), "immortall **powers**" (G1v), "**Powers** aboue" (G2^{v}), "nor Witch hath **powre** to charme" (B3^{r}); (2) murder, both instances describing poison poured into an ear, when the Ghoſt describes how someone "through the porches of my eares / Did **powre** the leaprous distilment" (C4^{v}) and when the same action is remediated by Hamlet through the players' dumbshow, "*Then enters Lucianus with poyson in a Viall, and* ***powres*** *it in his eares*" (F3^{r}); (3) a narrative of a jester's antics, describing how "He **powred** once a whole flagon of Rhenish of my head" (I1^{r}); and (4) Leartes's in-grave request to be buried with Ofelia, "Now **powre** your earth on" (I1^{v}). These may seem like disparate uses of dissimilar words, but they are part of the same powre structure, or as de Grazia and Stallybrass would call it, the same semantic field.

Power is powring, pouring is power. When two words converge homographically, they may expand semantic categories. And while the pronunciation may have been closer to a dipthong, the Ghoſt's description of how the poison was poured into the "porches" of his ears links it to the word group that includes poore (many instances), report (three instances), Porpentines (C4^{r}, taken as Porcupine), ſport (D4^{r}), poring vppon a booke (D4^{v}), opportunitie (E1^{r}), porrige (F2^{v}), portraiture (G3^{r}), Portall (G2^{r}).[10] Still staying away from arguments about intentionality, I want to suggest that the power of this specific anagram may have spoken to 1603 readers as a performative instance of powre's uncanniness and to show how letters poured into words in particular orders may generate particular effects.

The word group **do/due/doo/doe** in Q1 makes for a particularly interesting test set since Hamlet is concerned with doing, that is to say enacting his revenge, especially in the Hecuba soliloquy. Studies in early modern pronunciation have noted contemporaneous instances in which some or even all of these words may sound the same; Q1 also deliberately pairs some of them to riff off similar sounds as well as sights, as I note below.[11] The scholar of early modern English pronunciation, E.J. Dobson, cautions against basing arguments on pronunciation alone, as

> there were many variant pronunciations, many levels and styles of speech, co-existing at any time; and … the accepted norms of pronunciation of one generation were not merely apt to differ from, but were sometimes not even directly developed from, those of a previous generation.
>
> *(vii)*

Printed 20 years earlier than the First Folio on which David Crystal bases his recent study of Shakespearean pronunciation, Q1 contains orthographic options that Crystal does not identify – including **adue** for our present-day and First Folio **ado**, or **poring** for **pouring**.[12] In the case of the playtext, we must contend with a rich variety of speaking, writing, and printing practices shaped by the dialect-diverse natures of the play- and print-houses situated in metropolitan London.

To an eighteenth- to twenty-first-century reader, do flies under the radar as a normal spelling, but doe, due, and doo stand out. Jakobsonian linguistics calls the normalized form do unmarked and the other forms marked. Unmarked terms tend to hide important differences and privilege one member of a group over another, as in the oft-cited case of the unmarked lion, which encompasses both the female and male animals, and the marked lioness, which denotes a specifically female animal. Q1 is the marked *Hamlet* text.

Critics have frequently taken the Hecuba soliloquy as the articulation of Hamlet's famous delay in exacting revenge for his father's death: "What would he **do** and if he had my loſſe?" he exclaims about the actor who cries over Hecuba (F1ʳ). We might argue that the pace of Q1 moves so fast that Hamlet hardly has time to formulate a plan, but the play does link doing to duty both visually and aurally. This connection emerges explicitly in Roſſencraft and Gilderſtone's first speeches, appearing in response to the king's request to seek out what's bothering Hamlet: "**Doe** this, the king of Denmarke ſhal be thankefull" (D3ʳ). Roſſencraft describes them as "bound / By loue, by **duetie**, and obedience" (D3ʳ).[13] Gilderſtone further emphasizes the connection between doing and dutie: "So in all **duetie doe** we take our leaue" (D3ʳ).[14] The king's father-son-like intercourse with Hamlet's school friends recalls the previous one between the Ghoſt and Hamlet, wherein the Ghoſt departs by repeating "Hamlet **adue, adue, adue**: remember me" (C4ᵛ) after he has urged him on to a particular kind of doing and filial duetie—revenge. Hamlet also repeats these specific words as he records them in his memory tables although the text hardly carries as much weight as other parts of the Ghoſt's speech: "Now to the words: it is **adue adue**: remember me" (D1ʳ).[15] Crystal notes the shared potential spelling of **due** and **deaw** (our contemporary **dew**). While these seem semantically unrelated, a single speech of Horatio's contains doe/deaw/duetie, linking native beliefs about spirits' limitations on earth and the watchers' own duty to inform Prince Hamlet following the Ghoſt's limited interaction with them. The page B3ʳ is an echo chamber of that word group, with doe, deaw, duetie, doo't, do, dutie (twice) (see Figure 9.1). Ofelia's mad song tells of a false steward who "dupt the chamber **doore**" (H2ʳ),[16] emphasizing the symbolic virginal door with the comment that "Yong men will **doo't** when they come too't" (H2ʳ); this aural and visual connection between duplicity, doors, and sex augments the critical strand that suggests Ofelia has had intercourse with Hamlet. Both the tetrameter stress and internal rhyme reinforce the visual and aural connections. This cloud or cluster of do spellings slide meaning across the chain of signifiers, into which must also enter the Ghoſt's "**doomd** for a time / To walke the night" (C3ᵛ), Hamlet's **doome** as prescribed by the King's death writ, and the Gravedigger's "the gallowes **doth** wel, mary howe **dooes** it well? the gallows **dooes** well to them that **doe** ill" (H4ʳ). The king worries that Hamlet's actions doom Denmark itself: Hamlet will "**undoe** our ſtate" (G3ᵛ). In rare cases does the do/due/doo/doe word cluster include positive doings.

These particular results might emerge through a careful acoustic reading of normalized typography, but the typesetting of Q1 throws the play of visual and aural language into high relief. Evidence from within the play, from other Shakespearean texts, and from early modern English examples of writing, orthography, and typography more generally point to a readerly sensitivity to latent visual and aural word connections. The *Hamlet* editor puzzles over the fine lines separating typos, typographical contingencies like kerning and line justification, and deliberate spellings.[17] Kathleen Irace, editor of a 1998 Q1, points to Hamlet's comment, "Mouse-trap: mary how trapically" (F4ʳ), at the play-within-a-play: "With its pun on 'Mousetrap', Q1's reading seems intentional" (16). In the same play-watching scene, our protagonist comments, "This is myching Mallico, that meanes my chiefe" (F3ʳ), and Irace remarks that "'my chief' could be an error for Q2's and F's 'mischief', or it could link the king 'my chief') with 'mischief', at the same time emphasizing Hamlet's pretended madness" (16). Internal evidence comes from deliberate punning by characters; for example, Corambis comments that the players can play Plato (E3ᵛ), as opposed to the Q2 or F reading of Plautus (Q2, F3ʳ; F1, p. 263; oo4ʳ) that accurately refers to a Roman playwright but eliminates the pun. Other potentially deliberate puns for Irace include "ceasen" (B4ᵛ) invoking both cease and season; "beckles" (C3ᵛ) beetles and beckons; and "ghest" (H4ʳ) guest and Ghoſt (9). Other editors have struggled with additional individual words. Such ambiguities receive

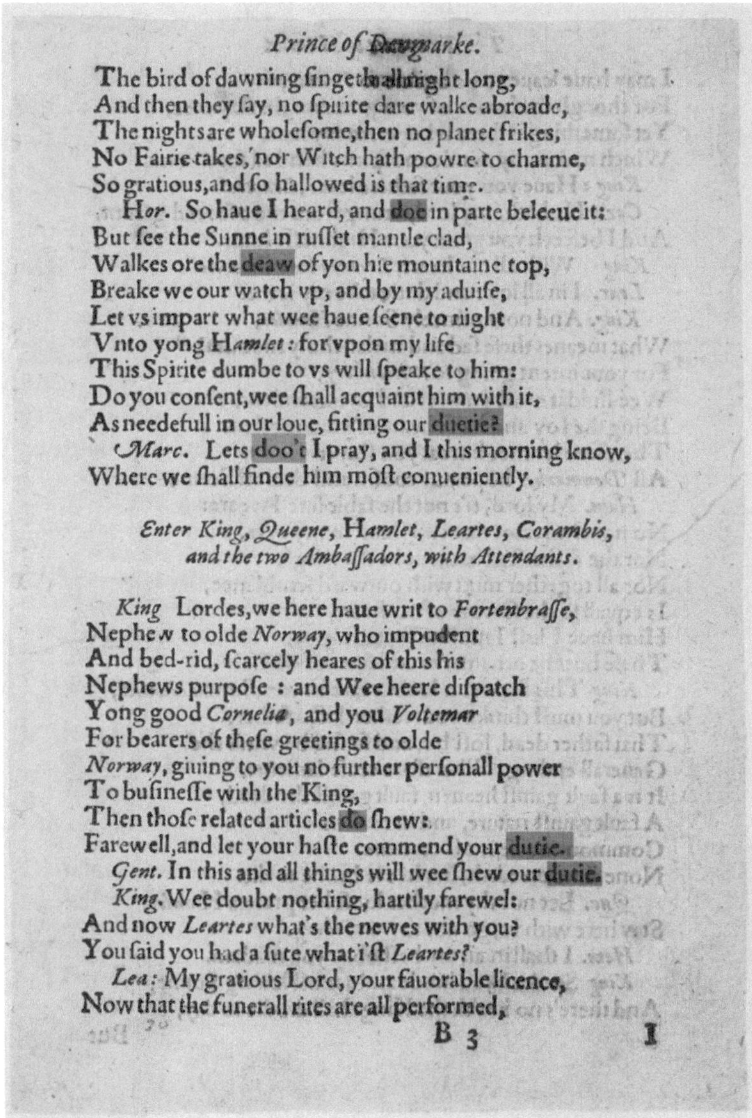

Prince of Denmarke.

The bird of dawning ſingeth all night long,
And then they ſay, no ſpirite dare walke abroade,
The nights are wholeſome, then no planet frikes,
No Fairie takes, nor Witch hath powre to charme,
So gratious, and ſo hallowed is that time.
Hor. So haue I heard, and doe in parte beleeue it:
But ſee the Sunne in ruſſet mantle clad,
Walkes ore the deaw of yon hie mountaine top,
Breake we our watch vp, and by my aduiſe,
Let vs impart what wee haue ſeene to night
Vnto yong Hamlet: for vpon my life
This Spirite dumbe to vs will ſpeake to him:
Do you conſent, wee ſhall acquaint him with it,
As needefull in our loue, fitting our duetie?
Marc. Lets doo't I pray, and I this morning know,
Where we ſhall finde him moſt conueniently.

Enter King, Queene, Hamlet, *Leartes, Corambis, and the two Ambaſſadors, with Attendants.*

King Lordes, we here haue writ to *Fortenbraſſe,*
Nephew to olde *Norway*, who impudent
And bed-rid, ſcarcely heares of this his
Nephews purpoſe: and Wee heere diſpatch
Yong good *Cornelia*, and you *Voltemar*
For bearers of theſe greetings to olde
Norway, giuing to you no further perſonall power
To buſineſſe with the King,
Then thoſe related articles do ſhew:
Farewell, and let your haſte commend your dutie.
Gent. In this and all things will wee ſhew our dutie.
King. Wee doubt nothing, hartily farewel:
And now *Leartes* what's the newes with you?
You ſaid you had a ſute what i'ſt *Leartes*?
Lea: My gratious Lord, your fauorable licence,
Now that the funerall rites are all performed,
B 3

Figure 9.1 Hamlet B3[r]

reinforcement in the text's own heavy symbolic accumulation that watches a word or image snowball into densely compacted meaning clusters, like the ear in *Hamlet* texts, or—to take an example from another play—the concept of the zero/nothing/whole in the *Lear* texts outlined by David Willbern (244–63). I find the German word *überladen* (literally meaning over-burdened or over-loaded) apt for describing this phenomenon with its semantic aura of individual terms as heavy nodes drawing in meaning from disparate parts of the lexicon.

Within the Ofelia-Leartes-Corambis plot, significant word clusters coalesce to emphasize brother-sister parallelism, represent the binary options for Ofelia's behaviour, and highlight Ofelia's own linguistic maneuvers. When we meet them, Leartes "must **aboord**" (C1[v]) and

Ofelia "keepe **a loofe**" (C2^{r}; later "walke **aloofe**"; D4^{v}): in the same opening, a parallel structure and visibly parallel activities unite the two as they part. These words appear in the same speech by Leartes, with "**aboord, aboord**" repeated again by Corambis within the same page opening (C1v and C2^{r}). Corambis's speech later picks up on the typographically slippery loofe and loofe (loose): with dramatic irony in light of her later madness, he comments about her that "that we thinke / Is fureft, we often **loofe**" (D4^{r}). Ofelia then becomes the "loofe" object who must "walke **aloofe**" (D4^{v}) in her father's plan to test his theory of Hamlet's lovesickness.[18] Later lines by Leartes reintroduce the word just before he lets loose in the fatal swordfight, noting he must "stand **aloofe**" (I3^{r}) in fully accepting Hamlet's apology.

A case can be made for the typographic—and the resultingly semantic—connection between **foule** (soule) and **foule** that dots C4^{r} (see Figure 9.2), for which readers have been primed with Hamlet's earlier alliterative rhymed couplet anticipating the Ghoft's appearance: "Till then, fit ftill my **foule, foule** deeds will rif / Though all the world orewhelme them to mens eies" (C1^{v}).[19] This typographic cueing appears in the Ghoft's periphrastic descriptions of his punishment; such a tale "Would harrow vp thy **foule**" (C4^{r}). A succession of references to soule/foule follow down the page in almost the same line position, "Reuenge his **foule**, and moft vnnaturall murder," "But mine moft **foule,**" "O my prophetike **foule.**"

The orthography and appearance of Q1 (and, indeed, of all early modern textuality) further encourage readerly connections across a narrative. Marcellus's famed comment that "Something is rotten in the ftate of ***Denmarke***" (C3^{v}) gets echoed in the same page a few lines later when the rotten thing, or the thing representing the "ftate of *Denmarke*," speaks his

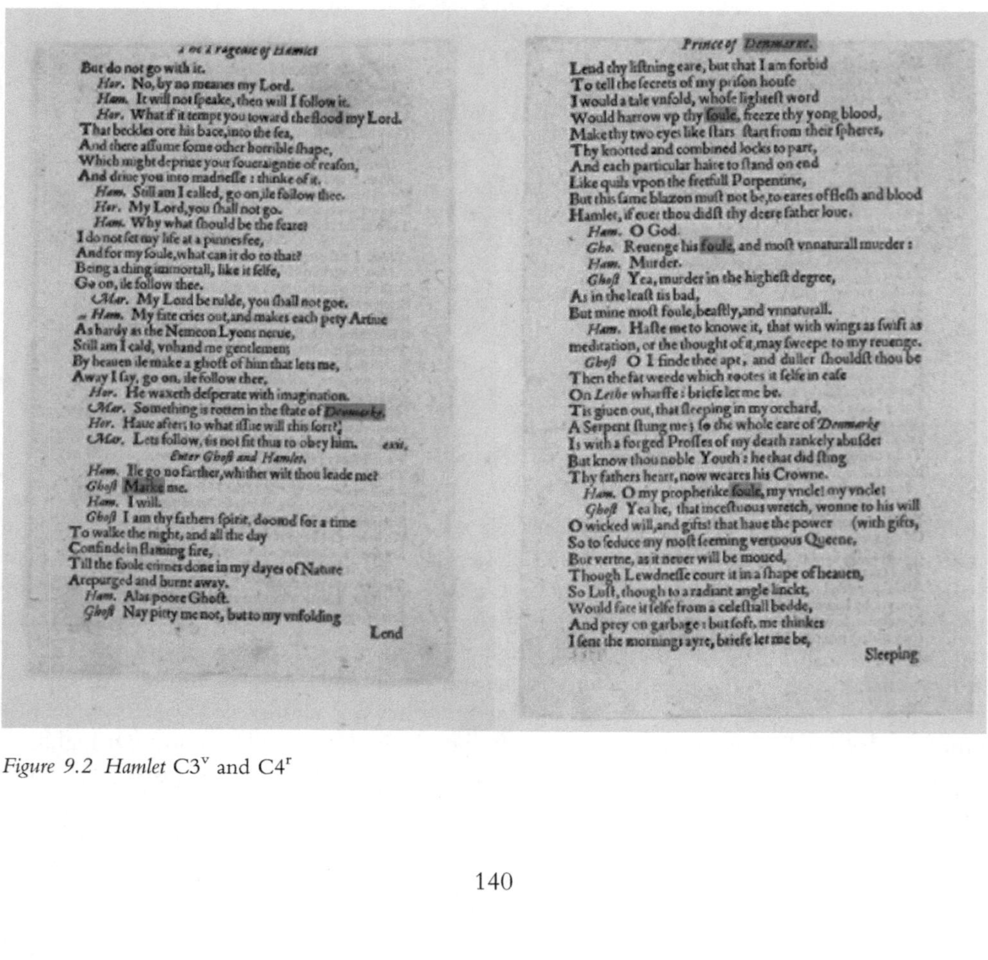

Figure 9.2 Hamlet C3^{v} and C4^{r}

first words of the play, "**Marke** me" (see Figure 9.2). The visual stress of italicization augments the acoustic; Q1 regularly italicizes place names, but here *Denmarke* appears prominently at the end of a line on the same page.[20] The visual impact of this interchange lingers on the recto of every page, where the running headline reads "*Prince of Denmarke*" (in conjunction with *The Tragedie of Hamlet* on the verso). In the same scene, the Ghoſt describes his siesta: "In the after **noone**, vpon my ſecure houre" (C4^{v}); the orthography of "noone" emphasizes the privacy of the ritual into which no one or none may intercede.[21] The secure hour refers not only to his regular seeking of this precious time away from the cares of state and its curative role, but also to the orchard's safety and security from human interruption.

Q1 visually prepares its readers for "to be, or not to be, I there's the point" from the beginning of the play. The exclusive printing of "I" for what we would render "Ay" in contemporary typography is a feature unique to, and consistent across, all of Q1 vis-à-vis Q2 and F. Its first appearance is remarkable within Corambis's palindromic response to Ofelia's description of Hamlet's gifts: "Tenders, **I, I**, tenders you may call them"—a chiastic sequence found only in Q1 (C2^{v}). In the same opening, C2^{v} and C3^{r}, Hamlet uses one word typographically but two words (ay and I) semantically in his preamble to the famed line about the king's partying habit: "**I** mary i'ſt and though **I** am/ Natiue here, and to the maner borne/ It is a cuſtome, more honourd in the breach" (C3^{r}). Soon thereafter, as Hamlet responds to his friends' request to tell what he heard from the Ghoſt, the page puts a series of negated Is in parallel with an affirmative (see also Figure 9.3) in rapid sequence.[22] In the breathless formatting of Q1, whose textual progress is only broken by stage directions or interrupted by other occasional passages in italic, isocolonic and other visual patterns can stand out.

Echoes of the exchange appear on the following verso as well. Corambis employs I in the sense of Ay a few more times leading up to Hamlet's iconic soliloquy.

From the very first line, this soliloquy's deviation from the expected Q2 or F versions' "That is the question" strikes contemporary readers. Viewed in the original 1603 orthography, the deviation appears all the more shocking with the estranging substitution of "I" in the supposedly deviant line "Ay, there's the point" (see Figure 9.4). The soliloquy continues in the same vein, with unexpected phrases and a series of equally unexpected uses of I in the next two lines. The Q1 speech itself admittedly presents serious syntactic challenges, as contemporary editors have noted. What sense might 1603 readers have made of it?

I think it matters that these three Is of affirmation visually mark the page in a vertically sequential, post-caesura isocolon. In a speech questioning why the I, the self, continues to exist in a world of pain, it matters that the I stands tentatively before its readers, for no first person pronoun appears in the entire soliloquy. The soliloquy truly presents, visually, a meditation on the I's (and eie's) existence and persistence in the face of erasure, on the inherent life-affirming qualities of the I that "makes vs rather beare thoſe euilles we haue."[23] The speech is simultaneously personal and general. Hamlet's divided self stands before us here, with the I absent in content but present in form. The capitalized "Iudge" links back to the series of I's above in a visual statement confirming that we have a share in divinity and a share in divine judgment, for we all have an internal judge in the "conſcience" that "makes cowardes of vs all."

Q1 renders visible Hamlet's struggle with and assertion of identity through this typographic subtext and by placing this speech within a framework of questions and assertions of identity and identification. In an exchange appearing quite differently in Q2 and F, Q1's first two lines ask and answer a question about identification (see Figure 9.5).

These two opening lines distinguish themselves typographically as a single unit both spatially and with a large capital S the height of two lines of type. Both of the lines follow with a uppercase T, the first as the second letter in the first word of the first line, "STand: who is

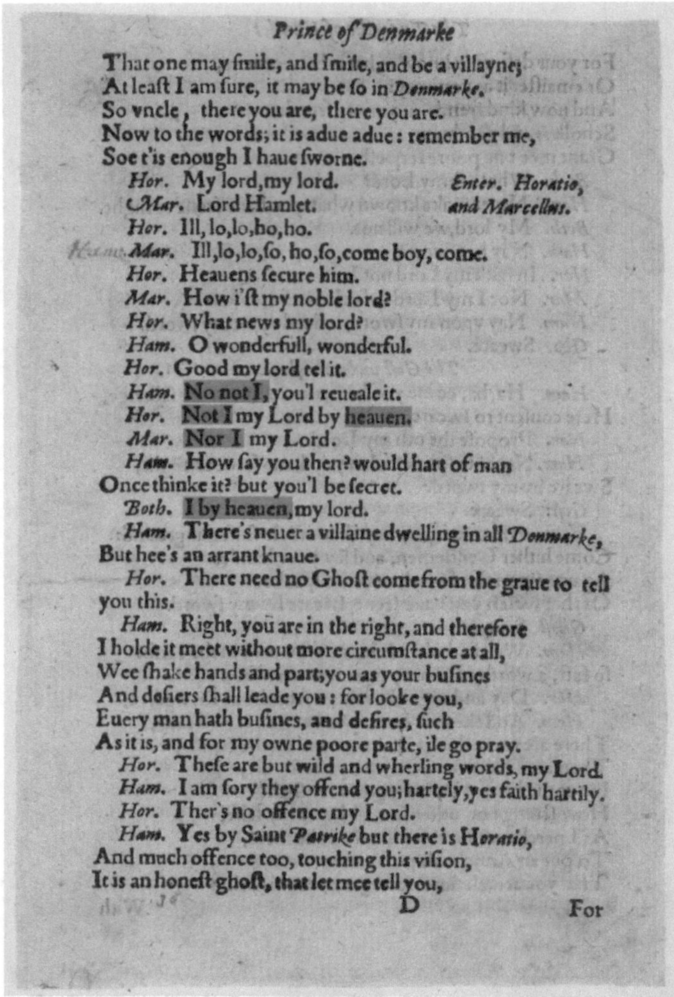

Prince of Denmarke

That one may ſmile, and ſmile, and be a villayne;
At leaſt I am ſure, it may be ſo in *Denmarke*.
So vncle, there you are, there you are.
Now to the words; it is adue adue : remember me,
Soe t'is enough I haue ſworne.
Hor. My lord, my lord. *Enter. Horatio, and Marcellus.*
Mar. Lord Hamlet.
Hor. Ill, lo, lo, ho, ho.
Mar. Ill, lo, lo, ſo, ho, ſo, come boy, come.
Hor. Heauens ſecure him.
Mar. How i'ſt my noble lord?
Hor. What news my lord?
Ham. O wonderfull, wonderful.
Hor. Good my lord tel it.
Ham. No not I, you'l reueale it.
Hor. Not I my Lord by heauen.
Mar. Nor I my Lord.
Ham. How ſay you then? would hart of man
Once thinke it? but you'l be ſecret.
Both. I by heauen, my lord.
Ham. There's neuer a villaine dwelling in all *Denmarke*,
But hee's an arrant knaue.
Hor. There need no Ghoſt come from the graue to tell you this.
Ham. Right, you are in the right, and therefore
I holde it meet without more circumſtance at all,
Wee ſhake hands and part; you as your buſines
And deſiers ſhall leade you : for looke you,
Euery man hath buſines, and deſires, ſuch
As it is, and for my owne poore parte, ile go pray.
Hor. Theſe are but wild and wherling words, my Lord.
Ham. I am ſory they offend you; hartely, yes faith hartily.
Hor. Ther's no offence my Lord.
Ham. Yes by Saint *Patrike* but there is *Horatio*,
And much offence too, touching this viſion,
It is an honeſt ghoſt, that let mee tell you,
D For

Figure 9.3 Hamlet D1^{r}

that?" and the second within an independent word in the second line, "Tis I" (B1r). The latter phrase is positioned such that, inclusive of the large S running into it, it takes up as much space as STand, with the I's ascender at the end parallel to the d. The two Ts visually evoke the image of the two "Centinels" standing in front of each other. Q2 and F (and the British Library version's marginal note) identify the speakers of these two lines as Francisco and Barnardo/Bernardo. Q1 significantly leaves unidentified these two speakers who initiate the play's concerns about identification, labeling them simply as 1. and 2., eventually distinguishing Barnardo in the dialogue but never in the character tag. The Q1 visuals force the reader into distinguishing the identities of the two sentinels.

In this moment's counterpart toward the end of the play, Hamlet responds to Leartes's grief by leaping into Ofelia's grave after him: "Beholde tis I, *Hamlet* the Dane" (I1^{v}). Where the first line of the play concerned itself with identification, this parallel moment moves beyond that to assert an identity. Q1's unique stage direction, noting that "*Hamlet leapes/ in after Leartes*" (I1^{v}), appears in the margin to indicate the simultaneity of action with Leartes's

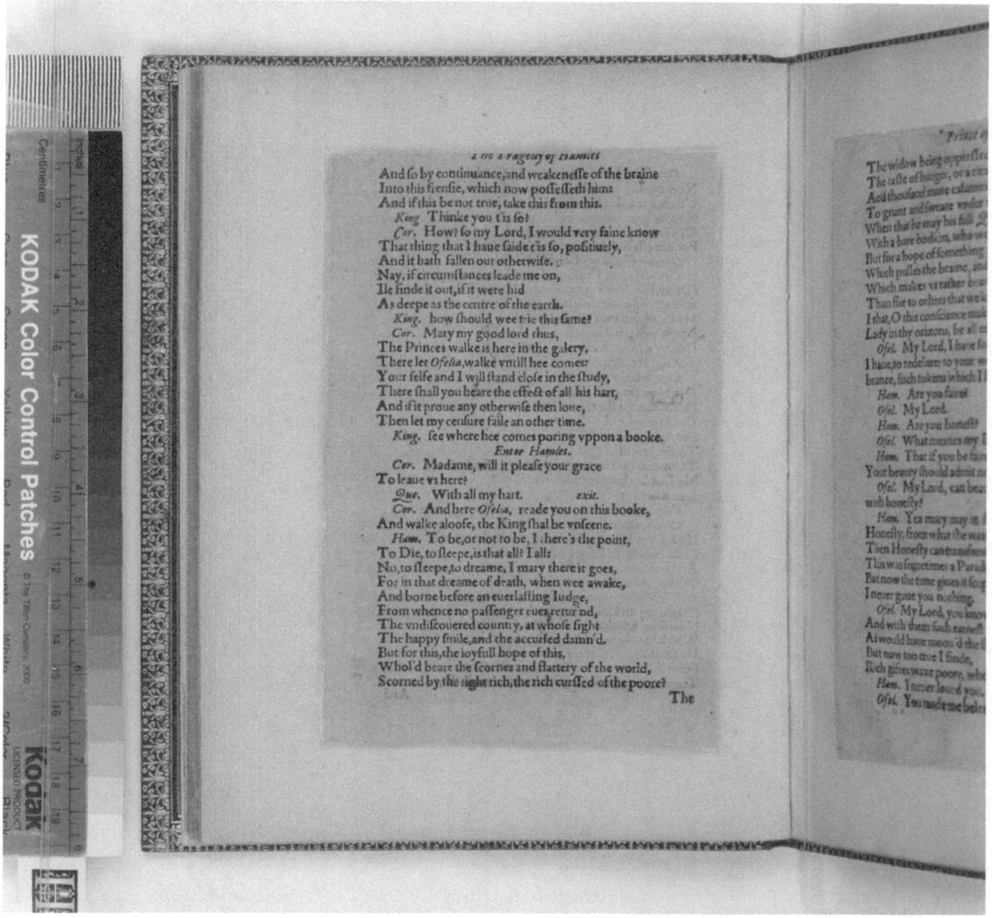

And ſo by continuance,and weakeneſſe of the braine
Into this frenſie, which now poſſeſſeth him:
And if this be not true, take this from this.
King Thinke you t'is ſo?
Cor. How? ſo my Lord, I would very faine know
That thing that I haue ſaide t'is ſo, poſitiuely,
And it hath fallen out otherwiſe.
Nay, if circumſtances leade me on,
Ile finde it out,if it were hid
As deepe as the centre of the earth.
King. how ſhould wee trie this ſame?
Cor. Mary my good lord thus,
The Princes walke is here in the galery,
There let *Ofelia*,walke vntill hee comes:
Your ſelfe and I will ſtand cloſe in the ſtudy,
There ſhall you heare the effect of all his hart,
And if it proue any otherwiſe then loue,
Then let my cenſure faile an other time.
King. ſee where hee comes poring vppon a booke.
Enter Hamlet.
Cor. Madame, will it pleaſe your grace
To leaue vs here?
Que. With all my hart. *exit.*
Cor. And here *Ofelia*, reade you on this booke,
And walke aloofe, the King ſhal be vnſeene.
Ham. To be,or not to be, I there's the point,
To Die, to ſleepe,is that all? I all:
No,to ſleepe,to dreame, I mary there it goes,
For in that dreame of death, when wee awake,
And borne before an euerlaſting Iudge,
From whence no paſſenger euer retur'nd,
The vndiſcouered country, at whoſe ſight
The happy ſmile,and the accurſed damn'd.
But for this,the ioyfull hope of this,
Whol'd beare the ſcornes and flattery of the world,
Scorned by the right rich,the rich curſſed of the poore?
The

Figure 9.4 Hamlet D4ᵛ

speech, rather than in text as Leartes's own stage direction leap does. Hamlet's italicized name as a result receives more visual emphasis than it would have had it appeared immediately after an italicized stage direction. Q2 and F, which do not contain the famous stage direction, let Hamlet ask a rhetorical question, to which the answer is "This is I, / *Hamlet* the Dane," spread across two lines (Q2 M4^{v}; F1 p278, pp5^{v}).[24] The 1603 readers received a unique typographic sequence that drives toward Hamlet's dramatic social re-emergence.

Contexts, Critics, Conclusions

There have always been literary texts crafted deliberately for the eie: a notable example is the substantial body of pattern poetry (figured poetry, concrete poetry, calligrams, technopaegnia, etc.) in continuous production from classical to present times.[25] Scholarship has appreciated how some early modern authors wrote for the eie in subtle ways; most critics readily identify Edmund Spenser as a poet of the eie as much as of the eare.[26] But this chapter is not about such deliberate inventions. I instead argue that a larger portion of more visually quotidian early modern literary production, including playtexts, ought to be situated nearer to such

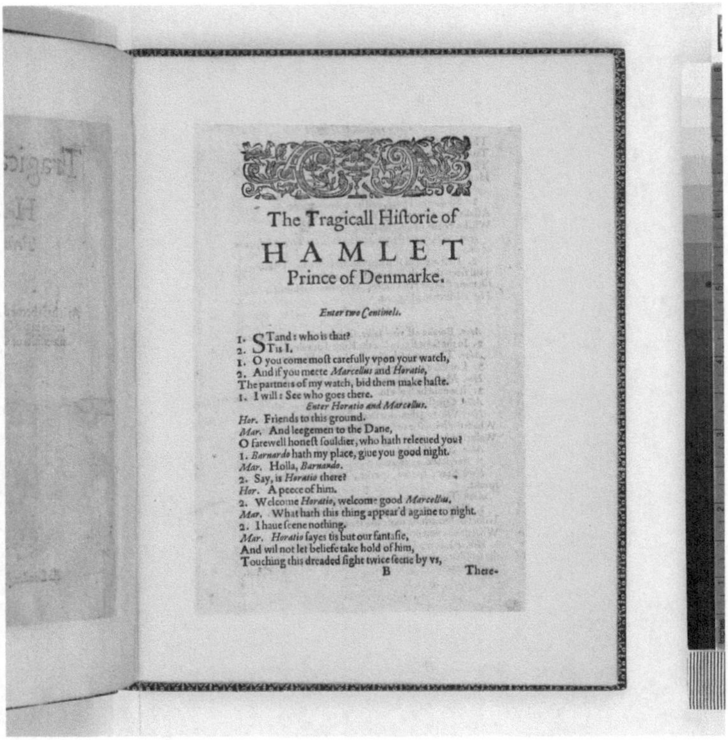

The Tragicall Hiſtorie of
HAMLET
Prince of Denmarke.

Enter two Centinels.

1. STand: who is that?
2. Tis I.
1. O you come moſt carefully vpon your watch,
2. And if you meete *Marcellus* and *Horatio*,
The partners of my watch, bid them make haſte.
1. I will: See who goes there.
Enter Horatio and Marcellus.
Hor. Friends to this ground.
Mar. And leegemen to the Dane,
O farewell honeſt ſouldier, who hath releeued you?
1. *Barnardo* hath my place, giue you good night.
Mar. Holla, *Barnardo*.
2. Say, is *Horatio* there?
Hor. A peece of him.
2. Welcome *Horatio*, welcome good *Marcellus*.
Mar. What hath this thing appear'd againe to night.
2. I haue ſeene nothing.
Mar. *Horatio* ſayes tis but our fantaſie,
And wil not let beliefe take hold of him,
Touching this dreaded ſight twice ſeene by vs,
B There-

Figure 9.5 *Hamlet* first page

works on the visual spectrum. In considering where Q1 *Hamlet* falls, we might turn our attention to its publisher, Nicholas Ling (a.k.a. Lyng), the preferred publisher of Spenserian poet[27] and sonneteer Michael Drayton and a publisher who valued Shakespeare more as a poet than a playwright, according to Terri Bourus.[28] She notes that the Q1 *Hamlet* is the only first edition play from the commercial playhouses published by Ling and, remarking on the text's few musical cues along with the absence of actors' names and duplicated stage directions, she agrees with Lesser and Stallybrass that this play looks more like a literary text than a typical playtext (Bourus 20–1).[29] How might the visual play noted above compare to Drayton's?

Drayton's sonnet sequences *Idea* and *Idea's Mirror* do not seem visually exemplary, and yet they illuminate how a typical early modern English poet and/or a publisher may deliberately draw on typographic effects. Drayton heavily curated the printed editions of his sonnets, which appeared in some 15 editions and reprints bearing one or neither of those two titles above over the course of 27 years. The sonnet "NOthing but no and I, and I and no" (initial publication, 1599; here cited in the 1602 edition, P1^{v}) hinges on the relationship between two key words: "no" and "I" (see Figure 9.6). The clever poem manages the typical sonnet addressee's resistance to the speaker's romantic advances through apophasis: what, ultimately, the no negates or even refers to is further complicated by the tensions generated in the typographically conflated I/aye. The mostly palindromic first line suggests immediately that the poem will be exploiting a reversal of the Faire's position; it concludes with the same chiasmus, suggesting the reversal worked. While the moments when the speaker means I or aye can be more or less distinguished (as modernized spelling editions demonstrate), it is quite

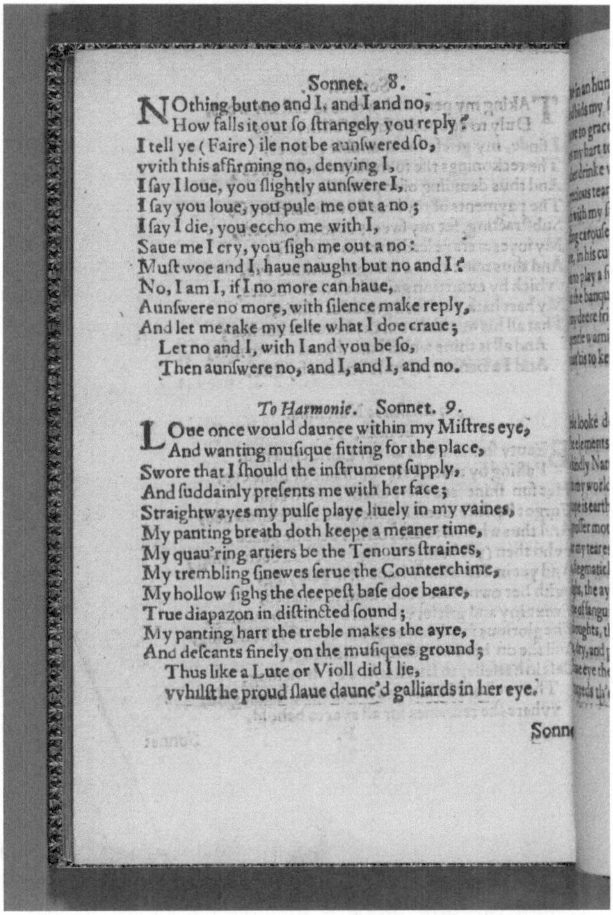
Sonnet. 8.
NOthing but no and I, and I and no,
How falls it out ſo ſtrangely you reply?
I tell ye (Faire) ile not be aunſwered ſo,
vvith this affirming no, denying I,
I ſay I loue, you ſlightly aunſwere I,
I ſay you loue, you pule me out a no;
I ſay I die, you eccho me with I,
Saue me I cry, you ſigh me out a no:
Muſt woe and I, haue naught but no and I?
No, I am I, if I no more can haue,
Aunſwere no more, with ſilence make reply,
And let me take my ſelfe what I doe craue;
Let no and I, with I and you be ſo,
Then aunſwere no, and I, and I, and no.

To Harmonie. Sonnet. 9.
LOue once would daunce within my Miſtres eye,
And wanting muſique fitting for the place,
Swore that I ſhould the inſtrument ſupply,
And ſuddainly preſents me with her face;
Straightwayes my pulſe playe liuely in my vaines,
My panting breath doth keepe a meaner time,
My quau'ring artiers be the Tenours ſtraines,
My trembling ſinewes ſerue the Counterchime,
My hollow ſighs the deepeſt baſe doe beare,
True diapazon in diſtincted ſound;
My panting hart the treble makes the ayre,
And deſcants finely on the muſiques ground;
Thus like a Lute or Violl did I lie,
vvhilſt he proud ſlaue daunc'd galliards in her eye.
Sonn

Figure 9.6 The Drayton sonnet

clear that altering the orthography severely compromises the full semantic effects of visual punning. The poem operates on an incredibly minimal visual vocabulary. Of the 125 words total in the poem, I and no (or no's variants: naught, not, nothing) make up roundly one third of them, and just four words— no, I, and, you—comprise 45 percent of the text. While this poem's efficiency is clever, it also does not seem to read itself as atypical. Meta-textual moments typical of early modern English sonnets appear within other poems of Drayton's sequence.

The best-known of all sonnet sequences, Shakespeare's *Sonnets*, shares a similar visual efficiency. The Will sonnets pun on both the sounds and the spellings of key words. In addition to playing with the sounds of will, fill, and full, these lines from Sonnet 136 also play with how full (or not ful) of lls the very words are:

Thus farre for loue, my loue-ſute ſweet fulfill.
Will, will fulfill the treaſure of thy loue,
I fill it full with wils, and my will one,
(*Sonnets, 1609 Q, I1r)*

In a poem invested in sophisticated linguistic number play, the orthographic account performs the way a single sound may be perceived when represented as either a single or double letter. Thus "wils" and "wills" are ful(l) of many wils/wills: semantically, acoustically, and graphically.

Some critics of *Sonnets* and other early modern lyric poetry have been reading visually and acoustically, acknowledging the significant contributions of the visual poetic experience of these works to their meaning-making. Helen Vendler sees words within words, for example, the sun's **car** in Sonnet 7 unleashes g**rac**ious, s**acr**ed, and **trac**t, and its aging spawns hom**age,** **age** (x2), g**old**en, and pilgrim**age** (B2^{rv}). Couched in more tentative language, she suggests that the golden sun (since the French word for "gold" is *or*) generates French-English puns in **or**ient, ad**ore**, m**or**tal, **fore** (Vendler 76).[30] She points to significant spelling choices unique to printed editions, characterizing Sonnet 9 as a "Fantasy on the Letter W" initiated by the near-palindromic properties of the Quarto spelling of "widdow" (B2^{v}) (Vendler 84). This reading appreciates the visual balances of words and even letters made manifest through spelling.

One might argue that, because these examples appear in the often more meticulously constructed, self-contained genre of lyric and because Shakespeare may have exercised more control over his lyrical work in print, there is stronger justification for attending to the particular orthographic choices of *Sonnets*. And yet these poems originate with the author of plays that naturalize sonnets or sonnet-like pieces in their dialogue and that feature characters composing sonnets for one another. The plays also include word anagrams like Thurio's "sonnet" and "onset" in *Two Gentlemen of Verona*, and name anagrams like Cordelia and Lear in *King Lear* as well as the anagrammatic triad Viola-Malvolio-Olivia in *Twelfth Night*. The readers of the plays may have also been (and likely were) also the readers of Shakespeare's poetry; some certainly came to his plays through his poetry as his name gradually achieved more recognition as that of a playwright, and many other contemporaneous poets also wrote plays.

The stakes of this approach involve the status of visual language as a bearer of information in the early modern era.[31] The gateway phenomenon for contemporary non-bibliographer critics into the challenges of early modern spelling has typically been the pun. Stephen Booth, the pun-sensitive editor of Shakespeare's *Sonnets* known for his exhaustive commentaries on the resonances of individual words, grudgingly admits in a long discussion about the spelling and punctuation of Sonnet 129 that "an ocular pun on *proud* (= modern "proved") and proud (= modern "proud") may have momentarily crossed a Renaissance reader's mind" (Sonnets, H3^{v}) (Shakespeare *Sonnets* 448).[32] For Booth, a spelling choice can potentially become an orthographic signal in the context of a line, maybe extending as far as an entire sonnet, but in the context of an entire playtext it achieves nothing more than an orthographic peculiarity.

What he had in mind with orthographic peculiarity was something like what Stallybrass and de Grazia point out in *Macbeth*, in which our contemporary words hair and heir appear as hair, heir, heire, and here and as heir, aire, are, haire, and here respectively (De Grazia and Stallybrass 265–6). These puns are not motivated by context. To early modern eies unaccustomed to ideal forms of vernacular words, what is the relationship of the things we now designate as hair and heir to all of those other spelled forms? What is the status of the physical form of the word on the early modern page as signifier? What does it tell us about the early modern understanding of written language?

Some critics like Jonathan Hope would have the eies imagining a single, platonic word realized orally with many different visual instantiations appearing in spellings, which he calls "signals." This approach contrasts with the contemporary eye's one-to-one sign-to-signifier, that is, one word to its one (occasionally two) fixed spelling correspondent (Hope 90–3). It also calls for the active participation of the reader in the text as she or he reads, overlooking the "surface level of spelling" and determining which "word" is intended.

This approach makes perfect sense in most cases. But early modern writers who so eagerly exploit the verbal pun also could turn to visual resources for semiotic expansion in the visually sensitive culture of the early modern world. Even the prescriptive George Puttenham, who deplores a weaker poet's use of "vntrue orthographie to wrench his words to helpe his rime," concedes that tweaking spelling might productively advance both visual as well as aural rhyme:

> [I]t is ſomewhat more tollerable to help the rime by falſe orthographie, then to leaue an vnpleasant diſſonance to the eare, by keeping trewe orthographie and looſing the rime, as for example it is better to rime [*Dore*] with [*Restore*] then his truer orthographie, which is [*Doore*].
>
> *(Puttenham 2.67)*[33]

The point here is not only that some rhymes may emerge—whether in sound or appearance—only through orthography but also that poets did selectively alter spellings for poetic purposes, and the visual appearance of the poem mattered. Rhyme in this formulation works on the eie as well as the eare. Puns, I argue, work the same way.

Margreta de Grazia has commented on the centrality of punning to early modern thought itself, speculating that Renaissance puns "literally made sense; that is, they constituted sense through their copious troping resources rather than representing it as something pre-existent in mind or world" (155–6). Critics tend to focus only on the aural pun. Even de Grazia's influential article begins with the centrality of the aural pun bear to *The Winter's Tale*, showing how it resonates from bearing a child, a "barne" (p288, F1 Aa6^{v}), to the famous "Exit, pursued by a Beare" (p288, F1 Aa6^{v}) stage direction (de Grazia 143–52). In Jonathan Hope's understanding of Renaissance linguistics, puns are oral because the written word or words only signal the appropriate (oral) referents involved and do not reference other similarly written words. According to his theory, the various punning possibilities already exist in the minds of readers when they see a written word, and, should the context call upon multiple such options, a pun is activated.

My claim is that orthographic puns are not mere surface play to be brushed aside in search of a holy grail word but rather one function in the literary work of the graphic letter as it links ideas. The visual effects of language materialized through orthography also constituted sense in the way de Grazia describes the sense-making of aural language. These effects may be local: proved (spelled "proud") and proud may be meaningfully linked in the tightly packed literary landscape of Sonnet 129. Effects may also be cumulative across a larger work, like the playscape of *The Merchant of Venice*, as Marc Shell has argued in his reading of the visual and verbal punning generated through "Iewes" and words including Jews, use/usury, ewes, jewels, etc. (47–92). Perhaps *Macbeth*'s early modern readers may have also located meaningful connections between heir and here since Duncan's heir is mostly not here, that is to say not in Scotland. A word might take many different forms on the page, and those forms constituted the word's presence in the physical world of the text. Words had both an aural existence that linked them to other words and a physical existence that linked them visually to other words in the text (and outside of it). But these associations only make sense contextually. I agree with de Grazia and Stallybrass that the single early modern word is always enmeshed in a semantic field of acoustic (and visual) cognates, but it is a semantic field that the physical, self-contained form of the text itself determines. Drama, poetry, and

Renaissance literary writing could toy with orthography to unlock and widen the semantic field and generate meaning. In the wilds of nonstandardized English orthography and typesetting practices aimed to preserve type and to physically fit pieces into a line, early modern printing was homophonic and homographic.

Rather than a barrier to close reading, I see particular spellings and typographic features—however they got there—as a gateway into the richness of early modern vernacular reading. Early modern readers and their texts reside at the intersection of four practices that encourage this approach: (1) an attentiveness to visuals within an ongoing manuscript culture and its medieval inheritance, and a visual approach to early modern printing that frequently involves pictorial elements such as printers' flowers, decorative borders, decorated initials, even varieties of type;[34] (2) a reading practice engendered in Renaissance Latin reading pedagogy that relentlessly cycles vowels through consonantal combinations and isolates phonemes from word contexts; (3) sixteenth-century inquiries into, and experimentation with, vernacular English as a literary language in all forms of literary expression; and (4) the influence of vernacular oralities in the playhouse and the mixed oral and written transmission of poetry, along with the lack of standardized orthography and other writing and printing practices (for example, abbreviations or the insertion of letters to protect serifs on type). Early modern writing itself was a highly self-conscious visual and material practice, exploratory of and interactive with both its physical material supports and its alphabetic ones. In a book dedicated to writing on a variety of materials from walls to pots to bodies, Juliet Fleming asserts that "paper was not necessarily the most obvious, or suitable, medium for writing in early modern England" (*Graffiti* 10). Wherever and however encountered, playtexts, poetry, and often other kinds of early modern texts encourage readers to read aurally, visually and for multiple meanings.

Poet John Powell Ward identifies such typographical and orthographical wordplay as a feature available to, and characteristic of, alphabetical languages due to the limited number of letters available for word making. He describes a "microscopic but perpetual stress in all our reading," modulated by what he calls the centripetal and centrifugal effects of spelling with only 24 letters (Ward 157). The contemporary poet must draw out the resonances, recognize and render meaningful the words within words. Ward suggests the potential psychological effects of daily reading's "nano-experiences" (156)—words within words, anagrams, near-misses like **cover** and **cower**—that must color our comprehension of contemporary texts. But the average early modern English readers had a readier eie and eare for such play. Cover might have been rendered covver, couer, or couuer, categorizing such words not as near-misses but as part of the same semantic grouping. The period's orthography and typography tend to foreground the materiality of words saturated with latent connectivity.

Scholars who take aim at literary interpretation through book history are continually confronted with the challenge of relating form to content as they grapple with what Jerome McGann has called the critical separation of the linguistic code from the bibliographic one (56). Without such multiple motivating factors as plot, context, rhyme, metrical stress, and repetition, the play of typography must register as visual background noise. In another era, this chapter might have taken a psychological approach, like Willbern's "Shakespeare's Nothing." But it is important to ground this inquiry in the Q1 text as a visual object engaging readers materially in its unique poetic resonances. The reading I offer here can certainly be performed on Q2 or F1 (or most early modern literary texts) with different, likely interesting, results. The First Folio, in fact, actively encourages a visual approach to the text in its prefatory materials. On its first printed page, Ben Jonson's verse "To the Reader" playfully places the visuals of image reproductive technology—copperplate engraving—on a spectrum with printed text as it encourages readers to look on the book—using ellipsis to highlight that readers engage in the same activity (looking on) with both pictures and books. Folio editors John Heminge and Henry Condell's prefatory "To the Great Variety of Readers" bills the book as available to anyone who can see letters: "From the moſt able, to him that can but ſpell." Looking irresistibly back on Q1, we can note that its title page and the first page both pair image with text, as is common printed texts of the period (see Figure 9.5). My choice to read Q1 visually rests in a desire to recoup some of its poetics for literary study by reading its texture as visually and acoustically effectual in generating its meanings.

Such textual performances of the play tend to nuance and enhance rather than radically revise our understanding of Q1. We see ideas clustering together through a potent mix of orthographic and acoustic equivalencies, or particular thematic strands highlighted through page layout and font. With the "to be or not to be" soliloquy, orthography renders visible the verbally suppressed first person. It is time to let typography and orthography speak, and update our critical practices by acknowledging the visual semantics of the early modern playtext interface.

Notes

1 Drucker describes interface as "a zone of affordances organized to support and provoke behaviors probabilistically" (157–8).

2 Originally given as a lecture, "Printing Should Be Invisible," in 1930, Warde's statement is best known though its inclusion as "The Crystal Goblet, or Printing Should Be Invisible" in *The Crystal Goblet: Sixteen Essays on Typography*. Not long before, Russian futurists, such as poet Velimir Khlebnikov, bemoaned the standardization of print and asserted that authors, or even better, artists, ought to hand-write, design, and publish authors' works so as to graphically capture the spirit within them, "The Letter As Such" ["Bukva kak takovaia"] (original publication, 1913). In contrast to "invisible printing," racial and ethnic minority-authored works are frequently subjected to what Giampietro calls "stereo-typography" through the regular assignation of particular, often histocially negatively-valenced, type-faces (Giampetro, n.p.).

3 Two notable exceptions are Masten's recent *Queer Philologies* and my *Playful Letters*.

4 As contemporary editions of the plays do not capture the play of early modern typography, I provide only signatures as citations. Facsimiles of the entire Shakespearean corpus are freely available online through *Internet Shakespeare Editions*, although I am mindful that variants always exist among single early modern editions.

5 For an overview of these histories and editorial responses, see Thompson and Taylor, "Introduction" and "Appendix 2." Indicative of how entrenched the bibliographic approach is, the 2017 Norton Shakespeare's online bibliography for Q1 includes only works treating genesis theories or editing issues.

6 Lesser and Stallybrass read the commonplace markers in the text as indicative of the intended literary reception of Q1. Since then, scholarship has begun to step away from bibliographic questions but still retains an interest in book historical ones. See also Bourus, *Young Shakespeare's Young Hamlet*, and Lesser, *Hamlet After Q1*, Character studies include Williams, "Enter Ofelia Playing on a Lute," and Melnikoff, "Nicholas Ling's Republican *Hamlet* (1603)."

7 Bourus reads this line as Q2 announcing its "freshness" (26).

8 Line four in the Drayton sonnet (reproduced in Figure 9.6) typographically articulates the letter, but as vv.

9 In its dual role as power and pour, powre is also a crux from the First Folio's *Anthony and Cleopatra.*

> And hauing lost her breath, ſhe ſpoke, and panted,
> That ſhe did make deʃect, perʃection,
> And breathleſſe powre breath forth
>
> (F1, p347, x4r; TLN 946–8)

Some editors have glossed the line as "And, breathless, pour breath forth" (Wilders, *Anthony and Cleopatra* 141; likewise Wells and Taylor, *Oxford Shakespeare* 1011). Eighteenth-century editor Edward Capell and his inheritors have unraveled it as something like "And, breathless, breathe forth power";

Capell calls it "power of charming" which "Cleopatra breath'd forth even by being breathless" (Capell Q1r). Others have offered "And breathe forth breathless power" (Blake, n. to 2.3.2, p.31).). Thanks to an anonymous reviewer who reminded me of this controversy.

10 On the variable pronunciation of "pour," see E.J. Dobson 2.688–9. David Crystal's entries for "power" and "pour" match the phonetics of these words in his *The Oxford Dictionary of Original Shakespearean Pronunciation.*

11 Taking account of spelling, orthoepists' writing, and rhyme and homophone lists among other sources, Dobson cites many examples in which the contemporary-spelled doe, do, dow, dough, or doo might be rhymed with our contemporary to, tow, two, toe, go, goo, shoe, who, woo (1,18, 418, and 433–4; 2.514–15). We typically pronounce due similarly with a "diu" sound, but one grammarian notes that ado and adieu are "near-alike" (ibid. 2.707).

12 The generational gap renders Crystal's excellent study of limited use for present purposes since his conclusions depend on "spellings, rhymes, puns, and observations by contemporary writers." Generally he considers "printer's rhymes" or "eye rhymes" to be infrequent, although he admits these exist and he comments that more research needs to focus on slant rhymes (Crystal xx, xxiii).

13 Note the king is unnamed in Q1.

14 Corambis immediately continues the connection between **duetie** and **doe** on the top of this same page's verso, and sig. E3v contains an exchange between Hamlet ("And **doe** you heare ſirs"?) and Gilderstone ("Our loue and **duetie** is at your commaund").

15 While **due** and **do** are not pronounced similarly according to Crystal's study of First Folio pronunciation, **adue** (which does not appear there) links the two.

16 While **dupt** may be part of this group, it seems unlikely. Crystal notes that it would have been pronounced differently in the First Folio.

17 Of special relevance here is McLeod, "Spellbound."

18 Resonances of this appear in Polonius's Q2 and F scheme to "looſe" his daughter on Hamlet. In Q1, this language applies to Hamlet as the king plots his death on the same page's recto and verso: his nephew "shall **aboorde** to night" (G4[r]) where he will "**looſe** his head" (G4[v]) at the King of England's hands.

19 Q2 prints "fonde deedes." F1 matches with Q1. This closing couplet about eies before Leartes and Ofelia's leave-taking is visually striking, with "till" and "sit" as partial anagrams of "still" and the base word ill as a common denominator.

20 Q2 and F1 emphasize the connection through capitalization only, with "state of Denmark" and "State of Denmark," respectively.

21 Q2 and F1 both print the combined "afternoone" (Q2, D3l; F1, p258, Oo1[v]).

22 D1[r] also toys with the "I" sound in its hunting calls ("Ill, lo, lo, ho ho") near the start of this stichomythic call and response.

23 On the I/eye dynamic, see Fineman.

24 I have used a slash to indicate a line break in the prose. Compare Q2's

> What is he whoſe grieſe
> Beares ſuch an empheſis, whoſe phraſe of ſorrow
> Coniures the wandring ſtarres, and makes them ſtand
> Like wonder wounded hearers: this is I.

Hamlet the Dane (M4[v])

25 See Higgins, *Pattern Poetry*. Of note in the late sixteenth century are Thomas Watson, *Hekatompathia* (London, 1582; STC: 25118a) and King James I, *The essayes of a prentise, in the divine art of poesie* (Edinburgh, 1585; STC: 14374).

26 Statistical computational analysis has recently challenged the actual archaism of Spenser's orthography, but that work does not address his strategic deployment of existing orthographic fluidity to emphatic effects—the unique *Faerie* in *The Faerie Queene* (London, 1590; STC: 23081) signals Spenser's commitments to this practice. See Basu; Woodcock; Eicholz 114.

27 At least some inheritors of Spenser's literary sensibilities vigorously engaged in exploring text-as-image, evidenced in the pattern and acrostic poetry of the Spenserian poets William Browne of Tavistock, William Drummond of Hawthornden, and George Wither. The deeper we move into the seventeenth century, the easier it is to locate other poets like George Herbert with clear commitments to the poem's image on the page.

28 Bourus emphasizes that Ling was Drayton's preferred publisher (18, 20). John Trundle also published the play, and he would go on to a larger investment in publishing commercial theater plays (23).

29 Ling also published the third edition of Ben Jonson's *Every Man Out of His Humour* in the same year as Q1. Perhaps Jonson's investment in the look of his plays (especially the use of tobacco smoke "as parenthesis") influenced Ling's work on Q1. See Helen Ostovich's note to 3.3.73, p. 10 in her edition.
30 I have retained Vendler's modernization of the typography here and in all subsequent modern critical quotations.
31 Masten insists that relational knowledge is importantly preserved in early modern orthography in *Queer Philologies*. For a pan-European view of how early moderns reimagined alphabetic letters, see my *Playful Letters*.
32 The full line reads "A bliſſe in proof and proud and very wo." (Most editors emend the second and to a.) For his take on how early modern readers saw orthography, see Shakespeare *Sonnets* vii–viii.
33 STC: 20519.
34 See Fleming, "Flower."

References

Basu, Anupam. "Spenser's Spell: Linguistic Change and Historical Stylometrics." 3 March 2016, guest lecture, Northeastern University, Boston.

Blake, Norman. *A Grammar of Shakespeare's Language*. Palgrave, 2002.

Boeckeler, Erika. *Playful Letters: A Study of Early Modern Alphabetics*. U of Iowa P, 2017.

Bourne, Claire M.L. *Typographies of Performance in Early Modern England*. Oxford UP, 2020.

Bourus, T. *Young Shakespeare's Young Hamlet: Print, Piracy, and Performance*. Palgrave Macmillan, 2014.

Capell, Edward. *Notes and various readings to Shakespeare, part the first; containing, All's well that ends well, Antony and Cleopatra, As you like it, Comedy of Errors, Coriolanus, Cymbeline, Hamlet, 1 Henry IV, 2 Henry IV*. London, 1774.

Crystal, David. *The Oxford Dictionary of Original Shakespearean Pronunciation*. Oxford UP, 2016.

de Grazia, Margreta. "Homonyms Before and After Lexical Standardization." *Deutsche Shakespeare-Gesellschaft West: Jahrbuch*, 1990, pp. 143–156.

de Grazia, Margreta. and Peter Stallybrass. "The Materiality of the Shakespearean Text." *Shakespeare Quarterly*, vol. 44, no. 3, 1993, pp. 255–283. doi:10.2307/2871419.

Dobson, Eric John. *English Pronunciation 1500–1700*. 1st ed., Oxford UP, 1968.

Drucker, Johanna. *Graphesis: Visual Forms of Knowledge Production*. Harvard UP, 2014.

Eicholz, Jeffrey Paul. "Play in the Poetry of Edmund Spenser." PhD dissertation, Yale University, 1970.

Fineman, Joel. *Shakespeare's Perjured Eye: The Invention of Poetic Subjectivity in the Sonnets*. University of California P, 1986.

Fleming, Juliet. *Graffiti and the Writing Arts of Early Modern England*. Reaktion, 2001.

Fleming, Juliet. "How Not to Look at a Printed Flower." *Journal of Medieval and Early Modern Studies*, vol. 38, no. 2, 2008, pp. 345–371. doi:10.1215/10829636-2007-029.

Giampietro, Rob. "New Blackface: Neuland and Lithos as Stereotypography." *Letterspace*, Type Directors Club, 2004, n.p.

Higgins, Dick. *Pattern Poetry: Guide to an Unknown Literature*. State U of New York P, 1987.

Hookway, Branden. *Interface*. MIT Press, 2014.

Hope, Jonathan. *Shakespeare and Language: Reason, Eloquence and Artifice in the Renaissance*. Methuen, 2010. doi:10.1017/CBO9780511617379.

Irace, Kathleen. "Introduction." *The First Quarto of Hamlet*, by William Shakespeare, edited by Kathleen Irace, Cambridge UP, 1998, pp. 1–27.

Jonson, Ben. *Every Man Out of His Humour*. Edited by Helen Ostovich, Manchester UP, 2001.

Lesser, Zachary. *Hamlet After Q1: An Uncanny History of the Shakespearean Text*. U of Pennsylvania P, 2016.

Lesser, Zachary, and Peter Stallybrass. "The First Literary *Hamlet* and the Commonplacing of Professional Plays." *Shakespeare Quarterly*, vol. 59, no. 4, 2008, pp. 371–420. doi:10.1353/shq.0.0040.

Masten, Jeffrey. *Queer Philologies: Sex, Language and Affect in Shakespeare's Time*. U of Pennsylannia P, 2016.

McGann, Jerome J. *The Textual Condition*. Princeton UP, 1991.

McKenzie, D. F. *Bibliography and the Sociology of Texts*. Cambridge UP, 2004.

McLeod, Randall. "Spellbound: Typography and the Concept of Old-Spelling Editions." *Renaissance and Reformation / Renaissance et Réforme*, vol. 3, no. 1, 1979, pp. 50–65. Available at: http://www.jstor.org/stable/43444248.

Melnikoff, Kirk. "Nicholas Ling's Republican Hamlet (1603)." *Shakespeare's Stationers: Studies in Cultural Bibliography*, edited by Marta Straznicky, U of Philadelphia P, 2013, pp. 95–111.

Puttenham, George. *The Arte of English Poesy*. London, 1589.

Shakespeare, William. *Hamlet*, London, 1603.
Shakespeare, William. *Hamlet*, London, 1605.
Shakespeare, William. *Mr. William Shakespeares Comedies, Histories, & Tragedies*. London, 1623.
Shakespeare, William. *Shakespeare's Sonnets*. Edited by Stephen Booth, Yale UP, 1978.
Shakespeare, William. *The Oxford Shakespeare: The Complete Works*. Edited by Stanley Wells and Gary Taylor, Oxford UP, 1988.
Shakespeare, William. *Anthony and Cleopatra by William Shakespeare* (Arden Shakespeare: Third Series). Edited by John Wilders, Bloomsbury, 2006.
Shell, Marc. "The Wether and The Ewe: Verbal Usury in *the Merchant of Venice*." *The Kenyon Review*, vol. 1, no. 4, 1979, pp. 65–92.
Thompson, Ann, and Neil Taylor. "Introduction." *Hamlet* (Arden Shakespeare: Third Series). Edited by Ann Thompson and Neil Taylor, Bloomsbury, 2006, pp. 1–137.
Thompson, Ann, and Neil Taylor. "Appendix 2." *Hamlet* (Arden Shakespeare: Third Series). Edited by Ann Thompson and Neil Taylor, Bloomsbury, 2006, pp. 474–532.
Vendler, Helen. *The Art of Shakespeare's Sonnets*. Harvard UP, 1997.
Ward, John Powell. *The Spell of the Song: Letters, Meaning, and English Poetry*. Fairleigh Dickinson UP, 2004.
Warde, Beatrice. "The Crystal Goblet, or Printing Should Be Invisible." *The Crystal Goblet: Sixteen Essays on Typography*, by Beatrice Warde, Sylvan Press, 1955, pp. 11–18.
Willbern, David. "Shakespeare's Nothing." *Representing Shakespeare: New Psychoanalytic Essays*, edited by Murray M. Schwartz and Kahn Coppélia, Johns Hopkins UP, 1980, pp. 244–263.
Williams, Deanne. "Enter Ofelia Playing on a Lute." *The Afterlife of Ophelia*, edited by Kaara Peterson, Palgrave Macmillan, 2012, pp. 119–136. doi:10.1057/9781137016461_8.
Woodcock, Matthew. "The First Sightings of Spenser's Faeries." *Notes and Queries*, vol. 50, no. 4, 2003, pp. 390–391. doi:10.1093/nq/500390.

10

DESIRING BODIES, DIVINE VIOLENCE AND TYPOGRAPHIC INTERFACES IN *CHAMP FLEURY* AND *VENUS AND ADONIS*

Simon Ryle

Throughout the sixteenth century, techniques of the body and the body's disciplinary control incorporate and are circulated by typographic print technologies. With the mass mediation of print, alphabetic letters and bodies intersect and form odd new compromises, couplings, pedagogies, and prostheses that reach to the heart of early modern culture. An explosion in the publication of English spelling reforms, dictionaries, alvearies and abecedaries, pedagogical treatises, abseys, primers, and hornbooks in the second half of the sixteenth century attests to a growing awareness of the material, alphabetic form of language in the era of print, and a desire to describe and reform the relation of language to its inscription—frequently linking questions of the alphabetic and the bodily in new ways. One of the most creative and influential examples is Geofroy Tory's *Champ Fleury* (1927 [1529]). Locating a letteral poetics of divine coercion common to Tory and Shakespeare's *Venus and Adonis* (1594), this chapter explores links between the proliferation of typographic interfaces and newly emergent subjectivities of the print era.

Writing on the increased prominence of calligramic forms in early modern poetics, such as Herbert's shaped verses, Anne-Marie Miller-Blaise argues that the era suffers a "poetic crisis of *mimesis*" and resolves this crisis "through a projection of the word into a space of visuality, which cannot be reabsorbed entirely by poetic textuality." As Lucian Febvre and Henri-Jean Martin describe, the availability of cheap books greatly increased general literacy levels across the sixteenth century, altering the process of mediation through media technological changes and subsequent forms taken by mass culture (216–22, 248–332). For D.F. McKenzie, the work of the writer fundamentally changes in the era of typographic print, which works upon "every detail of his works" (222). For Miller-Blaise, these social and aesthetic shifts mean that the era's poetics "can be understood as a *prolepsis* of sorts to a more recent shift towards what could be called a poetry of the 'impress'"—a strategy that might be read as an early example of the self-conscious poetics that Steven Connor terms "technography," or what, with reference to digital media, Katherine Hayles terms the "technotext." Connor describes "technography" as "any writing about any technology that implicates or is attuned to the technological condition of its own writing" (18). For Hayles, a "technotext" is a literary work that "interrogates the inscription technology that produces it ... it mobilizes reflexive

DOI: 10.4324/9780367821722-14

loops between its imaginary world and the material apparatus embodying that creation as a physical presence" (2002, 25).

Interfaces are central to the relation of early modern technography and its readers. Interfaces, as Benjamin Bratton observes, "locate competing master dogmas … about what the world does … what it is about" (246). This chapter describes a self-consciously technographic poetics of alphabetic interfaces in Tory and Shakespeare. Each in diverse ways uses the impossible relation of god and mortal in Ovid's *Metamorphoses* to explore their own recapitulation of the theological "dogmas" of typography. In early sixteenth-century Paris and late sixteenth-century London, respectively, both Tory and Shakespeare innovate a poetics of the material letter in order to chart the various subjective shifts associated with the development and increasing circulation of print typography.

Vital to the new dogmas that are encouraged and circulated by print are a reconceived conceptualization of faces, faciality, and the interface. This is in part due to the technotext's self-consciousness concerning mediation in times of technological change. One might consider the changing prominence of faciality in translations of Genesis 1.1–2 across the sixteenth century (all cited in Nicolson 192–4):

> In the beginnyng God created heauen and earth. The erth was voyde and emptye, and darcknesse was vpon the depe, & the spirite of God moued upon the water.
>
> *(Tyndale, 1534)*

> In the beginning God created the heauen and the earth. And the earth was without form and void, and darknesse was upon the deep, and the Spirit of God mooued vpon the face of the waters.
>
> *(Geneva Bible, 1560)*

> In the beginning God created the Heauen, and the Earth. And the earth was without forme, and voyd, and darknesse was vpon the face of the deepe: and the Spirit of God mooued vpon the face of the waters.
>
> *(King James Bible, 1611)*

Contrasting the increasing prominence of surface contact with the divine in these passages, Lucy Razzall links the growing theological gravity associated with faciality to the proliferating frontispieces of early modern books. As she notes, "face to face," is a phrase "which comes up explicitly, no fewer than eleven times, in the King James translation." This tropic concern is seemingly anticipated in *Venus and Adonis*, when the poem narrates the love goddess and mortal locked in embrace: "Incorporate then they seem; face grows to face" (line 561). George Coulter demonstrates how the Hebrew *al-pənê*, which literally means "on the face of," is commonly used in the Old Testament to convey the meaning "on" or "over." The choices of early modern translators regarding Genesis 1:1–2 might seem to increasingly favor literal translation, though elsewhere they retain the simpler sense of "on" (Coulter 2020, 207–8). For this reason, the poetics of faciality invoked in the literal translation might seem particularly to be used in early modern translation of Genesis 1 to describe the interfacing of the divine and worldly—a meeting of irreducible difference such as Tory's golden chain similarly theorizes, and from which Shakespeare's *Venus and Adonis* forges a narrative. Moreover, I would argue, this increasing literality is an effect of print letters. Writing on Lancelot Andrewes's 1611 translation, Nicolson observes divine reflection in the King James's increased emphasis on the face: "The face of the waters carries a subliminal suggestion that the face of God is reflected in them" (Nicolson 2003, 194). However, we might ask of

Nicolson and Razzall whether the increasing godly mystery of faciality in the period is solely, or even principally, due to the mystery of reflection, or the proliferation of frontispieces? Given that the majority of the literate early modern public would likely have spent their reading time perusing pages inside the increasingly available books and pamphlets of the era, might one rather locate the growing emphasis placed on faciality as a technographic registering of the increasing proportion of culture negotiated via the printed page, and subsequent emergent protocols of typography? Such a thesis would ascribe the "ghostly" mystery that Nicolson locates in faciality as arising from the new interface protocols of the period. The King James Bible's emphasis on surfaces of the divine and worldly that touch but do not intermingle in Genesis 1 would, in such an understanding, innovate a poetics of religious mystery in order to acknowledge the increasing significance of the page as interface to faith and self-knowledge.

Certainly, there are reasons to associate changes in theological aesthetics with cultural shifts in the meaning of the interface that emerge with print typography. As Branden Hookway states, the interface describes "a disputed zone, a site of contestation between human beings and machines as much as between the social and the material, the political and the technological" (1). Interfaciality describes the zone of touching or facing whereby two or more distinct entities come into a relation, as well as the channeling of activities in that space of relation "toward a resolution within a common protocol" while also opening "new vistas and capabilities to a now-augmented human sensorium" (4). Enabling the prosthetic enhancement of human sensory experience and fitting this enhancement to the demands of specific technological media protocols, the interface is simultaneously proximate to and at the heart of human becoming. This means we might expect shifts in information technology or media, such as the surge in printed pamphlets, broadside, sermons, tracts, and books in mid-late 1590s London to manifest changing cultural and individual forms. Elizabeth Eisenstein has detailed ways that the Gutenberg printing technology caused a revolution in European thought and knowledge by, amongst other effects, making modern scientific method possible, facilitating the Protestant Reformation, and guiding the path taken by modern capitalism. Significant changes in subjectivity and consciousness are also linked to effects of print as interface. "By removing words from the world of sound where they had first had their origin in active human interchange and relegating them definitively to visual surface," Walter Ong writes, "print encouraged human beings to think of their own interior conscious and unconscious resources as more and more thing-like" (129). Though Ong does not reference the concept of the interface, nevertheless his emphasis on surface intuits the "resolution with common protocol" that is internalized by the human sensorium in the era of print. For Eisenstein and Ong, the introspective melancholy of a figure such as Hamlet, and the individuated relationship with the God of Protestantism likewise ought to be conceived as epiphenomenal consequences of shifts in early modern interface protocols that arise with the massive increase in readers and printed pages of the era.

The interface is important because it is a place of negotiation—vital to understanding the dialectic of human agency and media determination always at play in the mass circulation of technology and associated technical protocols. For Benjamin Bratton, the desire to understand and negotiate the technicity is universal: "we are all probing our interfacial condition" (224). This chapter positions poetics as centrally involved in this negotiation. Connor's claim that "all literary writing is in fact technographic" suggests that the literary is continually alert to the protocols of mediation. For Vilém Flusser, this means poetics, especially after the printing press, which Flusser sees as "a precursor to the industrial revolution" (113), is continually a struggle for human agency against language's interfacial intersubjectivity:

> Language is apparently a medium for intersubjective communication, and yet the poet realises himself during the struggle against the deeply rooted rules and structures of language. No longer does he speak through language, but against it. He objectifies its intersubjectivity.
>
> *(108)*

Though Flusser's "intersubjective" does not name the interface, like Ong, it intuits the interfaciality of the "industrial" production of print communication. Rather than acquiescing to the interfacial domination of the human, poetics for Flusser is always minimally an act of resistance that pits itself stylistically against the compulsions of the linguistic interface's machinic protocols. Exploring the divine compulsions of typography in *Champ Fleury* and *Venus and Adonis*, this chapter locates a poetics of the material letter that charts and contests the newly emergent subjectivities of the print era.

1 Golden chains and fields of flowers

In the celebrated and influential early work of typographic design, *Champ Fleury* (1927 [1529]), Geofroy Tory uses Homer's tale of Zeus's golden chain to describe the divine and mortal powers drawn together in the interface of letters. From Book VIII of the *Iliad*, the golden chain is a classical depiction of Zeus's power, and the device by which he is able to constrain all the other gods to move at his will. Zeus, in Homer's telling, offers to challenge any god or mortal in a trial of strength: "I will drag you all hither and thither, by land and sea and destroy you utterly. And, far more, with this chain of gold I could draw the whole of the earth & sea to the topmost summit of Olympus" (cited in Tory 64). This classical golden chain becomes for Tory an image of the interface. As Bratton has it, "The interface could be a line that links two things together, or a line that cleaves them apart" (220); "Without coercing us the interface cannot properly interface anything to us" (221). As we will see, in various early accounts of the typographic interface, this coercive line both cleaves and binds the mortal in an embrace with divine power. The golden chain also describes the relation exerted in early modern typographic interfaces—and Bratton similarly notes the tendency for "Interfacial regimes [to] focus all mediation onto and into key switch points" (230). Tory cites both Homer and Macrobius, and in his Renaissance gloss the golden chain signifies how "every inspiration, spiritual and corporeal, that we can know here below, proceeds from the sovereign Creator" (64). However, rather than piety, Tory wants this image of an all-powerful Creator to inform his notion of letters in the age of print.

A printer and type designer by trade, Tory is always materially aware. In one set of images, the book includes backwards and reverse white-on-black images to archive and call attention to the printing practices that facilitate texts (Boeckeler 48). This is Tory's way of visualizing the series of mirroring reversals of interfaces that the mechanics of typography require of the letter. As Tory describes:

> Before the printed letter is complete it is made twice reversed & twice right. It is reversed the first time in the steel punches, in which the letter is to the left; the matrices have the letter to the right; the letter cast of metal is, like the said punches, reversed. And lastly, on the printed page, the letter appears in the right position.
>
> *(85)*

One might read the various processes here in Heideggerian terms, as disrupting the organic flow of writing from the scribal hand to the page. One of the epiphenomenal effects of the print shop, as described in the white-on-black images by which Tory figures the multiple mirror reversals that typography requires of letters, was a newly disembodied relation with the letter form. Yet alongside the disembodiment that typography brings to the letter, there is also a fascination and delight at the layering of the series of interfacial processes that materially enable typography, and which print memorializes and archives upon the page.

For Tory, typography is an opportunity to regularize letter forms, and print is the fulcrum of a creatively constituted genealogy and chain link between France and classical Greece. For Tory, the letters I and O describe the basic forms and spaces allotted to the Greek letters and encode the proportions to which the others should conform. The letter I describes the ideal height of letters, the proportion of width to height of the stroke, and serves as a model for the straight strokes that form the stems of many letters, the ratio Tory terms "the unit" (47). The letter O, on the other hand, describes the ideal width of letters, their symmetry and proportions, as well as the manner of forming the curved strokes and bowls of letter forms. In a series of memorable images, Tory overlays letters upon faces and bodies in Vitruvian man postures in order to put forward the claim that alphabetic letters derive from human forms, a claim that perhaps originates with Plato's *Cratylus*. The claim of 1:9 as the ideal ratio for the letter, based on the proportions of a well-made human body, had been made a decade earlier in Galeotus Martius or Galeotto Marzio's *De homine libri duo* (Basel, Froben, 1517), and repeated in a text that Tory may have known, Verini's *Luminario* of 1527 (Bowen 22).

Yet Tory is also playful in his illustration of "the unit," showing how letter forms specifically impose upon the human frame, making coercive demands upon the corporeal. As Erika Boeckeler has it:

> In exposing how the letters as pieces of language materially invade the senses, *Champ Fleury* explains in part how letters enter the world of things, how the mind is transformed by and expresses itself through letters, and how the ABCs act upon their literature subjects.
>
> *(38)*

Quite unlike the languid pose of Leonardo's Vitruvian man, the body of Tory's human form is stretched to maximum capacity upon the frame of the letter O, like a body tied to a breaking wheel. Tory perhaps originates the association of O and torture so vividly described in Shakespeare's *King Lear*, in Lear's declaration that he is "bound / Upon a wheel of fire" (4.7)—and it is also the case that Tory, in depicting the seat of Apollo, also depicts an "O" of fire. As Conley describes, "Tory's tortured human images" contain within them "the concern that language controls us" (49).

Another example is the censorship of human sex exercised by the letter A. The letter A is a significant letter for Tory, after I and O perhaps the most important. Concerning his serif designs, Tory writes, "A has its legs thickened and furnished with feet – just as a man has his legs and feet for walking and passing on ... we must pass on to B&C, and all the other letters." Letter A is a firm base and a peripatetic passage to the rest of the alphabet, but A also exercises constraint and closure:

> This letter A, because it is closed above and shaped like a pyramid, requires its said transverse stroke to be lower that the central line. Thus this cross-stroke covers the man's organ of generation, to signify that Modesty and Chastity are required.
>
> *(48)*

Layering, so fertile and generative in other instances, is also here a manner of blocking flow. This dialectic between the generative and constrictive capacity of layering, which one might associate with the contested zone of the interface, goes to the heart of many of Tory's ideas. For example, if the transverse stroke of the A facilitates "Chastity" by obscuring the place of genitalia, it is also the case that in Tory's images of I mapped onto the human frame, the foundational letter covers the whole bodily trunk. If covering is a censoring, as in the case of A, in Tory's image of I (which is the foundation of all letters), almost the whole being of man is blocked from view.

As Tory emphasizes, "to triumph in letters one must be moderate." This claim is figured in an image of a letter O, its circular form surrounded by leaping flames of fire, which forms a sun and a throne on which Apollo, the god of learning and moderation is seated. As exemplars of the ill-disciplined aspects of humanity, Venus, Bacchus and Ceres are led captive by Apollo's golden procession, keeping their intemperance in check by his golden strictures, just as the A of the letter's crossbar blocks human sexuality. Yet if the letteral interface blocks bodily desire and self-expression, in other accounts it also invokes desires of its own. The generative capacity of the alphabet is a feature of early typographic designs, perhaps most vividly pictorialized in Peter Flötner's *Menschenalphabet* ("Human Alphabet") (1534). A German designer, sculptor, and printmaker from Thurgau, Germany, Flötner's *Menschenalphabet* uses naked human bodies to depict the forms of the letters. Both apparently developing, but also significantly differing from Tory's conviction that the letters derive from human forms, Flötner models bodies in the form of letters. The alphabet presses upon Flötner's bodies, contorting them into the odd shapes of lettered humans, rather as Tory's golden chain stretches out his Vitruvius man on an O. But it is also the case that Flötner locates erotic energy in the lettered human—in his A, for example, two lovers press together, the sexual convergence of their bodies forming the two converging upstrokes of the capital A. Unlike Tory, the mutually mirroring hands of Flötner's joined lovers form the A's transversal bar by reaching across to the other's genitalia so that, rather than the letter censoring and intervening in human anatomy to enforce chastity as in Tory's image, it is the human replication of alphabetic forms in Flötner's A that indicates sexual union. Refuting Cratylist claims to originary bodily forms, Tory's constrictive golden chain has become an erotic impulsion.

Like the coercing and cleaving associated with interfaces by recent theorists, for the early printers the typographic interface is a place of both coercion and human desire; a site of divinely enforced chastity and sexual convergence; the loss of self-determination and potential site of becoming. At least in comedy, there is classical precedent for thinking of letters as choking constraints to human bodies. In Plautus's *Aulularia*, an old servant, Staphyla, laments her inability to keep the sexual liaisons of her mistress a secret with the exclamation: "There's nothing better for me to do, as I see, than tie a rope round my neck and dangle myself out into one long capital I" (cited in Tory 121). To hang herself is to render her body a long letter, a capital "I" stretched out from the noose to the toes. The letter that Staphyla imagines would be the transformation of herself into writing in the practice of self-elimination, and a silencing of scandalous discourse concerning eroticism with death. The claim is further diagrammed in Tory's depictions of the letter Y, in which Tory positions the branches of the letter as encoding a moral choice, such as the choice of Hercules at the crossroads. Tory perhaps borrowed from the depiction of Y in Jacob Locher's 1497 Latin translation of Sebastian Brant's *Narrenschiff*, which used a similar theme in emblematic form (Bowen 17). In one image of Y, a human figure struggles up the right branch towards a throne, whereas from the left branch a figure topples down towards hell fires. Tory's Y dramatizes the letter as both interface and site of potential, a place where agency can be enacted, and a control center where punishments are bestowed. Figuring the site of an agency not always clearly present in Tory's letters, the Y as another image of the golden chain indicates the typically Erasmine arrangement of Tory's arguments, which proceed by the copious layering of multiple positions.

Tory dwells at some length on the story of Hyacinth from Book X of Ovid's *Metamorphoses*. Within a humanist *copia* that takes Ovid's metamorphic world as its source of authority, Tory overlays the two alternative origin-of-letters tales. In Ovid's telling of the Hyacinth myth, one day while Apollo is throwing a discus, Hyacinth, the boy lover or admirer of the god, runs forward to retrieve the projectile. However, tragically, the god's discus bounces from the ground to strike his mortal lover in the forehead. The tale offers the typical Ovidian pattern of the failure and death that arise in the amorous meeting of gods and mortals, situating the metamorphic power of Apollo's grief, and the cruel fate that is memorialized and made good in the transformation of the mortal into a flower. As Apollo decrees:

> A new flower you shall be with letters marked
> To imitate my sobs, and time shall come
>
> ...
>
> And lo! the flowing blood that stained the grass
> Was blood no longer; and a flower rose
>
> ...
>
> Apollo (who had wrought the work of grace)
> Inscribed upon the flower his lament,
> AI AI, AI AI, and still the petals show
> The letters written there in words of woe.
> *(*Metamorphoses *X, 202–16)*

The transformation of Hyacinth into a flower offers a typical Ovidian motif of metamorphosis. In writing onto the body of this metamorphosis of Hyacinth, Apollo's writing of his grief emphasizes how the natural world memorializes and archives mourning in Ovid's tales. The field of flowers is written with blood—memorial and interface to the impossible meeting of god and mortal.

The Hyacinth tale also features in Tory's Preface, where he describes an ancient method of Lacadaemonian textual encoding, which involved writing on parchments scrolled around a truncheon:

> they wrote upon their parchment along and around their said truncheon in such wise that the greater part of the letters was a third or half or a very little way over either edge and place of jointure of said parchment; then they unrolled it and sent it to their said Prince, who, as soon as he received it, placed it upon his truncheon, and thereupon, because the truncheons were the same size, all the letters fitted together exactly.
>
> *(vii)*

This ingenuity for Tory makes metonymic and metaphoric reference to both the mythic secrecy of early texts, whose meanings were swathed in uncertainty, and the need for hermeneutic unscrolling (which *Champ Fleury* delights in)—as well as the material difficulty of obtaining and reading texts prior to the era of print. Yet if he borrows from the hermetic and hermeneutic, Tory also rejects Lacadaemonian textual closure. "Let us put aside these scrolls," Tory writes of his field of flowers, "and write on good open tablets ... to the end that your letters may be seen face to face" (viii). In this introduction to his designs, the elegant formation and spacing of letters are the newly decoded field of flowers as interface facilitated by print, and the openness of Attic lettering indicates a new era of faciality. Placing the secrecy and the singularity of Hyacinth's traumatic encounter under erasure, Tory bears witness to a new era in which multiplicity flowers, circulated by the mass dissemination of the printed page.

These constricting, connecting, and hierarchical powers of the letter are perhaps why Tory dwells on origin myths of the alphabet, and why he writes of Homer's golden chain:

> Let us, then, imagine and believe that we see this gold chain hanging down from heaven even to our feet, and this chain is of a length and breadth duly proportioned and adaptable to the symmetrical figure of our model I, and we shall perceive that Homer's conceit is to be referred to the inspiration and invention of letters.
>
> *(64)*

With the invention of letters, in Tory's telling, a chain—whose proportions are echoed in the "I" that serves as the basis for all letters—reaches from heaven to bind up the full length of our bodies ("even to our feet"). We are not so much transformed into a long letter in this telling, as Plautus's Staphyla imagines her death by hanging will effect upon her person, but stretched across a contested interfacial zone that reaches between the letter and the heavens.

2 V/A: Sharp and hollow bodies

If the rightly proportioned letter involves a golden typographic chain binding mortals and the divine, Shakespeare's *Venus and Adonis* dramatizes the violence of that coercive interconnection. Coming alongside other indicted or impossible loves from Book X of Ovid's *Metamorphoses* (including Orpheus's love beyond death for Eurydice and Hyacinth's love for the god Apollo), the tale of Venus and Adonis narrates the goddess of love wounded by Cupid's arrow, herself infatuated by the love that she governs. In Ovid's version, the Venus and Adonis tale is framed by Orpheus's story, and itself serves as frame for the narration of other tales of impossible love, so that a series of nested narratives perhaps formally expresses the short-circuiting involution of Love herself in love. Developing Ovid's brief account, for Shakespeare, on the other hand, it is the charged space between Venus and Adonis that is continually emphasized: the contested interface of their relation, wherein "face grows to face" (line 561).

Shakespeare's tragic plots often capture his dramatic and poetic characters in impulses that originate from outside or beyond them. Macbeth is drawn on by a series of portents, just as Tarquin is impelled forward to his crime by each instance of delay that he encounters on his path. With *Venus and Adonis*, Shakespeare remakes the uncannily externalized intimacy of desire's compulsions into the most popular poem from the final decade of the sixteenth century. Undergoing a record 16 re-printings during Shakespeare's lifetime, of editions likely numbering 800–1000 books, *Venus and Adonis* is at the epicenter of the first mass media age in England—the era of the widespread circulation of texts for the first time in history amongst large swathes of the population. Why was this era interested in the coercive impulsion of desire? For Russell Fraser, seemingly intuiting the awareness and resistances of technography, "Poetry menaces the referential role of language as it attenuates the characters of words as designation" (105). In its formal patternings, and its interplay of form and signification, poetry allows its material components to impinge upon the significatory function of language and in so doing opens a space between the desiring body and the interfacial protocols and coercions in which it is caught. As playful expression of this material interface, I want to claim *Venus and Adonis* similarly explores and contests the protocols of the print letter as channeling of desire.

First, one might note how in *Venus and Adonis* the physical forms of the letters of the alphabet are given unusual narrative and characterological prominence—in particular, the letters V and A. Letters "menace" the poem, in Fraser's sense, no longer merely contributing to word construction, but demanding and defining specific character and narrative possibilities due to their own material forms. In the initial impression that Adonis makes upon Venus, she envisions him bright as a sun: from his eye, she states, "darts forth the fire that burneth me" (196). She attempts to use rhetoric to position him as an advance upon her person, that is, to reverse his passive, restrained tendency with words. Replicating the Apollonian sun to be found in Tory's O, in her poetic image, flumes of fire issue from Adonis. But quickly his reticence causes her to revaluate. He is not Apollonian, but rather takes on qualities of the pyramid form of A that begins his name. Her rhetoric cannot simply redefine the letteral protocols at work.

Take the deathly aura of Adonis's dimples. One of the reasons why Adonis is so irresistible to the goddess of love is due to his dimples, in whose hollowed topography she seems to locate a prophetic imaging of his death:

> At this Adonis smiles as in disdain,
> That in each cheek appears a pretty dimple:
> Love made those hollows, if himself were slain,
> He might be buried in a tomb so simple;
> Foreknowing well, if there he came to lie,
> Why, there Love lived and there he could not die.
> *(258–63)*

The dimple and grave as topographic association point to a deathly element in Venus's desire. In his refusal of love, Adonis resists the generative possibilities of sexual encounter. He is deathly, his body a "swallowing grave" in Venus's words because, in an argument traced in many of the early sonnets, his refusal to procreate seems "to bury that posterity / Which by the rights of time thou needs must have" (780–1). If the deathliness of his resistance to desire renders him a "king of graves" (1013) in her later estimation, his coming death foreshadowed and seemingly hastened in his refusal of Venus's love, it is also the case that his refusals are openings for Venus's desire. Venus feels herself sucked into the hollows of his being and his death-to-come. Ultimately it seems that it is the topography of hollowed space that his face and his person, his resistance to her love, and perhaps also the physical imaging of death space in his body, that the goddess of love is unable to resist: "These lovely caves, these round enchanting pits,/ Opened their mouthes to swallow Venus liking" (267–8). The dimples are also caves in which she loses herself, and mouths that swallow Venus whole.

Adonis is a body of hollows, a series of openings that are both anticipations of his death and burial, and an enchantment: dimple, grave, cave, pit, mouth, and also, I claim, the letter A. With the hollow topography that Shakespeare attached to his depiction of Adonis, his absence of desire gives narrative manifestation to the shape of the letter A, just as Tory and Flötner earlier mapped human sexuality upon the letter A. To use the term that Katherine N. Hayles develops to read scriptive evolutions of digital literature, and associated shifts in digital poetics, the hollow A topology of Adonis is a "material metaphor ... a physical object that, through its construction and functioning, acts as a crossroad or a juncture point for the traffic between the physical and the verbal." As a verbal sign, A in the poem also takes on a physical, bodily manifestation. The letter refuses to stay in place, demonstrating the wide-reaching effects of the interface by stepping outside of its allotted role, and expressing the recurrent early modern anxiety concerning the relation of bodies and letters. As we have seen, for Tory, letters, and perhaps particularly the A, likewise take on architectural qualities. A is "shaped like a pyramid," and like the mysterious rebuses of Hieroglyphic writing that fascinate Tory and other Renaissance orthographers, it both impels and repels engagement. As the "gateway" to "all other letters" (Tory 48), A is a portal, and as such its sloping strokes against Tory's gridded plane lead the eye forward in a simulacrum of Alberti's 1435 treatise on the perspectival vanishing point, *Della pictura*. But the A also blocks the eye's forward movement, its "transversal bar" placed across the organ of generation in Tory's Vitruvian letter man expresses its functions as a "censor": "to signify the Modesty and Chastity are required" (48). A is interfacial in the combination of binding coercion and cleaving that it channels.

In an odd parallel that is similarly concerned with letteral interfaces, though originating in a Paris 450 years more recent than Tory's, with his celebrated essay "*Différance*," Jacques Derrida draws a similar matrix of architectural qualities from A. Coining his eponymous neologism to describe the "spacing" of difference and deferral that enables signification to occur, Derrida's *différance* is identical in pronunciation to the existent French lexeme *difference*. The unheard "a" of *différance* for Derrida therefore disrupts conventions of signification, while also exemplifying the spacing of difference on which signification depends. This lends the A what Derrida describes as the "economy of death":

> Now it happens, I would say in effect, that this graphic difference (a instead of e), this marked difference between two apparently vocal notations, between two vowels, remains purely graphic: it is read, or it is written, but it cannot be heard. It cannot be apprehended in speech, and we will see why it also bypasses the order of apprehension in general. It is offered by a mute mark, by a tacit monument, I would even say by a pyramid, thinking not only of the form of the letter when it is printed. as a capital, but also of the text in Hegel's Encyclopedia in which the body of the sign is compared to the Egyptian Pyramid.
>
> *(3–4)*

"A" is a monument to "the death of the tyrant," as Derrida describes, who is dependent upon the hierarchical organization of spacing to sustain power. Reminiscent of Tory's trickster capacity, in which the endless play of the field of flowers seems to revise or call into question the disciplining function of the typographic golden chain, "A" signifies the hierarchical and the deathly basis of power, and also the resistant letteral force that undergirds but also threatens this system of power relations.

Certainly, the bar as a chaining, or blockage, or a binding up of communication and consummation is a recurrent narrative antagonist in *Venus and Adonis*—foreshadowing a similar economy of death. Early on, the poem's narrative voice develops a theory of the dialectical relation of constriction and desire: "An oven that is stopped, or river stayed,/ Burneth more hotly, swelleth with more rage" (331–2). For this reason, the narrator counsels, "lovers say, the heart hath treble wrong,/ When it is barred the aidance of the tongue" (329–30). Paralleling the urging to procreate of the first grouping of sonnets, the narrator theorizes and foregrounds a violent outcome as resulting from Adonis's barred language and desire. Incorporating the common association of the bridle and chastity, Adonis's restrained horse offers another figure of sexual constriction. Spying a female horse, a "breeding jenny," Adonis's "trampling courser/ Breaketh his rein": "The iron bit he crusheth 'tween his teeth,/ Controlling what he was controlled with" (269–70). Envisioning the physical unloosening of constraint provoked by sexual desire, Adonis's horse wrenches itself free from the rein and the bit. For the narrator of the poem, language and control are intertwined, and the restraint of the horse is the cause of its attempts at communication: "Anon he rears upright, curvets, and leaps,/ As who should say 'Lo, thus my strength is tried…'" (280–1). Yet, while Adonis's horse's creaturely vigor can break free from the bar of the letter, and Venus's urges Adonis to recognize the parallel, Adonis cannot feel the same impulsion. Whatever comprises his rein, it is less obviously constraining, but also more deeply entrenched in his own identity.

Why is Venus impelled so irresistibly into the deathly hollow A of Adonis's character and physical features? I think the reason that she cannot resist his grave-like hollows is because they image an inverted topography of her own desire. His blocked desire manifests A, and in her character and impulsions she manifests the narrative representation of V. Adonis's dimples are both apertures and indentures that catch her own formal manifestation. He is constantly on the back foot: "like the froward infant still'd with dandling, / He now obeys, and now no more resisteth" (580–1)—a topographic manifestation of his inwardness, the inverse of Venus's forwardness. Like Hamlet's bookish introspection, or the interiorized spirituality of Protestantism that Eisenstein associates with the new mass reading at once solitary and net-worked across continental Europe, the contestation of the interfacial relation with divinity comes to define Adonis's froward interiority. Moreover, like Cleopatra, Adonis makes hungry where most he satisfies: "that sweet coral mouth, / Whose precious taste her thirsty lips well knew, / Whereon they surfeit, yet complain on drouth" (563–5). And the desire of Venus, defined by its advance, surges forward into this "drouth." As a "glutton," a "vulture," or a "conqueror," she is impelled toward her "prey" (568–72) by these retreating hollows. Her hunger for Adonis is appetite configured as angular attack, a violence that stabs and pokes its prey, and whose formal implementation echoes the point of her V. This is further seen in the way Shakespeare's poetics positions her as an eagle:

> Even as an empty eagle, sharp by fast,
> Tires with her beak on feathers, flesh and bone,
> Shaking her wings, devouring all in haste,
> Till either gorge be stuff'd or prey be gone;
> Even so she kissed his brow, his cheek, his chin,
> And where she ends she doth anew begin.
>
> *(55–60)*

Her kisses are an assault, comparable to the pointed "beak" of an eagle "sharp" with hunger and devouring its prey. In the strictly formalist sense of the letter shapes, Venus's attraction is both irresistible and unconsummated because it involves the alignment and convergence of her sharp-beaked V with the cave/mouth of his A: the forward hunger is impelled by the one shape finding its home and inverse proportions in the other. Yet, vitally, this symmetry and coming together are hindered by the transversal bar that, in line with Tory's "Chastity," rejects and blocks the consummation of her desire. Her desire might thus be diagrammed: >>, the impulsion of the V shape toward the similar pyramidal external form of the A, and his resistance or absence of desire: > I>, the transversal bar blocking both his desire and the consummation of Venus's love. As in Tory's image of Apollo, the unrestrained desire of Venus is constrained by the letter. The incompatibility of their dialogues and impulsions echoes the differential interfacial protocols by which letter forms inscribe the narrativization of their desire. As a triangular form that seeks to insert itself into a similar triangle, the V of Venus presses in and upon Adonis's A seeming to exemplify the proleptic "poetics of impress" that Miller-Blaise associates with typographic interface: "he with her plenty pressed" (line 562). But as with Tory's golden chain as a figure for the letters that hold humans in their thrall, the chastely resistant transversal bar of Adonis's A rejects all of her attempts at sexual/ typographic alignment. Reworking the impossible love of Ovid's book X, here the letter does not result from the inevitable failure of love between divine and mortal, but rather determines the condition of impossibility. As subtle late sixteenth-century media theory, Shakespeare's *Venus and Adonis* fashions the new constraints and impulsions of print interfaciality as sexual drama.

3 Queer letters and deathly economies

If in this reading, V and A would seem to take on distinctly erotic and phallic/vulvic connotations, it is important to note how Shakespeare develops the Ovidian theme of the reluctant swain in order to reverse the common early modern association of phallic forwardness with male sexuality and vulvic inwardness with female reticence. Since antiquity, women's bodies ha been characterized as a bottle or a jar, a result of the belief that female sexual organs were an inversion of the normalized model of male sexual organs, and that female anatomy involved an inside-out penis that resided in the abdomen (Fernandez 2015). In accordance with their organs, women were often as a result considered rightly to be passive, froward, and retiring concerning sexual matters. By assigning Adonis with feminine characteristics, and Venus with male forwardness, but in keeping the sense of each as an inverse of the other, Shakespeare makes a sweeping redeployment of early modern conventions. It is the case that recognition of the strange echo of their poses and motion has often in criticism been centered on their genitalia. For Richard Halpern, Adonis's froward inwardness touches on the erotic lack: "The strategic absence of Adonis' erection" (Halpern 42). But this is the very lack that others have attributed to Venus: as Kolin has it, "Venus's problem is that she can't actually rape Adonis, as Jove rapes Danae" (64); despite pressing against him and lying upon him, her feminine biology is too like the inward Adonis for her to be able to force a sexual encounter from her overbearing desire. Certainly, as she advances, she also seems to incorporate his person into the interface of her desire: "Her arms do lend his neck a sweet embrace; / Incorporate then they seem; face grows to face" (560–1). And it is the case too that Shakespeare supplies a proliferating excess of seemingly phallic forms. Foreshadowing Adonis's death, Venus fears the negation of Adonis's "javelin" in the hunt that he proposes:

> 'Thou hadst been gone,' quoth she, 'sweet boy, ere this,
> But that thou told'st me thou wouldst hunt the boar.
> O, be advised! thou know'st not what it is
> With javelin's point a churlish swine to gore,
> Whose tushes never sheathed he whetteth still,
> Like to a mortal butcher bent to kill.
>
> *(634–9)*

One might dwell on the scriptive capacity and significance of the boar's tusk. Parallel to the Cadmus myth from Greece, which associated teeth with alphabetic letters, "Indian legend ascribes the origins of writing to Ganesh, the elephant-faced god of wisdom, who broke off a tusk and used it as a pen" (Drucker 22). The tusk of the elephant god and the tusk of the boar reference the prosthetic reorganization of the bodily by media interfaces important to Derrida's grammatology, and in a parallel manner the phallic boar tusk involves a re-routing of desire, indicative of the long tradition of writing as deathly erotics. While it is unlikely that Shakespeare was familiar with Sanskrit literature, he seems to have intuited a similar link between the tusk, the pen, the phallus, and the grave. At the very least, we see that the poem proliferates objects and organs of the interface that echo the "V" and "A" of its protagonists: bits, beaks, tushes, dimples, lips, tombs—associating deathly futurity as the source of desire and reversing conventional accounts of gender identity.

However, in its specific organization of these materials, *Venus and Adonis* upsets conventional heteronormative accounts of the sexual interface. This is partly dialectical. The generative ambiguity of A simultaneously embodies the linear perspective of the eye's forward motion into the representation of depth, and the pyramid of death that Derrida associated with A. As a "material metaphor," or hieroglyph of both "Chastity" and the "enchanting pit" of desire, economies of A inscribe upon Adonis the deathly attraction that impels the "king of graves" toward the ending that his refusal of posterity promises:

> What is thy body but a swallowing grave,
> Seeming to bury that posterity
> Which by the rights of time thou needs must have,
> If thou destroy them not in dark obscurity?
>
> *(779–82)*

In this sense, A in the poem speaks to the brilliant way the criticism of Jonathan Goldberg and Jeffrey Masten has traced the relation between grave spaces and unproductive sodomitical erotics in early modern thought. Yet also, vitally, it positions print letters as the casual basis for this deathly erotics. Redeploying early modern discursive practices, Leo Bersani's question concerning whether the rectum is the grave of "proud subjectivity," which he saw literalized in 1980s responses to the AIDS crisis (222), Masten asks, "Is the fundament a grave?" In a parallel critical passage, Jonathan Goldberg, reading *Romeo and Juliet,* likewise teases out Shakespeare's deathly erotics of "the open arse and the open grave of transgressively (un)productive desires" (285). Can we, by the "illogical" "logic" (in Masten's analysis, 141) of Goldberg's brilliant critical frame *Sodometries,* the always-plural complication of gender, sexuality, and poetics so frequently put into (deadly) circulation by early modern writing, read an aspect of the posterior, or fundament, in the "posterity" of Adonis's "swallowing grave"? As "relational structures precariously available to prevailing discourses," sodometries describe the contingent linguistic circulation of homoerotic sexualities in a given era. Sodometries require historical care in reconstructing specific discursive relations. They suggest and resist lexical intercourse. As Masten reminds us, "*fundament* does not precisely mean … 'posterior'… *Fundament,* also spelled *foundament* and *foundment…* is closely related to a set of words that have remained in circulation in English: *foundation,* to *found,* and a bit later, *fund*" (133). On one level, sodometries might seem to function as closed to generation, "dislodged" from "transcultural meaning," and situated within a less than readily opened economy, their accessing requiring careful historical and etymological historicizing. They are in this sense cut off from posterity, in a double sense—removed etymologically, and themselves enclosed in their own historical time—rather in the same way that Adonis's refusal of Venus, "seeming to bury that posterity," renders his body a grave.

However, just as "a foundation" in Florio's 1611 definition, is "an offspring or beginning" (192), it is the case too that Goldberg's sodometries also find productive, generative textual relations. As Bruce Smith has recognized,

> In their androgyny, figures like Leander, Adonis, and Hermaphroditus embody, quite literally, the ambiguities of sexual desire in English Renaissance culture and the ambivalences of homosexual desire in particular. To use the categories of our own day, these poems are bi-sexual fantasies.
>
> *(136)*

In the specific context of the interface, and with regard to *Venus and Adonis*'s recurrent iteration of alliterative relations, I would locate a further layer of bi-textual intercourse by suggesting the addition of a further set of words to Marten's referenced terms, that similarly relate homonymically, orthographically, and etymologically to "fundament," and that are specifically linked with the grave of Adonis's posterity by Shakespeare: *font, fund*, and *fount.* In Joseph Moxon's *Mechanick Exercises: Or, The Doctrine of Handyworks* (1683), "*fount* (properly a *fund*)" (vol. I, 13) describes: "the whole number of Letters that are cast of the same Body and Face at the same time" (vol. II 377). Referring to the "complete set of characters of a particular face and size of printing type," the font, often referred to as "fount" or "fund" by early modern printers, seems to derive both from Middle French *fonte* ("a casting"), itself derived from Latin *fundere*, but also from "fund," referring to a supply or stock, from Latin *fundus.* Mixing these two etymologies, Moxon's use of fount "properly a *fund*" exemplifies the way the sonic and typographic similarities of words in early modern use pulled together diverse etymological roots into generative encounters. Exemplifying this cross-fertilizing early modern linguistic play, Venus, too, attempts to initiate a sexually generative consummation of etymological roots when, in comparing herself to a landscape, she seeks to erotically tempt Adonis:

> 'Fondling,' she saith, 'since I have hemm'd thee here
> Within the circuit of this ivory pale,
> I'll be a park, and thou shalt be my deer;
> Feed where thou wilt, on mountain or in dale:
> Graze on my lips; and if those hills be dry,
> Stray lower, where the pleasant fountains lie.
> *(229–34)*

In narrating the coming of the "fondling" to her "fountains," Venus attempts to configure herself conventionally as the passive terrain to his male exploration, rather as Donne will deploy in "To His Mistress Going to Bed": "O my America! my new-found-land." Punning on the uncovering of her body, and the discovering of Newfoundland, Donne positions his "Mistress" as a passive receptacle to his explorations and excavations. A similar discoverer of her "fondling," of which "foundling" and "fondling" were common spelling variants of the time (Duncan-Jones and Woudhuysen 231 n229), Venus's topographic sketch works against her active agency in attempting to position Adonis as grazing and straying upon her person. Seeking for generative consummation in conventional gender tropes, Venus seeks to forestall the lettered, interfacial channels that determine the impossibility and the violence of her love.

Her ploy does not work. Rhetoric and punning at the level of semantics cannot always alter the foundations of the interface though, significantly, her generative-etymological puns return in Adonis's death, though now darker and stripped of much agency. At the horrible sight of Adonis's gored body, Venus immediately finds in her own person the inward hollow spaces that attracted her to Adonis. Like a snail's eye stalks, her eyes recoil with horror "murdered with the view... / Into the deep dark cabins of her head ..." (1033–8). They shrink back from interfaciality, burying into herself as if deep into the earth, "imprisoned in the ground, / Struggling for passage, earth's foundation shakes, / Which with cold terror doth men's minds confound" (1046–8). The proliferation of font/fond sounds is here significant. Confounded by the foundational shaking of the earth precipitated by his death, the fondling's barred desire and subsequent refusal of her fountain have led him to his grave-fundament. The print technology of the interface continually sounds alongside this deathly erotics. As she perceives, when she is finally able to look:

the wide wound that the boar had trench'd
In his soft flank; whose wonted lily white
With purple tears, that his wound wept, was drench'd:
No flower was nigh, no grass, herb, leaf, or weed,
But stole his blood and seem'd with him to bleed.
(1052–6)

Sought out by every plant, the seeping wound exceeds the inscriptive metamorphosis of the tale of Hyacinth in Ovid's mythological account of the origin of letters. In a technographic registering of the typographic interface, Adonis's "blood upon the fresh flowers" replays, as general condition of the print interfacial zone between sight and page, the violent impossible meeting of god and mortal.

For Tory, the story of Hyacinth records a transition from "youth and self-indulgence" to "prudence and wisdom," "so that the letters, that is, the memory of the change ... remain written and manifest in the said flower" (26). Recasting as temporal progression the difference between the two branches of the Y, for Tory, the boy and the flower Hyacinth indicate the passage from youth to wisdom. Tory's is an ultimately optimistic vision of mankind newly matured by the aid of typography's field of flowers. At the other end of the sixteenth century, a less assured humanism is described by *Venus and Adonis.* In Shakespeare's alternative account of the typographic interface, the vulvic association of Adonis's "trench'd" wound further feminizes the homoerotic play of letter A, yet the generative play that impels and restricts early modern bi-textual intercourse foreshadows and is circumscribed by the deathly economy of the letter. As in Flusser's account of poetic resistance, *Venus and Adonis* depicts the bi-textual potentiality of print letters alongside the deathly closure impelled by the typographic interface.

***

There is no evidence that Shakespeare had any familiarity with either Tory's or Flötner's human alphabets, nor is it very likely that the majority of early modern readers would have perceived the impulsions of letters narrativized in *Venus and Adonis.* If a cultural transmission occurred that passed the diverse alphabetic imaginaries with which each were working into circulation in late sixteenth-century London, that transmission has a complex and perhaps not fully recoverable history, likely involving multiple Europe-wide intermediaries. Though the nebulous routes taken by cultural metaphors and metonymies of this kind are difficult to track with much certainty, what is certain is that print facilitated increasingly complex and far-flung passages of circulation, and increasingly complex and influential networks of transmission. One feature of these networks is increasing recognition that the print interface accelerates contact with irreducible difference. As in Levinas's theory of the transcendent compulsion of the face-to-face relation, interfaces always negotiate the meeting of sameness with radically irreducible alterity (such as expressed in the image of God on the face of the water in Genesis), so that ultimately reading with interfaces might involve questioning unexamined methodological assumptions: that interpretation perhaps ought not to be considered a matter only of that which commonly passes across the interface, as a historicism of normative regimes of meaning, but also of the depths of alterity that both linger beneath and are shielded by faciality. Moreover, the ideas themselves of Tory and Flötner—of the typographic letter as an inhibiting bar on human behavior, or as an influential or generational model that impelled new, and newly eroticized, human forms—contributed to a theorization of just this intersection of self and radical alterity. The medium, and its voluptuous and violent interfacing with human bodies, are the message. In Tory's and Flötner's alphabets, we find an incipit media theory of the new religious and sexual ecologies of print culture. It is the opposition of these two contemporary and competing media theories that feeds into Shakespeare's narrative. In *Venus and Adonis*, Shakespeare composes a narrative from the opposition of the erotic impulsion that Flötner attributes to letter forms, and the chaste golden chain that for Tory dictates lettered human constriction. As idiosyncratic exploration of typographic effects, *Venus and Adonis* maps poetic narrative upon the materiality of print letters.

References

Bersani, Leo. "Is the Rectum a Grave?" *AIDS: Cultural Analysis, Cultural Activism*, edited by Douglas Crimp, MIT Press, 1988, pp. 197–222.

Boeckeler, Erika Mary. *Playful Letters: A Study in Early Modern Alphabetics*. U of Iowa P, 2017.

Bowen, Barbara C. "Geofroy Tory's Champ Fleury and Its Major Sources." *Studies in Philology*, vol. 76, 1979, pp. 13–27.

Bratton, Benjamin. *The Stack: On Software and Sovereignty*. MIT Press, 2015.

Conley, Tom. *Graphic Unconscious in Early Modern French Writing*. Cambridge UP, 2006.

Connor, Steven. "How to Do Things with Writing Machines." *Writing, Medium, Machine: Modern Technographies*, edited by Sean Pryor and David Trotter, Open Humanities Press, 2016, pp. 18–36.

Coulter, George H. *How Dead Languages Work*. Oxford UP, 2020.

Derrida, Jacques. "*Différance*." *Margins of Philosophy*. Translated by Alan Bass, U of Chicago P, 1984.

Drucker, Johanna. *The Alphabetic Labyrinth: The Letters in History and Imagination*. Thames and Hudson, 1995.

Duncan-Jones, K. and Woudhuysen, H.R., editors. *Shakespeare's Poems*. Arden, 2007.

Eisenstein, Elizabeth. *The Printing Revolution in Early Modern Europe*. Cambridge UP, 1983.

Febvre, Lucian and Henri-Jean Martin. *The Coming of the Book: The Impact of Printing 1450–1800*. N.L.B., 1976.

Fernandez, Enrique. *Anxieties of Interiority*. U of Toronto P, 2015.

Florio, John. *Queen Anna's New Worlds of Words*. London, 1611.

Flusser, Vilém. *Vampyroteuthis infernalis*. Edited and translated by Rodrigo Maltez Novaes, Atropos Press, 1987.

Fraser, Russell. *The Language of Adam: On the Limits and Systems of Discourse*. Columbia UP, 1977.

Goldberg, Jonathan. "Romeo and Juliet's Open Rs." *Queering the Renaissance*, edited by Jonathan Goldberg, Duke UP, 1994, pp. 218–235.

Halpern, Richard. "'Pining their Maws': Female Readers and the Erotic Ontology of the Text in Shakespeare's Venus and Adonis." *Venus and Adonis: Critical Essays*, edited by Philip C. Kolin, Garland, 1997, pp. 377–388.

Hayles, N. Katherine. *Writing Machines*. MIT Press, 2002.

Hayles, N. Katherine. "N. Katherine Hayles Responds in Turn." *electronic book review*, 2 April 2004. Available at: https://electronicbookreview.com/essay/n-katherine-hayles-responds-in-turn/?bsearch_highlight=N.%20Katherine%20Hayles%20responds%20in%20turn.

Hookway, Branden. *Interface*. MIT Press, 2014.

Kolin, Philip C. "Venus and /Or Adonis Among the Critics." *Venus and Adonis: Critical Essays*, edited by Philip C. Kolin, Garland, 1997, pp. 3–66.

Levinas, Emmanuel. *The Levinas Reader*. Edited by Seán Hand, Basil Blackwell, 1989.

Masten, Jeffrey. "Is the Fundament a Grave?" *The Body in Parts: Fantasies of Corporeality in Early Modern Europe*. Edited by D. Hillman and C. Mazzio, Routledge, 1997, pp. 128–145.

McKenzie, D.F. "Typography and Meaning: The Case of William Congreve." *Making Meaning "The Printers of the Mind" and Other Essays*, edited by Peter D. McDonald and Michael F. Suarez, U of Massachusetts P, 2002.

Miller-Blaise, Anne-Marie. "The Iconic Word: The Theological and Rhetorical Sources of a New *Ut Pictura Poesis*." *Sillages Critiques*, vol. 21, 2016. doi:10.4000/sillagescritiques.4999.

Moxon, Joseph. *Mechanick Exercises: Or, The Doctrine of Handyworks Applied to the Art of Printing*. London, 1683.

Nicolson, Adam. *God's Secretaries: The Making of the King James Bible*. HarperCollins, 2003.

Ong, Walter J. *Orality and Literacy*. Routledge, 2012.

Ovid. *Metamorphoses*. Translated by David Raeburn, Penguin, 2004.
Razzall, Lucy. "'Like to a Title Leafe': Surface, Face, and Material Text in Early Modern England." *Journal of the Northern Renaissance*, vol. 8, 2017. Available at: https://northernrenaissance.org/like-to-a-title-leafe-surface-face-and-material-text-in-early-modern-england/.
Shakespeare, William. "Venus and Adonis." *Shakespeare's Poems*, edited by K. Duncan-Jones and H.R. Woudhuysen, Arden, 2007, pp. 125–229.
Smith, Bruce. *Homosexual Desire in Shakespeare's England: A Cultural Poetics*. U of Chicago P, 1991.
Tory, Geofroy. *Champ Fleury*. Translated by George B. Ives, Grolier Club, 1927 [1529].

11

"IF YOU CAN COMMAND THESE ELEMENTS"

TEI markup as Shakespearean interface

Sarah Connell

In the storm that opens *The Tempest*, there is a clash of authority between the mariners and their noble passengers in which the Boatswain demands of Gonzalo, "if you can command these Elements to silence, and worke the peace of the present, wee will not hand a rope more, vse your authoritie" (1.1.29–31).[1] The Boatswain's point is, of course, that Gonzalo's political authority has no sway over the storm. While this brief scene invokes the examinations of authority that are woven throughout *The Tempest*, it is an equally apt opening for this chapter, which discusses how encoded editions of Shakespeare's works can serve as interfaces that mediate distinctive forms of readerly access. Unlike Gonzalo, we *can* command the textual elements that encoded editions formalize, which means that we can also engage with these texts in ways that make their components manifest and manipulable.

Markup systems like the Text Encoding Initiative (TEI) are not just the frameworks behind digital publications that range from web interfaces to interactive visualizations. In fact, markup itself is a technology for accessing Shakespeare that makes a broad range of interactions possible. TEI editions enable readings that make the relationships between textual contents and structures as central as the words of the texts themselves. Shakespeare particularly rewards considerations of markup and interface because there are several TEI editions of his works, all of which provide distinctive textual models. In this chapter, I examine four TEI editions of Shakespeare's plays to show some of the ways that they function as reading interfaces. TEI editions, with their defamiliarizing syntax and operational legibility, provide textual access points in which the usual disappearing effects of interfaces are less pronounced than in modes of reading such as the codex or the web page.

Given its varied uses in a range of disciplines, I will briefly discuss the meanings of the term "interface" that are key for this chapter. The definition offered by Lori Emerson in her book, *Reading Writing Interfaces: From the Digital to the Bookbound*, is particularly applicable because it focuses on how interfaces provide access to writing:

> interface is a technology—whether it is a fascicle, a typewriter, a command line, or a GUI—that mediates between reader and the surface-level, human-authored writing,

 DOI: 10.4324/9780367821722-15

> as well as, in the case of digital devices, the machine-based writing taking place below the gloss of the surface.
>
> (x)

Also key to understanding interfaces is recognizing how readily they become invisible to users. Branden Hookway notes that the interface has a "tendency toward a seeming transparency and disappearance, even as it is undoubtedly a condition that demands to be worked through" (6). Emerson, following Alexander Galloway, sees interfaces as mutable transition points: "while interface does grant access, it also inevitably acts as a kind of magician's cape, continually revealing (mediatic layers, bits of information, etc.) through concealing and concealing as it reveals" (x). That this apparent transparency is an illusion is well accepted, as is the fact that such transparency often comes at the cost of user agency; as Galloway observes, "for every moment of immersion and connectivity, for every moment of volumetric delivery of inopacity, the threshold becomes one notch more invisible, one notch more inoperable" (25). The invisibility and inoperability of interfaces are tightly connected.

TEI editions undoubtedly provide less seamless reading experiences than web interfaces do, and so they are useful in considering how interfaces condition our encounters with Shakespeare. It is important to remember that TEI editions—and the tools we use to access them—are also subject to the same disappearing properties of all interfaces. Nevertheless, I hope to show that TEI editions, when treated as reading interfaces and not just data sources, offer distinctive modes of textual access that can even address some of the goals that Joanna Drucker outlined at the close of her article, "Performative Materiality and Theoretical Approaches to Interface." Drucker proposes several antidotes to "the familiarity that blinds us," including "engagement with fragmentation and partial presentations of knowledge that expose the illusion of seamless wholeness" (paragraph 42). She asserts that "more attention to acts of producing and less emphasis on product, the creation of an interface that is meant to expose and support the activity of interpretation, rather than to display finished forms, would be a good starting place" for addressing the concerns her article raises about the disempowering and underexamined functions of digital humanities interfaces (paragraph 42). Acknowledging with Drucker that "veils of maya are replaced with other veils of maya," I propose that TEI markup—which disrupts the apparent seamlessness of more familiar reading media, which explicitly articulates the conditions of its own production, and which can support a wide range of interpretive activities—is worth considering as a direct interface for readerly engagements (paragraph 42).

Modeling textual data

Modeling objects as complicated as texts necessarily involves many decisions, but the core activities of encoding can be expressed simply: using a standardized notational system, the encoder names, describes, and marks the boundaries of textual features. In TEI markup, that standardized notational system is currently expressed through XML (Extensible Markup Language). XML is a metalanguage that provides a syntax in which *elements* name and delimit content objects, while *attributes* provide more information about those elements. XML start tags are indicated with angle brackets and the name of the element, as in: <element>, while end tags are distinguished with a forward slash: </element>. XML attributes are indicated as follows: <element attribute="value">, where the name of the attribute is followed by an equal sign and the attribute value in quotation marks. If XML provides the syntax for text encoding, TEI provides a vocabulary and a grammar. The TEI schema governs the names of elements—for instance, that paragraphs are marked with <p> and not <paragraph>—as well as where they are allowed to go and what they are allowed or required to contain. For example, TEI has a <head> element for headings, which must appear at or near the top of a larger container, and an <lg> element for line groups, which must contain at least one verse line in <l>. Pulling this together, here is one possible encoding for a stage direction from *The Tempest*: <stage type="business">Solemne musicke.</stage>. The <stage> element is used to mark the presence and boundaries of the stage direction, and the @type[2] attribute further specifies that this particular stage direction can be categorized as stage business; the contents of the stage direction—"Solemne musicke."—are enclosed within the element's start and end tags.

This encoding is one of many possible approaches; potential variations include a further specification that this stage direction marks a sound or information to indicate how it appeared in the source text. Each TEI edition is thus not a *reproduction* of a documentary source but instead a *model* of those components that a project has elected to formalize. Different TEI editions will emphasize or elide different textual features. This expectation of variety is integral to the work that TEI editors do; the TEI is an international community standard that treats local customization as essential. Encoded texts carry their editorial interventions openly in the markup itself, which means that TEI files provide access to the textual models governing their production. This editorial legibility also has an important defamiliarizing function; there is no possibility that one could lose sight of the text as a constructed object resulting from a series of interventions. Editorial mediations are explicit, systematic, and written into the documents themselves in a language that both humans and computers can read.

Indeed, as Hookway observes, "in its drawing together of the capabilities of human and machine, the interface operates as a threshold condition through which both knowing and acting are enabled" (123). TEI editions provide conditions for knowing and acting in which both humans and computers speak the same language, albeit in different ways. XML does take some time to learn, as with any new language, but the core aspects of its syntax are straightforward enough and the naming conventions of TEI elements are commonsensical enough to make encoded documents accessible without necessitating the effort that would be required to read, say, a programming language like C++. Learning how an individual edition uses TEI requires much more time and attention, but also provides an opportunity to understand that edition's textual models.

While it is inarguable that most readers access TEI editions through mediations such as web interfaces, the encoded files include significantly more information than their HTML outputs. Web interfaces have a robust informational toolset, but the constraints of legibility within the current capacities of web display ensure that much of the detail formalized in the markup is suppressed or translated to typography for online publication. Our example stage direction suggests how this process takes place; the fact that this is a stage direction would be marked with some typographic distinction in most web interfaces, but the specific type of stage direction is less likely to be visible. And this is a very simple example; imagine how much more difficult it would be to display all of the information below:

```
<stage type="business" style="font-style:italic"><sound type="music">
Solemne <unclear reason="damage" resp="#editors" agent="mildew">
musicke</unclear> </sound>.</stage>
```

Due to this informational disparity, TEI editors often treat the encoded texts themselves as the significant scholarly output for their projects. Most readers may interact with encoded texts through the web, but TEI markup is not simply designed for producing documents to be read online (if that were the case, it would be far easier to work in HTML). TEI is instead a method for creating digital models of those textual features that a project has chosen to prioritize.[3] TEI editors can thus practice what Julia Flanders and Fotis Jannidis call a kind of "tool agnosticism" which asks data developers "to model our data to be as pure as possible an expression of the information we care about" ("Data Modeling in Digital Humanities" 15).[4] Scholarship on digital editions demonstrates the importance of focusing editorial energy not on a single publication output, but instead on the core textual model. Turska et al., for example, argue that "in digital editions the encoded texts themselves are the most important long-term outcome of the project, while their initial presentation within a particular application should be considered only a single perspective on the data" (paragraph 4). Given that web interfaces are necessarily impoverished translations of the information modeled within encoded texts, it is worth considering exactly what kinds of reading experiences become possible when engaging directly with TEI files.

These reading experiences are conditioned by both the XML data model and the TEI's schemas, which offer a set of textual insights generated through decades of discussion, testing, and refinement. The TEI markup language, as specified in the *TEI Guidelines for Electronic Text Encoding and Interchange*, is the product of the Text Encoding Initiative Consortium, an organization that has been working since 1987 to "develop and maintain guidelines for the digital encoding of literary and linguistic texts" (TEI "About"). As the publication of an international research community, TEI has received sustained scholarly attention.[5] XML and its predecessor SGML (Standard Generalized Markup Language) have likewise been studied as mechanisms for modeling documents in works such as the seminal "What Is Text, Really?" by Steven DeRose, David Durand, Elli Mylonas, and Allen Renear, which proposed that text is best understood as an "ordered hierarchy of content objects (OHCO)," a theorization instantiated in SGML. More recently, *The Shape of Data in Digital Humanities*, edited by Julia Flanders and Fotis Jannidis, includes several chapters that consider how XML functions as a model for textual data. Flanders and Jannidis outline some key aspects of the XML data model: the "structure is hierarchical, because elements nested within another element can be understood to be at a level subordinate to the enclosing element" and "the elements are ordered and the order is significant … thus, an XML document can be visualized as a tree" ("Gentle Introduction" 65).[6] That is, when we model documents in XML, we think about them as trees: compositions of objects in which both order and containment are essential.

Fundamental as it is, the tree structure is not the only textual model that XML provides, as John Bradley discusses in "Documents and Data: Modelling Materials for Humanities Research in XML and Relational Databases." Bradley notes XML's "strong preference for asserting associations between elements by hierarchy and containment" but also demonstrates that "the OHCO model itself is not the only modelling approach that XML markup provides" (133–4). In fact, as Bradley shows, XML is well able to represent linking relationships between content objects. Reading Shakespeare in the frameworks that XML and TEI provide, then, makes us aware of how documents comprise discrete units which contain and are contained by each other—and which also link to each other in ways that operate outside the tree hierarchy.

Given the expressiveness of TEI/XML, this chapter participates in current discussions in the digital humanities about how interfaces that prioritize seamless interactions may disempower users. For instance, Michael Whitelaw advocates for interfaces that provide access to cultural heritage materials not through restrictive modalities like searching, but instead by offering "multiple, fragmentary representations to reveal the complexity and diversity of cultural collections, and to privilege the process of interpretation" (paragraph 46). Emerson's book interrogates interfaces that attempt to erase themselves, which, she asserts, "share a common goal underlying their designs: to efface the interface altogether and also to efface our ability to read, let alone write, the interface" (2). These and other scholars have proposed several promising approaches to designing more generative web interfaces—and in no way do I wish to suggest that the solution is simply to replace web interfaces with their underlying data. But I do want to examine some of the ways that TEI documents can work against the vanishing nature of interfaces by making the conditions of their production and consumption explicit, and so highlighting both readers' and editors' acts of interpretation.

Reading in/with/through markup

But, what does it mean to "read" a TEI document? To clarify this question, consider the Bodleian First Folio encoding for another stage direction from *The Tempest* (XML line 5,646, sig. B2v):

```
<stage rend="italic center" type="mixed">Heere enters <hi rend=
"roman">Ariel</hi> before: Then <hi rend="roman">Alonso</hi> with
a franticke ge
<lb/>sture, attended by <hi rend="roman">Gonzalo. Sebastian</hi>
and <hi rend="roman">Anthonio</hi> in
<lb/>like manner…
</stage>
```

This markup makes several observations about the play explicit, including the presence and type of stage direction, the original lineation, and some aspects of the source document's appearance. The section also shows how this edition's policies are shaping the information that it formalizes. For example, several words are marked as shifting to a roman typeface with a <hi> ("highlight") element. <hi> specifies only that the appearance of the text has changed without offering any computationally formalized reason for that shift, but we human readers of the text can see that the distinctive words are all names. The TEI does have provisions for encoding named entities, but no digital model could include all possible details, and this edition focuses on other aspects of the text. This shows how editorial policies govern the readings that are made accessible in TEI documents while also providing a reminder that we are accessing not some unmediated original but the outcome of particular textual theories and priorities.

Since this chapter will consider several TEI editions of Shakespeare's plays, a brief digression to outline their distinctive approaches will provide useful context.[7] Most use standard encoding for marking core textual structures with elements like <div> (division), <sp> (dramatic speech), <stage> (stage direction), <p> (paragraph), and <l> (verse line), and all link from individual dramatic speeches to characters' unique identifiers. However, they also show substantial variations in their editorial theories, the objects of their encoding, and the markup that they use. As the example above shows, the Bodleian First Folio prioritizes recording the appearance and layout of its source document. The Shakespeare Quartos Archive, which publishes digital editions of more than thirty copies of early *Hamlet* quartos, marks many textual features in ways similar to the First Folio, but also has some distinctions. In addition to encoding named entities, the Quartos project makes more extensive use of markup for handwritten additions and deletions. The digital New Variorum Shakespeare (NVS) texts, based on the earlier NVS reference editions, focus on enmeshing the play texts in a broad editorial apparatus, linking to extensive commentary and annotation. The Folger Shakespeare project, which includes digital versions of Barbara Mowat and Paul Werstine's editions of Shakespeare's plays and poetry, encodes individual words within <w> elements and uses this fine level of precision to link extensively, not only for annotation but also to represent some document structures, such as verse stanzas.

Returning to our encoding sample: since XML is a tree, the contexts for this stage direction are as informationally powerful as its contents. The full path from the document's root element (<TEI>) to this stage direction, can be expressed as follows using "XPath," which allows for the precise description of locations within XML documents:

TEI/text/body/div/div/div/sp/stage.

That is, we have a stage direction contained by a dramatic speech, contained by several levels of textual divisions (a scene, an act, and the play itself), contained by the body of the text, contained by the text as distinct from its metadata, contained by the <TEI> root element. These elements also contain other elements; for example, the stage direction at stake has several "sibling" <l> elements marking the verse lines that precede and follow it, as well as another stage direction, all contained together in the same <sp>. This <sp> has a @who attribute pointing to the unique identifier for Prospero, indicating that this dramatic speech is spoken by him and that the stage direction is contained within one of his speeches. From this example, we can see how TEI foregrounds description, containment, order, and linking.

When we read a TEI file, we can do so linearly, starting at the first line of the text and continuing to the end. But it is important to remember that XML documents are structured not from the top to the bottom but from the outside in. We can see this in the example above; while the stage direction is the "first" textual item we read semantically, its end tag is the last thing we read in linear order. As humans reading through TEI documents, we need to focus on both order and containment to understand the full textual model. A reader with some light background in XML (very little more than is covered in this chapter) might sit down with an encoded edition of a Shakespeare play and read the XML from beginning to end to get a clear picture of how that edition is modeling containment, order, and linking. But, as valuable as it is to engage so directly with a text's editorial insights and interventions, readers of XML are not limited to such linear reading experiences. Tools like XPath make it possible to traverse the XML tree structure, writing descriptive pathways such as the one outlined above to access documents in some of the same ways that computers do. With XPath, we can identify "nodes" of an XML document that match certain criteria ("all stage directions that appear within dramatic speeches"), or we can jump to specific sections of a text ("the first verse line in the third act"), or we can extract and study language of particular interest ("all speeches attributed to Prospero").[8] When we write XPaths, we are thinking structurally about documents, examining the links between the precisely delineated textual phenomena that XML makes so visible.

Reading an XML document can thus involve both linear and discontinuous modes of engagement, making a reader highly aware of a text's structures and the relationships among its components.[9] With XPath, it is possible to act on the questions that arise when one is thinking critically about how documents are modeled. Below I offer three case studies that take up such XML-based readings to show how text encoding facilitates methods for reading Shakespeare that make editorial interventions and interpretations visible, offering access to the plays at many different levels and opening them up for further experimentation.

What's in a <name>?

TEI has several provisions for encoding named entities, which the NVS and Quartos projects apply using different standards. NVS uses the <name> element for names of people and places that are italicized in the source documents, while the Quartos use it for "all characters that occur within the fictional universe of the play" but not for "characters from fictional works within *Hamlet*'s fictional universe" ("Encoding Documentation"). If names represent the sort of repeated phenomena that TEI makes visible, their contexts and linkages are no less essential to a markup-based reading. Below is an example of how such linking and containment operates, simplified from the NVS edition of *The Winter's Tale*, line 555, signature 2A2[b]:

```
<sp who="#Camillo">
   <speaker>Cam.</speaker>
   <p>Businesse, my Lord? I thinke most vnderstand <name>Bohemia
</name>
   stayes here longer.</p>
</sp>
```

The <sp> element encodes the dramatic speech, which in this case comprises a speaker label and prose paragraph; the paragraph itself contains the name at stake. The @who attribute on <sp> points to an entry for Camillo in the play's cast list. This encoding can reveal which characters' speeches contain names, along with the contexts for those acts of naming—for example, in verse or in prose, at the beginnings or ends of scenes, alongside other names or in isolation. We also have access to the textual contents of these <name> elements and can, for instance, observe that "Camillo" is the most named entity in the NVS *Winter's Tale*, with 48 occurrences, followed by "Bohemia" and "Paulina" (22 occurrences each).

Taking up one of these possibilities, we can examine which characters reference names most often. An important aspect of XML-based reading is the need to navigate between concepts like "referencing names most often" and the precision demanded by computational processes. One way to express this concept might be to count the speeches that contain <name>s. The following XPath will first select only those <sp> elements that contain at least one <name> element, and then navigate down to the values of the @who attribute:[10]

```
//sp[descendant:name]/@who
```

This syntax provides a window into the tree structure of XML files and indicates how we need to think about documents when we author XPaths. In this case, I am navigating down the tree with the slashes, first from the root element to all <sp>s, at whatever level they appear (whether they are direct "children" of the root element or "descendants" contained within intermediary elements), and then down another single level to the @who attribute on those <sp>s. I am also, with the square brackets, providing further specification on which <sp>s I want to retrieve (those that contain <name>s at any level of nesting). Reading an XML document by writing XPaths that operate within its editorial model and then interacting with the results—whether that is by reading snippets of the document directly or by extracting, counting, or summarizing the nodes that are retrieved—requires one to engage critically and directly with the document's structure and with the editorial interpretations that are formalized through its markup.

Reading this way shows that Leontes has the most speeches that contain names (43) in this edition of *The Winter's Tale*. But, Leontes also has the most total speeches overall (126).[11] Looking at the character with the secondmost speeches containing names, Florizell, offers more interesting results: the young Bohemian prince has only 45 total speeches and 19 (42.2 percent) of these contain names. By contrast, the characters who have the lowest counts for speeches with names—Mopsa (0 percent), Mamillius (0 percent), the Old Shepherd (4.8

percent), the Clown (6.3 percent), Autolycus (7.5 percent), and Dorcas (9.1 percent)—are a more motley crew, comprising many of the lower-status characters, along with the child prince Mamillius.[12] Much as Camillo's role as a trusted confidant is indicated by the fact that he is the most-named entity in the play, Florizell's role as a bridge between nations and status groups is suggested by his tendency to pepper his speeches with the names of characters and locations—and this distinction is reinforced by the types of characters who tend not to use names.

These observations may not provide any ground-breaking new insights, but they do show some ways of reading with XML to investigate the types of questions that scholars might ask about Shakespeare's works, such as how agency and authority function in a play like *The Winter's Tale*. The Shakespeare Quartos Archive provides an example of how our readings will vary in a different edition, as well as another way of thinking about how names operate within these texts. In this edition, each <name> has a @ref attribute pointing to the unique identifier for that character. This encoding means that, in addition to examining which characters tend to use names, we can ask which characters are most named by others based on the contents of the @ref attribute. The XPath is fairly straightforward:

```
//text//name/@ref
```

navigates to the values for all of the @ref attributes on all the <name> elements within the text of the play.

To no great surprise, Hamlet has the most speeches in the full corpus of all 33 quartos (30.9 percent of the total speeches) and is also named most often by other characters (30.7 percent of the total names referenced). His antagonist Claudius has the third most speeches (9.1 percent) but is not directly named. By contrast, Laertes—who serves as one of Hamlet's foils—has only 5.6 percent of the play's speeches, but is the second most-named character in the play, at 12.9 percent. Looking instead at who tends to use names, 41.9 percent of the politically minded Claudius's speeches have <name>s in them, compared to 10.3 percent in Hamlet's (one is tempted to make a comment on solipsism here). The play's two main female characters diverge interestingly in their uses of names; like her husband Claudius, Gertrude uses names frequently, in 30.7 percent of her speeches. Ophelia's naming patterns are more similar to Hamlet's and only 5.5 percent of her speeches contain names. Considering *Hamlet* in this way suggests a complex interplay between the effects and causes of naming and being named.

Asking "how do names operate within Shakespeare's plays?" shows that there are many paths to investigating this question with TEI and XML, many possibilities for selecting from and examining the texts' contents. TEI editions can be queried minutely and subsetted precisely; thus, as interfaces, they call attention to how scholarly analyses of the plays are also inscribed into, and legible from, such discrete features as the locations and frequencies of names. The technical aspects that might restrict these editions' readerships also make their functions as interfaces distinctive: by formalizing editorial interpretations in a way that is directly legible within the documents themselves, these editions enable us not only to identify the various contexts in which naming occurs in Shakespeare's plays but also to consider the contexts that produced these editions' distinctive models of Shakespearean nomination.

Of question marks and queens: the interface at many levels

The analytical power of both linking and containment in TEI documents is particularly evident in drama because the form's structural units are applied at a fine grain and because editions typically incorporate links between characters and their speeches. As seen above, we can use this information to associate the textual features inside dramatic speeches with the characters delivering those speeches. XML-based readings can also act on any information that is formalized about the characters themselves. For example, the Folger texts establish unique identifiers for characters in the documents' metadata; each character has an entry as follows (*Hamlet*, XML line 183):

```
<person xml:id="Gertrude_Ham">
  <persName><name>Queen Gertrude</name></persName>
  <state><p>widow of King Hamlet, now married to Claudius</p></state>
  <sex value="2">female</sex>
  <death when-custom="ftln-4059"/>
</person>
```

We have basic details on the character's name and role in the play, but we also have two pieces of information that are designed for computational analysis: Gertrude's gender[13] and the milestone for the line in which her death occurs. We can follow these links in both directions to look at dramatic speeches not just on a character-by-character basis but also across traits that characters share, such as gender.

While many aspects of gender can be considered computationally, I will focus on punctuation characters, since they provide a clear view of the ways that editorial decisions shape our readings. The Folger Shakespeare project encodes not just individual words in <w> elements, but also punctuation characters in a <pc> element. This level of detail means that the Folger editions provide a particularly vivid example of how markup foregrounds the conditions of its production—in these texts, every word, every space, every piece of punctuation, is surrounded with encoding. Because of this precision, we can read across the Shakespeare dramatic corpus and follow the links between speech acts and character entries to consider whether these editions show any patterns in the types of punctuation ascribed to female and male characters.[14] One question we can ask is whether there are gender-related trends in how characters' speeches are punctuated. We do see some differences by gender for the full corpus, but only slight ones. Excluding speeches attributed to multiple characters, 7.7 percent of female characters' total punctuation characters are question marks, by contrast with 6.5 percent of male characters'; 4 percent of women's and 3.2 percent of men's punctuation characters are exclamation marks.

This summative analysis conceals substantial variety within individual plays, and must be considered in light of the great disparity between the numbers of women's and men's speeches. We must also determine what, precisely, we want our computational readings to assess. The discussion that follows focuses on those punctuation characters that usually end sentences: periods, exclamation marks, and question marks.[15] There are many noteworthy results for individual plays; for example, Florizell—who, as we have seen, references names frequently—tends to speak in statements over questions or exclamations, with much higher percentages of sentences ending in periods. I will focus here on *A Midsummer Night's Dream*, which is particularly interesting in that its punctuation intersects not just with gender and class but also with the differences between human and fairy characters. The markup shows that the fairies in this edition of *Dream* are far more likely to make statements than their mortal counterparts and male fairies are also less likely to engage in exclamations.

The least exclamatory characters in *Dream*, measured by the percentages of their "sentences" ending in exclamation marks, are technically Starveling, Philostrate, and Hippolyta, since they have no exclamation marks at all, but they also have very few overall sentences (9,

10, and 19, respectively). Of characters who speak more frequently, the least exclamatory are Oberon (0.8 percent), Theseus (4.8 percent), and Puck (5.5 percent). The most exclamatory characters are Titania's four attendants but they, again, have very few sentences: the next most rank as follows: Bottom (18.6 percent), Flute (16.3 percent), Hermia (16.1 percent), Snug (14.3 percent), and Helena (12.9 percent).[16] That is, the characters in *Dream* who tend toward exclamation are three of the mechanicals and the two women among the Athenian lovers. When one looks instead at the percentages of sentences ending in periods, the first by rank are again those who speak infrequently: Philostrate, Starveling, Hippolyta, and Egeus (who has 21 sentences). The highest among those who speak more often are Oberon (89.6 percent), Puck (84.5 percent), and Titania (83.6 percent). We see something similar in *The Tempest*, where the characters who have the fewest exclamations are Prospero, Gonzalo, and Ariel; those who have the most sentences ending in periods are Prospero and Ariel (looking at those with at least 25 "sentences").[17] These trends are not absolute, but they are suggestive of a relationship between status and punctuation in these two plays. High status male characters have more statements and fewer exclamations, in contrast with lower status male characters and female characters. That the fairies overall align with high status male characters in their tendency to make statements provides an interesting lens into how their roles are construed in this edition of the plays.

This punctuational exploration shows how TEI readings of Shakespeare encourage us to pay close attention to the components of his works at many levels, supporting navigation from the corpus as a whole to individual works and their contents. For example, examining the most exclamatory characters in *Othello* (Bianca at 27.8 percent, Emilia at 21.4 percent, and Cassio at 18.3 percent) might lead one to observe that the cast of this play appears to be highly exclamatory overall. *Othello* is indeed the most exclamatory play in the Folger Shakespeare texts, with 14.4 percent of sentences ending in exclamation marks (the average is 7.9 percent and the least exclamatory play is *As You Like It* at 1.5 percent). With 17.9 percent of sentences ending in question marks, *Othello* is also the fourth most inquisitive play, after *The Comedy of Errors, Two Gentlemen of Verona*, and *The Taming of the Shrew* (the average is 15.4 percent and the least inquisitive play is *Antony and Cleopatra* at 11.4 percent). Here, we might want to zoom out again and consider why there is so much greater variation in exclamation marks than in questions,[18] or we might zoom in to look at the ten of Bianca's 36 sentences that end in exclamation marks and investigate which aspects of her language triggered this punctuation when the plays were edited. Large-scale readings across plays and through conceptual domains like race and class are also legible in very small features, such as individual punctuation characters. If, as Galloway has observed, "the interface is a general technique of mediation evident at all levels," then the TEI edition is an interface that facilitates control over many levels of textual conceptuality (54).

(Re-)marking Shakespeare's plays: handwritten and digital annotation

Thus far, we have focused on the language of the plays, but markup can also formalize information about the physical condition of the source documents. This final case study considers handwritten annotations in the Quartos Archive texts. The markup at stake is as follows (spacing and bolding added to improve legibility; Bodleian fourth quarto (Arch. G d.41), XML line 4257, sig. H1v):

```
<subst xml:id="ham-1625-22278x-bod-c01.xml-5042">
<del type="substitution" hand="#aa" resp="#fol" xml:id="ham-1625-
22278x-bod-c01.xml-5043">& the thumb</del>
```

```
<add n="20" hand="#aa" place="mount-bot" type="intervention" resp=
"#fol" xml:id= "ham-1625-22278x-bod-c01.xml-5044">&amp; the vmber
</add>
</subst>
```

This shows a <subst> (substitution) element, wrapping both text deleted from the source document (in <del>) and a handwritten addition (in <add>). The substitution replaces the phrase "& the thumb" with "& the umber."[19] We can see here how much detail about editorial processes and analyses can be specified with markup, as well as how densely informational the links between elements can be. In this encoding:

- each element has a unique identifier specified with @xml:id;
- both the addition and the deletion have more information about their operations specified with the @type attribute;
- both have @hand attributes pointing to an entry for the hand that produced them;
- both have @resp attributes pointing to the editor responsible for applying and proofing this encoding;
- the <add> also has a @place attribute indicating where the addition appeared.

This example shows <add> and <del> together in <subst> but both elements can also appear independently.

Looking across the quartos, we can see the ways that readers have made their own marks on these texts.[20] The values for @type on <del> show key characteristics of how readers marked text for deletion—notable is how few of these involve direct deletion of the text on the page. By far, the most frequent mechanisms for "deletions," 459 in total, are substitutions, where "another reading is supplied with no other signal to delete the original text" ("Encoding Documentation"). The next most common form of deletion, at 184 instances, is underlining; in total, only 30 instances were struck through, 22 more were overwritten, 4 were erased, 3 were braced, and 3 obscured. These values indicate how readers intervened in the quartos: they are not reticent about writing in the books, but most of their interventions leave the original text legible. Thus, the substitutions form a dialogic relationship, in which reader-annotators are offering their own language, without removing Shakespeare's.

We can also look at the parent element, <subst>, to see how this dialogue functions. An important aspect of reading with TEI that we have not yet explored is its support of subsequent interventions. Markup makes it possible not just to read and interact with textual data, but also to extract textual materials *as* data and layer on additional information. In this case, I extracted the contents of the <subst> element and applied a taxonomy designed to characterize the relationship between the contents of <add> and <del>. To categorize several hundred items within the scope of this exercise, I did not examine the motives behind these substitutions (such as correction or regularization). Rather, I catalogued substitutions based on the difference between the addition and the deletion, for example, spelling changes, changes from one word to another, and additions of new words to a phrase.

In line with what we have seen, about 320[21] of the substitutions are simple spelling changes, for instance, from "command" to "commaund" or "springes" to "springs." Other minor changes include about 25 shifts between singular and plural ("watchmen" to "watchman" or "heele" to "heels") and about 30 variations in forms of the same word ("dulleth" to "dulls" or "labourer" to "labor"). There are also many cases in which words are replaced with different words, the most common being about 150 shifts from one word to another ("lap" to "cap" or "Maister" to "either"); in about 40 cases, annotators substitute a different word or words within a phrase ("Marry it is munching" to "Marry this munching"). There are about 50 additions to and 5 removals of words within phrases ("shall lie" to "shall I lie" or "I wil make you way" to "I wil you way"). As these examples indicate, the interventions are typically quite brief, and most of the shifts in words or phrases that I have investigated do function as corrections, bringing the text in alignment with the First Folio or with more accepted readings from other quartos.

Editorial transparency in TEI is imperfect—not all decisions are documented or formalized in markup—but, as the example above shows, TEI editions have substantial space for making editorial theories and the interventions that derive from them explicit. And this has an important impact on how the edited documents are conceptualized. As James Cummings has written, by "forcing us to formalise some of our assumptions, the structures and vocabularies of an encoded edition" help to "foreground the theories of text we use when creating scholarly digital editions" ("Opening the Book"). The visibility of editorial work, the documents' computational mutability, and the less "finished" appearance of TEI editions by contrast with print or web publication formats, opens up space for subsequent interventions such as those I have discussed here. TEI editions are fundamentally generative: editable, queryable, and able to support further informational density. Like the annotators who left their marks on the pages of the quartos, readers of TEI can participate in a dialogue with these texts, adding contributions to the layers of information they contain.

Commanding the elements

These are just a few examples that take seriously the idea that TEI/XML can function as a direct interface for reading in and across Shakespeare's plays. Other possibilities might consider the various values for @type on <stage>, or how stage directions' characteristics (types, numbers, locations) intersect with characters' traits. Enabling potential readings in the audial lexicons of the plays, the Folger editions have a robust vocabulary for sounds, including values for @type on <sound> that distinguish between flourishes, military sounds, and music, as well as a more precise list with @ana that includes values like alarum, trumpet, drum, and thunder. Markup also allows for subsequent interventions, which might include supplying and analyzing further information on other character traits (say, nationality and class as well as gender) or adding more precision to different types of names to distinguish between persons and places. Finally, any features made explicit in the markup can also be used to extract textual contents for further analysis, such as with word frequencies, keywords in context, and natural language processing. The potential here is very rich and, as I have shown, examining TEI editions as interfaces provides a useful lens for considering a range of productive readerly engagements with Shakespeare. If, indeed, we can command the elements, we gain a clear view of the processes, contingencies, and entanglements in these texts—and we can claim the authority to contribute to these ever-evolving editions ourselves.

Acknowledgments

I wish to express my gratitude to Ash Clark, Kevin Weiler, and James Connell, without whom this chapter would not have been possible.

Notes

1 *Internet Shakespeare Editions*. Folio 1, 1623 (Old-spelling transcription).
2 The "@" is a convention indicating that this is the name of an attribute.

3 Examining the difference between "descriptive" and "procedural" approaches to markup has deeply impacted the development of TEI—and, indeed, is much more complex than any straightforward opposition between HTML and TEI/XML. For an outline of this topic, see Flanders and Jannidis "Gentle Introduction," 71–3.

4 In pragmatic terms, TEI editors do have to take publication capabilities into consideration when modeling their documents. For more on the interplay between data models and publication interfaces, see Flanders and Jannidis "Data Modeling in Digital Humanities," 13–16.

5 For an introduction to the principles grounding the TEI and a discussion of its role in digital editions, see Cummings "The Text Encoding," 451–76.

6 Flanders and Jannidis outline and respond to some key objections to XML as a data model, one of which relates to its fundamental tree structure, which, "some regard as a serious shortcoming" due to the "difficulties arising around the representation of overlapping structures, which are common in humanities documentary contexts" ("Gentle Introduction," 73). For more on methods for overcoming the "supposed limitations of XML" in representing overlapping hierarchies, see Cummings, "Opening the Book," 179–93.

7 For the Bodleian First Folio, see https://firstfolio.bodleian.ox.ac.uk/. For the Folger Shakespeare, see: https://shakespeare.folger.edu/. The original site for the Shakespeare Quartos Archive has been withdrawn, but its contents can be viewed at: https://wayback.archive-it.org/org-467/20191016094633/http://quartos.org/. The digital editions of the New Variorum Shakespeare are not yet published, but Laura Mandell generously provided XML files for *The Winter's Tale, A Comedy of Errors*, and *King Lear*.

8 The examples that follow also use XQuery, an XPath-based query language for performing detailed searches and extracting data.

9 Exactly what one "reads" as the outcome of running an XPath will vary depending on how the XPath is run. In some cases, a human reader might remain within the XML document itself and simply navigate from one identified node to another to read their contents in the original context. In other cases, especially when working with XQuery, the outcome might be a separate document with results and their counts or with the textual contents retrieved by the XPath. In either case, the computer may be "reading" the document to produce the results, but these are based on the human's understanding of the encoded text as represented in the XPath.

10 See the resources developed by Ash Clark and published by the Women Writers Project at: https://github.com/NEU-DSG/wwp-public-code-share/tree/counting_robot/counting_robot.

11 Datasets used in this chapter are found at: http://sarahconnell.org/research/interface/.

12 Restricting to the characters who speak at least 10 times.

13 In addition to the <sex> element, the TEI also provides a @gender attribute; the *Guidelines* note that the "often used ISO 5218:2004 Representation of Human Sexes" in which 1 indicates male, 2 female, 0 unknown, and 9 not applicable "is widely considered inadequate" ("<sex>").

14 That the patterns discussed here are reflective of this specific edition is made particularly clear when one considers that there are 351 exclamation marks in the body of the First Folio texts and 6,059 in those Folger plays that also appear in the First Folio; question marks, however, are more similar, with 10,881 in the First Folio and 11,572 in the Folger.

15 This reflects again the importance of measurement and selection, not just in the decision to focus on sentence-ending punctuation but also in the specific punctuation marks chosen—I might have included em dashes, but a review of the Folger editions indicated that these are predominantly used to mark interjections between thoughts or in conjunction with other sentence-ending punctuation.

16 Notably, the author-figure Quince is distinctive among the mechanicals for having a relatively high number of periods (83.3 percent) and low number of question marks (4.4 percent). Titania is in the middle ground for exclamation marks, with 9.0 percent.

17 We see some of the same patterns related to gender and class here as well, with the most exclamatory characters being the Boatswain (33.3 percent), Trinculo (18.6 percent), Caliban (15.6 percent), and Miranda (15 percent).

18 This variation is particularly interesting when one considers the point above, that the Folger texts have similar numbers of question marks to the First Folio ones, but substantially more exclamation marks.

19 The string "&" is an entity reference, a way of referring to ampersands within XML documents where the character itself is reserved for use within the markup.

20 It is worth noting that <subst> elements are not evenly distributed among the quartos: out of 669 instances, 458 are in the Bodleian fourth quarto (Arch. G d.41) and 171 are in the Folger's third copy of the third folio (3 STC 22277). Independent additions and deletions are somewhat more evenly dispersed but still show a tendency to cluster in certain copies.

21 I am using approximate numbers to reflect the fact that these categorizations have not been through a formal review process; the overall patterns in scale here are more important than the false precision suggested by exact numbers.

References

Bodleian Libraries. "Bodleian First Folio." Available at: www.firstfolio.bodleian.ox.ac.uk/.

Bodleian Libraries. "Encoding Documentation." Shakespeare Quartos Archive. Available at: www.quartos.org/.

Bodleian Libraries. "Shakespeare Quartos Archive." Available at: www.quartos.org/.

Bradley, John. "Documents and Data: Modelling Materials for Humanities Research in XML and Relational Databases." *Literary and Linguistic Computing*, vol. 20, no. 1, 2005, pp. 133–151.

Cummings, James. "The Text Encoding Initiative and the Study of Literature." *A Companion to Digital Literary Studies*, edited by Susan Schreibman and Ray Siemens, Blackwell, 2008, pp. 451–476.

Cummings, James. "Opening the Book: Data Models and Distractions in Digital Scholarly Editing." *International Journal of Digital Humanities*, vol. 1, 2019, pp. 179–193. Available at: link.springer.com/article/10.1007/s42803-42019-00016-00016.

DeRose, Steven, David Durand, Elli Mylonas, and Allen Renear. "What Is Text, Really?" *Journal of Computing in Higher Education*, vol. 1, no. 2, 1990, pp. 3–26.

Drucker, Joanna. "Performative Materiality and Theoretical Approaches to Interface." *Digital Humanities Quarterly*, vol. 7, no. 1, 2013. Available at: www.digitalhumanities.org/dhq/vol/7/1/000143/000143.html.

Emerson, Lori. *Reading Writing Interfaces: From the Digital to the Bookbound*. U of Minnesota P, 2014.

Flanders, Julia and Fotis Jannidis. "Data Modeling in a Digital Humanities Context: An Introduction." *The Shape of Data in Digital Humanities: Modeling Texts and Text-based Resources*, edited by Julia Flanders and Fotis Jannidis, Routledge, 2018, pp. 3–25.

Flanders, Julia and Fotis Jannidis. "A Gentle Introduction to Data Modeling." *The Shape of Data in Digital Humanities: Modeling Texts and Text-based Resources*, edited by Julia Flanders and Fotis Jannidis, Routledge, 2018, pp. 26–95.

Galloway, Alexander. *The Interface Effect*. Polity Press, 2012.

Hookway, Branden. *Interface*. MIT Press, 2014.

Shakespeare, William. "The Tempest." *Internet Shakespeare Editions*. Folio 1, 1623 (Old-spelling transcription). Available at: www.internetshakespeare.uvic.ca/doc/Tmp_F1/index.html.

Shakespeare, William. *New Variorum Edition of Shakespeare*. Edited by Richard Knowles and Paul Werstine, Modern Language Association. 2021. Available at: https://newvariorumshakespeare.org/about/.

Shakespeare, William. *The Folger Shakespeare*. Edited by Barbara Mowat and Paul Werstine, Folger Shakespeare Library. n.d. Available at: shakespeare.folger.edu/

Text Encoding Initiative. "About." Available at: www.tei-c.org/about/.

Text Encoding Initiative. "TEI Guidelines for Electronic Text Encoding and Interchange." Available at: https://tei-c.org/guidelines/

Turska, Magdalena, James Cummings, and Sebastian Rahtz. "Challenging the Myth of Presentation in Digital Editions." *jTEI*, no. 9, 2019. Available at: journals.openedition.org/jtei/1453.

Whitelaw, Michael. "Generous Interfaces for Digital Cultural Collections." *Digital Humanities Quarterly*, vol. 9, no. 1, 2015. Available at: www.digitalhumanities.org/dhq/vol/9/1/000205/000205.html.

PART IV

Display, navigation, and functionality

12

"INTO A THOUSAND PARTS DIVIDE"

The Pursuit of Precision in Shakespeare's Interfaces

Rebecca Niles

In Shakespeare's *Cymbeline*, Iachimo bets Posthumus that he can seduce Posthumus's wife, Imogen. Seeking to win the bet, Iachimo attempts to prove Imogen's infidelity by describing her bedchamber. In his description, Iachimo correctly recounts various decorations in the room, but never in quite enough detail to convince Posthumus of his claim. To Posthumus, while Iachimo's proof is accurate, it is not precise enough. "More particulars," Iachimo realizes, "Must justify my knowledge."

Where in *Cymbeline*, exactly, does Iachimo make this declaration? Using the section markers in the First Folio of 1623, you may find it in Actus Secundus, Scena Quarta.[1] But since that section of the play spans five columns, you will have to do some scanning of the text to find the lines. One hundred and forty-five years later, you may find it a little quicker in editor Edward Capell's 1767–68 edition by using his proprietary referencing system: *Cymbeline*, p. 43, lines 6–7 (counting from the top of the page yourself, since the line numbers aren't marked). Another century later, reading the first Cambridge edition of *Cymbeline* published in 1864, you may locate the phrase in question at Act II, Scene IV, somewhere between lines 75 and 80—though, due to imperfect composition and lack of clarity regarding which lines count as individual lines and which count as continuations of previous lines, it is difficult to be more specific than this.

Today, you can find Iachimo's statement at 2.4.97–98 (that is, if you are reading the 2011 Folger Edition). But what if you are only interested in a single word from this phrase, say, "particulars"? For most purposes it is probably sufficient to say that it is found within line 2.4.97, but to be even more precise, you could say that the word is located at 2.4.97.2: the second word in line 97 of Act 2, scene 4. Or, if you are using the application programming interface (API) endpoint from The Folger Shakespeare online (formerly Folger Digital Texts), you could point straight to the word: folgerdigitaltexts.org/Cym/word/w0187720. And what if you were interested in an even more specific part of the text? Say, for instance, just the root of the word, "particula," from the Latin meaning "small part, little bit" (Whitaker)?

It is the little bits of Shakespeare with which this chapter is concerned—or rather, the systems that we use to interact with increasingly minute particles of Shakespeare's texts, and the editorial decisions that shape these systems. They lie on the borders of Shakespeare's texts

DOI: 10.4324/9780367821722-17

and yet are integral to how we think and talk about them. They are a form of textual interface technology, with a history and a future.

The present chapter will focus on the ways in which editors, printers, and programmers assign indicators to fragments of Shakespeare that let us order, find, reference, and reproduce them. This chapter will address the mechanisms of textual indexing that have taken one form or another since the advent of Shakespeare in print, mechanisms that form the basis of the texts' navigational interface. We will extend our view outside of Shakespeare's texts to look at other types of symbolic interfaces – the convergence points between information and the mechanical means of transmitting it – to see that it is not just Shakespeare's texts that favor fragmentation into smaller, more indexible units; that symbolic interfaces generally seem to flourish best when managing communication in the smallest possible fragments. If anything, what makes Shakespeare's texts unusual is not the ways in which they have been heavily fragmented for efficient handling by both man and machine, but rather the ways in which they have *resisted* fragmentation.

In the prologue to Shakespeare's *Henry V*, from which the title for this chapter derives, the Chorus begs of the audience to join in the conceit that a grand narrative can be told using only such miniscule stand-ins as can fit on a stage: "O pardon, since a crookèd figure may / Attest in little place a million, / And let us, ciphers to this great account, / On your imaginary forces work" (Pro. 16–19). Likewise, in this chapter, I hope to reflect on a seemingly universal principle – that in symbolic interfaces there is a direct correlation between fragmentation of data into the smallest possible meaningful unit and the efficacy of the mechanical/technological means of transmitting it – by examining the trajectory of fragmentation of a single corpus, Shakespeare's texts. Just as Shakespeare's stories have for centuries been read as microcosms of human experience, Shakespeare's textual interfaces are singular examples of a recurring motif in human communication. For the interface theorist or architect, the most important conclusion may be that in human-text interfaces there is a tension between mechanical optimization and human usability that must be thoughtfully navigated. For the Shakespearean thinker, it may mean that we must reflect on how the precision of our technologies of transmission shape our texts and either support or impede avenues of interpretation. It is up to you, the reader, gently to hear and kindly to judge.

Shakespearean Interface: A Definition

Settling on a definition for "interface" is challenging, in part due to the word's condition as a "productively open-ended, and cross-disciplinary term" (Emerson x). While some authors, such as Brandon Hookway or Leo Manovich, take a more theoretical approach, my own lived experience as an interface architect and web programmer engenders a greater love for the more concrete and specific definitions of interface offered by Florian Cramer and Matthew Fuller.

Cramer and Fuller provide a fairly straightforward definition of interface: "Similar to both its meaning in chemistry and to the meaning of 'language,' 'interfaces' are the point of juncture between different bodies, hardware, software, users, and what they connect to or are part of" (150). Cramer and Fuller, sensitive to how open-ended the term "interface" is, provide us with a five-item typology from which to draw. Discussing the technical role of referencing systems in Shakespeare, we can adapt Cramer and Fuller's interface type no. 4 to suit our purposes; namely, that interface is a set of "[s]pecifications and protocols that determine relations between software and software, that is, application programming interfaces (APIs)" (149).

This definition, and in particular its reference to a specific computing concept (that of the API), may appear too specialized to apply to Shakespearean referencing systems as a whole, which are systems of specifications and protocols that provide a point of interface not only between software and software, but also between human and software/hardware, and between human and human with the aid of software/hardware as a common platform between them. However, Cramer and Fuller open the door to more inclusive thinking about interfaces. They write:

> The distinction between a 'user interface,' an 'Application Program Interface' (API), and a computer control language is purely arbitrary. That more complex interfaces to computer functions tend to be called 'programming languages' and less complex, more specialized ones are known as 'user interfaces' is simply a nomenclature arising out of convention. Since the user interface to a computer program is always symbolic, and involves syntactical and symbolic mappings for operations, it always boils down to being a formal language.
>
> *(150)*

In this sense, textual referencing systems are a type of formal language that provide symbolic mappings for operations, whether the operation be compiling, navigating, or invoking the text.

Fuller and Cramer's interface type no. 5 also applies: "symbolic handles, which, in conjunction with [feedback devices such as screens], make software accessible to users; that is, 'user interfaces'" (149). This definition of interface is particularly relevant to this chapter in how the combination of symbolic handles and hardware provides the mechanical means of supporting the specifications and protocols that allow Shakespeare texts and their readers (human and nonhuman alike) to converge. Since the very beginning of Shakespeare interfaces, the material circumstances of the hardware – the book – have contributed significantly to the system used to navigate the software – Shakespeare's texts. The translation of the text into the material space of the book, with its built-in physical compartments such as page and typographical line, provided a foundation for a system of increasingly precise symbolic handles, such as page number and line number, pointing to progressively smaller fragments of text.

How does such fragmentation bear out in the design and shape the function of textual interfaces, and in particular, the textual interfaces of Shakespeare? We will first review the role that fragmentation plays in information technology generally, and then look in particular at the evolution of textual navigation that was made possible through the fragmentation of Shakespeare's texts into smaller and smaller units. Finally, we will examine the current state of textual precision in modern digital Shakespeare and theorize about the limits of precision in Shakespeare's texts.

Precision Shakespeare: The Evolution of the Navigational Interface

The fragmentation of Shakespeare's texts into ever-smaller indexable fragments for the purpose of facilitating the interface between texts and texts, texts and humans, and humans and humans through the medium of texts, is not unique. Breaking down a subject into increasingly fine units so that it may be more closely observed, articulately manipulated, and exactly reproduced is a hallmark of precision engineering, modern information technology, and, before that, print technology. This section will examine this commonality in more detail.

The extent to which a system of measurement is used to fragment a subject for the purposes of observation, specification, or reproduction is a useful way of defining the level of precision inherent to the use of that system. For instance, if one measures the diameter of a pipe to be 52 millimeters, this measurement is more precise than if one measures the diameter to be 5 centimeters. Both statements are accurate – the diameter is indeed comprised of five of one type of unit, or 52 of another – but the statement that uses more (and necessarily smaller) fragments is more precise, as it describes the object in greater, more explicit detail. While possibly trivial on its face, precision begins to matter a great deal when talking about interfaces. Say you want this pipe to fit into, or interface with, a pipe fitting. Measuring both in centimeters will provide only so much assurance that they will fit together, leaving the rest to chance, whereas the likelihood that the pipe and the fitting will interface correctly is much higher if one knows that both the pipe and the fitting diameters measure precisely 52 millimeters. Different interfaces require differing degrees of this sort of assurance. The pipe and fitting, for instance, may interface reasonably well if they are within a millimeter of each other in diameter. Components of a mechanical watch, on the other hand, need to fit much more precisely if they are to interface smoothly with one another, and might need to measure within a couple of micrometres of one another, i.e., to the 1/1000th of a millimeter. This is known as the *degree of tolerance* of a given system, and it describes how tiny the fragments need to be that one uses when measuring, specifying, or reproducing something within that system.

Fragmentation of the whole into smaller and smaller units resulting in an increase in available precision is a recurring feature of many interfaces – not just mechanical interfaces, such as the interaction of different parts of a watch, but symbolic interfaces as well, interfaces where symbols convey information, such as computing, and even written language.

In order to understand how fundamental the principle of fragmentation is to symbolic interfaces, it may be helpful to consider how information can be measured. We are all fairly familiar with estimating physical properties of objects, and with using physical measures, such as of size or weight. For instance, we can guess that a US penny weighs less than a US nickel, and we can verify this by using a scale that measures in grams. If we want to find out whether a US penny outweighs a Canadian penny, we can increase the precision of our measurement by a factor of ten to confirm that it weighs more by 2 decigrams, or increase our precision by a factor of one hundred to discover that the difference is actually 15 centigrams.[2] But how do we observe how much information is in a symbol, or set of symbols? For that, we will need to borrow a concept and an equation from Claude Shannon's "A Mathematical Theory of Communication."

Claude Shannon was a mathematician, electrical engineer, and cryptographer who, as part of a treatise on encoding information for the purposes of transmission, came up with the concept of Shannon entropy. In its simplest application, Shannon entropy can be used as a measure of how much information potential a message contains, by calculating the message's probability against its alternatives. As Alan Galey writes, "In Shannon's model, information is not a thing … but rather a measure of the disambiguation required to express an intelligible message" (303). The term "message" is used very inclusively, and could entail a single symbol, or a longer transmission of any complexity whatsoever. Take the example of flipping a coin, versus rolling a six-sided die. Imagine that your friend has flipped a coin, but hasn't shown you the outcome.[3] How many yes/no questions would you need to ask them before you know what side it landed on? Just one: "Is it heads?" Regardless of whether the answer is yes or no, that single disambiguation tells you what you need to know. Therefore, the outcome of a coin-flip has very low Shannon entropy, contains very little information potential. Now, consider the six-sided die. If your friend rolls the die and asks you to figure out which side it landed on, you might be clever and reduce the number of questions you'll need to ask by first inquiring, "Is the value less than four?" This one disambiguation, your friend's first yes/no response, cuts your options in half, but even if you now know "Yes, the value is less than four," that still leaves you needing to ask at least one more question to determine which of the remaining three options are right (say you ask, "Is it one?" and the answer is "yes"), with a good chance of needing to ask a third (if the answer to "Is it one?" is "no," you now have to ask a new question, either "Is it two?", or "Is it three?"). Because of this need for somewhere between two and three disambiguation statements in order to get our answer, we can say that each face of the die has higher Shannon entropy than each coin side – carries greater information potential.

We can actually translate this concept into a unit of measurement by borrowing a small portion of Shannon's entropy equation: the base-2 (or "binary") logarithm of the number of possible outcomes.[4] The resulting units are commonly called *bits*, the term being an abbreviation of "binary digits." For the two-sided coin, the equation is log2(2), or 1 bit. For the six-sided die, the calculation would be log2(6), or 2.585 bits. In other words, the outcome of the die roll contains nearly 2.6 times more information than the coin flip – but we already knew that from picturing how many yes/no questions we'd need to ask. Here, log2(n) is simply the mathematical way of saying "how many questions to arrive at the outcome?" By analogy to our thought experiment containing the coin and the die, we can extrapolate that systems of communication differ in the information value that each part within that system contains based on how many unique symbols the system uses, and, using what we've learned about Shannon entropy, we now have a way of calculating that information value.

Computing inherently relies on the principle of representing even the most complex data through a collection of units with the smallest possible information value: the single bit.[5] All computer data ultimately must take the form of binary digits, or bits, which are about as informationally simple as one can imagine, in that they exist in one of only two states: on/off, is/isn't, one/zero – just like the coin. The irreducible minuteness of the unit of information inherent to binary storage is what makes the interface between the mechanical and the symbolic possible – it provides us with the ability to use material states to represent binary values. Bits have been mechanically registered by punching holes in a punch card, switching the magnetic polarity on a miniscule portion of a floppy disk or hard disk drive, creating microscopic grooves on the polycarbonate surface of a CD or DVD, or charging the floating gate transistors of a solid-state hard drive. The physical substrate is immaterial; as long as there is a simple change we can make to it, we have the ability to create a pattern of changes by which to record data. By breaking data down into the smallest possible fragments, computing achieves a critical function of the interface, to "condition the asymmetry between the elements combined" (Cramer and Fuller 150). In this case, the asymmetry in question is between the limitations of physical storage, on the one hand, and the extraordinary complexity of the sort of data that humans tend to like to work with. Combining these minute particles of information into sequences, we become capable of representing any sort of data imaginable.

In the same way that using binary digits – practically speaking, the smallest possible fragment of information – gives computing the facility to process, reproduce, and display data of any sort or complexity, the relatively minute information value of the characters in phonographic writing systems makes them similarly well suited to function as part of a mechanical system for storing information: printing. While printing existed in Asia long before it did in Europe ("History of Printing"), it was printing of books using the Latin alphabet that first reached truly industrial levels. By looking at several moveable-type sets created during the early days of mechanical printing, we can see the fundamental difference. One of the first sets of movable type ever created was the Korean Gyemi set, consisting of over 100,000 hanja characters created under the rule of King Taejong in 1403 (ibid.; Lee 5). Meanwhile, in Germany, using the Latin alphabet, the number of unique types created to print the

Gutenberg Bible of c.1455 (including special characters like ligatures) did not exceed 290 (Lee 14; Man 164). The underlying reason for the drastic difference in the amounts of type in each set is that Hanja is a logographic writing system, meaning that each character represents a word or meaningful part of a word. The Latin alphabet, on the other hand, is phonographic, meaning that its characters represent sounds, and have no intrinsic meaning. Logographic writing systems typically contain far more unique symbols than phonographic systems, because the set must expand along with the language's vocabulary, while phonographic systems typically represent new vocabulary with novel combinations of existing symbols. We know from our coin and die example that symbols that are part of a system within which there are many alternatives to choose from have higher entropy than symbols in a system containing a very limited number of alternatives. Comparing the Gyemi type set against the Gutenberg set, we can say that the Gyemi set has comparatively high entropy – 16.6 bits – while the Gutenberg set has comparatively low entropy – 8.2 bits.[6]

Just as is the case in using bits to transmit data for computing, the low-entropy nature of the characters used in Western printing conferred distinct practical advantages. The small character set of the Latin alphabet meant that type foundries had to make fewer different matrices (the molds used to cast each letter), and could profit more substantially from mass production. Meanwhile, printers benefitted from the fact that sets of type were smaller (consisting at the very most of several hundred, rather than many thousands, of unique characters) and therefore were both manageable in size and affordable in price. Also, each piece of type was interchangeable and therefore easily replaceable ("Faith in Numbers" 25:42). In computing, using a system made up of the tiniest particles of information possible presents a distinct opportunity for overcoming the mechanical limitations of presenting complex information. Conditions that made printing in the West so proliferative, similarly, had to do with the fact that the interchangeable, low-entropy symbols used in Western printing provided distinct mechanical and industrial advantages. Mechanical printing in the East, while an unparalleled technological accomplishment achieved in several Asian countries many years prior to any similar achievements in Europe, required mechanical complexity at a scale only within reach of kings and powerful magistrates. Meanwhile, the low-entropy system of symbols that conditioned the interface between knowledge and the mechanical means of representing it in Europe established conditions to bring printing within the reach of the individual proprietor.

The progressive division of Shakespeare texts into smaller and smaller parts over time brings it increasingly in line with the trends we've observed in both computing and Western printing, of representing even the most complex information through combinations of minute fragments. Increasingly fine degrees of tolerance to which Shakespeare texts can be referenced facilitated new points of interface among various entities and agents – text and reader, reader and reader, text and apparatus, text and performer, performer and performer, performer and audience, text and other text.

Shakespeare's textual interfaces have contained some level of fragmentation for their entire existence by nature of their container – the book. It may be hard to envision the book as fragmentary in nature, but in a basic sense, it is; compare the book to its predecessor, the scroll. Whereas with a scroll, the text is laid out on a single, continuous surface, text in a book is partitioned into pages. The text of a scroll has no partitions inherent to the medium (though it may have symbolic partitions, such as section heads), whereas the text in a book is necessarily broken up into pages, which comprise discrete, navigable units. The written content of a book, practically speaking, cannot exist outside of this discrete system. In a book there are no interpaginal states, no inbetween-ness from one page to another. A word or phrase can always be located precisely (albeit to a very low degree of tolerance), on a specific page; conceptually, there is no gray area, no middle ground between one page and the next, in which text may exist.

This fragmentary condition of the book is simultaneously limiting and empowering. While the boundaries of the page space may impose a rigidity in how texts can be displayed, it also makes texts significantly more navigable. Peter Stallybrass suggests that the invention of printing might be thought of less as a disruption to textual practices of the time and more as a significant step in "the invention of the navigable book" (44), as several affordances of the book facilitate interfacing with the text contained therein. The first affordance is what Stallybrass describes as the "capacity for random access" (42) or the ability to easily access any part of the text by opening the book to any given page (as opposed to having to continuously unroll a scroll to find a particular location). The second affordance of a technology that stores information as a series of discrete, ordered containers (in this instance, a bound book containing pages) has to do with its inherent indexing capacity. The page, given some form of sequential label (page number, signature, what have you), allows the operator to both find specific information by knowing the appropriate label, and to point others to specific information by sharing the appropriate label. This particular innovation, the partitioning of a text into discrete, indexable units, is critical to what makes the book a revolutionary interface—in Stallybrass's words, it "allowed you to get your finger into the place you wanted to find in the least possible time" (44). The book's simultaneous ability to maintain the rational cohesion of the text through the (more or less) immutable order of the sequential march of pages while at the same time allowing access to any given part of the text when occasion calls for it, as well as making possible the user's ability to both find and share specific information by knowing and sharing a key to its location in the book, are frequently overlooked, but crucial, features of the book interface.

Occasionally, a text will become so widely used and disseminated that one finds it printed in many different editions, with many different page layouts and page numbering systems. Using page numbers to interface between one edition and the next is therefore untenable, and navigational partitions must evolve that are independent of the individual container in which the text may be put. The Christian Bible is one such example, divided into Old and New Testaments, then further divided into books, the books into chapters, the chapters into verses. Shakespeare's plays are another such example.

The first gesture toward an explicit navigational interface in Shakespeare's plays came in the practice of breaking up play texts into acts and scenes.[7] The first instance of conscious, explicit division within the early printed Shakespeare play texts was the *Othello* quarto of 1622, which contained divisions for acts 2, 4, and 5. Act and scene divisions were otherwise nonexistent in Shakespeare's early texts until the First Folio, where they were applied without much consistency. Subsequent editions paid increasing attention to these divisions, and, following Nicholas Rowe's introduction of act and scene divisions in *all* the plays in his *Works of William Shakespeare* (1709), nearly every major collected edition subsequently included these types of division. The editors of most of these editions also made a conscious effort to make such divisions more systematic and regular (Werstine 16:53–17:26; Murphy 61). Few early editors, however, show a greater level of attention to establishing a precise system of reference for Shakespeare than Edward Capell in his collected works of 1768.

The way Capell describes his sources in his editorial introduction shows his concern for precision:

> Division of acts and scenes, they have none; ... Entries of persons are extreamely imperfect in them, (sometimes more, sometimes fewer than the scene requires) and their Exits are very often omitted; or, when mark'd, not always in the right place;

> and few scenical directions are to be met with throughout the whole ... [T]he reigning fault of all is in the measure: prose is very often printed as verse, and verse as prose; or, where rightly printed verse, that verse is not always rightly divided.
>
> (4)

And in his measured praise of Heminge and Condell's work in compiling the 1623 First Folio, he remarks: "some of their plays are divided into acts, and some others into acts and scenes; and that with due precision, and agreable to the Author's idea of the nature of such divisions" (7). This matter of precise indexing of texts by act and scene is important enough to Capell that he even includes a table in his edition to illustrate which plays of the Folio receive such treatment, and to what degree.

The navigational interface that Capell constructed for his editions became a tool in both his working papers and his published efforts. His manuscript variant notes (*Various readings [to Shakespeare]*), written between 1768 and 1775, are organized into a table that locates each variant by play, page, and line number, corresponding to the 1768 edition. Likewise, his *Notes and various readings to Shakespeare*, the first part of which was published in 1774 (though subsequently withdrawn), uses the play/page/line number schema to guide readers to the specific parts of the text to which the notes refer, turning the edition into a pre-digital codec for deciphering Capell's editorial apparatus. While this may seem unremarkable by today's standards, this database-like management of Shakespearean reference was novel in its time. Capell's exploitation of the indexable nature of page and *mise-en-page* provides an interface that not only facilitated his own editorial labors, but also provided a base on which to append supplementary work, and supplied a guide for readers to interpret that work.

While Capell's technique of using the structure of the printed book itself as part of his navigational interface provided him and others with the ability to refer to fragments of the play texts with unprecedented precision, it was not until the first volumes of the Cambridge edition appeared in 1863 that line numbers started being printed in the margins of the plays, signalling the line number as an explicit component of the textual interface to be used as part of every reader's encounter with the plays. The Cambridge edition not only printed line numbering along the side of the type page, but also used these line numbers to link the notes to the text to which they refer. The Cambridge edition, whether its editors ever consciously recognized it or not, is a technological successor to Capell's edition, with its use of typographical line numbering as a system for more precisely referencing textual fragments in Shakespeare.

In digital Shakespeare editions, electronic markup, such as Text Encoding Initiative-compliant XML (TEI-XML) offers a mechanism for handling texts with still greater precision than that of the line unit. Through its exploitation of TEI-XML, The Folger Shakespeare's (FS) XML base texts, and its associated API, allow people and programs alike to navigate and manipulate ever smaller fragments of texts: acts, scenes, lines, and even words, punctuation, and white space – precision nearly to the point of absurdity.

"Thinking Too Precisely"? Limitations of Interface Precision

So far, we have explored the Shakespearean textual apparatus as an interface that has a clear evolutionary trajectory toward increased precision in how the text can be navigated, indexed, and manipulated. But to what end? As Simon Winchester writes,

> Does a race for the ever-increasing precision ... actually offer any real benefit to human society? Is there perhaps a risk that we are somehow fetishizing precision,

> making things to ever-more-extraordinary tolerances simply because we can, or because we believe we should be able to?
>
> *(17)*

In *Hamlet*, the prince wonders whether his own inaction is caused by "some craven scruple of thinking too precisely on th' event (A thought which, quartered, hath but one part wisdom, and ever three parts coward)" (4.4.42–46). His seemingly compulsive dissection of the idea of "thinking too precisely" into quarters is reminiscent of Zeno's dichotomy paradox, which holds that motion is impossible because anything traveling from one point to another must first travel half-way, and then half-way of what is remaining, and so on into infinity.[8] Precision, achieved through the act of dividing the whole into ever smaller fragments, is a similarly infinite, and therefore perpetual, pursuit. Hamlet, quartering his own thoughts, traps himself in the act of "thinking too precisely," resulting in the impossibility of ever reaching a decision and taking action to resolve the conflict of the play. Is there a risk that as editors and engineers attempt to achieve still greater tolerances of precision, we, like Prince Hamlet, may find ourselves thinking too precisely about Shakespeare?

Computationally, there is little, if any, use for units either as broad or as idiosyncratic as the act, the scene, or even the line. FS's XML corpus, for instance, encodes Shakespeare's plays and poems fundamentally as combinatorial units of words, spaces, and pieces of punctuation. Michael Poston and I, in our construction of the XML schema, created a series of documents that *could* be rendered in the familiar acts, scenes, and lines of the printed Folger Editions from which the digital texts are derived. But these divisions are not an inherent requirement of the document and are in many respects achieved only by means of special workarounds that are purpose-built to satisfy the human need for less exacting means of navigating the text. In the FS corpus, lines do not exist as elements in any formal sense but are rather programatically reconstructed through a @corresp attribute assigned to a placeholder element called a <milestone>, in which the value of the attribute is a list of the identifiers for the words, spaces, and punctuation that make up a given line. In other words, practically speaking, lines only exist in the XML corpus as a set of instructions that give the rendering document the information it needs to display the lines familiar to the document's human readers. This is not to say that, as far as the code is concerned, Shakespeare is merely a random collection of words, spaces, and pieces of punctuation; the textual elements of each play have sequential identifiers that allow a processor to recreate Shakespeare's plays in intelligible reading order, regardless of whether the output is to be printed in a book, displayed online, encoded into a synthetic strand of DNA, or shot out into space in the form of electromagnetic waves. The key point is simply that while FS's XML corpus *has* acts, scenes, and lines, they are no longer an inherent attribute of the medium in the same way typographical line breaks are in printed texts. Therefore, in the era of precision Shakespeare, lineation takes on a new life: it is now purely a synthetic system, not dictated by material necessity but only by the uses for it which the human reader has. In other words, it is now solely an interface mechanism.

If lineation in digital Shakespeare is exclusively a human-to-text interface mechanism, and numerous developments in Shakespeare computing have shown that there are many ways in which Shakespeare can be indexed with much greater precision than the tolerance of the line, then why in digital Shakespeare does the unit of the line still prevail as a means of interfacing with the human reader?

First and foremost, we must acknowledge that the line in much of Shakespeare is not only an indexical and typographical entity, but also a formal one; the concept of the line is built into the poetic structure of verse, and as such can be said to exist as more than either an arbitrary symbolic unit or as a typographical exigency. The formal concept of the poetic line impacts how we hear meter and rhyme in verse, and how we might interpret the interrelationship of short, sometimes broken lines, perhaps spoken by different characters, as forming a complete metrical line.

Another reason why Shakespeare documents may continue to favor the line as a unit is a consequence of the way that human beings *think*. Though computerized Shakespeare allows us to create and work with minute fragments of text, this also means that there are many more textual fragments to keep track of – 1,850,858 of them, according to the FS XML corpus. This may be fine for a computer, assuming that it has the required memory and processing capacity. But human brains seem to be partial to just the opposite, preferring to lighten the load on the mind by grouping data in a process known in cognitive psychology as "chunking" (American Psychological Association, "Chunking, n." Def. 1). This process has specific implications for communication, and more particularly for the interface mechanism of lineation and how it conditions the relationship of the human mind to the text. The chunking theory holds that

> effective communication between humans depends on sorting information into units that do not exceed the mind's capacity to chunk them (the *chunking limit*). This has implications for the content and layout of written documents, diagrams and visual aids, websites, and so on.
>
> (*Def.* 2)

Introducing the concept in 1956, psychologist George A. Miller famously argued that the number of chunks of information that humans can reliably recall is about seven, and that the "magical number seven" pertains across other types of cognition limits as well, such as the ability to distinguish among a number of tones, volumes, tastes, and visual indicators. It is interesting to note, then, that the average number of words per line in editions of Shakespeare often hovers around – you guessed it – seven.[9] Therefore, while there are certainly more precise ways to navigate and talk about Shakespeare's texts than at the tolerance of the line, ways that are surely more logical from a computational perspective, thinking at the level of the line may well be part of the innate processes of human cognition.

Here, we can observe a fundamental gap between computer storage, which handles text as strings of discrete, low-entropy symbols, and human information processing, which manages large amounts of units of information by clumping them into larger (and therefore, higher-entropy) groups. Lineation bridges that gap, thereby performing one of the fundamental functions of the interface. As we reflected on earlier in relation to binary data encoding, "[i] nterfaces describe, hide, and condition the asymmetry between the elements combined" (150). In this case, the asymmetry in question is the difference between how computational and human agents in the communication network process information. In this way, lineation, which might be viewed in digital contexts as a stubborn throwback to the limitations of prior technology (i.e., the printed text with its set page layout), in fact provides a remarkably effective way to reconcile two fundamentally different, possibly even opposing, processes for information management – that of the human and that of the machine.

Yet another reason why still greater precision in Shakespearean textual interfaces eludes us is the lack of one crucial component that is indispensable in precision engineering: standards. Truly, we see in Shakespeare a parallel process to one observed in the history of precision in the sciences and in engineering, of a gradual trajectory toward managing data in finer and finer units. Just as in measure of length there were "the cubits of the Babylonians … the unciae of the Romans, the grain, the carat, the toise, the catty – and the yard and the half-yard, the span, the finger, and the nail of early England" (Winchester 331), so too in Shakespeare did there develop the act, the scene, the line, and later still more precise encoding elements such as <w>, <c>, and <pc>, to identify and call up increasingly specific segments of Shakespeare's texts. However, as Winchester writes

> the later development of precision ... demanded not so much a range of ... units, but trusted standards against which these lengths and weights and volumes and times and speeds, in whatever units they happened to be designated, could be measured.

To this date, and perhaps endemically, precision in Shakespeare is missing the key element of standardization.

Some calls have been made for such a standard. Alfred Hart, as early as 1932, notes that without a commonly accepted number of words per line of Shakespeare, editions would vary greatly in the number of lines they contain due to the fact that prose lines were determined by layout, not by any inherent qualities of the text. "To arrive at some uniform method of counting lines of plays," he writes, "we need a 'standard' prose line comparable with the blank-verse lines in fixity of word-value" (24–5). Hart's campaign for a standard prose line clearly failed, as nearly fifty years later, in 1980, Fredson Bowers notes the same inconsistencies between editions on what constitutes a line, and makes his own recommendations for standardization. Both Hart and Bowers point out that the lack of a standard line unit invalidates efforts at quantitative analysis of Shakespeare's works. Many bibliographers of the earlier twentieth century, and perhaps most especially Bowers, tried to overhaul the practice (and perhaps just as importantly, the public image) of Shakespearean textual scholarship from a mere collection of aesthetic judgments to a scientific practice. The effort to enact standards for the line as a unit so that quantitative analysis could be performed was one way of establishing parity between bibliography and all the other sciences that already had standards upon which to form a foundation for analysis. To this date, I am unaware of any commonly accepted standard that comprehensively defines the line in Shakespeare (aside from the poetic definition of iambic pentameter, which only applies to verse, and inconsistently at that). A cursory glance at modern editions of Shakespeare tells us that even if such a standard exists, it is not followed.

The digital model that eschews the typographical concept of the line entirely in favor of more precise indexing of words, spaces, and punctuation seems to offer a new platform for standardizing textual units, but even there a standard eludes us. For example, there is great potential to disagree on a common definition of what constitutes a single word. Shakespeare's texts are resplendent with compound nouns, not only ones that existed prior to the writing of the plays, but also ones Shakespeare himself coined. How and where to separate these compound nouns into one or more words varies greatly, depending upon the modernization of the text, editorial intervention, or even the personal habit of the encoder. This variability introduces noise into the data and compromises quantitative analysis.

Is such a thing as a standard Shakespearean unit achievable? A unit more exact than the decidedly un-standard unit of the line, a unit perhaps based on some as-of-yet unestablished benchmark of precision for indexing Shakespeare's texts? And can we apply such standards to come to a more precise system that both human and nonhuman readers may use to interface with Shakespeare? As someone responsible for building and maintaining Shakespeare interfaces, I am inclined to believe that as engineers we can continue to experiment with ways of encoding the text to increasingly precise degrees for the purposes of improving the interface between the text and nonhuman readers (such as document compiling programs, internet clients, or machine learning algorithms), while still generating productively imprecise interfaces between the text and its human readers by suppressing unnecessary detail in the human-readable output of our encoding – the texts we all read on paper and on our screens. However, as we continue to refine, we must keep in mind the epistemological consequences of such a pursuit.

One of the central desiderata of both standards and precision in modern engineering is determinism – the ability to absolutely predict the behavior and outcomes of a system (Evans 3847). Precision, in other words, is a way to know the future by limiting as much as possible the potential for surprise. To manage Shakespeare's texts with ever-greater precision is to imply that we can know them absolutely. As the variability in defining the boundaries of both the line and the word demonstrate, precision Shakespeare requires a set text, wherein textual variants have been finally either accepted as canon or discarded, wherein further investigation of textual difference is foreclosed, and new interpretations are precluded. Such a state is not only unnatural to textual transmission, in which variation is a regular consequence of texts that travel from state to state across time, but also antithetical to Shakespeare studies, of which fresh and novel interpretation is its lifeblood.

Precision brings certainty – the ability to know the future by safeguarding against the unexpected. But with certainty comes the exclusion of new possibilities. In Shakespeare's *3 Henry 6*, the spiritually defeated King Henry laments the uncertainty of his fate and longs for a life he can measure precisely, and therefore predict:

> Would I were dead, if God's good will were so,
> For what is in this world but grief and woe?
> O God! Methinks it were a happy life
> To be no better than a homely swain,
> To sit upon a hill as I do now,
> To carve out dials quaintly, point by point,
> Thereby to see the minutes how they run:
> How many makes the hour full complete,
> How many hours brings about the day,
> How many days will finish up the year,
> How many years a mortal man may live.
> When this is known, then to divide the times:
> So many hours must I tend my flock,
> So many hours must I take my rest,
> So many hours must I contemplate,
> So many hours must I sport myself,
> So many days my ewes have been with young,
> So many weeks ere the poor fools will ean,
> So many years ere I shall shear the fleece;
> So minutes, hours, days, months, and years,
> Passed over to the end they were created,
> Would bring white hairs unto a quiet grave.
>
> *(2.5.21–40)*

Henry's longing for a simple, safe, precisely measured life begins as a death-wish, and every step in his fantasy leads him inexorably toward "a quiet grave." In this passage, precision, certainty, and oblivion are interconnected.

Herein lies the hidden power of imprecision: its capacity to resist certainty, and to accommodate, and even incubate, the unknown. Precision's natural enemy is indeterminacy, but indeterminacy is a constitutive element of challenging literature. Imprecise interfaces provide humans with the ability to navigate while also allowing the space needed to make their own interpretations. We *need* an interface that is forgiving, that is productively low-tolerance. It is the very imprecision of the common Shakespearean interface – which goes no deeper than the line, which differs from edition to edition, which resists consensus on the very definition of what a line, or even a word, entails – that acts as a constructive bridge, not only between the procedural handling of data in computation and the associative grouping of data by human minds, but also between what is actual and what is possible.

Acknowledgments

Support for the writing of this chapter was provided by the Folger Shakespeare Library. I am grateful to the editors of this volume, Dr. Paul Budra and Dr. Clifford Werier, for their thoughtful guidance and keen edits. This chapter is dedicated to Dr. Alan Galey, to whom I am forever indebted – both for his innovative approach to Shakespeare and Information Theory, and for his profound influence on my career as a Shakespeare technologist.

Notes

1 Our earliest witness to *Cymbeline*; see luna.folger.edu/luna/servlet/detail/FOLGER~1~1~1821~228030:Mr–William-Shakespeares-comedies,-?qvq=q:22273%20cymbeline&mi=10&trs=267.

2 Analysis based on coin weights specified by the United States Mint and the Royal Canadian Mint (United States Mint; The Royal Canadian Mint). This comparison assumes a US penny minted to 2019 specifications, and a Canadian penny minted to the specifications in place between 2000 and May 4, 2012, when the last Canadian penny was created in Winnipeg, Manitoba (Schwartz).

3 A visualization of this analogy can be found in the video "Information Entropy" by The Khan Academy. Available at: khanacademy.org/computing/computer-science/informationtheory/moderninfotheory/v/information-entropy.

4 This small excerpt of Shannon's entropy equation gives us a handy mathematical expression of the nominal entropy of a system of symbols, but intentionally leaves out the part that deals with variable probability (see note 5) for the sake of conveying the general principle as succinctly as possible. The equation in question, log2(n), is sometimes expressed as –(log2(1/n)), wherein one over n represents the chance of any one of the possible outcomes. But the result, for our very limited use here, is the same for either expression.

5 Again, we are leaving probability out of the question, but in reality it is possible for a symbol to have Shannon entropy of less than 1 bit, if there are only two outcomes and the probability is unbalanced.

6 Once more, the element of actual probability within a system is ignored for the sake of simplicity. In the actual *use* of these two type sets, many conventional factors in the two respective communication systems would govern the entropy of the actual printed messages; for instance, in English, factors such as the high probability of certain characters appearing together, for example "q" and "u," and the low probability of long strings of consonants, would considerably lower the entropy of the printed result. The general observation, however, that logographic systems are relatively high-entropy compared to phonographic systems, is true, regardless of the particulars of a given language that uses such systems.

7 The following four paragraphs are adapted from my original treatment of the subject in *Shakespeare Quarterly* (Galey and Niles 43–51).

8 For a more nuanced explanation of the Dichotomy Paradox, see Nick Huggett, "Zeno's Paradoxes: 3.1 The Dichotomy." *Stanford Encyclopedia of Philosophy* (2010). Available at: plato.stanford.edu/entries/paradox-zeno/#Dic.

9 The Folger Editions, for instance, has an average line-length of 7.318 words.

References

American Psychological Association. "Chunking, n."*APA Dictionary of Psychology*, American Psychological Association, 2020. Available at: dictionary.apa.org/chunking.

Capell, Edward. *Notes and various readings to Shakespeare*. London, 1774.

Capell, Edward. *Various readings [to Shakespeare*]. ca. 1775. Folger Shakespeare Library, Manuscript.

Cramer, Florian, and Matthew Fuller. "Interface." *Software Studies: A Lexicon*, edited by Matthew Fuller, MIT Press, 2008, pp. 149–153. Available at: ebookcentral.proquest.com/lib/amherst/detail.action?docID=3338867.

Emerson, Lori. *Reading Writing Interfaces: From the Digital to the Bookbound*. U of Minnesota P, 2014.

Evans, Chris J. "Precision Engineering: An Evolutionary Perspective." *Philosophical Transactions of the Royal Society*, vol. 370, 2012, pp. 3835–3851. doi:10.1098/rsta.2011.0050.

"Faith in Numbers." Performance by James Burke, *Connections*, BBC. Available at: youtube.com/watch?v=z6yL0_sDnX0.

Galey, Alan. "Networks of Deep Impression: Shakespeare and the History of Information." *Shakespeare Quarterly*, vol. 61, no. 3, 2010, pp. 289–312. Available at: jstor.org/stable/40985586.

Galey, Alan, and Rebecca Niles. "Moving Parts: Digital Modeling and the Infrastructures of Shakespeare Editing." *Shakespeare Quarterly*, vol. 68, no. 1, 2017, pp. 21–55. doi:10.1353/shq.2017.0002.

Hart, Alfred. "The Number of Lines in Shakespeare's Plays." *The Review of English Studies*, vol. 8, no. 29, 1932, pp. 19–28. doi:10.1093/res/os-viii.29.19.

Lee, Hee-Jae. "*Korean Typography in 15th Century*." Paper presented at World Library and Information Congress: 72nd IFLA General Conference and Council, 24 May, 2006, Seoul, Korea. Available at: origin-archive.ifla.org/IV/ifla72/papers/085-Lee-en.pdf.

Man, John. *Gutenberg: How One Man Remade the World with Words*. John Wiley & Sons, 2002.

Miller, George A. "The Magical Number Seven, Plus or Minus Two: Some Limits on Our Capacity for Processing Information." *Psychological Review*, vol. 63, no. 2, 1956, pp. 81–97. doi:10.1037/h0043158.

Murphy, Andrew. *Shakespeare in Print: A History and Chronology of Shakespeare Publishing*. Cambridge UP, 2003.

"Particula." *William Whitaker's Words*, U of Notre Dame. Available at: archives.nd.edu/cgi-bin/wordz.pl?keyword=particula.

Shakespeare, William. *The Tragœdy of Othello, the Moore of Venice As It Hath Beene Diuerse Times Acted at the Globe, and at the Black-Friers, by His Maiesties Seruants*. London, 1622.

Shakespeare, William. *Mr William Shakespeare His Comedies, Histories, and Tragedies: Set out by Himself in Quarto, or by the Players His Fellows in Folio, and Now Faithfully Republish'd from Those Editions in Ten Volumes Octavo; with an Introduction: Whereunto Will Be Added, in Some Other Volumes, Notes, Critical and Explanatory, and a Body of Various Readings Entire*. London, 1768.

Shakespeare, William. *The Works of William Shakespeare*. Edited by William Aldis Wright*et al.*, vol. 9, London, 1864.

Shakespeare, William. *Cymbeline*. Edited by Barbara A. Mowat and Paul Werstine, Simon & Schuster, 2011.

Shakespeare, William. "Cymbeline." *The Folger Shakespeare*. Edited by Barbara Mowat, et al., Folger Shakespeare Library, March 21, 2021. Available at: shakespeare.folger.edu/shakespeares-works/cymbeline/.

Shakespeare, William. "Hamlet" *The Folger Shakespeare*. Edited by Barbara Mowat, et al., Folger Shakespeare Library, March 21, 2021. Available at: shakespeare.folger.edu/shakespeares-works/hamlet/.

Shannon, C. E. "A Mathematical Theory of Communication." *Bell System Technical Journal*, vol. 27, no. 4, 1 January 1948, pp. 623–656. doi:10.1002/j.1538-7305.1948.tb00917.x.

Schwartz, Daniel. "Obituary: Canadian Penny, 1858–2013 | CBC News." *CBCnews*, CBC/Radio Canada, 4 February 2013. Available at: cbc.ca/news/canada/obituary-canadian-penny-1858-2013-1.1315144.

Stallybrass, Peter. "Books and Scrolls: Navigating the Bible." *Books and Readers in Early Modern England*. Edited by Elizabeth Sauer and Jennifer Andersen, U of Pennsylvania P, 2002, pp. 42–79.

The Royal Canadian Mint. "A National Symbol – the 1-Cent Coin." Available at: mint.ca/store/mint/about-the-mint/1-cent-5300004.

United States Mint. "Coin Specifications." Available at: usmint.gov/learn/coin-and-medal-programs/coin-specifications

Werstine, Paul. "Episode 31: Editing Shakespeare." *Shakespeare Unlimited from The Folger Shakespeare Library*, 9 September 2015. Available at: collections.folger.edu/detail/shakespeare-unlimited-editing-shakespeare/c3fff13c-2cc5–44f8–9fa6–705cf366878a.

Winchester, Simon. *The Perfectionists: How Precision Engineers Created the Modern World*. HarperCollins, 2018.

13

DOES JONSON BREAK THE DATA MODEL?

Interrelated Data Models for Early Modern English Drama

Meaghan Brown

> I am resolv'd
> To be a patterne to all Maides hereafter
>
> *(Heywood 1369–70)*

When Bess Bridges offers herself up as a "patterne to all Maides," like the factotum who appears on the quarto's title page (Figure 13.1), she invites young women to model their "constancy in love" after her actions in the wake of her lover's (presumed) death. As editors, we are able to deduce a different sort of pattern from *The Fair Maid of the West*: a model of the significant properties of a play in its earliest printed form. The creation of such models involves an iterative process, as the understanding of one early modern play is nuanced with information from others. In this process, we can begin to build a picture of the various ways the publishers of early modern English drama organized and represented textual and performance information. While the early printed playbook is an interface between the individual reader and the text of the play, a data model is an abstraction of that individuated interface: a way of marking certain elements of a text or set of texts that serves as a theory about their significant properties. Modeling the printed playbook allows editors to understand, mark, and reinterpret textual and performative elements of early modern drama in new interfaces, including digital editions and data visualizations.

Modeling the logic that underpins the interface of early modern printed playbooks and their transmission of performed plays requires analysis and testing. Extrapolating from a single example often cannot describe a set, as when Mullisheg, the King of Morocco and Fez, proposes Bess as a model for all English women—including Queen Elizabeth. Bess informs him that his model is misapplied: "You cast a blush upon my maiden cheeke, / To patterne me with her. Why Englands Queene / She is the onely Phœnix of her age"—in other words, a model built on Bess cannot adequately describe Elizabeth (Heywood 1945–1947). Data models are useful in how they can be applied to describe the semantic and visual information significant to the printed interface of early modern drama and to serve as the basis for interpreting and rendering that information in user interfaces for new editions. They can also be informative when they fail at describing an outlier, highlighting an example's differences from the rest of the dataset as it is currently described by the model.

DOI: 10.4324/9780367821722-18

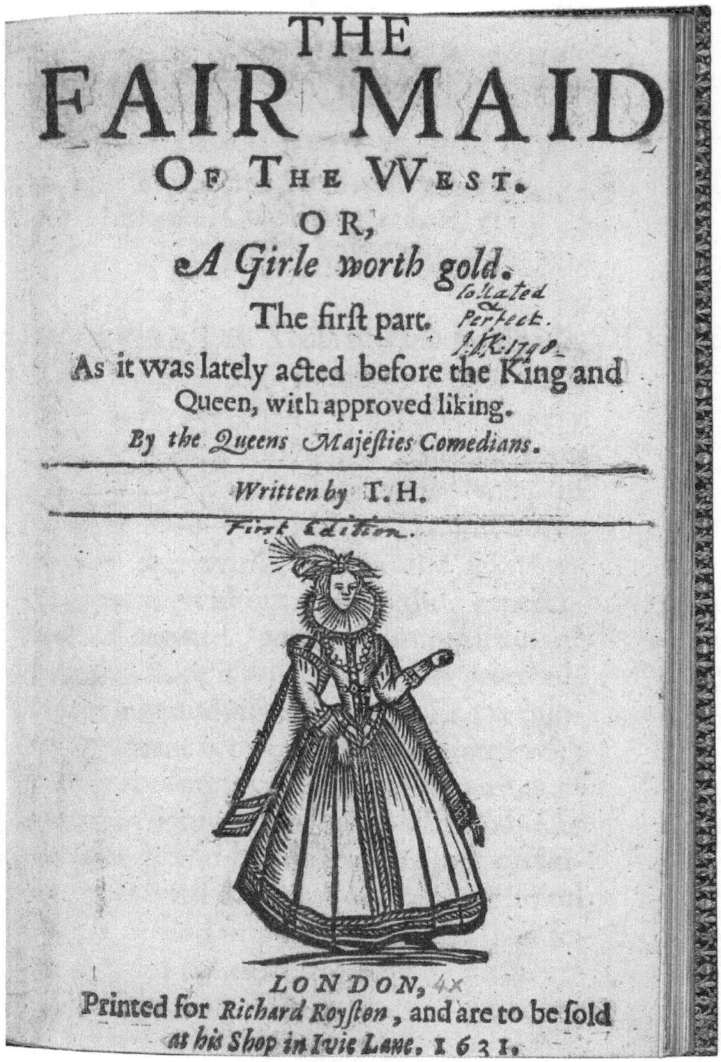
THE
FAIR MAID
OF THE WEST.
OR,
A Girle worth gold.
The first part.
As it was lately acted before the King and
Queen, with approved liking.
By the Queens Majesties Comedians.

Written by T. H.

LONDON,
Printed for *Richard Royston*, and are to be sold
at his Shop in Ivie Lane. 1631.

Figure 13.1 Thomas Heywood, *The Fair Maid of the West, Or A Girl Worth Gold*, 1 (1631)
Source: title page. Folger Shakespeare Library STC 13320 v. 1.

The early publishers of printed drama developed conventions for representing significant features of performative texts through systems of textual layout, font choices, symbols, and paratextual apparatuses. As Rebecca Niles and Michael Poston argue, editorial "strategies for transcribing, editing, and encoding a text are based on a perceived data model" of the instance being edited (121). In creating digital editions, we translate often implicit rules for information organization from print exemplars into explicit semantic and visual encoding. Layout decisions and typographic choices carry meaning but require interpretation: is a stage direction squeezed into a line because the compositor lacked room, or does that action interrupt a speech? Is that text italic because it's a header or a stage direction? Readers perform this interpretation of printed interfaces every time they read; in creating the encoding that permits flexible digital interfaces, the editor must be explicit about what the typography indicates.

Practical considerations in the print-house may have driven many of these choices—Tiffany Stern points out that the use of italic fonts for extratextual dramatic elements was "somewhat settled on" by the 1590s and that this predilection "preserved the full range of roman letters for the play's dialogue" (182). The trend taught readers to differentiate between spoken text and stage action through font and placement. The modern encoder must grapple with the interpretation of signs created in a print shop that was still developing a language for representing performative movement, sound, and speech, and translate those signs into markup that allows the signs to be consistently identified and represented. As Claire M.L. Bourne argues, "nothing about the way plays looked on the printed page *circa* 1600 was inevitable," but rather "by-products of more than a century of typographic experiments that tested the capacity of moveable type to articulate in textual form the most significant—and seemingly unprintable—dynamics of plays in performance" (1). Our subsequent need to translate the printed page to digital formats that are both machine-readable and legible to modern readers in digital interfaces adds a layer of interpretive complexity that is facilitated by theorizing the data model underlying the project.

In their "gentle introduction to data modeling" in the humanities, Julia Flanders and Fotis Jannidis explain that creating a "curation-driven" data model for a corpus of texts is a balancing act between "standardization and expressiveness, or, put another way, the fact that the better a model suits one specific case the worse it will fare in the general case, and vice versa" (88–89). The more consistent the data is, the easier it is to walk the line between specificity and wide applicability. Early modern plays, particularly in their earliest printed forms, are rarely consistent, either internally or across a corpus. Playbooks vary from printer to printer, or even compositor to compositor. New innovations in layout and paratextual features were introduced as the genre developed. Some authors and printers innovate to represent shifts in the performance practices on stage, to reference other genres, for expediency in production, or just for novelty. Nor is the data structure derived from the physical exemplar (even in aggregate) necessarily the only operative model needed to create a usable interface for a digital documentary edition. Editors must also take into account modern users' expectations for plays and for the affordances of the digital format. Finally, the encoded edition needs to be written in such a way that it can be transformed into something formatted for reading online or in print.

In 2014, the Folger Shakespeare Library set out to create documentary editions of non-Shakespearean early modern English drama. The Digital Anthology of Early Modern English Drama (EMED) was conceived as a comparative corpus to complement the Folger Digital Texts of Shakespeare, now known as the Folger Shakespeare.[1] Although the Folger Shakespeare (in both print and digital formats) are wildly popular modern scholarly editions of Shakespeare's complete works,[2] EMED was envisioned as a documentary corpus, a first step in making a number of plays by *other* playwrights freely accessible by creating rigorously accurate representations of a single printed witness. EMED texts represent a copy of the first printed edition of plays ranging from the famous—Christopher Marlowe's *Doctor Faustus*—to the rightfully obscure—John Fletcher's *The Faithful Shepherdess*. From a list of 403 plays roughly contemporary to Shakespeare's output, thirty-six plays were selected for editorial attention and twenty-nine documentary editions were eventually produced.[3]

The EMED team developed the data model for this project as we edited and encoded the corpus in eXtensible Markup Language (XML) using standards from the Text Encoding Initiative (TEI Consortium, "P5 Guidelines"). The encoded texts were then transformed using eXtensible Stylesheet Language (XSL) stylesheets into HTML and PDF reading copies.

The EMED project borrowed heavily from the encoding and stylesheets designed for the Folger Shakespeare—in essence, borrowing from the Folger Shakespeare's data model—which allowed us to leverage tools built for that corpus, such as those available through the Folger Shakespeare's Application Programming Interface (API), and enabled comparisons between the corpora (see Niles and Poston). In doing so, the team also encountered a second basic tenet of data modeling. As Flanders and Jannidis note, a model "can also be used to test whether a given set of data obeys these constraints" (6). The EMED team was able to craft consistent encoding and display rules for playbooks containing works by John Lyly, George Peele, Francis Beaumont, and others, but these rules were challenged by Ben Jonson's 1631 publication of *The Staple of News* and *Bartholomew Fair*. In what follows, I will explore some of the features captured by the EMED model, ways we adapted the encoding methods developed for the Folger Shakespeare to account for different descriptive needs, and the challenges presented by Ben Jonson's works, which ultimately were not included in the published corpus.

The mandate for the "featured plays" corpus was a broad one. This short list of plays emphasizes the variety of early modern drama: single-author works and collaboratively written plays; a range of genres, with an aim at proportional representation of tragedies, comedies, history plays, and less common types like pastorals; frequently taught plays balanced with a few more obscure ones. The corpus features a single author cluster—Christopher Marlowe—as well as several anonymous plays. Twelve playing companies premiered these plays, while ten companies are mentioned on title pages. Although no plays by (known) female authors made the cut, the work of two female Stationers, Joan Broome and Joan Orwin, are included. Some printers produced multiple plays—Valentine Simmes and Nicholas Okes both printed plays for multiple publishers and each is responsible for four plays in the corpus. Printing early modern playbooks was a collaborative process, and although our data model did not attempt to assign responsibility for various textual features, we documented the multiple responsible parties in the metadata.

The result was a corpus with a range of physical and textual features. Most were printed in quarto, although five on the short list first appeared in folio and three in octavo. Some were published in collections, as in the case of Christopher Marlowe's *Tamburlaine 1* and *Tamburlaine 2* and the substantial Beaumont and Fletcher folio of 1647. Some—but not many—featured lists of actors or characters before the play; more included dedicatory epistles or poems. Act and scene divisions are present in only about two-thirds of the texts and are not consistently indicated. In *Tamburlaine 1*, for example, act 2 has divisions clearly marked for scenes 1, 2, 3, and 6, but not for 4, 5, or 7. Characters speak or exit without stage directions marking their entrance, or they enter, but their exits are implied. Our task was to write rules to clearly describe these diverse plays in ways that helped researchers ask interesting questions, whether they were reading the play in a browser through our custom-built HTML interface, reading offline in PDF, or analyzing the encoded text in its XML format or through data visualizations.

The encoding team worked to create scrupulously accurate transcriptions and then layered in encoding that would allow these transcriptions to take advantage of display and analysis tools built for the Folger Shakespeare (discussed below). We were not starting from a blank slate. The project leveraged work by Martin Mueller's "Shakespeare His Contemporaries" (SHC), a corpus linguistics project that aimed to provide transcriptions of early modern texts annotated with part of speech tagging (Mueller), now part of the Early Print Project (Loewenstein and Mueller). The SHC project was, itself, built on transcription work done by the Early English Books Online Text Creation Partnership (EEBO-TCP), a project to transcribe early modern books from Chadwyck-Healey's Early English Books Online facsimile collection (*Text Creation Partnership*). The EMED data model integrated elements from the Folger Shakespeare and these precursor projects, while prioritizing changes to the model which helped us to accurately and consistently represent the physical playbook that was ultimately the source of each text. Our stylesheet transformed the XML encoding into an HTML interface that allows readers to switch between original transcription and lightly regularized versions of the texts, orienting themselves with references to the physical page, to the digital facsimile, and to the text.

Our first step was to check the SHC texts against Early English Books Online images of the playbook, and where those were illegible, against the microfilm Early English Books series from which they were digitized. By working back through this chain of remediation, the EMED team was able to fill gaps and correct the text to represent a single printed witness (Figure 13.2).

This working method influenced decisions about which layout features the project could accurately record and highlighted the difference between EMED's editorial goals and the efforts of previous projects. The exact relationship between the transcribed text and the facsimiles in EEBO is represented with the @facs attribute. EEBO images include both pages in an opening, so the @facs values include both the image number and an *a* or *b* to indicate the page, with *a* signalling the verso and *b* the recto; title pages are often "1-b" in this system because they are typically preceded by a blank endleaf. Another method of locating oneself within the text, printed signatures, were transcribed and encoded by EMED editors along with catchwords and running headers using the formework <fw> element. Not considered a significant part of the text in earlier projects like the EEBO-TCP and SHC—and thus not transcribed—formework can carry clues for understanding how a play was printed, as when changes to the running header might indicate that the skeleton forme was reset.

Unlike SHC and the EEBO-TCP it was in turn based on, EMED reintroduced line breaks, using the line beginning element <lb> in the encoded prose, as well as indicating turn-overs and turn-unders with their accompanying metamarks. This echoed the Folger Shakespeare's encoding, where line breaks are preserved so that line numbers match between the physical and digital editions. Preserving line breaks, turn-overs, and turn-unders in the "original" reading allows readers to easily compare the transcription to a digital facsimile or physical copy. Encoding these line breaks goes further: by pairing EMED transcriptions with extremely detailed digital images from the Folger's holdings, we were able to create a dataset that facilitated experiments with Optical Character Recognition (OCR). Being explicit about where turn-overs and turn-unders appear in the physical playbook offers other analytical possibilities, allowing for the quantification of long lines, the frequency of spacing challenges, or analysis of patterns based on where such challenges occur. Encoding turn-overs as their own milestone also made it possible to write flexible transformation rules for their display in the online interface. The regularized reading relineates the text and does not display

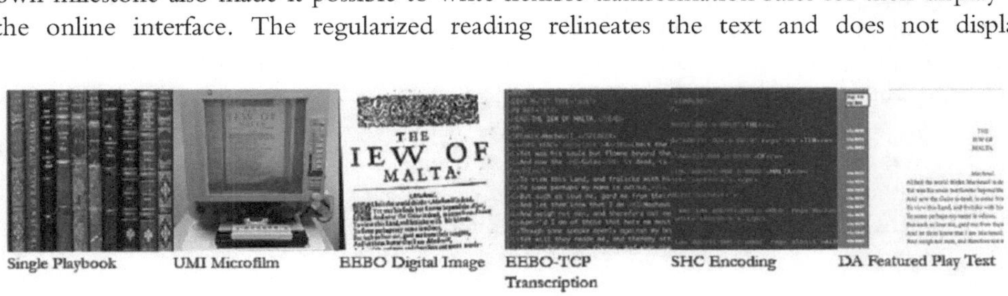

Figure 13.2 EMED's chain of remediation: single playbook, UMI microfilm, EEBO digital image, EEBO-TCP transcription, SHC encoding, EMED featured play text (Folger Shakespeare Library)

metamarks, typically single parentheses, prioritizing the logical textual structure over the physical layout.

The EMED team did not translate every aspect of a book's layout into encoding or replicate it in the reading interface. We acknowledged, for example, that it was impossible to record precise line spacing while working from digital facsimiles. For the same reason, no attempt was made to record the size of blanks used to fill out lines horizontally, although bibliographical scholarship on the use of em-quads demonstrates the importance of precise measurements (see Blayney). We could, however, choose to encode a feature but not render it. The Beaumont and Fletcher folio of 1647 is printed with two columns per folio page. Although the beginning of a new column is noted using the column beginning <cb> element, displaying the text as a single scrolling column works far better for readers with limited screen space. Similarly, we chose to standardize font distinctions, representing spoken text in a roman font and using italics for any text which varies from the primary font. These variations appear for a variety of reasons, including spoken names, foreign language passages, emphasis, or distinct textual units. *Tamburlaine 1*'s prologue is printed in roman, with the main text in blackletter; the font distinction is one of several signals that prologues were often less stable than other textual elements in a play. Replicating early modern blackletter with an updated blackletter font would not aid any scholarly question and would make the text more difficult to read for some of our target users; for *Tamburlaine*, the different textual units are wrapped in different <div> elements. The first edition of *Doctor Faustus* employs blackletter for spoken text, roman for names within the spoken text, and italic for Latin passages; in EMED both kinds of differentiated texts are rendered in italic, however, the Latin is wrapped in a <foreign> element, while in-text names are wrapped in the <name> tag. The semantics of the first edition are preserved, if not the font choices.

Because EMED's interfaces aimed to make the early modern texts not only more available but more *accessible* to modern readers and to computational manipulation, particularly search functions, we made an early decision to include regularized readings. Like the choice to forego the use of blackletter, the regularized reading provided a chance to meet the needs of targeted audiences such as students. We were not aiming to produce a fully modernized version. We updated u/v and i/j conventions but retained contractions and older word endings and forms: *doth*, not *does; think'st*, not *thinks*. We avoided over-correcting characters who purposefully misspeak or where language may be purposefully mis-represented: we did not, for example, correct issues in Faustus's Latin spells. We maintained elided syllables to avoid obscuring word choices that might affect meter or rhyme: *desp'rate, flow'ring, ne'er*. We were particularly conservative with representations of foreign languages, such as the "stage Dutch" in *Shoemaker's Holiday*.

Any change that went beyond this conservative practice, such as a reading that corrected a turned *u* or *n*, we marked with a footnote using the <note> element. When Lacy first introduces his disguise as a Dutch journeyman shoemaker, he enters with a mixed English and stage Dutch drinking song:

> Der was een bore van Gelderland, Frolick si byen,
> He was als dronck he cold nyet stand, vpsolce se byen,
> Tap eens de canneken drincke **scheue** mannekin.
>
> *(Dekker 453–455)*

The regularized reading corrects spelling on English words such as "cold" to "could" but leaves the stage Dutch, with the exception of "scheue," which is bolded and linked with a footnote: "The regularized reading schone is amended from the original scheue" (Dekker n.3). The *u* in this word may be a simple mistake, a missort or turned letter, or it may be part of the larger issue of transpositions and typographical errors identified by a number of modern editors, who characterize the mangling of the language as ignorance: "the compositor … was doubtless not familiar with Dutch" (Smallwood and Wells 106). Although writing about a different example, Robert Smallwood and Stanley Wells note that "In the circumstances the most honest editorial procedures seems to be to emend while admitting that obscurity remains" (107). While we did not correct other errors in Dekker's (or his compositor's) pseudo-Dutch, we had a policy of noting and offering alternatives to turned *u* and *n* characters, so in this case we adopted the reading prevalent in modern scholarly editions. Our stylesheet rendered <note> elements as hyperlinked footnotes in the final HTML.

One of the most interesting challenges to the regularization process was how to expand the abbreviated speech prefixes indicating which character speaks the line. The earliest surviving dramatic dialogue in English print, *Everyman*, published by Richard Pynson in 1515, indicates speakers by placing the character's full name in the outer margin of each page; on rectos, this means that the speaker appears to the *right* of the spoken text. Early printers also used "pilcrows to articulate discrete textual units"; as Bourne notes, this strategy for delineating sections of text was imported from scribal rubrication (3). By 1576, when the opening of the first purpose-built theater inspired new demand for printed drama, publishers were experimenting with ways to craft a reading interface that facilitated an understanding of dialogue as performance. The anonymous *Common Conditions* uses the outer margins for full speakers' names like *Everyman*, but the printer chose to indent the first line of each new speech. While the spoken text is set in blackletter, the speakers' names appear in roman (*Common Conditions*). In the majority of the texts chosen for EMED's edited corpus, the printers favored a more compact method: speakers are indicated by three to four letter abbreviations appearing at the start of their speech within the text block, sometimes indented and often distinguished from the spoken text by font choice: italic in roman texts, roman in blackletter. Each of these visual distinctions—font choice, placement of the speaker's name, and the use of either pilcrow or spacing—serves to mark the two types of text as having different functions in the reading interface. Because they have different functions for readers, they also needed to be encoded differently: with speech prefixes encoded using the <speaker> element and the spoken text encoded more flexibly, using the <ab> anonymous block element.

The abbreviations used for speech prefixes could sometimes lead an unwary compositor into trouble and, as a result, caused challenges for our efforts to provide fully expanded speakers' names in our regularized reading interface. In John Fletcher's *The Island Princess*, the titular character Quisara is often chaperoned by her aunt, Quisana. When they share the stage, the typical method of shortening the speech prefix to the first syllable, in this case "Quis" or "Qui" becomes problematic. The compositor solves this problem in most cases by expanding just enough to be distinctive. When Quisara interrupts a verbal sparring match between Quisana and Pyneiro, a Portuguese soldier, they become "Quisar" and "Quisan" respectively (Figure 13.3). On the next page, however, there's a problem. An ambiguous singular "exit" at line 1510 could be interpreted as Panura, a servant, leaving the stage, or—as is the case in Claire McManus's Arden edition—the exit of both Panura and Quisana (Fletcher, ed. McManus 3.1.217). The printer has no problem properly conjugating the plural "exeunt" where needed elsewhere in this play; it's used eighteen times. Creating a model for the text can help us see places where ambiguities—such as an "exit" that does not specify who leaves—can signal performance opportunities.

Many modern editors assign the subsequent speeches to Quisara, while the first edition not only uses "Quis" but the expanded "Quisan" at line 1526 (Fletcher, EMED). The scene

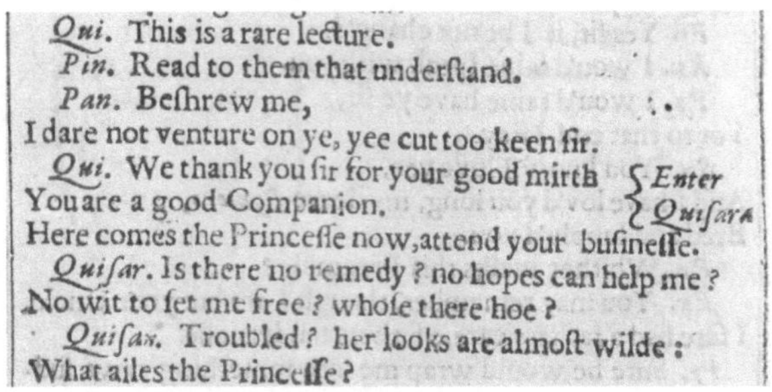

Qui. This is a rare lecture.
Pin. Read to them that underſtand.
Pan. Beſhrew me,
I dare not venture on ye, yee cut too keen ſir.
Qui. We thank you ſir for your good mirth { *Enter Quiſara*
You are a good Companion.
Here comes the Princeſſe now, attend your buſineſſe.
Quiſar. Is there no remedy? no hopes can help me?
No wit to ſet me free? whoſe there hoe?
Quiſan. Troubled? her looks are almoſt wilde:
What ailes the Princeſſe?

Figure 13.3 John Fletcher, *The Island Princess* in *Comedies and Tragedies* (1647), 301[v]
Source: Penn State University Libraries.

reads very differently if the chaperone overhears her niece hiring a hitman. As Niles and Poston argue, "ambiguities in the text require encoders to think like editors; not only because they choose how to describe the text, but also because successful encoders first need to recognize contentious areas even before they decide how to interpret them" (126). In EMED, our choice to expand speech prefixes to full names for the regularized reading meant we needed to indicate one character's name at this crux. We bucked the modern editorial convention to stick as closely as possible to the first edition and expanded "Quisan" to "Quisana"; however, we marked the regularized reading with a note. In this case, we did not want to imply that "Quisana" was the *correct* reading, simply that it was one of two alternatives chosen: "The regularized reading *Quisana* comes from the original *Quisan*, though possible variants include *Quisara*" (n. 9). Following the practice of the Folger Shakespeare, EMED assigns each speaker a unique xml:id and uses a pointer from a @who attribute to associate that xml:id with each speech. The @who attribute acts for computers the way a speech prefix acts for readers: it tells the computer who speaks that segment of text. Its value (the xml:id) must be specified in the header in a list of persons (wrapped in a <particDesc> participation description element) provided by the editors. For EMED, we based the xml:id on a character's name and the short code assigned to the play. Because we attributed the speech to Quisana using "who=#Quisana_IP," a program that counts lines by character would add it to her total.

The value of @who allows for the consistent identification of the speaker, even when their human-readable textual label might change over the course of the play, as in *Edward II* when "Prince" Edward becomes "King" Edward III upon the death of his father. While his printed speech prefixes employed his title, the xml:id used for the @who followed our policy of consistently identifying royalty by their reign name, in this case EdwardIII_ED2. In designing rules for these xml:ids, we benefited from prior work by Niles and Poston for the Folger Shakespeare. They designed a system that allowed for group attribution, including a method for labeling an unknown number of "servants," "soldiers," or other groups using a controlled vocabulary (Niles and Poston 127–35). EMED's encoders chose to make one significant innovation, which was to differentiate between ATTENDANTS, who might be lords, gentlemen, servants, or torchbearers, and MAIDS, who might be ladies, washerwomen, or chambermaids. Both systems have merit—the Folger Shakespeare, grounded in an imagined performance, perhaps better reflects the flexibility of casting, in which servants and cupbearers could be drawn from performers of either gender. The EMED system aims to offer a chance of capturing explicitly gendered depictions of speech in a manner that could be analyzed later, although further encoding would need to be done to identify all characters and groupings by gender.

The Folger Shakespeare's API demonstrates some of the ways encoding can facilitate alternative modes of reading or visualizing a text (Poston). Although ultimately building an API for EMED was outside the scope of the project, many of the extant tools could be employed on EMED texts. The Folger API transforms the encoded texts and renders them in alternate interfaces that allow users to interact with the plays in ways other than close reading. The "text" function, for example, returns just the spoken text in the play and is useful for linguistic analysis: the process strips out anything that is not part of the <ab> encoded "speeches," taking out speech prefixes, stage directions, and other non-spoken text elements. The use of @who on every speech allows for functionality like "charText," which provides a link to all speeches by a chosen character and "parts" which supplies the lines for a given character with her cues (both spoken and stage directions). Other functionality is based on simple counting: "monologue" provides a list of speeches longer than a specified line count. The "concordance" function counts each word in a text and arranges them by frequency. EMED's goal of transparent textual transmission complicated the simple adoption of some of these tools: where the Folger Shakespeare has a single reading for each word, EMED might have up to five: the original EEBO-TCP reading, an original and regularized SHC reading, and original and regularized EMED readings. To create the same tool, it would be necessary to include a selection function that specified which reading would be counted.

Ultimately, the EMED team experimented with making texts compatible with only one Folger API function, the popular "charChart." The "charChart" function provides a visualization of the text of the play based on whether a character is on stage or not, speaking or not, and is alive or dead (it is, in fact, quite possible to be on stage, speaking, and be dead). There were two challenges: When was a character on stage, and when was a character dead? Early printed witnesses often had ambiguous stage directions. In addition to "Exit" and "Exeunt" directions that do not name the characters involved, as in *The Island Princess*, there were moments when a character's exits are implied but not explicitly stated. In *Doctor Faustus*, a pious "Old Man" serves as a foil for one of Faustus's moments of despair. He enters at line 1299, only to enter again at line 1365. His exit in between is implied in the text: the reader must assume it happens shortly after he exclaims "I go sweet Faustus, but with heavy cheer, / fearing the ruin of thy hopeless soul" (Marlowe, *Faustus* 1329–1330). Many similar exits and entrances lack even this much indication, as minor characters speak without entering or are forgotten once they've spoken. While the editorial labor needed to encode entrances and exits for all characters in the corpus would be substantial and outside the scope of the limited project, as a proof of concept, we encoded entrances and exits for the works of Marlowe (Brown et al., "Data").

The encoding team employed <move> elements for entrances and exits that were not explicitly specified in printed stage directions. The <death> element provides the possibility of encoding a character's demise at either a specific line, such as line 1771 for Dido, or a range defined with @notBefore and @notAfter, as in the case of Gaveston from *Edward II*, who might have died any time between line 1379, when he is last seen on stage, and line 1482, when his death is reported to Edward II (Marlowe, *Edward the Second*). While in the Shakespearean version of this visualization characters appear in strict alphabetical order, Poston took the opportunity to experiment and in the Marlowe charts the characters can be dragged and dropped into new arrangements. A user might be interested in aligning political factions in *Edward II*, for example, or comparing specific characters side-by-side to consider possible doubling arrangements.

Although the full EMED Featured Plays corpus as a whole did not receive systematic encoded entrances and exits, we paid careful attention to the location of stage directions that were included in the printed text. We aimed to replicate the placement of stage directions in our reading interface since the location of an entrance, exit, or other business might have textual or performative implications, or may carry interpretive meaning for users studying page layout. While many entrances in the EMED corpus are centered, exits and stage business, such as sound effects ("the bell rings") and descriptions of motion ("they fight") or commentaries on delivery ("he reads," "aside") tend to be aligned right. The precise placement of stage directions on the printed page may represent performance choices or may be a relic of print house practice. In the first edition of Thomas Dekker and Thomas Middleton's *The Roaring Girl*, Ralph Trapdoor declares his discovery of the titular Moll Cutpurse, "Masse here she is," ahead of his entrance on the same line (816) (Figure 13.4). The generous spacing of dialogue and stage directions in this playbook suggest that this sequence is not compositional expediency. Instead, the placement may imply that Trapdoor has begun speaking before or as he enters the stage. His first two lines of this speech are clearly an aside, not meant to be heard by Moll. Alan Galey has noted a similarly rich moment in the First Folio's *A Midsummer Night's Dream*, when the four lost lovers may share a stage with an awakening Bottom ("Encoding as Editing as Reading" 4).

Because both speeches and stage directions are encoded, it is possible to query how often a stage direction of any kind happens, and, for each play, how often they occur juxtaposed with a speech act: in *Roaring Girl*, 18 out of 117 do, for about 15 percent of the stage directions in the play. This ratio places it about mid-range in the EMED corpus, where between 1.5 percent and 45.5 percent of stage directions appear within speeches. Raw numbers are of little statistical use in a sample size as small as the EMED corpus. Searching for the element <stage> within the element <sp> can, however, provide a list for researchers to quickly check their type (business, entrance, exit, location, or delivery) and examine them *in situ*, making it easy to find characters whose speech is interrupted by action; who linger on stage; who may be present or not present at key moments. Further encoding could facilitate other research questions: is there a type of character interrupted more or less? Are certain types of business, such as sounds, more likely to occur during speech acts? Marking stage business like "The clocke striks three" in *Roaring Girl* or the "Musick" called for in *Love's Cure* as a specific subtype (sound) would allow for tools like the Folger Shakespeare API "sounds" function, which displays the extratextual soundscape (*Roaring Girl* 1124–1125; *Love's Cure* 319).

We refined the EMED data model as we corrected transcriptions and layered in encoding that aimed to clearly represent the layout and physical quirks of the first printed witness for each play. Each new play allowed us to nuance our process; the detailed "encoding manual" we compiled was over 40 pages by the end of the project, filled with notes on challenging cases and plenty of examples. The model we built was not as nuanced or as full as the Folger Shakespeare, although it whistled the same tune; as Niles and Poston noted, "Imposing consistency and precision is difficult work for one edited play, let alone thirty-eight. Imagine the difficulty starting from hundreds of unedited works" (130). EMED imagined it and

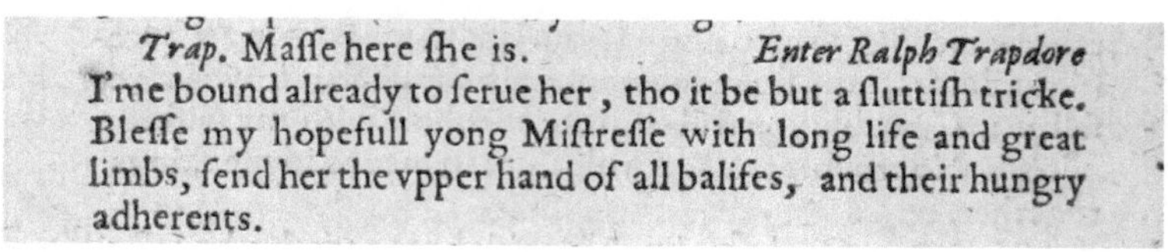
Trap. Maſſe here ſhe is. *Enter Ralph Trapdore*
I'me bound already to ſerue her, tho it be but a ſluttiſh tricke.
Bleſſe my hopefull yong Miſtreſſe with long life and great
limbs, ſend her the vpper hand of all balifes, and their hungry
adherents.

Figure 13.4 Thomas Dekker and Thomas Middleton, *The Roaring Girl* (London: [Nicholas Okes] for Thomas Archer, 1611), D3^{v}
Source: Boston Public Library, G. 3974.40 no. 1.

succeeded fairly well for twenty-nine. Along the way, several plays were cut from the short list to adjust the scope of work to accommodate more detailed encoding and the development of pedagogical materials. Although selected for the short list and encoded, Ben Jonson's *The Staple of News* and *Bartholomew Fair,* published in his 1631 folio, challenged both the data model and the stylesheets that interpreted the encoded plays for display. Given additional time, the team would have been able to adjust the model and rewrite the stylesheets sufficiently to integrate Jonson's plays into the project site. Although this wasn't possible, considering Jonson's idiosyncrasies in layout, typography, and format helped clarify the model and how it fits other plays.

Jonson's first innovation came in the location of many stage directions. In the Featured Plays corpus, the majority of stage directions were centered, a consistent enough pattern that we treated it as a default rather than explicitly encoding it. Enough were right-aligned that we applied a @rend attribute, which was interpreted by the stylesheet to consistently place those stage directions at the right edge of the textblock. When we encountered new placements, we created new @rend values. This is notably not semantic encoding: we were not making a claim about what function might be implied by placing a stage direction at center, inline, to the right of text, or, as in the case of John Marston's *The Malcontent* and Jonson's *Staple of News* and *Bartholomew Fair,* in the margins. The significance of these placements has been addressed by scholars such as Holger Schott Syme, who argues that both Marston's *The Malcontent* (1604) and the plays published in Jonson's 1631 folio employ typographic strategies that can be "conceptualized not as an escape into the autonomy of literary creation but rather as an attempt to construct an alternative mode of theatricality" (144). In *The Malcontent,* Syme equates the marginal descriptions of action with "both scribal and holographic scripts[, where] stage directions are commonly found in the margin, often sharply marked off with lines or even boxed in" (153) (Figure 13.5). By juxtaposing descriptions of action against the words being spoken simultaneously, Syme argues, Marston collaborates with his publisher (in this case, he argues, the Stationer Thomas Thorpe) to adopt "a specific strategy used in playhouse manuscripts, but ... radically changed its function, identifying a potential for printerly theatricality precisely in a visual proximity to an original manuscript from which the printed play appears to be straining away" (153).

Source: Folger Shakespeare Library STC 27479 Copy 1.EMED's encoding model was flexible enough to encompass Marston's (or his print shop's) innovations. A new value for the @rend allowed us to encode marginal placement and a tweak to the stylesheet placed the new @rend values outside the text block (Figure 13.6). Marston also used a marginal annotation that is *not* a stage direction. The Latin motto that annotates the play's title as it appears in the header above the opening scene is encoded as a <note> (Marston lines 1–3). *The*

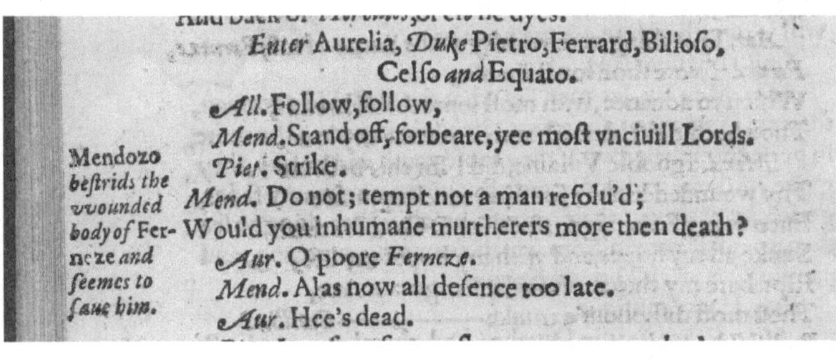
Enter Aurelia, *Duke* Pietro,Ferrard,Bilioſo,
Celſo *and* Equato.
All. Follow,follow,
Mend. Stand off,forbeare,yee moſt vnciuill Lords.
Piet. Strike.
Mend. Do not; tempt not a man reſolu'd;
Would you inhumane murtherers more then death?
Aur. O poore *Ferneze.*
Mend. Alas now all defence too late.
Aur. Hee's dead.

Mendozo *beſtrids the vvounded body of* Ferneze *and ſeemes to ſaue him.*

Figure 13.5 John Marston, *The Malcontent* (1604), D2v

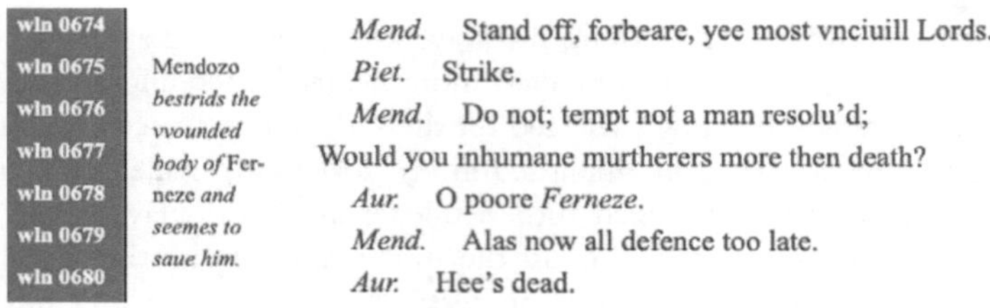

Figure 13.6 EMED's rendering of Marston's marginal stage directions

Malcontent contains the only primary-text <note> element in the published EMED corpus. With the exception of the Latin motto, Marston's marginalia are recognizable as either stage business or delivery, what Syme refers to as "all 'action' directions" which he observes "are placed outside the measure, only exits and entries (the most organizational and functional of stage directions) are noted in the body of the text" (153). Some of these directions are tied to precise placement within the text by asterisks (*), *signes-de-renvoi* that help place detailed action in the context of specific phrases and lines. These symbols mark how actions match words, rather than relying on the reader to connect them through context. The EMED team rendered the matched symbols as metamarks and created an <anchor> element to connect the two.

Jonson's 1631 *Works* took the marginal stage direction a step further, framing them (both figuratively and literally, with hard rules) as a different kind of text, but many of the same methods could be used to encode them. *The Staple of News* opens with a series of stage directions using the same *signes-de-renvoi* as Marston's *Malcontent:*

> * *His Shooe-maker has pull'd on a new payre of bootes; and hee walks in his Gowne, wastcoate, and trouses, expecting his Taylor.* * *He drawes foorth his watch, and sets it on the Table.* * *He throws off his gowne.*

The asterisks make it easy to connect Pennyboy Junior's exclamation "'t strikes!" to the stage direction describing him drawing forth a watch (Aa4[r]). The theatricality of this descriptive stage business is at odds with how the plays treat entrances and exits, which Tiffany Stern argues contribute a decidedly *untheatrical* register to the printed playbook. At the beginning of each scene, all the characters who will be present in that scene are listed as if they all trooped on stage at once: "the 'massed entrances' found in several early modern plays including some by Jonson," Stern notes, "in which every person who is to speak is apparently made to 'enter' at the start of the scene," are more literary than theatrical; they "would never work in performance" (185). Like Syme, Stern argues that many stage directions are the result of the collaborative process of bringing plays to print. These group entrances, she points out, "have been attributed to the habits of Ralph Crane, the scribe, as he tried to give plays on the page a classical aspect" (185).

The massed entrances never use the word "Enter," and the words "Exit" or "Exeunt" do not appear. In reaching for a generic convention borrowed from classical drama, either Jonson or Crane avoided the mixed Latin and English that typify most stage directions. As Stern explains, as vernacular drama overtook Latin plays in English performance, stage business appeared in English alongside the dialogue. Entrances and exits, however, retained Latin signal words and their word order "was firmly Latinate, irrespective of language, with the verb first and the proper noun second" (184). While Stern argues that this uniformity "added to the notion that these were unstable passages, open for anyone to write, moderate, or change and not tightly linked to the author," the uniformity also makes stage directions easy for readers to recognize and parse (184). Jonson's stage directions in *A Staple of News* firmly sidestep these conventions.

The basic rhythms of entering and exiting the hypothetical stage are missing, while stage business is set in the same visual space as other marginalia that are not stage directions at all. In act 3, scene 2, a series of news articles mentioned on stage are marked in the margin: "*Newes from* Rome." "*Newes of the* Emperor, *and* Tilly." "*Newes of* Spinola. *The fifith* Monarchy, *vniting the* Ecclesiasticke *and* Secular *power.*" One might suspect these marginal notes are meant to highlight weighty topics, until further down the list an item of news is glossed in the margin with "*His* Egges" (E3v). Clearly not theatrical actions, these marginalia challenge editors trying to fit them into an editorial model based on an imagined performance. Some modern editions, such as Anthony Parr's for the Revels series, include them as variant readings, but do not replicate them in the body of the play (158). In explaining Parr's suppression of these notes, Joseph Loewenstein provides a helpful summary of their function: "those untheatrical glosses ... summarize the action or render explicit the theme of a given dramatic moment" ("The Staple of News: a Textual Essay"). The EMED data model's focus on the printed playbook could accommodate these glosses but would require the extensive use of the <note> element not found elsewhere in the corpus.

Other elements of Jonson's typographical innovations were harder to accommodate in the model and its associated stylesheet. Where the majority of the plays in the corpus are smaller formats, quartos or octavos, Jonson's 1631 publication employs the full width of the folio page for lines of text. The other folio plays, drawn from the Beaumont and Fletcher folio of 1647, are printed in two columns, replicating the line length (even in prose) of a quarto. As a result, lines of prose in Jonson's plays were much longer than any other work in the corpus. In some cases, his shorter speeches share lines, condensing the space needed to print rapid back-and-forth exchanges, but complicating the reader's ability to quickly parse which character speaks which line or to assess whether a section is verse or prose; as Syme notes, "The layout grows extraordinarily complex at times and demands a great deal of visual literacy from the reader" (163). The EMED encoding could handle these rapid-fire changes in speakers, even when a speech header started midline and the speech wrapped around to a new line, because we employed <milestone> entities rather than <line>. The <milestone> entity is an empty tag. It does not wrap around textual data, but instead it lists the xml:ids for words, spaces, and punctuation which appear in that line. The length of the lines, however, created a problem. Texts in quarto, octavo, or the single column of a double-column folio could all be displayed in the fixed-width window designed for the Folger Shakespeare without much modification. However, Jonson's full-folio line either wrapped (an undesirable outcome in a project which emphasized fidelity to layout and line endings) or required the font size to shrink to illegibility.

Perhaps most challenging of all for our ability to model both the page and the scene described were instances of simultaneous speech, such as occur in the closing scene of act 2 of *Bartholomew Fair*. Four characters over-speak each other, described in the stage direction as "*They speake alltogether: and* Waspe *beats the* Iustice" (E4^{r}) (Figure 13.7).

The stage direction alone could be handled easily by the EMED data model, although it requires interpretation: it could be a single stage direction with a mixed type, or split into two stage directions, a "delivery" direction and "business" for the beating. But in addition to the stage direction, the printers arranged the overlapping speeches into two columns, connected by a curly brace. Wasp's final line wraps under the double column. Many modern editions move the stage direction, placing it within the text block prior to the section designated in the Folio (see Jonson, *Bartholomew Fair*, 2.6.144–145). While the Folio

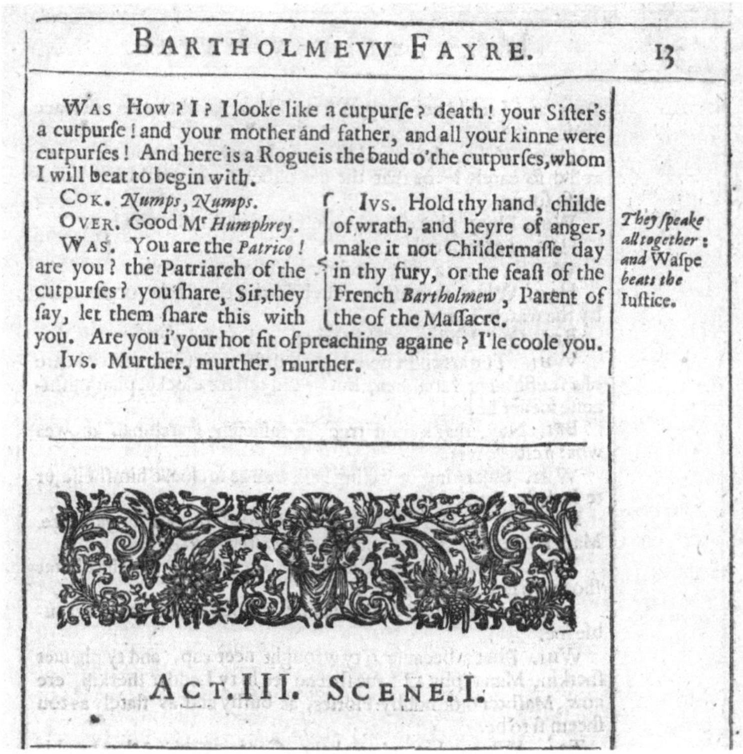

BARTHOLMEVV FAYRE. 13

WAS How? I? I looke like a cutpurſe? death! your Siſter's a cutpurſe! and your mother and father, and all your kinne were cutpurſes! And here is a Rogue is the baud o'the cutpurſes, whom I will beat to begin with.

COK. *Numps, Numps.*

OVER. Good Mr *Humphrey.*

WAS. You are the *Patrico!* are you? the Patriarch of the cutpurſes? you ſhare, Sir, they ſay, let them ſhare this with you. Are you i'your hot fit of preaching againe? I'le coole you.

IVS. Hold thy hand, childe of wrath, and heyre of anger, make it not Childermaſſe day in thy fury, or the feaſt of the French *Bartholmew*, Parent of the of the Maſſacre.

IVS. Murther, murther, murther.

They ſpeake alltogether: and Waſpe *beats the* Iuſtice.

ACT. III. SCENE. I.

Figure 13.7 Ben Jonson, *Bartholomevv Fayre* (1631), E3^{v}. STC 14753.5
Source: Houghton Library, Harvard University.

arrangement suggests that the final line in the scene is spoken by the Justice alone, without competition from other characters, the modern arrangement implies that the overlapping din continues to the end of the scene. The EEBO-TCP transcription—the source file for EMED—scrambles the scene further. Not realizing that the curly bracket connects the "simultaneous" speech, the transcribers place the Justice's final speech in the scene, "Murther, murther, murther," before his speech during the melee (E4^{r}) (Figure 13.8).

This textual arrangement is one of several examples of parallel dialogue and action which, Syme argues, "evoke the principle of multiple foci that is so central to *Bartholomew Fair*'s dramaturgical logic" (163). The challenges it caused for the transcribers meant that correcting the placement was more than devising ways for encoding a challenging passage; it would also require substantially correcting the original transcription.

Once we had a reliable transcription, there are several ways that we could have adjusted the encoding to accommodate the simultaneous speech. The <milestone> element could reconstruct the line regardless of where in the transcription the words occurred; we could have transcribed each complete speech in sequence and used the milestone to visually display their entwined layout. Or we might have worked through a way to introduce two columns in a text that typically has one. The switch back to a single column would have to occur within Wasp's speech, a move possible because the column beginning <cb> element is an empty tag that would not create overlapping hierarchy issues. Any outlier text challenges the editor to expand the model, change it, or exclude the outlier from the set; recognizing the amount of work needed to correct the transcriptions, on top of the work to adjust the data

WAS.
You are the *Patrico!* are you? the Patriarch of the cutpurses? you share, Sir, they say, let them share this with you. Are you i'your hot fit of preaching againe? I'le coole you.

IVS.
Murther, murther, murther.

IVS.
Hold thy hand, childe of wrath, and heyre of anger,

They speake all together: and Waspe beats the Iustice.
make it not Childermasse day in thy fury, or the feast of the French *Bartholmew,* Parent of the of the Massacre.

ACT. III. SCENE. I.

Figure 13.8 Ben Jonson, *Bartholomevv Fayre* (1631), Act II, Scene VI, EEBO

model and the stylesheets used to visualize the model, helped us make the choice to focus our limited project time on other plays.

Shakespeare's high profile ensured that his Works led the way in digital editions—and consequently, became patterns for how early modern drama would be encountered online. Niles and Poston found that "the underlying data model of the Folger editions is surprisingly consistent, given its twenty-year production process." The editors, Barbara Mowat and Paul Werstine, provided consistent editorial guidance, while "uniform typographical expression of the editions" came thanks to the lead production editor, Stephen Llano (Niles and Poston 123). The diverse decisions made by compositors, printers, and publishers involved in the production of EMED's texts, and the hands-on attention from authors like Ben Jonson or playhouse scribes like Ralph Crane, complicated the process of deciphering an underlying data model that could be consistently applied to this corpus. Choices made by prior projects, the transcribers for the EEBO-TCP and the machine encoding of the SHC, influenced the material EMED started with. With any large-scale editorial project, digital or otherwise, project priorities are regularly evaluated and occasionally rescoped to ensure project completion. Confronted with the need to retranscribe sections of the plays, rewrite substantial portions of the stylesheets, and rework, test, and implement changes to the encoding to properly display *Bartholomew Fair* and *Staple of News*, the challenges raised by Jonson were weighed against other project priorities. The project had a firm end date and the decision was made to save the Jonson files for a future round of editing, if additional funding could be found. A good editorial policy is like a battle plan: it rarely survives the first engagement with the full spectrum of texts. Each new text (or textual part) may fit or challenge the model: as Alan Galey puts it, "A model … provokes questions about its non-equivalence to the object it models; indeed, those questions are the point" (*The Shakespearean Archive* 242). Given Jonson's reputation as an interventionist author, the EMED team suspected that he would have taken delight in flummoxing the models that accurately described the work of other playwrights.

Notes

1 The EMED team consisted of Meaghan Brown, project manager; Elizabeth Williamson, encoding fellow; and Michael Poston, the Folger's data architect. The project director was Kathleen Lynch.

Funding for EMED was provided by the National Endowment for the Humanities and the Council on Library and Information Resources. I am deeply indebted to Elizabeth Williamson for many of the examples listed here, which we tracked during the process of encoding the EMED plays.

2 The Folger Shakespeare was first known as the Folger Shakespeare Library Editions, edited by Barbara Mowat and Paul Werstine (in print) and Folger Digital Texts (online); the new name signals the interconnected nature of the two outputs.

3 The larger bibliographic dataset was defined by a mix of features: plays had to be performed by professional players after 1576; be printed before 1660; and have at least one surviving copy (Brown, Poston, and Williamson, "About").

References

A pleasant comedie called common conditions. London, 1576, EEBO.

Beaumont, Francis, John Fletcher, and Philip Massinger, *Loves Cure, or the Martial Maid: Comedies and Tragedies*. London, 1647, EMED. Available at: https://emed.folger.edu/view/1932/LovCure.

Blayney, Peter W.M. "Quadrat Demonstrandum." *Papers of the Bibliographical Society of America*, vol. 111, no. 1, 2017, pp. 61–101.

Brown, Meaghan, Michael Poston, and Elizabeth Williamson, editors. *A Digital Anthology of Early Modern English Drama*. Folger Shakespeare Library. Available at: http://emed.folger.edu.

Brown, Meaghan, Michael Poston, and Elizabeth Williamson, editors. "About." *A Digital Anthology of Early Modern English Drama*. Folger Shakespeare Library. Available at: https://emed.folger.edu/about.

Brown, Meaghan, Michael Poston, and Elizabeth Williamson, editors. "Data." *A Digital Anthology of Early Modern English Drama*. Folger Shakespeare Library. Available at: https://emed.folger.edu/research-resources/data#mapping.

Bourne, Claire M.L. *Typographies of Performance in Early Modern England*. Oxford UP, 2020.

Dekker, Thomas. *The Shoemaker's Holiday*. London, 1600, EMED. Available at: https://emed.folger.edu/view/1662/ShoeHol.

Dekker, Thomas. *The Shoemaker's Holiday, The Revels Plays*. Edited by Robert Smallwood, and Stanley Wells, Manchester UP, 1999.

Dekker Thomas, and Thomas Middleton. *The Roaring Girl*. London, 1611, EMED. Available at: https://emed.folger.edu/view/1747/Roaring.

Everyman. London, 1515, EEBO.

Flanders, Julia and Fotis Jannidis. "A Gentle Introduction to Data Modeling." *The Shape of Data in Digital Humanities: Modeling Texts and Text-based Resources*. Edited by Julia Flanders and Fotis Jannidis. Routledge, 2018. doi:10.4324/9781315552941.

Flanders, Julia and Fotis Jannidis. "Data Modeling in a Digital Humanities Context: An Introduction." *The Shape of Data in Digital Humanities: Modeling Texts and Text-based Resources*. Edited by Julia Flanders and Fotis Jannidis, Routledge, 2018. doi:10.4324/9781315552941.

Fletcher, John. *The Island Princess in Comedies and Tragedies*. London, 1647, EMED. Available at: https://emed.folger.edu/view/1923/IP

Fletcher, John. *The Island Princess*. Edited by Claire McManus, Arden, 2012.

Galey, Alan. *The Shakespearean Archive*. Cambridge UP, 2014.

Galey, Alan. "Encoding as Editing as Reading." *Shakespeare and Textual Studies*. Edited by Margaret Jane Kidnie and Sonia Massai, Cambridge UP, 2015.

Heywood, Thomas. *THE FAIR MAID OF THE WEST. OR, A Girle Worth Gold. The First Part*. London, 1631, EMED. Available at: https://emed.folger.edu/view/1804/1FMW.

Jonson, Ben. *The Staple of Nevves: a Comedie*. London, 1631, EEBO.

Jonson, Ben. *The Staple of News*. Edited by Anthony Parr, Manchester UP, 1988.

Jonson, Ben. *Bartholomew Fair*. Edited by Ernest Alan Horsman, Manchester UP, 2000.

Loewenstein, Joseph. "The Staple of News: Textual Essay." *The Cambridge Edition of the Works of Ben Jonson Online*. Cambridge UP, 2014. Available at: https://universitypublishingonline.org/cambridge/benjonson/k/essays/Staple_of_News_textual_essay/6/.

Loewenstein, Joseph and Martin Mueller, editors. *Early Print*. Washington University in St. Louis/Northwestern University. Available at: https://earlyprint.org/.

Marlowe, Christopher. *The troublesome raigne and lamentable death of Edward the second, King of England: with the tragicall fall of proud Mortimer*. London, 1594, EMED. Available at: https://emed.folger.edu/view/1640/Ed2.

Marlowe, Christopher. *The Tragicall History of D. Faustus*. London, 1604, EMED. Available at: https://emed.folger.edu/view/1689/DrFaust.

Marlowe, Christopher and Thomas Nashe. *The Tragedie of Dido Queene of Carthage*. London, 1594, EMED. Available at: https://emed.folger.edu/view/1642/Dido.

Marston, John. *The Malcontent*. London, 1604, EMED. Available at: https://emed.folger.edu/view/2001/Malc.

Mueller, Martin. "Shakespeare His Contemporaries: Collaborative Curation and Exploration of Early Modern Drama in a Digital Environment." *Digital Humanities Quarterly*, vol. 8, no. 3, 2014. Available at: http://www.digitalhumanities.org/dhq/vol/8/3/000183/000183.html.

Niles, Rebecca and Michael Poston, "Re-Modeling the Edition: Creating the Corpus of Folger Digital Texts." *Early Modern Studies After the Digital Turn*. Edited by Laura Estill, Diane K. Jackacki, and Michael Ullyot, Iter Press, 2016, pp. 117–144.

Poston, Michael. "The Folger Shakespeare API Tools." *The Folger Shakespeare*, The Folger Shakespeare Library. Available at: https://www.folgerdigitaltexts.org/api.

Stern, Tiffany "Stage Directions." *Book Parts*. Edited by Dennis Duncan and Adam Smyth, Oxford UP, 2019, pp. 179–198.

Syme, Holger Schott. "Unediting the Margin: Jonson, Marston, and the Theatrical Page." *English Literary Renaissance*, vol. 38, no. 1, 2008, pp. 142–171.

TEI Consortium. "P5 Guidelines." Text Encoding Initiative. Available at: https://tei-c.org/guidelines/p5/.

Text Creation Partnership. University of Michigan. Available at: https://textcreationpartnership.org/tcp-texts/eebo-tcp-early-english-books-online/.

14

BROWSE AS INTERFACE IN SHAKESPEARE'S TEXTS AND THE WORLD SHAKESPEARE BIBLIOGRAPHY ONLINE

Heidi Craig and Laura Estill

Interfaces, both analog and digital, shape how we engage with texts, including how we search and browse their contents. In a recent article, noting the increasing importance of interactivity in textual studies in the last few decades, Gina Bloom argues that "2020 marks a critical time in the age of the interface," particularly when it comes to understanding early modern literature and drama. Bloom distinguishes "readers" who move through books from cover to cover from "human users" who explore digital texts interactively via the interface, which offers "new or more expansive opportunities for how to engage with a text" (9). Yet interactive experiments with textual form long predate the digital turn; early modern encyclopedias, William N. West notes, encouraged speed of access to and the "detached study and manipulation," of their ample contents (14–19). Textual interface technologies, from the codex form to alphabetization, from the manicule to subject headings, worked to make comprehensive texts such as encyclopedias more comprehensible.

The interface structures inherent in enumerative bibliography position it as the interactive genre par excellence. The compressed and ordered interface in traditional bibliographies enables the user to quickly manipulate and metabolize their ostensibly comprehensive contents. An interface consisting of some combination of section headings, indices, and alphabetical and chronological ordering allows a user to move through the text in different ways. One usually scans rather than reads a bibliography, as is typical of any list (Smith 127); the user might also follow the bibliography's system of organization to direct their attention to a particular author or publication venue. Given that enumerative bibliography provides an overview of publications in a given field, a print or digital interface that enables both targeted searching and undirected browsing will best serve the researcher. Indeed, modern scholarship would not exist without the functions of enumerative bibliography.

Interfaces that facilitate searching and browsing have long helped readers and users swiftly navigate the swirling eddies of Shakespeare's language and the ever-rising oceans of Shakespearean criticism. Shakespeare's First Folio (1623) featured a layout and paratextual catalogue that divided its thirty-six plays into Comedies, Histories, and Tragedies. Today, the *World Shakespeare Bibliography* (*WSB*), the premier annotated bibliography on Shakespeare, employs 117 tags to guide its users through over 132,000 entries (and counting) on Shakespearean

DOI: 10.4324/9780367821722-19

scholarship and performance. Clearly, interfaces shape how we understand both Shakespeare and Shakespeare studies. And while the digital affordances of *WSB* may seem like a far cry from staunchly analogue First Folio, the interface of the *WSB* is directly informed by F1's interface, and has been indirectly shaped by Shakespearean interfaces in the subsequent centuries. The *World Shakespeare Bibliography* has continued to evolve throughout the twentieth and twenty-first centuries to help users nimbly search and browse its contents. Generally speaking, Shakespeare's reception has continually moved towards ever-more specialized and professionalized approaches; as we will show, this story can be charted through developments in the Shakespeare interface.

This chapter moves from an investigation of historical notions of search and browse, using examples of browsing within and of Shakespeare's texts, to an analysis of how we search and browse Shakespearean scholarship digitally. We begin by demonstrating how print and digital browsing interfaces encourage different kinds of interaction with textual content—cursory overviews of an entire text, say, or targeted readings of selected extracts. No interface is neutral, and interface design influences interpretation and research directions. And although the twenty-first-century "user" of digital resources might at first glance appear to have more agency over the text than the "reader" of printed materials, digital interfaces also profoundly shape the user's experiences. After surveying the history of Shakespearean interfaces in print, this chapter proceeds to explore the influence and implications of digital Shakespearean interfaces focusing on the *WSB*, an annotated bibliography of Shakespeare scholarship and professional productions published or produced since 1960. In examining the browse and search interfaces of the *WSB*, we locate connections between the history of browsing and the current *WSB* interface design execution. The search and browse interfaces of the *WSB* allow users to access the site's thousands of entries in markedly different ways: from the empty textbox of the basic keyword search, to the multi-box advanced search interface which combines free text and dropdown options; to the browse interface's pre-set taxonomy which allows users to navigate eleven major categories, each with its own subgroups. The *WSB* interface mediates not only how scholars can find entries in the bibliography itself, but also how we interact with and understand the shape of Shakespeare scholarship. As this chapter traces, the long history of browsing Shakespeare leads directly to the browse and search interfaces' mediation of access to Shakespeare scholarship in the *World Shakespeare Bibliography*.

"Chanceable Hitting": Interfaces of Browsing Books

Today, "browsing" mostly refers to scanning digital resources, but its earliest definition referred to the feeding habits of deer, cattle, and goats, "cropping and eating young shoots, leaves and twigs from shrubs and trees (*OED* 1.a and b). It is with this definition that "browse" and its cognates appears in Shakespeare's oeuvre. In *Cymbeline*, "browse" describes humans' consumption of food before the main meal: returning with fellow hunters Belarius and Arviragus to prepare the deer they have killed, Guiderius offers "cold meat" to tide them over before dinner, stating "We'll browse on that / Whilst what we have killed be cooked." (3.6.38–39); upon entering the cave, they find the sleeping Imogen. At the beginning of the Bohemian section of *The Winter's Tale*, as the old shepherd looks for his lost sheep, he muses that they are likely "by the seaside, browsing of ivy" (3.3.66–67).[1] The old shepherd utters this immediately before he stumbles across the abandoned infant Perdita, exclaiming "what have we here? Mercy on's, a barne! A very pretty barne" (3.3.67–68). In both cases, "browsing" evokes leisurely, preparatory, even mindless eating bordering on animalistic consumption; in *The Winter's Tale*, the shepherd searching for his browsing sheep precedes and precipitates an unexpected, life-changing discovery. In this way, "browsing" in Shakespeare carries unexpected resonances for the modern researcher. For some, browsing is the appetizer before the main meal of search, as "cold meat" is to cooked venison. The old shepherd's casual search for his sheep and unexpected encounter with the "very pretty bairn" chimes with ideal browsing; in a pastoral academic fantasy, wandering across scholarly resources can lead to the serendipitous discovery of something "very pretty" we did not know we were looking for.

In the nineteenth century, "browsing" took on its more familiar meaning, the examination of books on shelves and stacks in bookshops and libraries, "especially in a casual or leisurely manner" (*OED* 4.a.). At the turn of the twentieth century, textual browsing started to refer to "perusing or glancing through the contents of the book" itself. Though "browsing" as a term became associated with texts only in the nineteenth century, as a practice it has been long in use, with readers leafing through texts in the hopes of making interesting and unexpected discoveries. Bibliomancy, a style of reading practiced in antiquity and in the medieval and early modern periods in which advice or predictions of the future are sought by random selections of texts, could be seen as a form of browsing. In *The Defense of Poesie*, Philip Sidney describes the powers of prophecy ancient Romans ascribed to the poet Virgil, such that

> they thought in the chanceable hitting upon any such verses great fore-tokens of their following fortunes were placed; whereupon grew the word of Sortes Virgilianae, when by sudden opening Virgil's book they lighted upon some verse of his making.
>
> *(Sidney 215–16)*

The outcome of the "sudden opening" of Virgil suggests the ideal outcome of browsing: a meaning manifests itself through undirected, discontinuous reading; the "chanceable hitting" on particular passages reveals and creates the reader's fortunes. It must be noted that previous interactions with the book will influence even this most seemingly random bibliographic encounter: a book frequently opened to a particular section will tend to open to that section unless a concerted effort is made to do otherwise. As the work in this volume attests (see particularly the chapter by Anne Burdick et al. (Chapter 16)), printed books have interfaces, too.

Scholars continue to debate whether readers thumbed through texts in early modern English bookshops prior to purchase. Some argue that books sold with folded and uncut leaves would make the practice impossible (Giddens 53), but Philip Tromans offers evidence of "in-shop, pre-purchase browsing" (112), demonstrating that people could "take books from open-access shelves and browse through the books' free-swinging leaves" (113). This could suggest that booksellers altered the interface of display copies, cutting pages so that readers would leaf through them. Indeed, the metaphor of "leafing through" a book as a form of casual reading, first cited in the 1660s, is suggestive of the physical changes to the text, which transformed folded sheets into turnable leaves. Again, the interface of the printed text—in this case, related to cut pages—shapes how the user interacts with that text, its effects expressed in emerging metaphors. Casual or cursory encounters with the text do not imply carelessness or idleness, however. Although D. R. Woolf refers to the "desultory browsers" who read in early modern bookshops without necessarily buying the book, he foregrounds the deep learning that could be gleaned from seemingly cursory encounters. Woolf cites Thomas Hearne's admission that he learned of recent "numismatic discoveries" in the 1708 *Philosophical Transactions of the Royal Society* solely from looking at the text in a bookseller's shop. Woolf continues that the notes of John Ward are "peppered with references to books perused only at booksellers, in libraries, or at friends' houses" (25). Clearly, browsing could then, as now, produce serious research.

While early modern readers "leafed through" and "looked on" books, the term "browsing" apparently did not yet refer to such activities. Metaphorical descriptions of reading as eating have long pervaded our discourse. As Jane Roberts notes, there is a "strong metaphorical crossover" between reading and food, evident in our metaphors of "devouring" books and "reading voraciously" (248–52). Yet it seems that "browsing" as reading—as the selective sampling of a broad field of material—does not emerge until there is a pervasive sense of an overabundance of reading material. Rolf Engelsing articulates an influential theory about a shift in reading habits that took place towards the end of the eighteenth century, largely due to the growth of the periodical press. Engelsing charts a move from the "intensive" reading of the pre- and early modern periods (characterized by focused reading and rereading of a small number of texts) towards "extensive" reading, more cursory encounters with a larger number and wider variety of texts, especially periodicals and reference books that seem to encourage discontinuous reading. Ann Blair, however, rejects the periodization and the suddenness of change implied in Engelsing's notion of a "reading revolution"; instead, she traces continuities of old forms alongside new forms of reading (59). As Blair notes, concerns about the glut of reading material and texts preceded not only the eighteenth century, but the onset of print: manuscript culture grappled with information overload. Yet with the advent of print, we see a raft of metaphorical language related to consumption as a way to move through and manage large tracts of material. Engelsing describes extensive reading as a way for readers to "consume" books then shelve them or pass them on (DeMaria 17). Practices recognizable as "extensive reading" are visible in the early modern period, when metaphors of consumption used to describe textual encounters become more varied and prevalent. Early modern reference works are often described as "digesting" larger amounts of material for greater ease of consumption. Though the metaphor remains unspoken in the early modern period, one can easily see how a reader would be envisioned as "browsing" pre-digested material to glean nourishment from the text.

The glut of printed material reshaped reading habits, as well as the textual interface. In order for the reader to make significant discoveries from cursory readings of one or more texts, the text needed to be arranged so that encounters could be quick yet meaningful. The interfaces of early modern texts and reference books were designed to deal with navigation through large amounts of material, as evidenced by the development of paratextual features (many carried over from manuscript culture), such as the index, tables of contents, commonplace markers, and manicules.[2] In other words, such paratextual interface features were designed to aid browsing, through the condensing of texts and ideas to a few lines of description or by means of alphabetized lists organized by subject or author, all of which encouraged superficial, discontinuous reading, allowing the reader to metabolize greater quantities of texts.

Browsing in Digital Spaces

The rise of the internet amplified the already-pervasive feeling that there is too much to know, too much information to organize, retrieve, and understand. As electronic references supersede print, targeted searches displace browsing. Yet the digital does still invite opportunities for browsing. Wikipedia has a "Random article" option, which amounts to a modern-day version of bibliomancy; instead of letting a book fall open, the algorithm chooses the page on which you land. Yet unlike turning to a random section in Virgil, the mechanics of arriving at Wikipedia's random article is largely concealed from the user. While Wikipedia offers other browse functionalities, in accessing the "Random article" button the user cannot influence serendipity.

The value of browsing has been recognized for the digital era, with critics embracing its unique ability to cultivate serendipity in electronic research contexts. Tammera Race and Stephann Makri's *Accidental Information Discovery: Cultivating Serendipity in the Digital Age* praises browsing without a specific aim in mind, and offers practical tips on how to cultivate serendipity in digital research contexts. Andrew Abbott likewise advocates non-linear, seemingly inefficient browsing over efficient searches where one sees exactly and only what one wants. Abbott contends that the serendipity produced by browsing is not a rare occurrence, but rather a key mode of effective research (116–19). He argues that successful browsing depends on an effective interaction between the browser's mind and the database (which could be an electronic list, a shelf of books, a single book, an article, or bibliography); this interaction in turn depends on the database's order and selection which enable a user to examine the "database's narrower, broader and related topics and even its somewhat arbitrary adjacent topics" (119). Although Abbott equates physical and digital databases, principles of selection and order are reconfigured in digital spaces, with concomitant effects on the interface. For example, the contents of printed reference books are fixed at the time of publication; they rely on various organizational systems—alphabetization, chronology, tables of contents, pre-defined keyword searches in indices—to order information spread across the physical space of the printed page (Lynch 30–1). By contrast, in digital spaces, hyperlinked tags and cross-references combine with traditional forms of organization to offer the user different ways of interacting with the material. Unlike the printed book, the digital contents may be constantly added to, with the result that it may outgrow its interface, or else impel it to adapt. This relationship is particularly evident in the case of Shakespeare, whose works and criticism have been organized in bibliographies analogue and digital, with interfaces that encourage different kinds of interaction that reflect a given era's critical and cultural preoccupations.

Browsing Shakespeare's Works

Texts of and about Shakespeare have long been the objects of browsing, with the text's interface guiding readers into different forms of interaction. For example, the extraction of passages as "commonplaces" is important in the history of early modern dramatic consumption (Estill, *Dramatic Extracts*). Early quartos of plays by Shakespeare and other early modern dramatists often included commonplace markers, an interface which encouraged cursory reading, with inverted commas printed in the text's margins guiding readers' eyes to the passages deemed to be useful for moral, intellectual, or linguistic improvement (Lesser and Stallybrass; Hunter). Readers might browse plays quickly, looking for commonplace markers indicating material to copy into their commonplace books, to relate in letters, or to repeat in conversation.

In the eighteenth century, Alexander Pope used commonplace markers and other forms of notation in his edition of Shakespeare (1725):

> Some suspected passages which are excessively bad … are degraded to the bottom of the page; with an asterisk referring to the places of their insertion. Some of the most shining passages are distinguished by commas in the margin; and where the beauty lay not in particulars but in the whole, a star is prefixed to the scene. This seems to me a shorter and less ostentatious method of performing the better half of

> criticism (namely the pointing out an Author's excellencies) than to fill a whole paper with citations of fine passages, with general Applauses, or Empty Exclamations at the tail of them.
>
> *(Pope xxii)*

Pope singles out the speed and elegance of this method for the writer. Instead of having to slog through a "whole paper with citations of fine passages," the interface streamlines the reading process for readers to quickly seek out the beauties of Shakespeare, which in the belle lettristic eighteenth century was a standard mode of literary appreciation and engagement.

While browsing allows for serendipitous discoveries, when the interface design attempts to curate the browsing experience, it can actually reduce the opportunities for happy accidents, precluding readers' judgement and depriving them of agency. Samuel Johnson, in *Proposals for printing the dramatic works of William Shakespeare* (1756), objected to Pope's habit of annotating the "faults and beauties" of Shakespeare. He condemned the distracting interface that impinges on the reader's own judgment: "I have never observed that mankind was much delighted or improved by their asterisks, commas, or double commas; of which the only effect is, that they preclude the pleasure of judging for ourselves" (57). To be sure, Johnson did not object to browsing; describing his own practice, he outlined four distinct ways of reading, ranging from "study" or "hard reading" of classical and sacred texts; the purposeful and careful "perusal" of treatises; and "curious reading" which refers to a trancelike immersion in the text (exemplified by Johnson's first encounter with *Hamlet*, where as a 9-year-old-boy reading the Ghost scene Johnson fled to the safety of the street). The fourth way is "mere reading" referring to quick, selective reading, which we might now recognize as browsing. As Johnson explained, not every book requires hard study: "One of the amusements of idleness is reading without the fatigue of close attention, and the world therefore swarms with writers whose wish is not to be studied but to be read" (Johnson 2: 94). This reading could be not only quick, but also partial. Robert DeMaria relates how Johnson "shocked [his] admirers by declaring openly that [he] did not read books through to the end" (14). Yet it would be wrong to equate unfocused and partial reading with bad reading; as Johnson indicates, it is simply reading with a different purpose.

And although Johnson associated "mere reading" with amusement, we'd like to suggest that discontinuous, undirected reading was well known to produce interesting results, akin to the "chanceable hits" described by Sidney. In bibliographical and academic contexts, browsing suggests opposite kinds of encounters with texts: on the one hand, it implies leisurely, casual engagement; yet browsing also enables one to look over vast amounts of material. This meaning is also informed by the earliest definition as cropping or grazing involves taking a little bit from each section over a large tract of land. For both eating and learning, then, browsing enables familiarity across a large field, whether of grass or of study; its value is owed to this duality.

Shakespeare, Bibliography, and Interface

An interface that facilitates the management of large quantities of reading material is important not only for anatomizing Shakespeare's corpus, but also for the ever-growing body of Shakespeare criticism. Browsing can be an integral part of information retrieval, especially when it comes to browsing bibliographies analytic, citational, and enumerative. In 1912, Clark S. Northup lamented that "it is regrettable that up to the present time no well trained scholar or group of scholars has undertaken and published an adequate, comprehensive bibliography of the ever-growing literature of Shakespeare." He continues,

> certainly if there is any one great author of whom we need a full analytical bibliography, it is Shakespeare. Year after year Shakespearean scholars and critics have gone on repeating themselves or others, ignorant of much that their predecessors have said, each writer playing the game in his own little corner of the university. Some of this waste, assuredly, a good bibliography might have prevented.
>
> *(218)*

A "good bibliography" depends on its contents, but also on its interface. Northup reviews three Shakespeare bibliographies published in the 1910s based on usability, that is, how scholars could interact with the interface and associated systems of organization in order to find relevant material. Northup advocates organization by alphabetization and play title; with reference to William Jaggard's 1911 bibliography, "if each article or book dealing with a single play were relegated to its appropriate sub-alphabet, the main alphabet would be so much the shorter and more easily scanned" (Northup 226). In other words, Northup finds the interface lacking for the bibliography's ideal function, namely that of easy browsing. Northup generally approves of the German *Bibliographie. In Jahrbuch der Deutschen Shakespeare Gesellschaft* (1865–1911), but questions the value of arrangement by region, commenting,

> It is of course interesting to see what the different countries are contributing to the literature of the subject: we think, however, that this is more than offset by the disadvantage of having to consult several alphabets instead of only one for each year.
>
> *(229)*

The Austro-Hungarian Empire ("Österreich-Ungarn"), one of the section headings in this bibliography published before World War I, ceased to exist by the decade's end, vividly exemplifying how taxonomies are a product of their time and are prone to obsolescence. In spite of defects of the reviewed Shakespeare bibliographies, Northup cautions that

> we must not expect to see anything better for some years to come. Publishers are not eager to risk capital in enterprises of this kind, and until bibliographical work is more fully appreciated, it is too much to hope that a band of expert bibliographers shall do the thing over and do it properly.
>
> *(227–8)*

Decades after Northup's 1912 call for a well-designed bibliography of works about Shakespeare that would better allow scholars to manage and retrieve information, Sidney Thomas edited the first *World Shakespeare Bibliography* in 1950 (then titled "Shakespeare: An Annotated Bibliography"), listing recent Shakespeare scholarship.[3] In the first *WSB*, items appeared in three broad categories—"Bibliographies and Surveys," "Collections, Editions, and Translations," and "Books and Articles Relating to Shakespeare"—with an index to help users navigate further. Such categorization recalls Shakespearean interfaces of the centuries prior, in which creators anticipated users' needs and framed and organized information accordingly: the First Folio divided Shakespeare's plays by genre, implying that a play's overall mood was most important for a reader's selection. Alexander Pope used commas to highlight beautiful passages for his aesthetically minded but seemingly time-pressed readers who want to quickly consume the "Author's excellencies." Sidney Thomas's interface for the first iteration of the *WSB* in 1950 reflected the needs of faculty and students in post-war academia to produce research in the burgeoning field of Shakespeare studies.

As with interfaces to Shakespeare's texts, the *WSB*'s interface to Shakespeare performance and scholarship continually evolved, reflecting the changing state of Shakespeare studies. The *World Shakespeare Bibliography* was first published in print in *Shakespeare Quarterly*: this meant that editors could simply introduce a new taxonomy category for one year without worrying about previous years. In 1961, Robert W. Dent began introducing new taxonomy categories slowly, adding "Selections and Adaptations"; by 1965, he was organizing the *WSB* by topic, including "Libraries and Collections" and "Shakespeare Around the World." His successors, Rudolph Habenicht, Bruce E. Nesbitt, and Thomas returned to a system that categorized not by topic but by format: book, article, dissertation, and so forth. In 1976, Harrison Meserole became editor and established the first version of the taxonomy that the *WSB* uses today, with its familiar categories such as "Language, Linguistics, Philology" and studies of individual plays. While prior topic categories such as "Libraries and Collections" and "Shakespeare Around the World" appealed to amateur and professional Shakespearean alike, Meserole's changes to the interface reflect the growing specialization and professionalization of Shakespeare studies. Just as commonplace markers helped seventeenth-century readers readily find and incorporate notable Shakespearean passages into their conversation and letters, topics like "Language, Linguistics, Philology" helped professional Shakespeare scholars write academic papers. As then-editor of *Shakespeare Quarterly* John F. Andrews explained to readers,

> a number of categories for compilation have been altered, (both in the listings and in the Indexes), with the result that it should now be easier for a scholar working, say, on a specific aspect of 'General Shakespeareana'—Biography or Palaeography, for example—to locate the entries that may be pertinent.
>
> *(387)*

The resultant academic papers and monographs would themselves eventually be incorporated into the *WSB*: the past use of *WSB*'s interface ensured the *WSB*'s continued success and growth just as its present interface affects current research practices and future publications. Grow it did, and with it the need to have a flexible, intuitive interface to manage the *WSB*'s continual increase. By 1977, Andrews notes that Meserole planned to move the *WSB* toward "full computerization" (387)—at least for the production of the bibliography if not for its interface. The taxonomy that drives the current interfaces (that is, search and browse) of the *WSB* was created as it moved from print to digital.[4]

Interfaces reflect the biases of their creators: Pope relegated "some suspected passages which are excessively bad" to the bottom of the page; such choices and typographical layouts, however idiosyncratic, nevertheless have enduring and powerful influences on readers' conception of Shakespeare. Likewise, any analysis of the taxonomy of the *WSB* must account for the fact that bibliographers are human, with different areas of scholarly expertise, idiosyncrasies, and preoccupations. *WSB* tags have been assigned by hundreds of human bibliographers over decades, and so, of course, can be inconsistent. As demonstrated above, the change in editorship, likewise, can often bring changes to not just the tags themselves but also to how they are applied. The work of substantially redefining the *WSB* taxonomy tags would be a Herculean, even Sisyphean, task: not only would it involve manually assessing and re-tagging hundreds of thousands of entries, but it would also require re-visioning the entire, ever-changing field of Shakespeare studies—a field that previous and present iterations of the *WSB* helped create.

The *WSB* currently uses 117 possible tags in its taxonomy, ranging from play titles to content descriptors,[5] to explore all the entries in the database. While search and browse are two distinct interface options in the *WSB*, both rely on the taxonomy to function, and taxonomy keywords appear in search results. All entries about *Double Falsehood*, for instance, are tagged "Cardenio," so that a basic search for the lost play *Cardenio* will bring up all the results for *Double Falsehood*, an adaptation of the lost play. This added tag is useful because *WSB* annotations on scholarship on *Double Falsehood* will likely mention *Cardenio*, but annotations of productions of the play might not. As such, users who search (or browse) the *WSB* for "Cardenio," will find all scholarship on *Double Falsehood*, and will learn that there were nine professional productions of the adapted lost play between 2010 and 2016. Users can also search the *WSB* for only "Double Falsehood," and the results for *Cardenio* will not automatically appear. Likewise, a search for "cardenio NOT double falsehood" will only return results on *Cardenio*, but requires users to be familiar with the Boolean operator NOT. In short, the *WSB* taxonomy default is that *Double Falsehood* is a subset of *Cardenio*: this is just one example of how the taxonomy affects search and browse results.

The 2016 update to the *WSB* interface enhanced the "advanced search" options so that users could choose more than one document type, language, or taxonomy tag.[6] For instance, users could now search for all French, Spanish, and Catalan complete works with a single search (which previously had to be undertaken by searching each language separately).[7] The *WSB*'s move online made multiple years of scholarship readily available with a single search; the ability to search multiple taxonomy tags in the updated interface likewise streamlined research. Although we might not readily admit it, the speed of search impacts the kinds of questions we ask about Shakespeare. Thomas Hearne's ability to learn about "numismatic discoveries" in the 1708 *Philosophical Transactions of the Royal Society* in a bookseller's shop required speed and focus, lest an annoyed bookseller boot the browsing researcher out of his or her shop; such work necessitated a well-designed interface. In the case of the *WSB*, research that previously would have taken hours (for instance, searching multiple printed *WSB* volumes or entering dozens of searches) now takes seconds with one well-crafted advanced search. The search interface of the *WSB* also allows scholars to easily expand from an isolated case study to multiple instances of a given type, facilitating more persuasive claims about wider cultural patterns. For example, instead of attempting to make general claims about a single production of *Hamlet* in Germany in 1995, with the advanced search, a researcher can see all professional 1990s German-language productions of *Hamlet* at single glance. Likewise, it is easier to expand searches beyond a single language, as one search can summon all Slavic language productions of a play. There is no such thing as a finished and comprehensive bibliography, particularly in a field as wide-ranging as Shakespeare studies; however, despite inevitable omissions in its extensive data, the *WSB* offers a key starting point for any study of Shakespeare.

The *WSB*'s "search and browse" interface, by default, takes users to a single search bar (Figure 14.1), following Marti A. Hearst's precept that the key to effective searching is "keeping the interface simple" (1). This allows users to work at their own level of search expertise: you can simply type keywords into the single blank box, a familiar research strategy from most web searches; you can use advanced Boolean operators;[8] or you can choose to click over to "Advanced Search" or "Browse."

Systems of organization and those systems' visual renderings can determine (or overdetermine) the ways users interact with the contents. In printed books, texts are organized and laid out by the creator (an order which the reader can then choose to ignore). In digital texts, however, the user has more control over sorting, but the categories are still preselected by the creator. Just as Samuel Johnson complained that Alexander Pope's commonplace markers deprived readers of agency over the material, digital searches likewise circumscribe

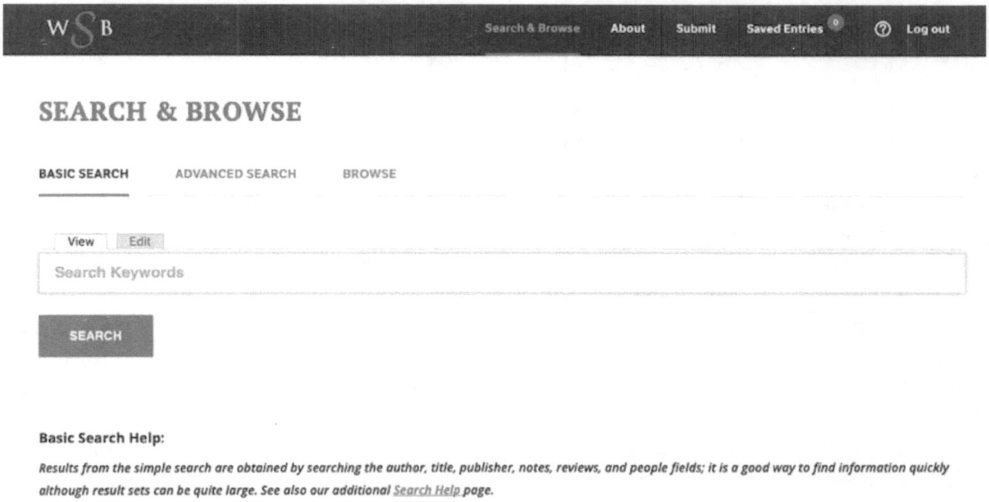

Figure 14.1 *World Shakespeare Bibliography* "Search and Browse" page (2020)
Source: worldshakesbib.org/basic-search. Courtesy of the *WSB*.

how results are presented. Indeed, it is even more important to critically approach digital results because a website's control can seem less intrusive and can therefore be more insidious.

The *WSB* interface allows users to sort their results in multiple ways: chronological and reverse chronological; alphabetical A–Z and Z–A for author or title; by document type; and by relevance. The last category, "relevance," is the default way results are returned, as weighted results are determined algorithmically,[9] with scholarship such as journal articles and book monographs appearing higher in the results. Likewise, having a word appear in the title of an entry will position it higher than if the word appears only in the entry. The weighted results usually privilege works *by* a person whose name is searched rather than *about* them: for instance, searching "Judi Dench" returns items where she is listed as the primary "creator" first, that is, the productions she directed and her autobiography; articles about her that feature her name in the title appear next; finally, entries that list her only in the annotation (such as productions in which she acted) appear at the bottom of the list. Search result weighting is never perfect because each user comes to the *WSB* with different research questions in mind (see Hearst Chapter 3). Algorithms that highlight creators reflect long-standing privileging of the author as a primary category of organization, which has in turn profoundly shaped the interface. In the literature sections of physical book stacks organized by the Library of Congress designations, the author reigns supreme; this is yet another connection between the physical and digital interfaces of textual study. The ability to craft more complex searches using Boolean operators or the Advanced Search options, combined with the multiple ways of sorting results, however, enable users to tailor what they seek and find—but require a few more clicks to retrieve and order the information.

Interface, Taxonomies, and Structures of Knowledge about Shakespeare

Just as the First Folio layout and paratextual interface reflect the state of reading and interests of Hemings and Condell in 1623, the current *WSB* tagset reveals the state of scholarship when it was created in the mid-twentieth century as well as the preoccupations of the editor who designed them. For instance, there are no taxonomy categories for theoretical approaches to Shakespeare's works, such as feminist criticism, postcolonial criticism, or race studies; yet more historicist approaches are included, with an entire taxonomy category devoted to "Shakespeare and His Stage," with tags such as "Shakespeare's Stage: Private Playhouses" and "Shakespeare's Stage: Acting Companies." These historicist categories are often themselves too narrow: for instance, the "Shakespeare's Stage: Public Playhouses" category is specifically about public playhouses in Shakespeare's day. Scholarship on current playing spaces and, for instance, remediations of performances, do not have a clear home in the taxonomy and so end up in the "Scholarship, Criticism, History of Criticism" catch-all tag.

The taxonomy tag "Scholarship, Criticism, History of Criticism" includes any journal article, chapter, or monograph about Shakespeare meant for an academic audience and so becomes too broad a category to be useful, except perhaps for differentiating performances and editions from secondary sources. Even this tag, however, suggests a value judgment on the types of publications we undertake as academics: translations and editions are usually not tagged as scholarship and criticism,[10] which suggests that they are somehow not "scholarly"—even if they contain rigorous scholarship with extensive introductions, such as Sukanta Chaudhuri's Arden 3 edition of *A Midsummer Night's Dream*. Likewise, the *WSB* style guide specifies that edited collections should not be tagged with "Scholarship, Criticism, History of Criticism," although the individual book chapters in the collection do bear the tag. Introductions to journal special issues and edited collections do not receive their own entries in the *WSB*, despite the labor and scholarship that often are undertaken with both. Indeed, although editors of special collection books are mentioned in the *WSB*, journal special issue editors are omitted altogether. These tagging practices have been inherited from previous editors and show how certain types of scholarship have been historically more valued in the academy.

The First Folio established (or warped) the boundaries of Shakespeare's dramatic canon for centuries, and its paratextual interface organized the plays into genres we still employ today. Alexander Pope relegated "suspected passages," i.e. what he deemed to be beneath Shakespeare or non-Shakespearean, to the bottom of the page; here, the interface separated Shakespeare from non- or unworthy-Shakespeare. The browsable taxonomy of the *WSB* continues to reify how we think of Shakespeare's work and canon. "Individual Works" receive priority on the "browse" page by being the first set of taxonomy tags listed. In order to keep the user interface more navigable, rather than listing all 117 tags (in, say, alphabetical order), the *WSB* offers them in a categorized list, which can be expanded as desired. With no ability to nuance taxonomy tags, co-written plays remain problematic: one need only turn to essays from and about the *New Oxford Shakespeare*, ongoing discussions on the SHAKSPER listserv, or the many publications that appear in the *WSB* with the tag "Stylometry and Stylometrics." The *WSB* taxonomy might seem innocuous, but, like the table of contents of any complete works of Shakespeare, it makes assumptions about what is part of "Shakespeare" and what is only liminal—the latter appearing with an "Apocrypha" tag. Listing *Sir Thomas More* under the "Apocrypha" heading of the taxonomy, for instance, separates it from the other items listed as "Individual Works," despite the widely accepted fact that Shakespeare had a hand in the play.

The First Folio set the initial bounds of Shakespeare's dramatic canon: thirty-six plays which were reprinted in the Second (1632) and Third Folio (1663). The second issue of the Third Folio (1664) reprinted these plays and added seven others: *Pericles, Locrine, The London Prodigal, The Puritan, Sir John Oldcastle, Thomas Lord Cromwell,* and *A Yorkshire Tragedy*. Despite their inclusion in the second issue of the Third Folio, the additional plays are nevertheless still separated from the original thirty-six Folio plays: the seven plays were included at the end of the text, and the second issue's title page distinguishes between original Folio plays and supplemental plays: "And unto this impression is added seven playes, never before printed in folio." Hence, F3's interface implicitly defines a "primary" and "secondary" canon of belatedly-added plays. The *WSB* "apocrypha" taxonomy tag likewise separates Shakespeare's primary and secondary canon, even as the overall site includes both kinds of plays. The "apocrypha" tag does not offer users an intuitive understanding of the kinds of apocrypha listed. For instance, in the *WSB, Sir John Oldcastle* is listed alongside *Arden of Faversham*, despite the fact that the former is non-Shakespearean and the latter is the subject of ongoing interventions about whether or not it is, in part, by Shakespeare. Of the seven plays added in the second imprint of the 1664 Third Folio, the *WSB* lists only *Pericles* in "Individual Works" because it is widely accepted to be in part by Shakespeare, and includes *The London Prodigal, Sir John Oldcastle*, and *Thomas Lord Cromwell* in the apocrypha category, but does not include tags for *Locrine, The Puritan*, and *A Yorkshire Tragedy*. A case could be made that these last three plays, by reason of their shared publication history, merit inclusion as tags in the "apocrypha" category as much as the others. A keyword search reveals 12 entries that mention *Locrine* and 14 that mention *A Yorkshire Tragedy*, both of which outnumber the 9 entries tagged with *London Prodigal*. Adding works to the "apocrypha" category of the taxonomy cannot be undertaken lightly, however, because the user's assumption would be that the *WSB* has included all professional productions, editions, and scholarship about the work.

The "apocrypha" category, furthermore, holds together works that are para-Shakespearean in different ways. And while established scholars will be able to look at the list of titles in the "apocrypha" category and identify *Vortigern* as an infamous forgery and *Cardenio* as a lost play, as it stands, the interface does not make clear how or why apocryphal texts are included in the *WSB*. As Peter Kirwan has demonstrated, debates about the Shakespeare canon are centuries-old and importantly shape how we think of "Shakespeare" not just as a writer but as an *oeuvre*. Continuing the notions of Shakespeare canon established by the interfaces of the First and Third Folios, Alexander Pope and others, the *WSB*'s taxonomy and interface participate in these debates by tacitly categorizing without offering the supporting arguments one would find in, say, the scholarship indexed in the bibliography itself.

Copious textual material—be it the works of Shakespeare or annotations of sources about and performances of Shakespeare—requires a clear and hopefully intuitive system of organization to be usable. The thirty-six plays of the First Folio were organized by its table of contents into genre; the German *Bibliographie. In Jahrbuch der Deutschen Shakespeare Gesellschaft* (1865–1911) organized its decades of scholarship by location. Similarly, the data in the *WSB* is only useful if it is findable; and to be findable, it has to be well curated (i.e. annotated, tagged, and edited) and accessible through an intuitive user interface. The "Basic Search" and "Advanced Search" interfaces are, perhaps, more intuitive than the "Browse" interface, but the "Browse" also allows for powerful results when users understand the taxonomy. For instance, the "Play Groups and Poems" considers Shakespeare's work by genre: with tags including "comedies," "histories," "poems," "romances," "tragedies." Entries with these tags do not cover all plays from a given genre or group—the "histories" tag, for instance, is not assigned to every study of a history play—but rather address the genre itself or the group of plays as a whole, such as Lena Steveker's "Englands dramatische Geschichte: Shakespeares Histories [England's Dramatic Story: Shakespeare's Histories]" or Vimala Pasupathi's "The King beyond the Clouds: Visualizing Statecraft in Shakespeare's History Plays." The *WSB*, however, does not include a category for "Roman Plays," another common grouping/genre explored in scholarship and performance—consider Ivo van Hove's production *De Romeinse Tragedies [Roman Tragedies]* and the over one hundred entries in the *WSB* whose titles include either "Roman Tragedies," "Roman Histories," or "Roman Plays."

Besides the generic categories highlighted in "Play Groups and Poems," there are two other small play groups tucked under the "Individual Plays" tag: *1 & 2 Henry IV* and *1–3 Henry VI*. This editorial decision is inherited from the plays' titles in the First Folio: the present tags reveal the powerful influence of Heminges and Condell four centuries on. If *3 Henry VI* had been titled *The True Tragedy of Richard Duke of York* in the Folio, as it is in quarto, it would not have been yoked together with those plays in a single taxonomy tag. Because the *WSB* currently has a single tag for *1–3 Henry VI* as well as individual tags for each play, it would make sense to also include a tag for each of Shakespeare's tetralogies. Having only some play groups, furthermore, complicates the interface, because users need to know to check both *1 Henry IV* and *1 & 2 Henry IV* in the advanced search box and look in both categories in browse (though basic searching would find all results).[11] The *WSB* browse and search interface is built on taxonomy tags, many of which descend from the First Folio.

Just as cultivating serendipity is an important goal in analogue research contexts, the *WSB* interface makes many fields such as author, journal title, and taxonomy tags clickable to encourage serendipity in scholarly contexts. The 2016 update and current *WSB* improved its interface to offer better access to its wealth of information about Shakespeare scholarship and performance by streamlining the presentation of information, making the information navigable in new ways, and even making the interface mobile-accessible. As this chapter has suggested, however, there is still much room for improvement, not least with regards to reformulating the taxonomy, or, as we argue, encouraging Shakespeareans to approach the taxonomy with an analytic eye. Shakespeareans, like all scholars, need to be aware of and actively engaged with how digital projects structure the information on which we build our research.

To search or browse in the *World Shakespeare Bibliography* is to explore all the entries in the database by their taxonomy tags which have been assigned by hundreds of human bibliographers over seven decades. Tags can be inconsistently applied, and certainly reveal the scholarly preoccupations of their moment of creation, as well as the particular interests of the editors who designed them.

The evolution of the *WSB* tags is an important chapter in the story of the ever-shifting Shakespeare interface, which began with generic divisions and commonplace markers in the seventeenth century, through the highlighting of favored passages embedded within a larger text (and banishment of lesser passages to the bottom), to bibliographies that divide criticism by country, textual format, or topic. In each case, the interface reflects the needs of the users, proclivities of the creator, and preoccupations of the culture at large. The Shakespeare bibliographies from the 1910s which divide scholarship by country ominously reflect the nationalism which descended in the countries into bloody wars in the decades that followed; the specialized taxonomy of the *WSB* in the earliest issues of *Shakespeare Quarterly* reflect the rising tide of academia in post-war contexts; critical developments in feminist, postcolonial and critical race studies reflect a pressing need for new tags, a need compromised by the realities of academic labor. The interface always mirrors our own interests and anxieties back to us; changes to the interface imply changes in scholarly thinking, and in turn make more changes more likely.

This chapter has explored how the interface (from printed books to digital platforms) informs the way we structure and access knowledge: from the sixteenth century's commonplace headings to today's browsable online taxonomies. Recognizing that anthologies, editions, and bibliographies mediate access to information by the categories they impose requires scholars to think beyond bibliographies as neutral information conveyances. This means, for Shakespeareans, exploring how interfaces define the very category of "Shakespeare" we study. Ultimately, interfaces, from the earliest Shakespeare publications to the *World Shakespeare Bibliography*, mediate not only how scholars can read Shakespeare, but also how we interact with and understand the shape of Shakespeare scholarship.

Acknowledgments

We would like to thank Kris May, Mark Kaethler, and the editors for their thoughtful feedback on this chapter. Thanks also to the team of scholars who make the *World Shakespeare Bibliography* possible.

Notes

1 Citations of Shakespeare refer to Orgel and Braunmuller's *The Complete Pelican Shakespeare* unless otherwise noted.

2 See, for instance, Duncan on the index, Sherman on the manicule, Hunter on various types of commonplace markers, and Blair on tables of contents.

3 In print, the *World Shakespeare Bibliography* 1949 appeared in 1950 and so forth. In-text references are to the year of publication, not the title year (that is, the year covered by the bibliography). Subsequent printed publications of the *WSB* are not listed individually in the works cited.

4 For more on the history of the *WSB* and its move from print to digital, see Estill, "Digital Bibliography."

5 The full taxonomy can be seen in the left-hand menu of the *WSB* browse page: worldshakesbib.org/browse.

6 The *WSB* rebuild was spearheaded by Laura Estill, Kris May, and Eric Johnson with generous funding from the Folger Shakespeare Library and the Texas A&M University College of Liberal Arts.

7 As the *World Shakespeare Bibliography* search help page (https://www.worldshakesbib.org/search-help) notes, the language and format searches assume an "OR" relationship: choosing "French" and "Spanish" as the option brings up all entries tagged with either language, not just entries tagged with both. Before 2016, entries were only allowed to be tagged with one language, so, for instance, facing-page translations would only be tagged with the non-English language. Likewise, selecting multiple document types (formats) such as "audio recording" and "production" will bring up items with either of those formats, because the *WSB* does not allow more than one format per entry. In these cases (language, document type, and *WSB* update), choosing more than one option will return more results. The "tag" section, however, functions with an AND operator, so choosing multiple tags will limit the number of results: a search for "*Hamlet*" "*Macbeth*" and "Music" tags must have all three, so would not return any scholarship on music in *Macbeth* only.

8 For an in-depth account of the importance and use of Boolean operators, see Mann, *The Oxford Guide to Library Research*, Chapter 10; on their functionality in the *WSB* specifically, see worldshakesbib.org/search-help.

9 The back-end of the *World Shakespeare Bibliography* search and browse uses Apache Solr. The browse results are technically generated using a search as well, by searching only for the requested tag(s).

10 As of May 2020, there are over 4,700 editions (tagged "Editions and Texts," "Selective Edition," or "Complete Editions") listed in the *World Shakespeare Bibliography*. Fewer than 200 also have the tag "Scholarship, Criticism, History of Criticism."

11 For instance, Arnáiz's "La Traducción Histórica de los Vinos Españoles en las Obras de Shakespeare" [Historical Translation of Spanish Wines in the Works of Shakespeare], which discusses translation choices specifically with regards to both *1* and *2 Henry IV* does not have the taxonomy tag "*1 Henry IV*" and so would not be visible if a user looked in "*1 Henry IV*" in the taxonomy. Arnaiz's essay, like over 1000 entries in the bibliography, bears the tag "*1 & 2 Henry IV*."

References

Abbott, Andrew. *Digital Paper: A Manual for Research and Writing with Library and Internet Materials*. U of Chicago P, 2014.

Andrews, John F. "From the Editor: The 'New' World Shakespeare Bibliography." *Shakespeare Quarterly*, vol. 27, no. 4, 1976.

Arnáiz, Laura Campillo. "La Traducción Histórica de los Vinos Españoles en las Obras de Shakespeare" [Historical Translation of Spanish Wines in the Works of Shakespeare]. *1611: Revista de historia de la traducción: A Journal of Translation History/Revista d'historia de la traducción*, vol. 11, no. 11, 2017. Available at: traduccionliteraria.org/1611/art/campillo.htm.

Blair, Ann. *Too Much to Know: Managing Scholarly Information Before the Scholarly Age*. Yale UP, 2010.

Bloom, Gina. "Theater History in 3D: The Digital Early Modern in the Age of the Interface." *English Literary Renaissance*, vol. 50, no. 1, 2020, pp. 8–16.

Craig, Heidi, editor. *The World Shakespeare Bibliography Online (WSB)*. Oxford UP and Folger Shakespeare Library. Available at: worldshakesbib.org.

DeMaria, Robert, Jr. *Samuel Johnson and the Life of Reading*. Johns Hopkins UP, 1997.

Duncan, Dennis. "Indexes." *Book Parts*. Edited by Dennis Duncan and Adam Smyth, Oxford UP, 2019, pp. 263–272.

Engelsing, Rolf. "Die Perioden der Lesergeschichte in der Neuzeit" [The Periods of Reading in the Modern Age]. *Archiv für Geschichte des Buchwesens*, vol. 10, 1970, pp. 947–1000.

Estill, Laura. "Commonplace Markers and Quotation Marks." *ArchBook: Architectures of the Book*. Edited by Alan Galey. Implementing New Knowledge Environments and the University of Toronto iSchool, 2014. Available at: drc.usask.ca/projects/archbook/commonplace.php.

Estill, Laura. "Digital Bibliography and Global Shakespeare." *Scholarly and Research Communication*, vol. 5, no. 4, 2014. doi:10.22230/src.2014v5n4a187.

Estill, Laura. *Dramatic Extracts in Seventeenth-Century English Manuscripts: Watching, Reading, Changing Plays*. U of Delaware P, 2015.

Estill, Laura. "Legacy Technologies and Digital Futures." *Doing More Digital Humanities*, edited by Constance Crompton, Richard J. Lane, and Ray Siemens, Routledge, 2020, pp. 7–24.

Giddens, Eugene. *How to Read a Shakespearean Play Text*. Cambridge UP, 2011.

Harmon, Robert B. *Elements of Bibliography: A Guide to Information Sources and Practical Sources*. Scarecrow Press, 1998.

Hearst, Marti A. *Search User Interfaces*. Cambridge UP, 2009. Available at: searchuserinterfaces.com.

Hunter, G. K. "The Marking of Sententiae in Elizabethan Printed Plays, Poems, and Romances." *The Library*, series 5, vol. 6, no. 3–4, 1951, pp. 171–188.

Johnson, Samuel. *The Yale Edition of the Works of Samuel Johnson*. Vol. 2, edited by Walter J. Bate, John M. Bullitt, and L. F. Powell, Yale UP, 1958.

Johnson, Samuel. *Proposals for Printing by Subscription the Dramatic Works of William Shakespeare: Samuel Johnson on Shakespeare*, edited by W. K.Wimsatt, Jr., Hill and Wang, 1960.

Kirwan, Peter. *Shakespeare and the Idea of Apocrypha: Negotiating the Boundaries of the Dramatic Canon*. Cambridge UP, 2015.

Lesser, Zachary, and Peter Stallybrass. "The First Literary *Hamlet* and the Commonplacing of Professional Plays." *Shakespeare Quarterly*, vol. 59, no. 4, 2008, pp. 371–420.

Lynch, Jack. *You Could Look It Up: The Reference Shelf from Ancient Babylon to Wikipedia*. Bloomsbury, 2016.

Mann, Thomas. *The Oxford Guide to Library Research*. 4th ed., Oxford UP, 2015.

Northup, Clark S. "On the Bibliography of Shakespeare." *The Journal of English and Germanic Philology*, vol. 11, no. 2, 1912, pp. 218–230.

OED (Oxford English Dictionary Online). "Browse, v." Oxford UP, June 2020. Available at: www.oed.com/view/Entry/23882.

Pasupathi, Vimala. "The King beyond the Clouds: Visualizing Statecraft in Shakespeare's History Plays." *Approaches to Teaching Shakespeare's English History Plays*, edited by Laurie Ellinghausen, Modern Language Association of America, 2017, pp. 179–184.

Pope, Alexander. "Preface." *The Works of Shakespeare in six volumes, collated and corrected by the former editions, by Mr. Pope*. London, 1723–1725.

Race, Tammera M., and Stephann Makri. *Accidental Information Discovery: Cultivating Serendipity in the Digital Age*. Chandos Publishing, 2016.

Roberts, Jane. "Silent Reading." *Mapping English Metaphor Through Time*. Edited by Wendy Anderson, Ellen Bramwell, and Carole Hough, Oxford UP, 2016, pp. 243–260.

Shakespeare, William. *William Shakespeare: The Complete Works*. Edited by Stephen Orgel and A.R. Braunmuller, Penguin, 2002.

Shakespeare, William. *A Midsummer Night's Dream*. Edited by Sukanta Chaudhuri, Bloomsbury Arden, 2017.

Sherman, William. *Used Books: Marking Readers in Renaissance England*. U of Pennsylvania P, 2008.

Sidney, Philip. *The Major Works*. Edited by Katherine Duncan-Jones, 1989, reprinted 2002, Oxford UP.

Smith, Bruce R. "Reading Lists of Plays, Early Modern, Modernist, Postmodern." *Shakespeare Quarterly*, vol. 42, no. 2, 1991, pp. 127–144.

Steveker, Lena. "Englands dramatische Geschichte: Shakespeares Histories" [England's Dramatic Story: Shakespeare's Histories]. *Literatur und Geschichte* [Literature and History]. Edited by Sikander Singh and Manfred Leber, Saarland UP, 2018, pp. 81–96.

Thomas, Sidney. "Shakespeare: An Annotated Bibliography for 1949." *Shakespeare Quarterly*, vol. 1, no. 2, 1950, pp. 97–120.

Tromans, Philip. "The Business of Browsing in Early Modern English Bookshops." *Buying and Selling: The Business of Books in Early Modern Europe*. Brill, 2019, pp. 111–135.

van Hove, Ivo, dir. *De Romeinse Tragedies* [Roman Tragedies]. Toneelgroep Amsterdam, Stadsschouwburg, Amsterdam, 2007, performance.

West, William N. *Theatres and Encyclopedias in Early Modern Europe*. Cambridge UP, 2002.

Woolf, D. R. *Reading History in Early Modern England*. Cambridge UP, 2000.

PART V

User experience

15

"MAKE YOUR BEST USE OF THIS"

User-Experience Design and the Shakespeare Interface

Kurt Daw

Serving Practitioners

This is not a theoretical essay. Rather, it is a case study of my personal experience working to create an edition of *A Midsummer Night's Dream* with a new digital interface in partnership with a user-experience (UX) designer and what I learned from it.[1]

I teach and direct in a theater department where my students encounter Shakespeare's plays as *scripts* that they turn into real or conceptual productions through performance, design, and dramaturgy. I undertook this project because I grew frustrated that the widely available editions from the major publishers, despite their many virtues as study aids for the plays as literature, did not address the production-related needs of my students. In fact, they sometimes confused the issues considerably. As Barbara Hodgdon famously noted, "Traditional codes of editorial commentary serve neither performers nor performance" (211).

In rehearsal, questions frequently arise around a handful of performance concerns: questions of scansion and rhetoric, textual alternatives and emendations, cutting and arranging, the practicality of doubling roles by a single actor, the conventions of constructing gender onstage and who can play what roles, the division of the script into rehearsal units, placement of scene shifts and light cues, and the authority and accuracy of stage directions. All of these point to places where a *script* (a starting point for a future production) differs from a *text* (a literary artifact), even if the words on paper do not change. The editions that dominate the market, aimed at literature students, understandably reference bibliography (or, occasionally, theater history) to "settle" matters when addressing these concerns rather than treating them as living questions. This settling is not due to editorial malpractice but is simply a matter of perspective: what are lacunae to practitioners creating a new production are irrelevancies to students or scholars studying the plays as fixed objects.

I initiated my project to assist theatrical practitioners whom I perceive as an underserved constituency in the universe of critical and scholarly Shakespeare editions. I did not initially conceptualize my work as a digital project, nor did I start with any intention of utilizing user-experience principles. Indeed, I did not even know about them. I simply wanted to make an edition to address the unmet needs of actors, directors, designers, and dramaturgs working on productions without sacrificing the valuable information they derive from editions for readers and literature students. That my edition eventually evolved in the direction it did is largely a

DOI: 10.4324/9780367821722-21

consequence of this desire to serve my students as both readers and practitioners. However, from the moment my design partner first asked, "Who are the intended users?" I found myself falling down the rabbit hole of app development to address what I believed were unmet needs—a problem that I came to understand was a central challenge of interface design.

The Locus of the Interaction

Interfaces, in the most fundamental sense of "a means or place of interaction," are properties of books every bit as much as they are of computer programs or applications (*OED*). We do not think about this very much only because, after a millennium of stability in the codex form, books and their pages are intuitively operable.

The quarto editions of the twenty Shakespeare plays that reached print before 1623—often in multiple editions—are all remarkably similar and good examples of this intuitive operability because of the simplicity of their design and layout. This is because they have almost no paratext. They all have title pages, but with two minor exceptions where stationers supplied a dedicatory epistle, no other introductory materials before the start of the playtext.[2] Not one of them has a list of *dramatis personae*. Running heads are nearly universal, with catchwords and signature marks (rather than page numbers) at the bottom of the page. Plays are not divided into acts and scenes, not even when they initially appear to be due to "*Actus Primus*" on the first page. These are books that one starts at the beginning and reads sequentially until reaching the end. Many printing conventions of the period are now unfamiliar to our students, but the page-as-interface remains clear and as readily accessible as ever.

Even the initial addition of paratextual content (like the author's biography, regularized lists of *dramatis personae*, and glossaries) by eighteenth-century editors did not muddle the standard playtext interface and reading experience because starting with Rowe (1709) and continuing through the editions of Pope (1725) and Theobald (1733), they arranged the paratextual material as front- or end-matter. However, the extensive placement of paratextual commentary on the same page as the text in the latter half of the eighteenth century significantly complicated the print interface's operation. Although he was not the first to use footnotes, Samuel Johnson's 1765 Tonson edition places his predecessors' lengthy notes at the foot of the page and then continues them with additional—often contradictory—commentary of his own.[3] As scholars, the operation of numbered footnotes is now so familiar that while the idea of interrupting one's reading to glance to the bottom of the page, find and read the note, and return to one's place in the text may *seem* intuitive, it is still far from evident to those encountering this convention for the first time. Nor is it frictionless even for those with extensive experience, especially the visual process of recovering one's place in the text after glancing away.

Over time, editors added or altered more page interface elements to accommodate distinctions among kinds of paratext. Suzanne Gossett traces the introduction of the modern "three-layer page" consisting of text, a concise collation line (aka the band of terror), and commentary below, that is now standard in editions like the Arden 3rd series and the Oxford Shakespeare individual editions, to nineteenth-century editor Howard Staunton (220). Some editions, for example, the Norton 3rd, add one more layer by treating glosses as a separate category from commentary, placing them in a narrow column on the right-hand side of the page. After the publication of Charles Hinman's facsimile edition of the First Folio in 1968, it became common practice to replace the consecutive numbering of footnotes with references to his through-line numbers. In most editions, there are no longer any markers in the line that indicate some or all of the text is subject to annotation. The reader must proactively check the commentary to discover any related to the line.

All of these devices require considerable sophistication to operate conceptually, all operate according to their own independent logic, and none of them can be said to operate in an intuitively obvious manner. Two or more types, like marginal glosses, notes in a collation line, and footnoted commentary (each with a different mode of operation) appearing on the same page, compound the problem. For any given line in the text, the reader might need to look to the right margin to find a column of glosses. Next, she might need to look to the collation line for instances of textual variants recorded in abbreviated form, then scan the bottom of the page to see what matters—if any—are discussed in footnotes, and finally, quickly check for the possible existence of endnotes treating yet other matters.[4]

There are no simple solutions to the problems of juxtaposing text and paratext in print, however, and so probably the best one can do (although it is regrettably infrequent) is to offer robust instruction in using the interface. In the current market, major critical editions do offer distinct differences in their page arrangements. The editions of David Bevington, for example, have a general glossary at the volume's end rather than placing specific glosses beside or below the text. Folger editions mix glosses and commentary on a facing-page where annotation aligns horizontally with the text it is illuminating. Although they are all essentially variations on the page interface that has been in use since the first Arden edition of *Hamlet* (1899), these subtle alternatives create a learning curve for even experienced readers every time they pick up a new edition.

The Limitations of Print

While my students routinely had difficulties learning the conventions of the printed three-layer page in Shakespeare editions, especially the meaning of the densely coded collation notes, that was not what motivated my project. My more significant concern was with information that was restricted or eliminated, presumably to keep the page legible or reduce information overload. My experience as an actor and director taught me that space restrictions often imposed limitations on how much information might be offered—and whether it was even offered at all. Important information for theater practitioners was only rarely—and inconsistently—included, as we were not assumed to be the users of most editions. For example, editors almost always note that they have emended the copy-text, but potential cases where they ultimately decided *not* to do so are often invisible even when a line is probably corrupt or is left metrically deficient. Similarly, diacritical marks and typographic indications of scansion (even when present in the early modern copy-text and informative about the meter) have been increasingly eliminated in favor of a cleaner, sleeker *reading* experience.

When I began working on my edition, I naively *thought* I would simply add an extra layer of notation about performance to provide practitioners with what I perceived was needed to address their concerns. I believed I could work within the confines of the print format, only with more notes. An initial draft of my experimental project, working on the first twenty lines of *A Midsummer Night's Dream*—a brief expository dialogue between Theseus and Hippolyta—showed me that static print forces selectivity. The Folger Shakespeare Library edition has eight notes about this section of the play. Peter Holland's Oxford Shakespeare edition has fifteen. The Arden 2nd, Arden 3rd, and the New Cambridge Shakespeare editions fall in between these extremes.

In contrast, I had thirty-eight notes for those same twenty lines. For example, I was very concerned about six elisions necessary to maintain the meter that *no* other edition referenced, in addition to sixteen examples of rhetorical devices (antitheses, alliterations, and similes) that had important implications for the actors' vocal delivery or physical performance. All twenty lines in my draft were subject to at least one note or gloss of some kind. A single glance at my overcrowded commentary section told me why standard editions do not even attempt to deal with scansion and rhetoric. The stack-up of notes at the bottom of the page was intimidating and unhelpful, as long explanatory notes addressing scansion and rhetoric are too dense to consult quickly in rehearsal.

Deeply dissatisfied with this overloaded page, I prototyped several attempts at sorting this jumble of information graphically. Perhaps the most visually successful placed all the paratext, arranged into four categorical columns (glosses, scansion, textual alternatives, and notes) on the versos across from the playtext on the facing rectos, but using it required so much eye-skipping that student volunteers giving it a trial run soon ignored the annotations altogether. In the next iteration, color-coding and typographical distinctions prevented the columns from blending into one indistinguishable heap and helped users determine what kind of annotation might be available but added to the visual overload, not to mention that printing it would be prohibitively expensive. I also found problematic the frequency with which words or phrases were subject to two or more notes, as often an individual word was both elided and in need of a gloss and sometimes needed a critical note in addition. When readers have to know typography and color theory to sort their options ("This bold-faced, italicized, green word must have both a blue elision *and* a yellow gloss"), usability has been defeated.

While I organized each iteration of my graphic experiment better than the last, it was always at the cost of creating a greater cognitive load. More operations with differing (and non-intuitive) rules vastly complicated the number of potential operations one had to hold in one's head, and even if I utilized standard conventions, many of the operations were still difficult to carry out. For example, I could eliminate one entire column (and its associated clutter) from my four-column annotation by treating the textual alternatives as endnotes and banishing them to the back of the book.[5] However, the user then had to be cued with an entirely new symbol or convention that the alternative existed, remember that it was in the endnotes instead of with the rest of the annotations, and interrupt their reading in an entirely different manner than glosses or scansion notes required to check it. I discovered first-hand that an interface is more than a container for, or location of, interaction. It is the means of interaction, and it can be tightly constraining.

Although I wanted to *prioritize* theatrical over bibliographic concerns, I soon realized that it was problematic simply to flip the traditional model and eliminate standard forms of editorial commentary to make space for information that served practitioners. Doing so made the page cleaner but not more useful since, at some point, the practitioner also needs access to the interpretive assistance traditionally included in critical editions. The new Arden Performance Editions from Bloomsbury would seem to confirm my concerns. These eliminate the standard annotation and commentary to create space for additional information. Although I admire the intent and their clean layout, in the end, I find them unsatisfactory because they achieve their sleekness by eliminating far too much. These performance editions use the critical texts established for either the Arden 2 or 3 series without including their apparatus. This elimination reduces clutter tremendously, but pragmatically, a practitioner needs to buy both the regular edition and the performance edition to get all the information I believe is necessary.

I also have reservations about how minimal the information which *is* supplied is. The editions note elisions, for example, with a marginal note giving the syllable count for the word but without explaining how the actor can accomplish the reductions. Notes that say only "given (equiv.1 syl.)," "Whether (equiv.1 syl.)" and "the Ath-**e**-nian (equiv. 3 syl.)," seem to me woefully under-informative about what an actor is supposed to say in these difficult, but not uncommon, cases. The editions rarely address contraction between words, like "th'impression," which still leaves about a third of the scansion challenges in the plays invisible to the actors. Issues of rhetoric are not taken up beyond two brief paragraphs in the introduction that list common types of devices. Performance practice (such as doubling roles, incorporating music, dance, and stage combat, or the increasing use of original practices/ pronunciation) is not addressed.

It was a casual observation from my digitally native son, reflecting on my observation that sooner or later, the theatrical practitioner still needed interpretive assistance, that the "at-some-point" factor was the crucial print interface complication. Although much of the paratext on the printed page is necessary and helpful only at a specific moment or for a limited amount of time, it is impossible to make it come and go. Once you place it there for potential use, it is *always* there. Conversely, if you choose not to include it, it is *forever* absent.

Of course, digital interfaces need not be bound by static print's limitations. Digital texts can be dynamic since they can be coded to display in alternative ways under different conditions. A very low-level example of this is how live internet links appear in many documents as blue text but change color (usually to purple) once a user has opened the link. It has one appearance in the unopened context, and in the "previously-opened" context, it has another. John Lavagnino notes that "the content of a digital commentary doesn't need to be fixed in the way a printed one is, and that suggests a useful kind of flexibility; in reading you could choose the sorts of notes to be displayed" (199).

The crucial breakthrough that ultimately enabled my project was to conceptualize the digital interface as the means of empowering users' choices where static print constrained them. Although I had understood my son's (and Lavagnino's) point about the flexibility inherent in dynamic text, I did not have a model for deploying it. Through experience, I learned that the key to creating the kind of edition I envisioned was neither just adding new stuff nor oversimplifying by throwing away old stuff. What was needed, I began to see, was a means for the user to interact with the edition according to their particular goals and needs.

Much of the actual or potential information overload in a standard critical edition is a consequence of static paratext being present before it is needed or lingering after it has outlived its usefulness. Glosses, for example, are immediately helpful when first reading a play if you do not know what a word or phrase means, but as soon as they have been consulted and you learn the meaning, they become obsolete. At the opposite end of the spectrum, notes about textual alternatives from the collation might be vital to a small number of people, but probably not until reasonably late in an investigation of the text. Until then, they are clutter.

This point might seem obvious, but it was not particularly clear to me, at least in the beginning. It was not clear to significant publishers, either, since several invested heavily in commercial digital initiatives, like the Folger Luminary and Cambridge UP's *Explore Shakespeare* apps for the iPad that have already come and gone from the market. That might be because their interfaces provided an unsatisfactory user experience to anyone who did not have a print paradigm in their head, and they operated with little attention to the conventions standard on digital devices. (These digital "apps" for tablets, in particular, generally seemed to reproduce the crowded look and feel of the printed page with side-by-side notes and text and attempted to "innovate" instead, through the addition of social media and multi-media.) Realizing these apps retained the all-the-information-all-the-time format of the printed page, even though this is not necessary for a digital environment, reveals that these apps were not designed to overcome the limitations of print but to transfer existing print editions to the digital marketplace.

The Cambridge University Press *Explore Shakespeare* app proved an instructive case. One of the earliest examples of digital transfer, this iPad app, created by the developer Agant, came to the market as a freestanding commercial product in 2012. Although it had some attractive and useful features, like a synching audio performance, and numerous full-color photos, it had striking operational weaknesses. In contrast to a familiar chronological table of contents, for example, the entire contents of the app were available only through a series of nested menus, some of which you reached by "clicking" and others that you reached with sideways "swipes," like a dating app. You had to hold the contents of the six menus in your head because their displays were mutually exclusive alternatives.

Viewing the playtext, you discovered that it was always shown in a window with a fixed size utilizing small type so that it fit in a portrait display, even when the tablet was rotated into the more verse-friendly landscape orientation. (The extra margin space created by the difference between portrait and landscape views was simply left blank.)

The app had three different operational modes, labeled Experience, Explore, and Examine, each of which used a unique interface of its own. The first of these was rather like a traditional print layout, albeit with embedded photos and an audio performance that could be played in the background while you read along. The second looked and felt entirely different, as it mostly contained non-text-based elements: it was focused on games and activities related to the play but also included graphic representations of the timeline of the play, maps of character relationships, and several other miscellaneous features like a word cloud generator. The third mode accessed a series of articles and essays that illuminated the play, like standard front- and end-matter, but it was also how you accessed commentary and notes, as well as the search function. The notes in the third mode were notoriously hard to consult. They came in several categories, not all of which operated in the same way, and appeared in frustratingly tiny print in small text boxes even when the entire width of the screen was theoretically available to display them.

The point is not to belabor criticism of a defunct product but to note that digital editions, which have capabilities that could potentially empower users, more often disempower them by offering too many features and options without an understanding of what to do with them. (I would soon learn that "feature overload" is a pervasive problem in software and app development, one which user-experience design was specifically created to address.)

The Folger/Luminary Shakespeare iPad app (2014), designed by Elliott Visconsi and Katherine Rowe for Luminary Digital Media, was markedly better than the Cambridge app but still confusing and difficult to use compared to the Folger print editions, so widely admired for their accessibility. It contained features that unexpectedly redirected users out of the app and onto the internet without warning, forcing them to close their browser, reopen the app, and navigate to their former place again. It crowded commentary into a narrow column that scrolled independently from the playtext, so it required constant effort to keep the notes and glosses aligned with the text they were elucidating. Oddly, the playtext was displayed in a tiny typeface that wasted much of the available screen space, while notes used a type size almost double that of the play itself. Long notes and essays were accessible only in a marginal column, in tiny type, while most of the page was taken up by the playtext that was (at that moment) irrelevant. Nothing in the playtext (such as an underline or ° symbol) alerted readers when a word was subject to a gloss. Instead, readers had to keep checking to see whether an annotation was available. The Folger Luminary Shakespeare is also no longer on the market, perhaps because it did not improve the experience already available from the Folger print editions.

Neither of these apps was trying to serve the audience of performers that I was focusing on, but they were both attempting something conceptually similar in that they aspired to provide more interactions with Shakespeare's texts. In both cases, it was not the apps' contents that I found lacking, yet the experience was unsatisfactory. The term "user-experience design" resonated with me the first time I heard it because I intuitively understood that to create a new kind of edition, I would have to find my way to a new kind of interface. UX design immediately sounded like the tool I needed.

User Experience

User-experience design is a still-emerging but widespread design approach which focuses on user interactions with physical and digital objects. The aim is to make those interactions intuitive, accessible, and enjoyable. It is an outgrowth of "user-centered design" developed and named by Don Norman, a cognitive scientist and usability engineer. Introduced in his 1988 book, *The Psychology of Everyday Things*,[6] the concept, simply put, is that design should communicate to the user how an object is to be used in a way that is both intuitive and pleasurable. His quintessential example is that doors on public buildings should have flat plates on the side meant to be pushed to open, with handles only on the side meant to be pulled. If you reverse that pattern, the door becomes unusable. If you put handles on both sides, you also have to put instruction on one side ("Push") that explains not using the handle as a handle. Doors, he argues, should have design features that make them intuitively functional without labels.

Focusing on ease and pleasurability of use may not seem particularly revolutionary until one realizes that traditional aesthetic design does not address usability at all. The problem with door design, for example, is usually a desire for architectural symmetry in a pair of double doors which is accomplished by making them mirror images of one another with handles in the center. While this looks balanced and attractive, particularly in a rendering, in practice, it does not give you the information you need to operate the doors if one or both does not pull open.

In user-experience approaches, what is being designed is not the product itself but the *interaction* with the product. It is a bonus if a door is both functional and beautiful, but what is paramount is that the user knows how to use it without trial-and-error attempts or even having to pause to think about it before opening the door. Norman's book, advocating for such "frictionless" relationships between users and objects, is still a best-seller in the field because, alas, the world is still full of counter-intuitive, or worse, dysfunctional, design in need of rethinking and correction.

Conceptually, user-experience design is grounded in mathematical psychology, systems design, and usability engineering. The practice, however, is far from rule-driven or theoretically fixed. It relies on empathetically innovating solutions for "pain points" in systems, which are unique to every new product or situation, and then iteratively testing solutions to eliminate perceptual blocks and unnecessary complexities.

In the early 1990s, Apple Computer, Inc. hired Norman to transfer his perspective on the psychology of usability of objects, with particular concern for end-users, to the realm of digital design. He joined Apple Research Labs, where his self-selected job title was "User Experience Architect" (Lyonnais). He helped the company develop and perfect the graphical user interface, in which users dropped graphic icons of "files" into "folders" or the "trash" on skeuomorphic "desktops" rather than issuing complicated text instructions on a command line. This change to simple, intuitive gestures from conceptually dense coded commands (with almost opaque semiotic relationships to the actions they were ordering) made computing accessible to the masses.

Although his user-centered principles are still important in almost all industrial design areas, they are nowhere more influential than in the design of human-computer interactions. Following Norman's lead, User-Experience Design is the preferred designation for this approach in digital fields. In the high-tech scene, demand is astronomical for designers trained in this discipline, as the ease of use and pleasure of the user experience are often the keys to product success in the crowded software and app marketplace.

Among designers who have significantly advanced the field since Norman's initial elaboration is Alan Cooper, the creator of the programming language Visual Basic, who developed an interaction design tool of particular importance to this project: Personas. In Cooper's formulation, a "Persona," is a hypothetical, archetypal user whose goals can be used to guide decisions about product development. A Persona does not represent an individual user but a class of users who will use a product in a particular way or follow a particular path through the options available (Cooper, "Long Road").

Personas were developed by Cooper just as personal computing was becoming widespread and put into use at his firm, Structure Systems Group, to help managers design software for a new class of computer users: non-engineers. Engineers had difficulty explaining what the software could do to laypeople and often had trouble imagining any use for their products beyond engineering applications. That spreadsheets might be helpful not only for mathematical calculation but for tracking home finances or creating textual databases was outside their imaginative realm. Personas are still powerful whenever one is developing a piece of software or an application for non-specialists because they help the developers see beyond their own biases and training. This sociologically based approach invites a human-scaled perspective about individual users rather than aspiring to serve one amorphous group. It is a counter to producing feature-heavy applications tailored *to please everybody* by piling every imaginable feature into a bulky and confusing product while simultaneously failing to suit any specific individual's needs. Personas, with their potential to illuminate ways to improve the usability of an object for specific classes of users, became particularly important to the design of the project examined in the rest of this chapter.

Conceptualizing the Digital Interface

Since I already knew that a traditional print interface did not work for my needs and I had not found any of my static print experiments successful, I decided to try a dynamic digital text. I was introduced to a digital designer who volunteered to assist with the programming necessary to enable the dynamic aspect. What she did, however, quickly encompassed far more than that.[7] The designer, Nicole Thayer, immediately began asking what I now know are *user-centered* design questions about who the edition I imagined was supposed to serve, how it needed to function to meet their needs, and intriguingly, *in what order the information offered needed to unfold over time*. What she did not ask was how it was supposed to look. The visual appearance of the interface would flow from its function rather than dictate it.

The design process for this edition followed a fairly standard protocol for user-experience designs. However, because we both saw the need for an actively empowering interface, it was quite different from what most print or electronic Shakespeare editions have followed. The five-step process is not complicated. Using terminology that had become standard across the UX discipline, the steps are empathize → define → ideate → prototype → test.

The first step (Empathize) asks who the users will be and what matters to them. In this stage of app development, the team is trying to understand the needs of the potential audience(s) and the "pain points" they experience in using current sources. In our case, I initially said that I wanted to serve theater practitioners—a viewpoint that, in the course of our discussion, I later amended to say that I wanted to serve both traditional audiences and practitioners. It was Ms. Thayer's crucial insight that readers, textual users (i.e., scholars and interpreters), and theatrical practitioners were not so much three different user classes but three successive stages in interacting with the play—i.e., three paths through the app, or (in

Cooper's terms) three Personas. From that intuition grew an assumption that has stayed with us as a crucial axiom:

- Practitioners' needs may be more extensive than casual readers or literature students, but they are not contradictory. (This principle probably applies to many other potential constituencies as well.) For users in the third stage of use, i.e., theatrical practice, the primary pain point is the absence of information about fundamental performance concerns or the difficulty of locating it in critical editions that relegate it to comparative obscurity.

The second step (Define) addresses what the users need, and it was at this point that we made several further conclusions:

- Very little of the paratextual information offered on a printed page is helpful to either readers or practitioners at any given moment, but its usefulness does unfold in a generally predictable order.
- Some of the information on the page (for example, the orthographic rendering of a word) needs to present differently, depending on where in the process of using the text you are, which implies using dynamic text to change what is displayed under different contextual conditions.
- Navigating the spatial relationship of text and paratext is more complicated for most readers of print editions than understanding their conceptual functions. Even when the reader understands what to do, it can be physically demanding to do it. This complication is especially true for young and inexperienced readers who have to learn strategies for tracking their place in the text while glancing away at the paratext. Dynamic digital options can alleviate this by reorganizing the layout to keep text and paratext both visible and juxtaposed closely.
- Eighteenth-century publishers designed the traditional print interface primarily to work within the constraints of print, much more than to meet readers' or practitioners' needs. Many design elements appear to have been instituted to save space, reducing the amount of costly paper needed. Others save ink, save the cost of added color, or otherwise make the project less expensive rather than making it more user-friendly. An example is how the collation is offered in a form so abbreviated that it is almost in code.

The third step (Ideate) was the richest part of the process for us. We created a problem statement to clarify how I had found standard editions unsatisfactory for my needs and those of my students, then brainstormed as many ideas as possible about how we might address our users' pain points if the print tradition did not constrain us. First, individually and then collaboratively, we tried to imagine multiple pathways through the text and paratext, and how we might make the app responsive to the users' goals. From that sprang the following conclusions:

- Many helpful design elements, especially color and shading, are expensive in print but essentially free in the digital realm. Since we were working in that realm, we had more tools than print interfaces use.
- The typical style sheet presumes that only one solution is possible. That the user might want to customize the order and nature of the information in the edition is such a recent possibility that it is usually not considered at all. To meet the users' shifting needs, however, we could make the text customizable. In the end, we arranged customizable

tabs around groupings that were related to archetypical pathways and goals of four types of Personas: readers, students, performers, and actors practicing memorization drills.
- Hyperlinked text, a long-favored digital solution, is useful only when the number of links is limited. In a Shakespeare edition with potential annotations to virtually every line, the solution cannot always be that you click and jump to editorial material.

The fundamental principle of ideation is to go for quantity of ideas without judgment. However, the next step (Prototyping) is when a designer begins to winnow ideas by mocking up the most promising possibilities. In this stage of development, our use of Personas was most prominent, and they were instrumental in winnowing design ideas to those that specifically served their needs. Our prototypes taught us several valuable lessons, some of which contradict standard practice:

- Users who most need glosses are often inexperienced readers, yet the placements of glosses can exacerbate their reading difficulties by forcing them to shift their focus from one part of the page to another quickly and frequently. Interlinear glossing puts the information directly under the words where it is needed but is untenable in print editions because it clutters the playtext block. "Just-in-time" dynamic glossing, however, is highly functional for the audiences who need it most.
- While modernization of spelling and punctuation is probably necessary for editions to be accessible to a broad audience, many other fairly standard orthographical practices (like the elimination of diacritical marks) improve the legibility of the text for casual readers at the expense of including information that will later have essential applications for scholars and performers.
- Directly indicating that a word or phrase is subject to some form of annotation (as opposed to passively placing the note in the margin or at the bottom of the page to be found by referencing line numbers or keywords) makes it far more likely that the notes will be consulted and used. The decreased legibility associated with numerous footnote numbers or symbols embedded in the text is no longer problematic, given that the indication can be accomplished through coloring, shading, or linking rather than by distracting typographical symbols.

After winnowing the design ideas to the most promising, Ms. Thayer and I began to settle on broad design principles that are now central to the edition. Paramount is keeping the web page's presentation as clean and uncluttered as possible, so paratext and commentary are grouped into categories that can be turned on or off as needed. While the groupings will be explained in more detail below, the principle guiding the development of the modes is that there is never a time that one needs all the layers of information typically contained in a scholarly edition at once. The interface needs to offer users a means to control their pathway through the text and paratext. The users' pain point with which I was most concerned (especially relevant to the Performer Persona) was that too much rarely needed information dominates the commentary space, squeezing out or obscuring performance-related information that one often needs or needs intensively at specific times, as in rehearsal. This problem is addressed by allowing the user simple and easy ways to customize which information is visible at any given time. In our interface, you can see only the information you need, and only for as long as you need it.

A second principle was that the playtext needed to remain centered, both literally and figuratively. Putting the playtext in a conspicuous serif font and all the paratext (including speech headings and stage directions) in a lighter-shaded san serif font makes the playtext visually prominent, serving the figurative purpose. The literal centering is accomplished by rather complex programming that keeps one's place in the text centered on the page even when pop-up overlays appear after clicking to bring up a note. The line in which the annotated text appears remains on the screen positioned prominently. The commentary pops up below it so that both are visible simultaneously. (This can be quickly contrasted with the typical operation of a hyperlinked foot- or endnote in an e-book, which causes the annotated text to disappear for the time one is consulting the citation. Hyperlinking is, to us, a less satisfactory arrangement.)

While this project is still a work-in-progress in its final phase (Testing), the interface has been in place for some time while the content is still undergoing refinement. Now called The Players' Reference Shakespeare, this open educational resource (OER), is available to users at the URL supplied in the notes. Although I describe its general features below, the most direct way to see and experience it is to go to the site and experiment with it.

Upon opening the edition, the most fundamental mode is simply a plain version of the playtext, similar to the Penguin editions heavily favored by actors for their clean look and light weight. When the app is first opened, the interface is not yet "unfolded" but consists of a single green dot with menu bars in the lower right-hand corner. (This icon, which designers call a "hamburger," is familiar to most users because it is an almost universal symbol to indicate the availability of a menu on a webpage.) In this print edition, subject to the limitations of static text already explored in this chapter, the look and feel of the app can only be approximated, but it looks something like Figure 15.1.

Clicking the hamburger menu icon reveals the interface bar, consisting of four equally sized, differently colored oblong rectangles ("tabs") stretched across the bottom of the page. The first is colored red and is labeled "Reader." The next one is blue with the word "Student" in it. A green box saying "Performer" follows. The last rectangle is olive, and it bears the label "Practice." The hamburger sits at the end of the row. It takes on the color of whatever mode a user happens to be in at any given time. This unfolded interface looks approximately like Figure 15.2.

The mode designed to serve inexperienced users, labeled "Reader" in the interface, displays short glosses interlinearly, along with marginal running line numbers, when a user clicks on that tab. Because the glosses are numerous, this universal activation avoids the tedium of

[THESEUS, HIPPOLYTA, and PHILOSTRATE enter the playing space, possibly with attendants.] ♫

THESEUS

Now, fair Hippolyta, our nuptial hour
Draws on apace. Four happy days bring in
Another moon. But, O, methinks how slow
This old moon wanes! She lingers my desires
Like to a stepdame or a dowager
Long withering out a young man's revenue.

Figure 15.1 The Players' Reference Shakespeare

Reader	Student	Performer	Practice

Figure 15.2 Interface bar

opening and closing links. Since the glosses are placed immediately under the words they are explicating, it also eliminates the annoying problem of glancing back and forth to the margins constantly. More experienced readers, even if they are simply students who have read and absorbed the glosses in a first pass, can turn the mode off again if it is no longer needed or becomes distracting, or never activate it in the first place if glosses are not required. (This is a distinct alternative to the widespread use of "facing page paraphrase" editions, like *No Fear Shakespeare*, which theoretically put annotation into a friendlier form, but in fact, incentivize skipping the playtext altogether in favor of just reading the modern paraphrase.)

The print model in Figure 15.3 demonstrates the look and feel of this mode, although, in the app, glosses are red.

The "Student" mode, unlike the mode for general readers, color-codes text that is subject to more extended notes (especially mythological references, classical allusions, and textual variants) and creates clickable links that bring up and dismiss full notes in a textbox that "floats" on top of the text, commonly described as an overlay. This mode has a general look like that in Figure 15.4, although the words in **bold** are instead colored blue in the app and are live, clickable links.

This arrangement does not command space unless the reader expressly opts to call up the note but allows the reader to see both the line of text being explicated and the note simultaneously if they do select it. Figure 15.5 is an approximation of how the annotated line with the open link overlay looks. The user clicks on the exponent x that has appeared behind the annotated word to close the note.

A third mode, "Performer," attempts to assist with the complex scansion process by indicating text subject to spoken contraction, expansion, or archaic accentuation. The specific words in the text display using a new color (green) along with diacritical marks and other typographical indicators (Figure 15.6). Such words also work as clickable links that open

[THESEUS, HIPPOLYTA, and PHILOSTRATE enter the playing space, possibly with attendants.] ♫

THESEUS

Now, fair Hippolyta, our nuptial hour
Draws on apace. Four happy days bring in
approaches quickly
Another moon. But, O, methinks how slow
This old moon wanes! She lingers my desires
obstructs
Like to a stepdame or a dowager
stepmother or widow
Long withering out a young man's revenue.
using up inheritance

Figure 15.3 Glosses

*[**THESEUS**, HIPPOLYTA, and PHILOSTRATE enter the playing space, possibly with attendants.]* ♫

THESEUS

Now, fair Hippolyta, our nuptial hour
Draws on apace. **Four happy days** bring in
Another **moon**. But, O, methinks how slow
This old moon **wanes**! She lingers my desires
Like to a stepdame or a dowager
Long withering out a young man's revenue.

Figure 15.4 Student mode

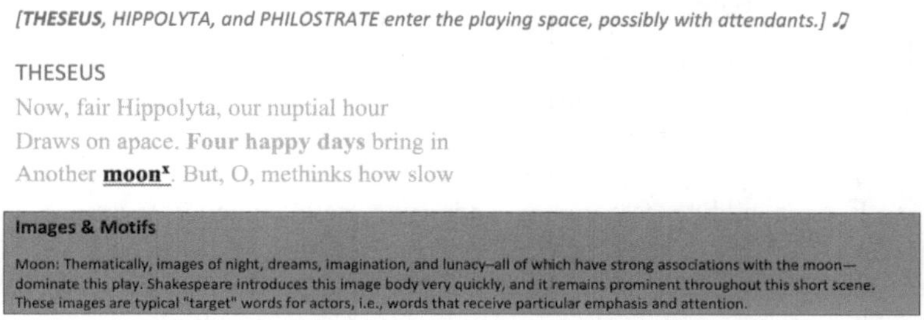

Figure 15.5 Open link overlay

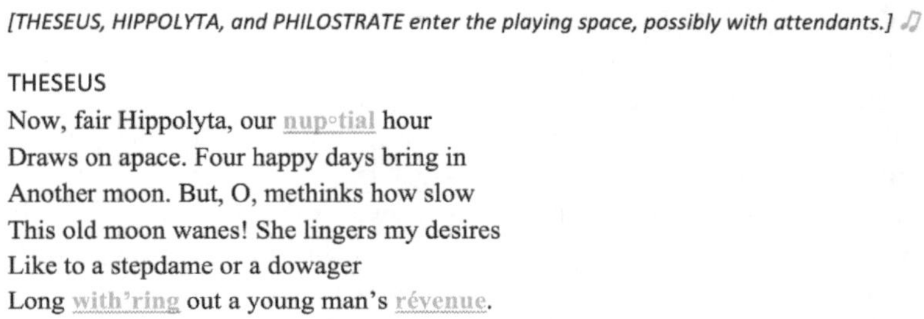

Figure 15.6 Performer mode

more extended explanatory notes as overlays, but the latter is optional. The musical notes in the stage direction line also change to green because there is a potential musical cue at this point, explained in a pop-up note, if desired.

In this case, you see a display change in the first line to indicate that "nuptial" is scanned as two syllables here, although it will scan as three later in the play. The final line also contains two annotations indicating that "withering" is subject to elision through the elimination of a medial vowel and that the word "revenue" is pronounced in its modern form, although elsewhere in the play, it will be pronounced "reVÉNue." All of these adjustments help with sight-reading the text. They are backed up with underlying notes describing the principle behind the scansion and further explicating the pronunciation in simple phonetics and, more precisely, using the International Phonetic Alphabet.

These four states of the text combined would produce an overwhelming jumble of annotation and color but separating them by function gives the user control over both the amount and the kind of commentary they access. A static page crowds too much into the visual field while still leaving too much out. This interface empowers the user to progressively select the level of detail they wish to see at any point, customized to the manner in which they are interacting with the text: as readers, as student literary interpreters, as speakers, or as performers.

An additional mode, Practice, gamifies the text (especially for memorization drills) allowing the user to highlight all of a character's lines by clicking on a speech heading anywhere in the play. A second click will hide all the text of the character's speeches. A third click restores the text to the original state.

Conclusion

The "three-layer" interface used in printed critical editions of Shakespeare was primarily designed by and for textual scholars, and it continues to serve that constituency well, assuming they are trained to understand and use it. However, after experimenting with several print options, we concluded that it could not easily be extended to serve more user groups. While it seems theoretically simple to expand the traditional conventions to a "four-, five-, or more-layer" interface to address additional needs, in practice, these become overwhelming, with unusably high cognitive loading.[8] Such information overload and conceptual confusion result from adding features or addressing new audiences without attending to usability.

However, our dynamic edition demonstrates that it is possible to add much more information to a Shakespeare edition than is standard and serve multiple user groups without overcrowding the page or creating information overload as long as users can control their experience. To do so, however, requires a new kind of interface. The text needs to display in alternate forms under differing circumstances. Annotation and commentary should selectively display when needed and disappear when not. While print cannot do these things, digital texts are easily capable of doing them. Ultimately, users must be able to customize a path through the text, paratext, and editorial commentary according to their current needs. User-experience design, especially the concept of Personas, can anticipate the primary paths and assist in creating an interface that is agile and adaptable.

Of course, there is no suggestion that this experiment is the only or even the best solution to utilizing digital interfaces. Many kinds of editions might benefit from dynamic text, but it seems a prerequisite to creating editions that are information-heavy, especially "performer-oriented" editions. Other editors might have different interests and categorize commentary differently. They might use the dynamic capabilities of a digital text for very different purposes. What our edition does do is provide a user-centered model as an alternative to the paradigm that the point of an edition is to create a single, stable, invariant text surrounded by fixed annotation. The digital interface can, itself, perform in a manner that destabilizes that undue certainty, a product of static print. The user can have a short learning curve after discovering the app and a frictionless experience using it thereafter.

Notes

1 For those who would like to explore this project before reading on, it is available as an open education resource rendered as a web app at https://www.PlayersReference.com/Midsummer. Interested parties can also contact the author at his institutional address for access.

2 The 1622 quarto edition of *Othello* is prefaced by a short letter entitled "The Stationer to the Reader," signed by the publisher, Thomas Walkley. One of the two 1609 editions of *Troilus and Cressida* also has an opening epistle, "A neuer writer, to an euer reader. Newes." It is unsigned, but it was penned by a "never writer" and not by Shakespeare, as clearly indicated by the title.

3 For example, the initial page of *As You Like It* in Johnson's first 1765 edition (there were two that year) contains only the first fifty words of the play but then dedicates the entire bottom half of the page to Warburton's 165-word note criticizing Shakespeare's grammar. Johnson defers fifteen additional words of Warburton's note to the next page *before* getting to his own 100-word commentary on why Warburton's criticism was excessive.

4 See Eggert "Apparatus, Text, Interface" 97–118.

5 The use of endnotes is the solution *The Riverside Shakespeare* uses. *The Oxford Shakespeare* infamously moved ALL its notes to a separate volume, *William Shakespeare: A Textual Companion*, to achieve its clean layout.

6 Norman's book was retitled *The Design of Everyday Things* in all subsequent editions. This new title more directly addresses his audience of product designers but loses the emphasis on the psychological aspects of designing inherent in the original. The book's topic is "the psychology *behind* the design of everyday things," but that is too clunky to be used as a title, presumably.

7 Ms. Thayer eventually assumed not just the user-experience design but the full range of design responsibilities. Much of her contribution, especially the aesthetic choices (such as the selection of

typefaces and sizes, layout, color, and flow), lies outside the scope of this chapter but is essential to the look and feel of the project.

8 Publishing practice would seem to confirm this limitation of layers. Recent attempts to expand user bases do so, instead, by creating separate editions, like the previously discussed Arden Performance Editions, or at least separate volumes, like *The New Oxford Shakespeare*, which utilizes a multi-volume approach to separate standard commentary from higher-order textual scholarship.

The New Oxford Shakespeare is a tremendously ambitious effort notable for its thoroughness, including a surprising amount of performance-related information. However, the three-volume set is, by far, the most expensive *Complete Works* on the market and is impractically large for anything but use at a sturdy desk. At the time of this writing, the complete set retails for over US $450 (£320).

References

Bevington, David, editor. *The Complete Works of William Shakespeare*. 7th edition, Pearson, 2014.

Brooks, Harold F., editor. "A Midsummer Night's Dream," *The Arden Shakespeare, 2nd Series*. Methuen, 1979.

Chaudhuri, Sukanta, editor. "*A Midsummer Night's Dream*," *The Arden Shakespeare, 3rd Series*. Bloomsbury, 2017.

Cooper, Alan. *The Inmates Are Running the Asylum*. Sams, 1999.

Cooper, Alan. "The Long Road to Inventing Design Personas." *OneZero*, 3 February 2020. Available at: https://onezero.medium.com/in-1983-i-created-secret-weapons-for-interactive-design-d154eb8cfd58.

Dowden, Edward, editor. *The Arden Shakespeare: The Tragedy of Hamlet*. Methuen, 1899.

Eggert, Paul. "Apparatus, Text, Interface: How to Read a Printed Critical Edition." *The Cambridge Companion to Textual Scholarship*. Edited by Neil Fraistat and Julia Flanders, Cambridge UP, 2013, pp. 97–118.

Foakes, R.A., editor. *A Midsummer Night's Dream*. Updated edition. Cambridge UP, 2003.

Foakes, R.A., editor. *Explore Shakespeare: A Midsummer Night's Dream*. iPad edition. Cambridge UP, 2013.

Gossett, Suzanne. "The Modern Editing of Shakespeare: The Apparatus." *The Arden Research Handbook of Shakespeare and Textual Studies*. Edited by Lukas Erne, Bloomsbury, 2021, pp. 206–224.

Greenblatt, Stephen, general editor. *The Norton Shakespeare*, 3rd edition, Norton, 2015.

Hinman, Charlton, editor. *The First Folio of Shakespeare*. 1st edition, W.W. Norton & Company, 1968.

Hodgdon, Barbara. "New Collaborations with Old Plays: The (Textual) Politics of Performance Commentary." *Textual Performances: The Modern Reproduction of Shakespeare's Drama*. Edited by Lukas Erne and Margaret Jane Kidnie, Cambridge UP, 2004, pp. 210–222.

Holland, Peter, editor. *The Oxford Shakespeare: A Midsummer Night's Dream*. Clarendon Press, 1998.

Johnson, Samuel, editor. *The Plays of William Shakespeare*. London, 1765.

Kidnie, Margaret Jane. "Staging Shakespeare's Drama in Print Editions." *Textual Performances: The Modern Reproduction of Shakespeare's Drama*. Edited by Lucas Erne and Margaret Jane Kidnie, Cambridge UP, 2004, pp. 158–177.

Lavagnino, John. "Two Varieties of Digital Commentary." *Textual Performances: The Modern Reproduction of Shakespeare's Drama* Edited by Lucas Erne and Margaret Jane Kidnie, Cambridge UP, 2004, pp. 194–209.

Lyonnais, Sheena. "Where Did the Term 'User Experience' Come From?" Adobe Blog, 28 August 2017. Available at: blog.adobe.com/en/publish/2017/08/28/where-did-the-term-user-experience-come-from.html#gs.1wpqnr.

Mowat, Barbara and Paul Werstine, editors. *The Folger Shakespeare Library: A Midsummer Night's Dream*. Simon & Schuster, 1993.

Mowat, Barbara and Paul Werstine, editors. *The Folger Luminary Shakespeare: A Midsummer Night's Dream*. Simon & Schuster, 2014.

Never Writer. "A neuer writer, to an euer reader. Newes." *The Famous Historie of Troylus and Cresseid. Excellently expressing the beginning of their loues, with the conceited wooing of Pandarus Prince of Licia*. London, 1609.

Norman, Donald A. *The Psychology of Everyday Things*. Basic Books, 1988.

OED (Oxford English Dictionary). "Interface, noun, 2A."Oxford UP, 2020. Available at: www.oed.com.

Pope, Alexander, editor. *The Works of Shakespear*. London, 1725.

Rokison-Woodall, Abagail, editor. *A Midsummer Night's Dream*. Arden Performance Series. Bloomsbury, 2017.

Rowe, Nicolas, editor. *The Complete Works of William Shakespear*. London, 1709.

Shakespeare, William. *The RSC Shakespeare Complete Works*, edited by Jonathan Bate and Eric Rasmussen, Palgrave Macmillan, 2007.

SparkNotes Editors. *No Fear Shakespeare: A Midsummer Night's Dream*. SparkNotes, 2018.

Staunton, Howard, editor. *The Gilbert Shakespeare. The Works of Shakespeare; Complete in One Volume. With a New Portrait and 511 Illustrations by Sir John Gilbert*. London, 1895.

Theobald, Lewis, editor. *The Works of Shakespeare*. London, 1733.

Walkley, Thomas. "The Stationer to the Reader." *The Tragoedy of Othello the Moore of Venice*. London, 1622.

Warburton, William, editor. *The Works of Shakespear*. London, 1747.

Wells, Stanley and Gary Taylor, general editors. *The Oxford Shakespeare: The Complete Words*. Clarendon Press, 1986.

Wells, Stanley, Gary Taylor, John Jowett and William Montgomery, *William Shakespeare: A Textual Companion*, 2nd edition, Norton, 1997.

16

USING DATA AND DESIGN TO BRING THE *NEW VARIORUM SHAKESPEARE* ONLINE

Anne Burdick, Katayoun Torabi, Bryan Tarpley and Laura Mandell

When digital humanists collaborate with scholarly editors to create an online digital edition, typically, it is not until after finishing all the coding and programming running behind the scenes that they begin thinking about the design of the web pages comprising the edition. There are indeed digital theorists and practitioners who argue that design is much more than mere decoration (McCarty; Ruecker, Radzikowska, and Sinclair; Drucker) and that visual interfaces create the subjects who view them—the readers or users of the digital edition (Brown; Suchman; Drucker). Builders of digital editions know from the field of information visualization that data and text can be presented in such a way as to "amplify cognition" (Ware 7), that presentation can help people understand better by organizing it visually in a particular way. And yet the digital humanists who emphasize design have seemed like voices crying in the wilderness. Given the amount of time and funding typically available, the producers of digital editions are constrained to focus on the laudable goal of creating editions that can be preserved and sustained, as described below. Generous funding from the Modern Language Association to create open-access, digital, variorum editions of Shakespeare's plays enabled the creators of the digital *New Variorum Shakespeare* (the authors of this chapter) to focus on interface design from the very beginning.

Project manager of the open-access digital version of the *New Variorum Shakespeare* (NVS) and co-author Katayoun Torabi gathered together a team that included designer-researcher Anne Burdick and programmer Bryan Tarpley, co-authors of this chapter as well. Over the course of two years of weekly meetings, the digital NVS design team worked to translate NVS print editions into user-friendly web pages, which is to say, an interface that invites user exploration and evokes research questions precisely by providing users with visual cues and visible paths for answering such questions. Of course, user/readers would need some instruction in manipulating the interface (Torabi, "How to Digital NVS"), but the learning curve needed to be gentle and the rewards great.

The research and discussions required to accomplish this task, described below,[1] involved understanding how the printed page functions as an interface to information about previously published editions of Shakespeare's works, and then thinking about medium: what does print "afford" to readers—what does it allow them to do easily? What kinds of thinking and research does a print edition make difficult for reader-users to do that a digital interface could make easy, even inviting? What, in short, are the possibilities, constraints, and tensions that can either be overcome or, sadly, are introduced by creating a digital interface? This chapter captures the

DOI: 10.4324/9780367821722-22

process of producing the digital NVS to date; the authors invite commentary and critique, which is to say *help*, as we continue this work.

About the *NVS*

In 2019, the Modern Language Association's Executive Council awarded the Center of Digital Humanities Research (CoDHR) at Texas A&M a grant to publish The New Variorum Shakespeare (NVS) editions online, making them freely available to readers, scholars, educators, students, and performers via as an open access, interactive web application. Working in partnership with the MLA, the NVS Board, and NVS editors, the NVS team at CoDHR has already published two complete volumes and plans to publish 16 additional NVS titles in the future. Each edition contains the complete text of each play along with a full collation of textual notes from the earliest editions to the present, including extensive previous commentary.

The word *variorum* alludes to the Latin phrase *editio cum notis variorum*, that is, "an edition with the notes of the various [editors and commentators]," a phrase indicating the chief purpose of a variorum edition: namely, to collect what has been written by various commentators, critics, and editors. A variorum is a work that sets all variations and emendations side by side so that a reader can track how textual decisions have been made in the preparation of a text for publication. As such, Shakespeare variorum editions help editors and scholars understand the historical evolution of Shakespeare's texts. The earliest variorum edition of Shakespeare was published in 1773. It was Horace Howard Furness, however, who published the first *New Variorum Edition* of Shakespeare, starting with *Romeo and Juliet* in 1871 (Werstine, NVS History). This publication set the design for subsequent editions which, after 1936, were published under the auspices of the Modern Language Association.

Based upon the meticulous work of book historians (De Grazia; De Grazia and Stallybrass; Orgel; Galey), one can envision all Shakespeare editors as partly creating the archive that their editions seek to represent. In 1733, Theobald wrote *Shakespeare Restored*—a book containing his editorial commentary on *Hamlet*, with the goal of "retrieving ... the *original Purity* of his text [by] rooting out that vast Crop of *Errors* which has almost Chok'd up his *Beauties*" (i). And although motivated by a more nationalist ideology—restoring one of England's literary "classics" (v)—Theobald's self-imposed mandate resonates with twentieth-century New Bibliographers invested in uncovering authorial intention. As Margreta De Grazia puts it, they wish to "distil the authorial essence from the scummy dross left behind by performance and publication." The problem, of course, is that there is no original manuscript in Shakespeare's hand, and so "the Manuscript" must always be an ideal version created by editors via inference: "The quartos and folios exist, their page and ink marks can be seen and felt, but the manuscripts supposed behind them, like the intentions supposed behind them, are hypothetical or inferential" (De Grazia 71).

What Furness wished to accomplish with his first Variorum edition, *Romeo and Juliet* (1871), was to "improve" upon the plan of the Cambridge edition of Shakespeare (1863):

> [W]hile it gives the readings of the old editions, [the 1863 Cambridge edition] omits to note the adoption or rejection of them by various editors, whereby an important element in estimating these readings is wanting; however uncouth a reading may seem at first sight, it ceases to be the "sophistication" of a printer when we learn that men so judicious as Capell or Dyce had pronounced in its favour; and in disputed passages, it is of great interest to see at a glance on which side lies the weight of authority.
>
> *(vii)*

Furness's goal was to make editorial decisions transparent, revealing their origins, uptake, and perpetuation, so that we may know who we agree or disagree with when we select a variation as valid—the "band of terror,"[2] discussed below, comes from Furness's desire to see the history of editorial decisions "at a glance," and thereby to record the acumen and ingenuity of various editors throughout history. The other goal articulated in this first "New" Variorum edition was "to abridge the labour and save the time" by collecting together all "the valuable notes … of such editors as Knight, Singer, Collier, Ulrici, Delius, Dyce, Hudson, Staunton, White, Clarke, Keightly, and Halliwell [that] are to be found only in as many different volumes" by placing them "on the same page" as the playtext itself (vi), in the form of "commentary notes."

A primary goal, then, of the variorum edition, is to create an interface adequate to visualizing "on the same page, in condensed form" (vi) the history of Shakespearean editorial scholarship organized by lines of playtext.[3] It was no small task for Furness to visualize and represent all the hands that have worked throughout history to create Shakespeare's plays.As shown in Figure 16.1, a typical page in a printed NVS volume includes three sections—the playtext, textual notes (which record any significant changes in later editions that are compared to the copy-text, which is usually the 1623 First Folio), and commentary notes (which are a condensed historical survey of significant attempts to interpret particular words, phrases, lines, and passages). Each page has a header which includes the title of the play, and each playtext includes act-scene-line numbers keyed to the *Riverside Shakespeare*. A variorum edition a modified diplomatic reprint of the copy-text. The textual notes will generally record only substantive and semi-substantive emendations, such as are relevant to the vast majority

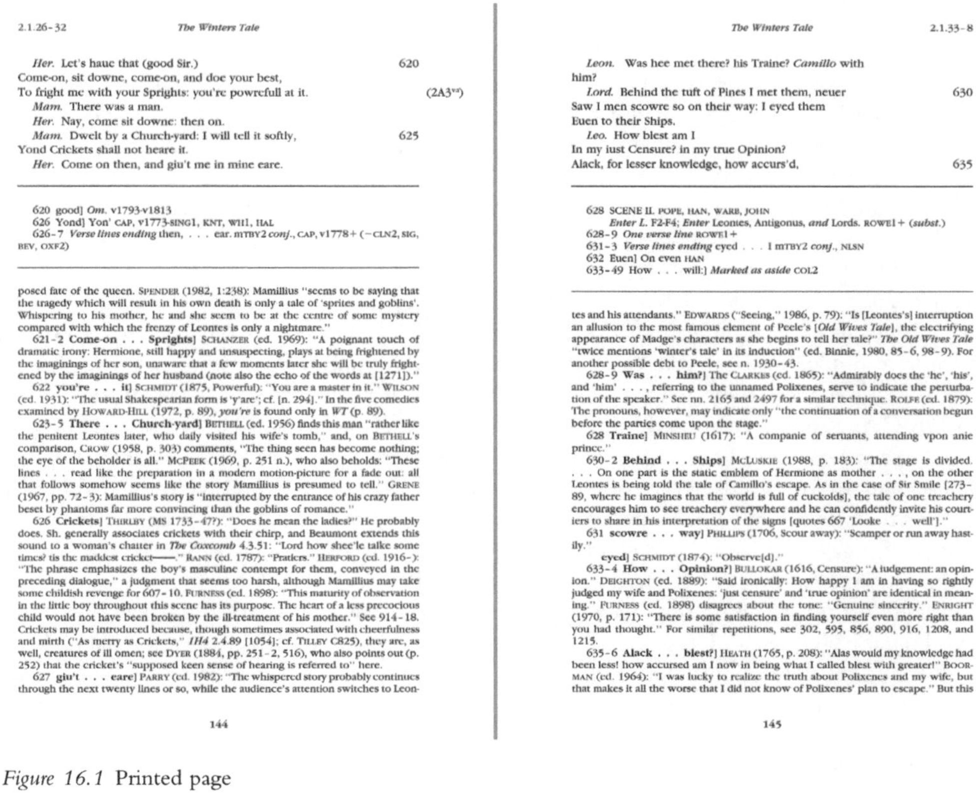

2.1.26-32 *The Winters Tale*

Her. Let's haue that (good Sir.)
Come-on, sit downe, come-on, and doe your best,
To fright me with your Sprights: you're powrefull at it. (2A3va)
Mam. There was a man.
Her. Nay, come sit downe: then on.
Mam. Dwelt by a Church-yard: I will tell it softly,
Yond Crickets shall not heare it.
Her. Come on then, and giu't me in mine eare.

620 good] *Om.* v1793-v1813
626 Yond] Yon' CAP, v1773-SING1, KNT, WH1, HAL
626-7 *Verse lines ending* then, . . . ear. MTBY2 *conj.*, CAP, v1778+ (−CLN2, SIG, BEV, OXF2)

posed fate of the queen. SPENDER (1982, 1:238): Mamillius "seems to be saying that the tragedy which will result in his own death is only a tale of 'sprites and goblins'. Whispering to his mother, he and she seem to be at the centre of some mystery compared with which the frenzy of Leontes is only a nightmare."

621-2 **Come-on . . . Sprights**] SCHANZER (ed. 1969): "A poignant touch of dramatic irony: Hermione, still happy and unsuspecting, plays at being frightened by the imaginings of her son, unaware that a few moments later she will be truly frightened by the imaginings of her husband (note also the echo of the words at [1271])."

622 **you're . . . it**] SCHMIDT (1875, Powerful): "You are a master in it." WILSON (ed. 1931): "The usual Shakespearian form is 'y'are'; cf. [n. 294]." In the five comedies examined by HOWARD-HILL (1972, p. 89), *you're* is found only in *WT* (p. 89).

623-5 **There . . . Church-yard**] BETHELL (ed. 1956) finds this man "rather like the penitent Leontes later, who daily visited his wife's tomb," and, on BETHELL's comparison, CROW (1958, p. 303) comments, "The thing seen has become nothing; the eye of the beholder is all." MCPEEK (1969, p. 251 n.), who also beholds: "These lines . . . read like the preparation in a modern motion-picture for a fade out: all that follows somehow seems like the story Mamillius is presumed to tell." GRENE (1967, pp. 72-3): Mamillius's story is "interrupted by the entrance of his crazy father beset by phantoms far more convincing than the goblins of romance."

626 **Crickets**] THIRLBY (MS 1733-47?): "Does he mean the ladies?" He probably does. Sh. generally associates crickets with their chirp, and Beaumont extends this sound to a woman's chatter in *The Coxcomb* 4.3.51: "Lord how shee'le talke some times? tis the maddest cricket——." RANN (ed. 1787): "Pratlers." HERFORD (ed. 1916-): "The phrase emphasizes the boy's masculine contempt for them, conveyed in the preceding dialogue," a judgment that seems too harsh, although Mamillius may take some childish revenge for 607-10. FURNESS (ed. 1898): "This maturity of observation in the little boy throughout this scene has its purpose. The heart of a less precocious child would not have been broken by the ill-treatment of his mother." See 914-18. Crickets may be introduced because, though sometimes associated with cheerfulness and mirth ("As merry as Crickets," *1H4* 2.4.89 [1054]; cf. TILLEY C825), they are, as well, creatures of ill omen; see DYER (1884, pp. 251-2, 516), who also points out (p. 252) that the cricket's "supposed keen sense of hearing is referred to" here.

627 **giu't . . . eare**] PARRY (ed. 1982): "The whispered story probably continues through the next twenty lines or so, while the audience's attention switches to Leon-

144

The Winters Tale 2.1.33-8

Leon. Was hee met there? his Traine? *Camillo* with
him?
Lord. Behind the tuft of Pines I met them, neuer
Saw I men scowre so on their way: I eyed them
Euen to their Ships.
Leo. How blest am I
In my iust Censure? in my true Opinion?
Alack, for lesser knowledge, how accurs'd,

628 SCENE II. POPE, HAN, WARB, JOHN
Enter L. F2-F4; *Enter* Leontes, Antigonus, *and* Lords. ROWE1+ (*subst.*)
628-9 *One verse line* ROWE1+
631-3 *Verse lines ending* eyed . . . I MTBY2 *conj.*, NLSN
632 Euen] On even HAN
633-49 How . . . will:] *Marked as aside* COL2

tes and his attendants." EDWARDS ("Seeing," 1986, p. 79): "Is [Leontes's] interruption an allusion to the most famous element of Peele's [*Old Wives Tale*], the electrifying appearance of Madge's characters as she begins to tell her tale?" *The Old Wives Tale* "twice mentions 'winter's tale' in its induction" (ed. Binnie, 1980, 85-6, 98-9). For another possible debt to Peele, see n. 1930-43.

628-9 **Was . . . him?**] The CLARKES (ed. 1865): "Admirably does the 'he', 'his', and 'him' . . . , referring to the unnamed Polixenes, serve to indicate the perturbation of the speaker." See nn. 2165 and 2497 for a similar technique. ROLFE (ed. 1879): The pronouns, however, may indicate only "the continuation of a conversation begun before the parties come upon the stage."

628 **Traine**] MINSHEU (1617): "A companie of seruants, attending vpon anie prince."

630-2 **Behind . . . Ships**] MCLUSKIE (1988, p. 183): "The stage is divided. . . . On one part is the static emblem of Hermione as mother . . . , on the other Leontes is being told the tale of Camillo's escape. As in the case of Sir Smile [273-89, where he imagines that the world is full of cuckolds], the tale of one treachery encourages him to see treachery everywhere and he can confidently invite his courtiers to share in his interpretation of the signs [quotes 667 'Looke . . . well']."

631 **scowre . . . way**] PHILLIPS (1706, Scour away): "Scamper or run away hastily."

eyed] SCHMIDT (1874): "Observe[d]."

633-4 **How . . . Opinion?**] BULLOKAR (1616, Censure): "A iudgement: an opinion." DEIGHTON (ed. 1889): "Said ironically: How happy I am in having so rightly judged my wife and Polixenes: 'just censure' and 'true opinion' are identical in meaning." FURNESS (ed. 1898) disagrees about the tone: "Genuine sincerity." ENRIGHT (1970, p. 171): "There is some satisfaction in finding yourself even more right than you had thought." For similar repetitions, see 302, 595, 856, 890, 916, 1208, and 1215.

635-6 **Alack . . . blest?**] HEATH (1765, p. 208): "Alas would my knowledge had been less! how accursed am I now in being what I called blest with greater!" BOORMAN (ed. 1964): "I was lucky to realize the truth about Polixenes and my wife, but that makes it all the worse that I did not know of Polixenes' plan to escape." But this

145

Figure 16.1 Printed page

of the commentary on the play. As shown here, NVS textual notes are presented in a condensed code that has been dubbed "the band of terror," due to its inscrutability to an uninitiated reader. The playtext, textual notes, and commentary notes ultimately form the core of the printed volume. This core is preceded by front-matter (including a plan of work), and is followed by the appendix, which includes information about irregular, doubtful, and emended accidentals in the copy-text, unadopted conjectures in the editions collated, the authenticity of the text, the reliability of the printer, early editions, sources for the play, criticism about the play's themes, genre, characters, language and style, historical performances, and music. The bibliography and index follow the appendix (Knowles).

As demonstrated above, each volume includes a great deal of information. The variorum edition of *The Winter's Tale*, for example, comprises 973 pages in addition to front matter. One can see how an editor might dedicate their entire life to a single volume and why many fail to complete a volume within their lifetime. The unusual page structure that the NVS developed over time was designed to maximize the use of printed space and enable the reader to move through the more than one thousand cross-references per volume (Werstine, "Past"). While the goal of making the NVS widely available on the internet was first proposed in 1996 by Phyllis Franklin, then-executive director of the MLA, the sheer scale and complexity of each edition have prevented the implementation of that goal until now. The first step of this journey was to hire Dr. Julia Flanders, professor of the Practice in English and the director of the Digital Scholarship Group in the Northeastern University Library to develop a TEI-XML schema to account for every aspect of an NVS edition. Julia and her team used this schema to encode the entirety of *The Winter's Tale, The Comedy of Errors, King Lear*, and *A Midsummer Night's Dream*.

TEI, or the Text Encoding Initiative, provides guidelines for using specific XML tags and attributes along with principles for applying them that are described by any TEI Schema (https://tei-c.org/release/doc/tei-p5-doc/en/html/index.html). These tags, attributes, and guidelines were developed by the TEI Consortium, "a large community of researchers from diverse fields" (Portela 286), as fully described by Elena Pierazzo in *Digital Scholarly Editing* (117–22). While the dream of the TEI may have originally been interoperability among all TEI-encoded practices, the code had to be malleable and customizable enough to be usable for any digital project, rendering that goal perhaps too complex to be achievable in practice (Brown 291). As a widely adopted community standard, however, TEI-encoding makes digital editions preservable far into the future: it is not the case that the TEI guidelines would never change— there have been five protocols to date, including the move from SGML to XML languages— but rather that everyone in the TEI community would need to upgrade to future protocols and could develop and share re-usable tools for upgrading, thus promising sustainability for carefully maintained projects.[4] Granting agencies, as well as the MLA Awards Committee for Scholarly Editions,[5] require either the use of TEI for digital editions or an explanation for why TEI encoding was not used. Using TEI ensures that a digital edition can be archived by university libraries or repositories along with the code that explains to software how its coding works, the schema. Theoretically, no matter how technology changes, archived TEI-encoded editions like the *New Variorum Shakespeare* can be displayed via the newest tools, platforms, and software.

In addition to providing sustainability independent of any current technologies, then, the encoding initially allowed each of the volumes to be made available as a searchable PDF version of the printed book that users could access using a CD attached to each book. From its inception, the XML schema combined both textual and documentary encoding in anticipation of a digital future beyond the production of a printed book.

CoDHR's job has been to take these XML-encoded editions and put them online so they are freely available to a wide range of users. For readers who are not familiar with producing web pages, web browsers (Firefox, Google Chrome, etc.) are software that creates what is seen on that webpage (the "front-end") by reading and rendering the code found in documents on a server which is controlled by the producer of the web pages (the "back-end"). The code that all browsers are able to render into a visual presentation is primarily HTML, HyperText Markup Language. (Javascript and CSS, Cascading Stylesheets, are other codes/programs used to create what people see when they visit a web page.) On the front end, a visitor would see, "The Winter's Tale," while the document on the server (the back end) would be sending to the browsers code that looks like this: <html><body><main><header><h2>The Winter's Tale</h2></header></main></body></html>. Visitors to a web-accessible digital edition (users of the digital NVS), of course, do not want to see that code, anymore than anyone would want to see the code running behind a Word document. To read a digital edition, one only wants to see the browser's *rendering* of back-end code as "The Winter's Tale." But browser software cannot translate XML into a readable web page. When a URL, http://newvariorumshakespeare.org, for example, takes a browser to a document that is TEI-encoded, it shows the TEI code itself (the XML encoding), along with a message at the top declaring, "This XML file does not appear to have any style information associated with it. The document tree is shown below." That means, in effect, "the software that is your browser has no information about how this code is supposed to look to the page's visitors." In the case of the NVS TEI, the playtext, textual notes, and commentary are encoded in three separate TEI documents that software on the back-end, on the server feeding code to the browser, must connect together and then display as HTML. Many web pages on the internet are produced by people who know nothing about coding by using software that presents a public-facing view as well as an interface that allows them to create content on the back-end without coding. (WordPress, for example). A common approach to producing online, digital editions using TEI is to transform it into HTML using XSLT,[6] resulting in one or more static web pages. Static pages, however, would not support the full gamut of features envisioned by the NVS design team (such as searching for a passage using modern spellings). Nor could a web browser running on a typical personal computer represent the full, densely interconnected textual apparatus without suffering from performance issues. As such, the decision was made to ingest the data encoded by the NVS TEI into a back-end system that could search, sort, and aggregate on-the-fly—a back-end that would in turn feed that data to a dynamic, interactive front-end, that is, the public-facing web presence of the NVS. For this back-end component, CoDHR chose Corpora, a "dataset studio for the digital humanities" whose main purpose is to ingest, transform, wrangle, and serve up big humanities data.[7] One of Corpora's strengths is the ability to define, using a simple web-based interface, idiosyncratic content types (like a play line, a commentary note, a textual note, etc.) and then handle the complexity of creating the underlying database schemas to store and retrieve that content. Once the NVS design team defined Corpora content types to reflect the kinds of data described by the TEI, a "task" (written in Python) was created to then extract that data and store it in Corpora. Once the data for an NVS edition "lives" in Corpora, it can be directly edited by the NVS project manager or volume editors using simple, dynamically created web forms, alleviating the need for them to become TEI experts. The data can also be queried (using Corpora's REST API) and displayed by the front-end website, itself written entirely in Javascript, HTML, and CSS.

This front-end that users see includes a home page, NVS information pages, and a set of pages for each of the NVS editions. Each edition features a separate page for the front matter, bibliography, and appendix, as well as a page for displaying the core features (playtext, textual notes, and commentary), which we refer to as The Variorum Reader.Figure 16.2 shows the structure of the Variorum Reader as a reader/viewer sees it—three panels similar to the three

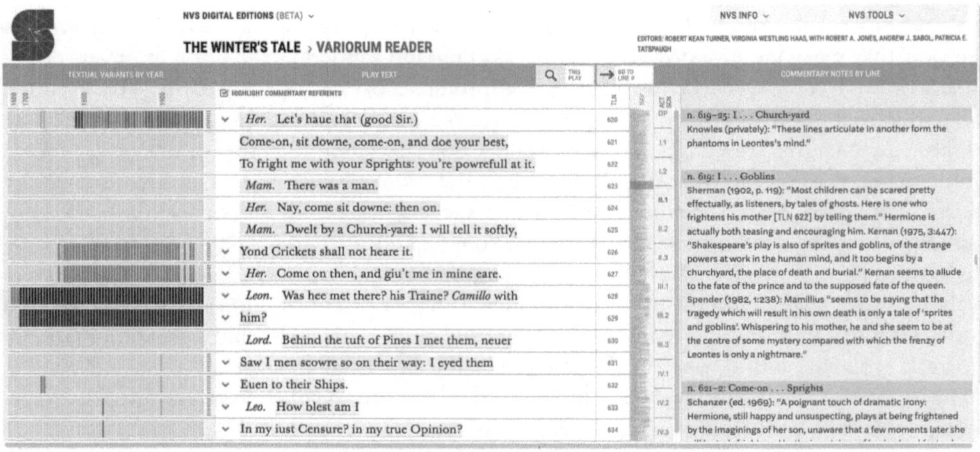

Figure 16.2 The Variorum Reader

sections of the page found in the book (Figure 16.1). The playtext and line numbers appear in the central panel, the textual notes are visualized as a histogram in the left panel, and commentary notes with cross-reference links are in the third panel, on the right. Unlike the print variorum editions, the Variorum Reader presents all core components of the variorum text in a single "space." For example, commentary notes in the Variorum Reader can scroll independently in their own frame or sync up to the playtext line they reference when the reader clicks on a commentary note. Also, clicking on a word or line in the playtext calls up the corresponding note in the commentary column. Commentary notes also include links to bibliographic entries, playtext lines, front matter, other commentary notes, and the appendix, which appear as pop-up modals. Users no longer have to go to the back of the volume, for example, to see references in the bibliography.

The NVS design team used an iterative, back-and-forth process for creating the Variorum Reader interface—a process we lovingly refer to as "chicken-and-egging." This was essentially a conversation between the designer and the web developer, where the designer would propose certain features, and the developer would attempt to rapidly prototype those features. Often, either the limitations of HTML and Javascript or the nature of the data populating the screen would force us to "re-iterate" the design in ways informed by the prototype. Certain design features were also so compelling that it prompted us to develop new functionality on the Corpora back-end to support them. In this way, the front- and back-ends were also subject to this "chicken-and-egging." Both Corpora and the Variorum Reader are designed to maximize the affordances of the web. The Variorum Reader enables readers to access textual notes, variants, sigla, commentary, and other references without the need to learn arcane nomenclature or lose their place in a play. Corpora allows new editors to create their editions more quickly and accurately by providing tools to help them check and collate texts with greater speed. Moving the NVS from its printed history to its digital future involved some direct translation, though it was mostly interpretative work that goes "beyond remediation" (Galey, et al.). The differences between media forms, formats, and practices meant that some elements would be lost in translation, for better or worse, while new ones would be introduced. In the sections that follow, we will show how acts of data and design interpretation that bring the history of Shakespeare publishing to the web reveal the inseparability of data structures, information design, and media affordances.

Textual Notes: From "Band of Terror" to Variorum Reader

At the heart of any variorum are the textual notes, which presented the biggest challenge to our team. Recall that a textual note records all of the variants across editions when compared line by line, word by word, and character by character against the copy-text. In the print editions, textual notes are written in a kind of shorthand to save space, which makes reading these notes difficult for anyone who isn't a Shakespeare scholar or who hasn't worked with a variorum before. This so-called "band of terror" uses an idiosyncratic coding system that requires a less experienced reader to reconstruct an entire passage—mentally, or on paper—in order to access each textual variation. The digital NVS edition simplifies the process of reading textual notes by allowing the reader to see both full text variants and complete references. The shorthand note format is replaced with interface features that allow the reader to easily control what is visible on the screen. A playtext line with variations displays an orange disclosure triangle at its left that can be used to expand and collapse the line's full set of variants. Each variant includes the full text with changes highlighted so the reader can immediately see and compare variations. To the left of each line, a simple yet elegant histogram shows markers that represent collated editions displayed from left to right in chronological order. Each color change indicates a different variation; when variants are expanded, the histogram displays sigla, shorthand for the name of each associated collated edition. Clicking on the sigla markers brings up pop-up modals that list all of the editions that include the variant in question. The histogram is both information visualization and navigational component, allowing the reader to quickly ascertain the quantity, frequency, and durability of editorial changes made across editions. The Variorum Reader is thus designed for close, distant, and all forms of reading in between—as an information interface, a reading space, and a scholarly tool.

Getting there was not easy and was not simply a matter of designing an interactive reader. Wrangling the textual notes exemplifies the kind of back-and-forth required between interface design and data structures. Consider the note for through-line number 2354 from *The Winter's Tale*, spoken by Florizell, which reads, "And most opportune to her neede, I have." Figure 16.3 shows the original textual note as it appears in the print edition. By parsing that note, a scholar can infer that there are two variant readings for this line, one appearing in a single collated witness, and another appearing in most others. As far as textual notes go, this one is pretty simple.

When it comes to parsing this textual note programmatically so as to display it in the Variorum Reader, however, there's nothing simple about it (Figure 16.4).

We start by identifying the through-line number to which this note pertains. We then identify the lemma for this note, which is ultimately the word or phrase belonging to the line in question that is modified by the readings. For this note, the lemma is the word "her" as it appears in the copy text. Having established the pertinent line and lemma for this note, we go on to establish the variant readings described by this note—in this case, there are two of them, highlighted in Figure 16.5.

Each variant reading specifies the collated witnesses in which those readings can be found, and aside from reproducing the sigla for those witnesses, we use that information to build the histogram visualizations for each reading, histograms which are in turn used to create an

2354 her] F1-POPE2, KNT1-HUD1, IRV, BUL, ALEX, SIS, SIG, EVNS, OXF2; the CAP; our mTBY2 *conj.*, THEOBALD (1729) *conj. in* NICHOLS (1817, 2:365), THEO1 *etc.*

Figure 16.3 Printed textual note

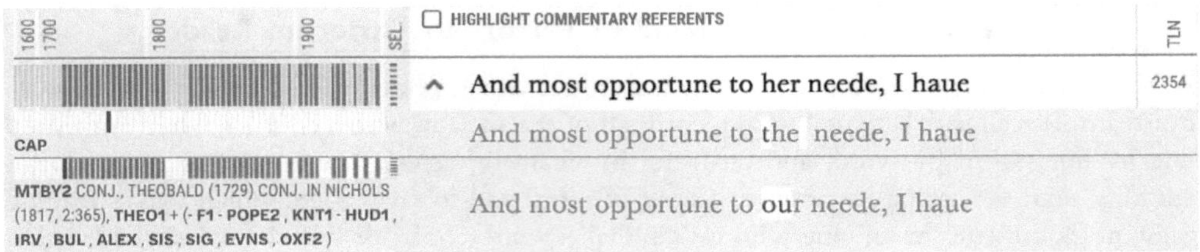

Figure 16.4 Variorum Reader textual note

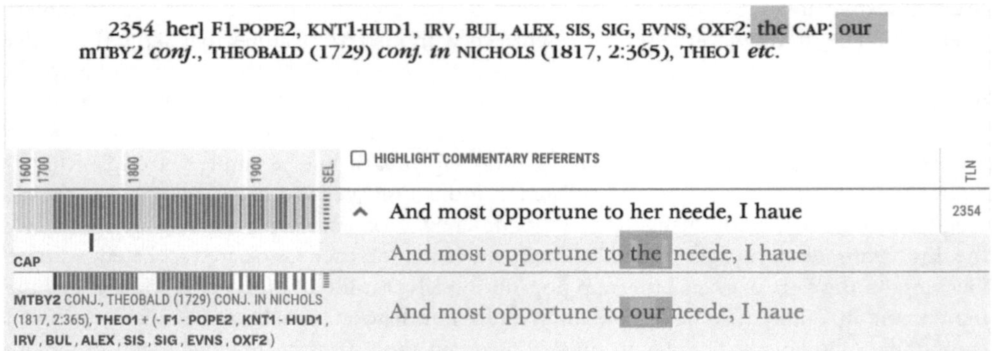

Figure 16.5 Two variants, print and online reader views

aggregated histogram for the entire line (top histogram, Figure 16.5). Finally, we capture the variant readings themselves and use them to modify the copy-text so as to synthetically reproduce how the line ostensibly appears in each of the collated witnesses associated with the readings. This process resembles the way a reader might have to reconstruct the lines from the clues held in the band of terror, which in turn is built into the XML schema. Flanders's TEI XML schema enabled translating the textual notes as an automated process. What you see in Figure 16.5, then, is that same textual note, as produced by the first act of translation from print to XML. This TEI encoding, more than anything else, is what makes the digital NVS possible, as it allows us to identify, programmatically, the various components of a textual note, a commentary note, etc.

Cross-References: Connecting Bodies and Spaces

The second major challenge in remediating the printed NVS to the web regards how a user understands the "space" of a variorum in media with distinctly different material and spatial capacities. In print form, the NVS takes full advantage of the discontinuous reading afforded by the random access and book-marking systems of the printed codex (Stallybrass, "Books and Scrolls"). Working with the book, a reader can leap from reference to reference, holding more than one place in the text with their fingers and other markers. The volume's varied contents occupy distinct spaces within the book body itself: front and back matter are named for their relative placement, as are headers and footers. The appendix is just that, a supplemental organ (even if more expansive than the variorum text itself), tucked away in the back. The general location of bookmarks, Post-its, and fingers inserted between pages can be ascertained in relation to the tangible body of the codex and the reader's own body—before or after, left or right, top or bottom, front or back. Textual components that are distributed across the spaces of the book are collated and connected through the physical interactions of flipping, turning, marking, opening, and closing. Thus, as Stallybrass claims, "men and women are crucially the indexers of actual volumes" engaged in "a practice of discontinuity" (46).

These spatial cues as to where you are in a text are greatly attenuated by the presentation of text on a web page. In most cases, at best, there is a scrollbar. While the scrollbar does try to give a sense of location, in many web browsers, particularly on Macs, the scrollbar vanishes unless the user is hovering over it. On web pages that are built dynamically, the scroll bar is useless as an index of a page's contents, updating endlessly on pages that seem to have no bottom. The scroll bar is also, critically, a *scroll* bar, which implies a linear orientation to content. Thus, the scroll bar is a weak substitute for the felt experience of traversing a codex, particularly when a reader is engaged in the discontinuous reading of a complex reference work such as a variorum.

Without the embodied, haptic cues available to the reader of a physical book, a digital variorum must rely instead on a different system of signification to indicate the position and relations between an edition's component parts. Adhering closely to the principle of a "generous interface" (Whitelaw), the Variorum Reader is designed to give the user a sense of the overall structure and scale of each edition. This is accomplished in part through the use of color coding to differentiate between information related to textual notes (orange tones), to commentary notes (yellow tones), and to the operations of the Variorum (blue). The Variorum Reader's three panels, or zones of activity, each perform according to the logic of their operations and relative to one another. Navigation is multi-directional and the interface allows the user myriad ways to move between its component parts in pursuit of research questions. Each section also includes controls that allow the user to hide and reveal components at any time, functionality that will be further developed in future versions. These features are designed to provide the reader with a sense of agency and location.

The vertical scroll of the copy text is the primary orienting feature of the Variorum Reader. Each line of the play aligns horizontally with its corresponding textual notes and through line numbers, all of which scroll up and down together. To their right, a vertical mini-map conveys at a glance where the reader is within the entirety of the play. The image that appears in that mini-map is generated on-the-fly by the back-end, an actual representation of the lines of the play built in proportion to the size of the user's screen. (Unfortunately, not every browser supports the ability to specify an image for the scrollbar track, for instance, the mini-map feature does not translate over to Mozilla Firefox.) This navigational element draws upon interface conventions found in coding software that allows one to get a sense of location within a long body of text. As with the histogram, the mini-map is both an information visualization and a navigational element which can be clicked or scrolled to bring the reader to a new location in the text. Similarly, to the right of the mini-map another vertical scroll titled ACT/SCN shows the reader which act and scene they are currently reading. When clicked, it allows them to jump to another act and scene, movement based on the logic of the play's narrative structure.

Above these columns, the reader can move through the play in a more targeted fashion by entering a specific line number in the "Go to Line #" box or a by entering a word or phrase in the search box for "this play." Rather than opening a separate box or page, search results are displayed within the Variorum Reader itself, moving from occurrence to occurrence within the body of the play or commentary notes. Thus the reader remains situated within the Variorum Reader and its three panels. The simple search is not as straightforward as it might seem in action. Bridging the gap between early modern and modern English required yet another act of translation based on the archaic and idiosyncratic spellings which occur throughout the playtext, variants, and material referenced by the commentary notes. Consider the spelling for the phrase "sleepy drinks," which appears in the F1 text as "sleepie drinkes." In order to make the NVS more accessible, users should be able to find such phrases using contemporary English search terms. We achieved this functionality by taking advantage of an Elasticsearch feature[8] which allows the user to specify a list of synonyms for search terms. The rather exhaustive list of synonyms was derived from work done by Martin Mueller, Stephen Ramsay, and the team that created MorphAdorner at Northwestern University.

Situating the reader within a single play that runs in a line from top to bottom is relatively simple. But allowing the reader to move horizontally, to jump around, and to make connections across disparate parts of a variorum is exponentially more difficult, particularly when the starting point is the spatiality of the printed book. Indeed, the beta version of the NVS site has not yet fully reconciled the remediation required to do this so effectively. Our workarounds are rough approximations; until we move to new editions that are entirely born-digital, our remediation will continue to be hindered by its print foundations.

The crux of the issue is that the main unit of the codex is the enumerated page, and cross-references in the NVS frequently rely upon page numbers. To locate a reference in a book, a reader flips around in order to "land" on a specified page. The conceptual relationship between the point of departure and the point of arrival is subtly informed by the distance and direction of movement between the two and by the location of each relative to the book body as a whole. Because we have years of practice with such an action, we may be unaware that a page number can be an imprecise indicator; while it narrows the field to a finite, manageable chunk, it is frequently left to the reader to locate the material they seek by scanning and following formatting or textual clues on the page. And while a line number may narrow down the terrain considerably, it still may not bring the reader to an exact word or phrase. Contrast this with a digital text in which a simple HTML anchor can be tied to a specific word or location without the need for larger organizational units such as pages or lines. But that precision gets lost when a link leads to an entire web page (which can be much larger than a print page), even if the anchored text scrolls to the top of the screen. Without navigational cues, landing in the middle of a new web page can feel a bit like exiting a subway station into a part of a city you've never before seen—it takes a moment to figure out where you are. The hyperlink offers word-level precision but it lacks the defined space of a printed page and the spatial orientation of a physical volume. It is this distance between reference and referent, literally and figuratively, that is experientially and operationally different in each medium.

Our workaround is a short-term fix with long-term implications. Within the Variorum Reader, each linked reference leads to a text that resides in one of the edition's sections—a line of playtext or a commentary note within the Variorum Reader itself (on that same "page"), bibliographic details or collated edition titles from the Bibliography or Front Matter, or longer passages from the Appendix. Rather than send the reader out to another page, we have introduced an intermediary step: when a linked reference in the textual notes or commentary notes is clicked, the referent appears first in a pop-up modal beside the link, at which point the user may choose to open it within a larger context in a new tab. Each modal remains open until the user closes it; multiple modals can accumulate and can be moved around the screen according to the needs of the reader. Such features allow for the kind of simultaneous juxtaposition of multiple components that is a recognized affordance of the digital environment (Portola).

Within an open modal, the reader sees an indicator of the source of the reference (Bibliography, Appendix, Front Matter), and can choose to open the reference and its source in a new tab. This feature works well for shorter texts but the sheer volume and the heterogeneity of an NVS appendix remain a bit of a compromise. Because the XML encoding of our current editions is both documentary and textual, meaning it was initially designed to capture topographic features of the printed text in addition to its structural and semantic features, many references in the commentary notes lead to page numbers, the logic of a material body that no longer exists. The XML does not always identify the precise word, phrase, or location that is being indicated; it can only bring the reader to the beginning of a segment of text but it cannot (at the moment) cordon it off as the edge of a page might. Without the contextual cues of page furniture and book architecture, finding the point of reference will require a very attentive reader. The work that would be required to stitch the references of the Appendix together in a way that works on the web would be enormous; therefore, we have to wait for future versions and future editions, those that originate through Corpora, to create a more direct connection. In the meantime, we plan to address how to break the appendices down into more navigable chunks.

New Digital Possibilities

After initial work was done on designing the front and back ends, the CoDHR team turned its attention to ingesting and displaying NVS volumes online by converting the XML-encoded variorum texts into HTML in Corpora. The project manager and developer corrected errors in the way that the back end read, converted, and displayed the TEI data as HTML. That process resulted in two digital NVS editions—*The Winter's Tale* and *A Midsummer Night's Dream*—that were made available online when the site was launched in Beta in early 2021. We are currently working on the next phases of the project: advancing accessibility and usability to move out of Beta; digitizing all NVS print editions, beginning with *King Lear* (2020) and working back through to *Romeo and Juliet* (1871); and assisting new editors with creating born-digital NVS editions, using Corpora.

Further "translations" involve usability, portability, and accessibility, and, lamentably, these translations have yet to occur, which is one of the reasons we consider the digital NVS to be in Beta. In the future, our accessibility experts on campus will evaluate and recommend ways in which the site can be made truly available for all of our users. We also hope to drastically reduce the amount of time it takes for the Variorum Viewer to load its content by implementing some caching and other methods.

We will soon be implementing an entirely new process for editors of new editions of the NVS to perform collations of witnesses. Historically, the collation process is the most time-consuming part of building a variorum edition. Performing optical character recognition (OCR) on all witnesses and then hand-correcting those automated transcripts, will allow editors to lineate those witnesses as they see fit, and once the lineation occurs, an automated process will compile every single variant reading of a line. The editors will then have the opportunity to determine which variants are meaningful enough to warrant a textual note and then create that note with the click of a button. We estimate that this will cut down the time it takes editors to perform the collation for an edition by a factor of ten at least, giving them much more time to focus on the other aspects of the variorum.

Proposing this new editing environment to the editors currently contracted for various plays has confirmed Susan Brown's argument about production interfaces: "With particular reference to editing and publication software, interfaces are the contact zones" within which "social tensions" are mediated. Digital workflows, she argues, have given rise to five types of tensions:

1 Individualism versus collaboration in relation to credit.
2 The shift towards dynamism versus stability in digital resources.

3 Swift dissemination versus scholarly quality control.
4 Simplicity versus complexity in data models and interfaces.
5 The benefits of standards versus disciplinary resistance to systematization.*(283)*

We are encountering these tensions as we work with the editors to design their workspace in the Corpora Data Studio: (1) Given the number of individuals who worked on *A Midsummer Night's Dream* (https://newvariorumshakespeare.org/front/mnd/), is there a way to visualize the contributions of collaborators so as to make their research and labor salient? Should more credit be given to editors who participate in the process of TEI encoding their editions? (Encoding, it should be stressed, gives rise to innumerable editorial questions calling for further research.) (2) Should we build in the possibility of switching the base text to any of the Folios or Quartos with the click of button?; and (3) Since compiling variorum editions can take a lifetime—or more[9]—should we allow publication of these editions in stages so that the editors do not have to wait for scholarly credit until the end of their careers? But, if we do publish in stages, portions of the digital interface (the commentary notes or appendices) could be blank, convincing the casual visitor to the NVS online that the site editors are not concerned with the quality of the scholarship. All of these tensions must be negotiated as we build the editing process.

On the horizon for readers in the not-too-distant future are search and discovery tools inspired by Mitchell Whitelaw's article cited above, "Generous Interfaces for Digital Cultural Collections." A generous interface abandons not only the search box, which requires knowing in advance what they wish to find rather than allowing for exploration, but also the dreaded long list of links pointing to search returns (Whitelaw, paras. 5–8). As Whitelaw points out, visualizing possible answers to queries has taken this form because of Google's success with it, but link lists do not promote discovery as well as other possible kinds of visualization. In fact, Helen Georgas has pointed out that users enjoy Google searching because they believe that only the top returns matter.

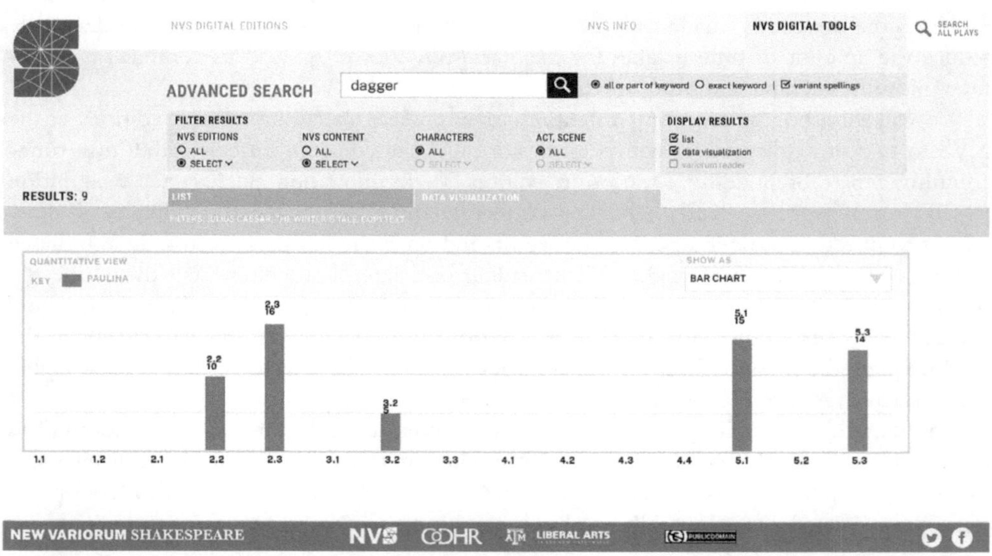

Figure 16.6 Options for visualizing search returns

We conclude our chapter with a mock-up search interface that will be implemented during Phase II of the New Variorum Shakespeare project, noting its implications for the concept of "interface," whether for research or reading, production or reception, and whether digital or in print (Figure 16.6).

Here, we imagine the user of the New Variorum Shakespeare online being able to search for all the speeches by character in *The Winter's Tale*: a list view offers links to the beginning of those speeches, but the visualization view shows when Paulina speaks (Act, Scene), and how many lines she speaks in each part of the play; searching multiple characters at the same time, whether in the same play or across plays, can allow students and researchers to discover interesting features of play structures, character development, similar or divergent patterns across plays, and more. The same could be done for word usage, as is visible in voyant-tools.org, the Trends tool displaying Shakespeare's corpus.[10]

In a trenchant summary of her own argument which appears throughout many of her articles and books, Johanna Drucker states that "technologies of knowledge production are not incidental but integral" to what we know and can discover.[11] A knowledge production interface could be constituted by a physical desk with books and papers scattered here and there, Post-it notes, 3x5 cards, handwritten notes, and printed articles. It can also be constituted by the Corpora Data Studio, and the challenge of developing digital interfaces for both editors and readers of the digital scholarly edition is to honor traditional scholarly practices—flipping pages, writing in margins—while introducing new techniques made possible by digitization.

Notes

1 One significant part of the process not discussed in this chapter was performed by Dr. Torabi. Instead of looking at our finished product and asking, "How could this interface be used to teach Shakespeare?" Dr. Torabi created numerous class assignments for a Shakespeare college course, as part of the research needed by Dr. Burdick and Dr. Tarpley to design and program the digital edition.

2 For the source of this phrase, see Rasmussen 211 and Marcus 72.

3 The concept of a Shakespeare edition as interface comes from Alan Galey's *Shakespearean Archive*. He argues that Teena Rochfort Smith's *Four-Text Hamlet* (1883) first used the medium of the printed book to imagine an "interface design" presaging the computer screen (29).

4 The TAPAS Project (https://tapasproject.org/) was developed to overcome interoperability projects, and editing-encoding platforms such as oXygen and CWRC-Writer (Brown) allow uploading any TEI Schema which formalizes any particular project's encoding decisions.

5 Please see the MLA Committee on Scholarly Edition's "Guiding Questions for Vetters of Scholarly Editions," 24.1 (https://www.mla.org/Resources/Research/Surveys-Reports-and-Other-Documents/Publishing-and-Scholarship/Guidelines-for-Editors-of-Scholarly-Editions#questions).

6 XSLT, or the eXtensible Stylesheet Language, is a Turing-complete programming language that is written in XML, used to transform XML documents into other kinds of code, including HTML. Why bother encoding a document in a language that web browsers cannot visualize for users, and then writing programs that turn the document into another kind of code which browsers can render? One thing that librarians, archivists, and digital humanists have learned—the hard way—is that technology changes. As mentioned above, TEI is designed to preserve digital editions against the tide of technological development. Now, at this moment in history, we render TEI XML into HTML so that people can see a readable document and, ideally, enjoy the way that it is presented. But ten years from now, we may be transforming that TEI into some other code for presentation on some other kind of device. As semantic markup, TEI code is much richer in information than HTML code can be, and all of that XML encoding that has been determined by the Text Encoding Initiative to be essential for creating a digital document will be needed. Web code tells you that this bit of text needs to be big, <h2>The Winter's Tale</h2>, but TEI XML tells you that this bit of text is a title, <title>The Winter's Tale</title>, and the programming required to transform it into the new technology can say, in effect, *make all titles big*.

7 Corpora is developed in-house by CoDHR, and is built using the Django web framework, allowing for its entire back-end codebase to be written in the Python programming language, which by many accounts is the most popular language in the world for software developers. CoDHR plans on open-sourcing and releasing this software in 2022.

8 Elasticsearch is one of the databases Corpora uses to store content. Elasticsearch is at its core a Lucene search index, and so it allows for the efficient retrieval of data via search terms.

9 After the death of her husband Richard, who had worked on creating the variorum edition over the course of a lifetime, Judith Kennedy finished *Midsummer Night's Dream* (https://newvariorumshakesepeare.org/front/mnd).

10 Voyant is pre-loaded with Shakespeare's corpus: via the "Open" icon that appears at the bottom left of the splash page at voyant-tools.org. One can get directly to the Trends tool via this link: (https://voyant-tools.org/?corpus=shakespeare&query=shall&query=lord&query=king&query=sir&query=good&view=Trends); a box at the bottom allows one to select the words one would like to see mapped throughout the corpus.

11 This summary of views expressed in her books from *Graphesis* (2014) to *Visualization and Interpretation* (2020), as well as numerous articles, comes from a telephone conversation: Johanna Drucker with Laura Mandell, November 20, 2021.

References

Bolter, Jay David, and Grusin, Richard. *Remediation: Understanding New Media*. MIT Press, 1998.

Brown, Susan. "Tensions and Tenets of Socialized Scholarship." *Digital Scholarship in the Humanities*, vol. 31, no. 2, 2016, pp. 283–300.

De Grazia, Margreta. "The Essential Shakespeare and the Material Book." *Textual Practice*, vol. 2, no. 1, 2008, pp. 69–86.

De Grazia, Margreta, and Stallybrass, Peter. "The Materiality of the Shakespearean Text." *Shakespeare Quarterly*, vol. 44, no. 3, 1993, pp. 255–283.

Drucker, Johanna. *Graphesis: Visual Forms of Knowledge Production*. Harvard UP, 2014.

Drucker, Johanna. *Visualization and Interpretation: Humanistic Approaches to Display*. MIT Press, 2020.

Galey, Alan. *Shakespearean Archive: Experiments in New Media from the Renaissance to Postmodernity*. Cambridge UP, 2014.

Galey, Alan, *et al.* "Beyond Remediation: The Role of Textual Studies in Implementing New Knowledge Environments." *Scholarly and Research Communication*, vol. 3, no. 1, 2012, pp. 1–9.

Georgas, Helen. "Google vs. the Library [Part III]: Assessing the Quality of Sources Found by Undergraduates." *Portal: Libraries and the Academy*, vol. 15, no. 1, 2015, pp. 133–161.

Knowles, Richard. *Shakespeare Variorum Handbook: A Manual of Editorial Practice*. 2nd edition. Committee on the New Variorum Edition of Shakespeare of the Modern Language Association of America, 2003.

Marcus, Leah S. *Unediting the Renaissance: Shakespeare, Marlowe, Milton*. Routledge, 1996.

McCarty, Willard. "Finding Implicit Patterns in Ovid's Metamorphoses with TACT." *CCH Working Papers*, vol. 1, 1991. Available at: https://projects.chass.utoronto.ca/chwp/mccarty/.

Modern Language Association, Committee on Scholarly Editions. "Guidelines for Editors of Scholarly Editions," 29 June 2011. Available at: https://www.mla.org/Resources/Research/Surveys-Reports-and-Other-Documents/Publishing-and-Scholarship/Guidelines-for-Editors-of-Scholarly-Editions.

Mueller, Martin and Ramsay, Stephen. "MorphAdorner." Available at: http://morphadorner.northwestern.edu/morphadorner/.

Orgel, Stephen. "The Authentic Shakespeare." *Representations*, vol. 21, 1988, pp. 1–25.

Pierazzo, Elena. *Digital Scholarly Editing: Theories, Models and Methods*. Ashgate, 2015.

Portela, Manuel. "Designing Digital Editions: Rev. of Elena Pierazzo." *Digital Scholarly Editing: MATLIT (Materialities of Literature)*, vol. 4, no. 2, 2016, pp. 283–287. Available at: https://impactum-journals.uc.pt/matlit/article/view/2182-8830_4-2_15.

Rasmussen, Eric. "Richly Noted: A Case for Collation Inflation." *In Arden: Editing Shakespeare. Essays in Honour of Richard Proudfoot*. Edited by Ann Thompson and Gordon McMullan, Thomson Learning, 2003, pp. 211–220.

Ruecker, Stan, Radzikowska, Milena, and Sinclair, Stéfan. *Visual Interface Design for Digital Cultural Heritage: A Guide to Rich-Prospect Browsing*. Ashgate, 2011.

Stallybrass, Peter. "Books and Scrolls; Navigating the Bible." *Books and Readers in Early Modern England: Material Studies*, edited by Jennifer Andersen, et al., U of Pennsylvania P, 2011, pp. 42–77.

Suchman, Lucy. *Human-Machine Reconfigurations: Plans and Situated Actions*. 2nd edition. Cambridge UP, 2007.

Torabi, Katayoun. "How to Digital NVS." Available at: https://newvariorumshakespeare.org/how-to/.nd.

Ware, Colin. *Information Visualization: Perception for Design*. Morgan Kaufmann, 2004.

Werstine, Paul. "Past Is Prologue." *Shakespeare*, vol. 4, no. 3, 2008, pp. 208–220.

Werstine, Paul. "NVS History." *New Variorum Shakespeare*, Beta Release, July 2021. Available at: https://newvariorumshakespeare.org/about/

Whitelaw, Mitchell. "Generous Interfaces for Digital Cultural Collections." *DHQ: Digital Humanities Quarterly*, vol. 9, no. 1, 2015, pp. 1–25. Available at: http://www.digitalhumanities.org/dhq/vol/9/1/000205/000205.html.

17

MEDIATING THE SHAKESPEARE USER'S DIGITAL EXPERIENCE

Stacey J. L. Redick and Eric M. Johnson

The *Oxford English Dictionary* (OED Online) offers a strikingly outdated definition of "interface," calling it "A surface lying between two portions of matter or space, and forming their common boundary," giving two illustrative quotations from the 1880s. Merriam-Webster, which is regarded by many as inferior but is frequently more nimble when it comes to new words and their uses, defines it as "the place at which independent and often unrelated systems meet and act on or communicate with each other." This is much closer to how the term is used in software development, where it serves as a catch-all for any point at which a computer system interacts with a human, whether that interaction happens in physical space or virtual space (Merriam-Webster). The interface is "what the user sees and operates; it sits between the machine and the person" (Murray 10). This notion of "interface" has sprawled past its digital boundaries and is now applied to books (Borsuk), automobiles (Black), and buildings (Mirti and Aprile).

At the Folger Shakespeare Library, the interfaces we develop often focus on Shakespeare-related content. In this chapter we discuss the Folger Shakespeare website (The Folger Shakespeare, April 14, 2020a), which shares a free, modern version of Shakespeare's works alongside contextual media related to the playwright and his life and times. Importing these works from artifacts related to the physical production of books has made them into digital texts.[1] Our team's labor centers on making these texts more widely available and accessible to our users who are mainly (though not exclusively) students, instructors, enthusiasts, and theater professionals around the world.

In this chapter we explain how we put users and evidence at the center of our work, and why that is so important for interface design. We start with an exploration and definition of "interface" and "digital experience design" (DX) before we discuss the activities and processes that we incorporate into the development of the Folger Shakespeare website and how they can support user-centered interface design for other Shakespearean interfaces.

Digital Experience Design of Interfaces

Shakespearean artifacts exist in every mass medium but began with the physical book. One of the main advantages that physical books have over digital interfaces is durability. Book interfaces have remained stable, which can be demonstrated when a modern reader picks up a sixteenth- or seventeenth-century book and is able to peruse it without training. Certain

 DOI: 10.4324/9780367821722-23

features such as catchwords and densely packed title pages might seem strange to those who are accustomed to modern book layouts, but they do not impede comprehension. Book interfaces have thus "eroded" in some of their particulars, but they offer an enviable level of stability that modern electronic media cannot match.

Digital interfaces, on the other hand, are more flexible and extensible than interfaces in printed or analog media. Online media and their interfaces also have a much broader reach than analog, printed interfaces. They also offer audiences more interactive environments and experiences than physical interfaces. A digital interface may enable a user to manipulate, contribute to, and influence digital content and computer processing (Murray 43). For instance, some websites will allow users to create their own annotations on top of the website content. Comments sections on blog posts enable readers to contribute to discussions about the post. Online content is often shareable across social media and website platforms. The digital medium can contain an extensive range of legacy and computational media formats and genres, such as text, moving and still images, audio recordings, three-dimensional models, databases, and more (Murray 418). Flexibility, reusability, interactivity, range of content types, and broad reach are affordances of digital media (and especially online media), defined as the "functional properties of objects or environments" that enable specific uses of or interaction with an interface. Such affordances offer many more possibilities than those that operate in books (Murray 409).

Though digital and physical media offer different affordances and opportunities for displaying content, media, or information, every Shakespearean artifact, regardless of medium, has an *interface*: the performance, the physical book that contains the play or its digital equivalent, and the website. And behind or within each media interface is the *content*: the lines within the play, spoken by actors; information about the play, such as title, actors, dates; the text of the article, its title and author; and, as in the Folger Shakespeare website, Shakespeare's works, scholarly articles, and webpages that contextualize the works. Once content has been included in or mediated by an interface, that content is automatically *organized*, advertently or inadvertently, by the interface. An audience member's interaction with an interface that contains organized content is a *user experience*.

The final element of the interface, although ontologically separate from the interface itself, is the *user:* the individuals or entities who experience the digital artifact. Robert Darnton describes a communication circuit that captures the essential relationships in the production of a book, which also applies to digital interfaces. The key to the circuit is the reader (or user), "whose influence on the author serves to 'complete the circuit'" (Howsam 29) because she "influences the author both before and after the act of composition" (Darnton 67). This approach highlights one of the strongest similarities between physical and digital design: there is always a user, and to optimize the user's experience that user must be considered in the creative process.

Digital experience design draws these elements into open, transparent discussions with team members, stakeholders, and users. Once revealed, internal design assumptions can be addressed so the interface efficiently and effectively delivers relevant content to users and stakeholders in ways that they expect. Designs can be tested against those user needs and expectations, and the interfaces can be built specifically to meet them. DX guides this process so that design decisions are deliberately chosen, instead of accidentally arrived at. DX focuses on the completion of the circuit, where the audience interacts with or consumes the content.

The principles of DX rely on common sense and on helping users to achieve their desired tasks without requiring them to figure out *how* to achieve them. They guide the creation of artifacts that fit within the work that users are already doing, instead of creating more work in order to accomplish their goals or complete their tasks. DX asks, who are the intended audiences and what are their information-seeking or computer-interaction practices? What assumptions do the creators or producers of the interface and its content carry? How does the infrastructure facilitate or hinder users in their journeys to reach goals and complete tasks? These goals, guidelines, and questions also affect information architecture, web usability, interaction design, and user experience design (Norman and Nielsen). The names of these fields and their definitions are important to know and understand, because they are often used interchangeably. At the Folger, we primarily talk about information architecture (the organization of content and navigational features) and user experience (what it is truly like for users to interact with the content on the website). The following definitions are useful:

- *Interaction design* is "an emerging discipline that structures people's relationships to artifacts and systems, especially but not only those that make use of the affordances of the digital medium" and focuses on the interplay between a human being and an automated system. Interaction design is particularly concerned with the ways in which digital interfaces interact with and are interpreted as being part of larger social and cultural systems (Murray 10–11, 426).
- *Information architecture* focuses on the structural organization, including navigation and classification, of an information space, whether physical or digital, to facilitate task completion, information management, and intuitive access to content. It is a discipline and a community of practice that apply principles of architecture and design to the digital environment. Information architecture starts with users and the reason they come to an interface in the first place: they have an information need (Rosenfeld and Morville 8). Information architects work to meet that need, as a physical building's architect is charged with meeting the needs of the people who will inhabit and use the physical structure.
- *User experience* "encompasses all aspects of the end-user's interaction with the company, its services, and its products" (Norman and Nielsen). The heuristics or guidelines for user experience of digital online interfaces include keeping visitors informed of what is happening within the interface, matching the interface to the real world and to familiar and common word and symbol usage, giving users the control and freedom that they need to do what they came for, preventing errors and enabling users to recover from them, and minimizing the user's memory load (Nielsen).
- *Usability* is "a design goal that … refers to the ease with which users of digital tools and informational resources can perform tasks" (Murray 443).

A product development team that applies DX principles performs a series of activities that center the product's human users and what they need from the product. We call these activities a development cycle. The DX development cycle for the Folger Shakespeare site was inspired by the Agile methodology, which enables incremental and iterative feature development and provides time to test assumptions, designs, and products with target audience members frequently.[2]

The development cycle iteratively passes from ideation to the codification of business and user requirements to the design, prototyping, and development of the digital interface itself. The interface is then tested to see if it was built according to the requirements, and if it has any flaws in its execution. This ideation phase brings all ideas, good and bad, into review. Conversations with stakeholders and target audiences (all potential users) in this phase teach us which of their needs are not being met by existing offerings, and what they will require in the interface. Based on the knowledge of our users that we gain from these conversations and from general trends in usage, we select the best idea to design and prototype.

When audiences have the opportunity to share how they work, what they need, and whether a system meets their needs, the interface will be more useful for those audiences. The design and prototype phase focuses on determining the essential functions and organizational and navigational schemes of the interface. The design may be low-fidelity (for example, a sketch drawn on paper) or high-fidelity (a clickable prototype in a browser or software program). Once the first prototypes have been designed, interviews with stakeholders and users who are members of our target audience groups (students, teachers, researchers, enthusiasts, and staff) validate the designs.

When the design or prototype meets with stakeholder and user approval, it moves into the development phase. Interface features, informed by the requirements and reception of users, are built into the existing structure and then tested for functionality and usability, just as the prototypes were.

About Audiences

Modern audiences for Shakespearean online and digital artifacts might be much more varied than for a physical artifact, such as a book, because these online resources are often free, often available to discover on a ready-to-hand computer or phone, and often fully available via search engines as opposed to being available for purchase. This means interfaces are discovered and used by geographically dispersed audiences, who use them at home, in the office, or while in transit between physical spaces. Included content and media types might be more diverse, broad, and numerous: visitors to a website can read text and watch a companion video of the text, while readers of a book are (at least for now) limited to consumption of text and images. Visitors to a website might also be able to interact more with the content than readers of a book, as when visitors to online shops and museum spaces can rotate 3D models of items by clicking and dragging their mouse over the model. Finally, the flexibility and dynamism of the digital interface make it potentially more engaging for repeat visitors. Most books have the same content and page design interface, no matter how many times their audiences re-read them, but digital interfaces may be updated, upgraded, or changed, based on evolving needs and content.

Common characteristics of how digital interfaces, such as websites, are used by their audiences inform DX principles and approaches. Widespread characteristics of website usage include glancing at pages and scanning some of the text instead of reading; selecting the first interesting or seemingly relevant link instead of finding and selecting the best choice; focusing on words, phrases, and images that seem to match the task at hand, current or ongoing interests, or trigger words like "free," "sale," and users' own names; and muddling through instead of figuring out how digital interfaces work. Many of these habits come from common user characteristics: we are often in a hurry, we do not need to read everything, and we are practiced at scanning. The penalty for choosing the wrong link instead of the best choice is light, weighing our options may not improve our chances, and sometimes guessing is more fun and even efficient (Krug 21–6). Understanding these characteristics, both of users and of usage, helps digital interfaces succeed.

Every digital interface has a specific audience or set of audiences that ought to be carefully anticipated, researched, and incorporated into design work. This remains true when a digital interface is built to conform to a narrow set of parameters, such as an interface that places content behind a paywall or avoids being crawled by search engines. Whether a digital interface is open to all or restricted to paying customers will affect user goals even beyond access: designers can reasonably assume that many users who have paid for content will be more deeply engaged with that content, by virtue of its monetary value. Whether content in different formats, such as 3D models or video recordings, are included will influence how digital interfaces will be used. Video content, for example, might be easier to digest in short chunks of time than text, and therefore will be more useful to audiences who are especially pressed for time.

Digital experience designers who understand the function of the interface and its social and cultural contexts, such as the customs, relationships, institutions, and value structures that it reflects or subverts, as well as the deeper, enduring human activities and values that it serves, will be able to design interfaces that support real-world contexts. Designers can also imagine how the digital interface would change if it were designed for people of a different social class, ethnicity, nationality, gender, age, profession, neighborhood, educational background, or physical or mental ability so that the interface works for users with different worldviews, experiences, abilities, and backgrounds (Murray 29).

A design is good or bad depending on how well "it serves a core human need whose value is larger than the immediate task" and is independent of the technology that currently supports it (Murray 40). One core need met by the Folger Shakespeare website is access to Shakespeare's works and supporting information that helps audiences understand his works, life, and times, while also serving the deeply human activity of understanding human nature, literature, art, and history. These aims and values, common to Shakespeare interfaces in any form, can be achieved through printed texts, online editions, full-cast audio recordings, and movie and television adaptations – all of which rely on different technology and media formats. Determining values, aims, and services will inform how the interface can best support its users and their needs.

DX helps identify and correct inaccurate or wrong assumptions about what users need. Often, these assumptions are based on designers' and developers' own experiences, which differ from those of a product's users. For the Folger Shakespeare site, users' experiences may relate to our impressions of who our visitors are and who reads Shakespeare, and to our own internal institutional needs and requirements. To make informed choices about the design of an interface, designers must identify and consciously examine the cultural biases, expectations, and value judgments that we all hold as a result of living in a particular society or subgroup (Murray 29).

We have discussed human users and how to ensure an interface succeeds for them, but the last kind of user that concerns DXers is not even human – but it is still a critical audience to consider when developing a digital interface. The majority of users start their web browsing sessions by querying search engines, of which Google is the most widely used.[3] While search engines cannot permit or prohibit content from being published based on their political, ethical, or religious suitability, a web page that has not been indexed by a search engine will not appear in the search results that the user sees. The page can still be accessed directly at its address if the user knows it, but for most users, the page effectively does not exist if it is not indexed.

Optimizing for search engine discovery is often simpler than serving humans. But to believe that modern search engines "index" by cataloging keywords as with traditional book production is a misconception, as they go well beyond the indexing of a book. Google "reads" web pages as human eyes do, as it "sees" text blocks with larger letter sizes (such as headlines) as important and places more weight on their words and concepts when it calculates search results and considers word frequency and related topics when it is deciding how to characterize a web page. Google's machinery will also penalize pages and entire websites if it suspects any attempt to deceive it or take advantage of its methods, and it will deprecate or outright ignore pages and sites that it considers particularly egregious.

Thus, odd as it might seem, DXers must think of how Google "reads" their pages prior to any humans reading them. Google reads a web page, not by considering how it might look in the interface of a web browser that has assembled all the page's elements into a visually integrated and scrollable image, but by looking at the page's underlying code. The code, to Google, is not used to build an interface but is the interface itself: an interface that communicates concepts, words, and meaning from machines to machines, instead of from humans to humans.

Search Engine Optimization, User Research, and Analytics

Since many users are searchers and many searchers use Google, we have tried to follow best practices for achieving high-ranking search results. Just as books have metadata that are used to catalog and organize and locate them within libraries and library search systems, web pages have metadata that Google can use to identify and rank them.

We begin by submitting the sitemap, or file that tells search engines that the web pages exist, to Google, which lets it know that our site should be added to Google's index and thus be findable in search results. Once the file is submitted and the search engine becomes aware of the site and its pages, Google tries to understand the pages by analyzing and cataloging the different content and media (Google Search Central 2017). We create meaningful titles for every page that are specific, succinct, and descriptive, and ensure that they and the page headings (content section headings) accurately describe the content that resides on each page. Titles, in addition to describing to users what the site and pages are about, also appear in search engine results, and therefore are critical pieces of the website architecture to help users and search engines understand the value of the website (Google Search Central 2021). We have also incorporated a strictly hierarchical URL structure that includes play titles in all the page URLs where they are relevant, to make it easier for search engines to crawl and collect the website structure.

Site rankings improve the more humans find a website useful and select it from the search results. There are additional ways to improve the ranking of a website in a search engine. Google's advice is to create pages that load quickly and are mobile-friendly, and to put up useful, relevant content and keep it updated (Google Search Central 2017). Throughout the design and development of the Folger Shakespeare site, we have focused on designing and organizing content so that it is not only useful but also will display well on mobile devices. Where possible, we try to keep content and text to one column, and where we have two columns, we ensure that they stack vertically when required by narrow screens.

We do this work continually as we build out new features in the website and create new pages that need to be succinctly named and nested within the hierarchy. Ultimately, guidelines for optimizing search engine performance and rank also benefit users, as they make content easy for machines to identify and understand. Often, when the metadata used to index and rank search results is easy for machines to understand, it is easy for humans to understand as well. Folger Shakespeare site users thus benefit from search engine optimization (SEO) practices that we put into place, although we do not rely on this to ensure that we are satisfying our users.

User research activities are built into the Folger's DX development cycle to discover and mitigate the effects of our biases and assumptions while uncovering real audiences' needs and contexts. We conduct these activities with two groups: internal stakeholders and users. Internal stakeholders are often Folger staff who serve customers who use the product. Our staff may not use the product themselves, but they may need to instruct their customers, who are the product's users, in how to use it, or they may need to conduct administrative tasks within a separate interface, such as identifying, verifying, deleting, or changing customer or catalog data. Often, these two groups partially overlap in their needs and goals but have different perspectives and knowledge of the content. Identifying internal stakeholders' needs (administrative-side systems and features to manage accounts, for example) separately from users' needs (which may be search features that help them find the digital items they're looking for, or features that allow them to save their preferred items to their account) helps to prioritize feature development that aligns with the goals of the project. User and internal stakeholder research activities could take the form of interviews and testing, analytics gathering, surveys, focus groups, prototype demonstrations to stakeholders, and more. In a case where the internal stakeholders and users are the same, as in the development of an intranet system for an institution, user research can help ascertain user needs.

Common user research activities include:

- *Contextual interviews*, which focus on audiences' current workflows, practices, and information-seeking habits and facilitate the identification of opportunities for development by revealing gaps or snarls in existing audience workflows.
- *Usability tests*, during which participants evaluate a prototype or website against specific tasks they are asked to complete and which help designers identify opportunities to improve an existing interface design.
- *Analytics*, which provide insight into trends that affect large numbers of users, and which, combined with qualitative user research, help designers identify trends and the reasons behind them.
- *Surveys*, which give users an opportunity to self-report their motivations for visiting a digital interface or website or their level of satisfaction with their experience on an artifact or website. Surveys may help development teams identify questions for future development.
- *Prototype demonstrations* with stakeholders that elicit feedback and questions from subject matter experts and power users which may help garner buy-in for the digital interface from decision makers and influencers.

These activities can be restricted by time, budget, or expertise; however, several compromises can be made to approximate the results these activities would have achieved. Designers may review best and common practices from experienced practitioners, use existing data from previous user feedback, and contact subject matter experts to solicit their feedback. These activities, in combination with a clear and thorough understanding of users, can illuminate and offset internal assumptions. When it is not possible to conduct user research activities and stakeholder interviews, gaps in knowledge can be filled later if assumptions are identified and recorded early in the process (Fessenden).

In addition to SEO principles and user research activities, DX incorporates digital analytics, which measure how users encounter and interact with an interface. Analyzing usage data for websites is a valuable and effective way to observe real-world user behavior. Further, the benefits of user research activities and SEO compliance increase when they are combined with analytics. When we observe from user research how individual users interact with a digital artifact and from analytics what types of usage are trending across and among demographics, we can better understand not only what is happening (from analytics), but why users engage with the site interface and its affordances (from user research). In this way, the analysis of larger, quantitative trends as demonstrated by analytics complements the qualitative results that derive from user research activities.

The most basic kind of digital analytics are the "counting metrics": how many users visited a site; how many times they visited (i.e., sessions); and how many pages they requested from the site (pageviews). These numbers show how popular a site is, what time of year it receives the most traffic, and which pages within the site are most popular. All else being equal, most site owners prefer these numbers to be higher rather than lower, because it means they are serving more people. Other metrics can show where users are located. Knowing where website visitors live can promote design decisions that consider users' cultural, linguistic, or economic contexts. We use these metrics and others in conjunction with user research activities as we move through the development cycle.

Putting It All Together

After engaging DX during site development, we can assemble what we have learned from subsequent user research and analytics to make informed decisions about future improvements to the Folger Shakespeare site and its interfaces. Placing Shakespeare's works online means that the site must adapt to the contexts and environments within which its users live, study, play, and work, in addition to adapting to the affordances offered by the internet and digital media. DX has given us the tools to do this, and to foster innovative design within the site. In the following examples, we demonstrate decisions we have made, and future decisions we may make, based on user research, analytics, and SEO results.

We have tracked years of website usage data and identified some seemingly adverse phenomena that have natural causes and do not need to be "fixed" by changes to site functionality or content. One perennial trend for the site, along with most of the Folger's other web properties, is that usage generally dips in the summer months in the Northern hemisphere. We have attributed this decrease to teachers and students not requiring the texts and related resources while they are not studying at school or university. (All of the data presented in this chapter is taken from Google Analytics and covers usage from July 2020 to June 2021.)

Other metrics can show where users are located. For the Folger Shakespeare site, three-quarters are from the United States, and the rest are from outside the US. Not surprisingly, the site is most popular in countries where English is widely spoken and taught. The five countries whose residents visit the site the most often are, in order: the United States, Canada, the United Kingdom, India, and Australia. Knowing that the site is most popular in English-speaking countries guides us in our use of web standards. For example, we design content and website architecture to start on the top left and run across to the right and then down because that is how English is read.

We have also found that users rarely enter the Folger Shakespeare site from the "front door": only 3.3 percent of the 3,158,481 entrances between July 2020 and June 2021 were through the home page. They were more likely to arrive on the main landing pages for *Macbeth* (6.3 percent), *Romeo and Juliet* (also 6.3 percent), or *Hamlet* (4.2 percent), the three most popular plays in the Folger Shakespeare corpus.

While the home page is not one of the pages through which most visitors enter the site, we try to avoid unnecessary confusion on the home page interface when we can. In a series of contextual interviews with members of our target audiences (Shakespeare/poetry enthusiasts, educators, and students), we discovered that a prominent feature on the home page was causing confusion. In our design, we put the most popular six plays at the top of the home page so that visitors could get to them quickly without having to scroll through the entire list alphabetically. We assumed that most visitors would want to read or investigate those top plays, since they are more studied and written about than the others. However, in one of these interviews, a participant mentioned that it confused her to see two differently ordered lists. Once she became familiar with the order of the popular plays on the home page, browsing on the "all plays" page was difficult because the plays were no longer in the same order (K.B., personal interview, November 13, 2020). One of our other testers did not notice the difference but struggled to find the play on the "all plays" list after looking at the list of the most popular plays on the home page (G.B., personal interview, November 18, 2020). In other words, users may not notice that the plays are ordered differently on different webpages. Without these contextual interviews of target audience members, we would still be working from the assumption that the visitors to the home page would want a shortcut to the most popular plays, while visitors to the main plays page would want the full list of plays. This demonstrates the importance of interface design practices that include real users.

When we look at the quantitative measure of home page entrances as well as this user feedback, we can make a rational decision about how much time we should spend on streamlining the home page, and how relatively important it is. It would be inefficient to spend a substantial amount of our time on a "fix" for relatively few users, or to prioritize it over other improvements which can deepen user engagement or remove more significant barriers for users.

What follows is a more nuanced look at user behavior which might reveal other improvements we could make to the interface. The top four exit pages (the last pages that users requested before leaving the site) are from the *Romeo and Juliet* section (Figure 17.1). A significant number of users left after looking at the prologue or the first scene; many of them left after viewing the play's main landing page.

Why do so many users leave the site after seemingly not getting very far into the play, or looking at any part of the play? This might represent a shortcoming of the interface, and as unfortunate as that might be, a designer would have to accept that outcome. But there are other possibilities: there is a brief plot summary on the primary page for each play, so some users might simply want to read that and move along. Instructors might be referring their students to the prologue and first scene as part of an assignment. Users might be checking out the site to see if it suits their needs, and then return at another time. They might also be downloading a copy of a text (which, as we relate below, is a very common occurrence).

Page	Exits ↓	Pageviews	% Exit
Site: Folger Shakespeare (all users)	3,258,564 % of Total: 57.02% (5,714,775)	10,029,763 % of Total: 66.29% (15,129,632)	32.49% Avg for View: 37.77% (-13.98%)
1. shakespeare.folger.edu/shakespeares-works/romeo-and-juliet/prologue/	**73,639** (2.26%)	157,722 (1.57%)	46.69%
2. shakespeare.folger.edu/shakespeares-works/romeo-and-juliet/act-1-scene-1/	**68,484** (2.10%)	153,142 (1.53%)	44.72%
3. shakespeare.folger.edu/shakespeares-works/romeo-and-juliet/	**59,999** (1.84%)	314,211 (3.13%)	19.10%
4. shakespeare.folger.edu/shakespeares-works/romeo-and-juliet/entire-play/	**58,935** (1.81%)	84,185 (0.84%)	70.01%
5. shakespeare.folger.edu/shakespeares-works/macbeth/	**56,873** (1.75%)	310,678 (3.10%)	18.31%
6. shakespeare.folger.edu/	**47,695** (1.46%)	176,550 (1.76%)	27.02%
7. shakespeare.folger.edu/shakespeares-works/macbeth/act-4-scene-1/	**46,157** (1.42%)	70,850 (0.71%)	65.15%
8. shakespeare.folger.edu/shakespeares-works/macbeth/act-1-scene-3/	**41,881** (1.29%)	102,303 (1.02%)	40.94%
9. shakespeare.folger.edu/shakespeares-works/hamlet/	**39,464** (1.21%)	211,738 (2.11%)	18.64%
10. shakespeare.folger.edu/shakespeares-works/romeo-and-juliet/act-2-scene-2/	**39,312** (1.21%)	77,678 (0.77%)	50.61%

Figure 17.1 The top ten exit pages for the Folger Shakespeare site between July 2020 and June 2021

There are sophisticated ways to test these hypotheses which go beyond the scope of this chapter, but this illustrates the truism that while analytics might identify a challenge, they do not always indicate a cause, much less a solution.

Examining the channels by which visitors arrive on the website can also suggest improvements. About half of Folger Shakespeare users arrive from a search engine (88 percent of the time from Google), one-quarter are referred from other sites, and one-quarter come directly to Folger Shakespeare after typing the address directly into their browser, or following a browser's bookmark or another link that cannot be tracked.

Because of the 2020–21 global pandemic, many classroom assignments were moved to learning management systems, accelerating a trend that we have been observing for the better part of a decade. The site referrals reflect this trend, with more than half of referrals coming from Google Classroom, and other learning management systems making up most of the rest (Figure 17.2). Social media is a distant second category of referring sites.

With more referrals coming from educational websites and learning management systems, we can confidently conclude that students and teachers are relying more on the website than they were in the past.

The Folger Shakespeare site is aimed at audiences from secondary school to undergraduates and their teachers and professors from around the world. As the number of student and teacher visitors grows in a time of increased hybridization of education models that incorporate digital and in-person teaching, we are committed to focusing even more on developing a website that meets their wide-ranging needs. We recently learned that there is a vast disparity among university students studying Shakespeare, ranging from students entirely unfamiliar with the language and the plays to those who have a developed understanding of both (D.

Site: Folger Shakespeare (all users)	906,369 % of Total: 11.67% (7,765,856)
1. classroom.google.com	**496,439** (54.77%)
2. course.apexlearning.com	**48,270** (5.33%)
3. s.brightspace.com	**9,803** (1.08%)
4. l.facebook.com	**6,321** (0.70%)
5. app.schoology.com	**5,662** (0.62%)
6. applications.itslearning.com	**5,273** (0.58%)
7. m.facebook.com	**5,273** (0.58%)
8. cn.bing.com	**4,411** (0.49%)
9. app.peardeck.com	**4,394** (0.48%)
10. docs.google.com	**4,141** (0.46%)
11. broadwayworld.com	**4,073** (0.45%)
12. schoology.dasd.org	**3,989** (0.44%)
13. mystudentdashboard.com	**3,701** (0.41%)

Figure 17.2 Online learning and educational websites that refer visitors to the Folger Shakespeare website

H., personal interview, November 13, 2020; A.W., personal interview, November 19, 2020). We discovered these differences through contextual interviews with five teachers, students, and scholars who have some previous knowledge of the Folger Shakespeare Library and the Folger Editions. We asked them to review the Folger Shakespeare website and two similar websites, one that was familiar to (and chosen by) them, and one that we selected. Each website has an online reading experience for Shakespeare's works. One of the undergraduate students we interviewed had much more experience with Shakespeare than another, which became more important than we expected.

Before our research, we might have focused only on developing features for students with prior Shakespeare experience under the assumption that they represent the "average" undergraduate student, an assumption based on our own interactions with a small segment of our users and on the knowledge that the Folger works with secondary school teachers around the United States to help them develop Shakespeare-related curricula. However, since even supposedly similar users (that is, undergraduate students) have very different levels of previous knowledge or familiarity with Shakespeare's works, we need to support a wider range of user needs, encompassing all types of students from all backgrounds. The Folger believes that everyone should have access to Shakespeare, and no one who wants to read his works should be impeded by a lack of prior knowledge or understanding. Without talking to these users, we would have undercut this belief by designing the website to meet the needs of only a segment of our users.

In addition to providing an intuitive navigation and reading experience that works for all experience levels, we have tried to make the site more than a reproduction of the printed editions. As Murray argues, the digital medium offers more than just a translation of content from an old medium into the container of the new:

> There is always a temptation to use the digital medium as a means of duplicating the appearance and behaviors of legacy media. We can make an excellent facsimile of the book in digital form, and in some circumstances, it can be helpful to do so. But it is a poor use of the affordances of the digital medium to create an artifact that must be paged through, and in which footnotes remain cryptic abbreviations, displayed separately from the items they are commenting on.
>
> *(43)*

Although it incorporates the pagination and lineation from the printed versions of the texts, we have avoided limiting the website to a strict facsimile of the printed editions in the site by adding multimedia annotations and downloadable versions of the texts for reuse, which engage users in different ways depending on their needs. More people around the world have access to these free, online versions than have access to the printed editions. For some of these users, more video and audio clips of performances would be welcome – and the online digital environment can support those types of multimedia annotations in ways that the printed editions cannot.

To that end, we are renovating a type of content that is present in the printed editions as "famous lines and phrases" (Murray 26). We call them Quotes now, after evaluating them and determining that "famous" implies an undesirable subjective value judgment. These "famous lines and phrases" are in the very back of the books, physically separated from the context from which they have been drawn. On the website, we have been able to re-locate them so that they are situated *within* their context. Audio recordings of these quotes as performed by actors are linked directly to the lines in the play interface, so that readers can experience them as they read the quoted passage.

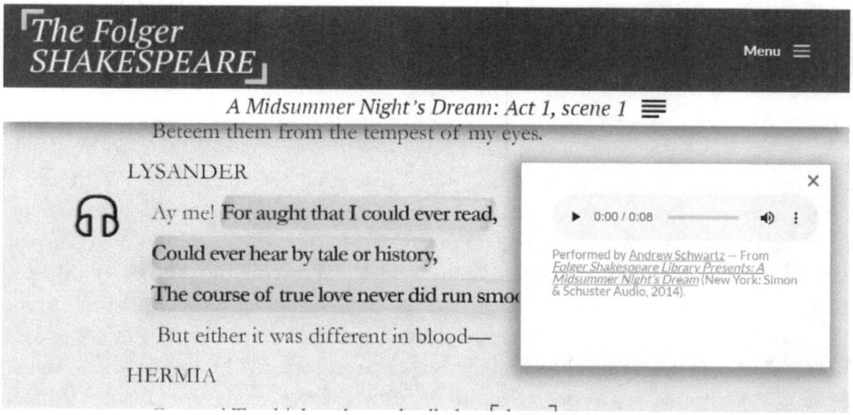

Figure 17.3 A quote from *A Midsummer Night's Dream*, highlighted in the scene text with a pop-up window of an audio recording that plays a Folger Theatre actor's performance of the passage

The lines where the quote is spoken in the play have been visually highlighted and have been identified further with an icon to the left of the text. These highlighting and framing features indicate to users that there is contextual content available. When selected by a user, the web page opens a small pop-up window with an audio player (Figure 17.3). When "play" is selected on the audio player annotation, the user will hear the line performed by actors hired by the Folger. Eventually, we will be able to augment these Quote annotations with video recordings as well. By virtue of their proximity to the play itself, more users will see and hear how these lines have been performed. This will help students and enthusiasts who are new to Shakespeare engage with the texts. Readers will also be able to use different senses to understand the cadence and language of the plays.

For those users who are interested in browsing popular or well-known quotes without reading the entire works (an activity that aligns better with the functionality of the list at the

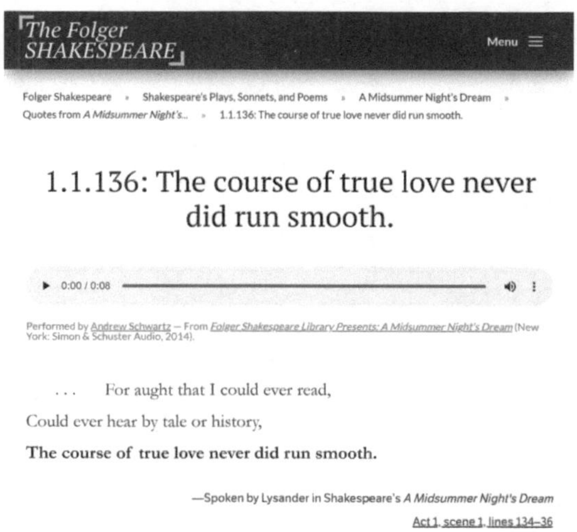

Figure 17.4 An example of a Quotes page for line 1.1.136 in *A Midsummer Night's Dream* with an audio player of an actor's performance of the passage and a textual representation of the passage

back of the printed book), we have added individual web pages to the site that can be browsed separately from the plays and poems from which they were chosen (Figure 17.4). By calling out passages which are likely to be searched by users, we assume that they will also appear in search engine results frequently, making them more findable than ever.

No longer are these popular quotes from Shakespeare's works relegated to the back of the book and separated from the surrounding lines that give them context. With the Quotes feature, the website offers a more comprehensive, contextual, and unified experience than the printed books, and it uses the affordances offered by the digital medium to do so.

As part of its content, the website also provides downloadable copies of Shakespeare's works that can be re-used by theater professionals to annotate the texts for performance and by teachers and students to conduct group annotation exercises by sharing a downloadable and editable Word or text file (The Folger Shakespeare, May 11, 2020b). The Folger team created these versions in response to requests from theater professionals and teachers who wished to take advantage of the flexibility and reusability of digital media for their work. Analysis of website usage metrics and feedback presented to us by user research participants

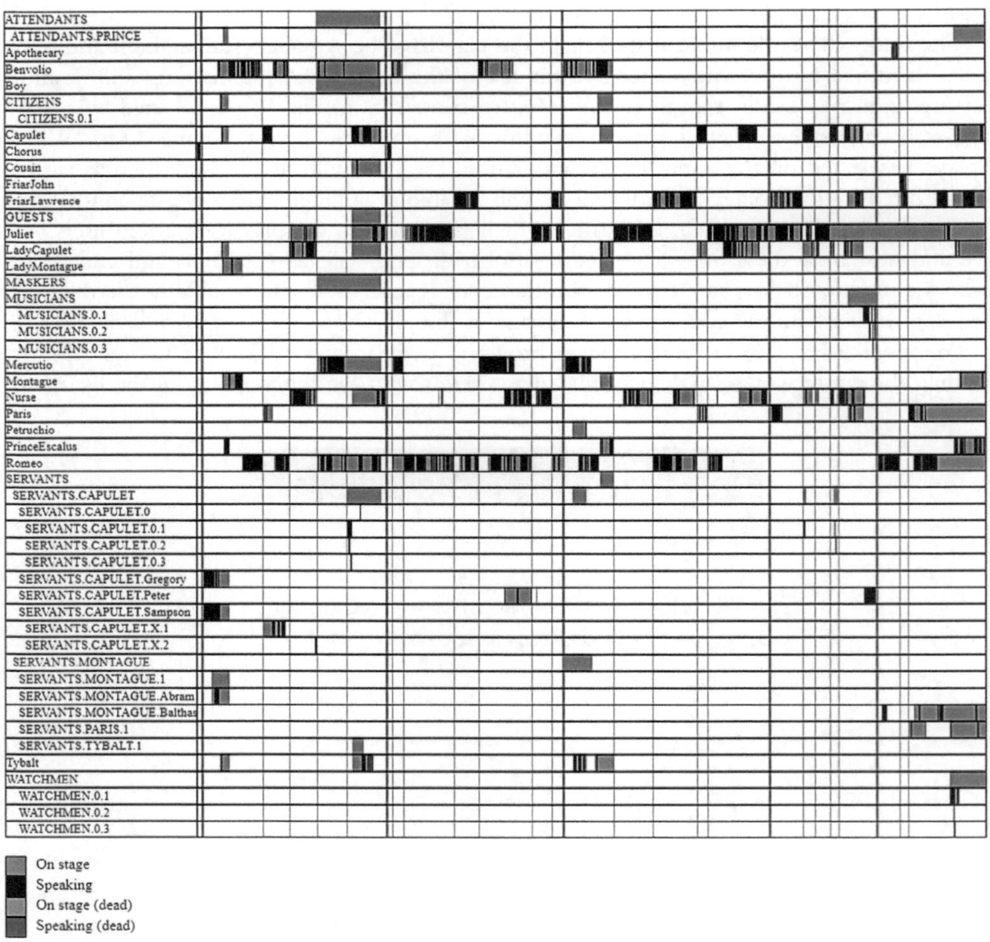

Figure 17.5 A character chart for *Romeo and Juliet* that shows who's on stage when, and whether they're speaking, either while alive or dead

has confirmed that these downloads are a valuable addition to the website. They have also shown us that a surprising amount of the traffic to Folger Shakespeare is from users downloading complete copies of the play texts – 3.2 million times in 12 months.

The contextual interviews that we conducted to understand users' online reading habits revealed that individual members of our target audience groups prefer to read the play in print format or on a document that they can mark up. In sum, the combination of results from these two research techniques led us to conclude that the PDF downloads are not an aberration in the analytics and that, for many users, PDF downloads are more important than providing the texts as web pages.

Finally, a small segment of the website is entirely focused on activities that require digital technology to perform: the Folger Shakespeare API suite (The Folger Shakespeare, September 1, 2021). In this instance, the API, or Application Programming Interface,[4] enables features such as concordances and character charts, among others. With the concordance feature, users can view every word spoken in a play, and with the character charts, users can identify which characters are on stage and/or speaking, even if they're dead (as ghosts) (Figure 17.5).

Much of the Folger Shakespeare site facilitates the most common activity (across media) related to the play texts: reading them. The ability to create links and contextual content across the site, such as audio recording annotations, downloadable files, and API features that support data mining makes the experience of reading the texts more flexible and usable for a wider audience than the printed books could manage. We could not have developed these features in ways that support user behaviors and needs without conducting user research and identifying analytical trends. DX offers many opportunities for Shakespeare interfaces to meet known and unknown needs. By centering the user in the design and development process, and by creating interfaces for specific spaces and audiences, designers can ensure that their interfaces succeed for their users. The Folger Shakespeare site will perpetually reflect this ethos of continuous improvement.

Notes

1 Other examples of Shakespeare's works in digital interfaces include, but are not limited to: Shakespeare.mit.edu, https://www.sparknotes.com/nofear/shakespeare/, https://www.opensourceshakespeare.org/, https://myshakespeare.com/, and https://shakespeareswords.com/.

2 For more on the Agile methodology, see https://www.agilealliance.org/agile101/.

3 Google's share of the global search engine market can be measured in different ways, but it is likely around 88 percent: https://www.statista.com/statistics/216573/worldwide-market-share-of-search-engines/.

4 An Application Programming Interface (API) sits between one software application and another, "allow [ing] services and products to communicate with each other and leverage each other's data and functionality through a documented interface." Typically, an API provides simplified mediation between the programs, so if application A wants to use application B, it can use the easily-understood methods provided the API. This is preferable to directly connecting A to B, which is typically more difficult and time-consuming. See https://www.ibm.com/cloud/learn/api

References

Black, Adam. "The Future Interface of the Automobile." *Medium, Design + Sketch*, 12 June 2016, Available at: medium.com/sketch-app-sources/the-future-interface-of-the-automobile-ef8a0f07e895.

Borsuk, Amaranth. "The Book as Interface." *The Book*, MIT Press, 2018. doi:10.7551/mitpress/10631.003.0007.

Darnton, Robert. "What Is the History of Books?" *Daedalus*, vol. 111, no. 3, 1982, pp. 65–83.

Fessenden, Therese. "Assumptions: How to Track Them in the UX Design Process." Video. Available at: https://www.nngroup.com/videos/tracking-assumptions/.

Google Search Central. "How Google Search Works (for Beginners)," July 21, 2017. Available at: developers.google.com/search/docs/beginner/how-search-works?hl=en%2F.

Google Search Central. "Search Engine Optimization (SEO) Starter Guide," August 10, 2021. Available at: developers.google.com/search/docs/beginner/seo-starter-guide.

Greg, W.W. *Dramatic Documents from the Elizabethan Playhouses; Stage PLOTS: ACTORS' Parts: Prompt Books*. Clarendon Press, 1931.

Howsam, Leslie. *Old Books and New Histories: An Orientation to Studies in Book and Print Culture*. U of Toronto P, 2006.

Krug, Steve. *Don't Make Me Think: A Common Sense Approach to Web Usability*. 2nd edition, New Riders, 2006.

Merriam-Webster."Interface." Available at: www.merriam-webster.com/dictionary/interface.

Mirti, Stefano, and Walter Aprile. "Building as Interface: Or, What Architects Can Learn from Interaction Designers." *Architectural Design*, vol. 75, no. 1, 2005, pp. 30–37. doi:10.1002/ad.10.

Murray, Janet H. *Inventing the Medium: Principles of Interaction Design as a Cultural Practice*. MIT Press, 2012.

Nielsen, Jakob. "10 Usability Heuristics for User Interface Design." Nielsen Norman Group. November 15, 2020. Available at: www.nngroup.com/articles/ten-usability-heuristics/.

Norman, Don, and Jakob Nielsen. "The Definition of User Experience (UX)." Nielsen Norman Group. Available at: www.nngroup.com/articles/definition-user-experience/.

OED Online. "Interface, n." Available at: www.oed.com/view/Entry/97747.

Rosenfeld, Louis, and Peter Morville. *Information Architecture for the World Wide Web*. 2nd edition, O'Reilly and Associates, 2002.

The Folger Shakespeare. Website. Folger Shakespeare Library, April 14, 2020. Available at: shakespeare.folger.edu/.

The Folger Shakespeare. "Download Shakespeare's Plays, Sonnets, and Poems." Folger Shakespeare Library, May 11, 2020. Available at: shakespeare.folger.edu/download.

The Folger Shakespeare. "The Folger Shakespeare API ." Folger Shakespeare Library, September 1, 2021. Available at: shakespeare.folger.edu/the-folger-shakespeare-api.

PART VI

Staging the interface

18

ACCESS POINTS

Stage, Space, and/as Interface in the Early Modern Playhouses

Laurie Johnson

The question with which I am concerned in this chapter relates to how audiences of the early modern playhouses *accessed* the plays of Shakespeare and his contemporaries. My choice of verb is deliberate, since it is meaningful within the computational discourse that shapes our contemporary understandings of interface as well as in the parlance of early playhouses—as when, for example, Stephen Gosson bewailed in *The Schoole of Abuse* (1579), "How many times hath accesse to Theaters beene restrained, and how boldly againe haue we re-entred?" (39). There is a potential risk in using interface theory to describe audience perception in the early modern playhouses—or, for that matter, any form of perception and in any context—as reference to an interface may convey the idea, promoted in communications studies, that computer-*mediated* communication (CMC) and face-to-face (F2F) communication are opposites. Where F2F is viewed in these terms as an unmediated presentation of one face to another, CMC is viewed by definition as a form of communication in which the interlocutors are not present before each other; instead, they communicate through the *medium* of the computer and the interface it presents. The risk is thus that the stage and the players performing upon it become flattened out by analogy with the computer screen as the proxy for a point of contact between interlocutors, one of whom is absent. The notion of access serves as a helpful reminder that even in computing, interface was initially used not to refer simply to a screen that separates interlocutors but to a point of contact through which complex systems interact or, better, act in unison. My aim here is to show that interface theory can indeed be used to explain important aspects of the experience of audiences in early modern playhouses beyond mere reception of the play, recognizing that the playhouses were themselves environments within which complex systems, including the audiences themselves, interacted.

To begin, I will consider two influential examples of using interface to describe the work of Shakespeare in a manner that, perhaps inadvertently, collapses the theatrical environment to a single surface analogous to the graphical user interface (GUI) in computing. With *Interfaces of the Word*, Walter Ong attempted in 1977 to demonstrate that the history of literacy was shaped by technological change in the dominant medium used to convey information—from clay tablets to papyrus, then parchment to paper, and from oral literacy to print culture, Ong argued that changes in the medium resulted in changes to the ways humans process words and then retain and order knowledge. Needless to say, Ong's historically-inflected

DOI: 10.4324/9780367821722-25

brand of technological determinism found favour with proponents of the new Media Studies that had emerged in the 1970s in the wake of debates over Marshall McLuhan's *Understanding Media* (1964) and its mantra that the medium is the message. Here was an argument, backed up by history, that the medium is more than the message; the medium provides the structure of thought itself. Yet Ong's history of change in communications technologies relied heavily on mistaking the transition to dominance of one technology for the absence of any other. While he argued that screen and then digital technologies had changed the way people process information in the twentieth century, he did not countenance the possibility that old technologies retain some place in the world, even as new technologies become dominant. His description of the television as an instrument that "takes a real presence from the place where it is real and present and represents it in other localities where it is neither real nor truly present" (315), for example, is valid but the complete transformation of the "human psyche" (316) that he associates with this mode of representation suggests total saturation of human communication by the television.

Even scholars of Television Studies recognize that television's presence in the home has an impact on people's lives but is by no means ubiquitous: "Because of television's primary (though certainly not exclusive) place within the home, reception studies have attempted to situate television viewing within the rhythms and routines of everyday domestic life" (Allen and Hill 457). The same is true of the home computing revolution, a thought not lost on me as I type this into my desktop computer while surrounded by piles of books and with occasional interruptions from my daughter to talk about her current obsession with musical theater—the presence of oral and print cultures are still strong in this household, for one. The same is also true of Shakespeare's age, which, for Ong, is typified by the Renaissance shift from orality to literacy as a result of the emphasis on visual culture and printed text, a shift "from the world of sound to the surface of the page, from the aural to the visual" (163). Shakespeare's sonnets represent the peak of this transition, according to Ong, because "his text consists so much of quotations—not grossly appropriated, but nuanced, woven into the texture of his work more tightly than is normally possible in any performance, no matter how sophisticated, in the oral tradition" (183). Yet, for Ong, Shakespeare's plays belong to that earlier oral tradition, which he characterizes as separating art (the fictional speech act or performance) from real life. Even a play that pushes at the limits of this tradition, like *Hamlet*, reinforces it: the *Murder of Gonzago* blurs the line between fiction and reality at Elsinore but Ong maintains that "the interface between the play-within-the-play and the encompassing play" is kept intact *within the play* (314). Here, the interface is the point of contact between two levels within what Ong considers a "closed system," which he then contrasts to the openness of the television in its capacity to bring the outside world inside our homes.

Robert Weimann countered Ong's bias toward print culture and the focus on plays as closed systems in *Author's Pen and Actor's Voice: Playing and Writing in Shakespeare's Theatre* (2000), by considering that the play is an interface between two other systems: "to explore the interface between pen and voice in terms of a more inclusive circulation of authority in Shakespeare's theater can help us … to qualify the sovereignty of the text of representation" (103). For Weimann, the play in performance consists of words that are both written and oral, thereby enabling two creative instruments (author's pen, actor's voice) to work together. The literary qualities of the author's work were based on "standards of Renaissance rhetoric and poetics," which Ong would concede were grounded in the oral tradition, and these qualities were not lost when the words were conveyed through the voices of the actors whose skillsets emerged instead across "a continuously viable tradition of common playing, jesting, and display" (79). The result is not some contested space in which these two traditions clashed for supremacy and with one emerging as the dominant medium; rather, "this disparity could be turned to good account in a hybrid practice of staging that, for its reference and function, encompassed both" of these traditions (Ong 79). Weimann's work has been instrumental in helping scholars of early modern drama to shift their focus from words on a page to words on a stage and, in the process, reverse the biases with which literary scholars have long maintained the view expressed by Samuel Taylor Coleridge in 1811 that the works of Shakespeare should be driven from the stage, "to find his proper place in the heart and in the closet" (563).

Yet even as Weimann overturns the print bias evident in both Ong's teleology and centuries of literary scholarship, the interface he depicts is the point of contact between player and playwright, which means that his version of an interface in the Shakespearean theater leaves the audience out of the equation. Represented in terms of the standard communications model of sender-message [via medium]-receiver, both Ong and Weimann situate their interface on the sender side, with the point of contention revolving around whether the sender is the playwright or the player. The answer each proposes then tells us something about the nature of the medium but not in a way that presents this medium as an interface with the audience. Ong's technological determinism reduces the audience to a receptor, but Weimann is more aware that the audience is a participant in the theatrical performance and yet he tends to reduce their presence to a feedback mechanism—of 15 uses of "audience" in *Author's Pen and Actor's Voice*, nine refer to their "scorne and laughter" (John Stephens, *Essays*, 1615, cited on 135), "response" (180, 234), "applause" (225, 242), or some other term for "reaction" to the play (203). The remaining six examples consist of Weimann invoking the social mobility of early modern Londoners as a pretext for their theatrical tastes, and this in turn acts as a point of reference for a key feature of early modern plays: metatheatricality. A "desire in the audience for upward mobility" (62) becomes, for Weimann, the touchstone for playwrights and players to shift the presentation of character from *locus* (characters located in fictional space, unaware of their fictional status) to *platea* (characters seemingly able to step in and out of the fiction, direct address to audience, and other metatheatrical devices). The early modern audience might perhaps thus be better understood in Weimann's model as the intended receiver (a concept used in communications models to refer to the person or group a sender had in mind when composing a message) rather than the present recipient (the persons actually in the room during the performance) of a play. To clarify the distinction, an intended receiver is a figure in the imagination of the sender, but my aim is to account for the physical presence of an audience in the space of a performance.

One of the successes of Weimann's model is the recognition that a play consists of more than a single apparatus. The interface between playwright and player is not reducible to either the page or the stage, book versus performance, but comprises interaction between both forms of expression. Yet in such a model the audience remains somehow *out there* beyond the stage as an amorphous set of ears and eyes toward which the play presents itself and whose feedback it anticipates. To extend Weimann's model gainfully, I propose that it is necessary to include at least one more apparatus: the playhouse. In doing so, I seek to make the same modification to models like Weimann's as I have argued elsewhere for CMC studies: a phenomenology of computer use requires an examination of how users gain access to the communications technologies that computers make available and this includes peripherals (keyboard, mouse, monitor) used to operate the computer (see Johnson, "Face-Interface"; "Spectral"). The idea is that while the user-interface on the screen interpellates me as a "user" without requiring me to know how to program the computer to perform its various functions, I must gain access to this interface in the first place by using each apparatus in the manner for which it is designed:

> The hand guides the mouse, caresses the touchpad, thumps the keyboard, but the engagement extends beyond digits and thumbs to cover the whole of my body in that I am situated vis-à-vis a chair, a bench, my lap, and most importantly, a screen. All of these technologies to which I make my body fit have evolved through various, not always altogether interconnected, pathways.
>
> *(Johnson, "Face-Interface," 51)*

While so much of the early focus of CMC studies was on the "user-interface" as the window into the soul of computer use, it seemed to me that a cultural material history was needed to give the fullest possible sense of the presence of the user and of the technology itself. Here, I want to make the same case for our understanding of the presence of audiences at plays in the early modern period: in attempting to apprehend the ways in which audiences took in plays, it is necessary to also comprehend how the play (vis-à-vis the playhouse) took in an audience.

The same modification should be applied to any model that uses the user-interface as a basis for an analogy with a process that is not directly related to computer use. Donald Hoffman's Multimodal User Interface (MUI) theory has, for example, been highly influential in studies of cognition and perception in the last decade, as it pivots the idea that our perceptions shape consciousness by arguing instead that our sensory perceptions constitute the MUI "between the perceiver and an objective world, an interface useful precisely because it does not match, approximate, or resemble that world" (95). Hoffman's analogy works because he aligns the functions of sensory perception with the operations of the user-interface, where access to and use of information stored in the computer's circuitry are undertaken through the manipulation of a graphical display involving icons, folders, a cursor, and so on (96–97). The icons seem to us like the objective reality because we manipulate them, out there, on the screen, but these icons "drastically simplify what they represent, and do so in formats designed for ease of use, not for insight into the true natures of what they represent" (97). Sensory perceptions do the same thing, enabling ease of use of the world around us rather than providing insight into the objective nature of that world and the objects in it. The issue with Hoffman's analogy is of course that *access* is viewed as the use of the GUI (aligned here with perception) to perform the unseen functions of the computer (aligned with objective reality), whereas computer use involves a physical process of fitting the body to each apparatus required to gain access to the GUI in the first place. The MUI model of perception need not be rejected on grounds such as these; the model may, however, require adjustment to account for an extension of the analogy to include the role of the body in gaining access to the interface and to sensory perceptions themselves.

It is with the same modifications that interface theory can be applied to the question of how early modern audiences gained access to plays. Some of this work has already begun under the guises of studies in distributed cognition and historical phenomenology. The former has been most consistently developed by Evelyn Tribble over more than a decade (see Tribble's *Cognition in the Globe* (2011) and *Early Modern Actors in Shakespeare's Theatre* (Tribble, 2017) for two of the most prominent examples of this work). This approach builds on the model developed by Edwin Hutchins, whose *Cognition in the Wild* (1995) used anthropological methods to tackle conundrums in cognitive science, focusing on issues of how teams can achieve complex tasks when none of the members of the team may be fully cognisant of the entire range of actions required to achieve a successful outcome. In this book and in subsequent studies, Hutchins examined cognitive processes in numerous examples, from air traffic control towers to naval vessels and many more, to develop a model of cognition in which the use of specific objects within a shared system of operations is a feature of shared cognitive processes in any instance of grouped performance: "All divisions of labor, whether the labor is physical or cognitive in nature, require distributed cognition in order to coordinate the activities of the participants" (176). As the model was developed to explain cognition in work teams, it was adopted by Tribble to examine the practices through which early modern playing companies could have collectively managed the intense cognitive load of repertory playing (a different play each day) using cue scripts, doubling, and other original staging methods. Yet Tribble does not confine her attention only to the players, and her model is extended—appropriately, for an approach that is consonant with "extended mind" theory—to account for how players and the cognitive artefacts of playing cater to the attention and memory capacity of the audience.

For the most part, though, Tribble's focus remains fixed on the players and their practices, and a distributed cognition model includes the audience only to the extent that a successful outcome of the players' performance involves the audience being able to follow the action. The distributed cognition model brings the instruments of performance into focus, thereby extending Weimann's interface between player and playwright to include the systems and objects used by the players but, as in Weimann's model, the audience tends to be present in the distributed cognition model only as an instrument of feedback. This need not be construed as a criticism, as both Tribble and Weimann are primarily concerned with understanding how early modern players and playwrights worked with the tools available to them. The audience has, however, been brought very much into focus by historical phenomenology, the approach developed by Bruce Smith to employ material cultural histories of objects and spaces used in early modern theater as a way to frame thought experiments designed to reveal something of what the experience of playgoing was like for early modern audiences by examining sensory perception (rather than merely reception) of a play. The method has most extensively been used to examine sound in the playhouses, as in Smith's *The Acoustic World of Early Modern England* (1999), although it is worth noting that such studies inevitably drift toward giving most consideration to the *production* of sound. Both the prominence given to sound in these studies and the focus on sound production are perhaps understandable since the plays of the period arguably provide more direct evidence of sound than of any other sensory stimulus, in the form of music, sound effects, and of course the actor's voice. Smith does, however, also describe the acoustics of different performance venues, with the polygonal wooden structure of the 1599 Globe, for example, creating "what acoustical science calls 'standing waves'—stationary patterns of vibration formed by many reflective surfaces, all superimposed on one another" (209). He then explains that listeners within such a space "experience these steady waves of energy as full, present sound, uniform throughout the listening space," an effect that is also "enhanced even by the energy the wood and plaster do happen to absorb" (209), since absorption presumably reduces the amount of echo from these waves of sound being reflected back again off opposite sides of the same building.

Knowing the differences in acoustics between venues can inform a greater understanding of how plays and performance practices were designed to make best use of these sonic effects, as, for example, in Sarah Dustagheer's *Shakespeare's Two Playhouses: Repertory and Theatre Space at the Globe and the Blackfriars, 1599–1613* (2017), which includes nuanced insights into how Shakespeare and others adapted their plays for the two principal venues used by the Lord Chamberlain's / King's Men: *Julius Caesar* takes full advantage of the standing waves made possible at the Globe by using sounds pitched at differing volumes to simulate the movement of armies (103–105), whereas *The Tempest* uses music and dispersed sound to fill the echo chamber of the Blackfriars in parallel with the confusion signified by the destruction of the boat at the end of the first scene (120). Our understanding of the plays of the period can thus be deeply enriched by knowing more about the perceptual environment for which they were written and within which they were performed. In the example of *Julius Caesar*, in particular, Dustagheer also provides a compelling case for how the architecture of the 1599 Globe contributes to the experience of the play for the listener. If we wish to extend this approach to apprehend more fully the experience of the audience, it becomes necessary to extrapolate out from one listener to many, which includes an acknowledgment that other listeners are also other noisemakers.

In Smith's explanation of how sound reflects within a polygonal structure such as the Globe, the sound is depicted as originating on the stage and moving out in multiple directions before being reflected back to a central point (211–13). This is suggestive not of a "uniform" distribution of sound, as he explained the phenomenon of standing waves, but a concentration of sound similar to the phenomenon of the whispering dish or parabolic reflector. Structural engineers acknowledge that this principle works well for spaces in which parabolic reflection is desirable to concentrate a single noise source for a relatively small audience, but in larger spaces, "concave surfaces will lead to strong late reflections that will be heard as a disturbing echo" anywhere other than in the focal point of the reflection (Vercammen 1). Here we must add that, of course, a polygonal structure is not a true concave surface, so the sound will be a little more dispersed than the science of sound concentration might indicate. It is unlikely that the builders of the playhouses were cognisant of the science involved since the earliest study published on the subject in Europe was Josephus Blancanus's essay on the echo phenomenon, "Echometria," in *Sphaera Mundi* (1620), but the existence of much older structures with echo and resonance effects, such as whispering galleries in cathedrals or echo halls in palaces and other large buildings, indicates a much older architectural tradition of using specific structural elements to concentrate or disperse sound (Crunelle 2–4). Whether the effect was intentional or not, nevertheless, in Smith's description of the Globe, only a small section of the audience, centrally located, is likely to experience the full, present sound projected from the stage; the experience will not be shared uniformly throughout. Instead of a more encompassing picture of an "audience," then, the subject of historical phenomenology may also resemble the intended receiver that Weimann's model posits.

Interface theory may be helpful in overcoming such tendencies to focus on the play and/or the production, or actor and/or author, thereby bringing us closer to the experience of the audience, because it begins with the premise that the subject is a "user" rather than just a receiver. The ascription of agency is an important step in achieving the reversal that Hoffman set out to achieve in describing the relationship between perception and consciousness. Just as he sought to reverse the formulation that perceptions create conscious experience, so I am seeking to reverse the tendency to focus on audience reception as the precursor to accounting for audience experience in the study of early modern theater. For Hoffman, consciousness is what shapes our perceptions, because it determines the manner in which we set out to use or engage with the world. As I have noted, because this model relies on a computational analogy of the user and a desktop, it also requires the adjustment needed to account for the embodied process through which the user gains access to the desktop. It is important to remember that computers had interfaces before they had desktop screens and icons, with the term initially used by computer scientists in the 1960s to refer to both the data transfer protocols and the physical connections required to enable computers to operate with other systems and with each other. The human-computer interface was merely one of the many interfaces a computer required to operate, and was originally understood as data input and retrieval, by push button, punch card, or other means of converting human languages and number systems into a code the computer could recognize. Even the early history of the internet involved an extension of the same concept, as Donald Davies wrote in his "Proposal for a Digital Communication Network" in 1966 that a network of interconnected computers needed "nodes" (that did the data transfer and processing) and "interface units" that were computers through which data was entered and retrieved by users (10–12); in other words, the internet originated with the goal of removing the clunky human connection from machines that could collectively process data more efficiently without it.

The GUI technology on which Hoffman's analogy is based is a relative latecomer, being first developed in 1973 for the Xerox Alto and not gaining traction in the domestic market until a further decade later. In both its initial development and in its wider commercial uptake, GUI technology relied on the development of the hand-held pointing device or computer mouse: first, a pointing device was necessary to enable a user to select and operate files or programs displayed as graphical icons, but the mouse was itself slow to achieve full marketability and it was not until Apple developed the simple one-button mouse in response to marketing results that the public embraced both the mouse and the GUI display on the successful Macintosh system in the mid-1980s (Douglas and Mithal 64–5). As Sarah Douglas and Anant Kartik Mithal observe, this history "demonstrates the tight coupling that sometimes occurs between physical design decisions and operating system software" (64). Interface theory must retain some sense of this history in which desktops, icons, and windows are a late development that hinged on design decisions that were more to do with the hands and fingers of users than they were to do with the symbolism of GUI icons to which Hoffman refers. By the same token, I will seek in the remainder of this chapter to describe the experience of the playhouse audience as a product of the embodied process of *gaining access*, and of design decisions in which "the play" was not a primary factor.

I have already noted Gosson's complaint in *The Schoole of Abuse* about "accesse to Theaters" being restrained only temporarily on numerous occasions (39). Perhaps what is most striking about this complaint is that it was published in 1579, with only the Playhouse at Newington Butts (1575) and the Theatre (1576) and Curtain (1577) in Shoreditch likely to be the objects of Gosson's complaint, if by "Theaters" he meant the open air amphitheater-style venues that are commonly associated with the Elizabethan and Jacobean stage. The Red Lion was built in 1567 at Mile End, but records suggest the site ceased to be used for playing after only a short period of activity. Restraints had been placed on playing in 1577 and 1578 due to the plague in London (Wickham, Berry, and Ingram 76–7), but Gosson's rhetorical "how many times" suggests that he has more frequent instances in mind and over a longer interval. Prohibitions against playing had in fact been enacted by both the City and the crown many times before the Red Lion was built, with two such orders—on 7 April and 16 May 1559—being among Elizabeth's earliest official acts in power (Chambers 4. 262–3). Of particular interest here is an order issued by the Lord Mayor of London on 26 September 1569, linking the plague to the "resort, access, and assemblies of great multitudes of peoples … to hear & see certain stage plays" (in Berry, Wickham, and Ingram 59), and which evidently referred to playing in inns within the city walls since no major playhouse was operating at this time. As the order indicates, authorities were concerned not just with the "assemblies," as is often the focus of studies of the impact of plague on the Elizabethan theater, but also with *resort* and *access*.

Although "resort" could at the time mean the same thing as both "access" (*OED* "resort, n. 3b") and "assemblies" ("5b"), its use here in conjunction with both terms indicates that the order is distinguishing the three terms sequentially: "resort" refers to the mode or frequency of travel to a specific place, "access" refers to the manner of ingress to that place, and the "assemblies" are the gatherings of people within. Preventing access is thus a key feature of sanctioned restraint, since the movement and assembly of people cannot be totally restricted without regimes of incarceration and policing that place significant stresses on the Treasury and the system of Justices of the Peace, Knights Marshal, and Sheriffs, but boarding up the building in which a play is to be staged requires minimal resources to be effective. In the 1569 instance, the order targeted the inns, so the keepers would have recognized the threat to their main business if their establishments were shut up for the sake of preventing occasional playing. The threat to "access" was thus a way to enlist the innkeepers themselves to assist in enforcing the restraint against plays. This method would not work with the proprietors of the large playhouses in later years, as any ban on playing would result in surcease of the primary business of the playhouse. Nevertheless, the language of access in relation to playing in the years before the rise of the major playhouses reveals that authorities understood the integral relationship between the regulation of playing and the control of a significant cross-section of the population who frequented the plays.

The advent of the major playhouses can be seen, then, as the development of a new apparatus through which the audiences could focus already established access to stage playing in early modern England. This development was very likely motivated on the players' side by a desire to obtain greater control over the takings from a performance, as it was far easier to obtain a fixed payment upon entry to the playhouse as it would have been in the earlier days of booth stages, those temporary elevated stages with a concealed rear offstage space which required the players to gather an income by circulating cap in hand through the throng of gathered spectators. It is also unlikely that the players would have enjoyed the ability to charge entry to an inn when performing. Yet the significant investment required to build a major playhouse—John Brayne and James Burbage initially invested £200 in building the Theatre, and then it cost hundreds of pounds more judging by their subsequent legal battle—indicates that those who paid for the early playhouses saw money passing hands in sufficient quantities at the booth stages and inns to justify the development. Like the computer mouse, the playhouses spent nearly a decade from development of a prototype (the Red Lion in 1567) to sudden upsurge once the market determined the commercial viability of a new instrument of access.

With the emergence of the major playhouses, the experience of attending a play will have shifted for audiences. I have already noted the distinctive acoustic effects of the polygonal structures, angling to achieve concentration of sound in a manner similar to that created by parabolic surfaces. Yet I also noted that the audience itself must be factored in when making arguments about the acoustic effects of different playing environments. While the diagram Smith uses to illustrate the focusing of sound at the Globe shows the sound originating from the centre of the stage, it is worth noting that the same effect will be achieved in such a space for sound emanating from all points within the same space. Thus, any crowd noise within the Globe, in particular, would also have been focused in the centre, potentially drowning out much of the sound from the elevated stage, but then this may well have been the point, and possibly explains why the optimal acoustic effect was centrally focused, since this is also where those who paid the least for entry crowded together during the performance. The patrons who shelled out more to gain access to the tiered galleries would have enjoyed much clearer sound from the stage over the heads of the rabble in the yard. Audiences crowded in front of the booth stage in earlier times undoubtedly found that nearer and central to the stage was optimal, but this was not to reduce noise from the crowd. Instead, with the booth stages usually being set up in street stalls or marketplaces, the players also faced competition from the noise of the township or city. As Maarten Walraven has argued, the history of the sound of a cultural practice is also defined by the residual noise of the neighbourhood, including the surrounding buildings, industries, and daily sounds through which the local population found a sense of community. With the early booth stages, then, those audience members nearest to the elevated stage not only enjoyed the performers' sounds most directly, but they were also able to put the rest of the crowd between themselves and the surrounding aural environment. By moving the audience experience into enclosed spaces, to halls, taverns, inns, and eventually amphitheater-style playhouses, this ability to block out surrounding noise was enhanced, albeit by creating the buffer in part by capturing the audience's own collective noise within an echo chamber.

The emphasis here has been on the audience experience as an aural one, but this is to some extent an artefact of the predominance of sound in studies of playhouse audiences during the period that the specifications for the Globe reconstruction were being worked out. As Gabriel Egan has observed, key scholars involved in the reconstruction described the early modern audience member as a listener, so Smith's focus on sound was understandable in this context, but Egan's search of the Literature Online (LION) corpus for references to "hearing" versus "seeing" a play revealed that the latter was far more prevalent (327–8). Notwithstanding the fact that the 1569 order refers to the multitudes of people going to "hear & see certain stage plays," it may be that line of sight was far more important to both audiences and playhouse designers than quality of sound. The evolution of the playhouse from the earlier booth and hall stages may have thus been inspired by the structure of the inns, with an open central yard surrounded by galleries used for entry to the rooms on the second and third floors. When the players erected their temporary stage within the yard, audiences would have quickly learned of the improved view afforded from these galleries, an argument that Joseph Quincy Adams proffered more than a century ago (1). From the perspective of the audience's experience, if sight was indeed the dominant sense perception, it is worth adding here that the addition of raked galleries in the evolution of the playhouses created clearer lines of sight for more of the audience members to see the performers on stage but also to see the rest of the audience. One of the great innovations of the amphitheater-style playhouses may simply be this capacity for the spectators to identify as such in a truly collective sense: to see *and to be seen*. Tiffany Stern makes this same point in her contribution to *Shakespeare's Theatres and the Effects of Performance*, but her attention turns to the stage: "Watching and being watched … were activities heralded by the space [the Theatre]—and the other round theatres that imitated it. Plays always had to fit around, utilise or add to what the stage was, visually, offering" (11–12). With the raked galleries and multiple tiers, the playhouses also invited the audience to fit around or add to what the whole internal space of the building offered.

By reminding ourselves that playing spaces are also audience spaces, we may thus begin to develop a clearer sense of what is experienced by the playgoer in the process of *being* a playgoer. Access involves a conscious act of fitting one's body to the space of the venue, but in the process the individual audience member will also become a participant in a collective act. When Antimo Galli wrote to Andrea Cioli to describe the Venetian ambassador's stupidity at the Curtain *circa* 1613 to 1614, he may have misunderstood Antonio Foscarini's actions as a playgoer:

> what made it worse, so as not to have to pay sixpence … [he chose not to] go to one of the boxes and not even to be seated in one of the degrees they have there but preferred to stand below in the middle, among the rabble of porters and carters, pretending that he needed to stay close by because he was hard of hearing, as if he really understood what was being recited.
>
> *(cited in Berry, Wickham, and Ingram 415; but for the date, see Orrell 13)*

What may have passed as an excuse for penny-pinching in the eyes of Cioli's agent should perhaps be better understood as a visitor's eagerness to embrace being part of an audience, knowing that he would be seen even, or perhaps especially, among the gathered throng. Foscarini's mistake was to join in with the crowd in shouting out the name of the play they wanted to see performed the next day, which he did in his native Italian, "frati, frati" ("Friars, Friars"—this was possibly a revival of Robert Greene's *Friar Bacon and Friar Bungay*), but the audience, thinking him to be speaking Spanish, "began to whistle in such a way that I cannot imagine that he would ever want to return to that place" (415–16). Undaunted, it seems, Foscarini did not give up attending at other playhouses, "almost always with a single servant" (416).

What the Foscarini episode reveals, I think, is something of the attraction of being part of the multitude and responding *en masse* according to specific cultural or communal norms. Just as he sought to join in their chorus of appeal to the performers, the crowd's reaction of whistling together at the outsider strikes me as a particularly theatrical response, as if he was simply a performer whose play they cared not to see again. There is no suggestion in Galli's account that the crowd sought to forcibly remove Foscarini and his servant. Instead, both Foscarini and the other members of the audience reinforced their collective identity in that moment as an audience. Thinking of this episode through embodied interface theory, we may apprehend what is at stake in gaining access to the play. By entering into the playhouse, each attendee is interpellated as "audience," and participates in a form of extended proprioception: awareness of being inside the space of the playhouse, but *with others*, filling out the space as one. In that sense, the audience does indeed become part of the apparatus of the playhouse, but inasmuch as the audience also contributes to the experience of the play and not just to its reception. The experience does not wait for the first flourish to announce the arrival of a performer on stage. Instead, the experience of the audience begins at entry, with the first sense of the space into which the playgoer has entered, the first hint of the hubbub of others' voices or shuffling of feet, the first sight of others finding a place above or below, a spark of recognition here and there—a neighbour, a familiar face from a prior play, or some such—and other sensations not yet touched upon here. Space prevents more detailed expansion along these lines, but I shall close with a brief mention of the impact of the olfactory environment to a sense of audience cohesion.

Holly Dugan describes the smell of the Hope Theatre as dominated by the stench of the nearby animal yards and markets in Smithfield, a reminder that the intrusion of the neighbourhood into a playhouse is not restricted to the aural environment as Walraven describes it. As Dugan points out, the double premiere of Ben Jonson's *Bartholomew Fair* at the Hope and also the cockpit at Whitehall "demonstrates not only how smells of urban life defined London but also how certain ones came to signify urban space in distinct ways, transcending clear-cut class differences between high and low entertainment venues" (208). Within the playhouses, there were specific practices for generating olfactory sensations, such as the sulphurous squibs that Jonathan Gil Harris describes in his landmark essay, "The Smell of *Macbeth*," and these will have contributed to the audience's sense that the playhouse environment was set apart from the olfactory world to which they were accustomed in their daily lives. Yet Dugan's work on the Hope may serve as a reminder that the smell of *Macbeth* was also partially the smell of the Globe. It was, after all, in February 1606 that Richard Burbage and John Heminges were ordered by the Surrey and Kent Commission for Sewers first to remove all of the props and posts under the bridge leading to the Globe on the northern side of Maid Lane, and, second, to board and fill up eight poles of the wharf there (SKCS 14 February 1605/6, ff. 434v–435r) and the order was reissued on 25 April (f. 438v), indicating that the adjacent sewer was blocked for some time and causing "filthie ayre" (*Macbeth* 1.1.13) indeed.

These final examples demonstrate what I think is the value of thinking about the playhouses using the analogy of the interface. While much of our way of thinking about early modern playing and playwriting continues to be shaped, however loosely, by communications models, the interface will remain a useful analogy for the playhouses because it will prevent us from sliding too easily back into a language that reduces audiences to being the passive end of a unidirectional reception model. Interface theory begins by positing the subject as a user and, as I have argued, the agency and presence that this notion should convey are only undermined when what counts as the interface is limited to the layout of graphical objects on a screen. It should always be incumbent upon us, in attempting to understand the experience of the user of any apparatus, to include an account of the body of the user and the physical environment to which this body must be fitted in order to access the interface. An embodied version of interface theory takes into account the full array of sensory stimuli that audience members experience in fitting their bodies to the playhouse environment, but in keeping with the key tenets of interface theory it acknowledges that these perceptions constitute the world rather than merely receive input from the world. The notion of "access" can help us to focus on the agency of the audience, whose collective consciousness of being an audience can shape how the sensory environment is perceived or can at least work in concert with the fictional world represented in the play (like the symbolic world of desktop icons) to refashion what smells, sounds, and other stimuli from outside the playhouse can represent within the playhouse.

References

Adams, Joseph Quincy. *Shakespearean Playhouses: A History of English Theatres from the Beginning to the Restoration*. Houghton Mifflin, 1917.

Allen, Robert C., and Annette Hill, editors. *The Television Studies Reader*. Routledge, 2004.

Chambers, Edmund Kerchever. *The Elizabethan Stage*. 4 vols. Clarendon Press, 1923.

Coleridge, Samuel Taylor. *Lectures 1808–1819: On Literature*. *Collected Works*, vol. 5. 16 vols. Edited by R. A. Foakes, Routledge & Kegan Paul, 1969.

Crunelle, Marc. "Is There an Acoustical Tradition in Western Architecture?" Translated by Andrew Vennet Tallon. The Tuning of the World, conference proceedings, Banff, 1993.

Davies, Donald W. "Proposal for a Digital Communication Network." National Physical Laboratory, UK, June, 1966.

Douglas, Sarah E., and Anant Kartik Mithal. *The Ergonomics of Computer Pointing Devices*. Springer-Verlag, 1997.

Dugan, Holly. "'As Dirty as Smithfield and as Stinking Every Whit': The Smell of the Hope Theatre." *Shakespeare's Theatres and the Effects of Performance*. Edited by Farah Karim-Cooper and Tiffany Stern, Bloomsbury, 2016, pp. 195–213.

Dustagheer, Sarah. *Shakespeare's Two Playhouses: Repertory and Theatre Space at the Globe and the Blackfriars, 1599–1613*. Cambridge UP, 2017.

Egan, Gabriel. "Hearing or Seeing a Play: Evidence of Early Modern Terminology." *Ben Jonson Journal*, vol. 8, 2001, pp. 327–347.

Gosson, Stephen. *The Schoole of Abuse*. English Reprints. Edited by Edward Arber, London, 1868.

Harris, Jonathan Gil. "The Smell of *Macbeth*." *Shakespeare Quarterly*, vol. 58, no. 4, 2007, pp. 465–486.

Hoffman, Donald D. "Sensory Experiences as Cryptic Symbols of a Multimodal User Interface." *Activitas Nervosa Superior*, vol. 52, 2010, pp. 95–104.

Hutchins, Ed. *Cognition in the Wild*. MIT Press, 1995.

Johnson, Laurie. "Face-Interface, or, the Prospect of a Virtual Ethics." *Ethical Space: The International Journal of Communication Ethics*, vol. 4, no. 1/2, 2007, pp. 49–56.

Johnson, Laurie. "Spectral Machinery (or Beyond Essence and System)." *Journal of Philosophy*, vol. 7, no. 17, 2012, pp. 40–59.

Korn, Granino Arthur. "Digital-computer Interface Design." *Simulation*, vol. 11, no. 6, 1968, pp. 285–298.

McLuhan, Marshall. *Understanding Media: The Extensions of Man*. McGraw-Hill, 1964.

Ong, Walter J. *Interfaces of the Word: Studies in the Evolution of Consciousness and Culture*. Cornell UP, 1977.

Orrell, John. "Antimo Galli's Description of *The Masque of Beauty*." *Huntington Library Quarterly*, vol. 43, no. 1, 1979, pp. 13–23.

SKCS (Surrey and Kent Commission for Sewers, 156–1606). London Metropolitan Archives. LMA: SKCS/018.

Smith, Bruce R. *The Acoustic World of Early Modern England*. Cambridge UP, 1999.

Stern, Tiffany. "'This Wide and Universal Theatre': The Theatre as Prop in Shakespeare's Metadrama." *Shakespeare's Theatres and the Effects of Performance*. Edited by Farah Karim-Cooper and Tiffany Stern, Bloomsbury, 2016, pp. 11–32.

Tribble, Evelyn. *Cognition in the Globe: Attention and Memory in Shakespeare's Theatre*. Palgrave Macmillan, 2011.

Tribble, Evelyn. *Early Modern Actors in Shakespeare's Theatre: Thinking with the Body*. Bloomsbury, 2017.

Vercammen, Martijn. "Sound Concentration Caused by Curved Surfaces." PhD thesis. Eindhoven University of Technology, 2012.

Walraven, Maarten. "History and Its Acoustic Context: Silence, Resonance, Echo, and Where to Find Them in the Archive." *Journal of Sonic Studies*, vol. 4, no. 1, 2013. http://journal.sonicstudies.org/vol04/nr01/a07.

Weimann, Robert. *Author's Pen and Actor's Voice: Playing and Writing in Shakespeare's Theatre*. Cambridge UP, 2000.

Wickham, Glynn, Ralph Berry, and William Ingram, editors. *English Professional Theatre, 1530–1660*. Cambridge UP, 2000.

19

THE HEURISTICS OF INTERFACE

Shakespeare's *Cymbeline*

Lauren Shohet

Interface and the Heuristic

The audience of Shakespeare's *Cymbeline* first meets the villain Iachimo as he articulately debates wifely fidelity with an international band of other verbally dexterous young men. The setting codes as Renaissance Italy: the characters contract a wager in "ducats" (1.4.130); they use the title "signor" (1.4.103, 1.4.174); and they broadly display "mercantile relations" (Wayne, *Cymbeline* 1.4n).[1] Among the men in the conversation is an exiled Briton named Posthumus, husband to the virtuous Innogen. Jarringly, Innogen is a princess of ancient Britain. Proposing a wager about her chastity, Iachimo resolves to persuade Posthumus that Innogen, still residing in her father King Cymbeline's court, is betraying him. To effect this, Iachimo travels to Britain and smuggles himself into Innogen's bedroom in a trunk. Having fabricated a story that the chest holds valuable "plate of rare device" (1.6.188) and requested that Innogen take it into her protection overnight, Iachimo stows himself inside. After Innogen falls asleep, Iachimo emerges from the trunk (2.2.10 s.d.). He records detailed information about Innogen's body, accessories, and private chamber; abruptly exits through a trap door; and reemerges on the stage two scenes later when, as Valerie Wayne remarks, "Iachimo's obscure language … conveys the temporal as well as national and ethical gap between this predator from the Italian Renaissance and his prey in ancient Britain" ("*Cymbeline*, Janus, and Folded Time" 250). Once back in Italy, Iachimo uses the information he has gathered to convince Posthumus that Innogen has welcomed Iachimo (and others) into her bed. Hereby, Iachimo not only wins the wager, but also transforms Posthumus from a loving husband to a bitter avenger.

The trunk in *Cymbeline* serves Iachimo as an interface. That is, it brings disparate realms into sufficient relation that action can be effected in one domain by manipulating elements in another. By means of the trunk, Iachimo undertakes adventures in Britain that change outcomes in Italy, and it lets him travel from the Renaissance to the Roman era and back again. It is also characteristic of interfaces that the trunk permits use without requiring that Iachimo (or the audience) comprehend the exact transactions between the systems it mediates. Designers describe computer-human interfaces in terms of "heuristics": the good-enough shortcuts that allow for use without full analysis. Word-processing programs offer familiar concepts like "folder" and "page" and "bookmark" that let writers set to work with only the most approximate sense of how the computer actually organizes, stores, or accesses their data.

DOI: 10.4324/9780367821722-26

Iachimo's breezy story that "some dozen Romans of us and your lord / … have mingled sums / To buy a present for the Emperor" (1.6.184–186) similarly serves his purposes of manipulating Innogen into taking the trunk into her chamber without anyone posing detailed questions about the purported gift, its aim, or its destination. Nor does the trunk's disappearance from the play after its purpose has been fulfilled cause any dramatic ripple. We need know no more than that mediation sufficient for the task at hand has occurred.

This chapter considers interfaces as liminal spaces where significantly different entities are functionally mediated: mediated, that is, to allow a user to undertake some work. Interfaces differ from relays insofar as the two entities are different in kind, and also insofar that work is unpredictable, subject to the agency of users and to potential swerves from the outcomes those users may desire or anticipate. The interface of the word processor, for example, lets us type into a machine, but does not determine what we write. The stylus on a record player produces audible sound from vinyl grooves—themselves produced through the mediations of a recording studio where sound waves are rendered as variable etchings in wax—but does not determine what the performer's intentions may have been, whether these are realized, or how the listener responds to the recording. The record player provides an interface between vinyl and the human body, and also between the place, time, and personnel of the performance and those of reception. The interface enables all of these encounters without defining any of them.

I also understand interfaces to constitutively keep their mediating operations out of the user's way. Interfaces do not demand that users ponder what happens within them. Indeed, interfaces are required precisely where deep analysis of mediating procedures would be debilitating: a writer could not effectively use word-processing software if she calculated the algorithms translating each keystroke into a letter on the screen. In the language of engineers, workable interfaces are "black boxes" that permit users to focus only on inputs and outputs, unconcerned with the technological operations that create one from the other. Philosopher of science Bruno Latour describes the necessity as well as the risks of black-boxing, which he understands to transpire in both technological and social contexts:

> When a machine runs efficiently, when a matter of fact is settled, one need focus only on its inputs and outputs and not on its internal complexity … the more science and technology succeed, the more opaque and obscure they become.
>
> *(304)*

Or, as a chestnut of user-experience designers has it, an interface is like a joke—if you have to explain it, it's not that good. Interfaces invite use, not inspection.

Although the earliest (1880s) uses of "interface" recorded in the *OED* concern the meeting of contiguous areas, proliferating *OED* examples in the 1960s and 1970s specify that the two things being interfaced are different in kind, referring to "stages where the work passes from one department to another" (n.1); describing "interfaces … from bus to train … city terminal to airport terminal, check-in counter to loading gate" (n.2); explaining that using "one of the IBM languages on an ICL machine [requires] what's called an interface to make the two different things compatible" (n.2). In the late twentieth century, "interface" becomes paradigmatically concerned with human-machine transactions, as computing develops from requiring humans to use punch cards to interact with batch computers, through command-line interfaces that accept linguistic input, to the inception of graphical user interfaces in the early 1980s. "Interface" becomes a common word and concept beyond the engineering community starting in the 1990s, as Windows and Apple operating systems are adopted by ever broader swathes of people. In 1997, Steven Johnson's *Interface Culture: How New*

Technology Changes the Way We Create and Communicate proposed interface design as the master narrative shaping entry to the digital age. "As it becomes more and more difficult to *imagine* the dataspace at our fingertips, to picture all that complexity in our mind's eye" (17), Johnson writes, "representing all that information is going to require a new visual language, as complex and meaningful as the great metropolitan narratives of the 19th-century novel" (18). Johnson identifies that requisite "new visual language" as graphical user interfaces.

As used colloquially since the 1990s, "interface" generally involves the interaction of computer and human, the mediation of digital and analogue codes. This occurs not only in the computer programs we use to write and bank and photograph, but also in the prostheses that replace missing limbs and the smart refrigerators that generate our shopping lists. As discussed elsewhere in this volume, designers of human-computer interaction frequently characterize the interface as a window (viz. Microsoft) or a door: a boundary that invites a user, conceived as a sovereign subject, to look in or to enter. Contemporary humanities-invested explorations, by contrast, tend toward more dynamic models that emphasize how users and systems reciprocally shape one another: how, in Branden Hookway's terms, the "distinct entities" of human and computer "enter into an active relation" (4).

Humanists frequently emphasize that the cognition entering into an interface is embodied. Johanna Drucker, for instance, understands interface as encounter between "the user/viewer, as a situated and embodied subject," on the one hand, and the "affordances of a graphical environment that mediates intellectual and cognitive activities" ("Humanities Approaches" 8), on the other. As the contents of this volume suggest, critics are beginning to adopt the vocabulary of "interface," initially used to describe computer-human interactions, for additional contexts where receivers encounter specific systems of mediation (print, theater, film) and theorists want to consider their impact on receivers' embodied cognition. A further step might come from broadening our understanding of "media" from the largely Anglophone tradition of Marshall McLuhan and Walter Ong, which focuses solely on systems of mediated communication, to also include the largely Northern European tradition of Walter Benjamin, Friedrich Kittler, and Sybille Krämer. This latter tradition understands media, in the words of the American media scholar John Durham Peters, as "vessels and environments, containers of possibility that anchor our existence and make what we are doing possible" (2). To this view, the conditions of embodiment (such as neural structures or sensory apparatus) are themselves mediations. For Peters, the ocean is a medium, as is a cloud, and different users enter into relationship with these media in distinctive ways, depending on how them themselves are situated. A more expansive notion of "media" would recognize interfaces at many kinds of boundaries where two distinct systems of mediation meet and act upon one another despite the irreducible gap between them.

First arising from human-computer interactions, interface theory has generated models and vocabulary that may be useful for exploring other encounters, earlier in history, that enable action at the boundaries of incommensurably mediated systems. Just as psychoanalysis and Marxism offered paradigms that could be fruitfully deployed in contexts predating the theories' articulation—and that could be skeptically tested against varying historical conditions to see what carried through, what was revealingly irrelevant, and where historical variation suggested alterations to the models themselves—interface theory is ripe for experimental use as an analytic tool. Hookway encapsulates interface theory in terms that indicate how widely applicable it might be by expounding on the centripetal pull of the prefix "inter" against the outward-facing force of "face." Hookway describes the interface as "both an interiority confined by its bounding entities and a means of accessing, confronting and projecting into an exteriority ... defined by its bounding entities at the same time that it defines them" (9). With a capacious focus that encompasses more kinds of interfaces, Alexander Galloway's *The*

Interface Effect considers interfaces "between subject and world, between surface and source, and between critique and the objects of criticism" (54).

Broadening always risks dilution, so I want here to clarify what counts as an interface for the purposes of this chapter. I have already argued that interfaces, designed to make something strange and complex usable, occupy the meeting point of two incommensurable systems; that they enable operations within one system to influence the other; and that they do not fully predict or constrain the transaction between systems (although they shape it). The incommensurability of the systems meeting in an interface differentiates it from hybrids, which directly conjoin what interfaces must bridge. The *mediated* transfer of action from one system to the other differentiates the interface from another adjacent concept, the node in a network. And, as noted above, both the ontological incommensurability of the abutting entities and the potential for the actions they sponsor to swerve—to exceed prediction or determination—differentiates the interface from the relay.

The final element I consider a *sine qua non* of the interface is the gap between the systems it bridges. Drucker calls interfaces the "space between human users and processes that happen according to complicated protocols" (*Graphesis*, 138). Where technical analysis would be interested in those "complicated protocols," students of interface think instead about what happens in that space *between* the "processes" and the user—a space that actually needs to remain unplumbed for efficient use. Like other black boxes that become "more opaque and obscure" the more they succeed (Latour 304), interface is "a productive moment of encounter embedded and obscured within the use of technology" (Hookway ix). When we spread apart our fingertips on the screen of a multitouch interface to expand the region we're exploring, designers of the interface have crafted a heuristic that lets us extrapolate from everyday experience to imagine that we're pushing apart the impulses on the inside of the screen producing the images. Actually, of course, changes in the detected capacitance of our fingertips moving across the glass connote instructions (which also could have been entered in command form) interpreted by an operating system to change the display and move visual objects further apart, *as if* responding to our fingertips. The pulses inside the computer don't know the story we are telling ourselves, and conversely we need not think about how the semiconductors are processing the input we provide. Instead, the interface offers a usable shortcut, a story that approximates reality closely enough to let us do what we need to. Johnson describes the digital-design revolution of the 1990s in terms of heuristics bridging the gap between user and computer system:

> We see almost nothing of … the great surge of information … that lurks in our microchips and our fiber-optic lines … because we have built such sturdy mediators to keep it separate from us, translators that make sense of what would otherwise be a blizzard of senselessness.
>
> *(236)*

The excitement, necessity, and risks of interfaces all inhere in the gap between interfacing systems. As a crucial tool for navigating that gap, the heuristic—the short-cut story, the good-enough plotline, the legible icon—invites exploration using tools of the literary humanities. Reciprocally, the analogous operations of the interfacial heuristic and other compressed, not-completely-denotative modes of representation—think rhetorical figures—suggest how interface theory might in turn prove useful to textual scholars. The similarity between the interfacial heuristic and figurations like the metaphor comes in the latter's requirement that language works cogently in the terms of both vehicle and tenor: that the explicit and implicit dimensions make sense on their own terms, that they are sufficiently distinct that they do not collapse into one another, and that they are sufficiently proximate that referring from one to the other provides some benefit. Similarly, in a computer-user interface, the logic interior to each of the abutting mediations must be sound. For the user to effectively add an event to an on-line calendar by tapping on the day where it should display, for example, the coding must give the computer bug-free under-the-hood instructions. Equally important, the graphical presentation of the calendar must feel familiar and sensible to the user. Once those conditions are established, the figurative realm (here, the icon evoking a paper calendar) enjoys a certain independence from its referential context. We don't tap on a square of our kitchen-wall calendars to record an event, but we nevertheless accept this mediated action as natural when we pull out our phones. Although derived from a paper referent, the heuristic has acquired its own logic: the calendar icon creates its own protocols that are workable even when they do not map perfectly onto analogue experience. The heuristic shares this semi-autonomy with figurative language. Students of rhetoric well know that figuration can acquire its own logic and heft, shaping response when a metaphor activates affective response (as Roderigo exploits in recasting Othello and Desdemona's love match as a bestial crisis) or replicates itself beyond good taste or good sense (as the mechanicals parody in their *Pyramus and Thisbe*). Metaphors matter both because they inflect response to their referents and because, once activated, they can generate their own energy.[2]

As Burdick et al. point out (and contributors to this volume explore), "graphical interfaces have been central to the humanities for centuries": "indexes, tables of contents, and foot- and endnotes [are all] ... information storage and retrieval strategies" (20). Part of this long history of how different media encounter human cognition and use, rhetorical figures such as metaphor and analogy are themselves heuristics that provide compressed stories about their referents and activate use (here, interpretation) without explicitly unpacking their logic. Corresponding to the operations of machine coding and graphical heuristic in my calendar app example above, effective rhetorical figures depend upon a balance of relation and separation. Jane Hedley, for instance, explains that metaphor "asserts [similarity], often in the face of a difference so great as to make that assertion surprising or bizarre" (5), "keep[ing] both of its terms continuously explicit, so that the vehicle does not displace the tenor" (67). Kenneth Burke's description of rhetorical figures and indeed referential systems more broadly suggests a long history for the kinds of mediations that interface exemplifies. Acknowledging that whatever is represented will always exceed its representation (a process he calls "reduction"), Burke takes metaphor as paradigmatic for broader semiotic systems when it "enables us to see one thing in terms of something else" (97). One aim of this chapter, and the present volume more broadly, is unfolding relationships between inherited and emergent ways of understanding the different vocabularies and protocols that can be used for "seeing one thing in terms of something else."

At the same time that the gap between mediations creates opportunities (to see one thing in terms of another, to act in a system whose alterity and complexity present barriers), it also carries risks. Because the two systems meeting in an interface remain distinct, Galloway calls interface "a medium that does not mediate" (52). Operating in, and despite, the constitutive gap makes interfaces powerful. But, like any black box, the interface creates a space where what we don't know (or examine) can hurt us: where questions can be foreclosed, interests can be obscured, alternatives can be tacitly pre-empted. Johnson's resolution is to lean into interface as "synthetic" in the double sense of the word: on the one hand "a forgery of sorts, a fake landscape that passes for the real thing"; on the other, "a form that works in the interest of synthesis, bringing disparate elements together into a cohesive whole" (238). Galloway, relatedly, writes that the "material distance or empirical falsity of [the interface's] simulation is at once foregrounded as a fatal flaw and then resolved as insignificant" (56).

Johnson's and Galloway's language of simulacrum and suture rather darkly casts the interfacial meeting of incommensurable ontologies as suspect. This chapter understands interface in a different key. Where Galloway argues that "the interface never admits [its] unworkability" (53), I contend that some interfaces cheerfully acknowledge an unbridgeable gap between elements and celebrate the effective arrangements whereby aliens can nonetheless collaborate, without requiring full mutual understanding or integration. Advantageously, those aliens need not lose their distinctive identities: because interfaces do *not* strive to conjoin or hybridize or fully mediate; they allow room for alterity. Herein lies one affordance of interface theory for Shakespeare studies. Understanding the text as itself an interface between past and present, between script and performance, or among realms like aesthetics and material culture and politics—these efforts can acknowledge disparity while still allowing engagement across the difference. Where New Historicism sometimes presumed that mere simultaneity implied relation (between, say, pantry inventories and dramatic tragedies of the same decade), interface theory provides a model for acknowledging the unintelligibility of the past, or the evanescence of the performance, or the imaginativeness of the fictional, while still maintaining grounds for understanding these in relation to the present, the playbook, or the historical.

Cymbeline

I take my test cases for cross-reading interface theory with early-modern drama from Shakespeare's *Cymbeline* because this play exuberantly and blatantly juxtaposes impossibly disparate realms in ways that still allow them to act upon one another in mediated ways, thus according with the working understanding of interface developed above. As remarked at the opening of this chapter, *Cymbeline*'s action plays out in chaotically different times and places. King Cymbeline and his daughter Innogen live in Roman-era Britain, which is an imperial client of the spatially removed but temporally coincident Roman Caesar. The play's antagonist Iachimo, on the other hand, lives in the same land as Caesar but (usually) inhabits a different time, early modern rather than ancient. Iachimo refers to "Italy" and its neighbor "France," for instance, where other (recognizably ancient) scenes cite "Rome," "Caesar," and "the Senate." The play makes no attempt to explain gaps like Iachimo's hiding in a chest in Renaissance Italy, then emerging in Innogen's ancient British chamber; nor does it apologize when, in an ancient British encampment, Iachimo anachronistically refers to "the [not-yet-invented] clock / That struck the hour … in Rome" (5.5.153–154).[3] The play's overabundance of sources, analogues, and characters (39 speaking parts!) cold-shoulders Aristotelian unities and suspensions of disbelief alike. Instead, *Cymbeline* boldly displays its logical aporiae.[4] This section of the chapter interrogates how some elements of *Cymbeline* work as interfaces, explores some specific resonances between theatrical romance (what contemporaries called "tragicomedy") and the interface, and concludes by considering implications of my *Cymbeline* readings for thinking about subjectivity and theater through interface theory.

If Iachimo initiates *Cymbeline*'s central plot of tragic calumny through the interface of a trunk, the resolution that rehabilitates Innogen's estranged husband Posthumus is effected by another interface: a prophetic tablet. A despairing Posthumus has returned to Britain as part of a Roman company dispatched to quell a rebellion. Although in the end he fights for the Britons, Posthumus reclaims Roman clothing after the battle in an effort at suicide-by-uniform, correctly surmising that he will be imprisoned and sentenced to death as a presumed enemy soldier. Manacled in a British jail, Posthumus falls asleep and is visited by apparitions of his dead father, mother, and brothers. The spirits appeal to Jupiter, who descends, promises that their "low-laid son our godhead will uplift" (5.4.73), and provides a "tablet" to be left on Posthumus's breast, "wherein," Jove promises, "Our pleasure [Posthumus's] full fortune doth confine" (5.4.79–80). Posthumus awakens to find this "rare" "book," whose "noble" cover contains a prophecy he deems inscrutable (5.4.103–115). Shortly, a messenger intervenes on the way to Posthumus's execution, bringing him before Cymbeline, where a soothsayer interprets the Jovian text. Jupiter's encoded message affirms that Innogen is virtuous and alive; identifies two rustic local youths as Cymbeline's lost sons; and excuses the British revolt as a machination of Cymbeline's wicked late queen. Cymbeline's family is reunited, as is Innogen with Posthumus, and Britain with Rome. "The fingers of the power above do tune / The harmony of this peace" (5.5.465–466), the soothsayer Philharmonus intones, and Cymbeline pronounces "Never was a war did cease, / Ere bloody hands were washed, with such a peace" (5.5.483–484).

In the British jail, the living, the dead, and the immortal find mediations that let them act on one another's experiences despite ontological divides between them. Ghosts gather around the living Posthumus, then pray for intervention from the divine. Jupiter responds with the tablet, transmitting prophecy that encodes input from the heavens to change outcomes on earth. Like the under-the-hood coding of computer interfaces, Jupiter's words do not require universal legibility to be effective: Posthumus is snatched from the hangman in advance of the prophecy being decoded. And, like a technical interface, the tablet *is* interpretable to an expert—the soothsayer—who remediates it from obscure written divine message to an oral proclamation comprehensible to mortals.

Harmonization of order across ontological realms: this is the project of romance. Genre theory describes romance as beginning with disequilibrium in the human realm (lost family members, alienated spouses). Often this radiates into nature or is intertwined with it (droughts, famines, tempests). Suffering and apparent or approximate death are ultimately overcome, with theophanies catalyzing rejuvenation, reconciliation, or rapprochement. Romance resolutions harmonize the disposition of human affairs with divine design; they recalibrate social, natural, aesthetic, affective, and providential orders.[5] The genre might be seen, then, as a mediating interface where action in one of these realms registers outcomes in another. Conventions of the form (shipwrecks, wicked step-parents, magical beasts, foundlings recovered) serve as heuristics. Bracketing the precise workings of the mediation (how does Hermione's statue come to life? How does Pericles survive his catatonia? Why does Jupiter relay the tablet to Posthumus's family to place upon his breast instead of putting it there himself?), the heuristic nonetheless enables plot resolution, character reconciliation, and audience satisfaction. An ear attuned to romance hears its echoes in theoretical descriptions of interface as an "in-between space … of communication and exchange … where two worlds, entities, systems meet" (Drucker, *Introduction* n.p.); a "mysterious zone … of interaction that mediate[s] between different realities" (Galloway vii). The mystery of interface—the remarkable capacity for profoundly different beings to communicate and collaborate even if they are unsure how they are doing it—resonates with experiences as different as magic, prayer, and data management. Remarking parallels in the operations of diverse interfaces situates present-day technologies in a long history, offering resources for understanding, living with, and shaping what otherwise might seem dauntingly unprecedented developments.

Cymbeline's two scenes featuring interfaces – the trunk in Innogen's bedroom and the tablet in Posthumus's jail cell—also, significantly, share an intense focus on media kinds. When Iachimo emerges from the chest, he finds that Innogen has fallen asleep just after setting aside Ovid's *Metamorphoses* ("She hath been reading late / The tale of Tereus" [2.2.44–45]). The materiality of her interaction with the codex is marked by her having turned down the corner of the last page she read ("here the leaf's turned down / Where

Philomel gave up" [2.2.45–46]). Iachimo records this observation in a different kind of text, a handwritten inventory:

> my design –
> To note the chamber. I will write all down.
> Such and such pictures, there the window, such
> Th'adornment of her bed, the arras, figures,
> Why, such and such, and the contents o'th'story.
> *(2.2.23–27)*

Beyond the material differences between Iachimo's list and Innogen's book, Iachimo's abbreviating gesture "such and such" draws attention to the different affordances of the two media: one an improvisatory aide-mémoire, the other a transmitter of Latin literary tradition. When Iachimo notes the "contents o'th'story" woven into the "arras" (which we later learn shows a scene of Antony and Cleopatra), he brings in the additional medium of tapestry.

Posthumus's jail cell lacks the luxury media of Innogen's chamber, but Jupiter's tablet similarly draws attention to media forms. The materialization of a book handed down from a god riding an eagle is dramatic, needless to say. The variable language used to refer to the item as a "tablet" (5.4.79), a "book" (5.4.103), and a "label" (5.5.429) arguably yields extra prominence as property directors and readers strive to visualize it. Posthumus's apostrophizing the tablet likewise elevates it in the attention economy, and his hope that the contents match its apparently opulent binding ("O rare one, / Be not, as is our fangled world, a garment / Nobler than that it covers" [5.4.104–105]) dwells on books' double existence as material texts and verbal transmitters.[6]

Maddalena Pennacchia argues that Innogen's book, the tapestries in her chamber, and Jupiter's tablet each becomes "a theatrical sign, which stands for a specific medium, [whereby] the stage is transformed into a hypermediated space, in which the dynamics of media relations becomes [*sic*] part of the story represented on the boards" (336). It makes sense for scenes featuring interfaces to stage hypermediation: Bolter and Grusin's term for the thematized, nested mediations that draw attention to the fact, modes, and operations of different media. Insofar as interfaces inhabit "the point of transition between different mediatic layers within any nested system" (Galloway 31), *Cymbeline*'s situating the trunk and the tablet within scenes of dense remediation shows the play's interest in the challenges, risks, and opportunities that arise at interfaces.

This interest in hypermediation characterizes romance beyond *Cymbeline*. *Pericles*, for instance, is narrated by the ghost of the fourteenth-century poet John Gower, who not only obsessively advises the audience which of the plot points unfolding on stage he's able to find in the written record, but also offers running commentary on what's too difficult to stage so will only be summarized verbally. In *The Tempest*, Prospero persistently, winkingly, refers to the rigors of public-theater production that dictates what time the anagnorisis is due, even as he deploys his magical book, Ariel's music, and the specialized stagecraft of masque to bring it about. Beyond theatrical tragi-comedy, romance in all its forms consistently indulges in metatextual play. Romances remark the genre's derivativeness, point to their source texts, and draw attention to multiple mediations of those texts. Mary Wroth's *Urania*, for instance, opens with the shepherdess Urania stumbling upon a cave set up with a writing desk and a book featuring … her own story! The heroine of Heliodorus's *Aithiopika* pacifies hostile bandits by telling them a story of a heroine pacifying hostile bandits. In romance, reiteration works like ritual, derivativeness affirming the tradition as it inscribes the present text into the corpus.[7] The romance imperative to sponsor commerce across ontological categories is one reason interfaces are central to romance; another is romance's explicit interest in nested remediation.

A second shared feature of the trunk scene and the tablet scene: both unfold around the sleeping body of the character they most directly impact. Sleeping and dreaming are of course venerable literary situations for allowing interchange across the boundaries of space, time, and logic that limit everyday experience. This is true of extra-literary experience as well. In Freudian thought, what is sleep if not an interface between the unconscious and the conscious, and what are dreams if not heuristic tools for representing a limited version of unconscious transactions to the conscious? In *Cymbeline*, Posthumus's jailhouse slumber leaves him with both solace from his past and a precious object from another realm. He retains a dream-memory of his dead family's visit ("Sleep, thou hast been a grandsire and begot / A father to me, and thou hast created / A mother and two brothers" [5.4.93–95]) as well as the material takeaway of the tablet, a text that he finds illegible ("a speaking such / As sense cannot untie" [5.4.118–119]) but still inchoately in "sympathy" (5.4.121) with his own bewildering experience.

The sleeping Innogen, by contrast, remains completely unaware of Iachimo's actions in her chamber, although he approaches her closely enough to note a mole on her left breast (2.2.37–38) and to steal a bracelet from her wrist (2.2.33 s.d.). In her deep sleep, what Iachimo calls Innogen's "sense"—her capacity to perceive—is immobilized: "a monument / In a chapel" (2.2.32–33). Indeed, figuring Innogen's sense as a memorial casts her as dead. Innogen's passive body contrasts with the lively interior life connoted by the accoutrements of the chamber that Iachimo carefully itemizes. Burning candles, paintings, the bracelet that was a gift from Posthumus (2.3.142), a "tapestry of silk and silver, the story / Proud Cleopatra when she met her Roman, / And Cydnus swelled above the banks" (2.4.69–71), and Innogen's bedside copy of Ovid's *Metamorphoses* all point to a cultured, independent subjectivity: a woman who (like Desdemona) has married without parental approval and who (also like Desdemona) seems unconflicted in her sexual life.[8] The scene stages the disparity between Innogen's body, vulnerably accessible to Iachimo's snooping and pilfering, and a mind whose activity we can infer but that remains private, closed off from Iachimo and from the audience by her deep sleep.

By emphasizing the distinction between outer bodily form and inner subjectivity, the scene constructs mind and body as disparate media (in Peters' sense, quoted above, of "medium" as a matrix that hosts being). Here, personhood is an interface at the boundary of mind and body. Innogen's sleeping body and vibrant but inaccessible mind show the amenability of interface models for thinking about dramatic characters—and perhaps extra-theatrical persons—more generally. While interface theory off-handedly wields phrases like "embodied cognition" and "human" as if these phenomena were unified within themselves, this assumption hardly accords with other accounts (or experiences) of subjectivity. This would be the usefulness of borrowing the notion of interface coined to describe mediated and partial transactions between human and non-human for designating the partial, unpredictable transactions among differently mediated parts of the self that are not fully accessible to one another—whether we think of these as unconscious, subconscious, and conscious; somatic, cognitive, and emotional; individually motivated and socially conditioned; or otherwise. A proper name, in this context, is a heuristic: a short-cut story that designates who someone "is" well enough for a given "use" (an interaction, a communication), but that could not hope to capture all the complexity within.

Cymbeline lends itself to exploring personhood as interface with its different forms of character doubling. These show aspects of personhood interacting with one another along boundaries of different mediations. The play also stages different heuristic shortcuts that make these transactions possible. One example comes in Cymbeline's doubled family. Innogen's two noble brothers, missing from court since early childhood, have been reared as Welsh rustics innocent of their heritage by a faithful retainer. The knowing audience watches the rough subsistence of the young men Polydore and Cadwal as they themselves perceive it, "warlike as the wolf for what we eat" (3.3.41). But we also understand their actions mediated by our knowledge of the play's courtly world: as the princes Guiderius and Arviragus, whose occluded noble heritage (think input) nonetheless shapes their behavior (think output). "How hard it is to hide the sparks of nature," their foster-father remarks (3.3.79).[9] The world of the court and the world of the cave cannot directly interact with one another, because the court believes the princes dead and their guardian vanished. Conversely, in the lonely Welsh cave, the brothers know of no connection to the court and their foster-father Morgan/ Belarius would put them in danger if he acknowledged it. Nonetheless, the princes' royal lineage acts on their rustic lives: "an invisible instinct … frame[s] them / To royalty unlearned; honour untaught, / Civility not seen from other, valour / That wildly grows in them" (4.2.176–179). In turn, their undertakings in Wales change outcomes at court when they turn the tide of battle against the Romans in a remote provincial lane (5.3.1–52). Within each prince, the rustic and noble identities act upon one another, but—as is characteristic of interfaces like computer graphics—not directly. The story their guardian has told them is a heuristic. "Cadwal" and "Polydore" are functionally serviceable identities; Belarius's story allows them to work as a foster family; the skills imparted by the old warrior serve for hunting in the Welsh mountains even if they derive from his experience in military campaigns.

A different kind of doubling comes in the twinned figures of Posthumus, Innogen's beloved and chivalrous husband exiled for their unauthorized marriage, and the doltish Cloten, son of Innogen's stepmother the British queen, whom the queen hopes Innogen will marry once Posthumus is banished. The two characters seem opposites. Posthumus is articulate, compassionate, and beloved of Innogen, while Cloten is coarse, violent, and repellent. But once Iachimo persuades Posthumus that Innogen has been unfaithful, Posthumus becomes misogynistic, violent, and crude … remarkably like Cloten. The plot carries the two men along a trajectory of increasing similarity: "both … obsessed with their identities … fearful of how others, and they themselves, will see and judge them" (Mazer, cited in Wayne, "*Cymbeline*," 86–7); "both are arrogant and self-confident, yet insecure and prone to violence. Neither has a father, both are given to wagers, and each desires Innogen but conceives violence against her" (Butler 33–34). After Cloten's death, Innogen herself mistakes his headless body for Posthumus's (4.2.307–309). The convergence between the two characters shows their initially different dispositions as mediations of the same masculine condition: of desire for a woman and the mistrust that apparently comes with it.

When a single actor is double-cast in the roles of Posthumus and Cloten (as was the practice in early modernity and, frequently, in recent productions), that actor's body is the heuristic.[10] Theatrical impersonation in general is a heuristic insofar as audiences agree to watch a production *as if* John Q. Actor were Cymbeline or Theseus or Hamlet. Doubling a role—and, with its 39 speaking parts, *Cymbeline* usually avails itself of ample multiple casting—intensifies the interfacial transaction between the embodied actor and the impersonated role. It also reveals that theatrical staging per se depends upon the "seeing one thing in terms of another" (to recall Burke's phrase quoted above) that interface depends upon. Impersonating a character, the actor's body works as an avatar: an icon originating in the analogue world that can enter the verbal/imaginative realm of the play-text.

The final mode of doubling in *Cymbeline* I will discuss here is amphibology: words with multiple meanings. This rhetorical figure works as a compressed form of interface. In amphibology, the signifier refers to multiple signifieds; the different lexical contexts for those signifieds connote different mediations; and the signifier is the heuristic visible at their boundaries. In *Cymbeline*, Innogen significantly initiates a meditation on this process as she mourns Posthumus's banishment: that is, she strives to connect realms of meaning as she contemplates her disconnection from her husband. Unable to bring herself to watch Posthumus's embarkation, Innogen demands a report from the friendly servant Pisanio. She complains that Pisanio should have watched the ship longer and insists that she would have gazed indefinitely upon the departing vessel:

> I would have broke mine eye-strings, cracked them, but
> To look upon him till the diminution
> Of space had pointed him sharp as my needle.
>
> *(1.3.17–22)*

The trifold sense of "point" mediates the separate realms of needlework, navigation, and punctuation. The first lexicon, of textile arts, evokes a practice that will occupy Innogen in her solitude. Needlework is furthermore the medium of the tapestry of Antony and Cleopatra decorating Innogen's bedroom (2.4.66–75). Remediated into Ovid's words on Innogen's nightstand, textile is also the medium of Philomela's revelation of her rape by Tereus. The navigational technology of the second sense of "point" pulls in the opposite direction from its textile associations. This meaning of "point" gestures to the compass of the ship carrying Posthumus away from Innogen. Using the same word for needle and compass puts into relationship the masculine realm of transportation (putting Posthumus into motion) and the feminine, domestic practice that marks Innogen's home-bound stasis. The third meaning of "point" indicates punctuation: a component of the letters the couple will use to communicate after the "point" of the compass guides Posthumus far away from the "point" of Innogen's needle. Drawing together textiles, navigation, and epistles, the single word "point" inhabits the "transition between different mediatic layers within any nested system," as Galloway describes the interface (31).

The amphibology of "point," then, shows a local affordance of Galloway's description of interface as "the state of 'being on the boundary'" (33). The heightened sense of boundary-dwelling that Galloway foregrounds also suggests how interface theory and early-modern theater might more broadly be useful to one another. Galloway calls the interface "that moment where one significant material is understood as distinct from another significant material" (33). At their shared dwelling on the boundary, interfacial components still acknowledge distinction. This resonates with theatrical boundaries between words and things, world and stage. Might an actor's body, for instance, be the interface between a living human and a scripted role? As an actor performs, neither aspect completely overwrites the other, and both are necessary to realize the character. Might a performance, to pose another question, be the interface between a specific moment in time and a reiterated drama, brought into relation but never fully harmonized? Are theatrical props interfaces, as they host the intersection of a real-world object's history and associations, on the one hand, and its stage function, on the other? Props become effective, after all, through both the relations between these contexts and their resistance to homogenized blending. Whatever our determination about these particular questions, theater as a performative and textual, historical and of-the-moment, narrative and embodied practice foregrounds that interfaces' mediations are only partial, that the logic of heuristics are incomplete—then lets us settle in to watch with satisfaction as they nonetheless gamely set to work.

Notes

1 All quotations of *Cymbeline* are from the 2017 Arden edition.
2 For examples of ways that figurative language can inscribe ideology into natural processes, see Fausto-Sterling or Martin.
3 As Wayne notes, there are "temporal convergences among characters in five of eleven scenes in the first two acts" of the play, with additional timeframes brought more fleetingly into the dramatic frame in multiple later scenes as well ("*Cymbeline*, Janus, and Folded Time," 248–9).
4 This artifice is essential to the play; McDonald notes that *Cymbeline*'s audience "enjoys being conscious of the managerial virtuosity of the dramatist ... [in] concealing, diverting, revealing, and above all controlling the multiple strands of the action" (40).
5 For this understanding of romance, see especially Frye, Jameson, Hunt, Fuchs, and Shohet, "Forms."
6 Pennacchia suggests that Jove figures the playwright abruptly altering Posthumus's fate, perhaps in response to audience preference that *Cymbeline* not be a tragedy: the tablet may be "a re-presentation of the play-text, that is, of a kind of impermanent writing that can be changed in performance according to many factors, not least the reaction of the audience" (339).
7 See Mowat, and Shohet, "Allusion."
8 Walter takes Innogen's reading material to assert self-determination. Walter describes Ovid as "material that might be considered inappropriate material for virtuous ladies by some" (125).
9 Readers of editions (including the Folio) and audiences with programs that give the princes and foster-father's birth names experience the dual names differently depending on the mediation of their encounter (stage, page, edition): the birth names are not spoken on the stage until after the anagnorisis in Act 5. The guardian Belarius/Morgan, however, informs all audiences of the princes' past.
10 See Wayne, *Cymbeline* 86–88 and appendix 3.

References

Benjamin, Walter. "On Language as Such and on the Language of Man." *Selected Writings*, vol. 1, 1913–1926, translated by Edmund Jephcott. Edited by Marcus Bollock and Michael W. Jennings, Harvard UP, 1996, pp. 62–74.

Bolter, Jay David and Richard Grusin. *Re-Mediation: Understanding New Media*. MIT Press, 1999.

Burdick, Anne, *et al.Digital Humanities*. MIT Press, 2012.

Burke, Kenneth. *A Grammar of Motives*. U of California P, 1969.

Butler, Martin. "Introduction." *Cymbeline*. Edited by Martin Butler, *New Cambridge Shakespeare*. Cambridge UP, 2005.

Drucker, Johanna. "Humanities Approaches to Interface Theory." *Culture Machine*, vol. 12, 2011, pp. 1–20.

Drucker, Johanna. *Introduction to Digital Humanities*. 2013. Available at: http://dh101.humanities.ucla.edu/.

Drucker, Johanna. *Graphesis: Visual Forms of Knowledge Production*. Harvard UP, 2014.

Fausto-Sterling, Anne. *Myths of Gender: Biological Theories about Women and Men*. Basic Books, 1992.

Frye, Northrop. *The Secular Scripture: Studies in the Structure of Romance*. Harvard UP, 1978.

Fuchs, Barbara. *Romance*. Routledge, 2004.

Galloway, Alexander. *The Interface Effect*. Polity, 2012.

Hedley, Jane. *Power in Verse: Metaphor and Metonymy in the Renaissance Lyric*. Pennsylvania State UP, 1990.

Hookway, Branden. *Interface*. MIT Press, 2014.

Hunt, Maurice. *Shakespeare's Romance of the Word*. Bucknell UP, 1990.

Jameson, Fredric. "Magical Narratives: Romance as Genre." *New Literary History*, vol. 7, no. 1, 1975, pp. 135–163.

Johnson, Steven. *Interface Culture: How New Technology Transforms the Way We Create and Communicate*. Basic Books, 1997.

Kittler, Friedrich. *The Truth of the Technological World: Essays on the Genealogy of Presence*. Stanford UP, 2014.

Krämer, Sybille. *Medium, Messenger, Transmission: An Approach to Media Philosophy*. Translated by Anthony Enns, Amsterdam UP, 2015.

Latour, Bruno. *Pandora's Hope: Essays on the Reality of Science Studies*. Harvard UP, 1999.

Martin, Emily. *The Woman in the Body: A Cultural Analysis of Reproduction*. Rev. edition, Beacon Press, 2001.

Mazer, Cary. "What Directors Can't/Won't Teach Scholars, What Scholars Can/Can't/Do/Don't Learn from Directions." Paper presented at Shakespeare Association of America seminar, 2008.

McDonald, Russ. *Shakespeare's Late Style*. Cambridge UP, 2006.

McLuhan, Marshall. *Understanding Media: The Extensions of Man*. Critical ed. Edited by Terrence Gordon, U of California P, 2003.

Mowat, Barbara. "'I Tell You What Mine Authors Saye': *Pericles*, Shakespeare, and *Imitatio*." *Archiv*, vol. 240, no. 155, 2003, pp. 42–59.

Ong, Walter. *Orality and Literacy*, 3rd ed., Routledge, 2012.

Oxford English Dictionary. "Interface." Available at: https://www-oed-com.ezp1.villanova.edu/view/Entry/97747?rskey=4JP6AM&result=1&isAdvanced=false#ei

Pennacchia, Maddalena. "Intermedial Props in Shakespeare's Roman Plays." *Shakespeare*, vol. 15, no. 4, 2019, pp. 335–343.

Peters, John Durham. *The Marvelous Clouds: Toward an Elemental Philosophy of Media*. U of Chicago P, 2015.

Shakespeare, William. *Cymbeline*. Edited by Valerie Wayne, Bloomsbury-Arden, 2017.

Shohet, Lauren. "Allusion, Temporality, and Genre in *Pericles* and *Troilus and Cressida*." *Temporality, Experience, and Genre in the Age of Shakespeare: Forms of Time*. Edited by Lauren Shohet, Bloomsbury-Arden, 2018a, pp. 97–120.

Shohet, Lauren. "Forms of Time." *Temporality, Experience, and Genre in the Age of Shakespeare: Forms of Time*. Edited by Lauren Shohet, Bloomsbury-Arden, 2018b, pp. 1–25.

Walter, Melissa Emerson. *The Italian Novella and Shakespeare's Comic Heroines*. U of Toronto P, 2019.

Wayne, Valerie. "*Cymbeline*, Janus, and Folded Time." *Temporality, Experience, and Genre in the Age of Shakespeare: Forms of Time*. Edited by Lauren Shohet, Bloomsbury-Arden, 2018, pp. 247–260.

20

SHAKESPEARE THROUGH THE BARE THRUST STAGE INTERFACE

Shoichiro Kawai

What is interface?

Let us first clarify what the term "interface" signifies and how it is different from "medium," as the two are often confused. In brief, an interface is the gateway through which we access a subject, while the medium is its container. As Steven Johnson states in *Interface Culture*, "The interface serves as a kind of translator, mediating between the two parties, making one sensible to the other" (14). Since Marshall McLuhan's *Understanding Media* (1964), we have become fascinated by the idea that media are not merely containers but modes of expression deeply interwoven with the content itself: "The medium is the message," as McLuhan succinctly puts it (7). This idea may be a variation on what William Butler Yeats famously implies in his poem, "Among School Children": "How can we know the dancer from the dance?"[1] The dancer's body (i.e. a medium), through which the dance is expressed, constitutes a significant part of the dance (i.e. the message). The medium transmits the content, but the two are interwoven; consequently, how can we separate the medium from the content?

On the other hand, an interface is a form of technological mediation whereby a user engages with or activates an entity which exists on the other side of the interface. The interface is differentiated from the media because we are always cognizant of how the specific interface with which we are engaging at any given time impacts our understanding. Interface theory explores how various interfaces necessarily affect the perception of the user of those interfaces.

Shakespeare's texts have been represented through various forms, such as Quartos, Folios, modern editions in physical and digital formats. They may be called media by which Shakespeare's texts are conveyed. However, when users are aware that these editions are not simply various containers of Shakespeare's texts but will greatly influence the users' understanding of the content, then they must be recognized as interfaces. Because reading Shakespeare, say, in Quartos will bring a different reading experience than when reading Shakespeare in modern editions, readers must be conscious of interfaces, through which they access the content. Interface theory is significant when we are conscious of the possibility that the content itself may be differently apprehended according to our deliberate application of particular interfaces.

DOI: 10.4324/9780367821722-27

Shakespeare's plays have also been represented through various genres such as theater, opera, ballet, film, painting, and manga. We may regard these genres as interfaces, through which we access Shakespeare's plays; we must be aware that different interfaces bring about different Shakespeares. All access through an interface involves some impact on the content caused by the user's choice and use of that particular interface. Like the "observer effect" in physics, whereby the observer's act of perceiving the object (via light hitting the object) influences the original status of the object, interface theory problematizes the process of perceiving the object. The tripartite relationship between the content, interface, and user does not allow us to presuppose the content *per se* until it is accessed via the interface. Because the user can only perceive through the interface, which affects the content, it is impossible to presuppose the existence of an unaffected true original. Thus, in interface theory, the *genuine* recognition of the original work is itself problematized.

The same thing can be said of Shakespeare on stage. Theater history tells us that the modes of theater have greatly changed since the Restoration period, when such new elements as actresses, curtains, and scenery were introduced to the modern proscenium arch stage, which is itself different from the Elizabethan thrust stage.

The bare thrust stage interface

We know that many of Shakespeare's plays were performed on the bare thrust stage in open-air theaters such as the Globe and the Curtain, although some were performed in indoor playhouses and halls. In the remainder of this chapter, I focus on the bare thrust stage as an interface.

An examination of Noh, a type of theater that uses a similar thrust stage, may be helpful. The remarkable resemblance between the structures of the Globe Theatre and the Noh stage is perhaps not a coincidence, as one could argue that "the open-air, bare stage [was] a kind of 'initial configuration' in world theater," as I mentioned in *The Cambridge Guide to the Worlds of Shakespeare* (1418). Both have a thrust stage and two pillars supporting a roof. Scenery was not employed with either type of stage. Since the Meiji period, when the Japanese became eager to adopt various aspects of modern Western culture, modern Noh stages have been housed in closed buildings; however, the Noh stage used to be a part of an open-air theater, like the Globe. Therefore, both had roofs covering the stage.

The Noh stage, with its 600-year history, has been a venue not only for Noh theater but also for Kyogen, its accompanying comic theater. Kyogen depicts humor in the everyday lives of the common people in a feudal society, and its acting style is much more natural than that of Noh and much simpler than that of Kabuki. Kyogen has many elements that are comparable to Shakespearean theater; for instance, as in Elizabethan theater, there were no female actors in Noh and Kyogen. The reader should note that because Kyogen has been performed on the Noh stage (the same stage for Noh theater), mentions of the Noh stage do not necessarily refer to Noh: in the following argument, the Noh stage is referred to as the stage for Kyogen. Noh consists mainly of chanting and dancing, whereas Kyogen utilizes mimetic acting. Therefore, we should turn to Kyogen, rather than Noh, for a comparison with Shakespearean theater.

The similarities of the stage structure produce similar staging. Kyogen usually begins with an actor appearing on stage and directly addressing the audience, saying, "*Kono atari no mono de gozaru*" (I am one of those who live around here). There is no imaginary "fourth wall" between the acting area and the audience. This direct address technique is frequently employed by Shakespeare in asides and soliloquies: For example, Shylock speaks of Antonio to the audience, "I hate him for he is a Christian" (*The Merchant of Venice* 1.3.42), and

Richard III confides in the audience, "I am determined to prove a villain" (*Richard III* 1.1.30), thereby making the audience accomplices to his secret plot. Because daylight illuminates both the audience and the actors, actors on a thrust stage cannot ignore the presence of the audience, which must be drawn into the performance.[2]

In Kyogen, the protagonist often announces that he is going to visit a specific place, such as a city or market. He will then walk in a circle on the bare stage until returning to his original spot and say, "Oh, here I am in the city." This technique is comparable to the one Shakespeare employs in *As You Like It*, whereby Rosalind, Celia, and Touchstone travel and arrive in the forest of Arden simply by stepping forward and announcing, "Well, this is the forest of Arden" (2.4.15).

Benedick tells his page to "bring [the book] hither to me in the orchard" (*Much Ado About Nothing* 2.3.3–4), and we are meant to understand that the locale is now "the orchard." Transitions between locales can occur in Elizabethan drama even in the middle of a scene. Alan C. Dessen provides examples, such as "the shoemaker who picks a fight with Jenkin in *George a Greene* asks: 'Come, sir, will you go to the town's end now sir?' and Jenkin responds (with no intervening stage direction): 'Ay sir, come. / Now we are at the town's end, what say you now?' (ll. 1009–1011)."[3] Presumably, the actor walks a short distance across the stage to indicate the trip, which is also a theatrical convention frequently used in Kyogen performed on the Noh stage.[4]

This theatrical convention of denoting a long trip simply by traversing a few steps on stage is possible on a bare stage where no specific locale is visualized. It is in accordance with the idea of theater expounded by the celebrated fifteenth-century Japanese dramatist, Zeami, in his treatise on theater, *Fushi-kaden*. Zeami regarded *mitate* (visual metaphor) as an essential means of expressing ultimate depth and beauty in theater, for example, by regarding falling cherry blossoms as falling snow. A similar function of theater is expressed by Philip Sidney in his *Defence of Poesy* as follows:

> you shall have Asia of the one side, and Afric of the other, and so many other under-kingdoms, that the player, when he cometh in, must ever begin with telling where he is, or else the tale will not be conceived. Now ye shall have three ladies walk to gather flowers, and then we must believe the stage to be a garden. By and by we hear news of shipwreck in the same place, and then we are to blame if we accept it not for a rock.
>
> *(65)*

Mitate is a metaphorical device used to imitate actual places or properties, and a common technique in Kyogen. Kyogen performers almost always carry a traditional Japanese fan which they use to represent various objects, such as a sake cup, sheet of paper, or knife. Although actual objects were used on Shakespeare's stage, the idea of *mitate* is not much different from the "as if" or "as from" techniques of Elizabethan stagecraft, some examples of which Dessen enumerates.[5] "Enter mariners wet" is declared in *The Tempest*, and the actors are simply to enter with a wet appearance on the thrust stage to signify their shipwreck; there is no need to introduce stage sets or special effects to simulate the shipwreck.

Immediately after Macbeth leaves the stage, crying, "I will not be afraid of death and bane, / Till Birnan forest come to Dunsinane" (5.3.59–60), Siward enters with Malcolm's army and asks, "What wood is this before us?" and receives the answer, "The wood of Birnan" (5.4.3). In an instant, the audience is transported from Dunsinane to Birnan wood. The bare thrust stage interface works "as quick as thought," as it is driven by thought. Everything changes so quickly "even with a thought" (*Julius Caesar* 5.3.19; *Antony and Cleopatra* 4.14.9) or "upon a thought" (*Macbeth* 3.4.54). The audience can be transported to wherever they want, "[f]or nimble thought can jump both sea and land" (Sonnet 44). Accordingly, in the second Quarto of *Romeo and Juliet*, Romeo has "love's light wings" to jump over or "o'er-perch [the] walls" of the orchard (2.266), for with his single line, "But soft, what light through yonder window breaks?" (2.2.2), he is transported from "A lane by the wall of Capulet's orchard," to "Capulet's orchard" for the balcony scene.[6]

In this way, the bare thrust stage is an interface – a cognitive technology that enables users (i.e. the audience) to engage with the play through their senses. This low-tech interface stimulates the user's imagination to such a degree that a scene change can occur in the blink of an eye. That Shakespeare himself was aware of this function is attested to in the prologue to *Henry V*, in which the speaker refers to his theater as "this wooden O" and implores the audience to work their "imaginary forces," asking them, "Piece out our imperfections with your thoughts" (Pro. 13, 18, 23). We should remember that through this interface, Shakespeare effectively invites the audience to enjoy a very swift and smooth theater experience around "the very casques / [t]hat did affright the air at Agincourt" in "[t]he vasty fields of France" (12–14). In contrast to the modern high-tech stage, where a scene change might take a minute or two or more, Shakespeare effects his scene changes in no time.

The bare thrust stage interface allows the user to enjoy the play in a different way from the reader's experience. In *King Lear*, for instance, when Kent is sleeping in the stocks, Edgar appears, and many modern editions demarcate the beginning of a new scene (2.3), given that Edgar "must not be supposed to be in the immediate neighbourhood of the castle" (Muir 80). Some modern editions designate the locale as "A wood." However, with the bare thrust stage, the audience is allowed to both listen to Edgar's monologue in the woods and see Kent asleep in front of Gloucester's castle at the same time. As soon as Edgar disappears, Kent wakes up at Lear's entrance, which means that Kent remains on the stage while the locale shifts back in an instant. Stanley Wells' commentary in his Oxford edition of the play is revealing: "Shakespeare's audience would have accepted the convention by which Edgar shows no awareness of Kent's presence and appears to be in a different place. Juxtaposition of the two men is emblematically fitting" (Wells 162).

Representing two locales simultaneously is easily done on the bare thrust stage, where no specific scenery is employed. When Benvolio, Mercutio, and Romeo march down the street to crash the Capulets' party, a stage direction in the second Quarto of *Romeo and Juliet* reads, "*They march about the Stage, and Servingmen come forth with Napkins*," to which Jill L. Levenson makes a suggestive note in her Oxford edition of the play: "In Q2 this direction indicating a transition from outside to inside the Capulet house is flexible" (189).[7] This suggests simultaneous staging: the maskers march around on stage to indicate their progress in the street towards the Capulet's house, and, at the same time, Servingmen come forth with napkins to show the busy preparations being carried out in the Capulet's hall as the maskers are marching in the street. There is no stage direction for the maskers' entrance in the next party scene, and the second Quarto simply reads "*Enter all the guests and gentlewomen to the Maskers*," suggesting that the maskers are already on stage, when the guests and gentlewomen enter to join them. It is natural to assume that the maskers' circuitous procession ends when they reach center stage. In other words, when the servants finish their brief scene and withdraw, the maskers complete their circuitous march to center stage to be received by Capulet as his guests. The user of the bare thrust stage interface can follow the movement of Romeo and his friends from the beginning of their march, with Benvolio's "Strike, drum" (1.4.114), all the way through until they are received by Capulet in the hall. Although the scene changes from the street to the hall (and the two locales are represented simultaneously, albeit briefly), there is no break in the maskers' movement on stage, as C. Walter Hodges points out (36).

The technique of representing two locales simultaneously is frequently employed in Kyogen as well, and it is by resorting to this technique that *The Kyogen of Errors*, an adaptation of Shakespeare's *The Comedy of Errors*, premiered at Shakespeare's Globe in 2001, represented both the inside and the outside of the door of Antipholus's house in Ephesus simultaneously. Dromio of Syracuse (within) and Dromio of Ephesus (without) were both performed by the renowned Kyogen performer Mansai Nomura, who, with a few steps and the use of a mask, changed locales and characters. The adaptation was created by Yasunari Takahashi, CBE (1932–2002), the former vice-president of the International Shakespeare Association. Takahashi also adapted *The Merry Wives of Windsor* into a Kyogen piece called *The Braggart Samurai*, featuring Falstaff. This was premiered at Tokyo's Globe Theater, for the International Shakespeare Congress held in Tokyo in August 1991, over which Takahashi presided as president of the Shakespeare Society of Japan. *The Braggart Samurai* was presented by the Mermaid Theatre in London in the same year and toured Hong Kong and Adelaide in 1994. Its text, translated into English by Takahashi himself, is included in *Shakespeare and the Japanese Stage*, edited by Sasayama and others, together with Takahashi's article on the relationship between Shakespeare and Kyogen.

After Takahashi passed away in 2002, it was left to me, his son-in-law, to create a third adaptation of Shakespeare in the Kyogen style. I decided to transform *Richard III* into a new play, *The Country Stealer*, using the techniques of Kyogen. In 5.3 of *Richard III*, Richard and Richmond enter at their respective tents, which are supposed to be far apart at the opposite ends of Bosworth Field, but the bare thrust stage interface allows us to envision them at the same time: the Ghosts of those who were killed by Richard come to curse Richard asleep at his tent and give blessings to Richmond asleep at his tent in the same scene. They curse Richard and bless Richmond alternately: The Ghost of Lady Anne, for instance, curses Richard, saying "Despair and die!" (5.3.163), and then immediately starts blessing Richmond as if the two were in the same place. I decided that there should be no time spent between cursing and blessing in my adaptation; we placed Richard downstage and Richmond upstage, so that the Ghosts, standing between them, only had to turn upstage to signify their transition from Richard's tent to Richmond's tent. Here we may confirm that one of the properties of the bare thrust stage interface is to facilitate the user's imaginative experience of the drama by disregarding locality.

In *The Country Stealer*, I made the most of the bare thrust stage interface and attempted to involve the audience in the plot. In a scene corresponding to *Richard III* 3.7 (in which Buckingham tries to induce the citizens to cry "God save King Richard!"), the audience members were treated as part of the play. Buckingham spoke directly to the audience as if addressing a group of citizens, and Richard insisted that he become king with the approval of the audience. The effect was hilarious: the audience became complicit in enthroning Richard. This was due to the effect of the thrust stage, which engrosses the audience's imagination and builds up the drama.

Conclusion

Theatrical structures channel attention through technological affordances (bare thrust stage), which can be read as interfaces. Shakespeare created his drama through his bare thrust stage interface, and if we try to access Shakespeare through this interface, we can understand how Shakespeare's imagination worked. The interface is a gateway, the necessary technology through which the audience engage, and by using it, we will be inevitably conscious of our use of it, for through this interface we are necessarily involved in the drama itself.

By far different from the CGI-enhanced RSC *Tempest*, which will entertain spectators with its stupendous visual effects, audiences at the Globe and Noh theater have to pick up textual cues to exercise their own imagination. And the users of this minimal stage interface will find themselves involved and immersed in the play's world, because this interface demands the users' positive participation. When we discussed media at the outset, we asked "How can we know the dancer from the dance?" but when we come to think of interface, we realize that we are not only observers of the dance but also a part of the dance.

Notes

1 Quoted from Finneran's *The Poems of W. B. Yeats* (Yeats 1983), p. 217.
2 Quotations from Shakespeare refer to Evans' *The Riverside Shakespeare*, 2nd ed., unless otherwise noted.
3 Quoted from Dessen, *Elizabethan Stage Conventions and Modern Interpreters* 86. See also Beckerman 175.
4 This convention of walking around on stage to signify a scene change is also found in Chinese Kunqu opera, one of the oldest extant forms of Chinese opera, which was dominant from the sixteenth to the eighteenth centuries and performed on a roofed thrust stage. In *The Peony Pavilion* (first performed in 1598), written by Tang Xianzu (1550–1616), actors are to gesture as if entering a gate to signify a scene change from a garden to the inside of a house (Swatek).
5 For a thorough discussion of "as if" or "as from" stage directions, see Dessen, *Elizabethan Stage Conventions* 93–5 and *Recovering Shakespeare's Theatrical Vocabulary* 139ff.
6 These "literary" stage directions were first given by W. G. Clark and W. A. Wright in their Globe edition (Cambridge, 1866).
7 Quotations from the Quartos refer to Allen and Muir's *Shakespeare's Plays in Quarto* (Shakespeare 1981).

References

Beckerman, Bernard. *Shakespeare at the Globe, 1599–1609*. Macmillan, 1962.
Clark, William George, and William Wright, editors. *The Works of Shakespeare*. London, 1866.
Dessen, Alan C. *Elizabethan Stage Conventions and Modern Interpreters*. Cambridge UP, 1984.
Dessen, Alan C. *Recovering Shakespeare's Theatrical Vocabulary*. Cambridge UP, 1995.
Hodges, C. Walter. *Enter the Whole Army: A Pictorial Study of Shakespearean Staging 1576–1616*. Cambridge UP, 1999.
Johnson, Steven. *Interface Culture: How New Technology Transforms the Way We Create and Communicate*. HarperEdge, 1997.
Kawai, Shoichiro. "PART XX: Changing Technologies of Stage Performance." *The Cambridge Guide to the Worlds of Shakespeare*, vol. 2. Edited by Bruce R. Smith, Cambridge UP, 2016, pp. 1417–1426.
McLuhan, Marshall. *Understanding Media: The Extensions of Man*. Routledge & Kegan Paul, 1964.
Sasayama, Takashi, J. R. Mulryne, and Margaret Shewring, editors. *Shakespeare and the Japanese Stage*. Cambridge UP, 1998.
Shakespeare, William. *King Lear*. Edited by Kenneth Muir, Methuen, 1952.
Shakespeare, William. *Romeo and Juliet*. Edited by Jill Levenson, Oxford UP, 2000.
Shakespeare, William. *The Riverside Shakespeare*. 2nd ed., general editor G. Blakemore Evans, Houghton Mifflin, 1997.
Shakespeare, William. *Shakespeare's Plays in Quarto: A Facsimile Edition of Copies Primarily from the Henry E. Huntington Library*. Edited by Michael J. B. Allen and Kenneth Muir, U of California P, 1981.
Sidney, Philip. *A Defence of Poetry*. Edited by J. A. van Dorsten, Oxford UP, 1966.
Swatek, Catherine Crutchfield. *Peony Pavilion Onstage: Four Centuries in the Career of a Chinese Drama*. Michigan Monographs in Chinese Studies. University of Michigan Center for Chinese, 2003.
Takahashi, Yasunari. "Kyogenising Shakespeare/Shakespeareanising Kyogen." *Shakespeare and the Japanese Stage*. Edited by Takashi Sasayama, J. R. Mulryne, and Margaret Shewring, Cambridge UP, 1998, pp. 214–240.
Wells, Stanley, editor. *The History of King Lear*. Oxford UP, 2000.
Yeats, William Butler. *The Poems of W. B. Yeats: A New Edition*. Edited by Richard J.Finneran, Macmillan, 1983.
Zeami, *The Spirit of Noh: A New Translation of the Classic Noh Treatise the Fushikaden*. Translated by William Scott Wilson, Shambhala, 2013.

PART VII

Interfacing with performance

21

SHAKESPEARE'S WALKING STORY

Site-specific theater in a Covid world

Gretchen E. Minton

The present volume brings together work that explores how the concept of interface can be applied to Shakespeare. As the chapters here demonstrate, interface theory readily lends itself to discussions about technologies—how mediations such as screens, recorded sounds, and the page function as portals through which audiences interact with Shakespearean texts. However, interface as a vehicle for understanding live performance adds layers of complexity that move us beyond the framework used to address issues of digital or typeface media. Stanton Garner notes that the cognitive processes necessary to create a narrative out of the unfolding of a theatrical presentation are dependent upon multiple factors:

> Narrative does not inhere in the materials of performance any more than it inheres in the words on a page; it constitutes an imaginative formulation, imposed upon the stage and its activities by actor, director, designer, and (more crucially) by the audience that assents to the fictionality of the dramatic world and constructs this world's temporal outlines.
>
> *(7)*

A full understanding of how narrative is constructed during live performances requires acute attention not just to the apparatuses of theater, but to the presence of physical bodies and minds that are immersed in a production's temporal unfolding. To center my exploration of interface on such physical components, I will be focusing more explicitly on immersive theatrical experiences, for such productions heighten the role of audience members and their movement—both physical and cognitive—toward the production of meaning.

The most famous immersive production of this century is undoubtedly *Sleep No More*, created by Punchdrunk in London in 2003 and an immensely popular show since its New York opening in 2011. *Sleep No More* takes its inspiration from *Macbeth* and is staged in a giant warehouse where audience members wear white masks and are encouraged to follow their own path through the space, interacting with characters when invited. Writing about this play, W.B. Worthen notes that

DOI: 10.4324/9780367821722-29

> Replaying *Macbeth* as an 'immersive' event, *Sleep No More* dramatizes the complex *affordance* of dramatic writing in contemporary performance. As theorists of both design and cognition recognize, an object's ability to be used, to do work, lies in its affordance, the interplay between the 'perceived and actual properties of the thing' that enables us to imagine its utility.
>
> (96)[1]

Worthen goes on to say that a text's ability to be instrumentalized in significant performance depends upon theatrical practices that are mediated by a variety of cultural, historical, social, and aesthetic factors. Such affordances are heightened in an immersive production such as *Sleep No More*, as Worthen rightly suggests, so I would like to extend the discussion to take measure of what happens when a production is ambulatory and outdoors, removed from all technology. What affordances remain as cues for the audience? And how does the unpredictability of the interface become part of the audience's embodied cognitive experience?

The case study at the center of this inquiry is an ambulatory outdoor production called "Shakespeare's Walking Story" that took place in Bozeman, Montana, on June 27 and 28, 2020. During this serial performance of Shakespearean monologues, the interface of human footsteps, music, facemasks, weather, and the overlay of natural and built environments all worked to intensify the audience's conviction that engagement with Shakespeare is a deeply personal—and present—matter.

The tour begins

"Shakespeare's Walking Story" was a concept borne out of a unique historical moment: the summer of 2020. Theater in Montana, as everywhere else, had been indefinitely closed, due to the Covid-19 pandemic. The most prized cultural organization of the state, Montana Shakespeare in the Parks (MSIP), had to cancel its season for the first time in its 48-year history. Normally, in mid-June, Bozeman audiences as large as 1000 would have gathered at Montana State University's duck pond to enjoy free performances, enhanced by professional choreography, sound design, and sophisticated lighting. In the absence of the usual theatrical opportunities over the summer and in the foreseeable future, a small collective of artists expressed interest in creating a piece of theater that could be performed outside for the citizens of Bozeman (a university town of about 50,000 residents in the Rocky Mountain West) in June. We sought to give audiences and actors a place that allowed for the creation and enjoyment of live art in a safe environment.

Part of the communal joy provided by MSIP's outdoor Shakespeare is crowding together on blankets to watch costumed actors move around an elaborate set. In "Shakespeare's Walking Story" we reversed this process: actors stayed at their stations and the audience came to them. The production consisted of a 45-minute guided walk around an extensive (60-acre) city park and nature preserve called Story Mill Park.[2] Along the walk the audience encountered six actors, each in an isolated place, who delivered a monologue. Group sizes were limited to 10 people, and the tours left every 20 minutes. We emphasized social distancing and encouraged the wearing of masks (which had not yet been mandated by the state and were not yet standard protocol, especially for outdoor gatherings).

Walking Shakespeare productions are not new, of course, including not just heavily adapted experiences such as *Sleep No More*, but a range of performances that capitalize on audience movement through spaces (both indoor and outdoor). As Rob Conkie notes in his "Reverie of a Shakespearean Walker," the chief benefit of such productions is that they allow for "a uniquely visceral and ruminative engagement with the chosen play" (232).

Ultimately, such site-specific ambulatory approaches to theater increase an awareness of being-in-the-world. "Shakespeare's Walking Story" was thus intended to offer a much-needed space for reflection on what such *being* meant in the summer of 2020.

As a pod of 10 people left the starting point, their designated guide gave a short introductory talk about this kind of theatrical experience, encouraging the audience to consider the natural spaces of the park as well as the speeches they would be witnessing during this short, ambulatory piece of theater. We challenged everyone to appreciate Shakespeare out of context, or rather, Shakespeare differently contexted. When I guided groups, I encouraged them not to worry about what play a speech came from, its plot or characters, but instead to focus on the words themselves, while being especially aware of their surroundings in that particular moment. The context that mattered in this production was not an imagined whole called "the play," but instead a site-specific environment that released Shakespeare from a conventional interpretive framework.[3] This differently contextualized Shakespeare was part of the joy of an organic, unpredictable production.

Rather than having actors deliver unrelated monologues, I designed the walk's Shakespearean speeches around the loose theme of prisons. The guides alerted the audience at the beginning that they should consider the prison theme while watching and hearing the actors. Such reflections, the guides explained, took little imagination, for we had all been experiencing a sense of imprisonment during the pandemic: a feeling of being trapped in our homes, unable to move about freely or to see and touch the people that we hold dear. Weeks after the George Floyd murder and attendant protests, this was also a time to be cognizant of other engines of imprisonment: economic and racial inequity, governmental and political systems, systemic oppression writ large. Walking through Shakespeare offered a chance to reflect upon different kinds of bondage. Migrating from one site to another would allow for silent spaces to digest numerous thoughts and emotions elicited by these performances. Because the format of "Shakespeare's Walking Story" was thematic rather than narratological, the emphasis was placed upon the audience's own ability to derive meaning from the production—a process impacted significantly by the physical environment and the temporal unfolding of the walk.

Step 1: The seven ages

Turning down a gravel spur early in the walk, the guide led the audience to a creek-side setting. Next to the water sat a young, bearded man (Keegan Grady) who was playing on a tin pipe. Catching sight of the audience, he leapt up and said excitedly, "A fool! A fool! I met a fool in the forest!" Jaques' lines from *As You Like It* morphed naturally, of course, into "All the world's a stage" and the seven ages of man speech (2.7.140–166). Using such a famous monologue as the production's opening was a deliberate choice: the audience would be familiar with these words and the metaphors described therein. But even more importantly, the reflection upon the seven periods of life established a rhythm that was central to "Shakespeare's Walking Story." The stages meant many things at once: not just the inevitable process of ageing and death, but the places where the actors stood to deliver their pieces and the stations along a progress of the audience's walk. In her masterful book about the history of walking, Rebecca Solnit notes that "Moving on foot seems to make it easier to move in time, the mind wanders from plans to recollections to observations" (5). Jaques' speech thus introduced a rhythm that was about both physical and imaginative exploration—the kind of uniting of the mind, body, and world that are aligned through walking.[4]

When Jaques ended his sorrowful meditation upon "mere oblivion" with the "sans everything" (l. 166–7) of the last stage, he distractedly wandered off. The guide motioned to the audience: follow this man. Grady's Jaques, seemingly oblivious to people treading the gravel path behind him, played upon his pipe and occasionally sang. This transition established an immersion into the experience of walking itself, for the progress down the path encouraged reflection, specifically during the "in-between" times that this ambulatory theater created. Reaching a bridge, Jaques motioned the audience onward with "There lies your way, due west" (*Twelfth Night* 3.1.132) and then retreated to his place by the creek. The passage over the bridge was a key use of landscape; this was a portal through which the audience would be entering a place both physical and imaginative. At this stage the guide took the lead again, but silently, thus modeling by example that this was a time for reflection upon journeys between the sites of performance.[5] The guides, like the walking paths in the park, became affordances that gave the production a physical structure, significantly supplementing the narrative one.

Step 2: This prison where I live

On the other side of the bridge, the audience entered the nature preserve section of Story Mill Park. This park was only a year old, but a welcome addition to public recreational opportunities for the residents of Bozeman. The town is known for its outdoor culture and proximity to natural spaces, but by locating this walk in the new park, "Shakespeare's Walking Story" took the audience into areas with which most were not familiar, inviting them into a "wild" space that was part of the urbanization plan for the fastest-growing area in Montana. The park's dedication to natural spaces never masks its anthropocentric dimensions, for walkways, bird feeders, interpretive signs, and sculptures are present throughout. Our production embraced this precedent, foregrounding an experience rooted in natureculture.[6] The movement at the production's core made binary thinking impossible, as is typical of the cognitive immersion created by walking: "On foot everything stays connected, for while walking one occupies the spaces between those interiors in the same way one occupies those interiors. One lives in the whole world rather than in interiors built up against it" (Solnit 9). An awareness of this "whole world" in the production meant recognizing multispecies entanglement; such thinking fosters a more nuanced sense of ecological systems that do not see humans as exceptional, nor as a destructive force set apart.

A short way into the nature preserve, a wooden structure emerged on the left of the path: a bird blind in the trees designed for bird-watching enthusiasts to observe the goldfinches, sparrows, and chickadees at the feeders that hung nearby. On the bare ground inside this structure knelt a ragged, barefoot man who seemed to be meditating. Opening his eyes, he explained, "I have been studying how I may compare / This prison wherein I live unto the world." Richard II's soliloquy about the nature of imprisonment (5.5.1–66) was unfamiliar to most audience members, but this estrangement enabled them to meet the language on its own terms. Richard's lines gained a powerful resonance in this environment, for the actor (Michael Goldstein) pounded on the walls around him, reached desperately through the slats, scratched the dirt beneath his feet. It was remarkable, in fact, that in a structure not closed off from the verdant nature preserve in any literal way as a prison cell would have been, the sense of isolation and terror at separation were nonetheless palpable.

Striving for a closer connection to contemporary events, Goldstein changed the phrase "unkinged by Bolingbroke" (l. 37) to "unkinged by Corona"[7] as he howled in despair about the loss of his fortunes and his friends. Such an unexpected reference to the most-used term of 2020 was designed to encourage audience awareness of their own lives as reflected/refracted in this moment of live theater. The emendation to "Corona" was powerful because it created a contact point based on the language of contemporary experience, thus drawing the audience into the predicament of a king whose situation would have elsewise seemed worlds away from theirs.

Meanwhile, the birds provided an accompanying soundscape, but one that necessarily changed with each iteration of Richard's speech because of the constant movement of these creatures. Bird cries can of course be dramatically effective, such as the recorded sounds of ominously cawing crows that were used by MSIP to great effect in the 2017 production of *Macbeth*.[8] Such artificially produced cries sounding on cue ensure that the performance is a tight loop of logical consequences. By contrast, the inflection of song birds by chance in Story Mill Park could elicit an experience of serendipity in the audience—by mere coincidence (or something beyond coincidence?), the more-than-human world was speaking to them.

The sounds of the actor's voice, of the bird songs, and of the audience's occasional shuffling were then joined, unexpectedly, by the sound of a guitar. Another actor (Aila Peck) sitting under a tree nearby, unnoticed until that moment, at first seemed to be an unrelated member of the public strumming her instrument and lost in her own reverie. These notes, however, came on cue, in response to Richard's hearing music from his cell partway through his soliloquy. In the play these strains occasion a reflection upon the inability of musicians and humans more generally to "keep time."[9] Goldstein used his arms and then his fingers to indicate the dials of the clock, allowing the audience to understand the full sorrow of his life. This realization reached its climax with the clear and profound utterance of "I wasted Time, and now doth Time waste me" (l. 49). The complexity of this moment serves as an example of what Rebecca Bushnell discusses in her article on tragedy and temporality: "Performance is tragic time made live, producing the strong illusion of present experience, still haunted by history and an expectation of what is to come" (788). Richard II's poignant expression of loss in times past inevitably became part of the spectators' contemporary sense of trauma, tangled into the "incalculable loss"[10] of humanity and its uncertain futures in the wake of coronavirus.

"Shakespeare's Walking Story" was designed intentionally to keep each actor in a solitary place for a solo delivery (partially to encourage social distancing between the artists, partially to allow for poignant reflections upon isolation and imprisonment). As Goldstein's Richard leaned out the window of the bird blind to address the guitar player, the production allowed one moment of possible connection between the characters, but the potential to reach across the divide was broken by Richard's complaints that "This music mads me! Let it sound no more" (l. 61). The musician's body language betrayed hurt feelings at that moment, then she slowly walked away. The damage was done and could not be repaired, thus it was too late when Goldstein delivered Richard's "Yet blessing on [her] heart that gives it me, / For 'tis a sign of love; and love to Richard / Is a strange brooch in this all-hating world" (64–66). The end of the soliloquy was sudden, leaving the audience hesitant about what they should do next.

Like *Sleep no More*, our production aimed toward a "dynamic foregrounding of text, character, space, and audience" which "open[ed] a series of questions about the emancipation of the spectator and about the character of cognition offered by theatrical immersion" (Worthen 84). However, "Shakespeare's Walking Story" did not offer the opportunity for spectators to roam in directions of their own choosing, which helped to heighten the production's emphasis upon imprisonment. One viewer wrote a poem after she saw "Shakespeare's Walking Story," giving voice to the personal connections she was making to the production's scenes: "In the midst of the monologue—myself / Wondering when I'll be free of this cage / If only to play my part. And if, what will it / Look like? How should I enter? How to exit?" (Chavez). The absence of an exit cue caused awkwardness, but the moment became an important one. That brief pause was just long enough to raise the specter of responsibility, requiring those present to take measure of their own movement and situatedness in space and time.

Step 3: There is a willow

The guitar player at whom Richard had railed slowly continued down the path, and the guide directed the audience to follow, until they arrived at a grassy spot along the East Gallatin River where she had stopped to play and sing Desdemona's willow song (*Othello* 4.3.39–56).[11] The words of mourning in this song were spliced together with Gertrude's speech describing Ophelia's death at the willow tree on another muddy bank ("There is a willow grows askant the brook" (4.7.164–181)). The transition from the song to the speech, which is of course also a transition between plays, was seamless and thus largely unnoticed by the audience. Peck, in fact, continued to play the same guitar underscoring as she delivered the first part of Gertrude's speech, until her voice quivered and her hands dropped from the strings with her explanation of how Ophelia "Fell in the weeping brook" (l.173).

The use of music in this environment created a specific framework for understanding and feeling the Shakespearean text. This type of sound is what Bruce Barton and Richard Windeyer call a "soundtrack"—a performative intervention that creates an acoustic journey.[12] At the same time, the site for Peck's performance offered the audience a "soundscape" as well, an acoustic ecology that included the gurgling of the creek, the swishing of the trees, and the falling of the raindrops. The dual acoustics of soundtrack and soundscape were paralleled by the visual features of the site, including stunning vistas of the Bridger Mountains. Yet this site's immediate backdrop was decidedly not bucolic: an old grain mill with giant silos. This post-industrial reminder of food production a century earlier ensured that it was impossible to become fully immersed in the Desdemona/Gertrude laments without considering the long history of the land on which the spectators stood while they engaged with this performance—a history that included settler colonialism, agricultural development, and industrialization. The performance in this site thus gave spectators a Shakespearean scene that elicited awareness of "folded time," which reflects "stopping points, ruptures, deep wells, chimneys and thunderous acceleration, rendings, gaps."[13]

The combination between the soundscape, the subject matter, and the folding of time made the affective experience at this spot pronounced. Multiple audience members said this performance moved them to tears because of the words and the song. What held their attention most was the way Peck deliberately made eye contact with the people who were watching her—a reminder of how much everyone was missing intimate human connection that was not mediated by computer or phone screens. Many audience members wore masks and were thus shielded from a full immersion in their environment, but Peck's performance gave them something for which they were longing. In fact, the audience sometimes came uncomfortably close to her, almost as if they were going to try to touch her.

The uncertainty about the boundaries between performer and spectator are typical of ambulatory performances, where "There is no fixed stage edge, the line between the fictional space and the real is fluid and unstable. The audience becomes dislocated in the sense of not knowing their proper place, position, or relation to the events depicted" (Collins 54). Sometimes, especially in urban productions, this dislocation includes close proximity of the audience to one another, as they're often moved into small rooms where they cannot help but rub up against each other.[14] *Sleep No More* capitalizes on these possibilities; the actors at times draw audience members to private rooms and speak to them, granting them a longed-for interactive experience. Given the constraints of performance in 2020, our situation was quite different, for distancing and not touching were the necessary physical arrangement. The white masks in *Sleep No More* function to "separate [the audience] literally and figuratively from the performers," resulting in "an eerie world in which each spectator is one of many specters watching the actions of the unmasked performers" (Flaherty 14). Sometimes actors in *Sleep No More* unmask audience members, creating a sense of deep intimacy. For our audiences, however, the barriers of facemasks and spacing between people during a speech about mourning intensified the sense of loss and despair. The enticement of breaking the fourth wall is integral to any theatrical performance (whether imagined or enacted), but "Shakespeare's Walking Story" unfolded in a way that made us painfully aware of what stands between the performer and the spectator. Nonetheless, the music and empathetic delivery temporarily created community across such barriers.

The words and ideas in the Desdemona/Gertrude speeches were not about literal imprisonment as the *Richard II* soliloquy had been. Instead, the imprisonment evoked here was primarily about gender: Desdemona's fear for the demise of her marriage (and herself), Gertrude's description of Ophelia weighed down by literal clothing and also, like Desdemona, by lost love. The most unexpected revelation about constraint came from the sense that Gertrude was trapped by her memories, unable to move beyond the horrific image of the young woman's drowning. Peck's delivery of the song and speech showed that she was caught as thoroughly as Ophelia, but by repetition. Having finished Gertrude's short speech, Peck began playing the same tune on the guitar again. This circularity was heightened (at least for me as a guide who saw the show several times in succession) by the knowledge that the actors were repeating the same short speeches again and again over this two-day performance period.

Here more than any stage in "Shakespeare's Walking Story," the audience stood frozen in place, not wanting to move on; Peck inserted Desdemona's line to Emilia, "So, get thee gone" (*Othello* 4.3.57), in order to direct the spectators to burden her no longer, and instead to continue on their walk. They gradually realized that the language of Shakespeare was giving direction: they had to proceed to the next station, even if unwillingly.

Step 4: Losing the name of action

The path continued past a crude wooden structure—an arboreal bower that would have made an ideal place for another actor. As the audience passed, they looked at it expectantly, assuming something would happen there. No scene was delivered in the bower, however, because a homeless man lives in that spot. At this stage in "Shakespeare's Walking Story," three sites had been transformed by performances, but the absence of performance here was, at least for those who knew the history of Story Mill Park, part of the point. The land on which the city of Bozeman had achieved this idyllic wetland restoration had formerly been a trailer park—one of the last remaining low-income housing areas in the town. This homeless man's ownership of the public space is rather thorough; a collection of his possessions is stacked in the woods behind the structure, and he often rests upon the bench and greets passers-by, as if he is sitting on his porch (though he was not present during the production itself).

Just past this bower the first of several sculptures in the park came into view. This one, called "The Flourish," is a 25-foot-high orange and blue welded steel piece designed to suggest both industrial windmills and the frames of boats. The sculptor, Jim Zimpel, constructed kinetically moving paddles that turn in the wind, recalling "traditional paddles from various cultures; the birds in the park's wildlife refuge, which include nesting sandhill cranes," as well as agricultural wheat. In an interview, Zimpel said that the sculpture was meant to address "historic uses of the area from the era of nomadic foraging through industrialization, urban housing (part of the site was once a mobile home park) and now leisure." He sees his piece as representing the site's "rich history, including use by indigenous populations," which is now "a public space for all people" (Schmidt). The sculpture and the indigent resident are both reminders that each site in the park comes with the residue of personal and communal history. We built upon these various hauntings, realizing that they would contribute to the possibilities of surprise, reflection, or absence, thus complicating the notion of what constitutes a stage.

It is always the case that spectators see stage action as filtered through their own experience as well as through the interface of a production's physical features and technologies. Such mediations keep an audience focused so that they can access the theatrical story in a prescribed way. Speaking of site-specific theater, Susan Haedicke observes:

> Physical site expands into the discursive realm. And, in fact, the more integral the actual public space is to the performance event, the more the discursive site wedges itself into the body of the spectator, as the experiential shock of being in a transformed familiar place reveals previously unimagined possibilities.
>
> *(104)*

This phenomenon gets at the heart of "Shakespeare's Walking Story," for in the unfolding journey of Story Mill Park, the levels of possible meanings were exponentially intensified because the spectators' gaze (literal and introspective) took in the various implications of this site. The accrual of lived experience carried by each spectator necessarily meant that, although they were all hearing the same words delivered by the same actors, the narratological progression was radically different for everyone.

Near the Flourish sculpture the next actor (Gabe Taurman) came into view, dressed in a hipster shirt and shouting into a megaphone, "Denmark's a prison!" (*Hamlet* 2.2.242). He stood on the sculpture's concrete base in an attempt to get the audience to join him in his anti-incarceration chant, displaying outrage that no one took up his cause. After some comments about being bounded in a nutshell,[15] Taurman launched into Hamlet's most famous speech. The delivery of "To be or not to be" (3.1.55–87) was most surprising in its unusual approach to this moment. No longer was this a private meditation about suicide, but instead a public speech delivered directly to the audience who stood on the path. Specifically, this interpretation of the soliloquy challenged the spectators to reconsider the political and ethical import of the Black Lives Matter movement (signaled by the megaphone) and their own complicity. Lines such as "conscience does make cowards of us all" (l. 82) and "lose the name of action" (l. 87) became the key moments in this delivery.[16]

The challenges of outdoor performance are myriad, due to the sources of distraction—everything from airplane and train noises to children running around the playing space to the discomfort of varied weather. How could Taurman create a sense of focused attention in such conditions, especially when the mosquitoes in this spot were troublesome, causing a constant shifting and swatting among the audience? Addressing this challenge required a shift in objectives. In "Shakespeare's Walking Story," the spectators did not need to be swept away from the surroundings and lost in the Shakespearean script; instead, we wanted them to focus on their present experiences (even the uncomfortable ones) as integral to this piece of theater.

The global pandemic had given us a precedent for this moment, because people worldwide were feeling fear and isolation, but of course experiencing these emotions in strikingly individual ways. The Hamlet station in "Shakespeare's Walking Story" used a famous speech as an avenue for the exploration of any number of thoughts related to personal and communal situations. The audience at this moment could have been considering George Floyd and Black Lives Matter, the discomfort of mosquitoes or rain, the drawbacks of spraying DEET on their skin, the indigenous history of this area, or the spread of Covid. Like the previous monologue, this one drew upon the generative possibilities of "folded time," but the tone was decidedly different. The unified feeling in the Desdemona/Gertrude delivery was made fragmented (in productive ways) by this Hamlet monologue. She drew us in and he made us uncomfortable.

Taurman's half-hearted return to "Denmark's a prison" at the end of the speech, without megaphone, was an expression of defeat. Unlike Peck's use of Desdemona's "So, get thee gone," Taurman's Hamlet did not bother to speak to the audience or cue them to the next station. They were left on their own, probably grateful when they heard the steps of the guide, leading them to the next station in the nature preserve.

Step 5: Like birds in a cage

A short walk from the Flourish sculpture took the audience to a shelter called Homestead Pavilion, where a woman was attempting to sing a song while wearing a facemask, until she stopped in frustration and ripped it off with a "No, no, no, no!" This outcry segued to Lear's speech to Cordelia about the pleasant nature of their shared imprisonment: "Come, let's away to prison; / We two alone will sing like bird i'th' cage" (5.3.8–25). In a field of native grasses behind the pavilion stood another sculpture: a 14-foot-tall, 8-foot-wide rendering of a Sandhill crane that was designed to be "highly visible at a distance by people exploring Story Mill Community Park." The sculptor, Stephen Fairfield, chose to call this piece "The Defender" because he envisioned the bird as being "high energy, charging, defensive, extremely alert creature seeking to keep interlopers from its turf" which "assume[d] an aggressive pose to defend its claimed area" (Fairfield).

Cara Wilder's delivery of Lear's speech with this sculpture in view was designed to invite a tangible consideration of what birds—from the song birds in the bird blind to the Sandhill cranes in the open field—have to do with freedom, or the lack thereof. Despite Lear's idealization of the idyllic shared cage, the language of retreat in this prison house (delivered in the most bulky and built site in the nature preserve) emphasized bondage most of all. Lear's desperate line about having "caught" (l. 21) his favorite daughter became unsettling, betraying that he would be another jailer, eager to constrict Cordelia's movements. The singing of a caged bird, especially in 2020, did not suggest notes of comfort. Indeed, during the rehearsal process we kept in mind Maya Angelou's poem on that very subject, with its poignant refrain:

> The caged bird sings
> with a fearful trill
> of things unknown
> but longed for still
> and his tune is heard
> on the distant hill
> for the caged bird
> sings of freedom.
> *(Angelou 31–8)*

On the second day of performance Wilder fell ill, and we had no one who was prepared to take her place with the Lear monologue. One guide, Kristin Hammargren, filled in, having prepared Duke Senior's speech with its famous exaltation of nature, which culminates with "tongues in trees, books in the running brooks, / Sermons in stones, and good in everything" (*AYLI* 2.1.1–17). This substitution meant that Sunday's audience witnessed a somewhat different performance from Saturday's, reinforcing the unpredictability of such ambulatory theatrical experience. But while the unexpected adjustment gave this station a very different emphasis from the Lear speech, it still offered a perspective on the (admittedly flexible) theme of imprisonment. The Duke's words as part of "Shakespeare's Walking Story" enacted what the Lear speech only imagined: the possibility of freedom. This freedom, importantly, was inextricably linked to nature. Hammargren's conveyance of this idea was achieved by her full immersion in the park's natural spaces. Rather than waiting in the pavilion, she scampered in the woods, encouraging the audience to look for woodpeckers; at one point even climbed a tree, calling out "Now my comates and brothers in exile" as if the subalpine fir itself were speaking.

The animistic thrust of the speech ("tongues in trees") infused the playing space with agency, sidelining the humans and encouraging the audience to make choices about how they would inhabit this space. Movement on foot ultimately resists ownership that would put birds (or anything) in a cage, for in Solnit's formulation

> Walking focuses not on the boundary lines of ownership that break the land into pieces but on the paths that function as a kind of circulatory system connecting the whole organism. Walking is, in this way, the antithesis of owning. It postulates a mobile, empty-handed, shareable experience of the land.
>
> *(162)*

Both actors' monologues enhanced the audience interaction with and consideration of the more-than-human elements of the park, creating the possibility of "smooth spaces"—places for walking and making holistic connections in the physical and imaginative world alike.[17]

Step 6: Virgil's progress

The longer walk from the last spot within the nature preserve back over the bridge was a logistical problem: how would we maintain interest and engagement up through the end? Until this moment the guides had given an introductory speech, but then mainly motioned to direct the audience onward.[18] Ultimately, however, the guides—along with the park itself—were the most consistent interface feature of "Shakespeare's Walking Story." In a sense, they were roving authors, recalling Solnit's point that "To read is to travel through that terrain [of the imagination] with the author as guide—a guide one may not always agree with or trust, but who can at least be counted upon to take one somewhere" (72). Like Dante's proxy guide, Virgil, the "Shakespeare's Walking Story" guides were characters who directed the imaginative journey through the production's narrative, while also directing the physical journey.[19]

We had not given the audience a map or foreknowledge of the route, but it was apparent that there was an established map in the guide's mind. Even though the walk was mainly in a loop, there was a prescribed way of proceeding from a beginning to an ending point. This marked divergence from *Sleep No More* and other choose-your-own-adventure theater experiences instead embraced the linear shape of journeys, thus our physical and narrative progression was much more like a pilgrimage than a treasure hunt.

As part of the return walk, the guides decided to share their own memorized Shakespearean speeches along the way. I recited Sonnet 29 in order to emphasize loneliness, but perhaps the most appropriate choice was from the guide who delivered Macbeth's famous "Tomorrow, and tomorrow" (5.5.18–27) while walking with her groups. The "petty pace" of life as uttered by Macbeth connected most naturally with what we had established at the beginning of the production. The continual motion of feet during this recitation echoed the pace of the walk and the pace of life—a point that had been running throughout the production, from Jaques' stages of life to Richard's dials on the clock and beyond. Writing about the passage of time in *Macbeth*, Bushnell makes the point that when encountering the text in different media, the degrees of control over time vary: readers can slow down or speed up at will, but viewers in the theater are "drawn forward relentlessly by the action, surrendering ourselves to the players' time and experiencing the character's anxiety about temporal distortion" (784). By providing only an excerpt from *Macbeth* and doing it while the audience members were in motion along a guided path, we both controlled time and encouraged individual reflection upon what temporal distortion might mean to each of us.

This stroll along the wider path where the "Virgil" guides delivered their surprise speeches also allowed an opportunity for audience members to participate in the creation of meaningful performance acts. When guiding, I asked the audience to freely share whatever Shakespearean words were in their heads. Though a handful of audience members were willing to contribute, ultimately few people chose to participate in this way, perhaps out of shyness, or reflection. More important than the verbal participation, however, was the invitation itself. Just as there were no boundaries between the playing spaces and the placement of the spectators, there was no ownership of these theatrical moments. The message was clear: everyone has a Shakespearean story.

Step 7: Released from the bands (an Epilogue)

As the audience re-crossed the bridge, they were returning to a more populated area typical of a public park, featuring manicured lawns, a playground, a climbing rock, and picnic shelters.[20] The material path echoed the change, for it was now pavement rather than gravel; meanwhile, the road noise could be heard again. It seemed as if there would be no more nooks, sculptures, or natural spaces for a stage. But there was one performance yet to come. A man carrying an umbrella rushed down from atop a grassy knoll to intercept the audience, noting that they "looked dismayed," as if they were in "a moved sort." The final speech was, of course, delivered by Prospero (a successive delivery of "We are such stuff" (4.1.148–158) and the Epilogue from *The Tempest*). As a companion to the initial Jaques speech, this well-known Shakespearean ending was a bookend to the performance. Jaques had led the audience into the depths of this embodied performative experience, but Prospero was leading them back out of it.

Ben Leubner as Prospero pointed back to the nature preserve when he referred to the "spirits" of the performance who had now "melted … into thin air." This famous reference to theater's ephemeral qualities was befitting here because it was easy to see that the actors would indeed leave no "rack" behind, for there was no set, no residue of our play. In the absence of constructed scenery or copious props, much ambulatory theater has incorporated technology—video projections, audio amplifications, handheld device apps—to enhance the experiences. Making the choice to eschew technological or physical additions to the production, "Shakespeare's Walking Story" focused mediations upon the actors' bodies, the words of Shakespeare, the direction of the guides, and the Story Mill Park settings.

Theater creates community, and people flocked to this production because they were longing for a public venue that filled this basic need.[21] As the rain fell steadily on the second day, we wondered whether the audience would come, but they did, carrying umbrellas and donning raincoats, trudging through the inclement weather to hear Shakespeare in concert with the sounds—both human and more-than-human—in this park. In fact, braving the elements and sharing discomfort helped to create bonds between people in various groups.

Prospero's language about confinement ("I must be here confined by you" and "release me from my bands / With the help of your good hands") offered a final way to think about imprisonment. Ultimately not cells or cages, but human relations are the cause of bondage, yet such bonds are not universally negative. The sorrow of letting Prospero go was apparent, for this also meant letting the imaginative realm of theater go. It was not possible to hold on to Prospero, any more than it was possible to hold on to the physically distanced performers or other audience members. Nonetheless, the concluding scene to the production gave the participants ways to think about their relationships to the performers, one another, and other local, regional, and global communities.

The physical spaces of performance in "Shakespeare's Walking Story" forged creative ideation, allowing for imagined communities that would far outlast the dispersal of spectators back into their warm, dry cars. Shakespeare was not a "solution" to the massive problems of 2020 (or of any age), but "Shakespeare's Walking Story" did create spaces for reflection as well as movement through those spaces. The continual steps on such pathways were a reminder that we must, and will, keep moving.

Notes

1 Worthen's internal quotation is taken from Norman's *The Design of Everyday Things* 9.
2 The "Story" of the production's title was thus a play on both a narrative and the name of this park.
3 See Conkie's argument that in ambulatory theatrical events "not just the text, but also the context, is imbued with renewed vigour" (232).
4 "Walking, ideally, is a state in which the mind, the body, and the world are aligned, as though they were three characters finally in conversation together, three notes suddenly making a chord" (Solnit 5).
5 One audience member wrote afterwards that "The promenade in between each performance was a time for inner reflection in a perfect setting" (Ilsa-Mari Lee, email, June 28, 2020).
6 See Haraway, whose coining of the term "natureculture" has proven useful as an anti-dualistic interrogation which instead illuminates multispecies histories.
7 Similarly, "Bolingbroke's proud joy" (l. 59) was altered to "Corona's proud joy." The etymological link between "Corona" and "crown" made this substitution especially apt.
8 See Minton 434–5.
9 "Music do I hear? *Music*
Ha, ha! keep time: how sour sweet music is,
When time is broke and no proportion kept!"
10 See the *New York Times*' article (March 24, 2020) on the "incalculable loss" of Covid-19.
11 Michael Goldstein composed the musical setting for the Willow Song.
12 See Barton and Wineyer 182.
13 The quotation is from Michel Serres in *Conversations on Science, Culture, and Time*; quoted in Bushnell 783.
14 "Audience members may rub up against other audience members, making the reading of the performance experiential in multiple ways, rather than limited to the approach prescribed by many forms of theatre architecture" (Tompkins 10).
15 Taken from *Hamlet* 2.2.252–254: "O God, I could be bounded in a nutshell and count myself a king of infinite space – were it not that I have bad dreams."
16 Collins notes a similar result of an ambulatory production of the *Duchess of Malfi* in which "Through their embodied engagement in the narrative, the audience was forced to confront their own conflicting responses to the reprehensible actions of the protagonists and examine their own complicity in the Duchess's suffering and eventual death" (55).
17 Deleuze and Guattari's concept of "smooth spaces" can be usefully employed as a way to consider walking as a nomadic pursuit that resists the striated spaces of civilization.

18 I joked that I felt a little like Dickens's ghost of Christmas future; we also joked that we resembled the guides that lead tourists through European tourist sites.

19 Solnit notes that the *Divine Comedy* is a book that resembles a walk (77).

20 Chavez noted this as a crucial moment of her experience: "Critch crunch – then a pause at the / Bridge, as the brook babbles by. The / Irony brings forth a laugh and anxiety / Dances in my stomach. Will I walk across?"

21 One audience member wrote to thank us for having "The insight and awareness of how much we, in the community, hunger for any type of theater" (Stephanie Campbell, email, June 28, 2020).

References

Angelou, Maya. "Caged Bird." *Shaker, Why Don't You Sing?* Random House, 1983.

Barton, Bruce and Richard Windeyer. "Immersive Negotiations: Binaural Perspectives on Site-Specific Sound." *Performing Site-Specific Theatre: Politics, Place, Practice*. Edited by Anna Birch, and Joanne Tompkins, Palgrave Macmillan, pp. 182–200.

Birch, Anna and Joanne Tompkins. *Performing Site-Specific Theatre: Politics, Place, Practice*. Palgrave Macmillan, 2012.

Bushnell, Rebecca. "Tragedy and Temporality." *PMLA*, vol. 129, no. 4, 2014, pp. 783–789.

Chavez, Lauren. "Another Dream." Unpublished poem, June 28, 2020.

Collins, Jane. "Embodied Presence and Dislocated Spaces: Playing the Audience in Ten Thousand Several Doors in a Promenade, Site-Specific Performance of John Webster's The Duchess of Malfi." *Performing Site-Specific Theatre: Politics, Place, Practice*. Edited by Anna Birch, and Joanne Tompkins, Palgrave Macmillan, pp. 54–68.

Conkie, Rob. "Reverie of a Shakespearean Walker." *The Oxford Handbook of Shakespeare and Performance*. Edited by James C. Bulman, Oxford UP, 2017.

Deleuze, Gilles and Félix Guattari. *A Thousand Plateaus: Capitalism and Schizophrenia*. U of Minnesota P, 1987.

Fairfield, Stephen. "New Media Public Art Sculpture." Available at: https://artrepreneur.com/p/newmediasculpture/art/C5JP2EdzN8cyijBxm.

Flaherty, Jennifer. "Dreamers and Insomniacs: Audiences in 'Sleep No More' and 'The Night Circus.'" *Comparative Drama*, no. 45, vol. 1/2, 2014, pp. 135–154.

Garner, Stanton. *The Absent Voice: Narrative Comprehension in the Theater*. U of Illinois P, 1989.

Haedicke, Susan. "Beyond Site-Specificity: Environmental Heterocosms on the Street." *Performing Site-Specific Theatre: Politics, Place, Practice*. Edited by Anna Birch, and Joanne Tompkins, Palgrave Macmillan, pp. 103–117.

Haraway, Donna J. *The Companion Species Manifesto: Dogs, People, and Significant Otherness*. Prickly Paradigm Press, 2003.

Minton, Gretchen E. "'The Season of All Natures': Montana Shakespeare in the Parks' Global Warming *Macbeth*." *Shakespeare Bulletin*, vol. 36, no. 3, 2018, pp. 429–448.

Norman, Donald A. *The Design of Everyday Things*. Basic Books, 2002.

Schmidt, Carol. "With a 'Flourish' – Jim Zimpel Sculpture Installed in Bozeman's New Story Mill Park." *Montana State University News Service*, January 7, 2019. Available at: https://www.montana.edu/news/18823/with-a-flourish-jim-zimpel-sculpture-installed-in-bozeman-s-new-story-mill-park.

Shakespeare, William. *King Lear*. Edited by R. A. Foakes, Arden, 1997.

Shakespeare, William. *The Tempest*. Edited by Virginia Mason Vaughan and Alden T. Vaughan, Arden, 1999.

Shakespeare, William. *King Richard II*. Edited by Charles R. Forker, Arden, 2002.

Shakespeare, William. *As You Like It*. Edited by Juliet Dusinberre, Arden, 2006a.

Shakespeare, William. *Hamlet*. Edited by Ann Thompson and Neil Taylor, Arden, 2006b.

Shakespeare, William. *Othello*. Edited by E. A. J. Honigmann, Arden, 2016.

Solnit, Rebecca. *Wanderlust: A History of Walking*. Penguin, 2000.

Tompkins, Joanne. "The 'Place' and Practice of Site-Specific Theatre and Performance." *Performing Site-Specific Theatre: Politics, Place, Practice*. Edited by Anna Birch, and Joanne Tompkins, Palgrave Macmillan, pp. 1–20.

Worthen, W. B. "'The Written Troubles of the Brain': 'Sleep No More' and the Space of Character." *Theatre Journal*, vol. 64, no. 1, 2012, pp. 79–97.

22
INTERFACING SHAKESPEARE ONSCREEN

Alexa Alice Joubin

Performance, as a medium, interfaces with textual variants, audience expectations, and site-specific arts—artworks produced and consumed at specific physical and social sites. Performances with screens as interface, in particular, create celluloid and digital pathways to various ideologies. As Alexander Galloway theorizes, "today interfaces are often taken to be synonymous with the media themselves" (936), but it is clear that the interface between humans (story-tellers) and machines (technologies of representation) governs the very logic of screened performance as a narrative medium, distilling "material flows [of representations] into concrete action" (Hookway ix). Live theater used to be a synchronous communal affair taking place in an architectural space, while performances on private screens are thought to be more asynchronous, intimate, and individuated. Theater, with modern playgoing conventions, may have a temporarily dampening effect, in that audiences in formal, indoor venues generally do not yell disapproving or appreciative comments during performance. In contrast, screened performances—film or digitized stage productions—can invite more immediate, if not voyeuristic, reactions in verbal or textual forms, since the audiences are physically separated from the space where dramatic action takes place. "Live" performances used to be distinguished from film—a more editorialized medium—by their cachet of being "ephemeral" and irrecoverable. However, these distinctions are going away, because more and more theatrical and filmic performances are mediated by the same screen interface. Through analyses of performances that call attention to filmic genres as well as (meta)theatrical operations in digital and digitized performances, this chapter argues that the screen is a self-reflexive, though often forgotten, interface that promotes collaborations across genres onscreen and onstage.

In the case of Shakespearean performance, the screen interface frequently evokes and reframes other media, including the interfaces of the codex book, television programming, and live or pre-recorded theatrical events. The interface of the screen is now a portal through which audiences experience Shakespeare's narratives with a range of associated artistic elements including costumes, sets, and music. That interface is itself shaped by modern ideologies and the structures of screen genres. Just as "the liberation of writing from the book in digital culture" has "changed the ways we make writing perform" (Worthen 217), the interface of the screen gives the concept of performance new, synchronous and asynchronous meanings. It offers variegated pathways to Shakespeare's plays and to other screen works; in turn, the efficacy of such interfaces is shaped by user participation and reception.

DOI: 10.4324/9780367821722-30

In fact, these dynamics extend from multiplex screens to the small screens of laptops, television, tablets, home cinemas, smart phones, and other personalized interfaces. The pandemic of COVID-19 has further blurred the distinctions between feature films intended for the multiplex and made-for-television, or made-for-streaming, films in terms of funding structures, aspect ratios, and scope of production. The interfaces and the channels of distribution are merging quickly. Netflix, a purveyor of streaming products, is now a global producer of original contents in the forms of both films and television series. These products are intended for streaming rather than collective consumption in multiplexes. Amazon, having acquired the Metro-Goldwyn-Mayer movie company in 2021, is also capitalizing on its Prime Video streaming platform. Amazon Studios have already (co)produced a hundred original films, including Richard Eyre's 2018 *King Lear*, starring Anthony Hopkins in the lead role and streamed as part of Amazon Prime. While "the smaller scope and intimacy of television" aided in the flourishing of television productions in the golden age of Shakespeare on television from 1944 to 1971 (Crowl 14), today's performances onscreen connect different modes of representation. In the golden era of television, most TV versions of Shakespeare were based on successful stage performances, but—due to the lockdown as a public health measure during the pandemic and due to the prevalence of streaming technologies already in place before 2020—there is no longer a hierarchical order of stage-to-television-to-film. Before the pandemic, more and more stage productions had been broadcast live, or in recorded formats, such as the RSC-Live series, to audiences in theaters. Now, an even larger number of born digital, or re-mastered, performances reached audiences directly on the small screen. It is no longer as meaningful to distinguish between "live" productions, multiplex films, and made-for-small-screen films.

It is now commonplace to integrate Shakespeare in traditional film format on the big screen into personalized experiences on the small screen for personal entertainment or for education. In Shakespeare criticism, there is therefore an urgent need to fully integrate the artifact of Shakespeare on the small screen (and screens within Shakespearean performances) "with an individuated integrity" into our overall understanding of Shakespeare's relationships to all kinds of interfaces from screens to the codex book (Desmet 2017). Competing digital interfaces, as Thomas Cartelli observes, "reduce the objective of feature film presentation in fixed screening spaces to one among many reception/display options" (48). With case studies showing how screens big and small have become more than "technologies of performance to concentrate the audience's focus" (Aebischer, *Shakespeare, Spectatorship and the Technologies of Performance* 4), this chapter reveals the central place of screen as interface between the differing universes of characters, performers, and audiences. The screen interface immerses audiences in an alternate universe in such a way that audiences rarely question the screen's aesthetic function. That interface often makes itself transparent even though it is generating the dramaturgical meanings central to the narratives. In some cases, as Richard Schechner predicted in the late 1960s, performance technologies have become "more important than the performers" (44), because the technologies of representation—in our case, the screen—is no longer merely a supporting mechanism but an interface generating new meanings for the narrative.

Interfacing Meta-Cinema

Interface is an important critical concept to understand Shakespeare in world-wide performances, because cinema operates not only as a medium to channel messages from the plays but as an interface among transhistorical and intercultural expressions. The ideological and aesthetic structures of that interface often create new meanings for Shakespeare's works.

Several meta-theatrical films draw on the "screen" as a framing interface between the films' fabula and Shakespeare's fictional universe. Stories told on the smaller screens within these films would not make sense independent of the stories told in the camera's frame. Full stories emerge from the juncture between the performance on the screen-within-the film, such a television set, and the performance within the film's frame.

Ralph Fiennes' 2011 film *Coriolanus* uses the fictional Fidelis TV channel as an interface to connect three key time zones of (1) the 1990s' setting of dramatic action that fuses (2) Elizabethan-era ideologies that are (3) mapped onto a Roman history inspired by Thomas Plutarch's *Lives of the Noble Greeks and Romans* (1579). Set "in a place calling itself Rome" in Serbia, a cinematic space created by the newsreels with references to the Yugoslav Wars, this film leans heavily on the screen-within-the-film as a framing device and interface. Protestors are shown filming, on their cell phones, Coriolanus' (Ralph Fiennes) speech vilifying the plebeians during a conflict at the grain depot. Jon Snow plays himself as a newscaster who interviews various characters while delivering breaking news in Shakespeare's blank verse. Multiple scenes show characters, such as Aufidius (Gerard Butler) or Volumnia (Vanessa Redgrave), glued to a television set in tense, pivotal moments. Appropriately enough, for a film bent on allegorizing the role of public media in modern political life, Coriolanus is banished during a live interview in a television studio. As Jennifer Flaherty argues, the co-presence of media coverage and on-screen action recasts "the viewer as a Roman media consumer" and fuses into one "the television screen and the movie screen" (236). The interface of television news goes far beyond their typical function of silent exposition to become the message itself.

Similarly, monitor screens of intercoms, hand-held video cameras, and television sets play a prominent role in Michael Almereyda's *Hamlet* (2000) which critiques consumer and media-dominated society. The film, set in twenty-first-century New York City, appropriates the trope of despondent urban youths and Buddhist spirituality. Personal memories are displaced onto and by various screens that function as mnemonic and surveillance devices. Hamlet roams around filming random footage using the Fisher-Price Pixel Vision, a toy camera. The First Player's speech about Hecuba in Shakespeare is replaced in this film by a clip of James Dean, a cultural icon of disillusionment, in *East of Eden* (dir. Elia Kazan, 1955), an adaptation based on John Steinbeck. Other examples of screens-within-the-screen abound.

The film contains multiple references to Buddhism through screens-within-the-film, including a clip from Ulrike Koch's documentary about a pilgrimage, *Die Salzmänner von Tibet* (*The Saltmen of Tibet*, 1997), which appears on the back-seat video monitor of Claudius's (Kyle MacLachlan) limousine as he prays. In the moment when the tribesmen pass through the boundary between the secular world and the sacred territory of the salt fields in the documentary, Claudius, who has been praying, covers the screen with his hand and laments the failure of his words to reach Heaven ("what if this hand be blacker than it is with brother's blood" in the film; "What if this cursed hand / Were thicker than itself with brother's blood?" in the play) as he is jolted by a nasty and dangerous swerve. Hamlet is driving the limousine, as chauffeur, without Claudius's knowledge. It is unclear if Hamlet pre-arranged for the screening of Koch's documentary on the back-seat screen, but the parallel story told on the small screen does ironize Claudius's half-hearted prayer.

The interface of screens in the film creates intertextual echoes. Notably in the "to be or not to be" scene, Hamlet's footage of his brooding self gives way to the pacifist monk Thich Nhat Hanh's lecture, trivializing Hamlet's self-indulgence while raising the Buddhist teaching of inter-connectedness as a nobler model. The echoes pitch the individualistic, existential question of being against the Buddhist, community-oriented mode of interbeing. On the television screen, Thich Nhat Hanh offers his teaching on "interbeing": "We have the word to be, but I propose the word to interbe. Interbe. Because it is not possible to 'be' alone. We must interbe with everything and everyone else—mother, father ... uncle." It is important to note the interplay among the many screens in Hamlet's room at this moment. Thich Nhat Hanh's words echo repeated video loops of Hamlet reciting the half-line "to be or not to be" while making suicidal gestures. Engrossed in his own footage of an erotic encounter with Ophelia on the hand-held monitor, Hamlet is not looking at the television or listening to Thich Nhat Hanh. The book Ophelia is reading, and with which she partly covers her face, is Jiddu Krishnamurti's *On Living and Dying* (1992) with a portrait of the sage on its cover. The book-on-screen within the film's frame contains intertextual commentary on Hamlet's "to be or not to be" speech. Krishnamurti advocates un-learning of preconceptions of the ideas of life and death. In contrast to Hamlet's apprehension of the unknown ("dread of something after death" in the "undiscover'd country"), Krishnamurti argues that the fear of death reflects the fear of losing essential parts of who we are.

Thich Nhat Hanh and Krishnamurti encode spiritualism as sources of wisdom that could redeem Hamlet. The Buddhist meditation highlights the contradictory nature of identities that can be constructed only in opposition to others. The "to be or not to be" speech is familiar enough to most audiences to have an impact and to allow for recognition even when rewritten as interbe. The fragmentary allusions to Shakespeare, via screens-within-the-screen, are part of a process of Shakespearization, the formation of social shorthand (Ridden).

Similar to Almereyda's film, several other films use television news as a framing device. The Singaporean film *Chicken Rice War* (dir. Chee Kong Cheah, 2000) draws its comedic energy from the stage rehearsals and performances of *Romeo and Juliet* and the off-stage life of the actors in the college production. The screen acts not only as an interface between *Romeo and Juliet* (with Singaporean twists) and film audiences but also between *Romeo and Juliet* and the actor-characters within the film's universe and between multiple versions of *Romeo and Juliet*. The film inserts an aspiring television news anchor into its opening sequence and several scenes as he reports on the conflicts between two families who own chicken rice stalls next to each other ("From forth the fatal loins of these two foes, / A pair of star-crossed lovers *choose their chicken rice*"). Against moments where the stage asserts its perceived Shakespearean or local authenticity (students performing in English; an elderly woman singing the story about the "feud" in Cantonese operatic tunes), camerawork and editing (cutting between shots of the failed stage performance and reaction shots of parents interrupting the performance) strive to reclaim the superiority of film over theater.

Chicken Rice War contains attenuated and explicit references to other films. Its opening and closing sequences, narrated by the news anchor, simultaneously parody both the now-clichéd chorus in Shakespeare and the news-anchor-as-chorus in Baz Luhrmann's *William Shakespeare's Romeo + Juliet* (1996). *Chicken Rice War* thrives on the tension between theatricalized presentation (such as play-within-a-play) and verisimilitude in cinematic representation.

In Luhrmann's film, after the composed, dispassionate, deliberately old-fashioned script reading by a female TV news anchor framed by an antiquated television set, a whooshing shot "sucks" the film audience through the mouth of the announcer into a second iteration of the Prologue in "fair Verona" in full action, complete with monochrome footage from police helicopters. The television screen within the film dramatizes the Prologue on three occasions: first, in a detached tone by a female news anchor, before a neutral background, reading from a script; second, by the voice of a male announcer in a low, overly dramatic, ominous but solemn tone against live-action shots; and third, as a print medium in which key words of the Prologue appear as headlines. A soundtrack of Craig Armstrong's "O Verona" accompanies the live-action shots in "fair Verona" in the second iteration of the Prologue. "O Verona" was inspired by Carl Orff's musical setting of the medieval poem "O Fortuna" (as part of his cantata *Carmina Burana*). "O Fortuna" was not available for licensing, and "O Verona," replete with echoes of the motif of "O Fortuna," served as a stand-in. "O Verona" is a spin-off and possibly a parody of "O Fortuna" for both pragmatic and metacinematic reasons.

Luhrmann's film was also parodied by the action-comedy *Hot Fuzz* (dir. Edgar Wright, Universal Pictures, 2007), which features Luhrmann's final scene in a village production staged by bumbling actors with the same soundtrack ("Lovefool" by the Cardigans) and the same costumes as those by Luhrmann. In this case, it is the stage-within-the-film, rather than screen-within-the film, that generates alternative meanings to the main plot. Set in Sandford, Gloucestershire, a fictional "model" village, *Hot Fuzz* is part of Wright's acclaimed tribology of parodies of police drama, zombie narratives (*Shaun of the Dead*, 2004), and apocalyptic stories (*The World's End*, 2013). Sitting on Juliet's "death bed" surrounded by copious candles and three neon-lit crosses, Romeo (Martin Blower, played by David Threlfall), still in his shining knight armor costume from the masked ball, states, with each vowel elongated, that: "A dateless bargain to engrossing death! / ... Here's to my love!" as he downs the poison. His unconvincing acting makes it seem as if he was taking a shot of liquor in celebration. After Romeo dies, Juliet (Eve Draper, portrayed by Lucy Punch) wakes up. As she sits up in the same angelic costume with white wings as Claire Danes' in Luhrmann's film, the feathers of her wings are glowing in backlight. She finds a pistol by Romeo's body and points it at her temple. As she pulls the trigger she yells in a cartoonish fashion, "Bang!", although there are no sound effects. The audiences in *Hot Fuzz* consist mostly of elderly villagers who sleep through it. The scene in the theater alternates between front shots of the audiences and long and medium shots of the action on stage. The production in *Hot Fuzz* draws attention to the over-the-top dialogues, stylized visuals, and campy nature of Luhrmann's *Romeo and Juliet*. Despite their incompetence, the actors take their performance seriously in front of audiences in the film's universe.

The trans-medial flow of content (Jenkins 2006: 18) among all of these screens, and screened stage productions, creates a point of convergence where Shakespeare's textual presence, in the forms of allusion and quotation, meets visual representations interfaced by screens.

Interfacing "To Be, or Not to Be"

Widely circulated speeches have also been used as an interface between the main plot and alternative universes to which the characters allude. Similar to screens-within-the-film, this artifact-as-interface operates in a liminal space to connect different narrative universes. For instance, *Hamlet* is merely one of the many sources of inspiration for Almereyda's film. The prince's "to be or not to be" speech itself—in verbal and visual forms—becomes an important interface in the scene analyzed above. Other screen works, such as Laurence Olivier's *Hamlet* (1948), have been deployed as a key interface between verbal and visual messages. In the Iranian film adaptation of *Hamlet* entitled *Tardid* (Doubt, dir. Varuzh Karim-Masihi, 2009), the archivist Siavash contemplates the parallels between his life and Hamlet as he hangs a framed Farsi text, "to be or not to be," on the wall of his depressing office in a basement. The speech becomes a tangible artifact and a key prop in this scene. The *mise-en-scène* interfaces the verbal message from the soliloquy with the sensation of being trapped in an interstitial space.

A poster of Olivier's film appears as an interface and a gateway in the French film *Ophélia* (dir. Claude Chabrol, 1963). Yvan (André Jocelyn), a spoilt scion of a wealthy family maps his life onto that of Hamlet. Overhearing the French dubbed conversations about the natural and necessary passing of generations (1.2.68–92) from Olivier's *Hamlet*, as he walks past a large poster of the English film, Yvan imagines himself to be mid-century Hamlet upholding some sense of morality amidst industrial actions by factory workers and intellectuals benefiting from the post-war economic boom (Figure 22.1). The film interfaces with French filmic and theatrical traditions, referencing *Hamlet*, Olivier, *Orphée* (dir. Jean Cocteau, 1950), and comedy of manners.

The nouvelle vague (New Wave) film director Claude Chabrol, known as "the French Hitchcock" (Miller 14–18), uses the film to comment on France's identity and economic crisis. In contrast to his *Les bonnes femmes* (1960) which depicts female sexuality through the misadventures of four young women in Paris, *Ophélia*—despite its title—focuses on the son of the factory-owning family Lesurf, Yvan (played by André Jocelyn). Ever so self-indulgent, Yvan wanders the mansion and its grounds reciting poetry. When he stumbles upon Laurence Olivier's film version of *Hamlet* in a local cinema, Yvan sets out to become a Hamlet himself—parallel to how James Joyce's Stephen Daedalus and Goethe's Wilhelm Meister embody select aspects of *Hamlet*. Yvan is a typical protagonist of the New Wave cinema which favors "spontaneous young characters" in "unpolished … film styles" (Neupert xviii).

Ironically, Yvan's arc marginalizes the tangential story of a woman who says repeatedly "Je ne suis pas Ophélia. Je suis Lucy." There is no plot parallel between Lucy's story and that of Shakespeare's Ophelia. The name Ophelia becomes a "free-floating apostrophe" (Peterson 22) in Chabrol's film, because the narrative refers repeatedly to the state of not being Ophelia. Teasing audience's expectations, *Ophélia* names its Shakespearean precedence in its title only to erase Hamlet and Ophelia. The Hamletian motifs—communicated through Olivier's film poster and the prince's speech—serve as an interface rather than originary texts for full adaptation.

It is not atypical to see films, such as *Tardid* and *Ophélia*, that use Shakespearean artifacts as an interface to have a cursory, and oftentimes evasive, relationship to Shakespeare. Hamlet's soliloquy features prominently in *My Left Foot* (dir. Jim Sheridan, Ferndale Films, 1989), a film that dramatizes the life of a character with cerebral palsy, Christy Brown, who struggles with daily speech. During a speech therapy session, Brown's therapist Sheila asks him to learn Hamlet's speech as a strategy to improve his speech impediments. Sheila motivates Brown to recite "to be or not to be" by asking him if he would like to one day be able to "say fuck off more clearly" without "impenetrable" and slurred speech. When asked for his opinion of the Prince of Denmark, Brown says Hamlet is "a cripple" who "can't hack it," before giving in and reciting the speech. Sheila frames Hamlet's speech as an interface, a gateway, to a new world. While Brown initially uses perceived disability (a cripple) to dismiss Hamlet as a possible source of therapy, he eventually achieves clear speech through the exercise.

Figure 22.1 Yvan walks past a poster of Laurence Olivier's *Hamlet* in Claude Chabrol's *Ophélia* (1963)
Source: Screen grab (DVD).

Eavesdropping on his therapy session, his mother is astonished by the miraculous clarity of his speech. She observes that "there's something in that voice that disturbs me. It's not like him. It has too much hope." Similar to other films about vocal disability, *My Left Foot* "plays the supercrip angle" with a reparative tagline that indicates it's a film "about life, laughter, and the occasional miracle" (Riley 84). The scene interfaces with a philosophical investment in Shakespeare's therapeutic value by dramatizing how even patients with voice disorder can recite the lines from Shakespeare.

In another film, the line "to be or not to be" is given a parodic spin. John McTiernan's *Last Action Hero* (1993) depicts the adventure of Danny Madigan (Austin O'Brien), a schoolboy who is a fan of the action film hero Jack Slater (Arnold Schwarzenegger). When Danny's English teacher screens the scene of Hamlet's soliloquy from Laurence Olivier's film, a bored Danny envisions the scene as it should be played, starring a Terminator-esque Slater in Olivier's costumes, who smashes his way through stalled moments in *Hamlet* without hesitation. Recast in the role of Hamlet, Slater asks himself, "to be or not to be?" Lighting up the cigar in his mouth, he declares "not to be" as he ignites explosives without hesitation, killing all the characters in *Hamlet*. The scene is an example of how films interface other modes of presentation. Olivier's psychological realism and clichéd theatrical style of performance on screen are overwritten by the schoolboy's imagination that draws on more contemporary cultural reference points. James Cameron's *Terminator 2: Judgment Day* made Schwarzenegger a bankable global star in 1991, two years before the release of *Last Action Hero*.

Screening the Penumbra

"To be or not to be" as an interface is one of the many nodes that narratives pass through; it is no longer a point of origin, or destination, for story-telling. The interface evokes a heterotopia (Foucault), a universe within the film's universe. As a gateway to parallel narratives, the interface mirrors and destabilizes the world within and without, giving multiple layers of meanings to the main plot. The interface creates a penumbra around the work.

These uses of screens-within-the-film or Shakespearean artifacts as an interface anticipate the Wooster Group's meta-media and multi-media stage production of *Hamlet* (dir. Elizabeth LeCompte, 2007), in which the actors projected onstage a filmed version of Richard Burton's performance in a 1964 *Hamlet* (dir. John Gielgud) on the Broadway. Burton's onscreen Hamlet ghosts Scott Shepherd's onstage Hamlet. In addition to the 1964 *Hamlet*, which is playing on a big screen upstage as pre-recorded material, another smaller screen is present downstage. The smaller screen, standing behind the actors but in front of the large screen, shows a live video stream of their action primarily in the form of close-up shots of their faces (Figure 22.2). Actors speak the same lines synchronously with Burton's performance. On some occasions, the soundtrack from Burton's video contributed to uncanny dual soundtracks of live and pre-recorded speeches. On other occasions, the actors appeared to be ventriloquizing, or mouthing, lines from Burton's video, because the louder soundtrack of the project drowned out the stage action.

An additional layer of screened meanings emerged during the pandemic, in April, 2020, when the Wooster Group streamed a 2013 video recording of their production online for free. The screen as an interface in 2020 did not work as well as its 2013 production when the concept was a novelty, because, in 2020, at-home audiences—easily distracted—lose connections with the characters and meta-characters. It did not help either that at-home audiences could only "watch through a single static camera." Juggling Shepherd's and Burton's now competing onscreen presence, some critics found that "the lack of emotion" became

Figure 22.2 Ari Fliakos's Claudius and Kate Valk's Gertrude in front of the two screens, with stagehands to the left, in Wooster Group's *Hamlet*, 2007
Source: Screengrab (freely available video released on Vimeo by Wooster Group).

"tiresome" despite the "striking spectacle's ... playful demonstration of control" (Wyver). This is a case of failed interfacing of Shakespeare onscreen.

Like a penumbra, Burton's performance forms concentric circles around the Wooster Group's production, befitting *Hamlet*, the "spectral play" (Callens 539). It also becomes a pretext, as the poster of Olivier's film does in *Ophélia*, for artistic recycling and creativity. The screen-as-interface evokes discrete plot elements in parallel universes and casts a penumbra around the film or production. When light is shed over an opaque object, it casts a shadow with a partially shaded outer region. Judith Buchanan theorizes that in this manner adaptations contain a "textual penumbra" (10), a body of extra-textual information that is closely associated with the work and enriches its meanings. An innocuous penumbra could be audiences' awareness of previous works by the artist, as in the case of Burton's Hamlet ghosting the Wooster Group's stage work. A more intrusive penumbra could be directors' statements on record or the significance of the venue.

All the World's a Digital Screen

Just as film screenings re-enact site-specific meanings connected to the works' historical contexts, digital video archives are also informed by their own site specificity in terms of the cultural locations of curatorial labor and the consumption of the archival materials at points of access (Lim 201). A digital performance video produced in London but consumed in, for example, Abu Dhabi, carries with it culturally-specific meanings of these locations. These meanings are filtered and enabled by the screen as interface. Building on the preceding sections on the screen-within-the-performance as an interface, this section turns to the dynamics of the digital screen itself as a screening interface on commercial and open-access platforms. Viewing digital Shakespeare as a performed event—whether asynchronous or synchronous—connects the concepts of re-play to liveness in performance.

Site-specific meanings of drama take a disembodied form in digital videos. As a form of instantaneous, inter-connected communication, the digital video is non-linear and non-sequential in nature. My research indicates that digital video has the unique ability to "support instant access to any sequence in a performance, as well as the means to re-order and annotate sequences, and to bring them into meaningful conjunction with other videos, texts and image collections" (Joubin 39).

The digital video as an interface gained increased significance when the outbreak of the global pandemic of COVID-19 closed live theater events and cinemas worldwide. Due to lockdown orders and restrictions on travel as public health measures, audiences—trapped at home—took to streaming to engage with Shakespeare as a familiar classic. The pandemic has led to a proliferation of born-digital and digitized archival videos of Shakespeare in Western Europe, Canada, the UK and the US. Key players included the Berliner Ensemble, La Comédie Française, the Globe Theatre in London, the Royal Shakespeare Company, National Theatre, Stratford Festival in Canada, and the Folger Theatre in Washington, D.C. Digital streaming—live or pre-recorded—has helped Shakespeare go viral on a global scale.

The Royal Shakespeare Company took digital performance one step further by enabling live, audience interaction with the actors through the screen as interface. In March, 2021, the RSC launched an innovative one-hour musical show online, *Dream* (dir. Robin McNicholas), which was inspired by *A Midsummer Night's Dream.* Using live capture and gaming technologies, the camera took online audiences backstage and onstage before going into a virtual reality environment (Figure 22.3).

Viewers follow an actor backstage in a motion-capture suit and witness her transformation into Puck, a digitally produced avatar onscreen. Her movements are transformed into the avatar's limb movements. The show draws on a kinetic, rather than verbal, energy, as actors do not speak. For *Dream*, the screen is the very venue and meaning-making agent where performative meanings arise; it is far more than a piece of technology to transmit performances to audiences. The movements of fairies generate live sound and music. Cobweb is represented as close-up shots of Maggie Bain's staring eyeball. Wearing motion capture sensors over her suit, E.M. Williams is transformed into Puck, a figure that wanders the night as an assemblage of pebbles in the shape of a human body. Audiences follow her through computer-generated forests and landscapes. On Tuesday, March 16, 2021, more than 7,000 ticket holders logged on to watch the show live, some of whom used the interactive feature by clicking on firefly icons to light up the path for Puck. The fireflies, however, were ornamental, as they did not have any direct impact on the performance or Puck's movement.

Figure 22.3 Dream, directed by Robin McNicholas, Royal Shakespeare Company Online, March 2021
Source: Screen grab (live streaming).

The highlight was the show's global reach. Questions came in from all over the world, from as far as Melbourne, during the post-show discussion session. The global visibility and huge turnout were welcome news for the RSC, but the technological wonders failed to woo some critics. *The New York Times* called it "a small copse of some really lovingly rendered trees." *The Guardian* acknowledges the technology could well be "a new arrow for the quiver of live theatre" while critiquing the show's lack of "an emotional dimension" (Clapp 2021; Soloski 2021).

COVID-19 accelerated the global processes of interfacing Shakespeare onscreen. Theater director Erin B. Mee writes optimistically that the pandemic has created "an exciting new performance environment," bringing artists and audiences together "from numerous nations" and creating "new possibilities for collaboration." Digital forms of video communication have enabled "artists from around the world" to gather in virtual spaces "playing to international audiences rather than … to people who can get to a particular piece of real estate" (Mee and TDR Editors 208–9). Thanks to Zoom, TikTok, and other platforms, any performance is now potentially a global event. For their participatory performance of *The Tempest,* Creation Theatre and Big Telly Theatre companies used the tagline: "live, interactive, and in your living room" anywhere in the world (2020), which is only possible through the screen as interface. When the Public Theatre in New York launched the *Brave New Shakespeare* Challenge (2020), they shared videos of their actors reading act 2 scene 2 of *Romeo and Juliet* in multiple languages, and invited the general public to share their own. The initiative has a global outlook, as evidenced by its emphasis of multilingual, user-created contents.

One reason for Shakespeare's global popularity on digital media, as W.B. Worthen surmises, is its status as comforting, familiar go-to-material for uplifting the spirits during the pandemic (cited in Soloski 2020). Shakespeare skyrocketed to the top of the list of digital performance events during the pandemic in the forms of memes, quotable quotes about Shakespeare and the plague, and performances of select scenes.

As measures to contain spread of the virus, the lockdown and stay-at-home orders have accelerated digital globalization with the screen as a key interface, redefining liveness along the way. As Pascale Aebischer suggests, as a "chronological order" that seems to slow down time ("Viral Shakespeare," 2020b), the lockdown motivates at-home audiences to break free of the limit of their temporality by engaging in escapism. Mobility is limited, even within one's own neighborhood. By late April 2020, 54 percent of the global population (4.2 billion people) were subject to complete or partial lockdowns (WHO). Audiences "bounded in a nutshell" (*Hamlet* 2.2.273) seek virtual connections that transport them beyond their now fixed geographic locations to an alternative universe.

Digital broadcasting is nothing new, for, in the past decade, prominent organizations such as the Metropolitan Opera and the Barbican Centre have broadcast their programming to theaters and cinemas around the world, both live and pre-recorded. In the summer of 2017, the John F. Kennedy Center for the Performing Arts broadcast in real-time Washington National Opera's performance of *Aida* (dir. Francesca Zambello) to the Nationals Park in Washington, D.C. (Midgette). Both the audiences in the Kennedy Center and those in the baseball stadium enjoyed the show live—the former in the same space as the singers and the latter synchronously in a different space. These indoor and open-air digital performances remained "live," communal experiences.

The new genre of born-digital performances has redefined the notion of liveness as "a temporal and spatial entity" (Sullivan). The global pandemic has further expanded the idea of liveness. Asynchronous digital videos do not so much replicate theatrical experiences as they enable experiential and affective immersiveness on personal electronic devices for private consumption. Blurring the boundary between film and theater, both genres are detached from the palpable bodily presence of actors. Notably, viewers' own subjectivity is also disembodied (Aebischer, "Viral Shakespeare").

Digital video has been a godsend for theater companies during the prolonged pandemic. Artists and fundraisers tapped into digital video to maintain their visibility and increase the arts' relevance to society. Their focus turned from playgoers in the physical playhouses to at-home audiences around the world. Some companies released pre-recorded performances on a time-limited basis on pre-scheduled intervals to drum up excitement. The sense of exclusivity paralleled the ephemerality and limited availability of live theater. Some events were free. Others sold tickets at a fraction of the price of live shows. In rural Virginia, the Blackfriars Playhouse, part of the American Shakespeare Center, moved their 2020 season online to their proprietary streaming platform called BLKFRSTV.

The pandemic has caused grief and damage to social infrastructures, but it has also helped a few theater companies reach mass, global audiences on an unprecedented scale. By May 18, 2020, the London Globe had already garnered 1.9 million viewers on their YouTube channel, which was cited by Neil Constable, chief executive of Shakespeare's Globe, as evidence of the "huge appetite for culture at a time of national crisis" when they bid for support from the UK's Department of Digital, Culture, Media and Sports during the lockdown (cited in Dams). The Globe is unique among British theaters in that it had a predominantly international, tourist audience base even before the pandemic.

Theater seating capacity was no longer a concern. The Donmar Warehouse's *Coriolanus* (dir. Josie Rourke, 2013), starring Tom Hiddleston, on "National Theatre at Home" attracted more than half a million views and raised US$20,691 between 4 and 11 June 2020. Significantly, this was a 2013, rather than a new, production that the organizers brought online during the pandemic. The number of online participants far exceeded the number of audiences a live production could ever reach within the same one-week period. The Donmar auditorium has only 251 seats; even the National Theatre has a total of only 2,417 seats across its three venues.

The key takeaways from digital theater in the era of COVID-19 are expanded notions of liveness and site-specific epistemologies. The site of live performance is distinct from the site where at-home audiences experience that performance—mediated by technologies of representation and their computer screens as interface. The rise of the screen as interface expands the notion of performance beyond brick-and-mortar buildings. Financial gains remain ancillary to online performances during the pandemic, because not all productions translate well to digital streaming. The theaters' global digital footprint is a symbolic means to connect with their patrons and to maintain the companies' cultural capital.

Conclusion

Three observations can be made about these instances of interfacing Shakespeare onscreen. First, the screen as interface has created deep structural connections among even works that seem to be isolated instances of artistic creation. The connections extend through the cultural practice of interfacing different media, such as film, theater, or visual arts. The cases above relate more frequently to one another, through the screening interface, than to Shakespeare as sanctified source material.

Second, these works are products of meta-cinematic and meta-theatrical operations and contestations among genres for primacy. The meanings of these narratives are shaped by the interface between disparate genres. Without reproducing Shakespeare's story or engaging directly with Laurence Olivier's *Hamlet*, Chabrol's *Ophélia* references a poster of Olivier's film as part of a network of cross-references. The archetype of Hamlet is deployed to capture the figure of the despondent in distinctively local contexts. The poster as an interface evokes Olivier's and Hamlet's universes and adds nuanced meanings about self-indulgence to the film *Ophélia*.

Third, as Terence Hawkes argues, phrases and ideas from *Hamlet* and *Romeo and Juliet* have been so deeply embedded in everyday speech that it operates simply as "a web of quotations" and a "universal cultural [and] social shorthand" (4). The "to be or not to be" speech is familiar enough to serve as an interface between a character's suffering and an index of intelligence. This interface culture has given rise to digitally enhanced global Shakespeare performances.

While in the 1990s, audiences typically encountered Shakespeare for the first time through film or theater, in our times the initial encounters occur predominantly on digital platforms in the form of video clips, memes, or quotes. It has become more common for non-professional readers and audiences to encounter Shakespeares in fragmented forms. "To be or not to be," even in fragmented forms and out-of-context quotations, carries weight and shifts the meanings of some characters' action. All of this is made possible by the screen as interface that connects what Linda Hutcheon calls the hypertexts, texts with embedded allusions, and hypotexts, texts that inspire subsequent works (121).

The screen as interface links the disparate meanings of Shakespeare in different locations. The pandemic has highlighted further the importance of networks of instantaneous cross references as well as localized, embodied knowledge about Shakespeare. The interfaces of screen-within-performances and digital screens further contribute to this repertoire of evolving, shared knowledge. The interface-driven screen culture has de-centered Shakespeare's singularity—the perceived infinite value of the canon—by turning Shakespearean artifacts into a heterotopia. To further our understanding of Shakespeare in the post-pandemic era, it is important to engage with this interface that informs many works.

References

Aebischer, Pascale. *Shakespeare, Spectatorship and the Technologies of Performance*. Cambridge UP, 2020a.

Aebischer, Pascale. "Viral Shakespeare: Binge-Watching Hamlet in Lockdown." The Royal Central School of Speech and Drama, virtual lecture on Zoom, May 20, 2020b.

Buchanan, Judith. *Shakespeare on Film*. Pearson, 2005.

Callens, Johan. "The Wooster Group's *Hamlet*, According to the True, Original Copies." *Theatre Journal*, vol. 61, no. 4, 2009, pp. 539–561.

Cartelli, Thomas. *Reenacting Shakespeare in the Shakespeare Aftermath: The Intermedial Turn and Turn to Embodiment*. Palgrave, 2019.

Clapp, Susannah. "*Dream* Review – The RSC's Hi-Tech Shakespeare Only Goes So Far." *The Guardian*, 21 March 2021. Available at: https://www.theguardian.com/stage/2021/mar/21/dream-review-rsc-royal-shakespeare-company-nick-cave-the-litten-trees-fuel.

Creation Theatre. *The Tempest*. 2020. Available at: https://www.creationtheatre.co.uk/shows/the-tempest-live-interactive-in-your-living-room/.

Crowl, Samuel. *Shakespeare and Film: A Norton Guide*. W.W. Norton, 2008.

Dams, Tim. "Shakespeare's Globe Could Close Permanently Due to Coronavirus, U.K. Legislators Warn." *Variety*, May 18, 2020. Available at: https://variety.com/2020/legit/uncategorized/shakespeares-globe-theatre-risk-closure-coronavirus-1234609264/.

Desmet, Christy. "Alien Shakespeares 2.0." *Actes des Congrès de la Société française Shakespeare*, 2017. Available at: https://journals.openedition.org/shakespeare/3877.

Flaherty, Jennifer. "Filming Shakespeare's Rome: The 'Preposterous Contemporary' Eternal City." *Interdisciplinary Literary Studies*, vol. 17, no. 2, 2015, pp. 228–240.

Foucault, Michel. "Of Other Spaces." Translated by Jay Miskowiec, *Diacritics*, vol. 16, no. 1, 1986, pp. 22–27.

Galloway, Alexander R. "The Unworkable Interface." *New Literary History*, vol. 39, no. 4, 2008, pp. 931–955.

Hawkes, Terrence. *Meaning by Shakespeare*. Routledge, 2012.

Hookway, Branden. *Interface*. MIT Press, 2014.

Hutcheon, Linda. *A Theory of Adaptation*, 2nd ed., Routledge, 2013.

Jenkins, Henry. *Convergence Culture: Where Old and New Media Collide*. New York UP, 2006.

Joubin, Alexa Alice. "Global Shakespeare 2.0 and the Task of the Performance Archive." *Shakespeare Survey*, vol. 64, 2011, pp. 38–51.

Lim, Alvin Eng Hui. "Thinking Virtually in a Distracted Globe: Archiving Shakespeare in Asia." *Documenting Performance: The Context and Process of Digital Curation and Archiving*. Edited by Toni Sant, Bloomsbury, 2017, pp. 189–202.

Mee, Erin B. and TDR Editors. "Forum: After COVID-19, What?" *TDR: The Drama Review* vol. 64, no. 3, 2020, pp. 191–224.

Midgette, Anne. "An *Aida* That Aspires to Give Street Cred to Grandiosity." *The Washington Post*, September 11, 2017. Available at: https://www.washingtonpost.com/entertainment/music/an-aida-that-aspires-to-give-street-cred-to-grandiosity/2017/09/11/aa47d17a-9700-11e7-82e4-f1076f6d6152_story.html.

Miller, D. A. 2010. "In Memoriam: The French Hitchcock." *Film Quarterly*, vol. 64, no. 2, 2010, pp. 14–18.

Neupert, Richard. *A History of the French New Wave Cinema*. 2nd ed., U of Wisconsin P, 2007.

Peterson, Kaara. "Framing Ophelia: Representation and the Pictorial Tradition." *Mosaic: An Interdisciplinary Critical Journal*, vol. 31, no. 3, 1998, pp. 1–24.

Public Theatre. *Brave New Shakespeare*. 2020. Available at: https://publictheater.org/news-items/buckets/Features/brave-new-shakespeare-v2/.

Ridden, Geoffrey M. "The Bard's Speech: Making It Better; Shakespeare and Therapy in Film." *Borrowers and Lenders*, vol. 8, no. 2, 2013–2014. Available at: http://www.borrowers.uga.edu/26/toc.

Riley, Charles A. II. *Disability and the Media: Prescriptions for Change*. UP of New England, 2005.

Schechner, Richard. "6 Axioms for Environmental Theatre." *TDR: The Drama Review*, vol. 12, no. 3, 1968, pp. 41–64.

Soloski, Alexis. "Is This a Livestream I See Before Me?" *The New York Times*, May 13, 2020. Available at: https://www.nytimes.com/2020/05/13/theater/shakespeare-online.html.

Soloski, Alexis. "Review: Living the 'Dream,' on Your Laptop or Phone." *The New York Times*, March 17, 2021. Available at: https://www.nytimes.com/2021/03/17/theater/review-dream-royal-shakespeare-company.html.

Sullivan, Erin. "The Audience Is Present: Aliveness, Social Media and the Theatre Broadcast Experience." *Shakespeare and the 'Live' Theatre Broadcast Experience*. Edited by Pascale Aebischer, Susanne Greenhalgh, and Laurie E. Osbourne. Bloomsbury, 2018, pp. 59–75.

WHO (World Health Organization). "Coronavirus Disease (COVID-19) Dashboard." 2020. Available at: https://covid19.who.int/.

Worthen, W. B. 2010. "Posthuman Shakespeare Performance Studies." *Postmedieval: A Journal of Medieval Cultural Studies*, vol. 1, no. 1–2, pp. 215–222.

Wyver, Kate. "*Hamlet* Review—The Wooster Group Resurrect Richard Burton's Dane." *The Guardian*, April 2, 2020. Available at: https://www.theguardian.com/stage/2020/apr/02/hamlet-review-wooster-group-richard-burton.

23
FRONT TO FRONT
Enactment as Interface

Mary Hartman

For several years between 1994 and 2003, Shakespeare & Company hosted a summer institute for teachers, sponsored by the National Endowment for the Arts, and I was privileged to work on it. The program brought scholars, theater practitioners, and school teachers together to develop the most dynamic, engaging ways of teaching Shakespeare. During these institutes the resident scholar, Maynard Mack Jr., would often talk about theater as a democratic art form. Unlike other literary forms, a play very rarely has an omniscient narrator as a mediating voice: the characters speak for themselves. This democracy is further realized by artistic interpretation, as different actors, directors, and designers put their personal stamp on the production. Sandy (as he was known to his friends) would then compare theater to film, a medium he thought of as rather dictatorial. The director of a film decides for us how we'll see things, determining the distance, angle, and length of each shot for what is a self-contained, finite work of art. On the other hand, every theatrical performance is subtly different, as every individual in the space, actors and audience alike, affects the experience.

But however democratic theater may be as an artform, for those who are not actively involved in the production of plays, it remains a largely passive experience. For most people, engaging with Shakespeare's text is done in stillness and silence. Whether we encounter it in the form of an actual First Folio handled with gloved hands in a carefully controlled room, or in a paperback Pelican edition pulled from a back pocket and enjoyed while lounging in a park, or through a hyperlinked digital edition on a tablet, or even in Braille, reading in the current practice doesn't involve much physical activity. Even consideration of Shakespeare in the context of performance is almost always from the passive perspective of the audience, leaving the actual performing to the professionals. This isn't surprising. Theatrical production is a huge, complex endeavor that usually showcases extraordinary skill and artistry. The actors are key, of course, but their art is aided and abetted by that of directors, designers, musicians, artisans, and technicians, all contributing their talents towards an immersive experience for a large, often paying, audience.

Now, as a line of inquiry and a mode of research, of course, experiencing Shakespeare in this way is invaluable. Theater artists collaborate to create a unique world for the play, offering their ideas and interpretations for us to consider. Our experience as audience can be invigorating and illuminating, and it can contribute to our individual and collective understanding of a play. However, our experience as audience is primarily passive and receptive. We have little agency in the experience beyond our response: whether or not we laugh, how

DOI: 10.4324/9780367821722-31

enthusiastically we applaud, whether or not we stand for the ovation, what we say or write about the production afterwards.

What happens when we shift our perspective from that of passive observer to that of active participant? What happens when we expand beyond exclusively intellectual inquiry to include the kinesthetic, the physiological, the intuitive, and the emotional? What happens when we consider the human machine in action *as* the interface that allows us to access Shakespeare? When our own bodies become the container for Shakespeare's text and our understanding comes through enactment, that is the bringing of text to life by actively personating it.

This is what I would like to explore in this chapter. My observations come from a non-traditional perspective. The first half of my career was spent at Shakespeare & Company in Lenox, Massachusetts, where I learned from and with Tina Packer, Kristin Linklater, Kevin Coleman, and others.[1] Since 2005, I've led community and education programming at Bard on the Beach Shakespeare Festival in Vancouver, British Columbia. The mission of this work is to inspire community through dynamic, engaging experiences with Shakespeare's language, characters, and plays.

I'm not an academic and I'm woefully under-read when it comes to the outstanding scholarly work that has been done in recent years. Instead for the past 30+ years I've done my research in theaters, rehearsal halls, and classrooms. As a teaching artist and education director at a Shakespeare theater, I've supported countless participants, both professional and amateur, as they have enacted Shakespeare's text. Sometimes this enactment is part of a rehearsal process with professional actors as they explore the text, making the most vibrant, nuanced contribution they can to the greater production. More often I've worked with amateurs of all ages and backgrounds, either in schools or recreational programs. We don't build sets or design the lighting. Costumes and props are often whatever's available. If there's music, we play it ourselves. The audience is sometimes family and friends enjoying the culmination of a project that has lasted a few weeks, but often it's just fellow students sharing what they've discovered in less than an hour.

But even in those restricted conditions, enactment provides greater engagement and demands greater commitment than either silent reading or auditing. Active communication is fundamentally different from reading or writing, as anyone who communicates through a signed language such as ASL or BSL can attest. For those who communicate through spoken language, speaking the text out loud with full commitment (not just mumbling or murmuring) is essential, as is getting away from the computer screen or desk and moving fully in the way each individual moves, for then we suddenly have what Gary Taylor has called "Feeling Bodies."[2]

In the context of professional theater, enactment can refer to a coaching session with an actor to help them explore their text in detail and discover how it resonates for them. This attention to the essence of the text and the actor's relationship to it supports the actor's contributions to rehearsals and ultimate performance. It's an early step in a complex process. By contrast, in the context of educational or recreational programs, enactment is often as far as we get, since we're usually not preparing a full production. In either case, professional or not, our attention isn't on a finished product. Rather, our attention is on the experience of the individual enactor and on what they can learn in the process.

Enactment, then, is our mode of inquiry; we become the interface between Shakespeare's text and our own cognition. Our physiological and kinesthetic processes become, according to Alexander Galloway's definition of an interface, "the mediating threshold between the self and the world" (viii). The first step in the process is simply acknowledging the presence of the body as more than a "mode of transport" to get your brain "to meetings."[3] Breath is essential, as I learned from Kristin Linklater through training with her and with her acolytes for more than a decade at Shakespeare & Company. Next is expressing the text fully in the ways that are unique to the individual. As the text lives in and is expressed through an individual's body, it comes to life in ways unique to that enactor. As breath connects with thought and with the impulse to express it, it changes. The breath might come more quickly, or perhaps it will deepen. It also connects with feelings. As the sound of the voice resonates through the body, that too, has an effect, and the different sounds in the text will resonate differently, producing different physiological effects and emotional responses. As the thoughts expressed in the text move us to action, that further enhances the experience. This process of allowing the text to affect the enactor's anatomy and physiology brings about what Alexander Galloway calls the "transformations in material states" (vii) that are key to understanding enactment as a type of interface.

Enactment shifts the perspective completely from that of observer to that of participant. It is impossible to remain objective when we personate a character by embodying their words. For example, when we look at Hamlet's dilemma from Hamlet's point of view, the struggle between action and inaction makes more sense. When Hamlet's words temporarily become our words; they resonate within us in a different way. I take this identification and ownership one step farther when working with enactors of Shakespeare's text. Although ordinary theater practice involves actors talking about their characters in the third person, I advocate using the first person. Of course, the actor or enactor is a separate entity with a unique personality, but when bringing to life one of Hamlet's speeches, that individual is Hamlet in that moment. It doesn't matter if they're not male or Danish or 30 years old, and they don't have to pretend to be. In recent email correspondence with accomplished professional actor Moya O'Connell I wrote:

> when we really dive into the words themselves, I like to think of it as entering an imaginative reality where Hamlet looks like you and sounds like you, has your sensibilities and imagination, in a sense is a version of you.

Because when we work on text, there is no other Hamlet but you and this taps into something very powerful about agency and ownership. When we say "I," then suddenly these are our words, not the words of a theoretical figure. It's temporary, transitory, provisional – we're not taking ownership of them forever – but isn't theater itself temporary, transitory, and provisional? And isn't that one of the things that makes it so powerful and so precious?

The spirit of this approach was summed up beautifully by two 10-year-old girls who participated in our digital summer camp on playmaking in Shakespeare in 2020. As part of their investigation of Hamlet's "Speak the speech…," they were asked to pen their own advice to actors. They worked in pairs, and Cora and Tesla gave this advice:

> Let your words flow through the river of your own nature, let your character become yourself, and still speak as yourself. Through the lens of your parts you may meld yourself so that you can live in both worlds harmoniously.

Enactment provides this open access because unlike performance, enactment usually takes the text out of context. In the case of coaching a professional actor, we explore the text pre-context, before the director's art brings together the myriad collaborative elements of theatrical craft to build a coherent world for the play. In the case of educational or recreational programs, the text often remains out of context, except in follow-up discussion. We often enact a single speech or a scene or collection of speeches and scenes, focusing on the depths and nuances of the text, moment to moment. Even when we explore an entire play with these non-professionals, it's a deeply abridged version, often with shared roles and ensemble casting. Our priority in these educational or recreational programs is the experience of participants and what they can learn from it, through the creation of a work of art. It is not the work of art itself.

Temporarily freeing Shakespeare's text from the context of plot or setting or tradition is deeply liberating on many different levels, but especially when it comes to casting. Approaching Shakespeare's characters and Shakespeare's text in this way makes it possible for anyone to identify with characters' thoughts and feelings, even if they don't have much in common with a particular character's situation. Hamlet doesn't need to be a man or Danish or 30 or non-disabled; Juliet doesn't need to be a girl or Italian or not quite 14 or non-disabled. The most moving experience I've ever had hearing Juliet's language was when it was spoken by a large, burly man in his fifties with a huge, bushy beard. He was a participant in a workshop for schoolteachers. He wasn't playing Juliet in the literal sense, but he'd just fallen in love for the first time in his life and when he enacted Juliet's lines,

> My bounty is as boundless as the sea
> My love as deep; the more I give to thee
> The more I have for both are infinite.

He meant it with every cell of his being. It still brings tears to my eyes just remembering it.

Shakespeare's text out of context can surprise and move us, and it can help us break free from the traditions and assumptions that have often limited our understanding of the text, the characters, and the plays. Taking Shakespeare's text out of context and inviting enactment disorients Shakespeare in powerful and empowering ways. And when the interface is enactment, the individual qualities of the enactor – age, gender, race, bearing, tone of voice, and/or way of moving – all have an impact on the delivery of the text, and therefore on our understanding of it. Every enactor is a unique container for Shakespeare's text and each enactor's unique agency and ownership place that individual at the center of the interpretation, reorienting Shakespeare's text and expanding its capacity for bold, new, unexpected interpretations.

Perhaps the clearest illustration of this phenomenon lies in one of my favorite introductory activities used in our school and recreational programs: the Sculpture Garden. I developed the exercise in the mid-1990s while at Shakespeare & Company, and I've shared it far and wide. The activity involves taking individual lines from a variety of plays and placing them on individual notecards. Participants choose a line of text and a partner, and they "sculpt" their partner into the perfect physical representation of what the line means to them. When the group is ready, the "sculptors" take a walk around the room to view the "sculptures" and hear them speak the Shakespeare lines they represent. Partners then switch roles and repeat the process. After everyone has been both sculptor and sculpture, we gather to share reflections on the text participants have sculpted, spoken, and heard. The text that works best for this exercise is brief, self-referential, and image rich. Here are a few examples:

> These words like daggers enter in mine ears
> I am a scribbled form, drawn with a pen upon a parchment
> My soul is full of discord and dismay
> I am a pretty piece of flesh
> I can hardly forbear hurling things at him

It's easy to imagine multiple physical expressions of each of these lines, and participants of all ages have thoroughly enjoyed this active, collaborative exploration. The final step in the exercise invites participants to reflect on the lines that particularly resonated for them, and these lines become our access into the material.

The exercise invites personal connection and subjective interpretation, encouraging participants to abandon any notions of "getting it right." Completely removed from context, the lines simply express an idea that participants are given free rein to explore for themselves. As a result of the participants' agency and ownership, the lines can resonate in unexpected ways. Two lines from *Romeo and Juliet* illustrate this phenomenon:

> You are too hot
> Thy lips are warm

Taken out of context, these lines conjure contemporary associations that inspire pleasure, especially given the mild naughtiness of thinking of such things in the context of a Shakespeare class. Participants delight in their interpretations of these lines and want to know more about them, about the characters who utter them, and about the stories they tell. When they hear that "You are too hot" is a warning about anger so extreme it may turn violent, or when they hear that Juliet says "Thy lips are warm" to a Romeo who has died mere moments before, participants aren't disappointed. Instead, they are interested, engaged, and want to know more. It's easy for participants to reorient their understanding when given additional information because they've been given an opportunity to care in the first place. Allowing participants the experience of connecting with these lines as they interpret them inspires a personal investment in the text, in the play, and in learning that so often proves elusive, especially with Shakespeare. Enactment provides ownership, which inspires investment.

Another recent example involves the line "My heart is heavy and mine age is weak." Perhaps because of my own middle age, or perhaps because I know that the line is spoken by the Countess in *All's Well that Ends Well*, I've always assumed that the weakness referred to is the result of old or at least advancing age. However, a teenage girl we worked with in a community program last year identified powerfully with this line. For her, it meant that as a young person she didn't have the agency or power of someone in a position of authority and decision making. As a result, she was stuck with her heart heaviness. Her insights didn't change the meaning of the line for me, but they have forever expanded its resonance.

When enactment does involve more of the story of the play, it can lead to greater understanding by arousing empathy through identification. Placing the learner inside the play gives them the perspective of the character they're playing. In the mid-1990s, I directed a production of *Romeo and Juliet* at a high school in Springfield, Massachusetts. The 17-year-old girl who was playing the nurse was very judgmental of her character, rejecting her advice to Juliet to marry Paris as her father demands, after Romeo is banished. This young woman thought that the Nurse couldn't possibly mean it; that course of action simply felt wrong to her, considering the power of Romeo and Juliet's love. After a few weeks' rehearsal, however, she started to see things more from the Nurse's perspective. She started to see that there was no other way out for Juliet, and what she cared about most was Juliet's survival. As she personated the Nurse and enacted her text, she adopted the Nurse's perspective on the story. Although she recognized that Juliet might think her a "wicked fiend" for offering this advice, she saw the wisdom in it. Enactment offered her a deeper, more nuanced understanding of the complexities of the play, and of the choices the characters must make.

This can also lead to a greater understanding of human behavior in general, again by arousing empathy through identification. In the late 1980s, I directed a production of *Hamlet* in a small town in western Massachusetts. A 16-year-old girl was cast as Polonius, and although she found some aspects of the character fun to play, she hated the way Polonius spoke to Ophelia, especially when providing advice about Hamlet's expressions of love. "I hate Polonius," she would say at our rehearsals, "This is just how my dad talks to me." But we persevered, continuing in the rehearsal process to discover how we would tell this story. One evening when we were working on the first scene Ophelia and Polonius share, the 16-year-old said, "I love Ophelia. I'm just trying to protect her." Her face suddenly changed as she said, "Maybe this is why my dad talks to me this way."

With agency and ownership come intriguing challenges with the more problematic, dated, and troubling aspects of Shakespeare's language. While the text provides wonderful opportunities for self-expression, it can also present serious problems. Ownership of the words, as we express them for others to hear, challenges us to challenge them. Shakespeare's writing reflects his situation: he wrote at a time and in a place in which the experiences of non-disabled white men were central, and those of everyone else were marginalized, ignored, or denied. The occasional language that displays both casual and overt racism, anti-Semitism, ableism, colourism, and misogyny cannot stand unchallenged. Ownership requires that we interrogate that language and collaboratively decide how to address it.

I've mentioned just a few instances of enactors struggling to engage with their text in a rehearsal process, but that process is the essence of enactment. Personating a character and inhabiting the text require deep critical thinking and careful close reading. When reading silently, learners can often get away with glossing over things, or reading in a generalized way. This doesn't work for enactors. It's clear when they are just saying the words as opposed to truly expressing the thoughts. There is a stark change in the physical processes of expression when the enactor makes sense of the words and they ring with meaning. This isn't a uniform response. Each variable of the individual enactor, time, place, circumstance, and the text itself will affect the experience. However, there is a palpable difference in heart rate, breath, blood flow, and sensation when a thinking, feeling body expresses a clear and cogent thought with authenticity and commitment. Enactors bring what's often experienced internally into the external realm – giving to airy nothing a local habitation, if not a name.

It's hard to imagine a more complex container for the text than an individual human body. After all, how many technologies are more intricate, complicated, and variable than the human machine in action? However, the complexity is compounded exponentially when considered in the context of a group of unique, diverse individuals. I've been discussing the experience of individuals embodying Shakespeare's text, but Taylor reminded us of that power of the presence of individual bodies, bodies enacting that text, especially when there are other bodies there to collaborate or bear witness.[4]

This brings another interface into play when enacting Shakespeare's text: the one between the enactor and others. Human beings are interested in other human beings, and we respond to one another empathetically. Whether through mirror neurons or some other mysterious mechanism of human physiology, transformations of our material states occur in the space between humans in a theater, rehearsal hall, or even a classroom when we enact a text. The layers of communication among enactors and between the enactors and auditors are subtle and complex. In the case of speaking and hearing people, the sound waves of the human voice literally resonate in the listener's body, inspiring emotional responses that are often difficult to articulate. If we're able to see one another, facial expression, gesture, and body language provide additional information as we read one another's complex, nuanced expressions. When we share space with one another, we pick up even more detail on an intuitive level about one another's energy, mood, and emotions. Attuned to one another through our shared humanity, we gather more information on a subconscious level in an instant, unable to identify it before it changes, like the lightning, which doth cease to be ere one can say, "It lightens."

Of course, these transformations are more frequent when the text is enacted by professional actors. Most actors spend years training and even more years honing their craft. Classes in voice, movement, and other disciplines of acting help these artists develop openness to sensation, availability to impulse and responsiveness to action that are essential to dynamic, compelling storytelling. The myriad subtle ways actor/enactors affect one another are central to the collaborative process of both rehearsal and performance. Often described as "chemistry" or "electricity," the interface between actors is alive with activity, providing fertile ground for Shakespeare's text to resonate for actor/enactors and audience/auditors alike. It is in this space between enactor and audience, in this interface that we find the process that effects a result (Galloway vii). Even amateur enactors and students can glimpse this phenomenon.

We are now painfully reminded of the power of such experiences by their enforced absence. As I write this, we've all spent more than a year deprived of this very interface, isolated from one another by a global pandemic. Film, television, and Zoom adaptations have provided options for engaging with enacted text, but this experience is fundamentally different from live theater. There is something uniquely powerful about sharing space, especially when we open ourselves up to one another and to an artistic expression of both our unique and shared human experiences. Those same mathematical models that have explained infection rates and made it clear why we can't gather can help us understand why it will be so important to do so when the danger has passed. Imagine that what is being passed between bodies isn't a deadly virus, but instead affective, collective, empathetic experience. In a theater, or even in a rehearsal hall or a classroom, each moment of interaction provides opportunities for "transformations in material states" as the experience resonates both individually and collectively (Galloway vii). These transformations are essential to a healthy society.

One of the recreational community programs offered by the Bard on the Beach Shakespeare Festival is called Bard for Life. In ordinary times, adult participants meet weekly to explore Shakespeare through performance, coached by professional actors. Each session begins with a "check-in," inviting participants to allow the distractions of the day to fade, bringing their attention to the present. Sessions usually end with a similar exercise which invites another moment of self-reflection to close the experience and transition back into whatever's next. The difference between participants' descriptions of their starting state and their state after a few hours of playing Shakespeare together is astounding. One participant described it this way, "I sometimes walk into the room, and I'm slumped; I've had a hard day. But by the end of the night I am floating on air, and that high continues all week."

In his Broadway show *American Utopia* (adapted for film by Spike Lee in 2020), David Byrne talked about this phenomenon. Referring back to earlier remarks about how human brains change from infancy to adulthood, he says:

> We're a work in progress, we're not fixed, our brains can change. Maybe those millions of connections in our brains that got pruned and eliminated when we were babies somehow get kind of re-established only now instead of being in our heads, they're between us and other people. Who we are is thankfully not just [in our heads], but it extends beyond ourselves through the connections between all of us.[5]

It is through these connections that we can address "the multiplying stimulus of the emotions of a group, emotions that are mutually and nonverbally communicated between bodies in a crowd, can overcome our socially constructed inhibitions against speaking certain feelings" (Taylor 267).

Enactment is one of the most accessible, immediate ways to challenge Shakespeare's longstanding position of cultural icon dispensing wisdom. When the text is expressed by enactors of all ages, races, genders, abilities, backgrounds, and personalities, his words become our words, and we can challenge as well as celebrate them. Shakespeare no longer has the answers, but rather raises questions. In a way, this interrogative energy and sense of possibility can be thought of as an interface as well.

Enactment is not likely to make any lasting contributions to what Shakespeare means on a theoretical or critical level; however, it can have a profound effect on our understanding of the text on personal and societal levels. Enactment empowers individuals, as participants of all backgrounds have ownership of the language, agency in their choices, and authority of their insights. A further collective empowerment comes from celebrating collaborative engagement and interpretation. Thinking about Shakespeare and personation as open, fluid, and kaleidoscopic is an extraordinarily effective way to nurture curiosity, increase understanding, and build community.

Notes

1 Founded in 1978 by Tina Packer, Shakespeare & Company presents a vibrant summer performance season, offers extensive professional actor training, and produces award-winning and nationally recognized theater-in-education programming.

2 I was in attendance at the Shakespeare Association of America/International Shakespeare Association World Congress in Los Angeles in 1996 and heard Taylor deliver that paper. I still remember the sensation of being a hearing body in that room, ready to jump out of my skin with excitement at hearing such an esteemed scholar not just acknowledge but celebrate my way of working.

3 Robinson 09:59.

4 See Taylor 263.

5 Byrne 1:30:00.

References

American Utopia. Directed by Spike Lee, music by David Byrne, HBO, 2020.

Galloway, Alexander R. *The Interface Effect*. Polity Press, 2021.

Robinson, Sir Ken. "Do Schools Kill Creativity?" TED, 2006. Available at: www.ted.com/talks/sir_ken_robinson_do_schools_kill_creativity?language=en#t-607946.

Taylor, Gary, "Feeling Bodies." *Shakespeare in the Twentieth Century: Proceedings of the Sixth World Shakespeare Congress*. Edited by Jonathan Bate *et al.*, U of Delaware P, 1998.

24

ZOOM SHAKESPEARE

Paul Budra

During Shakespeare's professional career, London saw two major outbreaks of the bubonic plague, in 1592–93 and 1603.[1] The city authorities issued a variety of edicts to slow the spread of the plague, including "That no Chirurgions, or barbers, which use to let blood, do cast the same into the streets or rivers" (Creighton 355). They closed the theaters as well as "beare-baitinges, bowlinges and other like assemblyes for sportes."[2] Theater companies responded to this edict by performing outside the urban centers where the plague was at its worst. They were given license to do so by the Privy Council in an act that explained that players could continue to "exercize their quallitie of playing comodies, tragedies and such like in anie other cities, townes and corporacions where the infection is not, so it be not within seaven miles of London or of the Court" (Dasent 212). Live theater in the early modern period continued during plague years.

In December of 2019, the Covid-19 virus was identified. The World Health Authority officially declared it a pandemic in March of 2020. Many countries around the world went into lockdown: people were urged to stay home, masks became a required fashion accessory, and public gatherings were banned. Cinemas, restaurants, sports arenas, nightclubs, and theaters were shut down. The Covid-19 pandemic did not allow contemporary theater professionals the option of touring: unnecessary travel was forbidden in many jurisdictions, and those in small communities were just as likely to spread the virus as those in large cities. Covid-19 killed live theater for two years.

But something unexpected happened during the lockdown: theater professionals repurposed a video-conferencing application called Zoom, a technology that experienced a surge in popularity as the pandemic forced people to take their business and social interactions online. This application, the brainchild of engineer Eric Yuan, was first developed in 2013 as a more user-friendly alternative to applications like Skype. It ran on different computer platforms; it was available for free; it allowed users to set their backgrounds; and it was operable even with unstable internet connections. Eric Yuan became a billionaire.[3] While the free version of Zoom allows people to host up to 100 people at once for 40 minutes, paid versions allow hosting of up to 1,000 people (https://zoom.us/pricing). The program also allows users to configure the screen in a number of ways and to control access and participation. Individual users may have the option of participating with their cameras and microphones turned on or off and a chat function allows meeting participants to share typed comments. Within months of the pandemic lockdown, theater practitioners repurposed

DOI: 10.4324/9780367821722-32

Zoom for performance and Zoom Shakespeare was born. The unprecedented adoption of Zoom by theatrical practitioners provides a rare opportunity to examine a new and emerging Shakespeare interface and its implications to performance, audience engagement, and the future of live theater.

Zoom performances can be recorded, but in this chapter I will restrict my discussion to *live* Zoom broadcasts of Shakespeare's works, for two reasons. First, the recording of any type of live performance introduces a secondary mediation which raises a different set of theoretical concerns around interface, many of which are addressed in other chapters of this book. Second, the essence of theater is live performance. In the words of Peggy Phelan,

> Performance's only life is in the present. Performance cannot be saved, recorded, documented, or otherwise participate in the circulation of representations of representations: once it does so, it becomes something other than performance. To the degree that performance attempts to enter the economy of reproduction it betrays and lessens the promise of its own ontology. Performance's being, like the ontology of subjectivity proposed here, becomes itself through disappearance.
>
> (146)

This insistence on both the live immediacy of theatrical performance and its ephemerality has been used as a selling point by the most enthusiastic theatrical adopters of Zoom technology. For example, according to zoomtheatre.com,

> Zoom Theatre is a theatre for our times. Using web based conferencing software, Zoom delivers live theatre to a live audience. Zoom is not a webcast of a recording of a traditionally staged production. Zoom is live every time. The shows are selected and staged specifically for webcam presentation. You'll see and hear every moment from the best seat in the house. And you are part of the event, just like in a real theater.

The website identifies three "components" of Zoom Theatre:

> Every performance is live for a limited, pre-registered audience; Shows are staged specifically for webcam presentation to take advantage of strengths of the medium; The audience can fully participate in the show by opening their microphones. This brings you into the event so that the actors can hear you respond, laugh and cry and clap right along with them.

I will confine my comments on Zoom Shakespeare to productions that follow these guidelines.[4]

The vast majority of people who have watched a Zoom Shakespeare production will have first used Zoom for a socially distanced business meeting or, perhaps, as a virtual classroom. They would be familiar with its features from having used it for work, education, or possibly to connect with family and friends. Indeed, during the height of the pandemic, they may have used all of those possibilities on a single day. Zoom theater productions, then, almost inevitably evoke the application's quotidian functions and design features. Let us begin with the most obvious of them: in Zoom theater, actors who are physically isolated from each other in their own environments, domestic or professional, speak into computers and look into those computers' cameras. The images of these actors are each framed in digital boxes on the audience members' computer screens in a virtual wall of faces displayed in a grid. The physical isolation of the actors from each other, then, is signaled in the boundaries of pixels that Zoom wraps around its performing participants. Depending on the complexity of the performance, the number of different "spaces" which the individual actors each occupy will vary and hence the grid will expand and contract in number of units. More sophisticated Zoom productions use single screen frames containing one actor for some scenes, and combinations of numbers of actors for others.

The appearance of actors on the screen, then, even though they are isolated in individual Zoom boxes, signifies as a stage entrance. "Signifies" is interesting here. In the theater, the actor physically enters onto the stage. In film, the actor is shown (usually) entering the scene's film set. Shakespeare scripts let the reader imagine the entrance of the character into the presence of the other characters when encountering the stage direction *enter*. In Zoom, since the actors are not physically moving, constrained as they are by the computer's fixed camera and their own, often domestic, environments, they "enter" when their faces appear out of nowhere, like late-comers to a video-conferencing business meeting. When their scene is over, their image disappears, and the Zoom grid reorients itself to accommodate the appropriate number of actors. Entrances and exits, then, like other stage directions in Shakespeare's playtexts, are made allegorical (screen appearance references character entrance) by a platform that has no stage and cannot offer an embodied experience.

Further, the audience members may be reminded that they are watching actors, not characters, in the Zoom grid because each unit within the grid contains a name label in the bottom left corner. In the majority of the Zoom productions I have watched, the actors' real names, not the names of the characters they were playing, appeared in that label. The effect—a rectangle with a close-up of a person's face and that person's name below—resembles a driver's license more than a stage performance. In some productions the actors *do* change the label to the names of the characters they are performing. This is a boon to actors who are doubling roles: their new characters are proclaimed for them; there is no need to put on a wig or adopt an accent. On the other hand, the label can undermine scenes of character revelation. Why don't the characters in the last scene of *Cymbeline* know the true identities of those around them? Can't they read? The labels can also undercut scenes in which knowledge is being withheld from the audience. In 1.2 of *Hamlet*, a silent character dressed in black skulks around a busy court. No one pays attention to him for over 60 lines. Is the ghost of the first scene back among the living? Well, no. The Zoom label tells us it's Hamlet, the eponymous character who, because the play is a tragedy, is going to die.

Whatever the number of actors present at any moment in a Zoom production, the webcam forces attention on the actors' faces within the grid. The dominance of the face means that there is little else that binds the actors together visually. If the actors are in costume, little of that costume will show unless the actor stands and moves away from the camera, an action made awkwardly artificial by the protocols of Zoom: we use Zoom to talk to each other, not to show off our new pants (if, in fact, we are wearing pants at all). Zoom *can* provide a digital background for the actors, and these can be synchronized so there is the appearance of some sort of shared environment, but the static nature of those backgrounds can create problems. In a Zoom production of *The Merchant of Venice*, all the actors may use an image of the Rialto bridge as their backgrounds, but this creates an obvious cognitive dissonance: all the characters they are performing cannot all be standing in the same place looking in the same direction. If each actor uses a different image from Venice, anyone who has been to that city would recognize the impossibility of inter-character communication: someone near the Rialto cannot be speaking to someone in St. Mark's Square. Many Zoom productions that I have seen have opted to use neutral backgrounds for their actors such as black screens. This is, perhaps, the closest analogy to the unadorned blank stage of the Elizabethan theater, but on that stage actors could move around to signify travel and different locations. For example, the Flint Castle scene in *Richard II* (3.3) requires Northumberland to cross, two times, from where Bolingbroke's army is arrayed to the castle where Richard abides. That walk across the stage conveys physical distance and it allows for the illusion that the characters in the two camps can speak among themselves unheard by the opposing forces. The Zoom grid does not permit such movement nor the imagined environment it evokes.

If the Zoom grid makes the representation of environments complicated, the use of a blank background makes the faces of the actors strikingly dominant. In the Zoom grid, actors do not have bodies; they have faces (or perhaps faces and torsos) and because the actors do not speak to each other, forced as they are to face the camera, they talk to the screen and, therefore, to the individual, isolated audience members watching those screens. This may create a form of intimacy—the actors each look into the virtual eyes of each individual spectator and deliver lines—but it transforms dialogue into soliloquy. Even if actors reply to lines of dialogue quickly, the visual effect is that of a series of isolated protagonists speaking directly to an audience member. If we use Robert Weimann's famous distinction between *locus* and *platea*, Zoom drama is all *platea* as the actors have no physical *locus* to step back into once they finish addressing the audience.[5] They are always, unless the director of the production turns off their individual cameras, in the (virtual) space of the audience member, a face staring outward. The physical isolation of audience members of a Zoom performance, then, is mirrored in both the isolation of the individual actors in their own living spaces or studios during a Zoom performance and the nature of the Zoom grid itself which *contains* the individual actors in their own frames.

Watching Zoom theater, then, requires new and unfamiliar cognitive processes. Because the actors are imprisoned and isolated in the Zoom grid, it is up to audience members to imagine the interaction between the characters that the actors are portraying. The audience members must discern which character is speaking to which character(s) and imagine the relationship of the characters' unseen bodies to each other. The audience must imagine the setting of each scene, a task made difficult by the boundaries of the grid and the often-eclectic backgrounds behind the actors. But more than that, the audience members must imagine any significant bodily movement—gestures, slapstick violence, deadly violence—for themselves because, with very few exceptions, those movements are impossible, or profoundly awkward, to represent. The final fight in *Hamlet* or Coriolanus' taking of his mother's hand are lost or represented in ways that are either unconvincing or which necessarily draw attention to their own ingenuity. Stanton Garner has argued that a dramatic performance is turned into "structured fiction" for audience members through a complex "conceptual process" (xvii), but that process is familiar and long established: most people intuitively understand the interface of live theater. The theatrical interface of Zoom is still being invented.

The forced intimacy of the Zoom interface can also create problems for actors. When Jack Lemmon made his first movie, the director, George Cukor, kept telling him to "give me less" (Bernard xiii). Lemmon, used to stage acting, was emoting on a scale too large for the minute attention of the camera. Experienced stage and film actors know that they must mediate their performance according to the medium: a large theater requires voice and movement that project to the back rows; a movie camera catches the smallest of facial nuances. For this reason, many filmed versions of stage productions can be painful to watch: the actors are performing in broad strokes (especially if their performances were recorded in a large theater) that are unnatural on the screen. Zoom Shakespeare, in part because it is new and in part because of its relentless focus on the actors' faces, has not yet, in my experience, established an appropriate scale of performance. It is not hard to understand why: the actors do not have an audience or a physical space to which they can attune their acting. They also do not have the bodies of the other actors present to react with and against. This can result in performances that are of different scales, all forced together into a grid of close-ups, for audience members who, because they are watching on screens, have the performance assumptions associated with television and film. But this is television with a difference, for the actors are staring at the audience members while *pretending* to be engaged with other characters in their shared scene. This makes asides doubly complicated because in asides characters step out of the *locus* to share a secret thought with the audience, looking directly at them, and then return to the world of the play. As mentioned, all dialogue appears as soliloquy, but it is also potentially an aside (the character *is* speaking directly to the audience members) so that *actual* asides are difficult to register. In a Zoom production of *The Revenger's Tragedy* (referenced below) that I watched, the actors tended to turn away from the camera to deliver an aside. This worked to a certain degree, but it removed the shared intimacy that an aside is supposed to foster.

If the design constraints of Zoom create challenges for both audiences and actors, they also pose challenges to directors, designers, and other theatrical practitioners. Imagine, by way of analogy, that you were told that the corporate boardroom you share with your colleagues is, for today, being used for a ballet. That room would not only be an awkward setting for a dance performance, it would frame the dancers with the associations of that room's original corporate function. This would both impact the understanding of the dance by you and your colleagues (each with her own memories of past corporate meetings) while simultaneously forcing the dancers to work around a meeting table and chairs. The latter inconvenience might be overcome with clever choreography, but that ingenuity itself would draw attention to the original function of the room. For example, if a dancer scooted across the space on a wheeled office chair, you might think, "what a cool way to incorporate office furniture into the dance," but that means you would be thinking about the furniture and its habitual use and placement in the work environment. At the same time, its use as part of the dance would draw your focus to the inventiveness of the choreographer in repurposing the object rather than to the dance itself. And remember that you would not be alone: every individual audience member would bring his or her own experience of that room to the performance and, depending on their engagement with the dance, would succeed or fail (or some combination of the two) in imagining the dance independent of that semiotically loaded space and their own embodied experience of having sat in that room for interminable meetings. Every individual's appraisal of the ingenuity of the performance in repurposing the space would be determined by personal experience of the space.

Perhaps it was ever thus. When the Lord Chamberlain's Men were called to perform before the Queen, they acted in palace rooms redolent of court politics and personal intrigue. How many of the courtiers in attendance were more focused on the politics of the space (who gets to be nearest the Queen or the most powerful peers?) than the play itself? But there was an established tradition of dramatic entertainment at court; there isn't one for Zoom. The virtual space of the Zoom Shakespeare performance inevitably bears the traces—at least for the near future and perhaps forever—of its intended functionality. Its efficacy as a container for Shakespeare's playtexts is in part dependent upon how successfully it throws off *or* incorporates the vestiges and associations of its intended functionality. Unlike the Globe Theatre, Zoom was not an environment intended for drama. There *have* been well-reviewed plays written for and performed on Zoom, plays that embrace the limitations and affordances of the Zoom interface, such as *What Do We Need to Talk About?* by Richard Nelson, but Shakespeare's works must be, like Bottom, translated to fit the emerging performance conventions of Zoom Theatre.[6] This can be difficult because, like the repurposed boardroom, Zoom is much more likely to be used on any given day for video conferencing than for performance (imagine if the Donmar Warehouse in London's Convent Garden was still used as a banana-ripening depot between theatrical events). One way to circumvent this problem is by playing *to* the associations of the space, performing Shakespeare's stories as though they were occurring during a Zoom meeting (imagine if the Donmar Warehouse produced a play about ripening bananas). A number of theater troupes during the pandemic presented adapted versions of *Romeo and Juliet* in such a way, calculating, perhaps, that young people are just as likely to carry on relationships online as in person and therefore the Zoom container would be, in a way, natural.[7]

The cognitive demands of Zoom Shakespeare and the unprecedented constraints it places on theatrical practitioners serve to underscore what many chapters in this collection have argued: interfaces are never transparent. They inevitably mediate the content to which they offer access. They are, at best, translucent, and the extent to which they cloud or distort the content of the medium that they mediate is, in addition to the restrictions we have already discussed, partly determined by the degree to which their use has become intuitive. If users bring their expectations from previous (or analogous) interfaces to a new interface, those expectations will necessarily impede their facility with the new interface, drawing attention to its particularities and away from the content to which it serves as a portal. A new interface needs enough cultural saturation or intuitive ease of use to establish its own conventions so that users, acclimatized to them, can forget or ignore them. That forgetting is important: when an interface is ubiquitous, its conventions of use become so intuitive that they barely, if ever, register *as* conventions. No literate adult has to be told how to work a book. The downside of an interface achieving that sort of universal acceptance is that users no longer recognize that they are engaged with an interface and assume they are receiving unalloyed access to content. The chapters in this book have, we hope, complicated such assumptions.

It is not just the users of a new interface who hinder its progression toward increased transparency with their physical or cognitive habits: in attempting to make a new interface user-friendly and shorten the learning curve, designers may take the features of familiar interfaces and graft them onto a new model, creating problematic hybrids. So, for example, the earliest printed books published in Europe had page layouts that imitated those of handwritten manuscripts, as printers copied an interface with which readers were familiar. While printed books gained cultural saturation, the layouts of their pages evolved: readers no longer expected the blocks of text, offset glosses, and blank columns of the handwritten book. The printed book developed its own conventions which readers, when acclimatized to them through use, assumed and forgot. This nostalgia for the pre-existing in interface design may, of course, not be a conscious decision. The creators of a new interface themselves might, just like the early adopters of many new technologies, be imaginatively bound by their own familiarity with established interfaces. As we have seen in other chapters in this volume, some creators of new interfaces did not initially understand the potential of the new technology they were wielding to create a fresh way to access Shakespeare's works; they tended to replicate that with which they are already familiar. The transparency of new interfaces, then, can be clouded by unarticulated technological nostalgia.

And so it is with Zoom Shakespeare. Let us begin with the obvious: despite Zoom Theatre's promise to audience members that they will be "part of the event, just like in a real theater," live Zoom theater is presented on screens. For contemporary theater goers, this may not be as significant a disjuncture as first appears. Indeed, an argument can be made that the Zoom theater format is the logical extension of a trend in theatrical performances to include screen technology. It is no longer unusual for an actor in a live performance to appear on a video monitor, as a projected image, or even as a hologram for at least certain scenes in a play. Johannes Birringer argues that "In the context of postmodern and postdramatic performance, after the recent decades of hybrid experimentation across all media and live art, the defense of the live actor onstage in mainstream theater is no longer urgent" (208). As Philip Auslander explains, this trend is in part driven by economics:

> the general response of live performance to the oppression and economic superiority of mediatized forms has been to become as much like them as possible. From ball games that incorporate instant-replay screens, to rock concerts that recreate the images of music videos, to live stage versions of television shows and movies, to dance and performance art's incorporation of video, evidence of the incursion of mediatization into the live event is available across the entire spectrum of performance genres.
>
> *(7)*

One might argue, then, that Zoom theatrical productions are the final expression of a trend. But, unlike the live theatrical events that incorporate screen technology in performance, Zoom theater takes place *entirely* on screens in the homes of individual audience members. It is not the final extension of screened media into theatrical performance, but rather the opposite: the restructuring of theatrical performance to fit screen technology. In this it more resembles filmed versions of live theatrical productions, Live-to-Digital productions, and live-streamed theatrical productions called "Event Cinema" (though many viewers watch them on home screens). This delivery model for theater has become so prevalent that the Arts Council England, UK Theatre, and Society of London Theatre commissioned a study in 2016 called "From Live-to-Digital: Understanding the Impact of Digital Developments in Theatre on Audiences, Production and Distribution." It surveyed a wide section of theater goers over their use of and reactions to digitally delivered theatrical productions. Perhaps not surprisingly, younger people (ages 16–24) were more likely to have streamed theatrical productions than those over the age of 45 (11). More importantly for our discussion of interface, the majority of those polled for the study enjoyed the digital experience but recognized it as something distinct from live theater.

> For audiences – and many creators and suppliers interviewed for this study – Live-to-Digital is seen not as a replacement for live, but as a distinct experience (66% and 77%) that opens up 'new ways of seeing theatre' (72% and 75%).
>
> *(AEA Consulting 12)*

At the same time, "Most survey respondents disagreed with the statement, 'Live-to-Digital work is more engaging than attending live.' In fact, 54% of Event Cinema participants and 36% of those who streamed stated that they prefer to attend live theatre" (12).

While most respondents to the survey may agree that live theater is more engaging than digital productions, the digital productions they were assessing were, for the most part, visually complex, using multiple cameras and sophisticated editing techniques. They drew on the visual vocabulary of contemporary film. Zoom theater, on the other hand, is a throwback to early television, which was, in essence, a primitive form of broadcasted theater because, before the invention of videotape, television productions were performed live before a studio audience using largely static camera shots. It was only with the advent of videotape that television shows could be pre-recorded and edited. Laugh tracks were then added to replace the reactions of live audiences. There is still live television, obviously, but except for news programs, award shows, and sporting events, viewers do not *expect* television to be broadcast live. Zoom theater, then, is a return to television's origins, but it is a fragmented return. Instead of the single, black-and-white, cathode-ray-generated image of early television, Zoom theater presents a series of individual screens *within* the screen frame, isolating performers in their own tiny performance boxes.[8] This grid emphasizes the lack of camera movement and stands in stark contrast to the kinetic and fluid camera work of modern film and television. In a Zoom performance the camera is resolutely fixed, more so than in early television. Ironically, given the name of the program, it cannot even zoom in or out. The only cinematic movement possible is the actor moving in and out of the frame, or closer and farther from the computer webcam.

The other heritage interface to which Zoom theater gestures is radio drama, a form of entertainment that has experienced a renaissance in the past few years through podcasting. Because Zoom theater is (so far) largely devoid of compelling visual content, a Zoom audience member may declare, like Puck watching the Mechanicals rehearse in the woods, "I'll be an auditor" (3.1.67).[9] Zoom Shakespeare, then, inadvertently recreates at least one aspect of the theatrical experience of the early modern period, insisting that audiences "hear" a play rather than watch it. Zoom theater *does* provide the grid of actors' faces, but because they are reduced, in essence, to talking and visually isolated heads, the chance for the actors to create significant visual theatrical meaning, through blocking and gesture, are, as we shall see, slim. The voices of the actors predominate.

We should recognize that there is an obvious demographic divide inherent in the technological nostalgia I am describing. Young people may have never seen one-camera live television or listened to a radio drama. On the other hand, these so-called "digital natives" have spent much of their lives staring into computer screens to communicate with their friends, not only in videochats, but in the digitally generated environments of multi-player video games.[10] Familiarity with the protocols of such virtual engagement and the constant use of digital technologies mean that younger audiences of Zoom theater will likely be more adept at accommodating, or ignoring, the interface's particularities. Steve Dixon has argued that

> Cyberspace exists between different physical locations, a rainbow bridge supported on all sides by site-specific physical hardware and the "wetware" of human bodies. Like a theater stage, it is a symbolic passageway to the imaginary (role-plays, narratives, and so on) building from and arising out of the physical and the tangible (bodies, sets, light, sound). But like events on a theater stage, the transformations of space remain primarily imaginary, metaphorical, and representational; suspension of disbelief is thus as crucial to the cyberspace participant's transportation or immersion into imaginary space as it is for the theater spectator.
>
> *(464)*

People who have spent significant time in cyberspace may be able to make the jump in imagination with more ease than those who have never engaged with a digital environment.

Even so, both the creators and users of a new interface may, at least in the early stages of its appropriation or development, be imaginatively bound by their experience of earlier interfaces. But, as mentioned in the boardroom example, the creators face a double bind. When they repurpose an interface in a clever way, they may draw attention to the ingenuity of that repurposing rather than to the content they are attempted to communicate. If they attempt to circumvent the limitations of the new interface by importing the conventions of a previous interface, they risk drawing attention to the restrictions that the new interface imposes. For example, in a recent Zoom production of Thomas Middleton's *The Revenger's Tragedy*, the actors appeared to pass items to each other. That is, one actor would take a letter, say, and hand it off to the left-hand side of his Zoom box while the actor in the Zoom box to the left of the first actor would pretend to receive a letter from the right side of his frame. Rather than create an illusion of the actors sharing a physical space and exchanging the item, the clumsiness of the exchange and its obvious impossibility (we all know that the actors are isolated in their homes) drew more attention to Zoom as an interface than it did to create the dramatic illusion of a shared playing space. As mentioned in the boardroom analogy above, repurposing an interface, especially a repurposing that attempts to import the conventions of another technology, necessarily draws attention to the intended original purpose of the interface. For an interface to maximize its translucency, it must establish its own conventions and those conventions must become familiar enough, through tradition or usage, that they are unthinkingly assumed.

Zoom has another unique problem as an interface: when the pandemic lockdown made the program the go-to platform for business, education, and social interactions, users complained of exhaustion after protracted Zoom meetings. The term "Zoom fatigue" was invented to label this condition.[11] What was so tiring about being in a Zoom meeting? Jeremy N. Bailenson has posited several arguments to explain this phenomenon. He points out that in Zoom meetings (and in some Zoom theatrical productions) participants (both actors and audience) see themselves on the screen—their computer cameras include them in the Zoom grid. As Bailenson explains,

> Imagine in the physical workplace, for the entirety of an 8-hr workday, an assistant followed you around with a handheld mirror, and for every single task you did and every conversation you had, they made sure you could see your own face in that mirror.

Even if audience members' video feeds are not included in the grid, performers, as mentioned, see themselves; they literally watch themselves performing. This means that

> Zoom users are seeing reflections of themselves at a frequency and duration that hasn't been seen before in the history of media and likely the history of people (with exceptions for people who work in dance studios and other places that are full of mirrors).

This enforced self-observation creates an unremitting self-awareness that is almost certainly, an impediment to naturalism in acting. Finally, Bailenson notes that "On Zoom, behavior ordinarily reserved for close relationships—such as long stretches of direct eye gaze and faces seen close up—has suddenly become the way we interact with casual acquaintances, coworkers, and even strangers." In Zoom Shakespeare that unnatural intimacy is focused on performers. For the first time in Shakespeare history, we have an interface that requires its users to stare at, and seemingly be stared back at, by *all* the characters in a play, be they ever so minor. It is hard to imagine any previous production that required the audience members to look in the eyes of the First Groom in *2 Henry 4* when he recites his immortal line, "More rushes, more rushes!" (5.5.1), but Zoom has made that not only possible, but inevitable.

Most of what I have discussed so far suggests that Zoom is a highly problematic interface for Shakespeare's dramatic works: it sets up complex cognitive expectations tied to its primary use as a video-conferencing utility and it forces directors and actors to perform Shakespeare's plays in ways that are radically different from those employed in live theater, either contemporary or early modern. But theater practitioners are nothing if not ingenious, and when the COVID-19 pandemic forced them to use Zoom as an interface for Shakespeare's works, they experimented.

The more successful of those experiments employed the limitations of the Zoom interface, making a virtue of enforced necessity and avoiding the trap of drawing attention to their own ingenuity. Laura Jayne Wright has described a production of *The Tempest* she saw performed on Zoom by Creation Theatre (an Oxford-based theater company). The production made use of Zoom's capacities in a number of ways. For example, it employed the microphones of the audience members for a special effect. As Wright explains,

> when the play began and Ariel conjured a storm, suddenly it became clear that – despite our isolation – we too were part of the action. The audience's microphones (muted while the actors spoke) were suddenly raised and we were asked to click our fingers to make it rain. The screen was full of audience members – and their pets, and their glasses of wine, and their pyjamas – and the storm was, even if I say so myself, convincing.

Wright also makes note of the choice of play, *The Tempest.* As mentioned earlier, there have been several Zoom productions of *Romeo and Juliet* that have tried to tie the use of Zoom as a social-media platform to the young lovers as prototypical teens addicted to their screens. But Wright speculates that,

> As site-specific, conference call plays go, *The Tempest* lends itself to such a production. It's a play about isolation and exile, about characters moving around a small island without ever meeting one another. Creation's performance did nothing to disguise its new medium. In fact, the most powerful part of the performance came as Prospero spoke the famous epilogue which begins: "Now my charms are all o'erthrown". The cast slowly and methodically packed up their bedsheet green screens and wiped off their makeup. They changed their onscreen identities from their character's names back to their own. By the time we were invited to stay on Zoom for a moment or two, to catch up with friends, thank the actors, and wave goodbye, the spell was broken.

Here we may have the first example of meta-Zoom-theatricality (to coin a term that I hope is never used again).

L. Lehua Yim notes that a Zoom production of *A Midsummer Night's Dream* by the Southwest Shakespeare Company that she watched was able to accomplish several things that a staged production could not. Going back to the earlier point about Zoom theater resembling radio drama, Yim reports that "the performers' voices could fill an audience member's headphones or speakers with a roundness otherwise not available in the playhouse" (121). And she could see a benefit in all of the characters appearing, in certain scenes, in the Zoom grid:

> the uniform window size for each performer's face made Titania and her faeries equal players, creating ample opportunities for the minor characters to convey their reactions to Titania's besottedness with Bottom in deliciously subtle eye-rolling and lip-pursing detail. Similarly, the more silent rude Mechanicals' good-natured head nodding and quizzical responses to the brilliantly over-the-top Bottom … got equal screen time and much-deserved attention.
>
> *(122)*

Kate Wilkinson reviewed a Zoom production of *The Duchess of Malfi* by the Creation Theatre company that used yet a different approach. Audience members were encouraged, before the show began, to "turn off the light and light a candle" (1), thus creating a mood and emphasizing the fact that the performance was being watched by individuals on their own, rather than by a gathered audience. As for settings,

> Each performer was also (presumably) in their front room (or other room in their homes), performing in front of either blank walls or drapes. Short video segments, reminiscent of the Eurovision Song Contest, of Rome and Malfi, for example, were used to indicate change of location.
>
> *(2)*

The Zoom grid was eliminated by a technical innovation, so that "the actors were seen on a single screen, a behind-the-scenes technical whizz merging the different images to great effect, in a way that – eventually – gave the impression they were in fact sharing the same space" (2) which, Wilkinson admits, though effective, did make the actors' speaking directly to the camera, rather than each other, especially jarring. The production used color washes on the screen as well as superimposed images to convey meaning and mood. Wilkinson's final assessment of the production and the experience of watching a Jacobean tragedy on Zoom is ambivalent:

> This was not theatre, but nor was it film or television, nor a flashy, sophisticated stream-on-demand theatre service. It had, because of the live performances, an immediacy that theatre in a theatre building has, but while I felt a shared experience with the performers, the shared experience that comes from being part of an audience watching theatre in the same physical space wasn't there.
>
> *(3)*

These, and other productions, are testaments to the creativity of theatrical practitioners. They are also evidence of the flexibility of Shakespeare's plays; their stories have, once again, proven to be affecting even in the most unlikely of containers: a videoconferencing program designed for business meetings. The restrictions and affordances of that platform have been a test case for interface studies as we have been able to observe, in real time, the adoption of this new medium and infer the nature and efficacy of the interface as it is being created. But will Zoom Shakespeare continue once the pandemic subsides or has the pandemic given us the most ephemeral of Shakespeare interfaces? There is no way of telling, but I suspect that once the pandemic is over (it is still running its course as of this writing), theatrical practitioners will regard it as something of a last resort, the digital equivalent to touring the towns outside London when the plague shuts down the playhouses.

Notes

1. For an assessment of the relative mortality rates of those plagues, see Cummins et al., especially 13.
2. Quoted in Knutson 453. See Knutson for a discussion of the impact of the 1593 closing.
3. See Konrad for Yuan's story.
4. Full disclosure: I helped produce a Zoom production of Djanet Spears' play *Harlem Duet*, which is based on *Othello*, in conjunction with Bard on the Beach, Vancouver BC's annual Shakespeare festival, in 2020.
5. See Weimann, especially 73–85.
6. See Schwartz for a review of the production.
7. This idea was explored before the pandemic in such movies as *Unfriended* (2014) which takes place entirely on the computer screens of a group of young people using social media.

8 This arrangement is redolent of a specific old TV show, *Hollywood Squares* (1966–81), a comedy game show in which celebrities sat behind desks that bore their names, facing the camera, in a vertical grid that resembled a Tic-Tac-Toe board.
9 All quotations from Shakespeare cite Greenblatt's *The Norton Shakespeare*.
10 Marc Prensky famously distinguished between digital natives, those who have grown up with digital technology, and digital immigrants, people who have had to adapt to the new technologies as they have appeared. See Prensky 1–2.
11 Nadler has argued that "computer-mediated communication" exhaustion is a better term because the condition is experienced by users of other video-conferencing platforms (2).

References

AEA Consulting. "From Live-to-Digital: Understanding the Impact of Digital Developments in Theatre on Audience, Production and Distribution," October 2016. Available at: www.artscouncil.org.uk/publication/live-digital.

Auslander, Philip. *Liveness: Performance in a Mediatized Culture*. 2nd ed., Routledge, 2008.

Bailenson, Jeremy N. "Nonverbal Overload: A Theoretical Argument for the Causes of Zoom Fatigue." *Technology, Mind, and Behavior*, vol. 2, no. 1, 2021. doi:10.1037/tmb00000301.

Bernard, Ian. *Film and Television Acting: From Stage to Screen*. 2nd ed., Routledge, 1998.

Birringer, Johannes. "The Theatre and Its Screen Double." *Theatre Journal*, vol. 66, 2014, pp. 207–225.

Creighton, Charles. *A History of Epidemics in Britain from A.D. 664 to the Extinction of the Plague*. London, 1891.

Cummins, Neil, Morgan Kelly, and Cormac Ó Gráda. "Living Standards and Plague in London, 1560–1665." *Economic History Review*, vol. 69, no. 1, 2016, pp. 3–34.

Dasent, John Roche, editor. *Acts of the Privy Council of England*, vol. 24, *1592–1593*. London: Her Majesty's Stationery Office, British History Online, 1901. Available at: http://www.british-history.ac.uk/acts-privy-council/vol24/pp201-225.

Dixon, Steve, Roger F. Malina, and Sean Cubitt. *Digital Performance: A History of New Media in Theatre, Dance, Performance Art, and Installation*. MIT Press, 2007.

Garner, Stanton. *Narrative Comprehension in the Theater*. U of Chicago P, 1989.

Knutson, Roslyn L. "What's So Special about 1594?" *Shakespeare Quarterly*, vol. 61, no. 4, 2010, pp. 449–467.

Konrad, Alex. "Zoom, Zoom, Zoom! The Exclusive Inside Story of the New Billionaire Behind Tech's Hottest IPO." *Forbes Magazine*, 31 May 2019. Available at: https://www.forbes.com/sites/alexkonrad/2019/04/19/zoom-zoom-zoom-the-exclusive-inside-story-of-the-new-billionaire-behind-techs-hottest-ipo/?sh=36e6a9fb4af1.

Nadler, Robby. "Understanding 'Zoom Fatigue': Theorizing Spatial Dynamics as Third Skins in Computer-Mediated Communication." *Computers and Composition*, vol. 58, 2020, pp. 1–17.

Phelan, Peggy. *Unmarked: The Politics of Performance*. Routledge, 1993.

Prensky, Marc. "Digital Natives, Digital Immigrants." *On the Horizon*, vol. 9, no. 5, 2001, pp. 1–6.

Schwartz, Alexandra. "The First Great Original Play of Quarantine." *The New Yorker*, 11 May 2020. Available at: https://www.newyorker.com/magazine/2020/05/18/the-first-great-original-play-of-quarantine.

Shakespeare, William. *The Norton Shakespeare*. 3rd ed., edited by Stephen Greenblatt *et al.*, Norton, 2016.

Weimann, Robert. *Shakespeare and the Popular Tradition in the Theater: Studies in the Social Dimension of Dramatic Form and Function*. Edited by Robert Schwartz. Johns Hopkins UP, 1978.

Wilkinson, Kate. "Review of *The Duchess of Malfi* (Directed by Laura Wright and Natasha Rickman for Creation Theatre), Performed via Zoom, 18 March 2021." *Shakespeare*, vol. 17, no. 3, 2021, pp. 362–364.

Wright, Laura Jayne. "Shakespeare on Zoom: How a Theatre Group in Isolation Conjured up a Tempest." *The Conversation*, 23 April 2020. Available at: https://theconversation.com/shakespeare-on-zoom-how-a-theatre-group-in-isolation-conjured-up-a-tempest-136974.

Yim, L. Lehua. "Review of Shakespeare's *A Midsummer Night's Dream* (Directed by Ty Defoe for the Southwest Shakespeare Company), Zoom, 11 July 2020." *Shakespeare*, vol. 17, no. 1, 2021, pp. 120–125.

INDEX

Note: Page references in italics refer to figures.